THE RESTORATION OF CHRISTIANITY

An English Translation of *Christianismi restitutio,* 1553
by Michael Servetus (1511-1553)

Translated by
Christopher A. Hoffman
and
Marian Hillar

Notes by
Marian Hillar

With a Preface by
Alicia McNary Forsey

The Edwin Mellen Press
Lewiston•Queenston•Lampeter

Library of Congress Cataloging-in-Publication Data

Servetus, Michael, 1511?-1553.
    [Christianismi restitutio. English]
    The restoration of christianity : an English translation of Christianismi restitutio, 1553
by Michael Servetus (1511-1553) / translated by Christopher A. Hoffman and Marian Hillar ;
notes by Marian Hillar ; with a preface by Alicia McNary Forsey. ; foreword by Ángel Alcalá.
        p. cm.
    Includes bibliographical references.
    ISBN-13: 978-0-7734-5520-7
    ISBN-10: 0-7734-5520-5
    1. Christianity--Controversial literature. I. Hillar, Marian. II. Title.

    BL2775.3.S4713 2006
    230--dc22

                                                                    2006052506

hors série.

A CIP catalog record for this book is available from the British Library.

Front cover: Copy of the print of Servetus found in *Iconica & Descriptio Praecipurum Haeresiarcharum*
by Sichem, dated 1609.

This publication was organized by Alicia McNary Forsey, Managing Editor and Project Director.

The Edwin Mellen Press   The Edwin Mellen Press
Box 450   Box 67
Lewiston, New York   Queenston, Ontario
USA 14092-0450   CANADA L0S 1L0

The Edwin Mellen Press, Ltd.
Lampeter, Ceredigion, Wales
UNITED KINGDOM SA48 8LT

Printed in the United States of America

Dedicated to Hardy Sanders, 1929-2003

THE RESTORATION OF CHRISTIANITY

An English Translation of *Christianismi restitutio,* 1553
by Michael Servetus (1511-1553)

This publication was organized by Alice McNary Forsey, project director.

Major References

Ante-Nicene Fathers : the Writings of the Fathers down to A.D. 325, edited by
Alexander Roberts & James Donaldson; revised and chronologically
arranged, with brief prefaces and occasional notes, by A. Cleveland Coxe,
(Peabody, Mass. : Hendrickson Publishers, 1994).

Apostolic Fathers, Greek Texts and English Translations, edited by Michael W.
Holmes, (Grand Rapids: Baker Books, 1999).

Biblia Hebraica Leningradensia, prepared according to the vocalization, accents,
and Masora of Aaron ben Moses ben Asher in the Leningrad Codex,
edited by Aron Dotan, (Peabody, MA: Hendrickson Publishers, 2001).

Biblia Sacra Iusta Vulgatam Versionem Vulgate Latin Bible, edited by R. Weber,
B. Fischer, J. Gribomont, H. F. D. Sparks, and W. Thiele, (Stuttgart:
Deutsche Bibelgesellschaft, 1983).

BibleWorks for Windows, version 4, (Big Fork, Montana: Hermeneutika Bible
Research Software, 1999).

Ioannis Calvini opera quae supersunt omnia, ediderunt Gulielmus Baum,
Eduardus Cunitz, Eduardus Reuss, (Brunsvigae: apud C.A. Schwetschke
et filium, 1870).

(Michaelis Servetus) *Christianismi restitutio. Totius ecclesiae apostolicae est ad
sua limina vocatio, in integrum restituta cognitione Dei, fidei Christi,
iustificatione nostrae, regenerationis baptismi, et caenae domini
manducationis. Restituto denique nobis regno coelesti, Babylonis impia
captivitate soluta, et Antichristo cum suis penitus
destructo.* M.D.LIII., (Reprinted by Graphischer Betrieb Heinz Saamer
Frankfurt am Main, 1968).

A Greek-English Lexicon, compiled by Henry George Liddell and Robert Scott.
Revised and augmented by Sir Henry Stuart Jones with assistance of

Roderick McKenzie and with the co-operation of many scholars. With a supplement 1968, (Oxford: At the Clarendon Press, 1983).

The Holy Bible containing Old and New Testaments with the Apocryphal/Deuterocanonical Books. New Revised Standard Version, (New York, Oxford: Oxford University Press, 1989).

The Holy Qur'an. Text, translation and commentary by Abdullah Yusuf Ali, Elmhurst, NY: Tahrike Tarsile Qur'an, Inc., 1987).

Walther Krantz, *Vorsokratische Denker: Auswahl aus dem Ünberlieferten.* Griechisch und Deutsch, (Berlin: Wedemann, 1949).

Moses Maimonides, *The Guide of the Perplexed.* Translated with an introduction and notes by Shlomo Pines. With an introductory essay by Leo Strauss, (Chicago: University of Chicago Press, 1963). vol.1-2.

The New Brown-Driver-Briggs-Gesenius Hebrew and English Lexicon, with an appendix containing the Biblical Aramaic, by Francis Brown, with the cooperation of S. R. Driver, Charles A. Briggs, (Peabody, MA: Hendrickson Publishers, 1979).

New Testament Apocrypha, edited by Wilhelm Schneemelcher, English translation edited by R. McL. Wilson, (Cambridge, UK, Louisville, KY: James Clarke & Co.).

Nestle-Aland, eds., *Novum Testamentum Graece,* editione vicesima septima revisa, (Stuttgart: Deutsche Bibelgesellschaft, 2001).

Nicene and post-Nicene Fathers. First series / edited by Philip Schaff, (Peabody, Mass.: Hendrickson Publishers, 1994).

Nicene and post-Nicene Fathers. Second series / edited by Philip Schaff and Henry Wace, (Peabody, Mass.,: Hendrickson Publishers, 1994).

Numénius, *Fragments,* texte établi et traduit par Édouard des Places, (Paris: Société d'Édition des Belles Lettres, 1973).

The Orphic Hymns, text, translation, notes by Apostolos N. Athanasakis, (Atlanta, GA: Scholars Press, 1988).

Oxford Latin Dictionary, edited by P. G. W. Gale, (Oxford: At the Clarendon Press, 1992).

PG *Patrologia graeca: Patrologiae cursus completus, series graeca,* accurante J.-P. Migne, Parisiis, 1857-1936.

PL *Patrologia Latina : Patrologiae cursus completus, sive biblioteca universalis, integra, uniformis, commoda, oeconomica, omnium SS. Patrum, doctorum scriptorumque eccelesiasticorum qui ab aevo apostolico ad usque Innocentii III tempora floruerunt* ... *[Series Latina, in qua prodeunt Patres, doctores scriptoresque ecclesiae Latinae, a Tertulliano ad Innocentium III]* Accurante J.-P. Migne, Parisiis, 1844-64.

Die Pseudoklementinen, (Berlin: Akademie-Verlag, 1953-1989), Vol. 1-3.
1. Homilien, hrsg. von Bernhard Rehm, zum Druck besorgt durch Johannes Irmscher.
2. Rekognitionen, hrsg. von B. Rehm, zum Druck besorgt durch Franz Paschke.
3. Konkordanz zu den Pseudoklementinen. pt. 1. Lateinisches Wortregister von Georg Strecker. pt. 2. Griechisches Wortregister, Syrisches Wortregister, Index nominum, Stellenregister / von Georg Strecker.

Pythagoras, *The Pythagorean Sourcebook and Library. An Anthology of Ancient Writings Which Relate to Pythagoras and Pythagorean Philosophy.* Compiled and translated by Kenneth Sylvan Guthrie with additional translations by Thomas Taylor and Arthur Fairbanks, Jr. Introduced and edited by David R. Fideler with a forward by Joscelyn Godwin, (Grand Rapids, MI: Phanes Press, 1988).

Registres de la Compagnie des Pasteurs de Genève au temps de Calvin, publiés sous la direction des Archives d'Etat de Genève par R.-M. Kingdon et J.-F. Bergier (Genève: Librairie E. Droz, 1962). Tome II 1553-1564.

Miguel Servet, *Restitución del cristianismo*, primera traducción castellana de

Ángel Alcalá y Luis Betés. Edición, introducción y notas de Ángel Alcalá, (Madrid: Fundación Universitaria Española, 1980).

Miguel Servet, *Treinta cartas a Calvino. Sesenta signos del Anticristo. Apología de Melanchton.* Edición de Ángel Alcalá, (Madrid: Editorial Castalia, 1981).

Table of Contents

Preface

During the early 1990s, while sorting through a card catalog at the Bodleian Library in Oxford, England, I found a card noting the translation of *The Restoration of Christianity* by Michael Servetus (1553) from the Latin into Spanish.

The most obvious, and probably most naive, question sprang into my thoughts: Why was there no complete translation available in English? How could we neglect to make accessible in English the central theological writings of a radical reformer and martyr credited for his significant contributions to freedom of conscience in matters of faith?

Thinking that an English translation of *The Restoration of Christianity* was an endeavor I could organize and oversee, I made a commitment to take it on. I did not know the magnitude of my commitment. Over the last decade, the translation project developed a fairly complex history of its own. Working with various individuals, there were differences of opinion over matters of style, the importance of preserving the tone of the original, how best to keep Servetus in his own Sixteenth Century context, and more.

After many setbacks and unexpected turns in the road, individuals who have now come together to work on the project possess the necessary scholarly abilities, agree on basic questions such as preserving the style of speech used by Servetus, and maintain friendly, helpful and gracious communication. Readers of this English translation are indebted to Chris Hoffman, Marian Hillar and Ángel Alcalá for their scholarship, dedication, patience and generosity of spirit.

Sadly, a great scholar, George Huntston Williams, who was committed to work on this translation project did not live beyond the initial stage of giving me his good advice and counsel. George Huntston Williams embodied the "Abiding Love whence alone cometh our hope"[1] and will always be remembered.

Special thanks to Claire S. Stelter (formerly Allen) for her meticulous and thoughtful proofreading of the text, to Javier Miranda for his help with technical matters, and to COLLEGIUM (Association of Liberal Religious Scholars) for their encouragement.

A little less naive today, I look to the readers of this text who will go on to expand our understanding of Michael Servetus and the context of his life. I look forward to increased awareness regarding the intense relevancy between The Radical Reformation (1517–1579) and current times. The connections are startling. Our grasp of their importance cannot be complete without understanding the pivotal position taken up by Michael Servetus.

Alicia McNary Forsey

Research Professor of Historical Studies
Core Doctoral Faculty
Graduate Theological Union, Berkeley, California

---

[1]Williams, George Huntston, *The Polish Brethren*, Part I, Harvard Theological Studies XXX, found in a line of the dedication of the text to his son-in-law who died in 1974

Foreword

Up to the present day, when at a friendly chat or an academic discussion Michael Servetus (1511-1553) is mentioned, this great Spanish genius might be remembered only as the early discoverer of blood circulation or perhaps, at least, as the author of its first description in the West. He might even be mentioned as the daring and dangerous enemy of the faith who, after being persecuted by the Spanish and French Inquisitions, was burned alive in Geneva on the initiative of John Calvin as a contumacious heretic. The apparent reasons for his death were his risky doctrines against the traditional concept of the Trinity (the most fundamental of all Christian dogmas), his denial of the legitimacy of baptizing children, and other proposals dear to his original brand of Radical Reformation.

Few theologians - Catholic, Protestant and even Unitarian - have bothered to go beyond these popular commonplaces and take seriously the overall intellectual system of his masterpiece, *Christianismi Restitutio* (Vienne, France, 1553), as one of the most outstanding theological contributions in the whole of Christian history. Even fewer have had the courage and the mental and spiritual objectivity necessary to delve into the doctrinal world of this monumental book. It is a work of truly oceanic proportions. It first questions the Biblical foundations of some of the post-Nicene Christian dogmas and of many ecclesiastical practices, such as the baptism of children; then, on the positive side, analyses and presents, with impressive profundity and immense personal vigor, a mystical doctrine of God's immediate presence in all beings and of Christ as the definitive divine "symbol" or footprint of God's intervention in human history; finally, points out the errors and abuses of the Christian churches, especially of the Roman

"Antichrist", and offers original ideas about the congregations and their communal role.

The Servetus theology is truly christocentric, and rests on three transcendental principles: 1. his insistence that Christianity is a religion of spirit and not of letter (and therefore, his obsession with the anti-evangelical character of established institutionalized churches); 2. his emphasis on the exclusively personal responsibility of each individual for his or her faith and salvation; 3. his defense of universal freedom of conscience as the highest divine participation, and thus the duty of mutual tolerance as the most essential of social ideals.

It is high time for scholars, and for the cultivated public in general, to familiarize themselves with Servetus. Many of us are convinced that, besides his radical reformist ideas and his mostly outdated scientific perspectives, the theological questions he posed, and the Biblical exegesis he advanced, are still awaiting for the long overdue technical answers that the so-called Christian orthodoxy owes him. It would be too much to expect the acceptance of some of his proposals by established churches, an improbable dream that – if granted – would undoubtedly overrun the subjective certitudes and supposedly sure riverbanks of the ecclesiastical consciousness. One could guess that this truly understandable, hesitant and suspicious refusal by all churches to approach Servetus as a theologian and reformer of merit is not only the natural consequence of his condemnation by all of them since the middle of sixteenth century, but also springs from some subconscious, uneasy fear that, should they acquiesce to his convincing conclusions, they would evidently be forced to close shop – so to speak – recognizing the lack of Biblical and rational grounds for the development of post-Nicene Christianity as it has taken place in history.

Born in Villanueva de Sijena, a little town in the Northern province of Huesca, where his father was a royal notary for its powerful medieval monastery, young Michael became a page and private secretary to Juan de Quintana, a local cleric and theology doctor of the Sorbonne a member of the Council of Aragon who would soon become the confessor of Emperor Charles V, King Charles I of Spain. He traveled with the Court through the country for several years, thus being exposed to its main political problems: the rebellious *moriscos* in Granada, quasi Evangelical sects such as the *alumbrados* around Toledo, the Inquisitorial examination of Erasmianism in Valladolid. This first personal contact with forms of religious and theological expressions other than the traditional Catholicism of his upbringing must have opened his mind. After spending almost two years studying law at the University of Toulouse, France, he was called back to accompany Quintana to the pompous imperial coronation by the pope in Bologna, Italy, on February 23, 1530. Only one page of *Restitutio* [462] makes a short although moving statement of the tremendous spiritual impact of that ceremony on him, but its meaning changed his life and colored most of his writings with abhorrence of ecclesiastical shows and external manifestations of piety.

He probably witnessed the fruitless discussions and disagreements between Roman and Lutheran (Philip Melanchthon) representatives at the Imperial Diet at Augsburg that summer. His hopes of reconciliation frustrated, he abandoned the Court, as well as Catholicism, and looked for spiritual refuge elsewhere. He first tried to meet Erasmus in Freiburg, but he had just left. Then accepted the invitation of Oecolampadius to stay with him in Basel as a student-in-residence. The result was Michael's *Declarationis Iesu Christi Filii Dei libri V*, a manuscript (not of his hand) now kept in Stuttgart, recently transcribed, translated into Spanish, and edited in our bilingual collection of his *Obras completas*. A first development of that draft that appeared in Alsace next year, the *De Trinitatis erroribus*, scandalized the political and ecclesiastical circles of both sides of European Christianity. The Spanish and French Inquisitions, and the Lutheran movement as well, declared its young author, just twenty, worthy of death. Having changed his identity to Michel de Villeneuve, he studied in Paris (where he met John Calvin), practiced medicine, edited with important original notes of Ptolemy's *Geography* and the new translation of the Bible into Latin by

Sante Pagnino, published some medical tracts, and lived in Lyon and Vienne of France for twenty years.

His temporary work as an editor and his medical profession were only a parenthesis and an outward façade for his secretly consuming theological passion. While nicodemitically hiding his true beliefs and living under the roof of the bishop as his personal doctor, he was slowly developing *Declarationis* and *Erroribus* into a complex system that tried to make the Biblical wisdom, the scientific discoveries and the Renaissance currents of Neoplatonism converge into a revelation rationally admissible by all "religions of the Book," including Islamics and Jews. It was Calvin who notified the French Inquisition from Geneva of his real identity and *Restitutio* authorship. Jailed and tried in Vienne, he was able to escape, only to show up four months later precisely in Geneva, of all places, where they put him to death on October 27, 1553.

Although Servetus studies are abundant, most deal with his description of blood circulation that he presents in theological *Restitutio* [169] context as proof of the presence and influence of the spirit of God in our most recondite dwellings. Due to the almost total destruction of its copies by Calvin (only three have survived: in Paris, Edinburgh, and Vienna of Austria), Michael's name rarely appeared except in adverse works by Calvin, Luther, Melanchthon, and a few others, until Leibnitz read the circulation section and started to call attention to it and Servetus for his own merit. No previous biography is comparable to Allwoerden's (1727) and Mosheim's (1759), their errors and misunderstandings notwithstanding. A century later, it was especially Voltaire (1756), who – as Castellio had done before against Calvin, although largely unnoticed – criticized his death as the supreme example of authoritarian absolutism, thus contributing, at the onset of Enlightenment, to Michael's fame as the modern source of the doctrine of freedom of conscience. The door was now open to continuing research on details of his biography and his theological position within the various streams of the Reformation. This was the task of several nineteenth and twentieth century scholars; while the former was mostly worked out by Spaniards, from de Pano and Arribas Salaberri to Barón in 1970, neither religious liberty nor academic tradition favored their concentration on Servetian heterodox ideas, witness the surprising lack of understanding shown by one of the greatest Spanish historiographers, Menéndez Pelayo (1877). In the theological realm we all must be forever indebted to the efforts of men like Tollin and his nineteenth century predecessors and contemporaries (Harnack, Pünjer, Trechsel, Willis), and, in the twentieth century, Earl M. Wilbur (1945) and the remarkable influence of Professors Roland H. Bainton and George H. Williams. All of them have recognized Michael's originality as one of the numerous branches of the prolific tree of the Radical Reformation, the title of the latter's 1962 seminal work.

It can safely be said that the definitive impulse to make Servetism a respected field of theological and historical research came from *Hunted Heretic. The Life and Death of Michael Servetus, (1511-1553)* (Boston, The Beacon Press), the 1953 book by Bainton, the late Yale University Professor of Church History, and his many revolutionary preparatory studies. Reprinted in 1960 and 1972, it is like a vademecum for Servetians, but also, due to its clarity and brevity, inestimably practical for the public in general, a useful companion for *Restitutio* readers. It is now available in a new edition by Peter Hugues (Providence, RI.: Blackstone Editions, 2005). When, in 1971, I was introduced by a common friend, in Hyde Park, NY, to Prof. Bainton, an instant friendship erupted; both he and I – although certainly on quite a different scholarly level – were fond of those intrepid sixteenth century souls who did not hesitate to foster risky ideas nor to rebel against unjustified abuses of power. He asked me to translate into Spanish and edit *Hunted Heretic* (*Servet, el hereje perseguido*, Madrid: Tauros, 1973), and do the same with *Restitutio*, which he kindly reviewed, and, separately, with its appendices: *Thirty Letters to Calvin*, the short tract *On the Antichrist*, and *Apology to Melanchthon* (Madrid, 1980). Belated fruit of Bainton's leadership is the above mentioned bilingual edition of Servetus works in six volumes (Zaragoza, 2003-2006).

While Servetus scholarship in English has not been meager, only some of his scientific writings and *De Trinitatis erroribus* were translated decades ago (by Charles D. O'Malley in 1953 and Earl M. Wilbur in 1932, respectively). The consequent lack of accessibility to *Restitutio* has hampered Servetus studies to a great extent, because of the growing scarcity of scholars fluent in Latin. Nothing but joy and a justified sense of accomplishment can therefore greet the publication, due to the initiation of the translation by Professor Alicia McNary Forsey, followed by her insistent determination to see the project through to completion. The text is translated by Professors Christopher Hoffman and Marian Hillar, edited and copiously annotated by the latter. The author himself of two fascinating books on Servetus (1997 and 2002), a Polish-born biochemist paradoxically renown as Biblical, Patristical and Socinian scholar, philosopher, and linguist living in Houston.

It is to be hoped that, with this masterpiece in their language and in their hands, English speaking readers and scholars will be able to improve their preconceptions of Servetus as a man and as a thinker. Many Protestant and Catholic historians still tend to obliterate him as an amateurish, fanatical theologian bordering on madness, and his works, as Mosheim wrote, as an obscure and boring model of disorder. They might learn from the respectful and admiring assessment advanced in 1897 by Adolf Harnack in his fundamental *History of Dogma* (Part II, Bk. III, Chap. III): "The most important representative of this coalescence [of speculative thinking and mystical experience] was the Spanish thinker – distinguished also for his deeply pious spirit – Michael Servede [sic]. In him we see a union of the best of everything that came to maturity in the sixteenth century, if the Evangelical Reformation be left out of account [of course!]. Servede had equal distinction as an empirical researcher, a critical thinker, a speculative philosopher, and a Christian Reformer in the best sense of the term. It is a paradox of history that Spain, the country that was least affected in the sixteenth century by the ideas of the newer age, and in which at the earliest date Catholicism was restored, produced this unique man." Well, if we also leave "out of account" Harnack's typically outmoded idea of Spain's backwardness in that century, his final judgment on Michael as a "unique man" sounds truly promising.

Ángel Alcalá
Emeritus Professor
Brooklyn College,
City University of New York

Note from Translators

When Servetus was burned alive in Geneva on October 27, 1553, all unbound copies of his major work, *Christianismi restitutio,* went up in smoke together with him. Today only three surviving copies of the original publication are known: 1. one in the National Library of Austria in Vienna; 2. one in the Bibliothèque Nationale in Paris and this copy was most likely used by Germain Colladon, attorney acting on behalf of Nicolas de la Fontaine during Servetus' trial in Geneva; 3. and one copy in the library of the University of Edinburgh. The latter lacks the first sixteen pages and the title page. These were replaced by manuscript pages reproduced in the sixteenth century from another manuscript.

Restitutio was circulated after Servetus' death in the form of copied manuscripts. In 1790 the German erudite, a follower of Unitarianism, Dr. Christoph Gottlieb von Murr made a handwritten copy of the exemplar from the National Library in Vienna and published almost an exact replica of the original book in Nürnberg. There are about 53 exemplars of this publication in various libraries. The Murr reprint was reproduced in 1966 by a new photographic technique and serves today as the research tool for Servetian studies. A reprint of the selected fragments from the *Restitutio* concerning the kingdom of Christ, the kingdom of the Antichrist, pedobaptism and circumcision, was also published by Giorgio Biandrata in Transylvania in 1569. The first translation of a small tractate attached to the *Restitutio* and titled *Sixty signs of the Antichrist* was made by Grzegorz Paweł in Poland in 1568. The book was translated into German in three volumes by Bernhard Spiess from 1892 to 1896 and into Spanish by Ángel Alcalá in two separate volumes in 1980 and 1981. The new Spanish translation by the same scholar is being prepared as volumes 5 and 6 of the ambitious six-volume edition of *Obras completas* of Servetus. Except for a fragment of a few pages concerning the famous discovery of the pulmonary circulation, the book was never translated into English.

For the present translation, we used the Murr reprint though it was compared with an identical handwritten transcript of the exemplar located in the Bilbiothèque Nationale in Paris. Servetus' Latin is not very elaborate or ornate, but rather could be characterized as a "staccato" Latin since it is very technical. Servetus also sometimes creates new words derived from his native Spanish. In contrast to the translation done by Alcalá into an ornate and elaborate Spanish we decided not to embellish the Servetus style, but rather reproduce it as closely as possible.

Servetus also uses many quotes in Greek and Hebrew and they were not altered except that they were corrected in one or two places. We did not make any attempt to modify the Servetus biblical quotes aligning them with the standard biblical translations. In the notes, however, we reproduced biblical quotes from the New Revised Standard Version of 1989 and the quotes from the Qur'an according to the edition and translation by Abdullah Yusuf Ali. Biblical Hebrew quotes come form the standard masoretic text, and the Greek from the Nestle-Aland 27th edition. Sources of other Greek citations are indicated in the notes.

We express our thanks to Professor Ángel Alcalá for permission to use his notes for his Spanish translation. They were of great help though they were not followed slavishly.

We hope that this long overdue English translation of the major Servetus work will stimulate new studies on this fascinating scholar, reformer, and visionist. Servetus was a unique and central figure in European history who originated or anticipated many later new developments and trends produced by xxv

the Enlightenment and modern times. His memory should be kept alive not only because of his ideas but also as a symbol reminding us about the twisted ways that humanity pursues its destiny.

Christopher A. Hoffman
Professor of Classics
University of Maryland
Baltimore

Marian Hillar
Professor of Philosophy
and Religious Studies
Center for Socinian Studies
Houston

Michael Servetus

The Restoration of Christianity.

The whole Apostolic Church is summoned to return to its origin
to restore the complete knowledge of God, of the faith of Christ,
of our justification, of the regeneration by baptism
and of the participation in the lord's supper.
And finally to restore to us the heavenly kingdom,
to end the wicked captivity of Babylon,
and to destroy the Antichrist with his host.

בעת ההיא יעמוד מיכאל השר [2]

καὶ ἐγένετο πόλεμος ἐν τῷ οὐρανῷ [3]

M. D. LIII.

.

---

[2] Dan. 12:1. "At that time Michael, the great prince, shall rise."
[3] Rev. 12:7. "And war broke out in heaven."

[2]⁴ Table of Contents

---

⁴ Numbers in brackets indicate the pagination in the original edition of 1553.

[3] Treatise Concerning the Divine Trinity
in Seven Books

The divine Trinity is not a mirage
consisting of three invisible entities,
but is the true expression of God's substance
in the Word and its communication to mankind in the spirit

Procemium

The purpose toward which we aim is as sublime in its greatness as it is easy to understand and demonstrate with certainty. There is nothing greater, reader, than to recognize that God has been manifested as substance and that His divine nature has been truly communicated to mankind. It is in Christ alone that we shall fully apprehend the manifestation of God Himself through the Word and His communication to mankind through the spirit. Both of these have been substantiated in him alone with the result that the complete divinity of the Word and the spirit are recognized together in a human being.[1] We shall explain the divine manifestation throughout time, and the manner of this great mystery which transcends the debate over piety; for, as God was once in the Word, ultimately He was incarnated, and, having being communicated by the spirit, He was made visible to angels and humanity: a vision that once was hidden, but has now been revealed. We shall detail for you in a plain, yet factual, manner the ways by which God has revealed Himself to us, making Himself outwardly visible through the

Word, yet internally perceptible through the spirit.[2] Though He remains a great mystery in either case, He is yet such that humanity may see God Himself and possess Him. God was previously not visible, but now we shall see Him with His face unveiled, and, so long as we open the gate and step upon the road, we shall gaze upon Him as He shines in ourselves. It is time that we open that gate and this path of light. For without it nothing can be seen, without it none can read the holy scriptures [4] or perceive God or become a Christian. This is the path of truth. The path that is sure, easy, and free from deceit, the only one that makes completely accessible the divine origin of Christ in the Word and the true perfection of the holy spirit, and identifies both with God substantively.[3] It is the one that places God Himself before our very eyes.

Now we have arranged in five books this path in its entirety, with the addition of dialogues at the end, in order that we might aspire through certain steps, as it were, to a complete understanding of Christ. The first book contains three axioms concerning Christ, three arguments from the Pharisees, as many from the Sophists, and their critiques, along with some absolutely ridiculous notions that derive from admitting these invisible entities.[4] The second book will set out twenty passages from scripture. The third book will focus on the prefiguration of the person of Christ in the Word, the appearance of God, and the hypostasis of the Word. The fourth is about the names and essence of God, and the first principles of all things. The fifth is about the holy spirit. Afterwards there is the first dialogue which, after showing how the Law was fulfilled, will elucidate how Christ is the culmination of all things, explaining also the substance of angels, souls, and hell. The second dialogue will explain the manner of Christ's

---

[1] Servetus refers here not to the human being in general, but to the specific man, Jesus.
[2] Servetus formulates here right from the beginning his doctrine of the Trinity: God unknowable to man revealed Himself in two "modes" as a Word and as a spirit.
[3] In the Edinburgh manuscript the word *Scripturas* is replaced by the word *litteras* and the *nec Deum intelligere* is replaced by *nec Deum recognoscere*.
[4] *Cum absurdissimis invisibilium illationibus.* The term used in reference to the three Persons of the traditional Trinity is "entities" because Servetus is, using most frequently the term *res,* negating their reality in the traditional sense.

3

generation by arguing to the effect that he is not himself a creature nor something of limited power, but rather is truly worthy of praise and the true God.

O Christ Jesus, son of God, who was given to us from heaven, You make manifest the revealed divinity that has been made visible in You, open Yourself to Your servant that Your manifestation may be truly disclosed! Grant me now, as I ask, Your good spirit and effective word; direct my mind and pen so that I can describe the glory of Your divinity and express my true belief concerning You. This is my case on Your behalf, and it sets out Your glory from the Father and glory of Your spirit. By some divine impulse this case presented itself to me as a task to be undertaken because I am concerned with Your truth. At one time in the past I began to handle it, but now I am compelled to do it again because, based upon my sure conviction about the matter and the signs of the age which have manifested themselves, the time has truly come for me now to make a showing to all who are pious.[5] The light must not be hidden, You taught us, and therefore I must spread the good news or pay the price. A case of concern to all Christians is being pursued, and we are all involved in it. It remains for you, reader, to keep yourself open-minded on Christ's behalf all the way to the end; you shall hear the whole subject presented truly and without any embellishment.

---

[5] *Quia completum est vere tempus.* Servetus believed that the apocalyptic time for the second coming was to be fulfilled soon, some 1260 years after the reign of Emperor Constantine.

[5] Book One

Regarding Jesus Christ the Human Being
and His False Representations

I shall begin my first book by presenting the facts about the son of God, in the manner of the first declaration of the apostles. That is, in order that this journey of ours may have a smooth start, I shall begin with the better known sources, being those things which are obvious to everyone who meditates upon them and which have been publicly proclaimed to everyone. Jesus himself, the human being, is the gate and the path, from which I shall with good reason take my starting point since the case will be presented concerning him and in order that I may refute the Sophists, who, by making their approach towards an understanding of the Word without this sort of basis, are diverted towards some other son and thereby abandon the true son of God to oblivion.[6] I shall endeavor to restore to their memory who that true son was. Starting with the fact that the personal pronoun when taken in context shows that he was a human being who was wounded with blows and whipped, I will candidly accept the following three propositions as being true, in and of themselves: first, he is Jesus Christ; second, he is the son of God; third, he is God.

First Proposition

The first proposition, namely, that he was called Jesus, is obvious by itself. You could show no more certain fact than this: that name was given to him

---

[6] By the term "Sophists" Servetus understands the "Trinitarians" who traditionally assume the Word as the second Person of the Trinity, thus the Son of God. The Word is for Servetus a substantial mode of God's expression and not a Person really distinct from the Father. The essence of Christianity is for Servetus the paternity of God with respect to the human Jesus.

as a boy on the day of circumcision (Luke 1 and 2)[7] just as you were given the name of John and someone else the name of Peter. The name, Jesus, as the ancients make clear, is a proper name of a man; Christ, on the other hand, is a title. All the Jews conceded that he was Jesus, but, denied that he was Christ. They asked "who is called Christ," and they "ejected from the synagogue those who would confess that Jesus was Christ."[8] The apostles were involved in frequent controversies with them over this point of whether Jesus was the Messiah. But there was never any doubt or question as to who Jesus was, and no one ever denied it. Consider the point of the statement Paul made when he bore witness to the Jews that Jesus was the Messiah in Acts 9.27 and 18.[9] Consider with what a passionate spirit Apollos, the Alexandrian, refuted the Jews and proved that this Jesus was Christ.[10] These things were said about Jesus, the human being, without any sophistry. Think then not about the Sophists, but about those Jews; think about the fishermen and the women who accepted with plain innocence that Jesus was Christ: this Jesus of Nazareth, Jesus the son of David.[11]

Yet by conceding that this man was Jesus, we must concede that this man was Christ, truly anointed by God. "For he is your anointed son whom you anointed" (Acts 4). "He is the Holy of Holies whom Daniel predicted would have to be anointed" (Daniel 9).[12] Moreover, in Acts 10 Peter says, "It is something

---

[7] "And now, you will conceive in your womb and bear a son, and you will name him Jesus." Luke 1:31. "After eight days had passed, it was time to circumcise the child; and he was called Jesus, the name given by the angel before he was conceived in the womb," Luke 2:21.

[8] "His parents said this because they were afraid of the Jews; for the Jews had already agreed that anyone who confessed Jesus to be the Messiah would be put out of the synagogue," John 9:22. "Nevertheless many, even of the authorities, believed in him. But because of the Pharisees they did not confess it, for fear that they would be put out of the synagogue, John 12:42. "They will put you out of the synagogues," John 16:2.

[9] Acts 9:22 and not Acts 9:27: "Saul became increasingly more powerful and confounded the Jews who lived in Damascus by proving that Jesus was the Messiah." "When Silas and Timothy arrived from Macedonia, Paul was occupied with proclaiming the word, testifying to the Jews that the Messiah was Jesus," Acts 18:5.

[10] Acts 18:25.

[11] Servetus emphasizes the simplicity of the original faith which is contrasted with the elaborate sophistry of orthodox Christianity.

[12] Acts 4:27. "Seventy weeks are decreed for your people and your holy city: ... to seal both vision and prophet, and to anoint a most holy place. Know therefore and understand: from the time that the word went out to restore and rebuild Jerusalem until the time of an anointed prince, there shall

manifest to practically everyone, you yourselves know,"[13] since it was publicly known about Jesus "how God anointed Jesus, the man from Nazareth, with the holy spirit and with power, for God was with him, and that he is the one whom God ordained as the judge of the living and the dead."[14] And in Acts 2 he said, "Let the entire house of Israel know with certainty that God has made him both Lord and Messiah, this Jesus whom you crucified,"[15] which means the anointed one.

Clement, Justin, Irenaeus, Tertullian, and all the other early authorities, asserted that this expression, "Christ," was a word that referred to human nature.[16] Similarly the connotation of the word itself indicates the same thing. For to be anointed makes no sense unless it concerns human nature. So who will deny that

be seven weeks ... After the sixty-two weeks, an anointed one shall be cut off and shall have nothing..." Daniel 9:24-26.

[13] Reference to Acts 10:36-37.

[14] Acts 10:37-42.

[15] Acts 2:36

[16] Clement of Rome, bishop of Rome (92-101) according to Eusebius (*Historia ecclesiastica* III.15.45). To his authorship were ascribed a series of Greek literary writings dealing with his life and classified as Pseudo-Clementines. Clement comes from an aristocratic Roman family. His mother leaves the city secretly with his two older brothers, directed by a vision. Then the father goes in search of her. Young Clement in the meantime busies himself with religious problems and not finding satisfaction proceeds on a journey hearing of the appearance of the son of God in Judaea. There he meets Peter and both go on a missionary journey. In the end the Clement family is reunited and the members recognize each other (hence the title *Recognitiones, Recognitions*). The purpose of the romantic story is to communicate the Christian doctrine. Also, to the romance were attached the letter of Peter to James (*Epistula Petri*), the Testimony of James Regarding the Letter (*Contestatio*) followed by the letter of Clement to James. The last one reports on Clement's ordination by Peter as bishop of Rome. In *Recognitions*, bk I. cap. 45, Clement explains the meaning of the words "messiah" and "christ" as the "anointed." He states that just as Arsaces (founder of the Parthian empire in 250 B.C.E.), the Caesars in Rome, and Pharaohs in Egypt, so among the Jews their kings were called "christs" because they were anointed by God "with the oil from the tree of life" (PG I.1233). Justin Martyr was a second century apologist (ca 100-165), who founded a catechetical school in Rome. In his *Second Apology* for the Christians, chap. 6, wrote: "But His [God's] Son, who is alone properly called Son, the logos who is with God and is begotten before the creation, ... is called Christ, with reference to His being anointed ... this name in itself ... is not a name, but an intuition implanted in human nature." St Justin Martyr, *The First and Second Apologies*, translated with introduction and notes by Leslie William Barnard (New York/Mahwah, N.J.: Paulist Press, 1997; PG VI.92). Irenaeus (ca 120-ca 202), bishop of Lyon, *Adv. Haereses*, lib. III, cap. 22, 1 (PG VII,219). Tertullian (ca 170-220), a teacher of rhetoric in Carthage, *Liber de bautismo adversus Quintilliam*, cap. VIII, (PL I., 1207); *Adv. Marcionem*, cap. XV: "The name of Christ does not derive from nature, but from the disposition" (PL II, 341). Servetus took the term "disposition" from Tertullian and applied it to the Word and the spirit; similarly, the term "christ-anointed" is a function of man.

8

it was a human being that was anointed? He who denies that this Jesus was Christ, is an Antichrist, but whoever accepts this, that he was anointed, is born of God (1 John 2 and 5).[17] In the first book of Clement's *Recognitions*, Peter explains that it was with this connotation in mind that kings were apt to be called christs. On that basis, because of the loftiness of his unction, he was called beyond all others Christ, the king. Just as God made one angel foremost among angels, one beast foremost among beasts, and one star foremost among stars, so He made one human being foremost among humanity and Christ. The authority of the Old Testament as well tells us quite simply that a human being is called Christ because even a worldly king is called christ (1 Sam. 12 and 24; Isa. 45).[18] We find the same thing in Matthew 1: ["and Jacob the father of Joseph the husband of Mary,] of whom Jesus was born, who is called the Messiah."[19] Take note that of the definite article combined with the name. He is a human being who was born from the holy spirit. Luke 3, plainly describes Christ, the human being, by saying "Jesus was about thirty years old when he began his work. He was the son, as was thought, of Joseph."[20] That very person "being, as was supposed, the son of Joseph" was Jesus Christ, the son of God. Also in Acts 13 Paul says to the Jews: "Of David's seed has God according to His promise sent Christ, this man who was killed by you."[21] Again in the same chapter and in John 2, John the Baptist said, "Do not think that I am Christ."[22] Would not John's denial have been utterly

---

[17] "Who is the liar but the one who denies that Jesus is the Christ? This is the antichrist, the one who denies the Father and the Son. No one who denies the Son has the Father; everyone who confesses the Son has the Father also" (1 John 2:22-23). "Everyone who believes that Jesus is the Christ has been born of God, and everyone who loves the parent loves the child" (1 John 5:1).

[18] In reference to Saul, "Here I am; testify against me before the LORD and before his anointed" (1 Sam. 12:3). "He said to them, 'The LORD is witness against you, and his anointed is witness this day, that you have not found anything in my hand'" (1 Sam. 12:5). "He said to his men, 'The LORD forbid that I should do this thing to my lord, the LORD's anointed, to raise my hand against him; for he is the LORD's anointed.'" (1 Sam. 24:6). In reference to Cyrus, "Thus says the LORD to his anointed, to Cyrus" (Is. 45:1).

[19] Matt. 1:16.

[20] Luke 3:23.

[21] Acts 13:23. The quote is not exact.

[22] John 1:20 and not John 2 according to Servetus. "What do you suppose that I am? I am not he. No, but one who is coming after me;" (Acts 13:25).

ridiculous if the term Christ did not apply to a human being? In Matthew 16, when Christ asked, "Whom do people say I am?" and Peter answered, "You are the Christ, the son of the living God," Christ's question and Peter's response would otherwise have been pointless.[23] The very one whom some thought was Elias and others Jeremiah, Peter said was Christ, the son of God. He did not say, "The son is made flesh in you," but "You are the son."

Given that Christ then directed them not to tell anyone that he was "Christ," what do you suppose he meant by this name? If he himself is not Christ, how does he make us christs? There would not be any need for Christ to dwell very long on so obvious a point if the minds of some were not deceived. In their failure to comprehend the mystery of the incarnation, they reckoned that Christ was an incorporeal being and as such a true Son, whereas in every age mere human beings had always been called christs. Hear the testimony of Christ himself as he calls himself a human being, "You are trying to kill me, a man who told you the truth" (John 8). Similarly 1 Timothy 2 refers to the "mediator between God and humankind, Christ Jesus, himself human."[24] If, however, that expression, "human being," offends you because the Sophists have tainted its connotations with their use of it, then use the word "man." Listen to Peter speaking in Acts 2: "Jesus of Nazareth, a man attested to you by God." We find this too in the last chapter of Luke, "The things about Jesus of Nazareth, who was a prophet mighty in deed and word".[25] And in John 2 "the one who is coming after me." In Isaiah 53 we read: "He was despised and rejected by others; a man of suffering." Zechariah 6 has: "Here is a man whose name is Branch." Acts 17: "He [God] will have the world judged ... by a man whom he has appointed" obviously referring to Christ.[26] If you have common sense, reader, and trust in the nature of the demonstrative pronoun, you will recognize manifestly that this is the true and original meaning of that expression. For just as this could be clearly seen,

---

[23] Matt. 16:15-16.
[24] John 8:40; 1 Tim. 2:5.
[25] Acts 2:22; Luke 24:19.
[26] John 1:27 and not John 2 as Servetus wants. Isaiah 53:3; Zechariah 6:12; Acts 17:31.

10

so it was pointed to him here and there "this man is Christ" or "you are Jesus."
Moreover, it is also conceded because he speaks, asks, answers, and eats, and
because they saw him walking on the waters. "Whom do you seek? Jesus of
Nazareth. I am he." "Whomsoever I kiss, that's him, detain him." "I am in person:
touch me and look at me."[27]

In Acts 2 when Peter is addressing the Jews, he says, "This Jesus whom
you killed God raised up, and of that all of us are witnesses."[28] To what would
you be referring with these pronouns in your debate with the Jews, if not the
humanity of Christ? Among them not a thing was ever heard about either the
Trinity or the invisible Son.[29] Are we of a lower order than the Samaritan woman?
In John 4 she said, "Come and see a man who told me everything I have ever
done! He cannot be the Messiah [Christ], can he?" And he himself then confirmed
the woman's understanding, though she knew nothing about incorporeal entities.
For, when she was seeking for the Messiah to come, who was called Christ, he
answered, "I am he, the one who is speaking to you." [30] He said "I am" and "the
one you see speaking;" He made no reference to some thing incorporeal; he
simply said, "I who speak, am the true and natural son of God." The blind man
who was cured held a similar belief concerning Jesus when he said in John 9:
""The man called Jesus made mud."[31] Because he had this belief about Christ he
recovered his sight; he did not have a false belief about Christ. The apostle's
statement: "Just as it was by the sin of one human being, so it is through the grace
of one human being, Jesus Christ, and just as death came through one human
being, so the resurrection of the dead comes through a human being,"[32] must be
understood as referring to a human being. Either he is speaking about a human
being in the absolute sense in both sentences or he is speaking in a connotative

---

[27] John 18:7-8. Mark 14:44. Matt. 26:48. Modified Luke 24:39.
[28] Modified Acts 2:23 and 32.
[29] This argument of Servetus is based on the simplicity of understanding of the Jews to whom
Jesus spoke. They never interpreted the son of God or Christ in the trinitarian orthodox sense.
[30] John 4:29, 26.
[31] John 9:11. The whole text is: "The man called Jesus made mud, spread it on my eyes, and said
to me, 'Go to Siloam and wash.' Then I went and washed and received my sight."

sense: otherwise there is no analogy. The first Adam and the second Adam are referred to there. Thus it is of no use for the Sophists to understand the term human being in a connotative way. Finally, according to John 20 he made signs in order for us to believe "that Jesus is Christ, the son of God."[33] The matter concerning Jesus has been made plain, and this has been done in order for us to believe that Jesus was born from God and anointed for our salvation. Nathaniel deduced that he was the son of God because Jesus told him: "I saw you under the fig tree." Similar inference is made in Matthew 14 based on the fact that he calmed the wind.[34]

Second Proposition

[9] Those inferences already make abundantly clear the second point that I had accepted as fact, namely, that this man whom I call Christ is the son of God. For it is based on the signs he made that it is inferred that this very man was the son of God. If it is established that this man is Jesus Christ, it is also established that the same man is the son of God since scripture consistently teaches that Jesus Christ is the son of God. Thus it asserts that God the father of Jesus Christ is God the Father of this human being. This human being is everywhere and openly shown to be the son of God, and with respect to him God is shown to be truly the father. He is truly the father because Jesus was born in substance from Him just as you are born from your own father. It was not by Joseph that Christ was fathered, but instead he was generated by the holy spirit from the substance of God. This Jesus was truly and naturally born of God without any sort of philosophical sophistication. In the following pages we shall explain in depth the manner of his generation.[35] For the time being we say simply in passing that the Word of God enveloped the virgin like a cloud. Like fertilizing dew, it settled on her like the

---

[32] This is not a literal quote but a contraction of several sentences in Rom. 5:12-19.

[33] John 20:31.

[34] Allusions to John 1:48 and Matt. 14:33.

[35] In Edinburgh manuscript the expression *corpus hoc* is used instead of *hic Iesus*. The manner of divine filiation of Jesus the man constitutes one of the most important points of Servetus's doctrine which can be summarized in these terms: *vere pater, quia ab eo est substantialiter genitus, sicut tu a patre tuo ... , vere et naturaliter genitus.*

rain that makes the earth germinate the seed (Ps. 71; Isa. 45 and 55).[36] It is on this basis, according to Matthew and Luke, cap. 1, that he is called the son. In Luke 1:35 the angel said to Mary, "The holy spirit shall come upon you, and the power of the Most High shall overshadow you." And he continues: "Therefore also that your holy offspring shall be called the son of God." Matthew provides the same line when he says that she was made pregnant by the holy spirit and that "what was conceived in her was from the holy spirit."[37] What was conceived in her was a son and Matthew was speaking simply, not philosophically. Jesus was born from Mary and was a son from Mary's substance. If Mary is the natural mother, she is herself the mother of her natural son, whoever he may be. Take note of what Luke says: "And now, you will conceive in your womb and bear a son, and you will name him Jesus. He will be great, and will be called the son of the Most High, and the Lord God will give to him the throne of his ancestor David."[38] Why did he not say, "He shall be called the son of the first person and the first person shall give unto him the throne" rather than "the son of the Most High" and "God shall give unto him the throne?" Or why did he not say that "the second entity, the incorporeal one, was generated by the holy spirit?" Is it not true that "what has been truly generated by the holy spirit is truly the son?" It is of no avail that a great many who twist the words of the angel, manipulate the expression "holy" so that may refer to a different son similar to Christ, [10] the first born, as if he were not worthy of it. This is all the more curious since in the very next chapter Luke makes quite clear why he had said "holy:" because he was a "male

---

[36] Servetus interprets literally the words of Luke (1:35) "the power of the Most High will overshadow you" which are suggested by Psalm 71:6: "May he be like rain that falls on the mown grass, like showers that water the earth." But it refers to the justice of King Solomon. In Isaiah 45:8: "Shower, O heavens, from above, and let the skies rain down righteousness; let the earth open, that salvation may spring up, and let it cause righteousness to sprout up also;" and in Isaiah 55:10-11: "For as the rain and the snow come down from heaven ..., so shall my word be that goes out from my mouth; it shall not return to me empty, but it shall accomplish that which I purpose, and succeed in the thing for which I sent it." The rain or the dew are used here as metaphor for the natural generation.
[37] Matt. 1:18, 20.
[38] Luke 1:31-32.

that opens the womb."[39] Moreover, every male creature that opens womb shall be called "holy" to the Lord according to Exodus 13 and 34, and Numbers 8.[40] As to the "power" or "strength" of the Most High which overshadowed Mary at the descent of the spirit, the trinitarians want it to be the metaphysical, invisible Son because the spirit and the "power" and the spirit and the "strength" are mentioned there in conjunction with each other. To this we say that by using the nouns "power" and "strength" Luke meant the same thing that he meant in Chapter 24 and in Acts 1 where he used the same words, saying, "You will receive power when the holy spirit has come upon you."[41] Luke likewise spoke with the same meaning when he said that John would come with "the spirit and power of Elijah," and in this too "he would be more than a prophet."[42] The other prophets did not have the power to make miracles in addition to the spirit of prophecy as Elijah did. It is for this reason that the spirit is said to be in him together with the power or perhaps the spirit together with the strength.

Just as Elijah, John had this power from his conception: the power of reaching him whom he had foretold and the power of turning the impious towards his God through the use of miracle. Just as the fact that when the waters had been poured upon the altar and fire came down from heaven at Elijah's call is seen as evidence of the truth in 3 Kings 18, so the fact that the holy spirit miraculously came down from heaven at John's baptism in water is seen as evidence of the truth of Christ (Matt. and Luke 3).[43] The joining of the power and the spirit signifies a particular strength rather than other metaphysical things. The difference between the spirit and the power lies in the fact that there is not in any given spirit an equal power or an equal strength. This is precisely the two-fold nature of the spirit of Elijah's which was sought by Elisha; namely, it is the spirit

---

[39] Luke 2:23. Not exact wording. .

[40] Exod. 13:12, 34:19; Num. 8:17.

[41] Acts 1:8; Luke 24:49.

[42] The phrase is "he is Elijah who is to come" not in Luke but in Matt. 11:14. This phrase refers to the myth about the return of Elijah reported in Mal. 4:5 and later in Matt. 17:11 and in Mark 9:12. "More than a prophet" and the whole situation is described in Matt. 11:7-19; Luke 7:24-35.

of prophecy and the power of miracles.[44] It is for the same reason that the apostles received the holy spirit and the power or the holy spirit and the strength in order that, inspired in this way, they might through the great force and power of miracles give witness to the resurrection of Christ (Acts 1 and 4).[45] This connection adds something when it is sometimes said: "with the holy spirit and fire." The addition of fire gives the force and zealousness to purify.

In Acts cap. 6 men are selected "full of the holy spirit and wisdom," and who, besides the shared gift of the spirit, would possess a wisdom suitable for their mission.[46] Based on this it is quite obvious why [11] Luke said that the holy spirit and the power were in Christ and the apostles. This point is made clearer by the fact that Luke himself also said that "God anointed Jesus of Nazareth with the holy spirit and with power," meaning with the holy spirit and the strength (Acts 10).[47] In this case the union does not mean that one may take metaphysically power for the incorporeal son, but rather that the spirit of Christ had all the strength. Consider, in addition, the fact that Luke did not say that the power was called the son. But the child that was conceived in Mary by the power of God will thus be called the son of God because Mary did not yet know a man. She was made pregnant through God's power when He overshadowed her and supplanted the seed of a man.[48] For that reason she herself is said to have been made pregnant by the holy spirit, and Christ himself, is said to have been conceived, sent, and anointed by the holy spirit (Isa. 48 and 61, and Matt. 1).[49] There is no mention

---

[43] In 1 Kings 18:38 the fire of God descended and consumed the offering. In Matt. 3:16 and Luke 3:22 "the Holy Spirit descended ... in bodily form like a dove."
[44] In 2 Kings 2:9, just before the disappearance of Elijah, Elisha is asking: "Please let me inherit a double share of your spirit."
[45] Acts 1:8, 22 and 4:31-33.
[46] Acts 6:3.
[47] Acts 10:38.
[48] Servetus excludes here the divine filiation of the second Person of the Trinity and exposes the natural divine filiation of Jesus as a human being.
[49] "And now the Lord GOD has sent me and his spirit" (Isa. 48:16); "The spirit of the Lord GOD is upon me, because the LORD has anointed me" (Isa. 61:1). Servetus applies these texts to Jesus Christ in view of Matt. 1:20. Servetus did not accept the existence of true prophecies in the Old Testament, only the existence of types or figures of persons and facts. He considers that they were fully realized in the person of Jesus. Thus the words expressed in the Old Testament historically

that the second entity was conceived by the third. Instead it is said that he himself, who was born from Mary through the holy spirit, is the son. That is how Irenæus understood this passage at the beginning of his fifth book, where he says that the son of the highest God was generated out of Mary. Augustine, who was similarly convinced, explains in his 99th *Tractate on John*, that it was the very power of God that acted as the holy spirit in the conception of Christ.[50]

The meaning of the word itself tells us that beyond being a human being, he was rightly also a son. For just as the act of anointing is appropriate to a human being, so being born and being conceived are also appropriate. That happened by the very power of the spirit; nevertheless, the body itself was truly born and truly conceived: the body that truly shares in the substance of God.[51] Who is that man "who was considered Joseph's son"? Who is the "fruit of the womb"? Or is not that fruit the son in substance? Who is that masculine issue that "opens the womb"? Or is not that male actually a son? Who is that little boy of whom mention is made in Matthew 2 and where Joseph took him up, brought him away, and brought him back home?[52] Is that one there not the son who was called out of Egypt? That little boy, that physical son, you will find, had no other father but God, no other sire, but God. Otherwise you will say that he is an illusion and not flesh. Yet if he is flesh, then he was produced by someone. Therefore, he is the son of some father. This is all the more so given the fact that God is called "the Father of this flesh" and "the Father of this bread" in John 6. [12] In John 15 God the farmer is called "the Father of his vine."[53] If then he is truly the son of God in the flesh, and there is some other real, though invisible Son, who is not in the

---

applied to Cyrus who was the figure of Jesus. These views were expressed by Servetus in the prologue to the Latin translation of the Bible by Santes Pagnini which was edited by Servetus in 1542.
[50] Irenaeus, *Adv. haereses*, lib. V, cap. 1, 2 (PG VII, 293). Augustine, *Tract. 99 super Ioannem*: PL XXXV, 1889.
[51] This statement is an example of the philological precision with which Servetus is using the terminology. What remains at the margin of the proper meaning of the term can be said only in the analogical or metaphorical sense. Thus only in the metaphorical sense one could say that the Word is the son of God, thus denying the reality of the second Person of the Trinity.
[52] Matt. 2:14-15.
[53] John 6:27, 48, 51; 15:1.

flesh, there are then two actual sons, no matter how you combine them into one heap: two sons were conceived, two were born.

We concede for the moment that the two births of the two sons are real. Therefore, we simply cannot deny that two real sons were conceived and born. Who would create such differences between the sons, who were thus conceived and born, unless he were bewitched? The holy scripture talks about Jesus, the only son of God. It does not say anything else about a son who was materially conceived by a human being. It is on this basis that all Christians ought to recognize that this Jesus of Nazareth is the son of God.

Christ himself openly declared to women and simple folk that he was the Messiah and the son of God. Come now, based on his straightforward declaration, what sort of Messiah ought a simple woman then to have pictured in her mind? All the more so, because the metaphysical inventions of our trinitarians were unknown in the Law. This other metaphysical and invisible Son was invented afterwards due to misunderstood interpretation of the text of John as I shall now demonstrate with all the evidence.[54] In John's day the belief in the son was different than it is now. This can be seen from a well known example. God said to John: "He on whom you see the spirit descend and remain, this very man is my son." "And I myself have seen," he said, and "have testified that this is the son of God" (John 1).[55] First take notice that John was ignorant throughout as to who was the son of God. Then take notice of his appearance and the other things that then came to pass. John would have been deceived by the opinion of the Sophists and with it he would have deceived others if he said that he whom he had merely seen, was the son of God. Instead, he said, "I myself did not know him." Once having received the sign from beyond, however, he said "this is the son of God and it has been clearly shown to me. Let me show all the Jews that he is truly the

---

[54] Not only the concept of the second Person or the Word as the Son of God is due to the misunderstood interpretation of the concept of *logos* of the fourth Gospel, but also the origin of this Gospel is due to a polemic with the group of Ebionites. The sixteenth century Unitarians, following Fausto Sozzini, developed their own version of interpretation.

[55] The word of John the Baptist. John 1:33-34.

son of God, by saying, 'behold the lamb, behold the son.'" Whom will you present to me as this lamb? This man, whom you see, is the lamb of God, the son of God. This man who can be seen with eyes, touched with hands, and perceived with all the other senses. Otherwise the heavenly voice would have been misleading since it had said "upon whom you see the spirit settle, this man is that one." It would have been misleading when it came down and said regarding what was present before the people, "this is my son" or "you are my son." Now, if it was pointing out some other hidden [13] entity with that expression, there was no clear testimony, and it was misleading the people. Likewise in John 9 when asked who was the son of God, by a certain man Jesus answered, "You have seen him, and the one speaking with you is he."[56] The very man you see is the son of God. Seeing the evidence before his own eyes a centurion said, "Truly this man was the son of God!"[57] Reckon that the evidence perceived by the senses has been reflected by those expressions. Next consider that the centurion was not a sophist, did not speak through sharing of idioms, neither did he use the word "man" in a connotative sense.[58] The centurion showed that he was a genuine human being when he said "this man was the son of God." Hear Paul, who as soon as he received his vision, entered a synagogue and preached about Jesus, since he was the son of God (Acts 9).[59] As to the locutions of the Sophists, not a word! The high priest gave no thought to that second entity made incorporeal when he said,

---

[56] John 9:37, Jesus talking to the blind.

[57] Matt. 27:54; Mark 15:39.

[58] It means in the implied, figurative, or indirect way. The expression *"communicatio idiomatum"* was introduced on the basis of the Council of Ephesus in 431 which treated the doctrine of Nestorius and was used in the Christological debates which originated from this Council and later was systematized by John of Damascus (676-ca 760), the last of the Greek church fathers and author of the work *Fountain of Wisdom* (*pēgē gnōseōs*), and by scholastics. This is a technical term which represents a certain theological method through which, due to the unity of person but duality of natures of Jesus, divine and human, the attributes of one nature, in principle exclusive, can be predicated of the other one. Thus one could say that God was born, walked, died, and was resurrected; similarly Jesus is the son of God; Mary is the mother of God, etc. Servetus interprets the terms in their philological acceptation; thus he understands the biblical text in its literal sense and rejects the "connotative sense" and the "communication or sharing of idioms" as simple sophisms. The word "idiom" comes from the Greek ἰδίωμα which means peculiarity, specific property, unique feature, characteristic.

[59] Acts 9:20.

"Are you the son of the blessed God?" And Jesus responded to his point, "I am" (Mark 14). "You say that I am the son of God" (Luke 22). Thus in their simple faith they said, "I believe that you are the son of God."[60]

You will say that it seems no great matter if Jesus, the human being, was himself called the son of God when even we are named sons of God. "It is of the greatest importance that he is the son of God," is my response. And I will demonstrate that more implications follow from that point which the world was ever able to understand. He is the true and natural son while we are adoptive ones. The fact that we are named sons of God proves that he himself was the true son. How would he make humans into sons if he, himself a human being, were not a true son? We are called sons by his gift and by his grace. Thus he is responsible for our adoption and is called "son" in a different, more sublime way. He is a natural son since he was born from the true substance of God. Others are not sons from the beginning. They are made sons of God, but are not born sons of God. By our belief in Jesus Christ we are made sons of God (Gal. 3 and John 1). Thus we are called sons by virtue of adoption (Rom. 8 and Eph. 1). He is not simply called a son, but rather a true son; he is not an ordinary son (Wis. 2 and Rom. 8).[61]

With equal justification is God called the father of Jesus Christ, just as earthly fathers are called the fathers of their own children. Otherwise God could not be called the cause— one that is uniquely effective and productive of a given and sure result. If God should choose individually for Himself some progeny, and by Himself work as much as possible and more than an earthly father can towards the birth of that progeny [14] by giving it even His own substance, why would He not with total justification deserve to be called the Father? "Shall I who give the

---

[60] Mark 14:61-62; Luke 22:70; Peter in Matt. 14:33 and 16:16; John 6:69.

[61] "In Christ Jesus you are all children of God through faith," Gal. 3:26; "But to all who received him, who believed in his name, he gave power to become children of God," John 1:12;   "You have received a spirit of adoption. When we cry, 'Abba! Father!' it is that very Spirit bearing witness with our spirit that we are children of God," Rom. 8:15; "He destined us for adoption as his children through Jesus Christ, according to the good pleasure of his will," Eph. 1:5; " He professes to have knowledge of God, and calls himself a child of the Lord," Wis. 2:13; " We are children of God, and if children, then heirs, heirs of God and joint heirs with Christ," "He who did not withhold his own Son, but gave him up for all of us," Rom. 8:17, 32.

power of procreation to others be sterile," said the Lord (Isa. 66).[62] Nay rather He is called the Father because "it is by Him that all fatherhood in heaven and on earth is named" (Eph. 3).[63] It is all the more reasonable because He not only fathered him, but He also adorned him with the substance, light, and fullness of His divinity so that in this respect the son would be likened unto the Father. Likewise by a different line of argument He is more fittingly called a Father than are human beings, because He is at work in the procreation of others, while humans have nothing to do with the birth of His own son. Therefore, if He is properly called the Father, Christ should be called the son in the sense much more proper than the others. We shall discuss other, more sublime issues concerning this filiation later on, if it is right to call this relationship "filiation."

The argument thus can be brought back to our main point as follows. The son of God shares his own relationship with us, while the relationship of that second entity has nothing whatsoever to do with us for ours is a relationship with mankind. But he calls us brothers because he is a human being. As a human being, he is "the first born of his brothers," just as he is "the first born of the dead."[64] Thus he is the first born human being, and having been born a human being, he is a son.

The Sophists think themselves so magnificent that they do not deign to direct their gaze to this son. They think the whole idea that a mere human being could be called the son of God a ridiculous and simplistic notion. They say that in order to be a son one should belong to the same special kind with the father. From where do they get this? It is absolutely impossible since parents are of divergent

---

[62] Isa. 66:9. Though the biblical text refers to the birth of the new nation of Israel, Servetus amplifies the meaning of it and uses it in a general sense.

[63] Eph. 3:15.

[64] "Nam quos praescivit et praedestinavit conformes fieri imaginis Filii eius ut sit ipse primogenitus in multis fratribus," Rom. 8 :29 ; "qui est imago Dei invisibilis primogenitus omnis creaturae," Col. 1 :15 ; "qui est principium primogenitus ex mortuis ut sit in omnibus ipse primatum tenens," Col. 1:18; "qui est testis fidelis primogenitus mortuorum et princeps regum terrae," Rev. 1:5.

natures.[65] Even the whole of scripture disproves this; Christ himself disproves it, since he showed that he was the son of God by analogy to other people. In John 10 he said, "If Scripture calls other people Gods and sons of God, you say that I blaspheme because I have said that I am the son of God because the Father has sanctified me beyond my other allies and comrades."[66] Behold he who was sanctified is the son of God. This is he who is called the holy son of God. This is he of whom the apostles said, "your holy son, Jesus."[67] Who is that holy man if not the male who opens the womb, the true and corporeal son of God?

Third Proposition

As my third proposition, I said that it was a fact that Christ is God. He is truly called God. He is called God in substance "because divinity is in him made flesh."[68] Because these matters will be completely explored in the following pages, suffice it to say for now [15] that he is called God because he is the form of God, the appearance of God, and he has the power and nature of God. He is called God by his nature just as a human being is called a human being by virtue of his flesh. The very power of divinity was given to him by the Father, and he himself is called mighty God (Isa. 9): "A child was born for us, and he will be called Mighty God."[69] Here the name and strength of God have been bestowed upon the new-born child and "He has been given all the power in heaven and on earth."[70] Likewise, in Isaiah 45 we find, "I am the Lord calling your name, God of

---

[65] This is a somewhat obscure statement unless Servetus refers here to the fact that parents belong to different sexes or species, a fact which, however, does not prevent them to be the parents of one and the same son. Thus according to Servetus there is no need that there should be the same species (or kind) between God and his son, the man Jesus.

[66] "Is it not written in your law, 'I said, you are gods'? If those to whom the word of God came were called 'gods' – and the scripture cannot be annulled – can you say that the one whom the Father has sanctified and sent into the world is blaspheming because I said, 'I am God's Son'? John 10:34-36 in reference to Ps. 82:6.

[67] This expression is not found as the expression of the apostles.

[68] Col. 2:9: "For in him the whole fullness of deity dwells bodily."

[69] Isa. 9:6.

[70] Servetus knew that Isaiah was talking about Hezekiah, but he considered him a prefiguration of Christ. The last words are from Matt. 28:18.

Israel."[71] In John 20, Thomas calls upon him by saying, "my Lord, my God." In Romans 9 Paul writes that Christ is in all things, and above all things he is called God worthy of praise, God who is blessed and worthy of blessing. His divinity is shown in many other passages, because he was exalted in order to receive divinity and a "name surpassing every name."[72]

But his adversaries look down upon him such that they say not only that he was not God, but that he was not even anointed. Indeed, they take from him the very things which are proper of his nature, and they deny that he was the son of Mary, that he was a human being, and they even deny his own humanity. They deny that he, a human being, was a human and they take for granted that God was an ass. Are they not true Antichrists and slanderers of Christ? Can there be any greater slander than for you to say that I do not exist while I am speaking or for you to say that the very attributes which are granted openly to me do not belong to me? These are all the qualities which the slanderers want to assign to the second entity of the Trinity. In order to confirm this absurd, the scholastic school has invented this sophism of "communication of idioms." They have added a certain new imposition to the expression, "human being," to wit: that it is to be understood metaphorically and is to have a force of meaning equivalent to the phrase, "something that maintains a human nature." Thus by virtue of this expression "communication of idioms" they concede the proposition "the son of God is a human being" as equivalent to the other proposition that "the second Person of the Trinity maintains human nature" and in this way this second Person is a human being in a connotative sense. By the same logic they concede that God could be an ass and that the holy spirit could be a mule, maintaining a mule's essence. Consider, reader, if Christ or his disciple, Paul, or any other of his disciples returned to preach again, could they tolerate such human conceits or would they declare that these forced expressions were satisfactory? Or rather, do

---

[71] The correct quote in Isaiah 45:3 is: "so that you may know that it is I, the LORD, the God of Israel, who call you by your name."
[72] John 20:28; other passages Rom. 9:5: *"Christus secundum carnem qui est super omnia Deus benedictus in saecula amen."* The last quote is from Philip. 2:9.

they not make Christ a master sophist when they say that the name, Christ, was applied by the prophets and apostles in order to signify the second Person in the divinity implying the fact that it maintains the [16] human nature? But is this meaning being invoked in those instances where we find the word, Christ, or in those instances where we see the expression "anointed?" Or will they refer strictly to that entity which was actually anointed and understand that it received the holy spirit and the power? Or would this entity say that all those things were bestowed upon it by its own Father? Or would the Father have been speaking sophistically about that entity when He said, "Behold my son, whom I chose, my beloved, I shall put my spirit upon him?" You will find that that expression obviously pertained to Jesus the human being (Matt. 12).[73] Whatever in any given passage in the Bible has been written about the son refers to him; everything refers to him and through him everything is fulfilled.

But precisely what is the nature of this "communication" of attributes? After all, the statement, "maintaining human nature," was never before applied to a human being. So just how does a human being impart his own attributes to God if they are not his own? We shall conclusively show that this was the situation with Christ and that his was a double nature, being both divine and human.[74] It is in Christ that God and the human are truly joined together in one substance, one body, and one, new human being (Eph. 2).[75] Because this divine nature of Christ depends on the subtleties of the word, we shall now say more simply that God can impart the fullness of his divinity to a human being and that He can give him His divinity, His grandeur, His power, and His glory. "The lamb that was slain is

---

[73] Modified Matt. 12:18. The words were taken from Isaiah 42:1-3 in which God speaks of his "servant."

[74] Servetian understanding of the double nature of Christ is not the same as the orthodox one. Christ is not the Word but a "mode" of God and not a Person of the Trinity. What is of God in Jesus is the Word which, by fertilizing Mary in lieu of a male, causes that other attributes of the divinity are equally imparted to him through mere biological inheritance, just as it occurs among humans.

[75] Eph. 2:15. But Paul refers to abolishing the Mosaic Law and uniting the Jews and the Gentiles in one human race.

worthy to receive divinity, power, wisdom, honor, and glory" (Rev. 5).[76] If Moses was made "the God of Pharaoh" (Exod. 7) and Cyrus was made "God of Israel" (Isa. 45), it is all the more likely that Christ be made "God and the Lord" of Thomas and of all of us, and in a far more excellent manner at that. Solomon too is literally called god (Psalm 44).[77] It was not by their nature, however, that they were all gods, but rather through a temporal gift; Christ, in contrast, is God through natural birth, having been naturally conceived from the substance of God.[78] Christ, the true God, is possessed of God's divinity in its entirety, possessed of God's adoration, and vision. Just as the Father is the true God, so through the unique gift of His true divinity to His only son, He brought it about that Christ was made the true God.

The First Argument of the Pharisees

Now that we have discussed the three axioms concerning Christ, it remains for us to dispose of the three arguments of the Pharisees which Christ himself disposed of on our behalf. This is the first argument: If Christ is God, there will then be several gods. His response to this argument, when the Pharisees accused Christ of making himself God, was "I said, 'you are gods'" (John 10).[79] At that moment Christ showed that he is God, sanctified by God the Father. He attempted to persuade the Jews that, if others who experienced death are called gods, He too could be called God. This was how ignorant people had to be induced step by step to recognize that Christ was divine by nature.

He continued: "if scripture calls those to whom God speaks gods, all the

---

[76] Rev. 5:12.

[77] Exod. 7:1: "The LORD said to Moses, 'See, I have made you like God to Pharaoh.'" But Servetus forgets that the term "elohim" strictly speaking does not mean "god" but "a powerful lord" and therefore it could be applied to God as well as to humans. The same applies to Isaiah 45:1 and 3. To Solomon would be referred erroneously the words in Ps. 44:4-7.

[78] In spite of his philological error Servetus is consistent in his doctrine. The fundamental difference from orthodoxy is that for Servetus, Christ is naturally generated from the substance of God. His theory excludes in a radical manner any danger of adoptionism with respect to Jesus.

[79] John 10:34: "Jesus answered, 'Is it not written in your law,' 'I said, you are gods'"? Jesus' quote refers to Psalm 82:6-7:
"I say, 'You are gods, children of the Most High, all of you; nevertheless, you shall die like mortals, and fall like any prince.'"

more ought the son, whom the Father sanctifies beyond others, be called not merely the son of God, but even God as well." Though there both be gods, there is nevertheless just one divine nature, and it has been imparted to the son by the Father through conception. God is unique and He is the source of all divinity. The Jews were not the least bit disturbed when Moses, Solomon, and Cyrus were called gods by this line of reasoning. The Jews not only ought to have conceded to Christ the divinity of Elohim, since they saw in him the great works and miracles of God, but they even ought to have recognized the fact that it was appropriate to him on account of his excellence.[80] Christ offered this explanation for his own outstanding divinity in John 5 and 10.[81] For this reason glorious epithets were applied to his divinity such that he was called God of all the earth, great God, strong, and blessed beyond all things. There were far greater epithets regarding the substantial divinity of Christ, which we shall more fully discuss later. This is agreed upon for the time being: we are not dissecting God nor dividing Him into parts as the Sophists do. It is quite certain that no such plurality in the divinity can be introduced from the foregoing, such as what is found in the conceptions of the trinitarians where there are three distinct and incorporeal entities. There is here a real and absolute plurality of gods as we shall soon show that.

The Second Argument of the Pharisees

The second argument is, "How can it be said that Christ descended from heaven and came into the world on a mission from the Father?" Those who make these objections clearly share in the delusions of the Pharisees. For in John 6[82] the Pharisees ask, "Is not this the son of Joseph whose father and mother we know? How then does he say, 'I have come down from heaven'?" In this passage Christ responds by explaining that we ought to live through the spirit in order to understand this descent, "For physical senses are of no use;"[83] the Word of God

---

[80] Here evident is Jesus' divinity as *Elohim*, but not as Yahwe, i.e., his substantive divinity.
[81] John 5:36 and 10:25: "the very works that I am doing, testify on my behalf that the Father has sent me."
[82] John 6:42.
[83] John 6:63: "It is the spirit that gives life; the flesh is useless."

has descended from heaven and is now on earth as the flesh of Christ. [18] You shall therefore concede that the flesh of Christ descended from heaven. The flesh of Christ is from heaven. It is heavenly bread from the substance of God and it has come out from God. Nevertheless, since these matters are better understood through the mystery of the Word, they shall be postponed until later books.[84] Meanwhile you can understand "from heaven", in other words, "from on high" in the way he explains it in John 8.[85] You can understand the words of Christ in a spiritual way: Christ preceded all times in the spirit of God and his spirit was originally in heaven. Only with the understanding that his words were heavenly ought it to have been conceded that he, too, was "from heaven," for "John's baptism was from heaven and "the second man from heaven was heavenly."[86] Whatever is beyond flesh and blood is both from and in heaven. Not only was Christ from heaven, but he even brought heaven itself to us, as you will see.

It is not difficult to respond to your objection that he was sent by the Father, since even John is said to have been sent by God in John 1: "There was a man sent by God, whose name was John."[87] All the prophets and apostles are said to have been sent by God. Christ declared this himself in John 17 where he said, "Just as You the Father sent me Your son into the world, so I am sending the apostles into the world." And in John 20 "As the Father has sent me, so I send you."[88] I am compelled to rely upon the comparisons which Christ himself made so that the truth may be more obvious. It is a fact that Christ's mission and departure from the Father is unique to him as shall be clear from the mystery of the Word.

Likewise it ought not to be a surprise when we say that Christ "came into

---

[84] Servetus is using the words flesh and bread in a convergent sense but distinct from the traditional one: *Verbum Dei de coelo descendens est nunc in terra caro Christi.* The Word for Servetus as a mode of God's manifestation descended on earth and became the flesh of Christ. Its humanization in the flesh is culminated in the Supper and Eucharist which is an instrument of the real divinization of a Christian.
[85] It is a reference to John 8:23.
[86] Matt. 21:25; Luke 20:4; 1 Cor. 15:47.
[87] John 1:6.
[88] John 17:18, 20:21.

the world," since this same situation applied to others. For example, in John 1 there is the statement, "every person comes into this world." John, who was responding against the two heresies that were gaining strength at that time, showed that Jesus Christ came in the flesh. The first heresy was that of Simon Magus's disciples who were saying that Christ was a phantasm without true flesh. To counter this he made a point of referring to "the flesh" specifically. The other heresy that soon followed was that of Ebion and Cerinthus who said that Jesus was a human being and nothing more and that he lacked divine substance and was nonexistent prior to Mary. To counter these John explained that Jesus came and was also previously the Word with God.[89] In [19] the coming chapters you shall plainly see the truth of this claim. You shall plainly see that the trifles of our trinitarians were not known to anyone at that time. Already Polycarp cites the statement of John against the aforementioned heresies in his letter to the Philippians. Ignatius did the same thing in a number of places as did Irenæus.[90] All these men neither documented nor contemplated the conceits of our trinitarians. They made the simple declaration that Jesus was the true Messiah, son of God, and that the same son was in His own person and substance "the Word with God" in a way that was unknown to all the sophisticated trinitarians, but must now truly be recognized.

The Third Argument of the Pharisees

Thirdly, who can explain how, in Philippians 9, Christ was not accused of usurpation when he said he was the equal of God?[91] Christ himself answered this, for the Pharisees made the charge in John 5 that he was making himself the equal of God. Responding to them, Christ did not deny this equality, but rather said that

---

[89] Servetus again indicates the polemical origin of the Gospel of John (see note 56).

[90] Polycarp in *Ad Philip.*, cap. VII, citing the anathema of 1 John 4:2-3, and 3:8. Ignatius, in various letters: *Ad Ephes.* VII, IX; *Ad Trall.*, IX; *Ad Smyr.* II. (*Apostolic Fathers,* ed., Michael W. Holmes, 1999).

[91] Philip. 2:6: "though he was in the form of God, did not regard equality with God as something to be exploited."

he possessed all the power and did everything that his Father did.[92] Just like the Father, so the son raised the dead, restored sight to the blind, cared for those afflicted with leprosy, and cured the deaf, the paralyzed, the possessed, and others as well. The Father gave His son all the right of judgment and all the power in order that everyone pay honor to the son just as they honor the Father. Notice how Christ bore witness that he himself was the equal of God. Consider the nature of His μορφή, in other words, the image of divinity that shined in him when he performed such miracles. As we shall say later, Christ had possession of the divine mark and the divine form from eternity. Now let's contemplate his divine mark and, together with the divine mark, his divine power. Paul joined a humble disposition of his spirit with that great power of Christ, and he set this before us as a model to imitate. He teaches us that Christ's humility is the greatest humility and all the greater in proportion to the greater majesty and power with which he was endowed all the greater the more he submitted and cast himself down.

Power is apt to turn other men into tyrants, but this is not so with Christ. By existing in the form of God, he did not consider it an act of usurpation to have such a level of divinity in himself. Christ did not want [20] to use his power for theft like a tyrant. He did not allow that theft when he realized that his followers were on the point of seizing him to make him king (John 6).[93] Instead, he conducted himself in a humble way since he did not want his kingdom to be from this world. Christ was able everywhere to maintain the divine mark or form that was seen on the mount and to interact with people as a heavenly king. For our salvation he preferred to conduct himself as a slave even unto the cross. He took no thought for theft; he was unwilling violently to defend himself against the Jews with the power which he held through the power of God, even if twelve legions of angels were enlisted to help. Instead, he wanted to suffer humbly. Therefore as

[92] Servetus interprets the term "to be in the form of God" in a diametrically different way from the traditional interpretation which considers it as meaning to be in the Person of the Trinity. Instead, Christ appeared in the "form of a slave." This form of God or of "Elohim" corresponded to Jesus, the natural son of God, as a human being, but was manifested often in his powerful works.
[93] John 6:15.

was said in Chapter 5, Christ is said to be equal to God by virtue of the power that was given to him to match God.

Everything the Father has belongs to him. Through him everything happens that happens through the Word of God because he is the Word of God. Christ himself pointed out this equality of power when he said, "The son of man will be seated at the right hand of the power of God" (Luke 22).[94] Paul explained this status of Christ and his exaltation to the right power of God in Ephesians 1 where he said that he was placed "above all rule and authority, power, virtue, lordship, and above everything that is named not only in this age, but also in the age to come." Finally "everything is placed at his feet, and he has been given above all things to the church as its head, as a fulfillment of all things in all things."[95] The equal status of God's power in him is noted in Daniel 7: "Behold, a son of man came, and he arrived until the Ancient of age, and all kingly power was given to him."[96] Jeremiah in Chapter 30 also gazed upon him who came in this way, and knelt before God that he might approach him on an equal footing.[97] In Zechariah chapter 13 the man, Jesus, is referred to as being עמית, *amith*, to God which means *ally* and *peer*.[98] At this point I shall refrain from mentioning those fantastic conceits which are based on the philosophical hypothesis that there are three invisible entities derived from both a theft in nature and a concession of equality as if happenings of this sort were common occurrences in such matters. I refrain all the more because Paul never had a thought about those things. He said, [21] "let the same mind be in you that was in Christ Jesus himself, who, being God in substance and being God in form, did not think about usurpation when he said that he was equal to God." It did not occur to him to direct his own divine power

---

[94] Luke 22:69.

[95] Eph. 1:21-23.

[96] Daniel 7:13: "As I watched in the night visions, I saw one like a human being coming with the clouds of heaven. And he came to the Ancient One and was presented before him."

[97] Jer. 30:21: "Their prince shall be one of their own, their ruler shall come from their midst; I will bring him near, and he shall approach me, for who would otherwise dare to approach me? says the LORD."

[98] Zech.. 13:7 : "'Awake, O sword, against my shepherd, against the man who is my associate,' says the LORD of hosts."

towards theft. Rather he conducted himself humbly even when he was later exalted through the resurrection.[99] Cyril in Book VIII of the *Thesaurus*, chapter 1, says that humility does not properly suit divine nature. "It is not in accordance with the nature of the Word," he says, "that Christ was humble, for humility is appropriate to the man to whom exaltation is also appropriate." Therefore, the divine nature in itself was neither made humble nor exalted, but the human being, Christ.[100] That is also Augustine's explanation in the beginning of the third book against Maximinus, but in other places he contradicts himself. He ignored, however, the logic of the term *person*, which we shall discuss later.[101]

Christ was a human being constituted in the form of God, but he had no intention to usurp when he said that he was the equal of God. He had no intention of using that strength of equality with God for some tyranny or theft. In fact it would have been theft if he had forcefully taken himself away from the task for which his Father had destined him or if he had seized the kingdom of this world as a tyranny for himself.[102] This is the proper meaning of the term ἁρπαγμός. Christ had no care for anything of this sort and he never violently seized anything from anyone.[103] The Greek definite article το confirms this opinion, and so does the adverb ἴσα, equally, which designates the disposition of a human being, not those transcendental and incorporeal, coequal natures. As Paul says, this statement that he was equal to God was not made by Christ in order to commit

---

[99] Phil. 2:5-8 : "Let the same mind be in you that was in Christ Jesus, who, though he was in the form of God, did not regard equality with God as something to be exploited, but emptied himself, taking the form of a slave, being born in human likeness. And being found in human form, he humbled himself and became obedient to the point of death – even death on a cross."

[100] Cyril of Alexandria (ca 360-444 C.E.), *Thesaurus de sancta et consubstantiali Trinitate*, lib. VIII, cap. 1 (PG LXXV, 72). This not an exact quote.

[101] Augustine, *Adv. Maximinum arianorum episc.*, lib II, cap. 2 (PL XLII, 759). Servetus placed the quote erroneously in lib. III. The Servetian concept of the person is not substantial or designating an entity, but rather phenomenalistic, designating a manifestation or aspect.

[102] Servetus is trying to explain more clearly the Latin expression found in the Vulgate *"non rapinam arbitratus est esse se aequalem Deo."* In the Greek original this is: "οὐχ ἁρπαγμὸν ἡγήσατο τὸ εἶναι ἴσα θεῷ." NRS translates this into "did not regard equality with God as something to be exploited." The Oxford dictionary translates the Greek ἁρπαγμός as "robbery," or "a prize to be grasped." The same translations are given for the Latin equivalent *rapina*.

theft. This is the most accurate sense. Paul did no violence with the expression "equal," but he inferred it from "the mark of divinity." For he said that Christ by having the mark of God did not think το εἶναι ἴσα θεῷ, in other words, did not think of that "to be equal to God," what he possessed, if he existed in God's form, would tend towards theft. Indeed the apostle said that Christ took up the "form or appearance of a slave," and he said this, in order to distinguish that state from the "form or mark of God," about which he had already spoken: for either notion could be rendered by the Greek word μορφή. And in this respect he expressed the greater humility. For [22] though he was powerful in either guise, he used the humbler. He did not appear in the guise and might of God, but just as one of the human beings. He, Jesus, a human being, who previously had the form of God, later took on the guise of a slave as you shall see. And he is said to have been found to be just like a human being as the psalmist says: "We shall die as men, even though you be gods" (Ps. 81). Samson too, because he was mightiest, almost inhumanly so — certainly greater than a human being — said, "I shall then be weak like anyone human."[104]

See how far removed from the debates of our age are the universal passages in scripture which talk about the equality of God. Moreover, that tension which results from the uncertainty of an unequal or equal nature among the invisible Persons, and which from the time of Sylvester has afflicted the whole globe, courtesy of the Arians, was an invention of Satan designed to divert the minds of people from a recognition of the true Christ and to make God a three-fold entity.[105] O Jesus, son of God, take pity on us now that we may acknowledge You as the son of God.

---

[103] In *De Trinitatis erroribus* (20r) Servetus is using in the same sentence a verb *"harpagare"*: *"Nam Christus nunquam harpagare curavit... "*

[104] Ps. 81:6-7: "You are gods, children of the Most High, all of you; nevertheless, you shall die like mortals, and fall like any prince." Judg. 16:17: "I would become weak, and be like anyone else."

[105] The theme of the Trinity was not a preoccupation of Servetus's contemporaries. Servetus states that the dogma of the Trinity, initiated during Sylvester's age by the Council of Nicea, was a reaction to the interpretation promoted by the Arians, which he himself did not share, and signals an invasion of the Antichrist, a new incarnation of Satan.

31

Now that we have considered the arguments of the Pharisees against Christ, we shall before coming to the arguments of the Sophists, explain two passages from scripture on the basis of which the belief in the Trinity is founded. One is 1 John 5 to wit: "There are three who bear witness in heaven, being the Father, the Word, and the Spirit, and these three are one." The other passage is in Matthew 28 where it says, "Baptize in the name of the Father and the son and the holy spirit."[106] The easy explanation of these is that the divine nature which is in the Father is one and the same as the divine nature that was imparted immediately and bodily to Jesus Christ. Next, with him as the intermediary and through the ministry of the angelic spirit, the divine nature was imparted spiritually to the apostles on the day of the Pentecost. Yet Christ alone possesses divinity by nature both in the flesh and the spirit. In turn, it is given by him to others as a holy breath of substance. Both means of sharing the divinity, in the flesh and through the spirit, we shall explain separately later by showing that the substance itself of the holy spirit is the same divinity that there is with the [23] Father and the son.[107]

Now, as to the first passage from John it is our opinion that its purpose is to show that Jesus is the son of God. To prove this John introduces six pieces of evidence, three in heaven and three on earth, which all agree that he is the son of God. In this passage the Word does bear witness concerning the son as a distinct thing, in order that Sophists might not identify it with the Son. Consequently, in order to make a point about heavenly evidence, John introduces the heavenly testimony in the Jordan when the holy spirit by an angelic ministry descended like a dove and a voice was made from heaven saying "This is my son." John cites obvious and manifest evidence; otherwise he would be proving nothing. The voice that was manifested there and the speech that was heard from heaven bear witness that this Jesus was the son of God. The Father is there offering evidence

---

[106] 1 John 5:7-8; Matt. 28:19. The text of 1 John 5:7-8 is the famous "comma johanneum" which was demonstrated by Erasmus to be a later interpolation by Christian scribes. The original text reads like this: "There are three that testify: the Spirit and the water and the blood, and these three agree."
[107] Thus Servetus cannot accept the presumed trinitarian meaning of these texts.

and bearing witness from heaven that this was His son. The spirit as well, when it came to him from heaven, was seen there bearing witness. Christ himself cites three similar pieces of evidence about himself in John 5. And all these three are one, because they unanimously bear witness about the same thing, namely, the unity of one and the same divine nature.[108]

John cites three other pieces of evidence "on earth which are the spirit, the water, and the blood": when as the blood and water was flowing out of his side, he gave up the spirit commending himself to God like a human being dying on earth. But what do these show? I for my part say that they show no separate incorporeal entity, but merely that he as a human being was the son of God and at his death those three witnesses went forth. You can get a glimpse into the mental processes of John, who left no stone unturned to prove that this Jesus was the son of God. The focus of all the scriptures is Jesus, the son of God. John urges us to believe this if we want to live in Christ. "Whoever believes that Jesus is the son of God, has been born from God" (1 John 5). "Who is there who conquers the world, unless he believes that Jesus is the son of God?" (1 John 5).[109] Whoever does not hold this belief is not a Christian. Whoever does not hold this belief has not laid his foundation upon that firm rock: "You are Christ, son of the living God" (Matt. 16).[110] The basis of our salvation and of the church is a faithful belief that this Jesus Christ is the son of God and our savior.[111]

[24] Regarding the other passage cited in support of the Trinity we say that, although baptism is correctly applied in the name of Christ in accordance with the teaching of the apostles, given that Christ holds within himself the Father

---

[108] Cf. John 5:31, 37. Servetus does not doubt the authenticity of the text of 1 John 5:7-8. Already Valla considered this text spurious and Erasmus excluded it from his first and second editions of the New Testament (1516 and 1519). But he included it in the 1522 edition. Pagnino includes it in his *Biblia*. Servetus, gives it a different from the orthodox interpretation considering it, in accordance with the suggestion of Erasmus, as a unity of consent.

[109] 1 John 5:1 and 5.

[110] Matt. 16:16.

[111] These are essential concepts for the Servetian system. To be a Christian means to believe that Jesus is the son of God as a human being. The famous text of Matt. 16:16 does not refer to Peter as the rock of the church, but to his expression of his faith that Jesus is the son of God.

and the holy spirit, that is, the anointed one holds the anointer and unction,[112] nevertheless Christ wanted to express everything broadly, to confer honor upon the Father, and to join the holy spirit to baptism since it is there that the gift of the holy spirit is uniquely made manifest. Therefore, he first says, "Baptize in the name of the Father," because the Father is first of all gifts, the true and original source (James 1). "Baptize in the name of the son," because it is through him that we have reconciliation nor is there any other name under heaven in which we ought to be saved (Acts 4). "Baptize in the name of the holy spirit," because the holy spirit is given as a gift in baptism (John 3 and Acts 2).[113]

In Clement's *Recognitions* in the third and sixth books, Peter said that this was the tripartite invocation of the divine name. There he said that the blessedness was threefold and the mystery trinary.[114] There are three modes of manifestation or three persons, but not through that metaphysical distinction of three incorporeal entities in God. Rather, they exist through a display of the sacrament or through the οἰκονομίαν of God as Irenæus and Tertullian teach.[115] Add to these the statement of Hilary in the beginning of his second book *On the Trinity*: "Christ bade us baptize in the name of the Father, son, and holy spirit, in other words, in recognition of the source, the only born, and the gift. The 'source' is the ungenerated God, the Father from whom all things are created. The 'only born' is Jesus Christ through whom all things are created. The holy spirit is the 'gift' in all

---

[112] This is an implicit allusion to the text of Irenaeus *Adv. Haereses*, III, 18 (PG VII, 934) which is cited by Servetus in his *Apology to Melanchthon* (in the original edition of *Christianismi restitutio*, p. 694): *"In hanc sententiam Irenaeus lib. 3. cap. 20: 'Uncti nomine contineri ait eum, qui unxit patrem, et ipsum unctionem, quae est spiritus sanctus in eo.'"*

[113] James 1:17: "Every generous act of giving, with every perfect gift, is from above, coming down from the Father of lights." Acts 4:12: "there is salvation in no one else, for there is no other name under heaven given among mortals by which we must be saved." John 3:5: "Very truly, I tell you, no one can enter the kingdom of God without being born of water and Spirit." Acts 2:17: "Very truly, I tell you, no one can enter the kingdom of God without being born of water and Spirit." In the last quote Jesus is quoting Joel 2:28.

[114] *Recognitiones*, lib. I, cap. 69; lib. III, cap. 1; lib. VI. Cap. 9 (PG I, 1244, 1282, 1352) : *"Sub apellatione triplicis sacramenti."*

[115] Servetus does not quote the texts of Irenaeus or Tertullian and their interpretation which is more amply discussed in his *Apologia*. In them the Persons of the Trinity are understood as dispositions, economies, administrations, or even presented graphically as the "hands of God." He did not refer to those texts when he wrote his *De Trinitatis erroribus*.

things, the singular gift of baptism. The infinite is in the eternal, the appearance in the image, the use in the gift."[116] Behold, the truest Trinity from ancient teaching: God, the Father, is invisible in the infinite, the seen manifestation of His image, and the gift proceeding thence. If only Hilary had always maintained this understanding! If only Augustine had not obscured these words in Book VI of his *On the Trinity* with those of the other crowd of Sophists as we see in the first book of *Sentences*, distinction 31![117]

But let us see what reasons the Sophists have for why they incorrectly conclude that these incorporeal entities are distinguished in God. They base [25] one of their arguments on what is written in John 10: "I and the Father are one."[118] Augustine explains this passage in sermon 56 in his *Commentary on John* and tracts 36 and 71, also in the same *Commentary on John*, where he was arguing against Arius who emphasized the word "one" and against Sabellius because he emphasized the phrase "(we) are." Therefore, against Sabellius he logically concluded the existence of those two incorporeal entities and against Arius that there was in them a single, equal nature. Hence he sings wonderful triumphs for himself.[119] But you, reader, imagine that Jesus himself is speaking in that passage and that he said "we are" because he was referring to God and to the human being, and that he said "one" because there is one divinity, one power, one unanimity, one will of man with God.

It supports the idea that there is one οὐσία and one ἐξουσία. We encounter *ousia* only once in the Gospel of Luke, chapter 15, and it properly refers there to household property, resources, wealth, and riches.[120] *Exousia* is found throughout and, when Christ talks about the power that was bestowed upon him by the Father, the word "*exousia*" is used. For Christ it means practically the

---

[116] These are the words of Hilary of Poitiers (ca 300-368), *De Trinitate*, lib. II, cap. 1 (PL X, 26).
[117] Augustine, *De Trinitate*, lib. VI, cap. 10 (PL VIII, 931) explained these words saying that the Father does not have a father, but the Son has a father and is coeternal with him. Also Peter Lombard in *Sententiarum*, lib. I, dist. 31,3 (PL CXCII, 604) comments on the same text of Hilary.
[118] John 10:30.
[119] Augustine, *In Ioannis Evang.*, tract. 36, 9 (PL XXXV, 1668); tract. 71, 2 (PL XXXV, 1821).
[120] Luke 15:12. "Ousia" in Greek is translated in the Vulgate as *"substantia."*

same thing as *ousia*, power, resources, wealth of power. All these things were abundantly in Christ's possession and were his one οὐσία shared with the Father or his one ἐξουσία. He is ὁμόουσιος with God the Father, being truly consubstantial and one with God.[121] This is the obvious interpretation of the old authorities when they explain the statement, "I and the Father are one." Origen explained it this way in the eighth book of his work *Against Celsus* as did Cyprian in his *Letter to Magnus*, both saying that the human being was one with God.[122] This interpretation is confirmed by the statement of Christ where he says that "we are one with him" just as he is "one with the Father."[123] True Christians are one with Christ not only by consensus, but also in substance as we shall demonstrate. Irenæus and Tertullian teach this in many places. Hilary in the eighth book *On the Trinity* and Cyril in his *Commentary on John* both say this.[124] Through the substance of Christ we are one just as he is one with God in substance.

The Sophists demonstrate the triad of three invisible entities by using a second argument, basing it on what is written in Exodus 3: "I am the God of Abraham, the God of Isaac, the God of Jacob." Nothing metaphysical is being

---

[121] Servetus exceeds here his philological analysis because the term *ousia* was a technical term in Greek philosophy designating essence, substance, being, nature. However, Servetus focuses his discussion on the biblical meaning of these terms which was diverted from use in the biblical text by the superimposition of the philosophical speculations of the church Fathers. He stated this clearly in *De Trinitatis erroribus* (76v): *"Universi erroris eorum causa erat, quia philosophi errant, et unum alium filium praeter Christum faciebant."* He also explains there more amply the problem (23r): *"Unum vero neutraliter, non ad singularitatem, sed unanimitatem et concordiam pertinet, ut duo crederentur in una virtute. Et hoc est quod antiquiores unam usiam recte dixerunt, quia est una potestas a patre filio tradita. Posteriores tamen vocem homusion, sicut et hypostasim, et personas pessime subsannarunt, de usia naturam facientes, non modo contra vocabuli proprietatem, sed contra omnes scripturae locos in quibus illa vox reperitur, nam Ioan. 17 et Matthaei ultimo, et ubique de potestate sibi a patre tradita loquitur Christus : ponitur dictio usia, quae Graecis non significat naturam, sed facultates, opes, fortunas, divitias et potestatem."* The same argumentation follows about the term *"unum"*: *"Et tam Latinis unum quam Greacis ἕν, unanimes, conformes, et omnes idem sapientes comprehendit, et capere in scripturis unum pro una natura, est potius metaphysicum quam christianum."*
[122] Origen of Alexandria (185-254 C.E.), *Contra Celsum*, lib. VIII, 12 (PG XI, 750). Cyprian of Carthage (d. 258 C.E.), *Ad Magnum Episc.* Epist. 69, V, 1. Servetus states in *De Trinitatis Erroribus*, 23v, that the same interpretation was given by Erasmus in his *Annotations to the New Testament*.
[123] These are allusions to various expressions in John 17:20-22.
[124] Hilary, *De Trinitate*, lib. VIII, 5 (PL X, 217). Cyril, *In Ioann. Evang. Lib.* IX (PL LXXIV, 267).

[26] noted there, and this is proven by the fact that, when speaking to Jacob, God said, "I am the God of your father Abraham and Isaac" (Gen. 29 and 30). No one would understand on this basis the existence of two separate, metaphysical entities. Even, when speaking to Isaac, God said "I am the God of your father Abraham" (Gen. 26). If those three entities are understood there, how can it be in Acts, "the God of Abraham, the God of Isaac, the God of Jacob is the father of Jesus Christ"?[125] Is that trinity called the father of the second entity or the father of a human being? In fact, Lombard in the first book of the *Sentences*, distinction 26, following Augustine and Hilary, explains that the human being is the son of the Trinity and the whole Trinity is the father of the human being. Hilary in the eleventh book of *On the Trinity* explains Christ's statement, "I ascend to my God, my father and your father," by saying that the entire Trinity is the father for that human being, Christ, just as Christ is a father for other people. For Augustine in the fifth book of *On the Trinity* the whole Trinity is the father of creation (*creaturae*).[126] For them it is the same to be the father of Christ's human nature and the father of his divinity: the whole Trinity is a father. Therefore, the Son is incorporeal, the human being is corporeal, and both are the son of the Trinity and begotten of the three.

If we put aside all these conceits, we realize, when we find "the God of Abraham, the God of Isaac, the God of Jacob", that God is taking steps to prevent the Jews from believing in a multitude of gods. For they were prone to that belief just as we are today. They were wont to multiply their gods in proportion to the number of communities (Jer. 2 and 11).[127] Therefore, God, who took measures

---

[125] Exod. 3:3, 16. It is Gen. 28:13 and 26:24.

[126] Peter Lombard, *Sententiarum*, lib. I, dist. 26, 5 (PL CXCII, 593): "Man who is the son and made by God, not only by the Father, but also by the Son and by the Holy Spirit is the son of the whole Trinity; thus the Trinity itself called his father." Hilary, *De Trinitate*, lib. XI, 14 (PL X, 383). Augustine, in *De Trinitate*, lib. V, 6, n. 7 (PL XLII, 94), distinguished the absolute predication from the relative one, which Servetus does not consider. His reading of Augustine may be correct, however, because in cap. 8 Augustine declares: "As far as the action is concerned, in the final analysis only God acts" (PL XLII, 94). Lombard cites these texts of Hilary and Augustine.

[127] Jer. 2:28: "For you have as many gods as you have towns," and Jer. 11:13: "For your gods have become as many as your towns."

lest they multiply the deities after the number of centuries or generations through believing that one God was the God of Abraham, another the God of Isaac, another the God of Jacob, declared that He was the same God of all those men as He showed from the words He uttered when He said "I am the God of your fathers, I am that God who led you out of the land of Egypt and out of Ur of the Chaldeans" In Exodus cap. 6 as well God says that He was the one who appeared to them: "I am the God who appeared to Abraham, Isaac and Jacob." At Isaiah 48 He said, "I am He, I am the first, I am the most recent." He said that He was the God of Abraham, Isaac, and Jacob for another reason, that reason being the fact that God at that time was starting to appear to the Israelites through Moses in order to [27] fulfill the promises which had been made to the prophets. There was also a third reason that He called himself their God, that is, in order to show that they all would return to life, indeed, even already living in the presence of God (Luke 20).[128]

For their third argument, the Sophists base their assertion of three incorporeal entities in God on the fact that three men appeared to Abraham, and, although Abraham saw three, he worshipped one (Genesis 18). My response is that the three were angels who appeared to Abraham.[129] The person of Christ was represented by an angel throughout the Law. An angel was tutor for Christ just like the Law itself. At that time the angel, like God, both spoke in the word of God and in him one saw the refulgence of Christ. The angel spoke like God in Genesis 16 and 22. In Genesis 31 the angel addressed Jacob directly saying, "I am the God of Bethel." The angel spoke to Moses saying, "I am the God of Abraham, Isaac, and Jacob" (Exod. 3 and Acts 7).[130] In all these instances there was an angel, like God, who was speaking before others, adumbrating the person of

---

[128] Exod. 6:2-6; Isa. 48:12; Luke 20:37-38.

[129] Gen. 18:3. In that scene many church fathers saw the announcement of the Trinity. The issue centers on the use of the plural and singular. In Gen. 19:1 there are mentioned only two angels and hence some conclude that there was a real theophany representing God accompanied by two angels. Servetus's interpretation of the text is more critical.

[130] Gen. 16:7, 17:15, and 22:16 where an angel of Yahweh talks to Sarah and Abraham. Gen. 31:13; Exod. 3:6; Acts 7:32.

Christ, bright in his reflection, as you will later see in the reflection of the Word. God made that angel chief of the other angels, chief of the synagogue, and he spoke like God to the Jews. Therefore, he is called מיכאל Michael, in other words, one like God. In Genesis 18, discussed above, he speaks to Abraham like God, but the two assisting angels who proceeded to Sodom, speak differently as the following chapter shows there. When God said "my angel will precede you," "my angel" means Michael as even the Hebrew words indicate for they spell the very name Michael. From these same Hebrew letters both מלאכי and מיכאל are spelled, and this is all the more fitting because that angel is especially called the chief of the Jews.[131] Augustine came to the wrong conclusion in the second book of *On the Trinity* because of how he interpreted the instance when Lot bowed in the presence of the two angels. For this was done out of politeness by a host, even if he did not know that they were angels (Heb. 13).[132] That Lot called them "lords" offers no support to Augustine's fantasies since the name of the tetragrammaton is not used there; rather we find the ordinary name by which we call people "lords." Both that and another name could have been [28] applied to angels, all the more so since the Lord Himself was present when Sodom was yet to be burned. Augustine is being an idiot when he asks whether the two guests of Lot were the Father and the son or the Father and the holy spirit or the son and the holy spirit. Ridiculous nonsense!

Lombard in Book One of *Sentences* towards the end of the section dealing with the second distinction, makes the following addition to the arguments already mentioned. He says that in the New Testament the "individual syllables

---

[131] According to Servetus then the chief of the three angels that appeared to Abraham was the highest angel of Yahweh, the one who is mentioned in Dan. 10:13, 21 and 12:1 as an angel of Israel, the God-like Michael. This is the first time that Servetus emphasizes the angel bearing his own name with whose function Servetus will progressively identify himself until adopting the apocalyptic role. Both, the expression "my angel" (מלאכי), *mal'khi*, and the name Michael (מיכאל), *mikhael*, have in Hebrew the same letters, but reading one for the other one is something arbitrary. The root of the word is מלח, *malach*, to send, to dissipate, just like the root for the Greek angel, ἄγγελός, messenger, is ἀγγέλλω, to send.

almost by themselves imply unanimously the existence of a Trinity of three invisible entities."[133] But to my mind, not the syllables but rather the individual letters, all the serifs of the letters, "the mouths of babes and infants," indeed, even the stones themselves cry out that there is only one God, the Father, and His Christ, the Lord Jesus. In 1 Timothy 2, we read, "For there is one God; there is also one mediator between God and humankind, Christ Jesus, himself human." At 1 Corinthians 8 we find, "For us there is one God, the Father, and one Lord, Jesus Christ." John too, for whom the heavens were open in Revelation, said that he saw only God the Father and His Christ. God alone and the lamb are praised and worshipped there. When heaven was laid open, Stephen, too, saw the glory of God and Jesus standing at God's right side. Likewise in Matthew 23 "The Father is one and Christ, the master, is one." In John 8 we have, "I am not alone, rather it is the Father and I. I am not alone because the Father is with me. They know neither the Father nor me."[134] Let them know that You alone are the true God and that whom You sent is Jesus Christ. When he said, "No one knows the Father, but the son nor does anyone know the son, but the Father,"[135] was the third entity unaware of this? John overlooked that third entity in his first letter because he wanted us to have a relationship with the Father and His son, Jesus Christ. Likewise in 1 Timothy 5 the apostle says, "I bear witness to You in the presence of God, the Lord, Jesus Christ, and the chosen angels."[136] Note that Paul's solemn declaration was made in the presence of God, Christ, and the angels, and not in the presence of that third entity. Yet the metaphysicians want to make that entity an equal to the second one, and have it seated on an equal footing at the table of the Trinity. Thus do they sing in their hymn: "On the seat of grandeur the three sit at the table." But Christ tells it differently in Revelation 3: [29] "I shall confess in

---

[132] Heb. 13:2 : "Do not neglect to show hospitality to strangers, for by doing that some have entertained angels without knowing it." Augustine, *De Trinitate*, lib. II, 11 (PL XLII, 858).
[133] Peter Lombard, *Sententiarum* , lib. I, dist, 28.
[134] Ps. 8:2; 1 Tim. 2:5; 1 Cor. 8:6; Acts 7:56: "I see the heavens opened and the Son of Man standing at the right hand of God!" Matt. 23: 8: "For you have one Father – the one in heaven. Nor are you to be called instructors, for you have one instructor, the Messiah." John 8: 16, 19, 29.
[135] John 16:32; Matt. 11:27.

the presence of my Father and in the presence of the angels." It is a serious affront to the third entity that Christ speaks in the presence of the angels rather than its presence. Christ makes mention regarding himself, the Father, and the angels in Mark 8 and Luke 9 and 12. John in Revelation 1 seeks grace and peace from God, the seven spirits, and Jesus Christ for us. He makes no mention of the third entity.[137] Irenæus in many passages of Book Three and in the beginning of his fourth book says that no one in scripture is called God except for the Father of everything and the son, Jesus. Neither Irenæus nor Tertullian nor any of the other, early authorities state that the third entity is God.[138] You shall later see the arguments of all of these as they pertain to the dispensation of the holy spirit, and then you will have an understanding of the holy spirit's divine substance, even though it is not manifested in substance as a visible person like the son.

Now allow us to demonstrate by means of argument and evidence that those three incorporeal and distinct entities cannot exist in the unity of God. I could first refute this imaginary triad with the same sixteen arguments which Robert Holcot presented in distinction 5, first book of his *On the Sentences*. Not one of these does he answer effectively nor could he, save by verbal sophistry as he himself admits.[139] Consider Augustine in the beginning of his books *On the*

---

[136] 1 Tim. 5:21.

[137] Rev. 3:5; Mark 8:38; Luke 9:26, 12:8; Rev. 1:2-5.

[138] Irenaeus, *Adv. Haereses*, lib. III, cap. 6a and the prologue to IV (PL VII, 180 and 228).

[139] Robert Holcot (ca 1310-1349), a Dominican monk who belonged to the first generation of scholars who followed the philosophy of William of Ockham (1285-1349). He studied at Oxford, commenting on Peter Lombard's *Sentences* in the years 1331-1333. He represents a reaction to a movement initiated by Richard of St Victor (native of Scotland, d. 1173), a mystical theologian, who attempted to demonstrate the existence of the Trinity by rational approach. Holcot reacted by presenting sixteen reasons against the doctrine of the Trinity and absurdities and incompatibilities which are associated with it. He concluded that this dogma opposed natural reason. William Ockham denied that the doctrine can be illustrated or demonstrated; he claimed that it can only be believed by the authority of the church. He represented a school known by the name of Modernists and which represented a nominalist philosophical position. According to it universals were denied and reality was considered as consisting of unrelated particulars. Thus, if the concept of one substance uniting the three person is retained, then it represents a fourth entity, and the Trinity becomes a quaternity as was postulated by Joachim of Fiore (1132-1202). Moreover, if the three persons are not held together by the one substance, then they become three distinct entities representing tritheism. Thus from a philosophical point of view, Ockham asserted that the doctrine of the Trinity means that there are three absolutes: "For the syllogism: God is a Trinity, the Father is God, therefore the Father is a Trinity, is sound according to Aristotelian logic, but fallacious

Trinity and the opening remarks of Pierre d'Ailly in Book I, question V, where they both acknowledge that that triad of three entities is not demonstrated through the holy writings, but rather is received from tradition.[140] Hear what in our own time John Major offers in Book One, distinction 4 of his *Commentary on the Sentences* as a response to the sixth argument, so that you can understand how bravely the Sophists defend the one God. They accept absolutely that those three persons are distinct entities.[141] Augustine in Book I of *On the Christian Doctrine* says that the three entities are things from which we derive benefit. Likewise they say that the word "person" is a noun of substance as Augustine explains in Book VII of *On the Trinity*, which everyone follows (Book I, distinction 23, *Sentences*).[142] Therefore, starting from this point and arguing from lesser to

---

from the point of faith..." And, "The diverse scientific disciplines (*scientiis*) are not able to establish that God is Three and One. This can be proved only in theology on the basis of faith" (*Quaestiones et distinctiones super IV libros Sententiarum,* II, 3, V, 1, VII, 13).

[140] Augustine, in *De Trinitate,* lib. I, 2 (PL XLII, 822), indicated that instead of getting involved in the rational investigation of the Trinity one has first to investigate the scripture and rely on the traditional magisterium of the church. He represented a moderate scholastic school which claimed that what the best human mind may do concerning the Trinity is to illustrate it using analogies. The school claimed that though the doctrine of the Trinity cannot be demonstrated, at least it can be illustrated. Augustine asserted that the doctrine can be known only through revelation, but not directly, as it is deducible from the scripture. It can be illustrated only by way of analogy with the human constitution. Thus he developed a number of similitudes of which three are most frequently quoted, namely, that of the loved, the lover, and love; that of mind, love, and knowledge thereof; that of memory, intellect, and will. Such an interpretation of the psychological Trinity, though illustrative, was treated as a proof because the human inner constitution was considered as an image of God (*imago Dei*). This approach was continued by others: Boethius, Peter Lombard, Anselm, Albertus Magnus, Thomas Aquinas, and John Duns Scotus. Pierre d'Ailly (1350-1420), a cardinal and an ex-counselor of Paris, represents the nominalist scholastic school. He participated in the Council of Constance which condemned Jan Huss to the stake. He conceded on the basis of the decrees of the Councils that some of the determinations of the church do not come from the deductions in the scripture, but by a special revelation to Catholics via a special gift of God. His claim was that the doctrine of the Trinity involves only verbal and not real inconsistency, thus we may say *personaliter* that there are three gods, but he stated "Such an expression though true and proper among experts is, nevertheless, not customary and should be avoided for the sake of simple believers" (*Quaestiones super I, III, et IV Sententiarum,* q. V).

[141] John Major (1469-1550), a Scott contemporary of Servetus, also professor at the Sorbonne in Paris. He repeated the assertions of d'Ailly and later Erasmus who wrote: "According to dialectical logic it is possible to say there are three gods, but to announce this to the untutored would give great offense" (*Opus Epistolarum Des. Erasmi Roterodami*. English version in *Opera omnia,* IX, 1217c, and V. Re-edited and revised by P. S. Allen and H. M. Allen, Oxonii in Typographeo Clarendomiano, 1924).

[142] Augustine, in *De doctrina christiana,* lib. I, caps. 4 and 5 (PL 34, 20-21), states that the Trinity is something to be enjoyed. In *De Trinitate,* lib. VII, cap. 4, 8 (PL LXII, 941) he admits that what

greater, John Major makes an absolute conclusion from the three persons that there are three hypostases, three substances, three essences, three beings, and, by extension, three Gods. Nevertheless he says that [30] just one being or one essence is to be understood. He says that he derives these expressions figuratively from those authors and they also are inferred from the Master in distinction 25, Book I, of the *Sentences*.[143] So is God merely figurative for us and not absolute? Are not genuine tritheists those who produce three gods really incorporeal and distinct as absolutely existing, three simple and incorporeal entities really distinct, three beings? An argument from lesser to greater concludes logically that there are three absolute beings and thus three essences because every being is an essence. This is accepted in the *Synods* of Hilary: there are three beings in God through the substance. This point is accepted by the Master in distinction 25, already cited, and everyone else follows it.[144] By the principle of convertibility three beings are naturally inferred from three entities. Therefore, there are three essences and three gods. The trinitarians support their Trinity in their argument against the Jews by pointing out that Elohim is the plural for the word God. Therefore, there are two gods or three gods or more. If there are gods by virtue of the Trinity, then they are three incorporeal and truly distinct gods. If they are truly distinct, applying argument of convertibility absolutely, they are also distinct in essence. Thus they are true tritheists and true atheists who do not consider God to

---

is meant in our usage by the term "person," for Greek it was "substance" or "essence." For that reason "they say three substances, one essence, as we say three persons, one essence or substance." Lombard follows Augustine, *Sententiarum*, lib. I, dist. 23 (PL CLCII, 583) citing Augustine: "There is the name "person" which is used substantively of every person." For Servetus, on the contrary, God is not a name of nature or essence which can be communicated logically, and person is not a name of a substance, but a manifestation, aspect, disposition, attitude, etc. Servetus accepts here the observation of Valla in his *Adnotationes* on Matt 22:16 (edited by Erasmus in *Opera*, I, 80-895) according to which the term *person* is not philosophically equivalent to a *substance*, against Boethius, by translating the Greek term πρόσωπον which means "face," "aspect" or appearance." Lorenzo Valla (1405-1457), an Italian philosopher and humanist, states the same in his essay "In Boethium in persona" in *Elegantiae linguae latinae*, VI, 34 (*Opera*, I, 215). Servetus, however, does not quote these sources.
[143] Lib. I, distinction 25, 11 (PL CXCII, 590).
[144] Hilary of Poitiers, *Liber synodalis seu de fide orientalium*, 12, indicates that the three Persons posses the same substance, but he adds that it is not proper to use this term because it does not

be one but only threefold and an aggregate. They understand God figuratively, not absolutely. They believe in imaginary gods— mere projections of demons.

For Athanasius, Hilary, Cyril, Nazianzenus, Basil, Augustine and all the rest, there is a certain God that is not begotten, one that is begotten, and one that is neither begotten nor unbegotten. Hence there are three gods. And in other words: one god is without birth, one is born, and one proceeds. The god that is not begotten is not the one that is begotten, and he that is begotten, is not the one that proceeds. Therefore, they are concerned with a different God, a different entity. One is a dead god, two are not dead; one person is dead, two are not dead; one entity is dead, two are not dead.[145]

If we take this line of reasoning in more directions relying upon their own principles, we may justifiably conclude not only that is it impossible for three entities to exist in one God, but furthermore that the entities are unimaginable. For, if someone had a notion [31] of the Trinity, he would have distinct notions of those three entities and, on that basis, would have a notion of one without having a notion of the other. But they all deny this, citing the passage, "He who sees me, sees the Father." Their response is that someone can have a notion of the Trinity because he comes to a notion of God by understanding the presence in Him of those three entities. But this response is obviously empty and smacks of sophistic conceits which are entirely based on metaphorical, connotative terms. It is unsatisfactory and contrary to their own premises that through one notion we can understand connotatively the three entities even though those cannot be absolutely indicated through the three other entities. This is because every metaphorical, connotative referent presupposes some other absolute entity. This point is

appear in the scripture. But he admits that "the essence is a thing that exists or through which something exists" (PL X, 466).

[145] With a series of such arguments Servetus concludes the discussion of the rational impossibility to admit the existence of the Trinity. This discussion is much longer and more audacious in *De Trinitatis erroribus* than in *Christianismi restitutio* and he ends it this way: "And do not tell me, as all claim, that it suffices to believe though one cannot understand the doctrine. For you show your stupidity in this that you admit something that is not intelligible without sufficient testimony of the scripture ... much more so that you confess that the obstacle to the faith is an intellection itself.

generally accepted by the terms of their own rules. Likewise, everyone is aware of Porphyry's rule that "A given concept that has absolute and simple signification can be derived from any of its given essential applications."[146]

If absolute concepts can be derived from divine matters, what is their nature? Is the Trinity known to Christ and the angels? If three distinct and absolute conceptions of the three entities exist within each of them, do they thus recognize distinctly three absolute gods? Christ plainly taught that the angels saw the face of his Father, but that they did not see any other entities. Today Christ himself sees nothing within himself but the Father in heaven.[147] Dream all you like, but direct your gaze towards the images and then you shall plainly see that your Trinity is not intelligible without three phantasms because the observer necessarily gazes upon them. In fact, you get a quaternity through your perception although you deny it in word. This is because you have four images, and the fourth is the image of the essence because in order to understand the essence itself, you must gaze upon some phantasm. If looking you direct your attention, you will find that your Trinity consists in the movement of false images that exist in the imagination, and this leads you astray.

Truly all the trinitarians are atheists.[148] For what else does it mean, to exist without God, than the inability to think about God because our intellect is assaulted by a certain dangerous confusion of the three entities, and it is by this confusion that we are deluded, when we think about God. [32] There are "three evil spirits" in the mind which thus trick people as John says in Revelation 16.[149]

Thus, if you believe, tell me: What is your ability to understand? Perhaps you take as a sufficient obstacle to your faith the confusion of your own brain?" (*De Trinitatis erroribus,* I Bk. 33v).

[146] As one can see Servetus approaches the logical analysis of the conceptual elements of the trinitarian doctrine using his knowledge of Aristotelian and Porphyrian logic (*Isagoge,* cap. 2:al)

[147] Matt. 18:10: "...for, I tell you, in heaven their angels continually see the face of my Father in heaven."

[148] This statement was considered an insult by Calvin and provoked his fury (*Calvini Opera* VIII, 501). In *De Trinitatis erroribus,* 21v, Servetus states that if the Sophists use the term constitution about God claiming that he is constituted from these three entities, then "It is clear that we are tritheists, we have a tripartite God, and atheists, that is without God."

[149] Rev. 16:10: "And I saw three foul spirits like frogs coming from the mouth of the dragon, from the mouth of the beast, and from the mouth of the false prophet."

"Belief is enough," they say, although the object of belief is not intelligible. It is here that they make manifest their stupidity because they admit that the thing is unintelligible. "They do not understand," he says, "what they say or the things about which they make assertions" (1 Timothy 1) and "They utter blasphemies in those matters of which they know nothing" (2 Peter 2).[150] This is all the truer because you admit, and they all admit, that the mental faculty in itself is an object of faith. So, if you have faith, show me what you understand to be your own capacity for understanding? Just what do you think has been understood by you? Is the very confusion of your mind an object of your faith?[151] Augustine, as he boasted in Book I of *On the Trinity* and Book I of *On Christian Doctrine,* could have seen that the Trinity is understood by him and discerned by a mind that has been cleansed.[152] But he was subject to various illusions as I shall show more clearly in later chapters. Augustine affirms in his letters to Fortunatianus and Paulina that God will not be seen by us in the future state of blessedness nor by the angels themselves.[153] Still, he imagines that his illusions about the Trinity are internal to us thereby overturning all the good fortune of people and angels, for he thus implies that our soul sees more now than the angels and all the saints will see in that future state.

Here is another argument against the false ideas of the trinitarians. Aristotle states that "In the understanding nothing exists which was not first in the senses whether the sense be a reflection of itself, something similar, or some sort of facsimile" (1 *Analytica Posteriora* and *De Anima* 3).[154] For example, a deaf man cannot learn music, and a blind man cannot learn perspective since what cannot exist in the sense, cannot exist in the understanding. Thus, concerning the

---

[150] 1 Tim. 1:7 and 2 Pet. 2:12.

[151] Compare note 148.

[152] Augustine, *De Trinitate,* lib. I, cap. 1,3 (PL XLII, 821). *De Doctrina christiana* lib. I, cap. 10 (PL XXXIV, 23).

[153] Augustine in *Fortunatiano episc. siccensi* (Epist. 148, cap. 1,1, PL XXXIII, 6222) explaining the expression "face to face" in 1 Cor. 13:12. In *Paulinae,* a long letter, almost a book, entitled *De videndo Deo liber* (Epist. 147, PL XXXIII, 596-622).

[154] Aristotle, *Analytica Posteriora,* I, cap. 17: 81a38. *De anima,* III, 4,7, and 8: 429b10, 431a16 and 432a4.

three entities which together make up a single one, no one has ever had any perception of these in the imagination since neither two nor three nor more entities that come together in such a way as to form one entity, have ever been discovered. Therefore, there is no sensory basis by which the intellect might form such an idea. On the contrary, the mind is exhausted and confused by the very effort to form a vision of that entity as if it were struggling over something ephemeral by constructing an idea of it without any sensory basis. [33] All that aside, let us imagine that the person of the Father exists separately, as our antagonists readily admit when they formally distinguish the persons from the essence. I ask, "since it is appropriate for a given entity to have its own essence and its own nature, how can I imagine a multiplicity of entities without a multiplicity of essences? How can I imagine the existence of a new entity without a new nature?"[155]

We are instructed to reject this plurality not only by logic, but also by innumerable authorities which are in both the New and the Old Testaments. In Matthew 19 we find, "God alone is good." In Mark 10, "No one is good but God alone."[156] Is it not true, therefore, that those who do not recognize one God, are satisfied only with the nominal concept of unity itself? Do they not, through their own constructed and connotative essence consign themselves to a plurality of entities and independent deities? Notice that it is the son who is speaking in those passages. On this basis it is clear that the entire structure of God's unity rests on the Father. "God the Father is one, and the Lord, Jesus Christ, is one (1 Corinthians 8). "God is one and the Father of everything" (Eph. 4). "God is one just as the mediator between God and humanity is one" (1 Timothy 2).[157] It is amazing that the apostles never said that the first entity or the first person is the father of the second. Instead, they said, "God is the father of Jesus Christ." They never said that the second entity was the son of God. Instead, they said that Jesus

---

[155] This is a response to the principle already declared that *"omne ens est essentia"*

[156] Matt. 19:17: "unus est bonus Deus," and Mark 10:18: *"nemo bonus nisi unus Deus."* Servetus interprets these expressions as indicating that "good God is one only.".

[157] 1Cor. 8:6; Eph. 4:6; 1 Tim. 2:5.

himself was the son of God. Likewise, when Ignatius, Irenæus, and the other early authorities declared that the one omnipotent God was the God of the Old and New Testaments, they also said that He was the father of Jesus Christ. So on this basis, reader, what would be your understanding? Tertullian, though he once followed the school of Montanus, made many straightforward and true declarations on this subject on the basis of apostolic tradition.[158] The book which is credited to Clement, the disciple of Peter, is an old one, and very straightforward declarations about Christ are made along these lines. In Clement, you will find the variegated scent of that common sense which marked the early authorities. In his letter to the Philadelphians, Ignatius, the disciple of John the evangelist, wrote thus: "Anyone who declares that the God of the Law and the prophets is one, but denies that Christ is [34] His son, is a liar. Whoever admits that Jesus Christ is a human being, but denies that the God of the Law and the prophets is the father of Christ, does not stand in truth." Furthermore, in his letter to the Tarsians he clearly explains that Christ is not above everything since that is God's place; rather Christ is His son.[159] You would find similar things in Justin as cited by Irenæus and others.[160] I wish the writings of all of those who lived then were extant.

Perhaps the God of the Law is not the whole Trinity for our trinitarians? Perhaps Jesus Christ is not considered by them to be the son of the whole Trinity?[161] Therefore, he is not the son of the God of the Law. Consider why the manner of speech used by the ancients is not found among our trinitarians and why instead we find another manner that is totally different and unknown to the

---

[158] Tertullian was partly affected by the teaching of the prophet Montanus who lived in the middle of the second century and founded, together with two prophetesses, Maximilla and Prisca (or Priscilla), a sect called variably Phrygians, or "those among the Phrygians" (*oi kata Phrygas*), then as Montanists, Pepuzians, and (in the West) Cataphrygians. The emphasis on tradition by Tertullian is exemplified by his *Liber de praescriptionibus*, cap. 21 (PL II, 33).

[159] Ignatius, *Epistula Ad Phladelphios*, VI. *Epistula Ad Tarsenses*, V. Both letters are considered apocryphal. Servetus probably read them in the edition of Lefèvre d'Étaples or in the Latin translation of Symphorien Champier published in Lyon in 1512.

[160] Servetus did not know the original Greek texts of Justin Martyr which were not published until 1531. He had access to his works through the citations by Irenaeus, e.g., in *Adv. Haereses*, IV, 3.111.27..52, and Eusebius of Ceasarea, *Historia ecclesiastica*, V. 8.

[161] Compare note 129.

ancients. Suffice it to mention one point only, if you really think about it: Irenæus' entire book *Against All Heresies* focuses on this very subject of the Trinity, yet never builds its case with this nonsense of the trinitarians. That is because these "facts" never occurred to people then.

Let us move on to the Old Testament. It is made clear in many passages there that we should acknowledge not a plurality in God, but only a unity. In Exodus 20 we find, "I am your God, and you shall have no other gods before me." In Deuteronomy 6 there is, "Listen Israel, Jehovah is our God and Jehovah is one." In the same book at verse 5 it says, "Know today and ponder in your heart that God is God in heaven above and on the earth below and is no one else but He. He is God alone" (Deut. 32, Kings 19, Ps. 85, Isa. 37, and John 17).[162] He alone is called God, yet the tritheists deny this by saying that He always had three partners. They add the argument that there is no complete solace in solitude. That is why three sat together at the table, as mentioned earlier. Through the prophet God Himself said "I am the Lord and there is none else. Beyond me there is no God and apart from me there is no Lord. I am the Lord and there is no other" (Isa. 43 and 45).[163] The Hebrews rely upon these many authorities, so they are justified when they wonder about our discovery of the tripartite God. They consider our testament to be schismatic [35] because they see that we have completely retreated from the unity and simplicity of their God and that none of their own principal authorities ever contemplated such a thing.[164]

What shall we say about the Mohammedans who disagree with us for the same reason? How wretchedly we are criticized by them! But they are justified and act with the just judgment of God because there is no one "who returns to his own heart."[165] The Trinity is clearly rejected in the Qur'an, Suras 11, 12, and 28

---

[162] Exod. 20:3; Deut. 6:4, modified verse 5, 32:39, 2 Kings 19:19; Ps 86:10; Isa 37:16, and John 17:3.

[163] Isa. 43:11-12, 45:21.

[164] It is characteristic for Servetus to insist on fidelity to the authentic original meaning of the Old Testament such as we can read in the original Hebrew and as it was understood by the ancient Hebrews to whom the text was addressed.

[165] This is an allusion to Isa. 46:8.

where Mohammed teaches that those three gods or parts of God were unknown to the patriarchs, that they are the children of Beelzebub, and that the trinitarians revere them instead of God.[166] In Revelation John plainly calls them three spirits of demons.[167] But let us listen more closely to what Mohammed says about Christ and the Christians. In the Sura of Imran, the chapter of al-Nisa and the chapter of al-Maida, and in many other Suras he says that Christ was the greatest of the prophets, the word of God, the spirit of God, the power of God, the very soul of God, the word breathed upon by God or by the breath of the holy spirit born of the eternal virgin, and that the Jews dealt with him dishonestly. Moreover, he says that Christ's first disciples were the best and purest men and that they wrote the truth without touching upon the concept of the Trinity. Rather, he says, it was the later adherents who added this element since they were corrupters of the holy teaching.[168] In the fourth Sura he says that innumerable disputes subsequently arose despite the fact that up to that point there was no debate or controversy concerning these things.[169] He makes the same point in Sura 20 when he says that the Christians were originally a single group, but that subsequently they were divided through various controversies because they concerned themselves with several Gods.[170] In Sura 12 and in other passages throughout he says that the source of error for those who posit the existence of three equal partners lies in the

---

[166] The first translation of the Qur'an into Latin was done by Robert Retensis in 1143 at the request of Peter the Venerable, abbot of Cluny. It was circulated in the Middle Ages in manuscript form. The first printed edition was published by Theodore Biliander in Basel in 1543. Servetus summarized the general ideas of the Qur'an but does not quote its text. Sura XI: 109: "Be not then in doubt as to what these men worship. They worship nothing but what their fathers worshipped before them." Sura XII: 39- 40: "Are many lords differing among themselves better, or the One God, supreme and irresistible? If not Him, ye worship nothing but names which ye have named .... The command is for none but God : He hath commanded that ye worship none but Him." Sura XXVIII:70: "And He is God: there is no god but He."

[167] Rev. 16:13 : "And I saw three foul spirits like frogs coming from the mouth of the dragon, from the mouth of the beast, and from the mouth of the false prophet."

[168] Servetus is summarizing Sura III Al-i-'Imram, Sura IV al-Nisãa (The Women), and Sura V al-Mãïda (The table spread).

[169] Sura IV:171: "O people of the Book! Commit no excesses in your religion: nor say of God aught but the truth. Christ Jesus the son of Mary was no more than an apostle of God, and His Word, which He bestowed on Mary, and a Spirit proceeding from Him : so believe in God and His apostles. Say not "Trinity" : desist : It will be better for you : for God is One God : glory be to Him : Far exalted is He above having a son."

fact that they are idolaters, worshipers of images, and, indeed, deprived of recognition of the true God.[171] In Sura 28 he says that the patriarchs were unaware of an incorporeal son and that those whom they call the partners of God, are sons of Beelzebub.[172] He says in Sura 29 that heaven is thrown into confusion, and that the mountains and earth tremble on account of this blasphemy.[173] Wherefore he concludes in Sura 50, "We believe in one God, not in the partners who have been suggested."[174]

Hear now with what other declarations he extols Christ. In Sura 4, which I have already mentioned, he says that God's [36] power and intelligence were granted to Christ who was raised high above everything.[175] In Sura 5 he says, "Christ came with divine power and potency; he is the face of all peoples in this age and in the future."[176] He says in Sura 11 that men of all the laws and the Jews and the Saracens will eventually believe in this Jesus, the son of Mary. In the same passage he says, "those of you who believe in God and his chosen, say not that they are three."[177] He says in Sura 12 that Christ has brought the good news

---

[170] Sura 20, Ṭā-Hā (Mystic letter Ṭ, H) , does not treat this subject.

[171] Sura XII:40, Yūsuf : "The command is for none but God : He hath commanded that ye worship none but Him : that is the right religion, but most men understood not."

[172] The closest text is Sura XXVIII:64-66, Qaṣaṣ (The Narration) : "It will be said to them 'Call upon your 'partners' for help : they will call upon them, but they will not listen to them; and they will see Penalty before them; How they will wish 'If they had been open to guidance!' That day God will call to them, and say : 'What was the answer ye gave to the apostles?'

[173] Sura XXIX, 'Ankabūt (On the spider). This Sura is about spiritual growth of men and begins with a differentiation of true believers from the false ones. Verse 41 compares those impostors to the spiders building their web : "The parable of those who take protectors other than God is that of the Spider, who builds a house; but truly the flimsiest of houses is the Spider's house." The Sura is summarized in verse 68: "And who does more wrong than he who invents a lie against God or rejects the Truth when it reaches him?" Servetus thus interpreted the Qur'an in his own way.

[174] Sura L, Qāf (Letter qāf), contains forty five verses which contain no such statement.

[175] Sura IV:171.

[176] Sura V:46 : "And in their footsteps [of the prophets] we sent Jesus the son of Mary, confirming the Law that had come before him : We sent him the Gospel : therein was guidance and light, and confirmation of the Law that had come before him : A guidance and an admonition to those who fear God." Verse 72: "They do blaspheme who say: 'God is Christ the son of Mary.' But said Christ: 'O Children of Israel! Worship God, my Lord and your Lord.' Whoever joins other gods with God, - God will forbid him the Garden, and the Fire will be his abode." Verse 75 : "Christ the son of Mary was no more than an Apostle; many were the apostles that passed away before him." Verses 110-116 continue the praise of Jesus but without any reference to his presumed divinity.

[177] The closest statement is in Sura XI:50: "O my people! Worship God! Ye have no other god but Him. Yet other gods ye do nothing but invent." There is no mention here of Jesus or Mary. .

to us because he is the light, the confirmation of the Law, the arbiter, and the right path. He says in Sura 13 that a pure and blessed soul was in Christ and that he offered a place at the heavenly table to his believers. In the book, *On the teaching of Mohammed*, Christ is called the word, spirit, and power of God. Mohammed called Christ Rohalla, which means, "spirit of God," since he was born from the very breath of God.[178] Finally, although he attributes practically everything to Christ, he does not recognize that he is the son of God. The tritheists of Mohammed's day regularly called him son. Indeed, Mohammed is offended by the notion of three divine incorporeal entities or three invisible, yet equal and distinct, entities that exist in one God. Because of the misguided teaching of the trinitarians, he dissented from Christianity, which was truly an unfortunate tragedy for the world. The incorporeal divinity that was made substantively distinct gave him a reason to deny that Christ was God. When Mohammed denies that he is the son of God, he is actually denying him who was at that time vaunted, namely, the invisible son, who is like his father. You can see this in Suras 100 and 122. Otherwise he would have readily conceded that Jesus Christ the man was the son of God since he concedes that he was born of God in the virgin.[179] Based on that public statement and based on the testimony of those opposed to Christianity, you can plainly see, reader, that that Trinity was unknown to the first Christians. You will find the same situation in the early writings of the Christians and in the curiosities which later followed. Now hear the curiosities which have followed the trinitarians so you may understand, based on one absurd example, that ever more absurdities follow.

Once this deluded idea of those three entities captured [37] the minds of people, the tritheists began to say that there were three gods, and this is what our own contemporaries actually admit, when they say that absolutely speaking they

---

[178] There is nothing about Jesus in Sura XII or Sura XIII. It seems that Servetus applies to Jesus what Qur'an says about the prophets who are designated as "apostles" (Sura XII:111) or the prophet Mohammed (Sura XIII:30).

[179] The Sura C says nothing about it and Sura CXXII does not exist. However, the Qur'an considers Jesus as purely a human being, the son of Mary and a prophet.

are three, but metaphorically they are one. The Arians created an inequality among those three entities by separating the second substance from the first substance. Macedonius said that the third entity, being unlike the others, was nothing but a creature and not God. So it is not surprising that those who err on this very principle, subsequently sink into the depth of the sea, since they are constantly seeing mirages all around them and are imposing a greater question onto a lesser one.[180] The Aetians and Eunomians made those entities so dissimilar that the third one was a creature of a creature, and was incapable of seeing the other two entities because it was written that "No one knows the Father but the son, nor the son but the Father."[181] On this point Aetius and Eunomius[182] differ

---

[180] Arius (ca 250-336) was ordained presbyter in 313 by bishop Achillas of Alexandria. He propounded the doctrine developed by Lucian, presbyter of Antioch, and based on his interpretation of the scripture. He described the Son as a second, or inferior God, positioned between the First Cause and creatures; as himself created out of nothing, yet as making all things else; as existing before the worlds of the ages. Thus Arius denied that the Son is of one essence, nature, or substance with God, he is not consubstantial (*homoousios*) with the Father. He was condemned for his views by the synod in Alexandria in 321 and exiled to Palestine where he continued his preaching and gained followers to his doctrine, among them Eusebius, bishop of Nicomedia. The Council of Nicaea was convened by Emperor Constantine in 325 in order to introduce unity of doctrine among Christians and it condemned Arius again and his followers. He was banished to Illyricum and his books were burned. Only fragments of his work entitled *Thaleia* (*the Banquet*) survived. In 328 Constantine recalled his exile and allowed a return to Alexandria where he even got an upper hand when the synod of Tyre in 335 deposed Athanasius in Alexandria. Macedonius (d. ca 364) was enthroned as bishop of Constantinople in 342 by Emperor Constantius and persecuted the opponents of arianism. His disinterment of the body of Constantine led to a conflict with Arians and anti-Arians and with the emperor; and he was deposed in 360. He developed his doctrine of rejection of the divinity of the Holy Spirit and founded his sect known as Macedonians.

[181] Matt. 11:27.

[182] Aetius, a goldsmith, physician, and grammarian, was ordained deacon at Antioch in 350. But he was deposed by Leontius and sought refuge in Alexandria, where he found a disciple in Eunomius of Cyzicus. They developed a doctrine that in substance and in all else the Son is unlike the Father: *animoios*, "unlike," as contrasting with the *homoousios* of the orthodox, the *homoioousios* of the semi-Arians (and the later *homoios* of the Acacians). Hence the Arian extremists came to be known as Aëtians, and later as Eunomians and Anomoeans. Their doctrines were received favorably by Eudoxius of Antioch and the Synod of Antioch in 358; but the formulation of their tenets was condemned by the semi-Arians at Ancyra and at the Third Synod of Sirmium, and were exiled for a short time to Pepuza. He was again exiled by the semi-Arian synod of Seleucia (September, 359), to Mopsuestia in Cilicia and later to Amblada in Pisidia. Julian the Apostate (361-363) allowed Aetius to return; he was rehabilitated in an Arian synod, and died c. 370. Meanwhile, Eunomius, supported by his friend Eudoxius, transferred from Antioch to Constantinople (January, 360), became Bishop of the Orthodox See of Cyzicus in Mysia. But at the request of his flock he was deposed and banished. Eunomius founded a sect of his own, ordained and consecrated some of his followers. Julian recalled both Aetius and

from Arius because, while he said that those entities were unequal yet similar, they said that they were unequal and dissimilar. This is how Epiphanius relates it in his description of the heresies; this is how Eusebius relates it in the *Ecclesiastical History*, Book X, Ch. 25.[183] Certain Donatists also differed from Arius who separated the substances, for the Donatists posited a son who was the same in substance yet unequal to the Father, as Augustine says commenting on the apostle's words in *Sermon* 31.[184] The Metangismonitans said that the son and Father were two containers with the lesser container being held within the greater. Others used to divide the three parts within God. Maximinus, because the Father was a part of God, suspected that any given person was a third part of the Trinity. Before Maximinus, according to Hilary in Books 4 and 6, Manichæus already declared that the son made up a certain portion of the Father's substance. Hieracas, again according to Hilary, made an analogy of separating light from light, thereby dividing the light of divinity into two parts like a lamp wick. Sabellius kept the unitary nature of God, but disregarded the manner of communication and dispensation.[185] He said that the Father and the son were one

---

Eunomius, who acquired considerable importance in Constantinople. The Synod of Antioch, 362, explicitly set forth the anomoean doctrine that "the Son is in all things unlike (*kata panta anomoios*) the Father, as well in will as in substance." The death of Eudoxius in 370 signifies the beginning of the end of Eunomianism. The sectaries were excluded from the benefit of Gratian's edict of toleration issued at the end of 378), and were condemned by the Council of Constantinople in 381. Eunomius died about 395.

[183] Epiphanius, *Haereses seu Panarion*: on Arius lib.II. t.II, 69; on Aetius and Eunomius lib. III. t. I, 76 (PG LXII, 222-334). Eusebius *Historia ecclesiastica*, there is no cap. 25 in Bk. X. Bk X ends with cap. 8 describing the victory of Constantine over Licinius in 323.

[184] Augustine, *Sermo 31. De verbis apostoli* (equivalent to *sermo* 183 in PL XXVIII, 930. Augustine discusses various heresies commenting on 1 John 4:2: "Every spirit that confesses that Jesus Christ has come in the flesh is from God,"

[185] Hilary of Poitiers, *De Trinitate*, libs. IV, 12 and VI, 4 (PL X, 80 and 134). He relates these various doctrines: "We believe that this God gave birth to the Only-begotten Son before all worlds,... so that He is unchangeable and unalterable, God's perfect creature but not as one of His other creatures, His handiwork, but not as His Other works; not, as Valentinus maintained, that the Son is a development of the Father; nor, as Manichaeus has declared of the Son, a consubstantial part of the Father; nor, as Sabellius, who makes two out of one, Son and Father at once; nor, as Hieracas, a light from a light, or a lamp with two flames." The name of metangismonitans is explained by Isidore of Seville (ca 560–636) in *Etymologiae* lib. VIII, *De Ecclesia et sectis*, cap. 5, as deriving from the Greek word *angos* (ἄγγος) meaning a vase: *"Metangismonitae ideo tale nomen acceperunt, quia aggos Graece vas dicitur. Adserunt enim sic esse in Patre Filium, tamquam vas minus intra vas maius."*

and the same, and that the Father Himself was the one who died. For this reason he was called a patripassian like Noëtius and Praxeas. Nestorius said that "the son of God" was one person and that Jesus, "the son of humanity," was someone else.[186]

But because these curiosities, as the Sophists say, arose outside of the church among the heretics, [38] I will not pursue them any further however innumerable they are. For the time being I will concern myself with the Sophists and their church, by showing that they are genuine Nestorians and that they actually admit two sons although they deny this in word just as Nestorius once did. For as it appears in the *Disputations* of Maxentius of Constantinople and as Liberatus teaches in the *Confession of Nestorius* which was preserved in Cyril, Nestorius never acknowledged that there were two sons, and in many ways by various ducks and dodges he defended this position just as the Sophists do who nowadays are in retreat. Read those sources and you will see these Nestorians as sophists who are hated by God.[187] In fact, even Athanasius, the very chief of the trinitarians, made two sons in his *Dialogues* when he said that truly two were born and two were begotten. In his book *On the Arian and Catholic Confession* he teaches that "the son of man" is to be understood as the human being that was assumed and not as God's actual son. He said that the son of man was filled with

---

[186] Isidore of Seville, *ibid.*: *"Noetiani a quodam Noeto vocati, qui dicebat Christum eundem esse et Patrem et Spiritum sanctum, ipsamque Trinitatem in officiorum nominibus, non in personis accipiunt. Unde et Patripassiani vocantur, quia Patrem passum dicunt"* (*Etymologiae*, VIII.V.41). Sabellius was follower of Noetius: *"Sabelliani ab eodem Noeto pullulasse dicuntur, cuius discipulum perhibent fuisse Sabellium, ex cuius nomine maxime innotuerunt; unde et Sabelliani vocati sunt. Hi unam personam Patris et Filii et Spiritus sancti astruunt"* (*Etymologioae* VIII.V.42). Tertullian wrote *Against Praxeas* ca 211. Nestorius distinguished two persons in Christ, and not as orthodoxy, two natures in one person: *"Nestoriani a Nestorio Constantinopolitano episcopo nuncupati, qui beatam Virginem Mariam non Dei, sed hominis tantummodo adseruit genetricem, ut aliam personam carnis, aliam faceret Deitatis: nec unum Christum in verbo Dei et carne credidit, sed separatim atque seiunctim alterum filium Dei, alterum hominis praedicavit"* (*Etymologiae*, VIII.V.64).

[187] It was not Maxentius but Maximinus. The deacon Liberatus of Carthage wrote between 555 and 566 a treatise *Breviarum causae Nestorianorum et Eutychianorum* on Trinitarian disputes. It begins with the ordination of Nestorius (428) and ends with the Fifth General Council (Constantinople II, 553). Servetus refers to the summary of the views of Nestorius written by Cyril, bishop of Alexandria (d. 444) for the Council of Ephesus (PL LXVIII, 986). The Council of

the son of God. He not only accepts that there are two sons, the one being the son of man, the other the son of God, but he even invents two sons of God, the one being metaphorical, the other being natural. As far as this whole man Christ is concerned, he is now through a communication of idioms the son of God, while the other one was previously the real, incorporeal son of God. Therefore, there are two sons of God.[188] Likewise, Athanasius in the dialogue, *On the Assumption of Man*, says that the assumed man whom some call humanity, was in accordance with the flesh "the first born son among many brothers," and that he is called the son of man: "If the assumed man is a man and was begotten, then he is a son." Our sophist nevertheless concludes that there is only one son because he is a person that has been augmented. Athanasius himself teaches about the augmented person in his *Letter to Epictetus* in which he denies that man in combination with the Word can make one substance.[189] Jerome in his letter, *On the Exposition of the Faith*, which is addressed to Pope Damasus, and Damascenus in the third book of *On the Orthodox Faith*, both say that in Christ there are two complete and whole substances of God and of man, and that the word, "son," refers to the substance. Therefore, he is through both substances the son, and whatever is in our own nature, God has taken it up entirely as the "whole idioms and whole properties,"

Ephesus was called when Celestine I was bishop of Rome and Theodosius the Younger was Emperor.

[188] Servetus alludes to a phrase in *Dialogi de sancta Trinitate quinque* attributed to Athanasius, but probably written by Didymus the Blind of Alexandria (ca 310-ca 398) : "Both are not made, since the Son is not made, but engendered, and the Spirit is neither engendered nor made but proceeds" (*Dialogi*, I. 19 in PG XXVIII, 1146). Didymus was follower of Origen and his pupil was Rufinus. The *Professio ariana et confessio catholica ad Theophilum* is equivalent to Bk XI of *De Trinitate* of the same Athanasius (PG LXII, 3024). In it he talks several times about the assumption of human personhood by the Word, which would assume complete and perfect humanship, engendered in Mary.

[189] Athanasius in *De assumptione hominis, contra Marcellinum haereticum*, lib. III of his *De Trinitate*. Here he states that the *"assumptus homo"* is God according to the order of the divinity which he assumed, and according to the order of flesh he is the son of man (PG LXII, 258 and 263). In *Epistula ad Epictetum* 2 and 4 (PG XXVI, 1053) he declares, in accordance with the Council of Nicaea, that not the body but the Son himself is consubstantial with God, while the body originates from Mary. And he asks a polemical question: "But who taught you that the body is consubstantial with the divinity of the Word?"

to quote Damascenus.[190] [39] Therefore, he took up the whole son.

Augustine denies that there are two sons, yet also admits it. For in the second book of *On the Trinity* he says that the assumed aspect was the son of man and that the assuming aspect was the son of God. "The seed of Abraham was assumed and the seed of Abraham is the son of Abraham. Therefore, the son of Abraham was assumed." In Book XIII of *On the Trinity* he says that "The Word is the true son of God and that the flesh is the true son of man." In the *Enchiridion* he says that "The Word is God born from God, but a man, in turn, is born from Mary." In *Against Felicianus* he says that in Christ the son of God is one thing, the son of man another, just as in a human being the mind is one thing while the body is another. A little later in the same tract he says: "Mary gave birth not to the son of God, but to the son of man."[191] I am horrified by this blasphemous notion that Mary did not give birth to the son of God and am unwilling to cite more evidence since it is obvious that each of these sources sees that two sons were begotten and two were born. I know that they excuse themselves by saying that this son may be called the son born of Mary by virtue of the communication of idioms, and through the same communication this man may be called the son of God. But these metaphoric processes fail to prevent the conception and birth of two sons by a genuine act of paternity. In fact, they really imply three sons. For if this assumed person is the son of Mary and the divinity is the son of God and both of those make a single entity, there is already then a third son composed out of the two sons. The Sophists deny that the substance of the Word and the substance of

---

[190] John of Damascus in *De orthodoxa fide*, lib. III, cap. 6 (PG XCIV, 1006) : *integra idiomata et integra propietates.* Jerome, *Epistula* 15, *ad Damasum, n. 3:* "If anyone does not confess three hypostases as three *enhypostata*, three subsisting persons, let him be anathema; moreover, if anyone understands *hypostasis* as a synonym of *ousia* or substance, and does not confess that in the three Persons there is only one hypostasis, he too is outside the flock of Christ" (PL XXII, 355).

[191] Augustine, *De Trinitate*, lib. II, cap. V, 9 and 11, *ad sensum*, as well as lib. XIII, cap. XVIII, 23 (PL XLII, 850, and 1032). In *Enchiridion*, cap. XXXVIII, 12 (PL XL, 251): "In both substances, the divine and the human, there is the only son of God, the omnipotent Father." In *Contra Felicianum arianum de unitate Trinitatis*, lib. I, cap. XI (PL XLII, 1166-1167): "Just as in man it is one thing his soul and the other his body, so in the mediator between God and men one thing is the Son of God and the other the son of man... Thus Mary conceived, but she did not conceive the Son of God, she only conceived when from her was born Christ according to the flesh."

the man are one in order to avoid the appearance that this substance would be a fourth person in the Trinity and thus create a quaternity among the divinities. This is the reason offered by Athanasius in the letter to Epictetus mentioned earlier.[192] Augustine in *Tractates* 27 and 99 of his *Commentary on John* and in his *Letter to Honoratus* makes a single aggregate of the person so there is no appearance of a quaternity. For, if the human aspect is a person, it is a fourth person.[193]

Now I shall show in contradiction to them and by another means that, given the three sons already demonstrated, there is a quaternity among the divinities. Joachim argued against Lombard for the existence of a quaternity among the divinities and thereby made God a collective entity as we see in his chapter entitled, "we condemn" (*damnamus*) of the *Summa de Trinitate et de fide catholica*. For, for Lombard as well as for anyone else, the divine essence is a certain nature that does not generate as the Father does, nor is it generated like the son, nor does it proceed as the holy spirit. Nevertheless, there is a certain reality, the sum of them all. On this basis thus he inferred that there was a certain [40] fourth aspect and thus that there was a quaternity.[194] On Joachim's behalf I have to add this argument: It is the opinion of all the trinitarians that the Trinity is no person whatsoever as Augustine says in Books V and VIII of *On the Trinity*. He goes on to say that "The Father is not a Trinity, nor is the Son, nor is the Holy Spirit, but rather that they are together a Trinity." They are therefore collectively called a Trinity. This is all the more clear because Augustine in Books II and III of his *Against Maximinus* said that these three were coupled together. Therefore,

---

[192] *Epistula ad Epictetum*, 7 and 8 (PG XXVI, 1062): "It is not flesh and bones, but only it possesses them, for the body in which the Word was contained was not consubstantial with divinity, but only truly born of Mary, and the Word did not make itself flesh and bones but only existed in them."

[193] Augustine in *In Ioannis evang.*, tract. 27, 4 and 99, 1: "One person is the Christ God and not two in order that our faith be the Trinity and not the quaternity. One Christ only in the unity of person" (PL XXXV, 1617 and 1888). In the *Epistula ad Honoratum catechumenum* cap. IV, 12 (PL XXXIII, 543): "That might be only one person in order to avoid a quaternity."

[194] The doctrine of Lombard is presented in *Sententiarum*, lib. I, dist. 5. 1 (PL CXCII, 535). It was declared orthodox since the Fourth Lateran Council in 1215. The Council condemned the opposition of Joaquin de Fiore (1139-1202) whose spiritualism and eschatological doctrine influenced greatly Servetus.

God, who is a Trinity, is a collective God. His essence, which is a Trinity, is a certain collection. On the other hand, if it is one thing on its own, then it is a fourth element.[195] Augustine was confused on this point in Book VII of *On the Trinity*, as were the Sophists after him, for they say that the essence is predicated on the person not in the manner of a material substance as when we say that three statues together form one sum of gold. Moreover, the essence is not like nature predicated on the temperaments as when we say that three men are of same nature, nor like a genus in terms of the species, nor like species from individuals, nor like a container from the contents, nor like the greater from the small, nor like the whole from the parts, nor like the total from the numbers.[196] Instead, it is like an illusion that is contingent on illusions. The question is doubtful as to whether God may be called threefold like a trine. For Isidore in the *Etymologies* says that God is a trine, being manifold and countable because a trinity is a unity of three elements. Augustine in *Tractate* VI of his *Commentary on John* says that he is "thrice God."[197] Hence the question arises, does the number grow from a unity into a trinity? No number can exist without there being more unities. Therefore, in God there are many unities. Did the Father in a single moment beget and then stop begetting? Does He continuously beget that Son? This is an illusory question. For they do not want this generation to have a beginning or an end, but rather to always be becoming like the procession of the third entity, which they say is continuously inspired in and of the second entity, which, they say, is likewise continuously born and generated.

Another question that is far more trenchant remains: What is the difference between to proceed and to be generated? Why is that third entity not said to be generated and why is it not called the son like the second one? Why is

---

[195] Augustine, *De Trinitate*, lib. V, cap. 11, and lib. VIII, proemium. *Contra Maximinum*, lib. II, cap. 10, 2 (PL XLII, 947, and 765) : "These three who are one, through the ineffable binding of the divinity through which they are ineffably united, are one God."
[196] Augustine, *De Trinitate*, lib. V, cap. VI, n. 11 (PL XLII, 943-945).
[197] Isidore, *Etymologiae*, lib. VII, cap. IV (PL LXXXII, 311): "The term Trinity is used because a total unity is made of those three entities as if one said Triunity." Augustine, *In Ioannis evang.*,

the second [41] entity not said to be inspired like the third? The logic that applies to them is the same since they are both incorporeal, like, and equal. On this question Gregory said that it was impossible for him to understand, though he could say that he had a belief[198] — as if true faith can exist without understanding and perception![199] As to this distinction between procession and generation, see the Scholastics in Book I, *Sentences*, Distinction 13 where they spew forth the amazing prodigies of the devil and the illusions of the demons which were instigated by those three sons of Beelzebub with their syllogisms and formalities.[200] Athanasius in the second and third books of *On the Holy Spirit* says that no reason can be given why the Son is not called the Holy Spirit or the Holy Spirit, the Son.[201] After him Augustine, despite engaging many points here and there in Books II, IX, and XV of *On the Trinity,* Book III of *Against Maximinus,* the tenth question of *Ad Orosium,* and *Tractate* 99 of the *Commentary on John,* in the end remains ignorant of the distinction between generation and proceeding, and he admits as much.[202] In John 3 the spirit is to have been born and begotten: "Whatever is begotten from the spirit is the spirit; whatever is born from the spirit, is the spirit." On this basis Athanasius in the third *Dialogue* reckons that the Holy Spirit is "born" from God. In the book *On the Profession of the Catholic Rule* he proves that the Paraclete spirit is God because it "is begotten and born"

---

tract. 6, 2: "I called him three times God, but not three Gods, since God is more thrice God than three gods" (PL XXXV, 1425).

[198] Gregory of Rimini (ca 1260 – 1358), an Augustinian monk and a nominalist, taught theology at the Sorbonne in Paris. He wrote *Lectura in primum et secundum librum Sententiarum,* He says in the second book, dist. 13, that this type of generation is ineffable and incomprehensible for us.

[199] Compare notes 147 and 153.

[200] Distinction 13 in bk. I of *Sentences* of Lombard is titled precisely "Why the Holy Spirit, though being of the same substance as the Father, is not called generated or son, but as the one who proceeds" (PL CXCII, 555).

[201] Athanasius, in *De Trinitate et Spiritu Sancto,* lib. II and III.

[202] Augustine, *De Trinitate,* lib. II, cap. 1, treats the three types of expressions used for the Persons of the Trinity. Bk. IX (entire) and bk. XV are devoted to the analogies of the Trinity in men, image of God (PL XLII, 845, 959, 1057). In *Adv. Maximinum,* lib. II (and not lib. III as Servetus wants) : "This I know that how to distinguish between this generation and this procession I do not know." In *Ad Orosiam,* X : The firm faith declares that the Holy Spirit is neither generated nor ungenerated" (Pl XLII, 770 and 670). Lombard quotes these two texts of Augustine. *In Ioannis evang.,* tract. 99, 9 (PL XXXV, 1890).

from God. In John 8 the Son as well is openly said "to proceed."[203] In this way the Spirit is born just as it proceeds, and the Son proceeds just as He is born. God is called the "father of the spirits," "the father of lights," "the father of glory," and "the father of the Holy Spirit which is born from God." If God is called the father of the Holy Spirit without a true distinction and without a metaphysical generation, then He is also called the father of the Word. Nevertheless, based on the prefiguration of Christ, without which the relational scheme of the Sophists is incomprehensible, we shall demonstrate that the condition of the Son is more suitable to the Word.[204] How John of Damascus feared that this distinction between generation and procession would be unintelligible!

The theory that three points are one point flowing randomly in every direction is unintelligible, and the theory that one simple essence contains three entities in itself, of which the first gradually comes to produce the second [42] so that the subsequent two gradually come to inspire the third, and that on the seat of majesty those three brothers sit at the table is also unintelligible.

At this point, since the derivations and mutations present no obstacle, the Sophists say that those three entities are equal and possessed of the same power. But as Augustine says in *Against Maximinus*, the Son is capable of producing another incorporeal son, and the latter is capable of producing another as the grandson and thus creating among the divine a quaternity and quinity. Even the third person can generate a son in substance. On this basis the equal, invisible gods can be infinite like the whole genealogy of Boccaccio.[205] Who can think that

---

[203] Comparing John 3:6 and John 8:42 Servetus mentions the third *Dialogue* of the *Dialogi de sancta Trinitate quinque* of Athanasius. These dialogues between an *orthodoxus* and a *macedonianus pneumatomacus* treat the mentioned texts of John (PG XXVIII, 1207). The same theme is treated in *Professio arriana et confession catholica ...* where he concludes that the technical terminology is not important since this process of generation is taking place in one only nature of the divinity (PG XXVIII, 283).

[204] Servetus concedes that God can be called father of the Word, but not in the traditional sense of the second and distinct Person of the Trinity. His understanding is that the Word, destined to be incarnated, will be substantively personalized in the man Jesus, the son of God.

[205] Augustine, in *Adv. Maximinum*, lib. II, cap. XV, 5 and XVIII, 1. Augustine expresses concepts somehow similar to those described by Servetus (PL XLII, 780, 784). Augustine, however, insists that the Son and the Father are equal, and that the inability of the Son to generate does not make him unequal to the Father. Servetus makes a joking reference to the title of a book by Giovanni

such horrendous thoughts could come from the good spirit? For Augustine even that third entity is able to inspire on its own, to render itself in the flesh, and to make another savior. Despite this, they say that now only the second entity can bear the body, that it alone can be united with humanity in a fundamental way. A whole flock of questions arise from this point: By what means does it happen that the second person alone makes, sustains, personalizes the connotative man and limits his dependence if all those entities exist simultaneously, each individual one in all individual ones, and all of them in every one, and if, as they say, the works of the Trinity which pertains to the external, are indivisible? Here God is clearly being divided or must exist in the manner of Scotus. The Scotist realists rejoice over this figment as Occam by positing these relationships is forced to admit the truth.[206] Athanasius in his pamphlet, *On the Unity of Faith addressed to Theophilus*, says that the Trinity was born from Mary and that the Trinity took up the body since the Trinity is ever unified and its actions are indivisible. The Trinity went down to the Jordan and the Trinity said, "Here is my son."[207] Augustine laid out this same doctrine at the end of the fourth book of *On the Trinity* and in other places throughout.[208] If the Trinity said, "this man is my son,"

Boccaccio (1313-1375), Italian novelist and humanist, *De genealogiis deorum gentilium* (written between 1350 and 1360, but published first in 1373), and to the polytheistic myths. However, Justin Martyr who represented orthodox doctrine equated the mechanism of Jesus' generation with that of the sons of Zeus (*I Apology*, 21).

[206] John Duns Scotus (ca 1270-1308), a member of the Franciscan order, taught at the universities in Oxford, Paris and Cologne. He was called "the subtle doctor" hence Servetus makes this remark *"gloriantur Scotistae Reales."* He did not write a *summa philosophica* or *theologica*, as did Alexander of Hales and St. Thomas Aquinas, he wrote only commentaries or treatises on disputed questions. He was founder and leader of the philosophical and theological system or school named after him, scotism. Servetus seems to identify the tendency of "exaggerated realism" of scotism with the nominalism of William of Occam who in his *Quaestiones et discussiones super I lib. Sententiarum*, dist. 26 "insists much on the various concepts, relations, formalities, identities, and filiations, about which Paul never thought" (*De Trinitatis erroribus*, 42r).

[207] Athanasius, in *De fidei unitate ad Theophilum*, lib. VIII *De Trinitate* (PG LXII, col. 285). Servetus does not relate faithfully ideas of this short treatise. Athanasius, without making reference to the baptism in Jordan, wrote: "Do you look for the birth of the Son of God? Read about his birth from the virgin Mary; the birth of the Son of God is from God before the beginning."

[208] Augustine, in *De Trinitate*, lib. IV, cap. XXI (PL XLII, 910): "The Trinity together produced the word of the Father and the flesh of the Son, and the dove of the Holy Spirit, since each of these things corresponds to each of the Persons of the Trinity."

62

then he is the son of the Trinity, but they deny this. Athanasius at the end of Book I of the *Dialogues* and in his book, *On the Faith addressed to Theophilus* said that the Father, the Word, and the Spirit are in Christ.[209] Likewise, John of Damascus in the third book of *On the Orthodox Faith*, chaps. 6 and 7, affirms based on Athanasius [43] and Cyril that the entire Trinity, the entire and complete nature of God, is united with the entire and complete nature of man.[210] On this basis it is impossible for them to make out which portion of that triune nature is in the human being, since the holy spirit is substantivized in man as is the Father. The man as son contains in himself, as a hypostasis, the Word and the spirit, that is, God's entire plenitude. Now let us consider other absurdities of theirs.

If the Word had assumed the form of a woman, then they would have said that the Word was the son of God and that the woman herself was the daughter of humanity what clearly points up the two children. The son of God would then have been a woman, androgynous or feminine with a masculine element. If the angels had assumed the bodies of asses in this manner, the Sophists would admit that the angels were asses, that the angels die in asinine hide, that the angels are quadrupeds, and that the angels have long ears. By this same reasoning they must acknowledge that God Himself is an ass, that the holy spirit is a mule, and that the holy spirit would be dead if the mule should die. What stupid beasts! Obviously it comes as no surprise if the Turks laugh at us more than at asses and mules, since we have been made like the horse and the mule which have no intellect.[211] Their greatest blindness is that they do not let themselves be convinced that a human being was born from God. The great Augustine in his *Exposition of the symbol* and in his book, *On the Predestination of the Saints*, said that Jesus Christ was

---

[209] There is no similarity of ideas attributed by Servetus to Athanasius and those expressed by the latter in the cited work. Athanasius deals with the internal relations between those three Persons of the Trinity. His Bk IX, *Libellus fidei ad Theophilum* of the *De Trinitate*, represents and enlarged formulation of the Nicean creed.
[210] John of Damascus, *De orthodoxa fidei*, lib. III, cap. 6 et 7, which are entitled, respectively, *"On how the entire divine nature in every one of its Persons is united with the entire human nature and not a part of the part;"* and *"On the composed and unique person of the Word of God"* (PG XCIV, 1002 and 1007).

taken up by the Son of God and that Jesus Christ was united with the Son of God. In the *Enchiridion* he failed to understand, whether Jesus the man ought to be called the son of the Holy Spirit inasmuch as he had been begotten from the Holy Spirit. He failed because he was deluded by his own philosophy. For, if there is a third, distinct entity that procreates, it is the Father.[211] The foremost Athanasius in his book, *On the Arian and Catholic Confession*, said that Jesus Christ was united to the Son of God and that Jesus Christ was filled of the Son of God.[213] The great Basil in the second book of his *Against Eunomius* bends over backwards with amazing vanity in an effort to say that the Son was begotten and not born as a result of procreation.[214] That great theologian Nazianzenus, following Athanasius, said that the second entity was begotten, but that the third entity was neither begotten nor not begotten, neither born nor not born, and Augustine follows this, as do others.[215]

[44] It is a most vexatious question whether, the third entity proceeds from the Father and the Son or from the Father alone, as the Greeks maintain, but I shall easily dispose of this later on.[216] I just have to wonder why they have not the slightest doubt about whether the second entity proceeds from the third such that as causes they would be reciprocal causes of each other. In fact in Isaiah 48 Christ says, "The Lord has sent me, and so has His spirit." Therefore, the Son is sent by the Spirit. That is how Ambrose explains it in the third book of his *On the Holy*

---

[211] Ps. 31:9 : "Do not be like a horse or a mule, without understanding, whose temper must be curbed with bit and bridle,."

[212] Augustine, *De fide et symbolo liber unus*, cap. IV, 5 : "The entire man was assumed by the Word." And 8 : "Through the temporal dispensation, our changeable nature was assumed by the unchangeable Wisdom of God" (PL XL, 184 and 186). *De preadestinatione sanctorum ad Prosperum et Hilarium*, cap. XV, 30 : "Let them respond to my argument, is it not that this man, as much as assumed in unity of person by the Word coeternal with the Father, did not begin to be the only son of God from the moment when he began to exist?" (PL XLIV, 982). Enchiridion, cap. XXXVIII, 12 : "Christ was not born from the Holy Spirit as from the father, but from Mary as if from a mother" (PL XL, 25).

[213] See note 191.

[214] Basil, in *Adv. Eunomium*, lib. II, accepting a challenge from Eunomius writes: "who are those who call Christ *genitura et factura* that is product of generation (procreation).

[215] Gregory of Nazianzus, *Oratio theologica*, V, n. VII, begins to respond to a question whether the Holy Spirit is "unbegotten or begotten" but later he prefers the expression "proceeding from" (PG XXXVI, 139).

Spirit: "He who comes from the Father as the Son, is sent by the Holy Spirit; according to the divine nature, the Son comes from the Father, and, therefore, according to the divine nature He is also sent by the Holy Spirit."[217] In Book II of *On the Trinity* Augustine gives the same opinion saying that the Son was sent by the Holy Spirit just as He was sent by the Father.[218] Hilary in Book VIII of *On the Trinity,* when explaining the line, "The Spirit of the Lord is upon me," said that in that same divinity the Spirit of the Father is upon the Son: "The Son is properly said to have been begotten by the Holy Spirit. He is wholly anointed with the Holy Spirit, wholly filled of the Holy Spirit, and thus it is said that the Spirit of the Lord is upon Him."[219]

Whether the Father and the Son are said to be two elements of the third entity or just one inspirer in a collective sense or one principle because they are one essence, and, furthermore, whether their essence is the principle of the inspiration, is a question the answer to which cannot be comprehended. The Sophists want that fourth mirage, which they call essence, to exist superfluously for everyone.[220] If, therefore, essence does not inspire, the Father and the Son are not a united entity that inspires. They do not know whether the Holy Spirit ought to be called a "light of light" or a "light of lights." They dare not concede that the substance or essence of God inspires the spirit or generates the generated lest the "substance" or "essence" be spoken of in relative terms. For Augustine, the master peddler of this brand of sophistry, gives us the following rule in Book V, chap. 7, of *On the Trinity:* "That which is spoken of in relative terms does not denote the substance."[221] Why do they concede that God begat the son? and that God begat God? If God is spoken of in a relative sense, already this does not

[216] This is an allusion to the famous polemics with the Greeks concerning the *"Filoque."*
[217] Ambrose, *De Spiritu sancto libri tres,* lib. III, cap. 1, commenting on the text of Isa. 48:16 (PL XVI, 811).
[218] Augustine, *De Trinitate,* lib. II, cap. V (PL XLII, 850).
[219] Hilary, in *De Trinitate,* lib. VIII, (PL X, 213-215) does not seem to comment on the text of Isa. 61:1 and does not refer to him.
[220] Servetus added in *De Trinitatis erroribus,* 42r : *saltem Moderni,* at least for the modern or nominalists.
[221] Augustine, in *De Trinitate,* lib. V, cap. VII, 8 (PL XLII, 916).

denote substance, and God is not substance. God begat, as they say, and He did not beget substance; therefore, He begat a quality. Herein lies the contradiction, which they concede: essence did not produce essence, but God produced God. [45] Substance produced substance and substance did not produce substance. Nature produced nature, light produced light, wisdom wisdom, reason reason, spirit spirit, love love, will will, they all produced and did not produce. The Father was wisdom and reason, and He produced them. The Father was not the *sophos logos* (σοφός λόγος) because He produced it. Read Augustine's doubts in the sixth and seventh books of *On the Trinity:* "If God is said to be from God, why we do not say essence from essence? If we say wisdom is from wisdom, why we do not say reason is from reason? If the person is from the person, there are two persons, so why in the case of wisdom from wisdom are there not two wisdoms? Or similarly with light from light. So then in the case of love from loves, do we have three loves?"[222] They say it is of great importance whether the notions are general or constituent parts of the person. With respect to the denotations of the terms, whether they are general or discrete. With respect to their distribution, whether they are pervasive or localized. Everything is everything, and not everything is everything. It is clear that in this matter all syllogisms are misleading. This *a* is *b*, and this *a* is *c*, and yet there is no conclusion that *b* is *c* provided that *a* is essence, *b* is the Father, *c* is the son! That is how I prove that God is not a Trinity, using Augustine, Book V, *On the Trinity:* "No person is a Trinity; every person is God; therefore, God is not a Trinity."[223] If you wish a negative universal to be the conclusion, it follows thus: Every God is a person; no person is a Trinity; therefore, no God is a Trinity. Every divine essence is Father, or Son, or Holy Spirit; no Father, Son or Holy Spirit is a Trinity; thus no divine

---

[222] Servetus is summarizing various problems which troubled Augustine and he attempted to resolve them in his *De Trinitate*, lib. VI, cap. II, 3 and lib. VII, cap. VI, 11 (PL XLII, 924 and 943).

[223] Augustine, *De Trinitate*, lib. V, cap. XI, 12 (PL XLII, 918). This principle is a conclusion of Augustine's deliberation according to which, because the term trinity is a relative term though collective, it cannot be applied separately to any of the three Persons, "thus as we say the Trinity is the one only God, one cannot say Trinity Father, Trinity Son.".

essence is a Trinity.

Regarding the individual properties of those three Persons, there are countless other insoluble syllogisms. The discussion about the persons in the first book of the *Sentences* from distinction 25 through 35 is long-winded. Here Scotus and Occam, the leaders of the schools, set the bases of our faith on certain notions, relationships, formalities, and *minutiae* for which neither Christ nor the apostles ever had a thought. Chaos is a confused and mortal chimaera in which there is no [46] order, but instead perpetual horror. Why at this point would I bring up the horrific illusions of Lombard, whom the Sophists revere as their teacher? Because in the *Sentences*, Book I, distinction 32, he engages questions taken up by Augustine, which neither author understood.[224] There is the first question: "Why is the Holy Spirit called the love with which the Father loves, while the Son is not the wisdom with which the Father was wise? What is the implication of the distinction, that the Father loves with that love which proceeds from Him, but is not wise with that wisdom which proceeds from Him?" Likewise, "Is the Son, who properly is wisdom, wise by virtue of Himself or by virtue of the Father? For one sort of wisdom is produced, while the other is not." "Through which Person will the Holy Spirit be wise? Through whom do the Holy Spirit and the Son love?" Later in distinction 33, where it says "but perhaps" Hilary presents an insoluble question. "What is the implication of this distinction that properties cannot be in Persons without defining them, while the properties are nevertheless in the essence, which can be determined because they define it?" Who but someone who is totally out of his mind, I ask, could endure this logomachy without laughing? Neither in the Talmud nor in the Qur'an are such horrifying blasphemies found. We have become so completely accustomed to hearing these things that we are unphased by them. Future generations will deem

---

[224] See the note 209. Referring to Lombard who was called *magister Sententiarum* Servetus wrote at the margin of *De Trinitatis erroribus*, 42r : "The Sophists, rejecting Christ, chose for themselves such a teacher." The questions of Augustine are found in his *De Trinitate*, lib. VI, cap. 1, dist. 32, no. 3 and 5, and dist. 33, no. 8, citing also *De Trinitate* of Hilary, lib. I, with the exact terms signaled by Servetus (PL CXCII, 607-609).

these ridiculous. They really are ridiculous, and more so than the discoveries of the demons which Irenæus attributed to the Valentinians.[225] Therefore, may the Lord, Jesus Christ, the true son of God, our Savior and liberator free us from these oddities. Amen.

---

[225] The Valentinians, described by Irenaeus in his *Adv. haereses*, were one of many sects classified under the term "Gnostic" which proliferated in the second century. One of their characteristics was that they multiplied eons or entities emanated from the divinity. Thus according to Servetus, these three divine Persons differentiated by the "Sophists" are an invention even more diabolical than the inventions of the Gnostics.

Treatise Concerning the Divine Trinity

Book Two

Wherein We Explain the Meaning of Several Biblical Passages

In the previous book, we considered the three basic notions about Christ, three responses of the Pharisees, and three arguments of the Sophists. Afterwards, additional points were introduced into the discussion by us, and nearly all the abominations of the trinitarian Sophists were exposed. Now in this second book, in our pursuit of that heavenly perfume, we shall expound upon a few biblical passages so that the scripture's statements about Christ will gradually be made plain to us. If at any time some difficulty remains, it shall be completely overcome in what follows. After all, not everything can be conveniently expressed in a given place, especially in a matter of this nature, which is difficult in itself and has been so confused by the obfuscations of our day.

The first passage

Pride of place in our discussion goes to that passage in the Gospel of John "In the beginning was the Word (λόγος)." Logos properly denotes both an internal faculty and external speech. At any rate, it is a true representation. This representation was an ideal conception or reflection of Christ in the divine mind just as in us the internal faculty and external speech are together a reflection or representation of any given thing that might occur to us.[1] Every logos is a

---

[1] John 1:1. Servetus, following Valla, Erasmus, and Papnini, makes an effort to interpret the term *logos* in its strict philological sense which eliminates any confusion with any type of real entity, supposedly divine or in God. In *De Trinitatis erroribus* 47r Servetus is more explicit: "Λόγος does not designate any philosophical entity but speech, voice, word, God's pronouncement."

particular representation, and a lucid one at that, just as there was "light and logos." Likewise, every type of wisdom is a natural reflection of a given item.[2] Therefore, just as Christ was chief of all things contemplated in the divine mind, so he flashed forth naturally and hypostatically. Hence the very wisdom of God was formerly called ἀπαύγασμα, that is, a reflection, and Christ himself, who flashed forth from there, is today called by the apostle ἀπαύγασμα, the glorious reflection.[3]

Now we shall shortly show how the reflection itself came forth, appeared visibly, and without any change of God "was made flesh." It truly was a divine brilliance bringing man from the eternity and offering him to the world. With John, [48] we rightly say that in the beginning of the world, λόγος was the extension of ideal reason, the external speech in its apparition, the expression, joined to the proper meaning of the verb λέγω, which means to say or to speak. Likewise, all the other passages in the scripture contain this locution: "God said" "God spoke" nor do they use this as an empty expression. Rather, the meaning is straightforward. This is all the more true, since God wanted to make Himself manifest to the world and to show an outward manifestation by means of this expression and this Word. The older tradition of the apostles also understood this Word to be an ordering principle (*dispositio*) in God; in other words, they saw it as an external governing (*dispensatio*) and visible ordering. Irenæus and Tertullian refer to this aspect as οἰκονομία, which means an act of disposition or dispensation.[4]

---

[2] This phrase illustrates Servetus's understanding of cognition which has its base in Aristotelian and Galenic speculations.

[3] Servetus refers to the biblical literature where Christ is described as the son of God and "reflection of his glory" (ἀπαύγασμα τῆς δόξης) (Heb. 1:3). In the Hebrew Bible wisdom is called "reflection of the eternal light" (Wis. 7:26).

[4] These are technical terms used by the early church fathers to describe the status and condition of the *logos* or *verbum* once Justin Martyr identified this Greek philosophico-religious principle with Jesus. *Dispositio* means orderly arrangement, development, organization, and *dispensatio* – management, direction, superintendence, administration. The meanings of these two Latin terms are combined in one Greek term, οἰκονομία, or *oeconomia* (or *economia*). Tertulian in *Adversus Praxeam* (caps. 2, 5, 21; PL II, 156, 160, 180) wrote that God since the eternity was planning and

The Word that constitutes the manifestation of God was located within God as a visible essence by means of a divine arrangement; it is an apparition in the clouds such that whoever hears and sees the Word does so by the grand design of God. There was the Word in substance, the apparition in fire, and a certain visible force, namely God, as a personality.[5] He was called Elohim, a God who was seen with a human appearance: the font of light, the font of life, Christ in God. From that appearance, from that Word, and from a God-given personality in the person of Christ, the spirit that gives life to everything, the one that breathed life's breath into Adam himself, went forth as if from the mouth of Christ. Adam was created after the image of Christ with respect to his body and soul, and Christ was personally in God, when he said, "Let us make man according to our own image and likeness." The Word that existed in God, when he spoke, was from time immemorial God Himself speaking and appearing in the mist of the clouds. After the utterance, it was the very flesh of Christ in which God is seen, since the misty shadow had been lifted away.

Jesus Christ himself as a human being is the Word of God, the voice of God, since he was uttered as substance from the mouth of God. This is just the same as if you were speaking in your voice or as if a cloud was sent from your mouth, subsequently settled upon a woman and, having become the dew of procreation, sank into her uterus and made her pregnant. This is how Christ was substantively conceived in Mary by the utterance of God.[6] John clearly states this in Revelation chapter 19, when he says that the Word of God became Jesus Christ himself, a human being. [49] Obviously, it was Christ whom John saw sitting

---

ordering what he would express by his word: *Sub hac tamen dispositione quam oeconomiam dicimus*. Thus God's Logos or Word is a certain disposition, but not a division.

[5] Servetus uses the term "person" in its etymologic meaning as πρόσωπον: aspect, face, mask, appearance. The Word of God is an aspect or manifestation of God.

[6] This is the most clear and realistic explanation of the meaning of the words pronounced by the angel in Luke 1:35 : "the Holy Spirit will come upon you, and the power of the Most High will overshadow you;" and of John 1:14: "And the Word became flesh and lived among us, and we have seen his glory, the glory as of a father's only son, full of grace and truth." But this is exactly the Greek meaning of the "son of God," not the Hebrew meaning. Moreover, the process of generation of such a son is the same as described for the generation of Zeus's sons.

upon a white horse: "And his name is called the Word of God."[7] Truly he is the Word because he was uttered with God's mouth. John saw the Word of life and touched it with his hands when he saw and touched the body of Christ in whom the divine essence was made flesh.[8] Irenæus likewise proclaimed, once "the Word became flesh," that Jesus himself, who was born from Mary, Jesus the body, who was hanged on the cross, was the Word of God. The body itself is called "the bread of life" and the heavenly flesh.[9] We do not need the idiom of the Sophists to accept that Christ's body and flesh are the Word of God, for that which was uttered from the mouth of God was the Word of God; it was the pronouncement of God. The very Word of God is the seed for the generation of Christ which sprouted in Mary and yielded fruit in accordance with the prophets who taught that the seed had thus sprouted.[10] One can find the illustration of this matter in the mystery of regeneration. "The Word of God is the seed," just as the seed of the sower is the word of the evangelist. The word of Christ's gospel was sown in our heart, and there it spawned a new, inner man through the potency of the holy spirit in resemblance to Christ, who was conceived through the Word of God by the holy spirit. The evangelical word in us is truly fertile being a resemblance of that word which was the Word of the generation of Christ.[11]

Concerning what was stated earlier, the following observation must now be made as well: in the expression, "the Word was made flesh," many ideas are encompassed, and these are more than can be considered here. First, there is the fact that God wanted to make Himself manifest and in His own flesh in order to glorify the flesh. The entire mystery of the Word was the glorification of man to

---

[7] Rev. 19:13: "He is clothed in a robe dipped in blood, and his name is called The Word of God."

[8] Allusion to 1 John 1:1:" We declare to you what was from the beginning, what we have heard, what we have seen with our eyes, what we have looked at and touched with our hands, concerning the Word of life."

[9] Irenaeus, *Adversus Haereses*, lib. I, cap. 1: "I am the bread of life." John 6:14: *"ego sum panis vitae."*

[10] For example Ps. 21:31; 88:37; 111:2; Isa. 44:3, and in the application which is made of the parables in Matt. 13:38 and Luke 8:11.

[11] Servetus, referring to the parable of the sower (Luke 8:5-8), makes a comparison between the generation of Christ for which the Word of God was a seed and the generation of the new man in us humans for which Christ's gospel as the word (or teaching) of God is the seed.

come, just as man himself already was at one time glorious in God, as in John 17.[12] Everything which God previously performed by His Word or Hs own voice, Christ now performs as the flesh, and to him "the kingdom has been transferred together with all the power." The answers which Moses received from that oracle are now taken from the mouth of Christ. "I shall put my words in his mouth, and in my name he shall speak," Deuteronomy 18. "I do not speak," he said, "on my own initiative, but just as my Father instructed me, that is how I speak."[13] He is called the very Word of the Father [50] because he announces the mind of the Father and makes Him recognizable. Yes, indeed, he is even the likeness of the Father, His taste, His touch, His smell. In reality we also understand that "the Word was made flesh" because that flesh was generated "from the beginning" when the Word was uttered. God on high was made known when His voice was given expression as fire, cloud, and rain. We understand that "the Word was made flesh" in the person because that face, the person of Elohim, that creates everything, existed in the flesh, and the very face of Christ is the face of God that was once visible to all. The Word was made flesh in substance because that shining oracular cloud which was the glory of the Lord, "was made flesh" in substance like the dew of Christ's birth; in the same way the essence of this flesh is the same as the essence of that Word. For the formal light itself is the essence of the thing as you shall see. Thus the process of incarnation has a place in the spirit. Just as the Word of God was made man, so the Spirit of God was made the spirit of man as a hypostasis and as substance.[14] This idea will be given more clarity later along with other subtle matters concerning Christ. This mystery of Christ is great and sublime, and it was widely, but not rashly spread in the time of the apostles. John, facing questions from many sides, urging him to oppose Ebion

---

[12] In John 17:5 Jesus prayed in this way: "So now, Father, glorify me in your own presence with the glory that I had in your presence before the world existed."

[13] Deut. 18:18; John 8:28 and 14:10.

[14] Servetus signals here several of his doctrines: identification of the Word of God, of God-Elohim revealed in the Old Testament, with the body of Christ; formal representation of the essence as light; incarnation of the spirit of God in the man Jesus. He gives here a summary of his parallel doctrines which he developed earlier in his *De Trinitatis erroribus* published in 1531.

74

and Cerinthus, and after fasting and prayers decided to write that phrase, "In the beginning was the Word."[15] For salvation it was enough to believe that Jesus was the anointed one or that he was the Messiah, son of God, the savior. It was by this faith alone that uneducated commoners were justified although they did not fully appreciate Christ's divinity. Therefore, when it was known to a few, and at the time there was a dearth of writers and a lack of familiarity with the holy language, the genuine tradition soon gave way to the metaphysically focused Sophists who were crashing down upon Christianity and savaging God. Based upon the traditions attested in Irenæus, it is easy to see how sterile was the perception in that era of this issue which degenerated from day to day as it is also shown by Tertullian. At just about this time Clement of Alexandria was already lamenting in the first book of his *Stromata* that in the tradition of the blessed doctrine few people resembled the fathers and that many details had already fallen away. Finally, in Book 6 he said that [51] proper understanding had survived from the apostles for but a few people.[16] So you, pious reader, if you fail to comprehend

---

[15] Compare Bk. I, note 57. It was suggested that the Gospel of John was written in response to the doctrine of the Ebionites and Cerinthus who claimed that Jesus was only a human being and did not believe in his virgin birth. Ebionites or Nazarenes were the first followers of the cult of Jesus, whether a real person or a universal Savior, or of the messianic movement in the first century. The term Ebionites (from the Hebrew *'Evyonim*) means "Poor Ones," and was taken from the teachings of Jesus: "Blessed are you Poor Ones, for yours is the Kingdom of God" based on Isa. 66:2 and other related texts that address a remnant group of faithful ones. The term Nazarenes may come from the Hebrew word *Netzer*, found in Isa. 11:1 which means a Branch—so the Nazarenes were the followers of the one they believed to be the Branch. The term Nazarene was likely the one first used for these followers of the Jesus cult, as evidenced by Acts 24:5 where Paul is called "the ringleader of the sect of the Nazarenes." Cerinthus is mentioned for the first time and his doctrine described by Irenaeus in *Adv. Haereses*, I, cap. 26; III, cap. 3, cap. 11, written about 170. He is supposed to be contemporary with the author of the fourth Gospel. His doctrines were a strange mixture of Gnosticism, Judaism, Chiliasm, and Ebionitism. Cerinthus distinguished between Jesus and Christ. Jesus was a mere man, though eminent in holiness. He suffered and died and was raised from the dead, or, as some say Cerinthus taught, he will be raised from the dead at the last day and all men will rise with him. At the moment of baptism, Christ or the Holy Spirit was sent by the highest God, and dwelt in Jesus teaching him, what not even the angels knew, the Unknown God. This union continued until the Passion, when Jesus suffered alone and Christ returned to heaven. Cerinthus believed in a millennium which would be realized here on earth before the resurrection and the spiritual kingdom of God in heaven.

[16] Irenaeus, *Adv. Haeres.*, lib. III, cap. 3 and 5, defends the tradition, especially of the Roman church. However, among the most ancient doctrines he does not cite the doctrine of the Trinity, but that of "the one only God the Father creator of all" (PL VII, 176). Tertullian in *Adv. Marcionem*, lib. I, cap. 21: "And if this question were discussed, it would be found in the apostle,

the manner of Christ's conception and the plenitude of his divinity in every detail, always keep the faith that he is the Messiah who was born of God to be your savior. This detail, if any, you must believe in order to live in Christ. As for me, in making my ardent prayer with all possible love, of the anointed one who alone has been given us as a sign, I asked for some knowledge of this truth and through his grace I obtained it even though I am neither perfect nor have perfect understanding. Now, as to what concerns our theme, because we deal here with the mystery of Christ, who is the light and the *logos*, that is the shining representation, I shall thus give a suitable explanation of the language of John.

"In the beginning, there was the "*logos*;" in other words, the reflection of Christ, an expression referring to Christ, a pronounced expression for the generation of Christ. That reflection of Christ was "the Word with God" that consisted of God Himself, shining brightly in heaven, "and it was God Himself." But, for the Sophists to say that "the Word was with God" is the same as if you were to say that the second invisible entity was with the other primary one, in some metaphysical sense, in the second seat at the table (lit. *triclinium*) just as the third was in the third seat.[17] They do not want the second entity to have been with the divine essence, for this would argue for a distinction from the essence; so they prefer that it was with the first entity. Thus, either the divine essence is something else than God, or John infelicitously expressed himself in saying that "the Word was with God." I am talking about essence as understood in their language, which tends towards an understanding of it as a certain fourth element which includes the other three. If, in fact, it is accurately expressed, the Word was the very essence of God or the manifestation of God's essence, and there was in God no other substance or hypostasis than His Word, in a bright cloud where God then seemed to subsist. And in that very spot the face and personality of Christ shone bright.[18] Also, according to their metaphysics, "God made everything by His

had it been so important" (PL II, 270). Clement of Alexandria, *Stromata* lib. I, prologue, indicated that even in his time few traditions resembled those of their ancestors (PG VI, 118).
[17] This is a reference to the discussion in Bk. I, note 140.
[18] Servetus insists on the observations made already before, note 14.

Word;" in other words, the first entity created through the second, but this is a ridiculous absurdity. Rather, scriptures teach that all things were made by the Word of God because God said, "let there be," and "it was done." And "The heavens were made by the word of the Lord because He spoke, and they were made."[19] Irenæus clearly states as much in Book 1, chapter 19, Book 2, chapters. 2 and 56. [52] Before him Justin explained this along the same lines or it was some other earlier student of the apostles that was cited by Irenæus himself in Book 4, chapter 52.[20] Likewise, scriptures show us that God's choice of words was an expression for Christ whereby God called him "from the very beginning" and whereby He pointed him out by calling him, as, for example, in Isaiah 41, where He is referred to as the generation from the beginning: "From the beginning of the sun He called my name." And in chapter 46 when "From the east He called the bird from a distant land, calling for the man of my counsel; I have spoken and I shall bring him." In Chapter 49 "The Lord called me from the womb and caused my name to be remembered."[21] On this basis Irenæus said in Book 2, chapter 48, that the generation of the son of God was called the announcement.[22] On account of this expression or turn of phrase it is said that the name of Christ was produced in the beginning. Psalm 71 is typically cited in support of this: "His name will be generated before the sun – or it will be filiated – before the sun." As long as the sun lasts, ינון שמו *(innon shemo)*; [his name will be propagated].[23] The literal sense of the verse refers to Solomon: "His name

---

[19] Ps. 33:9 and 148:5.

[20] Servetus is citing Irenaeus in the 1527 edition of Erasmus (Basel, Froben, 1527) and hence the discrepancy in the numbering of the chapters. *Adv. Haeres.* lib. I, cap. 22.1; lib. II, cap. 2 and 4, and 30.9. (PG VII, 98, 118, and 163). Irenaeus makes reference to Justin in Bk. IV, chap. 32 of the edition of PL.

[21] Isa. 41:2; 46:11; 49:1. Servetus does not give the exact literal quotes.

[22] Irenaeus, *Adv. Haeres.*, lib. II, cap. 31, n. 1 of PL VII, 823. Perhaps Servetus refers to an obscure antignostic phrase of Ireneaus: "There is no other God but the pronouncement of the Omnipotent."

[23] Ps. 71:17. Its text in Latin is: *"sit nomen eius benedictum in saecula ante solem permanet nomen eius et benedicentur in ipso omnes tribus terrae omnes gentes beatificabunt eum."* Servetus is using the term of the Vulgate *ante solem* which could be misunderstood as "before the sun was created." It is the original meaning of *ante*, but it also means, and is used in the literal sense of the verse, "in front of." And as Servetus explains, the literal meaning of the verse refers to Solomon

shall be united to the face of the sun; so long as the sun lasts, it shall be spread by his generation." But the true sense of the verse makes reference to the true propagation of Christ's filiation among his own [people]. In this way it is not a question of priority in time, "prior to sun," but "in the presence of the sun," "while the sun lasts." The Hebrew word ליפני, *liphne*, has both meanings. It can be said concerning Christ, that his name is or will be joined while the sun lasts. The verb "join" is being used with future reference, and before the sun was created there existed already the origin of his filiation: His filiation was existing from the beginning in the seed which was the Word.[24]

The Second Passage

We comprehend the primacy of Christ by considering an analysis of the apostle's statement in Colossians 1 and by deeper inquiry into how Jesus Christ is said to be "the first born of creatures."[25] The philosophers attribute this primacy to that second entity and say that his generation is inexpressible as Isaiah said in chapter 53, "Who will express his generation?" In fact, Isaiah's words are being violently misinterpreted here. For he says "Cast out among men, a man of pain will be led to the slaughter like a lamb, he will fall silent like a sheep in the face of the shearer. Who will express his age or his manner of birth? He has, after all, been cut off from the land of the living." [53] Philip in Acts 8 shows that all these refer to Jesus himself.[26] Isaiah is not talking there about the manner of Christ's generation from his Father as the Hebrew term makes clear, but about the wicked age of the murderous Jews and about the good lineage of the Christians, which he

---

whose name will last and will be propagated as long as the sun lasts. In the original Hebrew, the text of Ps. 71:17 reads "His name shall be forever, his name shall continue before the sun ..." (יהי שמו לעולם לפני־שמש ינין שמו).

[24] The Hebrew word לְפְנֵי (liphne) is derived from the preposition לְ (li) and the word פָּנִם (panim) which means face, faces. The term *liphne* is used in both meanings of "before" as "in front of," "in the presence of," as well as in reference to time, "prior to," "before."

[25] Col. 1:15.

[26] Isa. 53:8. The text too which Servetus is referring is:in NRSV : "Who could have imagined his future?" The Hebrew text is : מֵעֹצֶר וּמִמִּשְׁפָּט לֻקָּח וְאֶת־דּוֹרוֹ מִי יְשׂוֹחֵחַ (He was taken from prison and from justice; and who shall consider his generation?). Servetus correctly points to the Hebrew word דּוֹר (generation). Acts 8:32-35.

engendered by his own death, and it will be a new, heavenly lineage the likes, greatness and abundance of which it will be impossible to express. As to what we were just discussing, we are similarly to understand "in the presence of the sun, his name will be propagated among the sons." And if the Hebrew term דור, *dor*, were to indicate the creation of the son, we might say along with Isaiah, "who will express the creation of Christ?" Clearly no one is capable of this much. The creation of Christ is unknown to the world: "He is that Melchisedek, of an unknown race," Hebrews 7, "whose origin no one knows," John 7.[27] Melchisedek is to have been likened to the son of God,[28] not the imaginary son, but the human one. There is in God no metaphysical generation of a distinct entity which cannot even be called a generation. It is called the utterance of the Word and the generation of a man. The utterance of the Word for the generation of Christ is from the Father the eternal generation; in the mother it is flesh and temporal. That which is created in a human being has a limited duration. What is of God has an everlasting eternity in itself.[29]

Now consider this next point in order to understand the primacy of Christ's birth. For we are gravely mistaken when we think in terms of the flesh regarding temporal priority and posteriority in God. God touches everything without any interval of time. No decay is to be found in Him, but always the essence. For Him nothing has gone before; all things are in the present, all things are alive for God. All things are bare and plain before His eyes. He names those things which do not exist just as those which do. With Him 1000 years are as a single moment, and the length of a single day is as 1000 years. The prophets teach that in God there are no distinctions of time because they also substitute one time for another, declare the future as the past, and consider everything as being

---

[27] Heb. 7:1-3; John 7:27.

[28] Heb. 7:3 : "Without father, without mother, without genealogy, having neither beginning of days nor end of life, but resembling the Son of God, he (Melchizedek) remains a priest forever."

[29] Servetus states clearly that the generation of Christ does not refer to the second Person of the Trinity, but to the man Jesus Christ who is generated by God from eternity intentionally by the utterance of God's Word. But he is generated in time being actually born of Mary and in this way the Word was temporized by this human condition.

present. The reckoning of time, the designation of which is determined by the heavenly bodies, was not created as something so much necessary for God as for man so that they would fit into distinct times, days, and years. Therefore, He [54] who made time has no time before time nor does He who made the beginning have a beginning before the beginning. This is a firm, solid system. For God has not so much subjected Himself to time as by creating it. Numenius's logic is powerful: "Whatever is taken alternatively as past and future has a certain admixture of privation since the future is not yet and the past is no more."[30] Moreover, in God, because He is the first being and the prime mover, there is no privation. Therefore, in His presence there is no distinction of time. On the basis of these facts the mistakes of many have gathered, and many argue based on the passage of time that a change has taken place in God, though He is immutable, because before a given thing existed, He willed that it be, and now He does not want it to exist since is has already existed. Therefore, since, as they say, the object in the proposition "a given thing will be" is fixed, they concede that God with regard to this thing wanted to have it and later no longer wanted it. From this point, certain people wickedly conclude that, inasmuch as the bases of God's prior knowledge about the future have been advanced, the will of God itself is but a slave, and in everything there exists a certain fatalistic necessity.[31] This is my response to all these points. In the case of God, there is no distinguishing between what is predestined and what actually is. In God there is no discovering his will past or future, no discovering the future or past itself. Rather, for Him a given

---

[30] It is not a literal quote but rather a summary of a paragraph (Fragment V, 9-13 in Numénius, *Fragments*, texte établi et traduit par Édouard des Places (Paris: Société d'Édition "Belles Lettres, 1973)). Numenius of Apamea (fl. ca 150), Syrian Middle-Platonist philosopher, contemporary with Justin Martyr. Fragments of his works were preserved by Eusebius of Caesarea, Origen, Macrobius, Calcidius, and Porphyry. He was acquainted with the Hebrew and Christian traditions. He developed the concepts of the Greek philosophical tradition such as One, Demiurge, Father, Logos, Mother, World Soul into a theological system of hierarchical cosmic entities. Justin Martyr developed his logos doctrine and the three *pneumas* by transposing directly the concepts of Numenius's metaphysics onto the Christian interpretation of Christ and the Holy Spirit. Servetus probably read in *Praeparatio evangelica* of Eusebius, lib. XI, cap. 9 (PG XXI, 871) summaries of the Numenius treatise *On the Good.*

[31] This is an allusion to the doctrine of predestination of John Calvin and in general to deterministic doctrines.

thing comes to pass thus, thus it comes to an end, and thus He wills it. And just as He freely wills something and is capable of it, so He allows man freely to want and be capable of accomplishing his own desire within certain limits. God achieves this through a divine technique just as in man there is a divine technique. The divine intellect itself is reflected in man. To be sure Adam himself or Christ or the angels had a free will. Free will is the property of everyone, and thus clearly demonstrates that predestination is not fatalistic nor does it constrain anyone through necessity.[32] Therefore, those who think, based on God's preordination, that everything turns out a certain way by necessity and measure God's power by their own inherent quality and thus limit Him, are under a false impression. This sort of necessity is anathema to God because it encompasses the sense both of privation and time. Because they think that everything must come about by necessity, they do not realize that God is beyond all time and beyond all necessity. They do not think that the disposition of God [55] is beyond their own comprehension. If the past was and no longer is, and God then preordained it, then He has bound His own hands with the result that not only is the will of God a slave, but even His power is limited. Thus it was the very faulty reasoning of Lucian and Valla in their dialogues, being, as it is, dependent on the understanding of the flesh, and many people today follow their error.[33] This logic

---

[32] Servetus will treat the question of the free will also in the *Twenty Second* Letter to Calvin and in his *Apology against Melanchthon*.

[33] Lucian of Samosata (125-ca 200), a Syrian rhetorician who satirized the decadence of Rome. The vocation of a rhetorician was to plead in court, to compose pleas for others and to teach the art of pleading; but in practice he was traveling from place to place, from country to country displaying his ability as a speaker before the educated classes. Lucian traveled through Ionia and Greece, to Italy and even to Gaul, and won much wealth and fame. His dialogues had a great influence on the literature of the Renaissance and were translated from Greek into Latin by Erasmus (1466-1536) and by Thomas More (1478-1535). Lorenzo Valla (1405-1457) is one of the most influential and original humanists of the Renaissance. Servetus refers here to his work *De libero arbitrio* which was edited in Basel in 1543. In it Valla describes a certain psychological determinism, but Servetus could read a reference to his doctrine in Calvin's *Institutes of the Christian Religion*, Bk. III, chap. 23:6: "But Valla, though otherwise not greatly skilled in sacred matters, seems to me to have taken a shrewder and more acute view, ... If God merely foresaw human events, and did not also arrange and dispose of them at his pleasure, there might be room for agitating the question, how far his foreknowledge amounts to necessity; but since he foresees the things which are to happen, simply because he has decreed that they are so to happen, it is vain

alone has tackled the problem of that necessity and subservient will, which is said to be possible regarding that which neither is, nor was, nor will be. Christ could have requested legions from the Father, which he did not. David could have killed Saul, which he did not. Paul could have received financial support, which he never did. Others could have done many things, which they did not do as the Ecclesiasticus states.[34] This, therefore, is a free ability which is given by God Himself to man: and in no way do those who believe that the predestination of God is bound to necessity see this. God could have saved Christ from death, Hebrews 5. And thus Christ says, "Abba father, it is possible for you" (Mark 14).[35] Therefore, where is the necessity of predestination? If that act, which was so certainly preordained and predicted so many times, could have turned out otherwise, then why not the same thing with other acts as well? God could make him who has fallen stand. He could make a camel pass through the eye of a needle. He can make men from these stones. He can make in us everything we seek or contemplate, Ephesians 3.[36] It was in the power of the soul not to sell its property; when it was sold, it was in its power to retain the whole price as Peter says. Because he abused his power, he was justly punished. But if it were otherwise, it would have been unjust, had there been necessity because, according to scripture, necessity would exonerate.[37] Nevertheless, we are able to act when we want, Mark 14.[38] This, too, is a gift from God: we are capable in proportion to our own will. Paul teaches that men are not constrained to act, but have the power of their own will (1 Cor. 7 and 2 Cor. 9 and to Philemon). He says that we ought not to abuse this power; it is therefore a power. When we have to unite with

---

to debate about prescience, while it is clear that all events take place by his sovereign appointment."

[34] Allusions to Matt. 26:53; 1 Sam. 24:1-12; 1 Cor. 9:12; 2 Cor. 12:14, Ecclus. 31:10.

[35] Heb. 5:7: "Jesus offered up prayers and supplications, with loud cries and tears, to the one who was able to save him from death." Mark 14:36: "Abba, Father, for you all things are possible."

[36] Various allusions and to Eph. 3:20.

[37] Servetus refers to the punishment of Ananias and his wife Sapphira, Acts 5:1-10.

[38] Mark 14:7: "For you always have the poor with you, and you can show kindness to them whenever you wish."

Christ, he himself gives the power (John 1).[39] [56] On account of this, the unbelievers and those who blaspheme the spirit will be more severely punished than Sodom because they were able to believe and refused, thus abusing the power they were given. God led us through his beneficence to penitence, and He grants the opportunity for penitence, yet we increase His anger when we refuse (Rom. 2 and Wisd. 12). He extends His hand and gives us the ability to recover our senses, yet we refuse (Prov. 1, Matt. 23 and Rev. 2 and 3).[40] I admit that some people are totally denied the possibility of coming to Christ. To them Paul makes the response that such is the will of God. Nonetheless, in their case God's judgment will be just as we shall later show.[41]

Now to satisfy the first question, we say that for God all eternity is the image of the present moment and in that moment of eternity before He creates the world and, at the same time, by the very process of that creation God produces from His own substance this son in Mary. We shall declare that the very manner of God's substance is a display and an extension of what was conceived previously in His mind. Thus, if we remove the veil of the middle time, then the very hour when the body of Christ is produced and conceived is something that is eternally present for God prior to the origin of the world. When you have made this concession, you will even allow that God has uttered from time immemorial

[39] 1 Cor. 7:37 : "But if someone stands firm in his resolve, being under no necessity but having his own desire under control, and has determined in his mind to keep her as his fiancée, he will do well." 2 Cor. 9:7 : "Each of you must give as you have made up your mind, not reluctantly or under compulsion." Philem. 14 : "but I preferred to do nothing without your consent, in order that your good deed might be voluntary and not something forced." John 1:12 : "But to all who received him, who believed in his name, he gave power to become children of God."
[40] Rom. 2:5 : "But by your hard and impenitent heart you are storing up wrath for yourself on the day of wrath, when God's righteous judgment will be revealed." Wis. 12:2 : "Therefore you correct little by little those who trespass, and you remind and warn them of the things through which they sin." Prov. 1:24 : "Because I have called and you refused, have stretched out my hand and no one heeded." Matt. 23:37 : "Jerusalem, Jerusalem, the city that kills the prophets and stones those who are sent to it! How often have I desired to gather your children together as a hen gathers her brood under her wings, and you were not willing!" Rev. 2 and 3 refer to the seven churches in Asia Minor and their ingratitude.
[41] No specific reference to Paul, but it may refer to Phil. 1:28 where Paul admonishes them not to be intimidated by their opponents because: "For them this is evidence of their destruction, but of your salvation. And this is God's doing."

the Word as substance and that by uttering it He produced from His own substance in Mary this son. Christ is, therefore, the first born man and one that was born from time immemorial since that utterance, made from time immemorial, is itself the creation of the flesh of Christ. You may again ask whatever was that utterance of God. We shall thoroughly explain that in the following pages. For by a fixed method God advanced, exhibited, manifested, and communicated Himself to the world. Now it would be enough if we should say that from time immemorial the origin of this man in terms of substance arose from God's generative act which was consumed substantively in Mary. But not that alone, rather the creation of him too is the cause of the creation of other things so that he himself is the first principle of all things. Along with the arrangement of time, God retained in His presence the Word that was the Christ-generating act, and used various figures [57] to designate many things in order to manifest the greater glory of Christ. The craft of creation is marvelous! God did everything on account of Christ's glory, and He generated him as the head of everything. For now you might regard these things concerning the primogeniture of Christ as absolutely true. You will plainly see in what follows that he existed in substance prior to everything else and that he has an eternal substance. By another mode of reckoning Christ is said to be the first born since primogeniture is a noun expressing marks of dignity and more gracious benediction, just as David is said to be the first born in Psalms 88. Joseph is called the first born in 1 Para. 5 and so is Israel.[42] By a third argument, Christ is, according to the flesh, the first fruit of all creatures and thus the first born. For our flesh derives from a second flesh of sin whereas the flesh of Christ is from that first, purer mass which existed prior to sin. Thus his flesh by this reasoning is prior to ours and, just like the first fruits, he is the first born of men, even without the mystery of the Word whereby he has another, more divine claim to primogeniture.[43]

---

[42] Ps. 88:27, 1 Chron. 5:1, Gen. 27:36.

[43] With these concepts of a "celestial body" of Jesus Christ Servetus is connected to certain doctrines typical of the Anabaptism of his time, especially to those of Melchior Hofmann (1495-1543) whom he most certainly must have met in Strasburg during his stay there at the end of 1530

The Third Passage

Most people think that the passage in Psalm 2 concerning David relates to this primogeniture: "You are my son, I bore you on this day." In other words, "I bore you before the ages" as they explain when they say that the second entity was at that moment really generated. Augustine has a different explanation concerning this passage since he says that the generation of the Son always existed and that by the phrase, "on this day," the on-going process of generation is indicated, as if the Son of God were some transient entity produced on a daily basis. This is pure nonsense. For that passage pertains not to the act of generation, but of regeneration as Paul shows in Acts 13. Christ has been resurrected just as was written in the Psalm: "Your are my son; today I have born you." Here he clearly shows that the word "today" pertains to the day of Christ's resurrection, and he is correct.[44] Likewise, Paul in Romans 1 says the same thing, that Jesus Christ "was declared the powerful son of God since he rose from the dead."[45] Today the declaration of the son is made glorious and immortal. If he had not risen, no one would have believed that he was the son [58] of God. At that time

---

and the beginning of 1531. Hofmann, originally a furrier, was attracted to the doctrines of Luther and became a traveling preacher in Sweden, Denmark, and Germany. He developed a Zwinglian view of the Eucharist which alarmed Luther. At a colloquy of preachers in Flensburg (8th April 1529) Hofmann, John Campanus and others had to defend their views. Hofmann maintained, contrary to the Lutherans, that the function of the Eucharist, like that of preaching, is an appeal for spiritual union with Christ. He refused to retract and was banished. Next he traveled to Strasburg and founded a community at Emden (1532) in East Friesland, securing a large following of artisans (Melchiorites). He returned in the spring of 1533 to Strasburg, where he preached a vision of resurrections of apostolic Christianity. In May 1533 he and others were arrested; under examination, he denied that he had made common cause with the Anabaptists, claiming to be only a witness of the Most High. He refused, however, to accept the articles of faith proposed to him by the provincial synod. He and Claus Frey, another Anabaptist, were detained in prison. The last notice of his imprisonment comes on the 19th of November 1543, and he probably died soon after. Two of his writings in 1530 influenced Menno Simons and David Joris.

[44] The text of Ps. 2:7 was interpreted in many writings of the New Testament as messianic as in Acts 4:25, 13:33; Heb 1:5, 5:5, and in Rev. 2:26-27. Servetus, though he always interprets the Old Testament within its historical context, does not doubt that it has also a prefigurative messianic meaning, but he rejects the interpretation that it refers to the eternal generation of the second Person. The commentary on Augustine refers to his statement about the continuous and eternal generation of the son in *Enarrationes in Psalmos* (PL XXXVI, 71), where he discusses the term *hodie: "Jesus Christus secundum hominem natus est; tamen* hodie *quia praesentiam significat ... .* Ego hodie genui te, *quo sempiternam generationem virtutis et sapientiae Dei."*

[45] Rom. 1:4.

Christ was glorified, was made a son anew, and for that reason given to us as a new spirit causing us to rise again in Christ's place. This is the spirit of υἱοθεσίας, the spirit of filiation (sonship) that makes us sons by adoption through resurrection. The brotherhood of Christ or its very mechanism exists through the power of the resurrection which has been impressed upon us as brothers: the brotherhood is granted and declared through this new spirit. On this basis Paul said in the passage cited that Jesus Christ was at that time declared the son of God through the spirit of sanctification. Likewise all the power was at that time given to Christ in heaven and on earth (Matt. 28). Indeed it is said that he was declared the son with strength and power. David refers to the same strength and power of Christ's resurrection in a prediction at Psalm 2 where he says, "Ask of me, and I shall give you nations as your inheritance and as your possession, the ends of the earth and you will wear them down with an iron rod." In Revelation 2 and 19 Christ himself recalled this same iron rod and power which he accepted in the resurrection.[46] This agreement of words shows that the psalm harmoniously refers to the day of the resurrection. Christ showed this day when he said, "Immediately, from this moment the son of man will be sitting on the right side of God's strength," (Matt. 26; Mark 14; Luke 22).[47] At that time comes the kingdom of God "with power" just like the son of God "with power," (Mark 9 and Rom. 1). For in both passages the phrase ἐν δυνάμει, i.e., in strength or with power is used. Twice in his letter to the Hebrews, the apostle cites the same passage of the Psalmist in order to show the great power of Christ after the resurrection because at that time he was exalted above the angels at God's right hand and was made pontiff for eternity since it was said to him, "Today I have born you," (Heb. 1 and 5).[48] The apostle proves the priesthood of Christ on the basis of that statement because he says that Christ did not glorify himself in order to be made pontiff, but

---

[46] Servetus makes allusions to Matt. 28:18, Ps. 2:8, and Rev. 2:27 and 19:15.

[47] This refers to what Jesus said during his judgment. Matt. 26:64; Mark 14:62; Luke 22:69.

[48] Mark 9:1; Rom. 1:4; Heb. 1:5, 5:5. As indicated in note 44 Servetus interprets "today" of Ps. 2:7 as referring to the resurrection. He explains this in a note in his edition of Pagnini's Bible: "The

it was He who addressed him, "You are my son, I have today born you." Thus was made a true handing over to Christ of the priesthood because by offering himself as a victim for suffering, he immediately entered into the Holy of Holies by his resurrection. Therefore, Christ is said to have been born "today" because "today" he is made the son, powerful in his glory, as if he were "today" brought forth. The Chaldean tended towards this opinion, "You are my son [59] as if I had created you on this day."[49] He is said to have been born "today" because he was reborn "today," a new man born anew with full power, a new son, one that was made king anew. We are born again in his image through baptism and by rising again with him we are said to have been born anew (John 3 and Col. 2).[50] On the day of our baptism, God says to us, "You are my son; I have born you today." This sense is made clear from the story. For that psalm, just like the following one, was composed when the princes formed a conspiracy with Absalom against David, who, once he regained the throne, said "I know that today I am made king over Israel" (2 Kings 19).[51] In this way when we have avoided a great danger, we, too, are apt to say, "today I am born, especially since today a new dignity has accrued to me." Today were born a son and a king, and yesterday they were not of this sort. Today the immortal sonship was handed over to him. Today the incorruptible son was born, an image of the incorruptible father, such that you would say that previously he was not the son of glory. Indeed, truly yesterday he

apostle Paul refers the expression 'today' to the day of the resurrection of Christ, because, just as about David, who escaped his enemies, one can say that he was born 'this day.'"

[49] Servetus refers here to the interpretation found in Targum (in Aramaic it means "translation") of the first or second century Aramaic version of the Hebrew Bible called the Targum or Bible of the Chaldean Onkelos. Onkelos is the name of a proselyte who is mentioned as a contemporary of the elder Gamaliel, but it is not known who actually made this translation. Some identify Onkelos with Aquila, who made a literalistic Greek translation of the Hebrew scriptures in the second century. This Targum was first printed in Bologna (1482) together with the Hebrew text of the Bible and the commentary of Rashi; later, in the Rabbinical Bibles of Bomberg and Buxtorf, and with a Latin translation in the Complutensian Polyglot (1517). L. I. Newman, *"Michael Servetus, the Antitrinitarian Judaizer,"* in his *Jewish Influence on Christian Reform Movements,* (New York: Columbia University, 1925, p. 556. Bruce M. Metzger, "Important Early Translations of the Bible," *Bibliotheca Sacra* 150 (Jan 1993), pp. 35ff.

[50] John 3:4 in a conversation with Jesus Nicodemus asks: "How can anyone be born after having grown old?" And Col. 2:12 : "When you were buried with him in baptism, you were also raised with him through faith in the power of God, who raised him from the dead."

who is now the son, was not the son. Truly the son of God was dead for three days, and, having been brought from nonbeing to being, he was made the son anew. With the renewal of Christ's body the new son was created there, thus being born as a new son. The entire act of Christ's generation, which was accomplished at the beginning of the world, which fell in death, is repeated today: today all things are renewed, and today the new kingdom of Christ is established so that Christ truly says with David, "Today I am made king."

It would not be irrelevant at this point to consider the responses which the Jew, David Kimchi, made against the Christians in his commentary on this psalm.[52] The Sophists were trying to force the man with such blind arguments that he would ridicule them as asses and lunatics. They wanted to force the Jew to believe in a certain arithmetical and invisible son by explaining "today" as meaning "I produced you before the ages." He acutely responded them by saying "If in those eternities there were two distinct, incorporeal entities, like and equal, on equal footing, they were two twins, not a father and a son." And [60] therefore, "if a third, similar entity is added there to the two equals, you will be speaking of the triple Geryon."[53] The notion put forward by the Sophists, that there was in

---

[51] Servetus lists 2 Kings but the quote is from 2 Sam. 19:22.

[52] It is not possible to determine how and which edition of the *Commentaries on the Psalms* of David Kimchi Servetus knew. Rabbi David Kimchi (1160-ca 1235) of Narbonne in southern France was a Hebrew grammarian and wrote biblical commentaries in which he attacked Christian misunderstandings of the text. He also wrote a separate grammar/lexicon called Michlol, in which, among other things, he introduced the idea of long and short vowels. But he is best known for his defense of Maimonides' *Guide For the Perplexed* during the second Maimonidean Controversy. The editio princeps of his *Commentaries* was published in Bologna in 1471. Servetus could have known the doctrine itself from the medieval summaries of the rabbinic and Talmudic literature or through the conversations with the Hebraists with whom he interacted such as Capito in Strasburg and Pagnini in Lyon. In any case, he must have had a good knowledge of David Kimchi's texts considering Kimchi's influence on Servetus' interpretation of the many texts of Psalms and Prophets and his radical divergence form the traditional accepted interpretation by the Catholic exegetes.

[53] In *De Trinit. error.* 56v Servetus comments: *'Non possum hic continere a gemitu, dum video responsiones quae super hoc fecit Rab Chimihi contra Christianos. Video tam caecas rationes quibus eum compellabant, ut non possim non flere.'* The text of Kimchi was translated by R. G. Finch, *The longer Commentary of R. D. Kimchi on the First Book of Psalms*, London, 1919. Servetus also in his *Apology*, p. 700 of the *Restitutio*, compares the three Persons of the Trinity to "the triple Geryons, the three-headed Cerberus and the Chimaera of Belorofon." Geryon was a mythological monster giant with three heads and three torsos; he ruled over the island of Erythea

God Himself this real generation operating like rays from the sun, was a monstrosity in God that he found abhorrent. This was particularly the case because from that arises the argument for the notion of a division within God, the argument for a change and distinction just like the separation of solar rays, a change and distinction between the sun and the ray. The Sophists are clearly wrong regarding this expression, and the Jew obviously recognized it because in Hebrew we find there a demonstrative adjective which indicates a specific day, "You are my son, on this day I have created you." Even the Chaldean made this observation.[54] The Sophists are likewise mistaken because they provide the Jew with no literal interpretation. What can be crazier than to deny a literal understanding of what was said about Solomon, "I shall be a father for him, and he shall be a son for me"? The passage concerning this one is very plain (1 Para. 22 and 28). Otherwise Solomon would not be said to be a type of Christ, nor would David, nor would the others.[55] Jesus Christ's testimony is the spirit of the prophecy in Revelation 19 although it would be a different literal sense.[56] We grant a literal interpretation to the Jew; nevertheless we warn that there is a hint of the mystery of the future Messiah, and even they concede this since throughout the text often appears the speech which is florid or hyperbolic: "the property of the king" is extended up to the ends of the earth; he shall wear out the kings of the earth "with an iron staff;" "his scepter is eternal;" "over the throne of God sits the

---

and was killed by Hercules. Cerberus was a vicious beast that guarded the entrance to Hades and kept the living from entering the world of the dead. He was a strange mixture of creatures: he had three heads of wild dogs, a dragon or serpent for a tail, and heads of snakes all over his back. Chimaera was a monster with three heads - lion, goat, and snake. Its body was also mixed having the front part of a lion, the middle of a goat, and a snake for the tail. It breathed fire. It ravaged Lycia, killing cattle and setting fires until it was killed by Belorophon.

[54] Compare note 49. Servetus already in the notes on the translation of the Bible by Pagnini commented on the traditional interpretation of the expression *hodie* of the Vulgate text.

[55] 1 Chron. 22:10 : "He shall build a house for my name. He shall be a son to me, and I will be a father to him, and I will establish his royal throne in Israel forever." These are the words of God addressed to David talking about the future son of David, Solomon. A similar idea is expressed in 1 Chron. 28:5 where David reports what God had told him: "And of all my sons, for the LORD has given me many, he has chosen my son Solomon to sit upon the throne of the kingdom of the LORD over Israel." Servetus emphasizes that without a historical or literal sense one cannot talk about the typological sense of the scriptures.

[56] Rev. 19:10.

king, priest," and everything else. These statements were made about the kings after a certain manner but more generously than could suit the kings themselves so that it is easily apparent that the spirit was implying something else, especially because words unsuited to them were introduced. As in Psalm 109, which was cited by Christ against the Jews, there are these three points: the true Messiah is a priest and the son of David; his throne and priesthood are eternal; he is called Lord by his kings and his own parents (Matt. 22). These are the terms that we need to debate with the Jews regarding the image of Christ so that they may understand the mystery of the elements which underlie those statements because they themselves [61] all admit that in the holy tongue nothing is written without mystery.[57] From these statements it follows that son is properly a man as a type of man. The true filiation of this man, Jesus Christ, was formerly manifested through a shadow in the filiation of another man. But the inference drawn from the type of man, Solomon, called a son, that there is a filiation of this invisible entity, is a chimeric filiation unknown to scripture; neither can the condition of type nor some other similarity of representation be applied here. Neither would the truth of that resurrection nor the declaration of the filiation through which Jesus was himself declared the true son of God and not that invisible entity, stand firm. Regarding the true Solomon, the Christ, it is said in Chapter 28 already cited, that this man was chosen before others as "my son."[58] There is no entity that has thus been chosen in the heavens before other entities; rather that man himself, Jesus Christ, is the truly chosen son, the most cherished from eternity.

The Fourth Passage

After coming in the territory of the conflict between the rabbis and Sophists, I shall come to another passage in which the amazing delusion of the former as well as the latter is always seen. It is clearly something to be rejected by

---

[57] Matt. 22:43-45 discussing the Ps. 109:1-2. Servetus takes a middle position between that of the traditional Catholic interpretation and that of the Jews which does not accept an interpretation other than literal and historical, though at times mystical. Servetus by no means proposes a Judaic Christianity, he only aspires in discussion for an eventual conversion of the Jew.
[58] 1 Chron. 28:5.

anyone who fully perceives how devastatingly against Christianity that treacherous Jew, Baal Nizaon, treats that passage, though not even he reaches the proper meaning. The passage is Genesis 49 where it reads in Hebrew:

לֹא־יָסוּר שֵׁבֶט מִיהוּדָה וּמְחֹקֵק מִבֵּין רַגְלָיו עַד
כִּי־יָבֹא (שִׁילֹה) [שִׁילוֹ] וְלוֹ יִקְּהַת עַמִּים:

It is properly translated into Latin as "The scepter will not withdraw from Judah nor the legislator from the midst his feet, until verily he comes to Siloh and a mass of people unto him." Whoever understands the significance in Hebrew of those diacritical marks, *athnach* and *zakeph*, will readily concede that this passage ought thus to be marked.[59] Everyone agrees that the scepter here is understood as David's. What is said regarding Siloh is completed in Joshua 18 where practically the same words are found. In Siloh a tribe of the Israeli people used to gather up till the transfer of the ark. In Siloh the wealthy people first came to rest as the name שׁילוֹה (Siloh) implies, for it does mean quiet and opulence such as the Israelites had at that time when they [62] were by chance portioning out for themselves the whole earth. Therefore, Siloh came before David, and, when Siloh faded away, the kingdom of David began, that being in the days of Samuel. God repelled Siloh and chose David (Ps. 77) just as He repelled the synagogue and chose Christ from whom the scepter would never be taken. Here you see that the mystery and the florid speech suits Christ alone. Indeed, Jacob says that the scepter would never have been taken from Judah as was proven (2

---

[59] Gen. 49:10. The Hebrew text transliterated is as follows: "Lo yasur s(h)ebet mihudah umehoqeq mibben raglav 'ad kiyabo Shiloh velo yiqehat 'ammim." *Athnach* and *zakeph* are important punctuation signs in the Hebrew sentence which divide it into logical parts. Servetus spells Siloh instead of Shiloh. Servetus refers to Baal Nizaon as to a person. But the work Sepher ha-Nitzachon (*The Book of Victory*) is a complex anti-Christian and anti-karaite treatise containing many biblical quotes as well as many quotes from various Jewish scholars who were known to Servetus [Maimonides (1135-1204), Ibn Ezra (1089-1164), Nachmanides (1194-1270), Saadia (?), Rashi (1040-1105) and others]. This work was written before 1410 by the rabbi form Prague Yom-Tobh ben Salomon Lipmann-Müllhausen. It was not printed until 1644 at Altdorf, so it was known to Servetus probably in manuscript form as attached to the *Commentaries* of Kimchi (*Jewish Encyclopedia*, New York: Funk, 1904, vol. VIII, p. 97).

Sam. 7, Ps. 88 and Jer. 33).[60] On the basis of these passages, the Jews are clearly refuted, for, if the scepter is not to be taken from Judah, where is it now if not with Christ? From this passage therefore, the prophecy is evidently concerning Christ and his perpetual scepter after the rejection by the synagogue, and it does not deny the literal meaning concerning Siloh. The words which Jacob used there manifestly show this sense: "Binding his hen to a vine and the child of his ass to a palm tree, he shall wash his clothing in wine and his coverlets in the blood of grapes. His red eyes from wine; his white teeth from milk." All these things came together in Siloh. Then at Joshua's arrival the land of promise presented itself to them as something fierce so that people could bind and load their asses with grapes to the last vine. So great was the abundance of wine that they stained the clothing of the vintners with its must and their eyes turned red from the good quality of the wine which they had drunk. So great was the abundance of milk as well that their teeth turned white from consuming it so often. Thus spoke the good father Jacob when he was bestowing a benediction of the flesh upon his people, who were of the flesh. Nevertheless, he praised before all others the tribe of Judah and he said that the scepter would remain with it because that tribe maintained the kingdom with more stability while all the others were giving way, and because the scepter was not transferred from them to another tribe. Siloh was also praised at times because on account of its double portion, it was the primogeniture of Joseph himself, as it states in 1 Para. 6 and Genesis 48, and Joshua, who placed the tabernacle in Siloh, who came from his stock. The Lord, however, spurned the tabernacle of Joseph, i.e. Siloh, as was said in Psalm 77.[61]

---

[60] Ps. 77:60-70. Texts on the election of David: 2 Sam. 7:14; Ps. 88:27; Jer. 33:15-16. In Shiloh Joshua put down a camp upon his return from Egypt. Here the neighboring tribes cast lots for the adjoining lands.
[61] Gen. 48 and 1 Chron. 6 treat the primogeniture of Joseph and his second son Ephraim and the partition of the land, respectively. Ps. 77 mentions in various passages that God "[He] abandoned his dwelling at Shiloh, the tent where he dwelt among mortals .... He rejected the tent of Joseph, he did not choose the tribe of Ephraim; but he chose the tribe of Judah." Servetus links the three different historical scenarios trying as usual to recover the literal sense of the texts demonstrating

The Fifth Passage

The fifth passage shall bring us back to the psalmist, to that word, "today," which reflects the day of the resurrection: "If you hear today his voice" [63] (Ps. 94).[62] We have that psalm in particular as well as most of the others David sang at the renewal of his kingdom, which was already mentioned as a metaphor for the resurgence of Christ. He sings there a new song and about a new kingdom. The word, "today," refers to the day of Christ's resurrection which we also understand as the day of our regeneration. The prophet, rejoicing with great joy, today calls everyone to Christ. The apostle instructs us similarly in his letter to the Hebrews, when he uses the same word, "today," in chapters 3 and 4. Today we are granted entry into the peace of the Lord just as today Jesus has entered into his own peace. Today the true sabbath finds its completion in us. Today finding respite from all things which he suffered on our behalf, Christ obtains the eternal peace of heaven, and he obtains for us the same peace so that when we have been revived with Christ we may today and together find respite from the works of the flesh, and the day shall every day be called "today" in us. In the passage cited, it is about this matter that the apostle is speaking thus: "We are made claimants of Christ if we hold firm to the beginning of the substance up to the end inasmuch as it is said, 'today if you hear His voice.'"[63] Many people understand "the beginning of the substance" to be the faith by which we principally stand. This is certainly correct. Nevertheless the underlying implications must not be overlooked when it is said, "today if the voice," and, "if they will enter into my peace." The apostle explains that peace must be understood sometimes as referring to the past as in the beginning and sometimes as nowadays to the end of the ages. Chrysostom fully explains this passage in his *Commentary on John*, Homily 13, as "A grace for a grace." He says that one old grace was made for the Jews, and a new grace was made for us just like a new peace. In the past, one glory was given, but now a new

---

that it does suggest only a remote typological but not strictly prophetic sense as is believed by the Catholics or the exclusively literal as is believed by the rabbis.

[62] Ps. 94:7-8: "O that today you would listen to his voice! Do not harden your hearts."

[63] Paul in Heb. 3:7-15 and 4:7, citing and stating the same words of Ps. 94.

glory has been given. As Paul says, we cross from glory to glory (2 Cor. 3), from justice to justice (Phil. 3), from faith to faith (Rom. 1), from the Law of the letter to the law of the spirit (Rom. 8), from the spirit of servitude to the spirit of freedom (in that same chapter, Rom. 8). Chrysostom explains that there is a double adoption, a double testament, a double sanctification, a double justification, a double temple, a double sacrifice, a double baptism, a double [64] circumcision, and all the other things are double as well. Once this was figurative; now it is true.[64] The apostle calls the former the beginning, but the latter he calls the end. Christ consumed and completed everything from beginning to end in order to make us partners in the substance of God. On this basis the apostle wants us to pay attention to the essence of this entire process, which he calls hypostasis, to keep it with a firm faith, and to weigh the substance of the undertaking with a living spirit. The essence, basis, and hypostasis of this consists in that, we, made partners of his substance and glory, may bring back the universal process of the Law to Christ as to our end. That aspect which concerns peace, however, we shall thus relate to Christ with the understanding that the day of Christ's resurrection and of our own is always a day of today, and that that day is correctly said to be among us today. Today in the completion of the ages is the seventh day from the beginning of the world, the day on which "God rested from the works" of the Law, the day on which we, rising today together with Christ, ought to retire from the works of the flesh. To this peace, into which the Jews have not entered because of their disbelief, we today enter because of our faith in the son of God. We maintain one, true and spiritual sabbath, a sabbath of sabbaths, without distinguishing between one day and another; and, because our eternal priest always has peace within the tabernacle of heaven, he too finds peace in us. This is a genuine and perpetual sabbath which was left to the people of God as the

---

[64] John Chrysostom, *In Ioannem,* homil. 13, 2 (PG LIX,93), commenting on John 1:16 and the Ps. 94 distinguished "between what is ancient and what is new; between the type and truth, children and adults, humans and angels, number and reality, slaves and sons, mere lack of idolatry and a spiritual life, beginning and perfection." Servetus embraces this attitude referring to 2 Cor. 3:7-8; Phil. 3:9; Rom. 1:17, 8:2 and 15.

apostle put it: a truly continuous respite of the spirit and a sanctification just as the sabbath was a sign of sanctification. By this logic the apostle says that we have been made Christ's partners in peace. For that continuous and perpetual peace which he has with the Father, is the one which we taste here together through the spirit which was given by him.[65] Prior to Christ's resurrection God did not in this way extend this peace of the spirit to our fathers. But today he shall extend it to you, today to the one who believes in Christ and rises today with him. Today, I say, if you hear his voice today. The voice of God, however, which you ought to hear, is a heavenly voice, [65] "This is my son." Therefore, today, O Christian reader, do not harden your heart but trust the son of God who has risen. He is not some incorporeal entity that dies and rises again, but the very body which truly died and rose, was truly born from God and was truly the son of God. You ought to believe this and have the faith thereby in your salvation because for your salvation he was born from God, was revived, and today was made the son of glory.

The Sixth Passage

The sixth passage will be from Psalm 109: "The Lord said to my lord, sit at my right hand." The Sophists conclude from this passage that there is a metaphysical equality among those incorporeal entities because it is expressed with an equal rank: Lord to lord. Still we must forgive those who, without knowing the original language of the holy scripture, are ignorant themselves. Yet you, reader, if you know Hebrew, shall find the prophet saying נאם יהוה לאדני, "Jehovah spoke to the Adon himself." This passage is noteworthy because it distinguishes between the Father and the son.[66] This same distinction is inserted in Psalm 96: "Before

---

[65] One could look under this concept of the "eternal Sabbath" for a certain influence of spiritualism on Servetus. In fact, Servetus formulated the Christian spiritualism which rejects all forms which might resemble a new legalism: all ceremonies, as few as possible, should be observed "not as a form of the law, but as a form of the doctrine." He opposes the Sunday or sabbatical rest formulating the extreme view that the Jewish Sabbath was a mere type of eternal Sabbath in which the Christian is already immersed (*Apologia*, in *Christianismi restitutio*, p. 709).

[66] Ps. 109:1: "The Lord says to my lord." In the margin of his edition of Pagnini's Bible Servetus commented that the text "Refers to Solomon whom David calls lord as a type of Christ" in accordance with the interpretation of Kimchi.

Jehovah and before the Adon." Here Christ is that Adon, in other words, heir or lord whom the angels worship there just as in Hebrews 1. Here is the Adon, whom the church, the queen, worships in Psalm 44. Here is the Christ, the Adon, whom Malachi predicted in chapter 3, who sits at the right hand of God as was stated in Psalm 109. At the resurrection, this was said to Christ, and then he himself sat at the right hand of the Father (Mark 16).[67] A similar expression will be found many times in 1 Samuel 25: "The Lord shall make a house for my lord; my lord shall fight the battles of the Lord." "When the Lord has acted for my lord, the Lord has acted well for my lord." Wherever Jehovah is placed in the first position, the Adon is placed in the second. On this same point, in Genesis 24: "The Lord God of my lord is blessed;" "the Lord led me to the brother of my lord." Besides, beyond the old, literal or historical meaning, that psalm referred to Solomon when the kingdom was handed down to him by David during his lifetime (1 Para. 29).[68] At that time [66] as David handed over the kingdom during his own lifetime to Solomon to whom it was owed based on the revelation from God, he sang as follows: "God spoke to my heir." When he sang in the spirit, David gazed upon Christ, understanding that Christ was in the person of Solomon. David literally announced the one, but the spirit indicated the other. For the testimony of Jesus Christ, as we were saying, is the spirit of prophecy. This is how the prophets should be read: as if by gazing upon one thing with your eyes, you will see something more profound with the spirit. In this way "the word of God is called a sword that cuts both ways" (Heb. 4). Indeed betimes an expression is ambiguous so that the sense be more fruitful, the true sense be manifold. David called Solomon "lord" as a figure of Christ, that is "in a shadow." In truth, however, he called Christ himself "the lord." By this argument, as I have previously said, Christ roused the Jews to understand the mystery and the divine nature of the Messiah (Matt. 22).[69] In the passage cited, 1 Para. 29 Solomon is

---

[67] Ps. 96:5; Heb. 1:6; Ps. 44:9; Mal. 3:1; Mark 16:19.
[68] 1 Sam. 25:28 and 31; Gen. 24:27 and 48; 1 Chron. 29 narrates the festivities organized for this occasion of the transfer of the kingdom.
[69] Heb. 4:12; Matt. 22:43-45.

literally said to be seated upon the throne of God in order that it would be appropriately said of him who, as it were, held Christ's position, "Sit at my right." Solomon sat there upon the throne of God, according to the strength of God, at God's right, and, hyperbolically, in the shadow of Christ. The holy language is entirely replete with hyperbole since it was not rendered fully in a literal sense but in the mystery of Christ. As to the following words, "Until I render your enemies as a stool for your feet," Solomon is literally referring to himself (3 Kings 5).[70]

The remaining words of this psalm are also literally attributed to Solomon as the next section will soon show. For he is the one to whom the people made their spontaneous oblations. He was called the priest according to the order of Melchisedek, who was obviously both king and priest at the same time. On this basis Solomon too undertook the priestly office for the building and dedication of the temple, but as the shadow and symbol of the true king and priest, Christ. Just like Melchisedek, Solomon undertook the priestly office by making offerings and blessing the people (3 Kings 8). [67] Moreover, Solomon is said to have drunk from the torrent on the road, from the torrent, Gihon, when they anointed him king in the Gihon. He drank water while Adonijah was becoming drunk elsewhere (3 Kings 1). Therefore, he raised his head while the other was cast out of the kingdom.[71]

Concerning the name, Jehovah, we shall have more to say later. For the time being, this should be sufficient: while Christ was on earth, the name was not applied to him by the prophets as was the case with Elohim and Adon. But certain ignorant persons so far have inferred those equal entities, and they say that the name Jehovah was applied to Christ by Thomas when he said, "My lord and my God" (John 20). They are ignorant of the Hebrew tongue in which the possessive, "my" is never joined with the name, Jehovah. Never is the tetragrammaton or the name, Jehovah, added when we read "my lord." Thus Thomas neither used it then nor could he have used this name, only Adoni and Eli. Whoever shall handle the

---

[70] This is quote from Ps. 109:1. Also the similar theme in 1 Kings 5:3.
[71] 1 King. 8:14; and 1:38-53.

holy scriptures without a knowledge of the holy tongue will fall into pernicious errors.[72]

The Seventh Passage

In turn, the seventh will be the passage of the same psalm which is commonly read as follows: "With you is the beginning in the day of your virtue among the splendors of the holy, from a womb before Lucifer I bore you."[73] Regarding the explanation of this, the ignorant are hallucinating because they neither understand the Greek translation nor the Hebrew original. The "principate of the people," they have rendered as "beginning" (*principium*) although in the Greek translation αρχη is used not for "beginning" (*principium*), but for "principate" or "magistracy of the people," which the Hebrew original clearly shows. It is written in Exodus, "the princes and people willingly brought gifts in order to improve and decorate the temple," (Exod. 25, 35, and 36), and similarly for the dedication of the altar (Num. 7).[74] The expression in the passage under consideration says something similar. And since it relates to history, David speaks there about the spontaneous largesse of the people for the building of the temple and the decorating of the house of holiness, and this largesse or offering was made at the time when Solomon's reign was secure as appears in the passage already cited (1 Para. 29). Under this type of historical figure, David predicted in the spirit the spontaneous offering of the peoples to Christ with a greater [68] splendor of holiness. Indeed, the people themselves will constitute the very offerings. Thus it reads in Hebrew:

---

[72] John 20:28. In Hebrew there are two words to express the meaning of the term "lord." One is Adonai used exclusively for God and the other is adoni used for any human lord. Moreover, Servetus here makes use of his theory of divine names whose progressive use in various epochs was supposed to suggest a progressive revelation of God in the Old Testament which he discussed already in his *De Trinitatis erroribus*, Bk I, 13v-15v, and Bk V, 96v-98v.

[73] Ps. 109:3. Servetus follows the text of the Vulgate.

[74] Exod. 25:2 : "Tell the Israelites to take for me an offering; from all whose hearts prompt them to give you shall receive the offering for me." Exod. 35:5 : "let whoever is of a generous heart bring the LORD's offering." Exod. 36:2 : "everyone whose heart was stirred to come to do the work."

עמך נדבת ביום הילך בהדרי קדש מרחם משחר לך טל ילדתך

In other words, "Your people are a spontaneous offering on the day of your strength, among the beauty of your holiness, from the womb, from the dawn: for you are the dew of your youth." That is how it is expressed in Hebrew, and it is the correct sense.[75] Those spontaneous offerings of the people were made on the day of strength or power of Solomon, because on that day his kingdom was strengthened and affirmed as the most powerful just like the kingdom of Christ at the resurrection. On the same day Solomon was made king anew, a symbol of Christ, and for the second time he was anointed king as is said in chapter 29.[76] Just so the same the kingdom of God came anew with power on the day of Christ's resurrection. He said above that these offerings were made "among the beauty of your holiness" because they were made for the beauty and ornament of the holy temple. Just so we sanctify and decorate our temple by offering ourselves to our own Solomon. He stated there "from the womb" and "from the dawn" since children born from the womb and from the beginning of day were offering gifts. He later added, "yours was the dew of your youth" because that offering was made to Solomon in his youth and in the youth of his reign. Likewise, in terms of the spirit, the offering of the peoples was made to Christ at the beginning of his reign with far greater splendor of holiness and far greater beauty: not by children of the flesh, but by children of the spirit, and from the dawn of Christ's resurrection. These were the people offering their property along with themselves to Solomon, as is clear from the Acts of the apostles. Moreover, he said "spontaneous largesse" to distinguish the offering, as the word, נדב, *nadab,* (to donate), differs from נדר, *nadar* (to vow) (Lev. 7, 22, 23; Num. 15, 29; and Deut. 12).[77] Christ's people are spontaneous and constrained by no promises. Regarding

---

[75] The exact literal translation of this verse is: "Your people shall be willing in the day of your power; in the majesties of holiness from the womb of the dawn, to you is the dew of your youth."

[76] 1 Chron. 29:22 : "They made David's son Solomon king a second time; they anointed him as the LORD's prince, and Zadok as priest."

[77] Lev. 7:16 : "But if the sacrifice you offer is a votive offering or a freewill offering, it shall be eaten on the day that you offer your sacrifice." Lev. 22:23 : "An ox or a lamb that has a limb too

this spontaneous offering, the scripture speaks throughout with a similar mystery by means of the same word, *nadab*, as in Psalms 46, 53; Ester 1, Ezekiel 44, 45, 46, and 48.[78] Regarding the same offering, David himself spoke in Psalm 71, where gifts are offered to Solomon by various kings. [69] Nor does the fact that the gold from Arabia and Ethiopia was not similarly given to Christ present any difficulty. For in the phrasing of the Law or history the prophets typically prophesy. Offerings in the literal sense belong to history; the offering of the spirit and the spiritual offerings look to Christ. It is sufficient that those material gifts were given to Solomon and that the gold of Arabia and Tharsus was offered (3 Kings 4 and 10 and 2 Para. 9).[79] What is said by the expression "in the splendors of holiness" is made clear by the same David in Psalms 28, 95 and 1 Para. 16. The place that is holy, beautiful, and full of glory, they call the "beauty of holiness" and the "glory of holiness."[80] In this instant it is expressed in the plural, beauties or splendors, in order to emphasize the meaning because the splendor of glory is manifold. Psalm 67 goes in the same direction: "In your temple in Jerusalem, kings will offer gifts to you."[81] Even if in that earthly Jerusalem and in that temple none of these things was offered to Christ by the kings. Christ demands greater things of us since on this question he teaches us about the temple of his body, and, speaking about Sheba, the queen who offered gifts to Solomon, he said "behold,

---

long or too short you may present for a freewill offering; but it will not be accepted for a vow." Lev. 23:38 : "apart from the sabbaths of the LORD, and apart from your gifts, and apart from all your votive offerings, and apart from all your free will offerings, which you give to the LORD."
The same differentiation is presented in other texts: Num. 15:3, 29:39; Deut. 12:6. The word *nadab* means to give or donate voluntarily, whereas the word *nadar* means to make a vow or offering. Both words, however, meant voluntary or spontaneous offering. Servetus, though he always adhered strictly to the philological meaning of the text, goes beyond the meaning of the Hebrew text and here we can find the basis for his rejection of vows, especially of the monastic vows.

[78] In these texts the term *nadab* is used in the meaning of offering which Servetus interprets as voluntary.

[79] That is 1 Kings 4:21 and 10:10-22 where the visit of the queen of Sheba is narrated. Parallel narration is in 2 Chron. 9. Important is the formulation of Servetus's hermeneutical principle: *"in terminis legis, seu historiae solent prophetare prophetae."*

[80] Ps. 28:2, Ps. 95:9, 1 Chron. 16:29 : "in holy splendor" (Latin *"in decore sancto,"*). The Hebrew term which is used in all these instances is: בְּהַדְרַת־קֹדֶשׁ

[81] Ps. 67:29.

this is more than Solomon."[82] Christ does not seek what belongs to us, but rather our very persons.

The Eighth Passage

Isaiah 7 will be the eighth passage: "Behold you are a pregnant virgin and will give birth to a son, and, as his mother, you will call him by his name, Emmanuel. He shall eat curds (*butyrum*) and honey that he may know to reject evil and choose good because before the boy knows to reject evil and choose good, the land which you hate shall be freed from the face of its two kings, Rezin and Pekah."[83] According to history a sign was then given to Ahaz in his moment of fear for him to understand that soon his two enemies, Rezin and Pekah, would be destroyed and the kingdom of Judah would be freed of them. Ahaz clearly was at that time very afraid of these two kings because he had already suffered many ills at their hands (2 Para. 28). And Isaiah had predicted this earlier in chapters 3 and 4.[84] And much later he became afraid when he saw them come into the very city of Jerusalem after the kingdom of Judea had been almost entirely destroyed. And then a sign was given to him, one that suited that age [70] and held the mystery of Christ. Isaiah portrays literally the king's wife, Abijah, who was present there, the daughter of Zechariah whom he even called a prophetess because she had prophesied when giving the divine name to her son. Mothers are apt to honor their sons with great names: so Isaiah then directed his speech to the

---

[82] In Matt. 12:42. The reference to the temple of his body is in Col. 2:17.

[83] Isa. 7:14-16. Servetus interprets this crucial text strictly in its historical sense which he explained on the margin of his edition of Pagnini's Bible. The prophet refers to a young woman who will conceive and bear a child. This woman is Abijah, wife of the king Ahaz, who was to give birth to his son, the future king Hezekiah, the strength of God and Immanuel (God is with us), and before he began his reign those two kings, Rezin and Pekah, enemies of Judea, were defeated as it is recorded in 2 Kings 16 and 18.

[84] 2 Chron. 28:1-3 : "Ahaz was twenty years old when he began to reign; he reigned sixteen years in Jerusalem. He did not do what was right in the sight of the LORD, as his ancestor David had done, but he walked in the ways of the kings of Israel. He even made cast images for the Baals; and he made offerings in the valley of the son of Hinnom, and made his sons pass through fire, according to that abominable practice." King Ahaz deviated from Jewish righteousness and for this he was defeated. He probably sacrificed his sons ("made his sons pass through fire") and would die childless if it were not a special favor of God to give him another son, Hezekiah, about whom Isaiah is prophesying. Isaiah 3 and 4 describe in a poetic manner all the calamities which have fallen on Judah.

mother. Thus the son was properly called Hezekiah, in other words, the "strength of God;" and he said that he was properly called by him Immanuel "god is with us." Hezekiah was called Immanuel just as Solomon was called Lemuel in Proverbs 31 because at that time God was with them. Solomon's mother called him Lemuel just as Hezekiah's mother called him Immanuel.[85] While a girl and a virgin, the said Abijah, as if by a great miracle, conceived Hezekiah. Ahaz was only 11 years old when she became pregnant with Hezekiah as the history of the kings says. Realizing this, the prophetess gave her son a divine name. He was conceived in the womb of a virgin as a symbol of Christ Jesus. Through a sort of hyperbole and figurative expression he could be said to have been conceived within a virgin, especially since the Hebrew expression indicates a "young girl" as well.[86] She could even be called a virgin on account of her youthful age. Abijah did not conceive without the seed of a man as Mary was the mother of Jesus: nonetheless Isaiah indicates that a miracle was adumbrated somewhat in the conception of Hezekiah, who, for that reason, was called "the strength of God" and "God is with us" because in his day God was with the people against all enemies, and especially against the Assyrians, and, in this case, powerfully so. On the basis of that miraculous sign, Isaiah teaches the greater miracle of the true virgin. The evidence of history ought not to be spurned even though it does not contain the complete truth. Hence chapter 9 about Hezekiah himself is consequently written: "Every battle of a warrior is with struggle and goriness of clothing, and that will be burned as fuel for the fire in a miraculous consumption of fire" by the angel against the Assyrians, just as Christ through a fiery sword destroyed the enemies and the Antichrist himself, who was symbolized by the

---

[85] Prov. 31:1 : "The words of King Lemuel." Prov. 1:4 : "It is not for kings, O Lemuel, it is not for kings to drink wine."

[86] The Hebrew term 'almah (עַלְמָה) (= young woman) appears four times in the Bible and never with a clear connotation of virginity or lack thereof (unless it is the meaning of the passage in Prov. 30:19). The Hebrew word for virgin is בתולה (b°tulah). The Greek version of the LXX translated the term 'almah into παρθένος, the virgin, or young girl. The exegetes saw in the text of Isaiah a prophecy of the virginal birth of Jesus and, especially, that this text was utilized in

Assyrian (Isa. 11).[87] Hence like the third day of Christ's resurrection, [71] through the speeches of Hezekiah there occurred on the third day the miraculous liberation of the people, and on the third day Hezekiah himself, as if rising from death, ascended to the house of the Lord like a true symbol of Christ (Hos. 6 and 4 Kings 20).[88] Finally everything that Isaiah said about Christ from the beginning to the fortieth chapter is typified in the history of Hezekiah. In the fortieth chapter he starts to talk about Cyrus who also was a symbol of Jesus Christ as a liberator from captivity and for that reason was also called christ just like Immanuel or Lemuel. Notice moreover, how precisely in chapter 7 Isaiah says הרה וילדת, *hara veioledeth*, meaning, pregnant and about to give birth or conceiving and about to give birth, so that the phrase reaches for the future and the past like a sword that cuts both ways. For Hezekiah was already born at that time as Isaiah explains by repeating the same words in the following chapter. "I have approached," he said, "that prophetess who conceived and bore a son: in whose childhood destruction of Damascus and Samaria took place."[89] But why did he say, "he shall eat curds and honey in order to know to reject evil and choose good?" The prophet sets this out in the same passage when he says that they shall eat curds and honey for their poverty of cattle and the destruction of their beehives. Such bounty will God soon give after these wretched depredations of the enemy so that in eating curds and honey even the children will see the goodness of God and learn to choose good and reject evil. And at that time Hezekiah, as a boy, will know this. For that is the food of children, so it is there

---

Matt. 1:23. Servetus preserves the literal sense of this passage with a possibility of its typological use.

[87] Isa. 9:5 and 11:16.

[88] Hos. 6:2 : "After two days he will revive us; on the third day he will raise us up, that we may live before him." And similarly in 2 Kings 20:5-6 when narrating the illness of Hezekiah : "Turn back, and say to Hezekiah prince of my people, Thus says the LORD, the God of your ancestor David: I have heard your prayer, I have seen your tears; indeed, I will heal you; on the third day you shall go up to the house of the LORD. I will add fifteen years to your life."

[89] Isa. 8:3-4 : "And I went to the prophetess, and she conceived and bore a son. Then the LORD said to me, Name him Maher-shalal-hash-baz; for before the child knows how to say "My father" or "My mother," the wealth of Damascus and the spoil of Samaria will be carried away by the king of Assyria."

given to the boy. And he even makes allusion to the fertility which was so unexpectedly given, and for that reason God is especially to be praised. In this matter even Ahaz was restrained because he had chosen evil and rejected good without considering the great gifts of God because the curds and honey have so quickly become abundant after the destruction of the cattle and beehives by the enemy. A sign like the bounty which next is to come is given in chapter 37 of Isaiah.[90] The prophet even provides another example of a sign. [72] Because, before the boy knows to reject evil and choose good, "the land of those two kings, Rezin and Pekah, the land which you abhor, Ahaz, will be abandoned by them." For they both shall be killed before this boy reaches the mature age that brings the knowledge of good and evil. And this came to pass a little later (4 Kings 15 and 16).[91] "Therefore you, Ahaz, accept this sign that God will save this kingdom for your son. For behold a girl, though a virgin, miraculously conceiving and bearing a son, whom you, the mother, shall justly call, Immanuel. And through him God shall make miracles among the people, and he shall save the people. He, yet a boy, because of the fertility which God shall so quickly give, will know the good path of God and reject the wicked one. Indeed, there is another thing. Because before the boy reaches that point, those two kings whom you fear will be destroyed." All these things were fulfilled to the letter and must so be explained. We must not overlook the meanings of the old history through which the mysteries of Christ are particularly illustrated. For it is he alone whom the virgin truly conceived and bore. He alone is the true Hezekiah, the true Immanuel, the strong God, the father of eternity, the prince of peace.

The Ninth Passage

Now the ninth passage, which is John 3, must be explained: "No one has ascended to heaven, except he who has descended from heaven, the son of man, who is in heaven."[92] It is something amazing that Christ, who exists on earth, is

---

[90] Isa. 37:30-32. Servetus commented on the passage in his edition of the Bible of Pagnini using *Commentary on the Prophets* by David Kimchi which he could read in the Pisa edition of 1515.

[91] 2 Kings 15:29-38, 16:7-9 with the help of the king of Assyria.

[92] John 3:13, in a conversation with Nicodemus.

said to be in heaven, and yet to have both ascended into heaven and descended. But we touched upon the notion that Christ descended from heaven in the previous book, and we shall expand upon this again. For the heavenly Word made flesh on earth expressed the substance of flesh so that the flesh itself is said to be from heaven: because that flesh in itself actually has the divine substance from heaven. Indeed, that Christ has already ascended into heaven, I shall show in the following way. For man's ascent to God follows from the incarnation of the Word. The Word that descends to earth from heaven brings earth back to heaven by making us all heavenly. We say that Christ has already ascended to the bosom of the Father and that at that time heaven was for him the unapproachable light, [73] which the Father inhabits. Truly he who brought heaven to us, was then already in heaven. He alone then ascended to heaven. For neither had the soul of Abraham nor have the souls of the patriarchs been received into the celestial regions at that time. Indeed, he truly said, "No one." It was he alone who was in heaven, since we were not yet "born on high," as he said there. However, when we are "born from above," we are then said to ascend into heaven, having been made heavenly men engaged in the intercourse with heaven.[93] We are even said to descend from heaven, having been born from heaven, since the spirit was given to us which descends from the heavens; and having been born in the heavens, since the spirit was given to us which descends from the heavens and transports us into heaven. Therefore the saying of Christ that then suited him alone and after the supernatural regeneration will apply to us, is always true: no one is said to ascend into heaven save whoever descends from heaven, being born from heaven and transported thereto even through the holy spirit, which descends from heaven. Thus through Christ the heavenly and terrestrial are joined together and the heavenly descends to us in order to transport the earth to heaven. Therefore the holy who were born from heaven descended from heaven, not just Christ himself.

---

[93] Though this doctrine is based on the baptismal formula of John 3:4-7, there is here a certain neo-Platonist tone. The basic concepts were already treated by Servetus in his *De Trinitatis erroribus* 44v & ff. at the beginning of Bk. II in a much less systematic manner. Here Servetus wrote: *"Nec considerant quod coelum illic est, ubicumque Christus est"* (Bk. II. 44v).

But he alone descended through natural birth and all "the fullness of divinity."

The Tenth Passage

The tenth passage shall be that of Paul when he says to the Colossians, "In Christ inhere all the fulfillment of the Law and all the fulfillment of divinity as flesh."[94] The whole fulfillment of the Law is in Christ. For the shadows of the Laws represented different mysteries which were all fulfilled in this body, realized actually and physically. Even the fulfillment of divinity simultaneously with the fulfillment of the Law is completely in Christ and is visible and tangible in the manner of a body as a body. The very body of Christ is the very fulfillment in which all things are fulfilled, come together, are regathered and reconciled, God and man, heaven and earth, Jews and Gentiles, circumcision and foreskin, kingdom and priesthood, Law and prophets. The very body of Christ and the body of divinity, his divine flesh, the flesh of God, the blood of God, the [74] very flesh of Christ is heavenly, born from the substance of God. As it was in the tomb, it had form as substance from the substance of God's light and the higher elements from the substance of God's Word, as we shall say later.[95] Divinity is said to be in that flesh bodily, a thing which did not happen in the shadow of the Law. So the body is appropriately opposed to the shadow. Moreover, based on the fact that Paul said it "inhabited," it is shown why divinity was in it. The *rabbinim* called divinity שכינה, *shechina*, which comes from the word שכן, *shachan*, which means to "inhabit." Therefore the divinity of Christ is God's act of dwelling. In Christ there is not some portion of God, but the whole totality of God, the whole fulfillment of the Word and the spirit. From the same word that refers to God's dwelling, the tabernacle where God lives, is called in the Law מישכן, *mishchan*, the "dwelling of God."[96] It is the dwelling of God in which Paul says, "in Christ

---

[94] Col. 2:9.

[95] This is another of the Servetian doctrines, the doctrine of the "celestial body" of Christ. He might have been influenced in this doctrine by Melchior Hofmann (1495-1543/44).

[96] In the rabbinic literature the term *shechina* is used to designate the presence of God or of his spirit in the community of Israel. Though Servetus is using the term in a different meaning, it is useful for the purpose of opposing the doctrine of the double nature of Christ in the traditional

God was reconciling the world to Himself" (2 Cor 5).[97] Christ's divinity is God in Christ, as in His image His divinity was in the tabernacle. Adapting Himself to this understanding of His divinity and at the same time accounting for the Law, Paul clearly teaches us that the divinity of the tabernacle and the angels who were seen there, was the shadow of His truth, which is in the body of Christ. "These things are, he says, the shadow of the future, but the body is of Christ."[98] There the divinity was figured, without a true body, and here it is truly the body of divinity. The true divinity figured through those shadows is manifested bodily in Christ, in the very body and flesh of Christ. In Christ there is the whole divinity of the Father and the angels. The entire fulfillment of God, the whole God the Father, with the totality of their properties, of His entire substance, the fulfillment of power and divinity, and splendor, He completely dwells in this body. The total hypostasis of God, the nature and essence, the complete apparition of God, the worship, and mien, whatever God has, adheres in Christ as substance and bodily so the Christ truly is ὁμοούσιος with God, the Father, truly consubstantial.[99] In Christ himself alone God subsists and is seen. There is no other face, nor person, nor hypostasis of God [75] except him himself. Throughout the scriptures teach about the splendor of His face whereby the heavens themselves are illuminated and will be illuminated in the age to come. The light itself by which God is light is observed in the face of Jesus Christ alone. So completely is the divinity and glory of the Father in him that the angels may marvel at this and learn the future through him and see it in him. Not only is God present in him but the entire power of God has been given to him. All things are accomplished through Christ in the

---

orthodox sense which claimed the preexistence of the second Person which later would inhabit corporally in the man Jesus.

[97] 2 Cor. 5:19.

[98] Col. 2:17 : "These are only a shadow of what is to come, but the substance belongs to Christ" (*quae sunt umbra futurorum corpus autem Christi*). The concept of the shadow (*umbra*) is equivalent to that of the type (*typus*) which is fundamental for the theory of Servetus.

[99] But one should not ignore a totally different sense of the term understood by the Nicene fathers who claimed that the Word was consubstantial with the Father, and that by Servetus. The man Jesus, being son of God, is consubstantial with his father, the concept which has a strong affinity with realism.

spirit and virtue. All things are accomplished through Christ in the person. All things are accomplished through Christ in the substance. All things through Christ and in Christ are seen and exist in essence.

The Eleventh Passage

Our eleventh passage: "The Father is in me, and I am in the Father" (John 14).[100] Hilary said at the beginning of his third Book *On the Trinity* that the nature of human intelligence does not comprehend through what way those three entities may exist each one in the other one.[101] Augustine made a contribution in his *Commentary on Peter Regarding Faith* and at the end of Book 6 *On the Trinity* by adding that those three entities are total in each other.[102] Athanasius in Book 3 *On the Holy Spirit* makes an amusing statement about the invisible images to the effect that those entities are all in all.[103] It really takes the breath away, the fact that they allow him to be alienated from himself and that they have no regard for the straightforward interpretation of Christ. For in the same chapter Christ addresses the apostles saying, "The Father is in me, and I am in you: I am in the Father and you are in me." Christ is in the Father, and he is substantively united with Him. The Father is in him as far as it is said, "God was in Christ," because all divinity was in him both bodily and spiritually. "God was in Christ reconciling the world to Himself" (2 Cor. 5). Thus Peter explains that "God was with him" (Acts 10). The works which this man did, the Father did in him. "The Father who is in me, performs the deeds." Hence, said Christ, he did what he saw his Father was doing.[104] Just as the artisan does with his hand what he sees his soul doing within, so it is with Christ. Likewise he said that the Jews did what they saw the devil doing within them because the devil was among them acting and fashioning the image of evils just as God was fashioning the image of good in Christ. In his

---

[100] John 14:10.

[101] Hilary of Poitiers, *De Trinitate*, lib. III, 1 (PL X, 49): *Natura intelligentiae humanae rationem dicti istius non capit.*

[102] Augustine, *De fide ad Petrum, liber unus*, I, 4 (PL XL, 754) and *De Trinitate*, lib. VI, cap. X, 12: "And each one is in the other one, and all in each one, and each one in all, and all in all, and all are one" (PL XLII, 932).

[103] Athanasius, *De Spiritu sancto*, lib. III, (PG LXII, 328).

tractate *On John*, chapters 18, 19, 20 and at the beginning of Book 2 *On the Trinity*, Augustine expounds upon this passage regarding the Father's acts in Christ in a ridiculous manner [76] by offering the three-fold sophist distinction lest it be said that the Father is inside a human being. They want the son alone to be within man, not the Father nor the holy spirit lest there be a blending of their substances.[105] Who but someone deluded by the demon, would deny that the holy spirit existed as substance in Christ, the man? Likewise, that the Father existed in the man, they deny, as if this were the patripassianism.[106] These are absurd dreams with their "communication of idioms." I am not saying that He who was in the son suffered, but that the son suffered. Just as birth is the experience appropriate to the flesh, so also beating, crucifixion, death, and resurrection are experiences appropriate to the flesh. But these matters do not relate to the incorporeal elements. The soul is not said to die when a man dies, nor is the angel that is placed within the man, nor is any incorporeal thing. The idea of the death of that invisible entity, which could not sense any suffering of death, is ridiculous. I shall never acknowledge that anything that does not suffer the pains of death truly dies. For fanatics and those deluded by demons there are other manners of death which were never mentioned in the scriptures as if the holy spirit could thus have died in another person. Clearly God would be undermining the notion of the world's redemption through the death of that invisible entity because it is not truly a death. The redemption of the Sophists is deceptive just as is the death of that invisible entity upon which they set the basis of their salvation. By this logic, the son of God is, as far as they are concerned, mortal just as they say that angels die within the hide of asses.[107] There is another obvious deception among the

---

[104] 2 Cor. 5:19; Acts 10:38; and John 14:20.

[105] Augustine, *In Ioannis Evang.* tract. 19, 19, 20 (PL XXXV, 1535-64) and *De Trinitate*, lib. II, cap. 1,3 where he differentiates between three classes of expressions: those predicating about the father and the son, those that indicate the son as inferior as a man and servant, and those that demonstrate him neither inferior nor equal but as the one who comes from the father (PL XLII, 846).

[106] Servetus is expressing the same thing in *De Trinitatis erroribus* 58v and 76r-v.

[107] On the margin of *De Trinitatis erroribus*, 58 v, Servetus expressed the same idea even more emphatically: *"Hoc ipsi concedunt si corpus asininum angeli induant, et tunc angeli erunt asini."*

Sophists because among them even Christ's as a man sufferings are not genuine. For Augustine in commentary on Psalm 21, Jerome commenting on Matthew chapter 26, and Hilary in his commentary on Psalm 68 say that Christ though a man, was not saddened, and never feared death.[108] In fact there was no suffering from his wounds or death nor did he sense pain, affirms Hilary in Book 10 of his *On the Trinity*. "No more, he says, in the passion did the flesh of Christ feel pain than if you were to wound fire or water with a sword." With similar idiocy in Book 9 of *On the Trinity* [77] he admits that the Father is greater, but says that the son was not less: he says that he suffered no more than the Father Himself.[109] Augustine in his sermon *On Faith* anathematizes those who say or believe that the son of God is dead.[110] Indeed, because of Augustine, Lombard also believed that the man himself was not dead. For in Book 3 of *Sententiarum*, distinctio 22, on his own authority he grants that Christ during those three days in the grave was a human being.[111] But if, in fact, he was a human being, then he really lived as a human being. Who could keep up the fight with these comedians? He is moved by this logic because Christ was said to be in the tomb and Christ was in hell. But those things can be said by a synecdoche, as we say that Saint Peter is in Paradise. Now, if the man was truly dead, he must necessarily have stopped being a man. If the son was truly dead, he must then have ceased being the son, granted that those aspects survived which belonged to the son. For genuine death leads from existence to nonexistence. If he truly ceased being the son, it immediately follows

---

[108] It is not clear what Augustine and Jerome thought about it in the indicated passages though Jerome wrote in his *In Matthaeum*, lib. IV, cap. 26:39: "There should be ashamed those who think that the Savior was afraid of death and spoke with terror about the passion, 'My Father, if it is possible, let this cup pass from me'....." (PL XXVI, 197). Hilary of Poitiers, *In Psalm 68* (PL IX, 242).

[109] Hilary of Poitiers, *De Trinitate*, lib. IX, 56 and lib. X, 23 (PL X, 303 and 336).

[110] Augustine, *Liber de fide ad Petrum* (PL XL, 757), but not exactly in the terms used by Servetus.

[111] P. Lombard, *Sentenetiarum*, lib. III, dist. 22,1, entitled "Whether the Christ in his death was a human being." It did not seem to him that way, since a dead man already is not a man, for if he were, would he be mortal or immortal? He could not be mortal since he was already dead, nor immortal because then it would be possible only through the resurrection. Thus Lombard responds that with the death of Christ God was truly a man though dead; but a man neither mortal nor immortal, because he was united with the soul (PL VXCII, 803).

that the son was actually not the divinity per se.

The Twelfth Passage

Our twelfth passage: "Before Abraham was born, I am."[112] That expression, "I am", indicates a certain essential character of being. The substantive form of the Word gives the essence of this body, just as it is the form that gives being to a thing: and this is from the beginning. Indeed, as we shall show, Christ existed already from the beginning in the elemental essence as well as in the essence of the soul. The essence of the body and soul of Christ is the divinity of the Word and spirit. Christ exists from the beginning equally according to the character of the body as to the character of the soul.[113] The flesh of Christ holds the beginning of being based on the Father's articulation of the Word. So Christ, too, preceded all times in the spirit of God. Likewise, he who was the spirit of Elohim, is now the spirit of Christ. And only by this character of the spirit, could he, possessing the unworldly spirit, say, "I was there, I saw, I did," not as if a man were talking, but as if the spirit itself were talking. In this manner Simon Magus, who was imbued with the evil spirit, caused himself to be summoned as he stood and claimed that he was standing from the beginning as an image of Christ. He had heard these things from the apostles and in this way by imitating the truth of [78] Christ, he fought it with the result that they neither believed him nor Christ. Notice this aspect in particular, that Simon Magus, the first heresiarch of all after the good news and a particularly notorious adversary, never impugned the faith by means of the Trinity because no one had heard of such ideas in that era. The question was solely concerned with the visible person of Christ, who bore the everlasting spirit before himself.[114] Truly is the spirit of Christ eternal, and it is that spirit which, from the beginning, breathed life into Adam. Regarding this eternal spirit of Christ, the apostle says in Hebrews 9, "who

---

[112] John 8:58. The theme is discussed in *De Trinitatis erroribus* 67v-68v.
[113] This means that Christ is virtually, intentionally eternal because the Word and the spirit of God which are the two substantive modes of his manifestation and communication, respectively, were from eternity destined to be the substantive form and spirit of the body of Christ.
[114] On Simon Magus, Acts 8:9-24.

through the eternal spirit offered himself." Therefore, Christ was correct when he said, "Before Abraham was born, I am." I am that eternal Word of God, which was articulated before Abraham, and heard and seen by Abraham himself. By the visible Word articulated before Abraham and Adam, Christ went out from eternity from God's mouth (Mic. 5).[115] Not only do we say that Christ went from God, but also that he is in God. "I am existing in the substance of the Word." My being exists from eternity, from the articulation of the Word by the eternal Father that was made in eternity. I who grant essence to other things existed then in essence. "He, whom we see, existed from the beginning" (1 John 2). "He exists before all things, and all things exist through him" (Col. 1). This son is born eternally from the Father, temporally from man.[116] Accept this relationship. If I were given the ability to father a son in a woman through the mouth's breath, and then if I were to withdraw, having emitted the breath, I could say to the woman, "I have fathered a son; I leave the son in you, who after he has become a human being, in the coming fullness of time will be born from you." This breath is not a real son, but we say that the son was then generated by virtue of its seminal character. Thus in the case of God, there was no fathering of an invisible son among those entities, but by the articulation of the Word the conception of the subsequently appearing flesh, which is the son of blessed God, took place.

The Thirteenth Passage

From the foregoing, what the Baptist, the precursor, said in John 1 is understood: [79] "He who comes after me, was made before me because he existed before me." Interpreters of our own era translate the passage along these lines, but ineptly so. For after the phrase, "was made," there needs to be a period with the result that ὅτι should be the beginning of the next phrase like this: "He who comes after me was made before me. For he existed before me and we have all a share in his fullness." And later John repeats that passage when he says: "He who comes after me was made before me." And likewise repeating the statement

---

[115] Heb. 9:14 and Mic. 5:2.
[116] 1 John 2:13 and Col. 1:17.

a third time he says, "This is he about whom I was saying, 'after me will come a man who was made before me; for he existed before me, and I did not know him.'"[117] This man was said to have been formerly made. Notice the phrase "formerly made" or "previously made." What will the Sophists say to this? For they do not grant that the second entity was made, but the Arians granted this. Long before the Arians, Ignatius, Irenæus, Tertullian, Clement of Alexandria, Asterius Thyensis, Dionysius of Alexandria, and other authorities clearly said that the son was made. This is what the apostle teaches not only in other places but also in his letter to the Hebrews although neither Arius nor Athanasius ever understood his intention.[118] I would have wanted to ask this one question of them all: does the conception of this man from God seem to them to be divine? If divine, this man will be called the only son of God. If Jesus of Nazareth was fathered through this manner of conception, he who was conceived and born, is the son. You see that this man is that Melchizedek whose conception was unknown to people. This son is known after the manner of his conception.

The Fourteenth Passage

We said that Christ's spirit was eternal, and Peter spoke about this in chapter 3 of his first letter: "He was made alive by the spirit by which upon departing he preached even to the spirits who were in prison, who had been disobedient in Noah's time."[119] I shall set forth this passage here because in an amazing way it relates to the knowledge of Christ's mysteries. Speaking about the

---

[117] John 1:15 and 27-30. The trinitarian use of this passage conflicts with the philological interpretation which is proposed by Servetus. New Revised Standard Version translates this passage this way: "After me comes a man who ranks ahead of me because he was before me."

[118] Servetus attempts to demonstrate the nonexistence of the second Person, who is supposed to be "not made." But the texts to which he refers do not contain the phrases such as "made from a woman," "was made" or "became as we are in order for us to become as he is" (from Irenaeus, *Adv. Haereses*, lib. V, prologue; PG I, 399); from Tertullian (*Adv. Praxeam*, cap. VIII), from Clement of Alexandria (*Stromata*, lib. III, cap. XVI: PG VI, 168)), from Dionysius of Alexandria, (perhaps fragment *Adv. Sabellium*: PG X, 1269). The mentioned Asterius Thyensis (d. 341), called "the sophist" is not the ascetic of Amasea whose homilies are in PG XL, but the disciple from the school of Lucian of Antioch, a theologian of the Arian school who was opposed by Athanasius. Bishop Marcellus of Ancyra wrote a treatise *Against Asterius* fragments of which are preserved in Eusebius work *Against Marcellus*. Servetus could obtain this information only indirectly from other sources not from his work.

prison, Peter related his statement to that time when the giants were destroyed by the flood together with the wicked angels who were cast headlong into the prison of the abyss; [80] and in this same place he related another mystery of Christ, who went down to the infernal prisons, and he pointed out the reason for imprisoning the angels.

In his discussion of hell, he introduced the story of the giants as an important one because never is such a crowd of men and angels read to have been cast into the prison of hell. Moreover, he does it also on account of the similarity because in their disbelief when the church through preaching and baptism was being built, they were like those who did not believe the prediction when the ark was being built.[120] Peter shows that Christ through the eternal spirit was already once a savior of believers through water just like now through baptism. Certain words of his were taken from Psalm 89 based on the translation of the Septuagint's interpreters, which at that time was the only Greek one in use even as the apostles themselves were writing in Greek. In that psalm mention is made of the time of the flood.[121] Peter and Jude say, "the angels." In Revelation John assigns the prison of the abyss to the angels, and Luke does the same in his gospel. The interpreters of the Septuagint say "angels" in Genesis 6, which Josephus mentions in his *Jewish Antiquities*.[122] The angels were the sons of

---

[119] 1 Pet. 3:18-20. In *De Trinitatis erroribus*, lib. III, p. 70v-73r.

[120] It is a biblical source of the analogy between the ark of Noah and that of Peter, a symbol of the church. Servetus treats the same matter in his fourth letter to Calvin, *Christianismi rest.* pp. 582-585.

[121] Ps. 89:4 : "For a thousand years in your sight are like yesterday when it is past, or like a watch in the night."

[122] 2 Pet. 2:4 : "For if God did not spare the angels when they sinned, but cast them into hell and committed them to chains of deepest darkness to be kept until the judgment." Jude 1:6 : "And the angels who did not keep their own position, but left their proper dwelling, he has kept in eternal chains in deepest darkness for the judgment of the great Day." Rev. 20:1-3 : "Then I saw an angel coming down from heaven, holding in his hand the key to the bottomless pit and a great chain. He seized the dragon, that ancient serpent, who is the Devil and Satan, and bound him for a thousand years, and threw him into the pit, and locked and sealed it over him, so that he would deceive the nations no more, until the thousand years were ended." Luke 8:30-31: "Jesus then asked him, 'What is your name?' He said, 'Legion'; for many demons had entered him. They begged him not to order them to go back into the abyss." Servetus knows from Gen. 6:4 the popular tradition of the *nephilim* or giants identified in LXX with the fallen angels, or with the tribe of Seth in other Jewish sources. Flavius Josephus (37-ca 100) says: "For many angels of God accompanied with

114

Elohim, deceiving spirits, who by recalling the angelic life among the human race held sway over the world. The angels themselves, when they saw the beauty of women, excited men more strongly by that means to lust, for they fashioned themselves as men and forced themselves into the bodies of great men. For this reason, says Jude, those angels abandoned their origin or they degenerated from their natural origin out of their desire to reproduce through jealous mimicry of people. For the impulses of demons are particularly depraved, and they mesmerize men with wondrous tricks. Hence it is said that Enoch was transferred lest that enchantment of the angels affect his mind (Wis. 4). For Enoch himself took part in a legation to the angels, as Irenæus says; he addressed the angels and preached to them just as Paul made his preaching known to the angels, which they did not previously know (Eph. 3). Preaching penance, Enoch disputed with the wicked according to Ecclesiasticus 44 and [81] Jude's Epistle. For that reason, when the tyrants wanted to tear him apart, God transferred him lest he see that violent death (Heb. 11).[123] They made women common property choosing from all of them those whom they wanted as wives. Berossus tells that they were punished on account of illicit sex, not on account of just marriage, and even Moses said this much. They filled the earth with luxury, tyranny, rapine, and iniquity. Because of the size of their bodies the ancient Hebrews called them great demons.[124] With that common word, *"elohim,"* they referred to angels, demons,

women, and begat sons that proved unjust, and despisers of the all that was good, on account of the confidence they had in their own strength, for the tradition is that these men did what resembled the acts of those whom the Grecians call giants" (*Antiquities of the Jews* I.III.1).

[123] Servetus interprets the allusions made in Wis. 4:11 as referring to Enoch. Gen. 5:24; Sir. 44:16; Heb. 11:5: "By faith Enoch was taken so that he did not experience death." Paul in Eph. 3:10: "So that through the church the wisdom of God in its rich variety might now be made known to the rulers and authorities in the heavenly places." Irenaeus, *Adv. Haereses*, lib. IV, 2 (PL VII,146).

[124] Moses in Gen. 6: 2-4. Berossus (ca 340 ca 270 BCE) was a Babylonian historian, priest of Bel, cited by the church fathers and by Josephus (*Against Apion*, Bk. I; *Jewish Antiquities*, Bk. I, IX, and others). He was the author of *Chaldean History* written in Greek and preserved only in fragments (Gerald Verbrugghe and John Wickersham, *Berossos and Manetho, Introduced and Translated: Native Traditions in Ancient Mesopotamia and Egypt*, (Anne Arbor: University of Michigan Press, 1996). K. Müller, *Fragmenta historicorum graecorum*. Auxerunt, notis et prolegomenis illustrarunt, indice plenissimo instruxerunt, (Parisiis: A. Firmin Didot, 1849-1884) vol. II, pp. 495-510). It describes the Mesopotamian myth regarding creation and history. The church fathers cite him especially in relation to the biblical stories of the Babylonian exile:

and remarkable people. By sending the bodies and very spirits that were imprisoned there into the abyss, Christ went against all those who were involved in such a crime of the spirits. Hence Satan's prison is said to be in the abyss of the waters (Luke 8, Rev. 20, and 2 Pet. 2).[125] Tartarus is the proper name for the place, τάρταρος, from the word ταρταρίζειν, because there is stiffness there and a cold trembling from the waters. Therefore, it was fitting that Peter and Jude said that those angels were cast down into Tartarus and that they were bound and saved there for the final judgment.[126] Hence the giants and demons who inhabit them are said to be pressed under the waters and to tremble (Job 26, Prov. 9 and Isa. 14).[127] Job has a fine passage: "The giants are pressed under the water, and those who inhabit them are nude before God in hell." They were deservedly cast down into the abyss with men because they were the cause of men's perdition, an image of the serpent that was cursed from the beginning for that reason. In that prison even now with the souls of the giants they are detained in some way to be punished more harshly by fire in the final judgment. Now the words of Peter are more easily explained. Christ's spirit πορευθείς, having approached those imprisoned spirits, after reaching them, proclaimed and preached. Just as God set out and went into Egypt, crossed over there, and, having thus approached them, killed the first born (Exod. 12), so in the time of Noah, he went, and, thus having approached them, he preached to those spirits. Through the declaration of Noah himself that they would receive a terrible judgment, Christ's spirit proclaimed just

---

Clement of Alexandria, *Stromata*, lib. I, cap. 21; Eusebius, *Praeparatio evangelica*, lib. IX, cap. 40. His *History* was edited for the first time in 1497 by Giovanni di Viterbo and later in Paris in 1510 with a title *De his quae praecesserunt inundationem terrarum.*
[125] Compare note 122.
[126] Luke 8:31; Rev. 20:1; Jude 1:6 talk about dwelling, darkness, and abyss (pit). It is only in 2 Pet. 2:4 that the Greek term *tartaros* is used in a verbal form of ταρταρόω meaning "to cast into hell (underworld)" and not the one Servetus is using. ταρταρίζω, which means "to quake, to shiver with cold." Servetus explains the etymology of the word *tartaros* and finds a support for it in the Old Testament.
[127] Job 26:5-6: "The shades below tremble, the waters and their inhabitants. Sheol is naked before God, and Abaddon has no covering." Prov. 9:18: "But they do not know that the dead are there, that her guests are in the depths of Sheol." Isa. 14:9: "Sheol beneath is stirred up to meet you when you come; it rouses the shades to greet you, all who were leaders of the earth; it raises from their thrones all who were kings of the nations."

as he preached penitence to them through Enoch. [82] But they were disobedient, as Peter says. The sleepy spirits of the giants and the deceiving angels disdained to hear the voice of the herald. What our version has "he preached" is ἐκήρυξεν in the Greek, which means "to make a public declaration" or "to proclaim." It was properly said of Noah's time, wherefore Peter likewise, retaining the same expression and sense in his second epistle, calls Noah himself κήρυκα, "herald," "emissary," "one making declaration of war."[128] There Christ having approached those spirits with his own eternal spirit declared his judgment through Noah.

What we call "a prison" is φυλακή in Greek, in other words, a ward, a watch, a detention. Just as Babylon is called φυλακή, "the ward of every impure spirit" (Rev. 18),[129] so the bodies of the impious were the wards of evil spirits who, as Job said, inhabited them. Those wicked spirits were held in the bodies of men, and they were sent into the stronger hold of the abyss where they were kept when Christ descended to the underworld after his suffering. He, too, preached to those there. Peter, implying both senses with his ambiguous expression, teaches all these things. His words, which are inexactly articulated, sound thus: "Made dead in the flesh, made living in the spirit, having approached the spirits that were in prison, He preached to the ones that were disobedient before when God's leniency was expected in the days of Noah when the ark was being readied." Therefore, not only did the spirit of Christ previously preach to spirits of this sort through Enoch and Noah, but also later, when he went to the underworld, he preached to them himself, proclaiming another judgment to come. Hence Peter himself in the following chapter says that "the Gospel was preached to the dead" by Christ.[130] It was the gospel of Christ's coming and resurrection made manifest to hell itself after Christ, having gone down there, rose again and led out most

---

[128] 2 Pet. 2:5 : "And if he did not spare the ancient world, even though he saved Noah, a herald of righteousness (δικαιοσύνης κήρυκα), with seven others, when he brought a flood on a world of the ungodly."
[129] Rev. 18:2 : "Fallen, fallen is Babylon the great! It has become a dwelling place of demons, a haunt of every foul spirit, a haunt of every foul bird, a haunt of every foul and hateful beast.".
[130] 1 Pet. 4:6.

with him and proclaimed to the rest that another judgment would come. Yet, not only in the time of Noah, but also in the eras of others Christ's spirit always acted through the prophets as Peter also says in chapter 1. This is Christ's greatest glory. All God's actions, [83] of which we have read before, were actions of Christ himself because he alone was the divine display. "From ancient times he is the king working salvation upon the earth" (Ps. 73).[131] Both Christ's person and Christ's very eternal spirit were truly active there. But regarding the other evil spirits, this point, too, must not be left out: that in calling them spirits Peter is marking out thoughts that are oppressed by wicked spirits. "God saw that every intent of the heart was devoted to evil."[132]

Paul, too, in the question about capturing the minds of men for following Christ's faith says that the fight is against worthless spirits (Eph. 6) because "they hold those minds captive" (2 Tim. 2).[133] By this fight we must now fight against worthless angels. They were made stubborn by the evil spirits. For the spirit, the one that operates in stubborn sons, is evil (Eph. 2).[134] Not wishing to argue often with stubborn spirits of this sort, by preaching penitence to them through Enoch, God preached their destruction through Noah and visited it upon them. In this way God said, "My spirit will not contend forever in man" (Gen. 6). Nevertheless does there seem to be a contradiction because God says, "my spirit in man," if they were besieged by wicked spirits?[135] My answer is that God's spirit was placed in man from the beginning (Gen. 2). The serpent that invaded the flesh and our own

---

[131] Ps. 73:12 : "Yet God my King is from of old, working salvation in the earth."
[132] Gen. 6:5 : "The LORD saw that the wickedness of humankind was great in the earth, and that every inclination of the thoughts of their hearts was only evil continually." References to it are found in Matt. 24:37 and in Luke 17:26.
[133] Eph. 6:12 : "For our struggle is not against enemies of blood and flesh, but against the rulers, against the authorities, against the cosmic powers of this present darkness, against the spiritual forces of evil in the heavenly places." 2 Tim. 2:26 : "And that they may escape from the snare of the devil, having been held captive by him to do his will."
[134] Eph. 2:1-2 : "You were dead through the trespasses and sins in which you once lived, following the course of this world, following the ruler of the power of the air, the spirit that is now at work among those who are disobedient."
[135] Gen. 6:3 : "Then the LORD said, "My spirit shall not abide in mortals forever, for they are flesh; their days shall be one hundred twenty years." The same topic is covered in *De Trinitatis*

sin everywhere blocked Him lest He dominate man's mind. Regarding this the inner struggle is constant. For from time to time or at certain moments God's spirit wakes us and advises us against the goads of the evil spirit, and it keeps us in a state of freedom. But, when He sees that we are in no way willing to obey Him, then He hands us over for destruction or makes our mind stubborn for the greater display of His own glory as when He hardened the Pharaoh and the Canaanites. And so, given that the spirits of men are under siege and that evil spirits are taking up residence in the body's storehouse, [84] they have, therefore, been consigned all the way to the abyss.

The judgment was against the spirits and, while the bodies were untouched, the spirits were pressed with suffocation, and the evil spirits, having entered them, were held bound in the abyss. Peter said that those angelic spirits were cast headlong into the tartarus of waters with the chains of night. The word, φυλακή, confirms this since it properly means a nightwatch. It is used most often in the holy literature in this sense, even in the Gospels as in Luke 2.12 and Matthew 24.[136] It is therefore acknowledged that the cataclysm took place at night time or later at night or when they were submerged in darkness. By way of comparison with this, the final judgment will come to pass at night time like a thief at night (Matt. 24, Luke 17, 1 Thess. 5 and 2 Pet. 3).[137] Psalm 89, already cited, also recalls night time because it mentions there φυλακή, the nightwatch, and calls it the prison of the soul. In sleep, the senses of the soul seem to be more imprisoned. In the silence of night the first born of the Egyptians were killed, and here even φυλακή, is used for the nightwatch. In Exodus 12 and, more fully, in

---

erroribus, but Servetus there is using the Hebrew term, לא־ידון which means "shall not plead" (or judge, or strive).

[136] Luke 12:8 : "In that region there were shepherds living in the fields, keeping watch over their flock by night." Luke 12:38 : "If he [the master] comes during the middle of the night, or near dawn, and finds them so, blessed are those slaves." Matt. 24:43 : "If the owner of the house had known in what part of the night the thief was coming, he would have stayed awake and would not have let his house be broken into." Servetus probably followed Valla in his interpretation since he quotes him in De Trinitatis erroribus, 72r, as giving the meaning of the word φυλακή, "the nightwatch."

[137] Matt. 24:43; Luke 17:24; 1 Thess. 5:2; 1 Pet. 3:10.

Wisdom 17 similar words referring to a prison watch without iron and chains of darkness.[138] At night, in their drunkenness, the Babylonian chieftains were killed together with their king Belshazzar (Isa. 21, Jer. 51, and Dan. 5). Those Babylonian chieftains slept a perpetual sleep with the giants, never to wake (Isa. 26), just as the giants of our Babylon now sleep a perpetual sleep.[139] They were thus given over to an attitude of refusal with the result that God did not want for them to be awakened from their sleep, but in their drunkenness and whoring to perish. Therefore, the far reaching sentence clings well to the spirits that are so evilly oppressed with sleep and are imprisoned during night time.

From all this let us therefore learn that the far reaching sentence against the spirits in Noah's time ought to be feared, and it has become anew an object of fear to us thanks to Christ and not without foundation. For you would correctly say that God passed sentence against our bewitched spirits because there is a guard of demons in our Babylon as was prophetically repeated by John [85] in Chapter 18, which has been mentioned. There the spirits truly are deceivers because they once before called themselves spiritual and angelic although they had not even a scintilla of the good spirit. The sons who have been consecrated to God "come together there with the sons of men." For that reason Babylon, the mother of whoring and of the world's abominations, must, as John said, be destroyed anew. Today, you would obviously see nothing in the church of Babylon but the sons of *elohim*, decorated with royal purple heroes, great demons, adulterous shepherds, all seduced by empty thoughts, whose entire spirit snores "in prison." And, just like those, they eat, drink, have many wives, and want their women to be common. There is none of them that seeks Christ, and they say that they cannot be wrong. So blind is the world today that it believes that the church

---

[138] Exod. 12:29. Wis. 17:2.

[139] Isa. 21:9 : "Fallen, fallen is Babylon; and all the images of her gods lie shattered on the ground." Jer. 51:57 : "I will make her officials and her sages drunk, also her governors, her deputies, and her warriors; they shall sleep a perpetual sleep and never wake." Dan. 5:30 : "That very night Belshazzar, the Chaldean king, was killed." Isa. 26:14 : "The dead do not live; shades do not rise – because you have punished and destroyed them, and wiped out all memory of them."

of God can be governed by rakes of this sort! With great hypocrisy they display a certain outward piety with which they cajole us whether by appeals to our humility or to superstition (2 Tim. 3 and Col. 2). Read Isaiah 56, and, if you fail to find that our shepherds are like this, call me a liar. Read Jeremiah 8 and 23, and Ezekiel 22 and 34, and Micah 5. If those who ought to be "the salt of the earth" have gone bad, with what will the others be seasoned?[140]

The Fifteenth Passage

Next comes one passage in particular out of many that deserves explanation: "Just as God established all things through Jesus Christ" (Eph. 3, Col. 1, Heb. 1 and 2 and 1 Cor. 8).[141] This man Jesus is, in essence, the Word "through which all things were made." Thanks to him the Word was articulated and the world was created; on account of him everything exists, as the apostle said, "Because of him and through him all things exist." He himself was thus the end and the purpose through which all exists. He is thus the one through whom God made everything. For the very act of pronouncement or Christ's generation was the cause for the creation of everything, and through that articulation of the Word or manifestation of Christ, which was accomplished by that act of articulation, all things were created at once. Thus, everything exists truly through him.

Because these issues will be further clarified in subsequent chapters, [86]

For Servetus and for the reformers in general, Babylon was a symbol of Rome and the Catholic church.

[140] Servetus refers to the texts: 2 Tim. 3:2-5: "For people will be lovers of themselves, lovers of money, boasters, arrogant, abusive, disobedient to their parents, ungrateful, unholy, inhuman, implacable, slanderers, profligates, brutes, haters of good, treacherous, reckless, swollen with conceit, lovers of pleasure rather than lovers of God, holding to the outward form of godliness but denying its power." Col. 2:8: "See to it that no one takes you captive through philosophy and empty deceit, according to human tradition, according to the elemental spirits of the universe, and not according to Christ." Col. 2:23: "These have indeed an appearance of wisdom in promoting self-imposed piety, humility, and severe treatment of the body, but they are of no value in checking self-indulgence." Servetus refers to the beautiful texts of the prophets of the Old Testament in which they treat the fight against the external cult devoid of the authentic spirituality. The last sentence refers to Matt. 5:13: "You are the salt of the earth; but if salt has lost its taste, how can its saltiness be restored? It is no longer good for anything, but is thrown out and trampled under foot."

it will be sufficient for now, if by the expression, "the Word was made flesh," you understand that such force was present as the same nature of God by which the ages were created; such was then as now there is in Christ, having been made his own, so that it was just as he said, "Whatsoever the Father has is mine." The power of the Word was made the power of the flesh just as the Word was made flesh. So Christ was able to say with complete justification that by his own virtue the ages were made. Moreover, it is the same thing whether he says, "it was made through me," or "it was made by my virtue." Along these lines Paul repeated himself many times saying "through the son," "through Christ," "through whom," "through him," that is, through that great virtue of God which is in him. In the Letter to the Hebrews he said, "everything is made and is governed by the word of Christ's power."[142] By the word of the son you hear that all things came into being in order to avoid confusing the Word with the son in a metaphysical sense.

Likewise, from another perspective, you could say that that which formerly was done through your spirit, if your spirit preceded the flesh, was done through you. But in Christ that was the nature of the eternal spirit, which was the spirit of wisdom that once held the forms of things. Because there was no material distinction, that very Wisdom was once simultaneously the Word and the spirit as Irenæus and Tertullian teach in many passages. That same wisdom was the spirit and the mind of the living Christ that makes everything in such a way that everything is said to be made through Christ himself. Like this, Simon Magus, aping Christ, used to claim that the ages where made through himself and by his own virtue. Therefore, if that eternal spirit of Christ's wisdom and the form of things were in you, then, when speaking through the spirit, you would say that you were there; you would be aware of all things; you would gaze upon the creation of all things face to face, in your presence, within yourself; and you would say that all those things were made through you. This discussion is enough

---

[141] Eph. 3:9; Col. 1:16; Heb. 1:2, 2:13; 1 Cor. 8:6. The same subject is treated in *De Triniatis erroribus*, 73r-75r.
[142] Heb. 1:3.

for you to say that the ages were made through the power of Christ's virtue. Indeed, later you will easily understand that all things, in that they were substantively placed within him, were made by Christ himself, and that Christ himself created everything, and that he was [87] once the creator in his own substance and person.[143]

The Sixteenth Passage

Since the divine virtue and power of Christ is known, we understand that what he said is true, that he has "the power of giving life and taking it back" (John 10).[144] The substantive divinity and the same divine power exist not only in the soul, but also in the flesh of Christ. This man fully possessed within himself the life and power of God. Because the divinity was entirely in the man, "all the fatherly power is in me and belongs to me." Thus do I have the power of making everything. The power of divinity which will urge this corpse from the grave and lead back the soul, is mine and is in me. Thus do I have the power of raising this body; I have the power of giving this soul and taking it back. The son has the power of life and death. The spirit of Elohim which filled the whole earth is now in Christ. His breath now sustains the whole earth. The living Christ holds the entire life of the world in himself, and, therefore, through this power of the spirit of the one who gives life, I in myself have the power. But after I die, when I am no longer, according to the reckoning of time, it will not correctly be said "I revive myself," but "the Father revives me." You will read this through the scripture, that the Father raised this son of His, Jesus, from the dead.[145] If God actually raised His dead son, He actually led him from nonexistence to existence. Then in this way he was not at that moment the living son. For true death destroys life; it leads from existence to nonexistence, and true resurrection leads from nonexistence to existence. Indeed, the person of the son was always living; his

---

[143] *In propria substantia et persona.* Christ is substantively God as he received from his father his total being and the creative Word of God, the formal cause of his substance is substantively identical with God. This Word of God is a person, a manifestation of God as well as Christ, the man, in whom God manifested himself corporeally.

[144] John 10:18.

was the divinity which raised the body and introduced the soul so that you could say that he raised himself with that power which is now within him.

The Seventeenth Passage

In the seventeenth passage not one, but many passages will be explained, if we consider this: Whether the man, Christ, be called the wisdom of God, the power of God, and the splendor of glory? The question of abstract names will cause the followers of Scotus difficulty, but none for the Hebrews. Among the latter there are innumerable nouns that end [88] in *el* or *iah* which have this meaning. It is the very essence of Hebrew that, when some property of God suits something by surpassing it, the thing is named for that aspect, as something strong is called the strength of God, something wise, the wisdom of God, the medicine of God, the health of God. A big tree is called the tree of God, a great wind, the wind of God. Something beautiful and holy is called the beauty of holiness, the glory of holiness, the splendor of holiness.[146] Often we call a man "the outstanding honor of his country," "the flower," "the glory," "the splendor," because these things by their excellence suit Christ. Regarding John the Baptist Christ said, "he was the burning and shining lamp," and he said that the apostles were "the light of the world."[147] Regarding Simon Magus they said, "He is the power of God which is called great" (Acts 8). Judith was called "the glory of Jerusalem, the joy of Israel, the honor of the people."[148] Therefore Christ, shining in the splendor of glory, is the true burning lamp. He is the light of the world, the light of nations, illuminating everyone and looked for by everyone. The brilliance of his face illuminates the entire sky, and it will shine in the coming age. He is the wisdom of God that holds all the wisdom of God entirely within himself and, "In him are all

---

[145] Peter in Acts 2:24, 3:15, 16, 4:10, 5:30, etc.; Paul in Rom. 4:24; 1 Cor. 6:14.

[146] These are abundant biblical examples. Servetus wanted to emphasize that these Hebraisms accentuate the excellence of a certain quality, but they cannot be taken as evidence, that, if applied to Christ, they designate the existence of his power, wisdom or spirit as persons. This is the way Calvin understood this proposition among those he objected to concerning Servetus's doctrines during the trial in Geneva and in his *Defensio orthodoxae fidei* (*Calvini Opera*, VIII, 502. n. XI). The subject is treated in *De Trinitatis erroribus*, 77r.

[147] Matt. 5:14.

[148] Acts 8:10; Jth. 14:10.

the stored up treasures of wisdom and knowledge."[149] He is the power of God through whom God made all things, and now continues making all things, for he possesses entirely the power of God and is capable of everything.

The Eighteenth Passage

The eighteenth passage: "The Lord rained down form heaven sulphur and fire from the lord upon Sodom and Gomorrah" (Gen. 19).[150] Because he is called the lord by the Lord, most people gather that there are two equal entities, the Father and the son, as if the writer were saying, "the Father from the son." For a straightforward interpretation of this passage, first we must notice that the phrase is in the Hebrew language just as it is said: "Solomon has brought together all the tribes of Israel to Solomon," that is, to himself (3 Kings 8). And "Roboam brought together his tribes in order to restore the kingdom to Roboam," in other words, [89] to himself (3 Kings 12 and 2 Para. 11). Or "Moses said to Hobab, relative of Moses," in other words, his own relative (Num. 10). Likewise in Genesis 1, 5 and 9 "God made man after the image of God." In the same place God said, "I shall remember the pact with God," that is, between me and man. God said to Jacob, "let him make an altar to God" (Gen. 35). "The Lord heard your murmur against the lord" (Exod. 16). And a little later, "The Lord said to Moses, 'the Lord has given you the Sabbath.'" And in Chaps 31 and 35: "God filled Bezeleel with the spirit of God."[151] It is common among the Hebrews for the antecedent to be used instead of a relative. This first answer on the basis of the idiom of the language is fairly obvious. If only all the Sophists knew how to speak Hebrew! That holy language alone which God Himself spoke contains the true mysteries of God.[152] The second implication of his statement is gathered from the

---

[149] Col. 2:3.
[150] Gen. 19:24.
[151] Here Servetus again explains these strange expressions as the typical Hebraic forms of speech devoid of any systematic significance. One should recall here previous explanations of Servetus regarding the various names of God.
[152] Regarding this issue there is an important statement of Servetus in *De Trinitatis erroribus*, 78v-79r: *"Omnem philosophiam et scientiam ego in Biblia reperio, nonne clare vides quomodo Paulus ibi Graecorum sapientiam reprobam et mundanam esse dicit. Nec te seducat quod filii huius seculi prudentiores sunt filiis lucis. Lege obsecro milles Bibliam, nam si eam legendo gustum non capias,*

idiom of the language just as the fire from the Lord is called "a great fire," sleep from the Lord, "a great sleep," wind from the Lord, "a great wind." They are Hebraisms as we just now were saying. However, it is said "fire from the Lord from heaven" because the fire in *empyreum* is on high and from there the fire is sent thither, as we shall say about the fire that has been already prepared for the demons. The final mystical implication, in which we recognize the mystery of Christ, is that the true Jehovah was the Word among men, the person of Christ represented by the angel; the angel, having then the name Jehovah, rained fire from the great and supreme Jehovah, the Father of our lord, Jesus Christ.

The Nineteenth Passage

In the nineteenth passage we shall not explain, but rather ask whether that Word of John was once the son as reality or the son as person. My answer is that among the prophets it was always foretold that there would be a son. "The sun of justice shall rise for you" (Mal. 4). "The land shall open and nurture a savior" (Isa. 45). "A branch shall come from the stock of Jesse" (Isa. 11). "his leader will rise from him, and the prince shall be led forth from his presence" (Jer. 30). "A star shall rise from Jacob" (Num. 24). "From Bethlehem the leader shall go forth" (Mic. 5). "You will call him Immanuel" (Isa. 7). "He will have me as father, and I shall have him as son" [90] (1 Para. 17 and 2 Kings 7). "He shall be called the son of the Most High" (Luke 1).[153] Do you think that John said that the Word rather than the son spoke with human will? Whence so great a misuse of nouns? Whence such a license to imagine sons? You could not show a single word or a single iota in the Bible whereby scripture ever would call that Word the son. Whoever will properly regard God's word, when "word" is said in scripture, will also say "the Word," when "son," "the son:" once the Word, now the son.[154] In fact, eternal generation is attributed to the son, Jesus Christ. This son, this man, this Jesus, we

---

eo est quia perdidisti clavem scientiae Christum, quam sine intermisione pulsando facile recuperabis."
[153] Mal. 4:2; Isa. 45:8, 11:1; Jer. 30:21; Num. 24:17; Mic. 5:2; Isa. 7:14. Servetus applies these texts in a typological sense and not prophetic. 1 Chron. 17:13; 2 Sam. 14; Luke 1:32.
[154] Crucial statement for the theology of Servetus: *Olim verbum nunc fiulius.*

say, from the beginning was with God in his own person and substance. The Word was once the son as person, in the person and the substance of the son to be. For the person of Christ with God was that oracle. From eternity is this Jesus Christ with God in person and essence according to the substance of the body and spirit. Therefore, one must grant that the Word was once the son as person and not as reality.[155]

The Twentieth Passage

The last passage is from the Epistle to the Hebrews, Chapter 2: "He took not the angels but the seed of Abraham."[156] From the hypostasis of the Word and the person we will grant that, coming from heaven, he took and put on the flesh. Although we grant this much, that the man took flesh and was clothed in the flesh, in the words of Job, "I clothed myself in hide and flesh,"[157] nevertheless, this passage about the "assumption" will be explained differently now. The apostle was not comparing the seed of Abraham to a single angel as to a single humanity, but to the entire assembly of angels, as if he were saying, "He did not come to free the angels and to take them unto himself, but rather mankind." The apostle was speaking there as a certain corrective not about the totality of mankind gone by, but about the present and daily assumption of men unto himself as the present tense verb clearly shows there: ἐπιλαμβανέται. The "seed of Abraham" was taken in a collective sense as is established by many passages of literature, especially John 8, Psalm 104, and Isaiah 41, where this assumption was declared.[158] Exodus 19 is on hand regarding this same assumption: "You see how I carried [91] you and took you to myself." And 3 Kings 12: "Moreover I shall

---

[155] This paragraph is decisive with respect to the doctrinal system of Servetus since it clearly explains his position concerning the interpretation of the scripture. Servetus uses his terminology in a precise and technical meaning. Calvin could not or did not want to grasp the meaning of these terms and for that reason he could not understand Servetus (*Defensio orthodoxae fidei*, in *Opera Calvini*, Vol. VIII, 502-503, n. V, n. XII)..

[156] Heb. 2:16.

[157] Job 10:11.

[158] John 8:52-59; Ps. 104:6 : "O offspring of his servant Abraham, children of Jacob, his chosen ones." Isa. 41:8: "But you, Israel, my servant, Jacob, whom I have chosen, the offspring of Abraham, my friend."

take you." 2 Kings 22: "He took me and drew me from many waters."[159] In this way, our faithful pontiff, Jesus Christ, took, not the angels, but us, thereby freeing us from the slavery of the devil and drawing us from death to life. He took us into his bosom, into the heavenly kingdom and the glory of God. "I shall take you," he says (John 14). "Take yourselves in turn, just as Christ took us into the glory of God" (Rom. 14). Likewise Deuteronomy 30: "He will take you, he will gather you, and he will lead you to his peace."[160] And into this peace, reader, today you may arrive, today born from heaven and taken into the heavenly kingdom, if, nevertheless, today you have heard his voice, that heavenly voice: "This is my son." Woe to the Sophists who labor away in hairsplitting (*cavillis*) and tricks. Woe to those who dissect God, tear Him apart, and parcel Him up in their imagination.

---

[159] Exod. 19:4; 2 Kings 22:17.
[160] John 14:3; Rom. 14:1, 3; Deut. 30:3-5.

On the Divine Trinity

Book Three

Which Shows the Prefiguration of the Person of Christ in the Word,

Being the Vision of God and the Hypostasis of the Word

Jesus Christ, our lord and God, having already been made plain in so many places, adds a spur to us and strengthens our mind in order that we finally bring forth other greater matters, which remain regarding him. Indeed, it is the entire purpose and end that has been set for us to explore the true manner of God's manifestation and to put forth Christ as the ultimate end in all things. Therefore, in this third book, we shall first discuss the person of the Word in order to reach the vision of God, by showing in the Word itself the person of Christ so that the whole mystery of the Word may be the glorification of Christ.[1] We say that the first chapter of the Gospel of John goes in this direction so that we all see the glory of God in the face of Jesus Christ like Paul says: "This glory is seen in the face of Christ" (2 Cor. 4).[2] John himself also said, "That Word became flesh, and we saw his glory" (John 1). "We saw the same divine Word which in the beginning was with God" (1 John 1).[3] The Word was λόγος, ideal reason, and it already indicated the man. It was already secretly indicating that that in which it was to pass would

---

[1] The Servetus concept of person is not the same as the orthodox one: for him a person is an aspect, a mode of manifestation. This paragraph represents a change with respect to the doctrine exposed in the work *De Trinitatis erroribus* in which Servetus did not develop yet this eternal personal relationship between the Word and the human Christ. It will be developed on the basis of an original explanation of the doctrines of the Old Testament.

[2] 2 Cor. 4:6.

[3] 1 John 1:1.

be seen openly as "we have seen and witnessed." We saw that glory in the face of Jesus Christ, "the glory which at one time the darkness failed to seize" as it was shining above the cherubim between mist and cloud. We saw that glory of Christ, which he possessed from eternity "with God" (John 17).[4] Already in the past the model, the person, and the image of Jesus Christ, the future man, was with God in the Word. And τὸ πρόσωπον, this person, this expression, this face, this representation [93] of man in God lay mysteriously hidden in all the passages of scripture which spoke about image, face, and person. The prophets, called also visionaries, formerly saw God in no other way except that they saw Christ in God and they saw God through Christ just as he himself said: "He who has seen me, has seen God." The prophets once saw the face of Elohim, they saw in the oracle of God that prototype and model of the man that would be. For what else could they have seen face to face in God? They saw there the very substance of Christ just as we see the substance of God in Christ.[5] Jesus Christ, the man, was the first model in that archetypical, superior world. About this image, figure, and depiction in God, Moses spoke in Deuteronomy 4 and 5, Numbers 12 . In Exodus 20 he says: "These people heard him speaking, but did not see the image of Christ who spoke to them." And there תמונה temunah, indicates, the very shape, the figure, the effigy, and the image of Christ which Moses saw.[6] David confirmed this by using the same expression in Psalm 16, which is for the Hebrew, Psalm 17: "I shall see your face and I shall be satisfied when your face appears." Balaam saw this image at a distance (Num. 24): "I shall see him," he said, "and not now; shall I gaze upon him, and not near." All the prophets wanted to see this brilliant face.[7] In his desire

---

[4] These texts are in John 1:14 and 15; 1 John 1:1 and again in John 17:5.

[5] The same theme, but less developed, we find in *De Trinitatis erroribus*, IV, 86v.

[6] Servetus refers to Deut. 4:16, 5:8; Num. 12:8, and Exod. 20:4. In these texts the Hebrew *temunah* signifies an image. But Servetus cites these texts in an indiscriminate way though Maimonides in his *Guide* I,3, whom Servetus knew very well, differentiates its three different meanings in these same texts: form, likeness, essence.

[7] Ps. 16:15; Num. 24:17.

for this, David said in Psalm 79: "You who sit above the cherubim, shine forth and appear with your splendor. Show your face, make your face shine, and we shall be saved." Psalms 4 and 43 related the same thing about this face and expression. In the same way, Psalm 88 portrays the face and expression of Christ in God.[8] Isaiah saw this face sitting high above the throne, and, nonetheless, the face was veiled with flaming wings (Isa. 6).[9] What face would you say was there, and what feet, if not those of Christ? Of course, they were not material limbs, but theirs was the brightness in the light of God and the prefiguration of Christ. The very same thing is proven in that vision of Ezekiel in chapters 1 and 10, and in the vision of Daniel, chapter 10, and in the vision of the seventy old men in Exodus 24. [94] Compare all these visions with the vision of John in Revelation, chapters 1 and 4, and you will say that the same thing and the same face was seen by all of them in Christ, the person.[10]

It was not just a specter, not only was a figure created there, as the Sophists fashion out God Himself wanted to show Himself in that way, for the glory of Christ.[11] In truth they recognize no display of God's substance and therefore not even the true communication of the spirit as if God were incapable of this by Himself, as if He did not father Christ by Himself, and as if He were deceiving the viewers solely as a trick. Or was this figure which the prophets called upon, worshipped, and saw, which was sitting over the cherubim, which they

---

[8] Ps. 79:1-3. Ps. 4:6: "Let the light of your face shine on us, O LORD!" Ps. 43:24: "Why do you hide your face?"

[9] Isa. 6:1-2.

[10] Ezek. 1:1: "I saw visions of God." Ezek. 10:1: "Above the dome that was over the heads of the cherubim there appeared above them something like a sapphire, in form resembling a throne." Dan. 10:5: "I looked up and saw a man clothed in linen, with a belt of gold from Uphaz around his waist." Exod. 24:9-10 "Then Moses and Aaron, Nadab, and Abihu, and seventy of the elders of Israel went up, and they saw the God of Israel." On the margin of *De Trinitatis erroribus* Servetus explains the difference between these visions found in the Old Testament and the visions of John in the Revelation 1 and 4 of the New Testament: *"Obscure semper videbatur olim, nunc vero clare"* (87v).

[11] According this text the hidden God has the visible aspect which is his Word and which since eternity had the same human aspect adopted by the face and body of Christ.

wanted to come forth only created? God explains most clearly in Numbers 12: in that face-to-face vision of Moses there was not some enigma nor even some inserted illusion, nor a specter, nor the figure that was everywhere sought, but it was God Himself, although His face was covered. In that very Word was the representation and image of Christ says Irenæus in book 4, chapters 15 and 17.[12]

The Sophists also deny that God could disclose Himself in any vision through an angel because they say that any form that would be seen is impossible for an angel. But we shall show that it was an angel and that it was Christ. Besides the angel there was the true face of God as is quite clear from Exodus 33 and the already cited chapter, Numbers 12.[13] It was the shining face of Christ that was once the face of God. In His own virtue the face was outshining the sun's brightness: it was not shining through a created light, but a light that was not created. The same face was shining then in the angel, because the angel was draped with the light of the Word.

It is a fact that on account of sin a certain cloud or veiling mist was placed before the vision of God, including Christ. There was not some open vision earlier as now because at that time God dwelt in the mist and somehow veiled Christ. Hence, Daniel saw the image of "the son of man" under a veil and cloud (Dan. 7). Zechariah saw the same thing [95] under the obscurity of night (Zech. 1).[14] "This face," as Christ said, "the prophets and kings once desired to see, but they did not see it entirely" (Matt. 13 and Luke 10). Indeed, this desire is clear from the passages cited and Psalms 23, 26, 66, 67, 79, and 2 Para. 9.

In fact, it is a precept of the Law that those wishing to greet Him, say, "Let

---

[12] Num. 12:6-8: "Hear my words: When there are prophets among you, I the LORD make myself known to them in visions; I speak to them in dreams. Not so with my servant Moses; he is entrusted with all my house. With him I speak face to face – clearly, not in riddles." Irenaeus in *Adv. Haereses*, lib. IV, cap. VII, 1 and 4 (PG VII, 235-236).

[13] Exod 33:11: "Thus the LORD used to speak to Moses face to face, as one speaks to a friend." Ex. 33:14: "My presence will go with you."

[14] Dan. 7:13; Zech. 1:8.

the Lord show His face to us" (Num. 6).[15] Isaiah looks for this face (chapter 8).
For, inasmuch as he had seen the face veiled and hidden in chapter 6 and later in
chapter 8, he said that it would happen that the face be revealed. Habakkuk looked
for the same face (chapters 2 and 3). With John as witness, Isaiah and the other
prophets said these things and others besides when they saw the glory of Christ
(John 12). Was Christ's glory in God only a manufactured specter? The Arians
would say this. In God, Christ, the man, had his glory before the world existed
(John 17).[16] Isaiah plainly speaks about Christ's divine glory and splendor and he
proves that Christ is the splendor of glory or a glorious reflection in God (chapters
60 and 66), just as Christ is called the "refulgence of glory" in Hebrews 1, as his
splendor shines (Hab. 3). The shimmering splendor of Christ's face appeared to
Paul above the splendor of the sun (Acts 9 and 26).[17] The fact that the Lord is said
to have appeared face-to-face before, we consider it stated in the gospel as being
Christ's face. For the Gospels teach, "God was seen through Christ: neither was
He seen nor could He be seen otherwise" (John 1, 5, and 14; Heb. 11, 1 John 4,
and 1 Tim. 6).[18] Jacob's vision most clearly shows the same thing in Genesis 32,

---

[15] Matt. 13:17 and Luke 10:24. The Psalms listed contain a tone of expectation and as such they
were considered in the New Testament as messianic. 2 Chron. 9:23 says that "All the kings of the
earth sought the presence of Solomon to hear his wisdom" as also desired the Queen of Sheba.
Num. 6:25 is a formula of benediction.
[16] Isa. 8:17: "I will wait for the LORD, who is hiding his face from the house of Jacob." Hab. 2:3:
"For there is still a vision for the appointed time; it speaks of the end, and does not lie. If it seems
to tarry, wait for it; it will surely come, it will not delay." Hab. 3:2: "O LORD, I have heard of
your renown, and I stand in awe, O LORD, of your work. In our own time revive it; in our own
time make it known." In John 12:38-41 there is an allusion to Isa. 53:1 and 6:10 in the sense that
God blinded the eyes of the ancient and hardened their hearts "so that they might not look with
their eyes, and understand with their heart and turn." In John 17:5 Jesus refers to his glory he
had before the creation of the world: "So now, Father, glorify me in your own presence with the
glory that I had in your presence before the world existed."
[17] Isa. 60:1-3 and 66:15 mention future "light," "brightness," "glory," "fire," and "flame of fire"
of God. This is the Servetian interpretation of these texts and collation with Hab. 2:3 and Hab.
3:4 : "The brightness was like the sun." Acts 9:3 and 26:13 mention this detail in two narratives
of the conversion of Saul.
[18] John 1:18 : "No one has ever seen God. It is God the only Son, who is close to the Father's
heart, who has made him known." John 5:37: "And the Father who sent me has himself testified
on my behalf. You have never heard his voice or seen his form." John 14:9 : "Whoever has seen

where he said that at night he saw Elohim Himself, face-to-face. He teaches that the same face was the face and expression of the man, Christ, when in the following chapter he says to Esau, his brother: "I saw your face as if I were seeing the face of Elohim, the expression of Elohim, whom I saw tonight."[19] [96] Christ teaches the same thing with a verb in the past tense: "He who has seen me, has seen the Father," not a ghost, not a false specter. Once the prophets saw the Word of God as Irenæus and Tertullian said.[20] God laid open His Word to His times. The grace which has now been made open, was given to us through Christ before the eternal ages because God before the eternal ages was the model of Jesus Christ, and contained the substance, the light, and the spirit within Himself, as He would give this grace to us through him. Peter and John said that Christ himself was made manifest as the Word in 1 Peter 1 and 1 John 1 because that same Christ was previously adumbrated in the Word within mist and cloud.[21] There was the Word representing Christ, and he was represented there; he was God's face. Paul said that Christ, the man, was an εἰκόνα, the true image of invisible God, and that God's very glory was discerned in the face of Jesus Christ (2 Cor. 4).[22] He is discerned, I say, because that glorious face of Christ [seen in the cloud was the face of the Word itself which since eternity] was shining in God.[23] Note Paul's

me has seen the Father." Heb. 11:3 : "By faith we understand that the worlds were prepared by the word of God, so that what is seen was made from things that are not visible." 1 John 4: 12 : "No one has ever seen God." 1 Tim. 6:16 : "It is he alone who has immortality and dwells in unapproachable light, whom no one has ever seen or can see."

[19] This reference to Gen. 32:30 : "For I have seen God face to face, and yet my life is preserved." And Gen 33:10 : "For truly to see your face is like seeing the face of God – since you have received me with such favor."

[20] Servetus nowhere gives the reference to this statement. .

[21] 1 Pet. 1:25 : "'The word of the Lord endures forever.' That word is the good news that was announced to you." 1 John 1:1: "We declare to you what ... we have ... touched with our hands, concerning the word of life."

[22] 2 Cor. 4:4 : εἰκὼν τοῦ θεοῦ. For Servetus the image, aspect, person are the synonymous terms.

[23] The phrase in the parenthesis is omitted in the printed copy of the *Christianismi restitutio*. It is found in the Manuscript of Paris and was probably inadvertently omitted during printing since without it the sentence loses its sense.

135

statement that, if the face of Christ has been seen, glorious God is seen. That very thing, he says, "is the glory which I had with you before the world came into existence" (John 17).[24] Now ponder this, the fact that not the divinity but the man himself sought to be exalted to this level of glory which he once had in God's presence. This man was already at that time glorious in God and desirable for everything, but not a ghost created in God. Moses and the prophets desired to see His face. To some extent "they did see Him, and they were joyous" as Christ said about Abraham himself (John 8). "They saw the back, but did not see the face" (Exod. 33). Therefore, it is possible to see Him from behind or to see His veiled face. Terror overcame them when they directed their eyes to this face, and they were afraid that they might die (Exod. 3 and 20, and Judg. 13). Because God's face was obscured on account of Adam's sin, there was in front it a flaming sword which was earlier visible to Adam and later made invisible (Gen. 3). The sin caused God's face to be hidden with something like a cloud of His anger cast over Him (Isa. 59 and Lam. 3).[25] The vision was terrible in the Law being [97] fearsome and terrifying because it forced Moses and Elias to hide their face according to Exodus 3, and Kings 19. But Christ graciously speaks to us: the terrible sights having been removed (Heb. 11).[26] God has shown Himself once angry, but now placated through Christ. The cover not only of the internal oracle, but also of the face of Moses indicated the glory of God and the true path of the saints that had not yet been made manifest (Heb. 9). Indeed, with the tearing asunder of the temple curtain, the face was revealed, and we were permitted to attain the *sancta*

---

[24] John 17:5 : "So now, Father, glorify me in your own presence with the glory that I had in your presence before the world existed."
[25] John 8:56. Ex. 33:23 : "You shall see my back; but my face shall not be seen." Ex. 3:6 : "And Moses hid his face, for he was afraid to look at God." Exod. 20:19 : The people said to Moses: "You speak to us, and we will listen; but do not let God speak to us, or we will die." Judg. 13:21-22 : "Then Manoah realized that it was the angel of the LORD. And Manoah said to his wife, 'We shall surely die, for we have seen God.'" References to Gen. 3:24; Isa. 59:2 and Lam. 3:43.
[26] Exod. 3:6; 1 Kings 19:13. In Heb. 11 Paul opposes that which Jews were able to achieve to the fulfillment of the promises with the Christians.

sanctorum, that is, the heavenly face of Christ, which had been covered from them (2 Cor. 3 and 4). For us there is no other covering than the very flesh of Christ, which in itself holds entirely the Father's divinity in its substance (Heb. 10 and Col. 2).[27] Like a sail, the flesh was torn asunder by the Jews at the passion, laying open the true divinity and the heavenly glory through the resurrection. Therefore, Moses saw the veiled visage of God, but not the true face. "They desired," Christ said, "to see what you see, and they did not." "That light shone in the darkness, and the darkness did not grasp it" (John 1). "He established the darkness as His hideout around Himself" (Ps. 17 and 2 Kings 22). "At that time God dwelt in mist" (2 Para. 5 and 6).[28] Wherefore, because that glorious face shining within the mist had been hidden from them, John indicated that they were all in darkness when he said, "even the darkness did not grasp it." The whole of human nature being, because of Adam's sin, dependent upon the darkness of hell, was comprehended there by the word, "darkness." In that respect Luke in chapter 1 said: "to give light to those who sit in darkness." The people that sat in the darkness "saw a great light" (Matt. 4). In John 12 even Christ said, "I have come as light to the world that all who see and believe in me, will not remain in darkness." The face of God, which had been hidden from them, was made manifest to us so that it is accurately said that "God was manifested in the flesh" (1 Tim. 3).[29] Isaiah goes in the same direction when he calls upon the hidden God in chapter 45 because Christ's visage lay hidden within the shadow of the Father. At that time Christ dwelt in "the hiding place of the Most High and in the shadow of the Omnipotent" [98] (Ps. 90). In that place there

---

[27] Heb. 9:8 : "By this the Holy Spirit indicates that the way into the sanctuary has not yet been disclosed as long as the first tent is still standing," that is before "a new covenant, not of letter but of spirit" described in 2 Cor. 3 and 4. Heb. 10:20 : "By the new and living way that he opened for us through the curtain (that is, through his flesh)." Col. 2:9 : "For in him the whole fullness of deity dwells bodily." This is an original idea of Servetus to connect the veil of Moses and of the temple (Matt. 2:51) with the one remaining, that is that of the body of Christ.

[28] John 1:5. Ps. 17:15 and not 2 Kings 22 but 2 Sam. 22:12 : *"Posuit tenebras in circuitu suo latibulum."* 2 Chron. 5:13 : *"impleretur domus Domini nube."* 2 Chron. 6:1 : *"Dominus pollicitus est ut habitaret in caligine."*

was the "concealment of his strength" (Hab. 3 in agreement with Deut. 33).[30] For, at the time when the Law was given, there was a concealment, while the visage of Him who was speaking, was not seen; nevertheless, He has been made brightly manifest to us because, as was predicted, "The glory of the Lord will be revealed, and all the flesh shall see." "Behold I am here, the one who was talking," and "They shall see eye-to-eye." This same Christ was previously hidden away, but later "made visible on earth, and he interacted with men, the God of Israel" (Bar. 3).[31] Baruch speaks about God's wisdom, about the visible Word that "appeared on earth and interacted with men" in the times of the patriarchs and Moses. The light and the man's face were divine just as the face of the man, who was seen, is in the light of your mind. That light is the glory of God, which was the light of the Word, and the shining Word itself is now the visible radiance of the Christ's face, as Paul teaches (2 Cor. 3 and 4). David taught the same thing, calling it "the light of Elohim's visage" or "the light of Christ's face" (Pss. 4, 43, 66, 88, and 89).[32] Who is so out of his senses that he would say with the Sophists that this entire light and the glory of Christ was a false ghost, a trick, an imposture? If the phantasm alone was created there and it was to be revealed, it follows now that Christ is the phantasm.

If you want a broader understanding of Christ's glory, ascend to the cherubim and seraphim and contemplate the wheels and animals of Ezekiel. For the image of Jesus Christ, which is the very glory of God, is represented in the person in all those things and in them he appears in substance. Ezekiel saw Christ, a vision

---

[29] Luke 1:79; Matt. 4:16; John 12:46; 1 Tim. 3:16.
[30] Isa. 45:15; Ps. 90:1; Hab. 3:4 and Deut. 33:25-26.
[31] Servetus cites here Isa. 40:5 and 52:6, then Bar. 3:37.
[32] 2 Cor. 3:7-13, 4:4-6. Ps. 4:6 : "Let the light of your face shine on us, O LORD!" Ps. 43:3 : "O send out your light and your truth." Ps. 89:15 : "Happy are the people who know the festal shout, who walk, O LORD, in the light of your countenance." Ps. 90:8 : "You have set our iniquities before you, our secret sins in the light of your countenance." This is Servetus interpretation that the light of the face of the Lord is the Word which later will become Christ.

of the Lord's glory, above those wheels and animals.[33] The animals that were seen, and the sound of "many waters" in Ezekiel and in the Revelation of John are the same. Wherefore, it is proven that the reference is always to Christ. The angels were the heralds of Christ's glory as the repeated expressions indicate (Isa. 6, Luke 2, and Rev. 4). The angels adumbrated Christ with a human face. When Christ is seen in an angel, the messenger of the Father is shown, and [99] the true messenger-to-be, "the angel of the great council," is prefigured there.[34] After Adam's sin, God placed the cherubim before the oracle of Christ's face just as they were covering both the face of the oracle and their own or just as those who were seen in heaven, were hiding the cherubim, one of whom was made manifest to Moses for the construction of the tabernacle, just as was the case for Solomon that he might make golden cherubim.

Cherub generally means an excellent figure, and the figure that is understood through its excellence is a human one, to which its wings add even an angelic excellence. According to Hebrew etymology, because of the presence of the first auxiliary letter, they are called cherubim כרובים, just like *litigants*, like *great* and like *famous* ones, just as a king is called a *great cherub*. The cherubim were always shown in heaven where there was some struggle, and with their fiery faces they indicated that God was angry at that time. The anger of God burst into flames, then, in the likeness of fire. On this basis even the seraphim are said to be fiery, flaming, burning.[35] These Cherubim, just like the seraphim that were seen by

---

[33] The same paragraph is in *De Trinitatis erroribus*, 89r.

[34] Voices of the angels are mentioned in Isa. 6:3; Luke 2:10-14; Rev. 4:1. Servetus compares the visions of Ezekiel and those of the Revelation. E.g. the sound of the wings with the "sounds of waters" (Ezek. 1:24: "I heard the sound of their wings like the sound of mighty [many] (*aquarum multarum*) waters;" Ez. 43:2 : "the glory of the God of Israel was coming from the east; the sound was like the sound of mighty [many] waters;" and Rev. 1:15 : "and his voice was like the sound of many waters."

[35] *Cherub, cherubim* (is the Hebrew masculine plural, כְּרֻבִים), is a word borrowed from the Assyrian *kirubu*, from *karâbu*, "to be near", hence it means *near ones, familiars, personal servants, bodyguards, courtiers*. It was commonly used of those heavenly spirits, who closely

Isaiah, were in the image of man that was concealed with a certain flame, covering the face with wings and shading it over because without Christ at that time, not even the angels were allowed to see the divine splendor, especially at that time lest that fiery light of Christ's face be seen then by the Jews. Moses described all the things according to the image and model of Christ that he had seen in God (Exod. 25, Acts 7, and Heb. 8). For that model, to which Exodus 25 relates, is that thing about which mention was made in the preceding chapter, namely, Elohim Christ, whom he had seen there.[36] David saw the same image of Christ above the cherubim (2 Kings 22), whose model and likeness presented to his own son, Solomon (1 Para. 28).[37] He called what he had seen with the spirit, a model and likeness of everything. And he said, "He made me understand all the works of the model." "Indeed, everything," he said, "that was written by the hand of God." But what can be said more properly to have been written by the hand of God than the very thing which had been expressed and portrayed in Himself? Nevertheless, it had been portrayed to them under a covering, with which the cherubim with their wings were covering and shading the very oracle of Christ (Exod. 25 and Heb. 9).

surrounded God and paid him service. Hence it came to mean an "angelic spirit." Servetus follows the interpretation of the vision of Ezekiel given by Maimonides in his *Guide*, Part III, caps. 1-7, in which it is also identified with the seraphim of Isa. 6:3. Servetus speculates suggesting the etymological component of the word *cherub*, namely the prefix כ (the "first letter") which means "as" "like as," "the like of," and the root of the word which he confuses with "rab," (רב) *great*, also *a chief*, and with "rib," (ריב) other Hebrew term which means "to litigate," "to strife," "to contend." Thus he derives the meanings *like litigants, like great ones*, with the suffix indicating the plural.

[36] Exod. 25:40 talks about a model shown to Moses on the mountain: "And see that you make them according to the pattern for them, which is being shown you on the mountain" where "Moses and Aaron, Nadab, and Abihu, and seventy of the elders of Israel went up, and they saw the God [Elohim] of Israel" (Exod. 24:9-10). Servetus interprets Elohim as the face of the Word-Christ. Stephen in Acts 7:44 and Paul in Heb. 8:5 allude to this model or pattern of the sanctuary seen by Moses: "They offer worship in a sanctuary that is a sketch and shadow of the heavenly one; for Moses, when he was about to erect the tent, was warned, 'See that you make everything according to the pattern that was shown you on the mountain.'"

[37] 2 Sam. 22:9-13 and not 2 Kings as Servetus wants. 1 Chron. 28:14-18 : "Then David gave his son Solomon ... his plan for the golden chariot of the cherubim that spread their wings and covered the ark of the covenant of the LORD."

Nevertheless, although the letter and shadow had [100] there the picture of the stone temple, "the body of Christ is the true temple" (John 2). And the comparison of this example, as it relates to Christ, is proven in Hebrews 9.[38] In sum, everything that is in the Law, is the shadow of the body of Christ as the apostle teaches in the epistles to the Colossians and Hebrews. As far as the Jews were concerned, everything happened through the angels, in the shadow of Christ, and Christ was represented through them. For the Jews, the angels are often called divine, although, nonetheless, the fact that they are called divine actually refers to God and Christ (1 Cor. 8) and not those tripartite invisible divine entities.

To say that the glory of God sits above the cherubim means that Jesus Christ is superior to the angels because he is "the lord of glory" and he sits "on the seat of his glory" (1 Cor. 2 and Matt. 25). And he shall come with that "splendor, majesty, and glory" (Mark 8 and Matt. 16).[39] That very glory of God and majesty, regarding which it is said in Exodus 40 to be receding from the cherub and coming to Christ, and is said to be elevated above the cherub and located much higher (Ezek. 9). The throne was above the head of the cherubim and the spreading seat of Christ (Ezek. 1 and 10)[40]; that is because Christ is far superior to the angels. By

---

[38] Heb. 9:13-14 compares the unique sacrifice of Christ with sacrifices of the Jewish temple: "For if the blood of goats and bulls, with the sprinkling of the ashes of a heifer, sanctifies those who have been defiled so that their flesh is purified, how much more will the blood of Christ, who through the eternal Spirit offered himself without blemish to God, purify our conscience from dead works to worship the living God!" In John 2:21 author of the gospel indicates that Jesus in conversation with the Jews "was speaking of the temple of his body."

[39] 1 Cor. 8:5-6 : "Indeed, even though there may be so-called gods in heaven or on earth – as in fact there are many gods and many lords – yet for us there is one God, the Father, from whom are all things and for whom we exist, and one Lord, Jesus Christ, through whom are all things and through whom we exist." Next Servetus quotes 1 Cor. 2:8, Matt. 25:31, Mark 8:38, and Matt. 16:27 where there is allusion to the second coming of the son of Man. Before Servetus made allusion to the use of the term *elohim* as meaning *angels*, interpreted often as gods according to Maimonides, Guide, Part I, cap. XXVII.

[40] Ezek. 9: 3 : "Now the glory of the God of Israel had gone up from the cherub on which it rested to the threshold of the house." Ezek. 1:26 : "And above the dome over their heads there was something like a throne, ... and seated above the likeness of a throne was something that seemed like a human form." Ezek. 10:1 : "there appeared above them [cherubim] something like a sapphire, in form resembling a throne."

this logic Christ is compared with angels in the Epistle to the Hebrews so that on that basis the Jews, who understood the angels as representatives of God, could understand that Christ himself, who was portrayed in the Law as higher than the angels, was above the angels as the true God. Indeed, the divinity of the angels only suited the logic of the ministry in the shade and prefiguration of the true divinity of Christ. Hence it came to pass that Paul labeled it a superstition if anyone inferred a religion of angels on the pretext of his divinity (Col. 2). With the same thinking, John said that we must be wary of all images though they have some appearance of divinity because Christ alone is the true God (1 John 5). "There is no other name under heaven in which we ought to be saved" (Acts 4).[41] The truth of Christ, shining forth for us, destroys those shadows. The glory of the Lord, which appeared so many times through the angels in the cherubim and in the cloud, is now revealed in the face of Christ (Isa. 40 and 46). Now that Christ is known, [101] all of us by directing our eyes to him, now that his face has been revealed, see the glory of God (Isa. 66 and Hab. 2).[42] The very thing which among the Jews was once overshadowed through the angels, is known by us in the face of Jesus Christ. The Jews saw the angel in God and God in the angel; we see Christ in God and God in Christ. They saw the angel managing everything in the Law and speaking like God with the whole Law (Acts 7, Heb. 2, and Gal. 3). The angel is at that point called the face of God (Exod. 33). Upon seeing the angel, Jacob is said to have seen the face of God, *Peniel*, (Gen. 32), because the face and the person of Christ were represented in that place by the angel. At that time, among the angels

---

[41] Col. 2:8; 1 John 5:1; Acts 4:12.

[42] Isa. 40:5 : "Then the glory of the LORD shall be revealed." Isa. 46:1 : "their idols are on beasts and cattle" and Isa. 66:15 and Hab. 2:3 and 3:4 cited in notes 16 and 17. In these references the final triumph was prophesied. It is interesting that Servetus ascribes the prophetic meaning to the pronouncements against his doctrine concerning the meaning of the biblical prophecies which he expressed in the prologue to his edition of Pagnino Bible and in the notes on the margin of various chapters of Isaiah (41, 43, 53, etc.). In there Servetus indicated that Isaiah was referring to the historical Cyrus who allowed the Jews to return from the Babylonian slavery and to the events of his life.

under the person of Christ dwelt the name of God, whose act of dwelling among the cherubim indicated the same thing. The name of God at that time lived in the angel (Exod. 23), but at that time in a shadow; now it is in Christ through the body (Col. 2).[43] The angel that prefigured Christ assumed the person of God and was called God, just as the angel said to Jacob, "I am the God of Bethel" (Gen. 31). And the angel said to Moses, "I am the God of your fathers" (Exod. 3). The angel appeared and spoke to Abraham himself in the person of God (Gen. 18 and 22), and to Agar herself (Gen. 16 and 21).[44] On this basis Origen in his eighth homily on Genesis, on the basis of his opinion on the aforementioned chapter 22, said, "I think that, just as Christ was found among us men as a man in his manner, so he has been found among angels as an angel in his manner."[45] This statement is quite true because the angelic substance partook of the light of the Word, and in the Word it was the person of Christ borne through an angel. In fact, the angel about whom Ezekiel spoke in chap. 43, was Christ. "A man stood next to me and said to me, 'the atrium within is the place of my throne, the place of the soles of my feet where I will reside among the sons of Israel for eternity.'"[46] That man was the figure of Christ, by which the angel made himself God and man, just as Christ is

---

[43] In Acts 7:38 and 53 Stephen explains that the Jews "received the law as ordained by angels" and it was the angel who spoke to Moses on the mount Sinai. In Heb 2:5 and 9 the author states that God made Jesus "for a little while lower than the angels," but God subjected everything to his authority and not to that of the angels. Gal. 3:19 : "It [the Law] was added because of transgressions, until the offspring would come to whom the promise had been made; and it was ordained through angels by a mediator." Gen. 32:30 : "So Jacob called the place *Peniel*, saying, "For I have seen God face to face, and yet my life is preserved." In Hebrew *Peniel* is פְּנִיאֵל, a composition of פָּנִים, (*panim*) *face*, and אֵל, (*el*) *God*. Ex. 23:23 : "When my angel goes in front of you." Col. 2:17: *"quae sunt umbra futurorum corpus autem Christi."*

[44] Gen. 31:13; Exod. 3:6; Gen. 18:1, 22:15 (sacrifice of Isaac), 16:7, 21:17 (angel speaking to Hagar). .

[45] Origen, *In Genesim*, hom. 8 (PG XII, 208).

[46] Ezek. 43:7. Important is for the Servetus view a statement in *De Trinitatis erroribus*, 90v, in which Servetus explains that all the celestial creatures are called "spirits" and "angels" only when they are sent to us, because we perceive them in that way. "However, neither 'angels' nor 'spirits' are the natural names." It means that they are names which express a function not a nature, a mode of existence.

God and man living in the interior atrium of our heart. The angels with their human faces allowed themselves to be worshipped at that time (Num. 22 and Josh. 5). But now it is the contrary, [102] because Christ, whom they prefigured, has been exposed, and they now worship him and are our fellow slaves to him (Rev. 19 and 22).[47] God was once worshipped via an angel, but now He is truly worshipped in Christ alone, and among the angels He was then worshipped under the shadow of Christ. Just as the Jews, by hearing the voice of the angel, heard the voice of God (Exod. 23), for us Christ's voice is God's voice (Acts 12). Christ speaks the words of the Father (John 3). Just as by seeing him so by hearing him the Father is heard (John 14). The bread of Christ's body is the "bread of God" (John 6), and his blood is "the blood of God" (Acts 20).[48] We have been made justified through Christ by the justice of God: made the body and limbs of Christ, we are the congregation of God.

The fact that he is called a man, having been made in the "image and likeness of God," or to the form and figure of God as the words put it in Hebrew, corresponds very nicely with the proposed prefiguration of the person of Christ in the Word. He says, "to our image and our likeness," that is, to the form and figure of that image that is common to God, the Word, and the angels (Gen. 1). "Our," he said, as if in the plural, and "image," as if in the singular, not "images" because the personal image or face was one alone, which was the person of Christ in God communicated even to the angels. Recall what we said: representation is a property of speech and wisdom. The Word was the representation of Christ. The personal "Word was with God and was God Himself." Among the angels was the

---

[47.] Num. 22:1-41 narrates the story of Balaam and his donkey, how they reacted to the sight of "the angel of the LORD." Joshua 5:14 recounts how Joshua prostrated himself before the angel, "The commander of the army of the LORD." Rev. 19:17 and 22:9 present an angel who is "a fellow servant" worshiping God.

[48] In Exod. 23:22 God announced to Moses that he would send an angel "in front" of Israelites and that they should be attentive to him and obey his voice. In Acts 12:21-23 when people declared that the voice of King Herod was the voice of God, angel of God struck him down. John

ministry of representation with the participation of the light of the Word. Therefore, the model was genuine, and the image was primary, or the prototype was Christ Jesus himself in whose image we were once made, just as when we are born again in baptism, we are regenerated in his image. I am talking about the true image, the one that is visible because of the internal man, as I shall show.[49]

For the moment our discourse is concerned with the external image. The ancient Hebrews maintained from scripture, where it is quite plain, as Philo, Eusebius, [103] Jerome, Petrus Alfonsus, Paul of Burgos, and many other Jews who converted to Christ teach, that the image appeared visible in God Himself.[50]

3:34 : "He whom God has sent speaks the words of God." John 14:9, 6:33; Acts 20:28.

[49] This Servetian interpretation of Gen. 1:26: "Let us make humankind in our image, according to our likeness," is highly original. Servetus avoids here completely any trinitarian allusion and the image mentioned here is not that of God, but of his Word which was from eternity in the human figure, that of Christ, in whose image a man will be made. The same figure is partaken by the angels in the theophanies, but only as "the ministry of representation" since there is only the "personal Word," a concept which Servetus ascribed also to Tertullian (Kingdon, pp. 8, 10, 14).

[50] Demonstration of this human form and visible "person" of a man, future Christ, in God should be one of the principal goals of Servetus. But he does not quote specific references neither in Philo, nor in Eusebius or Jerome. Philo of Alexandria talks about the Logos as an image of God and about visions as the visions of this image, e.g., in *De somniis*, I, 25.157: "But the dream also represented the archangel, namely the Lord himself, firmly planted on the ladder." II, 6.45: "For God gives to the soul a seal, a very beautiful gift, to show that he has invested with shape the essence of all things which was previously devoid of shape. and has stamped with a particular character that which previously had no character, and has endowed with form that which had previously no distinctive form, and having perfected the entire world, he has impressed upon it image and appearance, namely, his own word [logos]." Servetus quotes only once famous Spanish converts Petrus Alphonsus of Huesca (Moses Sefardi, 1062-1110) and Paul of Burgos (Pablo de Burgos, 1351-1435), father of Alonso of Cartagena (Salomón ha-Levi). Peter Alfonsus was baptized in 1106 in the presence of King Alfonso I of Aragon and became his physician. He published twelve dialogues between a Jew and a Christian which were first printed in Cologne in 1536 as *Dialogi lectu dignissimi*. He also published a second work based on Arabic sources, entitled *"Ecclesiastical Discipline"* (*Disciplina Clericalis*). It has been translated into several languages and is preserved in numerous manuscripts. The text of both works of Petrus Alfonsus may be found in Migne, PL, CLVII, 527-706. Servetus perhaps makes reference to the loci in *Dialogi* which explain the passages from Exod. 33 to Isa. 62 (PL CLVII.541). Paul of Burgos was the most wealthy and influential Jew of Burgos, a scholar in Talmudic and rabbinical literature, and a Rabbi of the Jewish community. He was baptized in 1390 together with his brothers Pedro Suares and Alvar Garcia (and his family). The wife of Paul, Joanna, died a Jewess shortly after. Paul of Burgos, who became known as Paul de Santa Maria, spent some years at the University of Paris, where he took his degree of doctor in theology. In 1405 he became Bishop of Cartagena; in 1415, Archbishop of Burgos. In 1416 King Henry of Castile named him lord

The first Christians maintained this, as is clear from Irenæus and Tertullian, who said that in the Word itself was the human form and figure.[51] Even before Moses and among Gentiles this was accepted as Job and his companions teach. Job saw the form of God with his own eyes, as he says in the last chapter, "With the power of my ears I heard you; now it is my eye that sees you." What is that, "now it is my eye that sees you?" "I saw the King Himself, God, with my eyes," said Isaiah (Chap. 6). And Micah said: "Jehovah Himself I saw upon His throne," at the end of 3 Kings.[52] About this matter see Eusebius Pamphilius in the fifth book of the

---

chancellor. After the king's death Archbishop Paul was a member of the council which ruled Castile in the name of the regent Doña Catalina, and by the will of the deceased king he was tutor to the heir to the throne – later John II of Castile. Servetus may refer to published writings of Paul of Burgos: *"Dialogus Pauli et Sauli contra Judæos, sive Scrutinium scripturarum"* (Mantua, 1475; Mains, 1478; Paris, 1507, 1535; Burgos, 1591); *"Additiones"* to the *"Postilla"* of Nicholas of Lyra (Nuremberg, 1481; 1485; 1487, etc.; Venice, 1481, 1482, etc). Both works were well known to Servetus who makes use of them in his second edition of the Pagnini in 1545.

[51] Irenaeus uses in various places expressions that might support Servetus's view: *Adv. Haereses*, lib. III, 18.1: "For I have shown that the Son of God did not then begin to exist, being with the Father from the beginning; but when He became incarnate, and was made man;." lib. IV, 6.3: "For no one can know the Father, unless through the Word of God, that is, unless by the Son revealing [Him]; neither can he have knowledge of the Son, unless through the good pleasure of the Father. But the Son performs the good pleasure of the Father; for the Father sends, and the Son is sent, and comes;" lib IV, 20.1: "It was not angels, therefore, who made us, nor who formed us, neither had angels power to make an image of God, nor any one else, except the Word of the Lord, nor any Power remotely distant from the Father of all things. For God did not stand in need of these [beings], in order to the accomplishing of what He had Himself determined with Himself beforehand should be done, as if He did not possess His own hands. For with Him were always present the Word and Wisdom, the Son and the Spirit, by whom and in whom, freely and spontaneously, He made all things;" and lib. IV,20.6 : "Thus, therefore, was God revealed; for God the Father is shown forth through all these [operations], the Spirit indeed working, and the Son ministering, while the Father was approving, and man's salvation being accomplished" (PG VII, 234.256). But he interprets "Let us make" as directed by the Father to his two "hands," the Word and the Spirit. (lib. V, 1.3 : "For never at any time did Adam escape the *hands* of God, to whom the Father speaking, said, "Let Us make man in Our image, after Our likeness;" lib V, 5.1: "For in Adam the *hands* of God had become accustomed to set in order."). Tertullian is more explicit, e.g., in *De resurrectione carnis*, cap. VI (PL II, 802) : "For, whatever was the form and expression which was then given to the clay (by the Creator) Christ was in His thoughts as one day to become man, because the Word, too, was to be both clay and flesh, even as the earth was then. For so did the Father previously say to the Son : 'Let us make man in our own image, after our likeness.' And God made man, that is to say, the creature which He molded and fashioned; after the image of God (in other words, of Christ) did He make him. And the Word was God also, who was being in the image of God."

[52] Job 42:5; Isa. 6:5 . The quote from Micah seems to be erroneous; it could be a result of a bad

Evangelic Demonstration, and the seventh book of the *Evangelic Preparation.*[53]

Adam's body was formed in the image of God before the soul was added; therefore, it was the image of a body. Man, and afterwards woman, was first shaped according to the face, in the image of God, Paul teaches when speaking about the image of the face (Cor. 11).[54] The image and likeness at the first creation of man in the image of God contained the image and likeness of the soul and body. Although, in a moral sense the first man is called the image and likeness of God in his innocence and justice; although, likewise the soul in the manner of God is a certain mentality with understanding, nevertheless, in the fashioning of man, as the meaning of the words clearly shows, צלם *zelem* (image) and דמות *demuth* (likeness, similitude) is the image of the whole man and the visible figure. All the more so because Christ himself is said to be entirely the copy of God and the figure.

Regarding *zelem* Daniel 3 is proof where it is said about Nebuchadnezzar, *zelem*, in other words, "The form of his face was unchanged." And Psalm 72 which is Psalm 73 for the Hebrews, says *Zalmam*, that is, "their face" or "expression you shall despise." It is plainly shown there that *zelem* is the outward form. *Zelem* also means the form and physical image of a statue as in Numbers 33, 4 Kings 11, and elsewhere throughout.

As to *demuth* the same thing is proven in Ezekiel 1 and 8 and Isaiah 40. That is the same model according to [104] which man was constructed; it is *demuth* which Ezekiel saw in this passage. Or was *demuth* referring to that made-

---

reading of certain words in 7:10.

[53] Eusebius of Caesarea, *De demonstratione evangelica,* lib. V, cap. 4 and cap. 9 (PG XXII, 370, 382). Here Eusebius comments various passages in Gen. 1:26 on the "image and likeness;" 12:7 on "Then the LORD appeared to Abram." The one who appears, says Eusebius, is neither angel, nor God the Father, who is invisible, but the Word of God, who appears *"revestido de humana specie ac figura."* Similarly, in *De preaparatione evangelica,* lib. VII, cap. 11 (PG XXI, 538).

[54] 1 Cor. 11:7-11.

up ghost in the image of which man was made?[55] Through the true form and figure of Christ, which was in God, man was likened unto God even physically so that even the body of a dead man is called the image of God. Through these words, *zelem* and *demuth*, Adam produced sons "in his own image and likeness" as he himself was formed in God's image and likeness (Gen. 5). Therefore, he was the likeness of the figure of God.[56] The very body of Adam is fashioned after the image and likeness of God, so teach Irenæus and Tertullian. Following the ancient Hebrews Philo together with the first Christians taught the very same thing in Book 1 of *Questions on Genesis*, and Eusebius Pamphilius cited him in book 7 of the cited work, *Evangelical preparation*: "No mortal being," he said, "can be compared to the supreme Father as an image, but a comparison is made through the Word as through God being a type of intermediary." In his book *On Agriculture*, Philo as well said that the soul of man was made and figured in the form and image of the first model, the Word. He teaches the same thing about the form of the soul and the image of the face in his book, *On the Unsuitability of Women Acting Shamelessly* and in the book *On the World*. He said that the expression was old, that the divinity very often appeared in human form, which made man even after his own image.[57] There according to the model, the form, the

---

[55] In Dan. 3:19: "Nebuchadnezzar was so filled with rage ... that his face was distorted." Ps. 72:20 : *"imaginem ipsorum ad nihilum rediges."* Num 33:52 : "cast images." 2 Kings 11:18 : "his images [of Baal]." Ezek. 1:10 : "the appearance of their faces." Ezek. 1:13 : "something that looked like burning coals of fire." Ezek. 8:2 : "a figure that looked like a human being." Isa. 40:19 : "what likeness compare with him? An idol? – A workman casts it." Both terms are explained by Maimonides, *Guide*, Part I, cap. I..
[56] Gen. 5:1-3.
[57] Eusebius, in *De praeparatione evangelica*, lib. VII, cap. 13 (PG XXI, 546) cites the text of Philo, *Quaestiones in Genesin*, lib. 2, 62, in which he calls the Logos "the second God." Eusebius says of Philo: "Why as if speaking of another God does He say, 'In the image of God I made man' (Gen. 9:6), and not in the image of Himself? With consummate beauty and wisdom is this oracle expressed. For nothing mortal could be made in the likeness of the Most High God and Father of the universe, but in the likeness of the second God, who is the Word of the former. For it was right that the rational character in the soul of man should be impressed on it by the divine Word." There are other two places where Philo calls the Logos God: LA 3.207, Somn. 1.229-230. And Eusebius also quotes another passage from Philo's *De agricultura* (XII, 51): "'All these

figure, and the image of Christ, Adam was made in terms of body and soul.

In fact, although when it is said, "Let us make" and "our," it is taken literally to refer to angels since even the angels possessed a certain idea of man, nevertheless, Christ, as adumbrated in the angels, is always understood to be in mystery. Regarding them, it is said that in the person of Christ, just as in regard to David and Solomon many things are said more excellently than could suit them; it is because of the subconscious understanding of the mystery and not because of them that these are said about them. It is literally said about the angel, "my face shall precede [105] you" (Exod. 33), even though the true face is nonetheless Christ, who was the son of Israel, the companion of the journey (1 Cor. 10).[58] Indeed, he who said, "Let us make man," was Christ, was Elohim, the person of the Word, which was the person of God. And he was speaking to the angels just as even the angels were speaking throughout as gods. He said to the angels, "Behold, Adam like one of us," and again, "Come, let us descend, and leave." Everything in the Law comes about through the angels and the angels are called gods.[59]

Hence some were taught regarding the gods of the Old Testament that they were other gods. Hence the heresy of Simon Magus, Cerdo, Marcion and others who, because they had a wicked understanding that the God of the Law was an angel, denied that the God of the Law was the father of Jesus Christ.[60] Others

---

things then God the Shepherd and King guides according to justice, having set over them as a law His own right Reason (Word) and First-born Son, who is to receive the charge of this sacred flock, as a lieutenant of a great king." Servetus probably does not refer to the passage from *De agricultura* but from *Quaestiones in Genesin*, lib. 1, 4. The title which Servetus cites *Quod mulieres non decet indecore agere* does not exist in the known lists of Philo's works. The quote on the creation of man in the image of God comes from *De opificio mundi*, cap. 6.

[58] Exod. 33:2 : "I will send an angel before you." Exod. 33:14 : "My presence will go with you, and I will give you rest." 1Cor.10:4 : "For they drank from the spiritual rock that followed them, and the rock was Christ."

[59] Gen. 3:22. Maimonides wrote about the ministry of angels in the Old Testament, (*Guide*, Part II, cap. VI), and some of his ideas were taken by Servetus. Calvin and his ministers in Geneva could not understand nor admit the theories of Servetus (*Calvini Opera*, VIII, 511; Kingdon, pp. 14, 34

[60] Servetus suggests that these gods of the Old Testament are a philological misunderstanding due to the bad translation of the Hebrew terms. Marcion ca 140 C.E. developed further the school

imagined that God, in fact, is corporeal and according to His nature possessed innate corporeal bodies which had been attributed to Him in the entire Law. Concerning this subject, Onkelos the Chaldaean, in his translation, and Rabbi Moses of Egypt in his *Books of the Perplexed* exercise themselves over this matter in order to free God from His forms.[61] But all those things are proof for us that all that perplexity is easily disposed of through Christ. Because he truly is the face, image, copy, and figure of God, who in reality has within Himself the corporeal forms. He is the God of gods and the God of the angels.

Now in this matter the craft of the diverse style of the scriptures comes for due consideration. It is not without mystery that in the Old rather than in the New Testament the scripture attributes such things to God. It is not without significance that in the Old Testament ever so often you read of hands, eyes, face, and feet of God, [all] seen with corporeal eyes, yet none of these things are found in the New Testament, but the opposite, to wit that God is a spirit. The reason for this is because at that time the person of Christ was indicated as being with God. There was then no actual distinction between the Father and the son but, corporeal forms were attributed to God Himself, which now exist in the son.[62] By the same reasoning the angels were introduced in the scriptures' mode of speaking in the form of God and Christ. If Cyprian simply understood this fact, he would have

---

of Cedro which goes back to Simon the Magus of the first century. Marcion founded a peculiar type of Gnosticism which lasted until the fifth century. He differentiated the God of the Old Testament, who was according to him a malicious and belligerent being, from God the Father and the Creator. Jesus appeared in a human form without a real body in order to free us from all the Judaism and conquer the God of the Law.

[61] Servetus differs in here from the explanation which is given by Rabbi Moses ben Maimon, Rambam, known as Maimonides, to the Hebrew term *zelem*, which for him means a "specific form," a form of his intellectual perception, and to *demuth*, likeness, "but far from conceiving the Supreme Being as corporeal and having any material form" (*Guide*, Part I, cap. 1). But Servetus does not cite the *targum* of Onkelos the Chaldaean. Servetus, against the authentic Hebrew tradition wants to attribute to these terms the meanings of *image* and *face*, which he thinks is found in many ancient Christian texts.

[62] The real distinction between the two began when Jesus was born as the son of God, who, however, in his mode of existence as the Word, had already the corporeal forms which he would posses as the son. This interpretation is bold and highly original.

correctly applied the ancient truth and said [106] that God, the angel, and Christ were all speaking there. For in the second book of his, *Against the Jews,* he shows in many ways that God and the angel were the same thing, as was Christ, who addressed Abraham and others, and was seen.[63] All of this is inferred also from one passage in Exodus 3. For Christ said, "I, who shall be, shall be." It was the angel who appeared and spoke, but it was God's voice.[64] Paul emphasized the same point in his third letter to the Galatians. "The Law," he said, "was given by God through the angels in the hand of a mediator."[65] Such was the glory of Jesus Christ that his person is depicted in God, the angels, men, the lamb, the calf, the serpent, wood, rock, and other things. These mysteries of Christ being such, had they been understood in the past, no one would have said that the angels created the world and that they were the gods of the Old Testament. For they acted as the shadow of Christ alone in their ministry and not in the creation itself, but in the other activities that later followed. Some have made God and the idea two principles since the idea was the appearance of the Word and the divine form. Amazing logic; amazing Word.[66]

With the Word God created, and it was the person of Christ that was

---

[63] Cyprian, *Testimonium adversus Iudaeos,* lib. II, cap. 5 (PL IV, 728), where he comments on various texts of the Old Testament (Gen. 22:11 on the vision of Abraham; 31:13, on the vision of Jacob; Exod. 13:21 : "The LORD went in front of them in a pillar of cloud by day, to lead them along the way, and in a pillar of fire by night, to give them light, so that they might travel by day and by night;" and 14:19 : "The angel of God who was going before the Israelite army moved and went behind them; and the pillar of cloud moved from in front of them and took its place behind them;" on the "pillar" of fire or "cloud") as well as of the New Testament, especially John 5:43 : "I have come in my Father's name, and you do not accept me."

[64] Exod. 3:14 : "God said to Moses, 'I AM WHO I AM.'" Thus Servetus deviated from the usual interpretation of this text as defining the essence of God.

[65] Gal. 3:19.

[66] The originality of the Servetus thought becomes more emphasized if one considers that Servetus not only rejects the traditional Hebrew interpretation and, of course, any materialistic concept of God, all political and Gnostic views, but also the Platonic distinction between the ideas and the demiurge or creator God. The ideas, in the peculiar Servetian Platonism, which is more Augustinian in this respect, are identical with the Word of God, his reason or mind, his pronouncement, which has the same form and figure, and as a man has the same "image and likeness."

151

creating. God created through the Word by creating through Himself, namely, through a certain display of Himself that was manifested through utterance. There was at the creation a certain display of God, and a communication of the creature with God, with the result that Adam before the sin gazed upon that form of God and received the pure spirit. After the sin God's face was hidden to man under an engraved veil (*caelatura velaminis*) that was to remain unopened until the advent of Christ. As if Christ exhibited himself through shutters of a window to be gazed upon in the Law, though not openly (Prov. 7 and Songs 2). In chapter 3 Zechariah teaches that this engraved veil of Christ is to be opened for us when God says concerning Christ, "I engrave him; I open his inscription." *Patach* פתח properly means here "to engrave by opening" and "to uncover the hidden image as with a chisel." Thus, by showing Christ, God opened Himself. Along nearly identical lines does the Chaldean translator render it as "the face of Christ is revealed" or [107] "opened." For thus is the *targum* of Jonathan there: אה אנא גלי כזיי תהא, *ha ena gele chezijathaha*, that is, "behold, I reveal," or "I open his vision."[67] In summary, as all the prophets, along with stories and prophecies of Christ, very frequently mix the words, "face" and "image," "hidden" and "removed," "dwelling" and "hideout," so does the Law. That is because the spirit of the Lord by sculpting very skillfully engraved all those things which have been written in the Law and in all the prophets about him, as Luke 24 and Matthew 11 said "Christ,"[68] so that under a silver filigree the golden Word would lay hidden. The whole of this, as by a certain protective covering, was adumbrated by God's secret plan in historic and ceremonial symbols just as Christ himself was adumbrated in God. By

---

[67] Prov. 7:6 : "For at the window of my house I looked out through my lattice." Songs 2:9 : "Look, there he stands behind our wall, gazing in at the windows, looking through the lattice." Zech. 3:9 : "For on the stone that I have set before Joshua, on a single stone with seven facets, I will engrave its inscription."

152

analogy to higher mysteries, the display within the lesser mysteries of the Law was also under the shadow of prefiguring Christ. Therefore, the function of the shadow had come from above to lesser matters.[69] There was in God a certain bright Word that was, nevertheless, shining in mist and shade. And the beginning was as a shadow of Christ at that time because it foreshadowed Christ and because the shadow is called a diminished light. There was a light there that had, so to speak, been diminished because of Adam's sin and because it was not shining for the Jews, as it does for us. The ancients called it the "corporeal word." For there was substance, shining with the image of a corporeal thing in the cloud, although there was in it no "corporeal material."[70] You shall know presently the manner of divinity in the cloud and the manner of Christ's conception from heavenly dew on the basis of what follows once God's universal and omniformed essence is known. If you could believe that God really fathered from Himself a man as His son, then you will easily believe these things. There with plain and simple reflection is Jesus Christ in God, the Father, being now the subject of inquiry. In the preaching of Paul and the other apostles never is anything heard but that there is the one God, who is the Father and that Jesus Christ is His son. All differences and manners of speaking are worthy of your attention: namely, when they say, "Word" and when they say, "son." For the meanings [108] of those expressions are different. If you show me some passage where "Word" was at some point called "son," I will admit that I am beaten. Therefore, I shall say with the scriptures "once the Word, now

---

[68] Luke 24:27 : Jesus "Then beginning with Moses and all the prophets, he interpreted to them the things about himself in all the scriptures." Matt. 11:13 : "For all the prophets and the law prophesied until John came."

[69] These are two basic concepts in the system of Servetus's thought: *analogy* and *shadow*.

[70] Facing an enormous intellectual challenge Servetus is forced to coin an adequate terminology such as *corporale verbum* (corporeal word) though which is not *materia corporea* (corporeal material). Among the ancients mentioned by Servetus one has to list Tertullian whose various passages Servetus cites during his trial in order to show that Tertullian shares his theory of the "identity of the face of Christ then and now," or of the "person and form of man Christ who always shone in God." Kingdon, p. 14.

the son," and "once in the Word was the person of the son."[71]

The person of the son was correctly described to the ancients even though the Sophists who fail to understand this have wrenched free from elsewhere "persons." They make bodiless, metaphysical invisible persons that are stupidly called persons.[72] It would be a small abuse of language if they were not abusing God Himself, too, by splitting Him up, tearing Him apart, and cutting Him to bits. Moreover, notice what scripture hands down about the person so that you may understand their level of abuse. The outside aspect of man is always called appearance, face, representation, and person both in scripture and elsewhere, as when we say that this man's person is beautiful. Person is taken in this sense in Romans 2, Colossians 3, Acts 10, and 1 Peter 1. "God does not consider person" nor these outward aspects whether it be masculine or feminine, slave or free, Jew or Greek, rich or poor.[73] Thus is it taken in 1 Kings 17, Leviticus 19, Deuteronomy 1, and James 2, when we are taught that the person of a pauper is not to be considered nor the face of a powerful man. Likewise is 2 Corinthians 1, 2, 3, 4, 8, 10, and 11.[74] Even outside of the scripture, the meaning of the word, πρόσωπον, for the Greeks, like *persona* for the Latins is *per se* evident that it had to be some wicked demon who encouraged all the trinitarians to force on us those made-up, invisible entities as persons. The matter is obvious in Hebrew: what we call *person*, they call *face*. Check here, reader, from the start what those first

---

[71] This is very succinct in Latin: *"Olim verbum, nunc filius. Et olim in verbo persona filii."*

[72] Servetus rejects the ontological concept of a person which constitutes one of the basic points of his intellectual system. He believes that the original biblical sense was recognized by some early Christian writers before the formulation of the trinitarian dogma.

[73] Rom. 2:11: *"non est enim personarum acceptio apud Deum;"* or in Greek "οὐ γάρ ἐστιν προσωπολημψία παρὰ τῷ θεῷ." The same expression is used in Col. 3:25; Acts 10:34, 1 Pet. 1:17.

[74] Not 1 Sam 17 as Servetus says but 16:7 : "'Do not look on his appearance [*ne respicias vultum eius*] or on the height of his stature." In Lev. 19:15; Deut. 1:17; James 2:9 are used the terms: face (*facies*), person (*persona*), and persons (*personae*), respectively. The citations from 2 Cor. 1:11, 2:10, 3:7, 4:6, 8:24, 10:1, and 11:20 refer to the term *persona* (πρόσωπον), always used in the sense of external appearance, and never in the philosophical sense deduced adopted later.

Christians felt about the person of the Word and the reasons why.[75] Likewise in scripture there is a method for talking about the person so that one thing is said to bear the person of another; in this manner the comrades of Job want to speak and judge, assuming the person of God, as if they themselves were gods.[76] The angel in the person of God speaks in the whole Law. The pseudoapostles used to speak in the person of the apostles. Satan speaks in the person of a good angel when he transforms himself into the angel of light. Wisdom, the angel, [109] David, and the other prophets often speak in the person of Christ. In this way we say that the Word in the person of Christ was once the son and that this Christ once was in the person of the Word with the Father. Christ is the person of the Word, and the Word is the person of Christ, and they do not exist save as one person and one aspect. The very thing which shone forth in Word and Wisdom, is Christ himself. Just as if you should see me face-to-face and even in a mirror, you do see but one person. From the foregoing the parable about Wisdom is plainly understood (Prov. 8). The person of Christ is shown there, saying that he was formed from before time. It was the foreshadowing of Christ, a brightness, a certain expression. In God the act of generation was His very thought and display directed towards the act of generating Christ. Wisdom speaks there in parable and in figurative language because Wisdom was bearing the person of Christ who was formed in God from before time, having been conceived and created by a certain expression. But he is said to be created because He partakes of creation. Conceived in terms of personality, he is the personal son, and so in this way was also formed in terms of personality.

---

[75] This point was discussed with Calvin during the trial in Geneva. Servetus insisted that such a biblical interpretation of the term was used by Irenaeus and Tertullian.

[76] Job 13:8 : "Will you show *partiality* toward him, will you plead the case for God?" The Hebrew original text is : הֲפָנָיו תִּשָּׂאוּן אִם־לָאֵל תְּרִיבוּן׃ which translates as: "Will you lift up His *face*, or will you contend for God?"

Regarding the Vision of God

Now that the person of the Word is clear, and the manner of its manifestation is
known, those details which remain to be said about the vision of God shall be
straightforward. The vision of God, which the world did not know, I am compelled
by Christ's instruction to bring to the fore in such a way that I shall call them blind
that "fail to see God, although they see Him, and those that fail to understand God,
although they perceive Him." In fact, you, Christian reader, shall realize that
through Christ you are obtaining the knowledge and vision which you truly acquire
about God, and you shall consider it entirely received thanks to Christ. In and of
Himself God is utterly incomprehensible because He can neither be seen nor
understood unless, as Christ himself teaches in John 5, you observe in Him a
certain image.[77] This is, as it already has become clear, the face of Christ and the
person of the Word. Because He desired great things in that face, the divine
majesty appeared not only on the mountain, but in the temple and elsewhere, so
that His aspect alone with great strength moved His witnesses. That very thing is
now in heaven, as in Paul's vision, far more glorious because he [110] is a man
glorified for the glory, which the Word once had with God (John 17).[78] The Word,
which was with God and was God Himself, was the person of Jesus Christ through
which the God of glory wished to be seen, is and will be seen ever more. As you
see light in the body of the sun, so in the body of Christ the apostles with their
physical eyes saw God shining, and you see Him with your inner eyes. For what
other light could be seen in the face of Christ, once it was transfigured and shining
above the sun, if not the uncreated light itself? The subtle notions which the
Sophists claim hold themselves separate from God, are absolutely nothing or rather
illusions in the presence of God. What Christian of sound mind would make the
Turks, the Saracens, or other foreigners our equals in the vision of God or

---

[77] John 5:37 : "And the Father who sent me has himself testified on my behalf. You have never
heard his voice or seen his form" (Latin: *speciem*; Greek: εἶδος).

conceptions about God? Peter in Book 2 of Clement argues similarly about notions which he had formed about Jerusalem and Caesarea before he had seen the cities. Subsequently, after seeing them, he realized that all his preconceptions were false.[79] We, who see God through Christ, clearly sense the manifest falseness of others' ideas about him. For what could a man ever conceive about God before He made Himself visible? He is more removed by far than these very cities that confounded Peter's ideas. The mind that thinks about God fails because He is incomprehensible; the eye does not see Him because He is invisible. The ear does not hear Him nor has it ever heard Him unless He has spoken in a human voice. The hand does not touch Him because He has no body. The tongue does not explain Him because He is ineffable. A place does not contain Him because He is not circumscribed. Time does not measure Him because He is immeasurable. Finally, He transcends everything and surpasses every intellect and mind. Certain people have taught that God can be defined by denial alone.[80] For, if you consider this light and these other things that are known to us, you will say, "of course," because God is not the light, but above light, nor is He essence, but above essence, [111] nor spirit, but above spirit, above everything that you can think of. This is not an accurate conception about God because it fails to teach just what God is and instead it teaches what God is not. No one knows God save someone who knows the way in which He has chosen to manifest Himself to us. That manner has obviously been presented to us through the holy oracles, and the Sophists do not believe it because they do not want to see God in Christ. Nevertheless, this is the surest truth of Christ's doctrine, a truth that is essentially in agreement regarding the vision of God: we cannot form a true idea about God Himself or any other

---

[78] John 17:5. Allusion to the vision of Paul on the road to Damascus, Acts 9:3-5

[79] In *Recognitiones* of Pseudoclement, lib. II, cap. LXII (PG I, 1277).

[80] Servetus rejects the validity of the so-called *via negativa* in the theological speculations by which some attempted to define God. Servetus accentuates the transcendence of God affirming that the only way we can know God is through the mode of his manifestation; and this substantial mode of God's manifestation is his Word, one of his "persons."

thing unless we look upon its aspect or some image in it. No idea is said to change the mind itself merely by representing some thing except insofar as the image of the thing in question meets the faculty of perception through a certain "phantom." Thanks to Aristotle everyone knows that the person who perceives necessarily gazes upon a reflection.[81] Paul likewise teaches that "we now see through a mirror" (1 Cor. 13).[82] For him seeing through the reflection of a mirror is the same thing as understanding. Now let our adversaries answer Paul: "In what mirror do they see God?" Let them tell us what image it reflects or what likeness that reflection upon which they gaze it presents when they form their idea about God? For it is a fact that that reflection (*phantasma*), whatever it is, represented a perceptible image or depiction. If they were all themselves to be taught the correct philosophy, nay, the correct wisdom about God, they would sooner feel the urge to call it a vision of God as it is in the holy and divine statements wherein mention is regularly made regarding the vision of God. It is called a vision, even an internal one, which occurs in the mind's eye. It has nothing to do with God or the angels or any conception which is not the same thing as a vision.[83]

Some may object that there was a notion of God among the philosophers because Paul says, "The invisible aspects of God, such as His power, divinity, justice, and the other things that are attributed to God, are recognized through His creatures" (Rom. 1).[84] Here there is no need for any other answer because Paul himself specifically [112] teaches what those invisible attributes of God are, and

---

[81] Servetus applies here the Aristotelian empirical principle of the *"conversio ad phantasmata"* or reduction of the sensory perception to the sensitive images which we produce in our senses (*De anima* III,2. 425b) in order to acquire a true intellective knowledge. This was the empirical Aristotelian principle *Nihil in mente quod non prius fuerit in sensu.*

[82] Paul in 1 Cor. 13:12 : "For now we see in a mirror, dimly (per speculum in enigmate), but then we will see face to face." Servetus combines in his doctrine the philosophical formulation with the biblical datum found in Paul. Thus for Servetus the Word is the face, image or *phantasma*, a person, of transcendent God who through this way makes possible for man to know him.

[83] Servetus wants to say that the authentic knowledge of God is in the vision, including the mental vision; and this type of knowledge of God is always mentioned in the scriptures.

[84] Rom. 1:20. Paul asserts knowledge of God through the knowledge of natural things.

that they are known through common ideas. It is a fact that we have some general knowledge about God and share some ideas about Him, although, as Paul concluded, they have been culled on the basis of other things. From the sheer size of creation we argue for the power of the creator, from the manner of His reign, for His justice and other, similar things which are in us. From those things which indicate here a certain divinity or hidden virtue, we argue that there is something else more divine, more wise, more powerful. These are the "invisible aspects of God," which are known by people in general, which Paul introduced in that passage. From the results we conclude by way of syllogism that there is one prime cause; from the movements, we reckon that there is some prime mover. Nevertheless, Aristotle never held the conception of Him as something odd, singular, or abstract. These things, says Paul, are the things which can be known about God; nevertheless, they do not constitute something by which God is known in actuality because His will in particular is unknown; in fact, Aristotle's entire discussion about cause and movements is nothing but a comparison by analogy to visible reflections in the brain. In this way they, too, are said to know God because by that syllogism they convince themselves of the reflection of a certain mover, and because they gathered certain predicates which are accurately ascribed to God.[85]

Indeed, besides all these things, whoever has become accustomed to drink water from the divine fonts, will recognize more quickly than has been said, the truth that flows like light from there because God wishes Himself to be manifested to the world through His Word and to be seen; whoever sees Christ, sees the Father; and no one sees Him, but in Christ. If the Jews, Turks, and other pagans

---

[85] Servetus in this paragraph scorns the so-called *via rationalis* or philosophical for demonstration of the existence and knowledge of God. This procedure was initiated by Plato and Aristotle and was formulated in definitive ternms by Maimonides and Thomas Aquinas. Aristotle did not attain the true knowledge of God, the creator. This approach gives us only a relative knowledge of God and says nothing about his most important aspect, namely, his will. But this initial and natural knowledge of God is sufficient for the stimulation of the natural moral conscience, the fact which will be emphasized by Servetus at several occasions.

now like us see God in this way, what vision of God did Christ bring to us? Therefore, Christian reader, you ought to recognize this visible appearance of God as a genuine θεοφανίαν in order that you may know the glory of God in the face of Jesus Christ (2 Cor. 4).[86] Thus you will then know God, "whom you never knew before, nor have you seen His face" (John 5). [113] In this passage he used the word, εἶδος, appearance, shape, figure, and face, so that we are there taught that God cannot be seen by us except in Christ's face. There the divine educator alludes to what is written in Exodus 20 and Deuteronomy 4. For, because the people of Israel once heard voices, and many of them saw a certain appearance of the speaker through Christ, it follows that those who did not recognize Christ under those circumstances, neither heard God's voice nor saw Him through the appearance just as the Sophists today neither see nor hear anything with any profundity.[87] For Christ's voice is God's voice just as the vision of Christ is the vision of God. In Christ's face God is known and seen for those who believe, and, if with that visible face with which He appeared face-to-face to Moses, He were to show Himself to me without the veil. If God were to show me clearly that face which Moses did not see, I would see nothing but the glorious face of Jesus Christ. This is the manifestation of the invisible God through the visible Word, and it is called the visible image of the invisible God. In this way Christ is called "the face of God." The thing through which a given thing is seen and recognized as such, is called its face. Therefore, we must purely and sincerely grant that God is seen in the face of Christ just as Paul said: "God is seen through Christ." "Whoever sees Christ, sees the Father, and none ever saw Him except through the son" (John 1, 5,

---

[86] 2 Cor. 4:6 : "For it is the God who said, 'Let light shine out of darkness,' who has shone in our hearts to give the light of the knowledge of the glory of God in the face of Jesus Christ."
[87] John 5:37 : "et qui misit me Pater ipse testimonium perhibuit de me neque vocem eius umquam audistis neque speciem (εἶδος) eius vidistis." Exod. 20:22 : "The LORD said to Moses: Thus you shall say to the Israelites: "You have seen for yourselves that I spoke with you from heaven." Deut. 4:12 : "The LORD said to Moses: Thus you shall say to the Israelites: "You have seen for yourselves that I spoke with you from heaven."

6, 8, 12, and 14).[88]

We are always speaking here about the vision of God, which can touch upon mortals in this era; for in the future era we shall see God differently. Then we shall see Him just as He is. Now we see Him just as He shows Himself to us. Neither the present intellect nor the human heart can aspire to attain to that future vision. Now we refer to the internal image, not to an invisible illusion.

Our opponents maintain by a certain imaginary illusion that the first entity is now seen through the second. Fine, but by what logic? How on earth will that invisible and unintelligible entity which is more unknown than the Father Himself lead us [114] to a genuine knowledge and viewing of the Father? The trinitarians have never understood the aim of the evangelic language, whenever mention is made about the vision of God, who is seen eye-to-eye through Jesus Christ, who never was seen or known before: how is it to be understood that "God was truly manifested in the flesh"? Why is it that God promised that we would all see Him eye-to-eye? God seen on earth? Take heed, reader, lest you suffer from a misapprehension by abusing together with the Sophists the word for "vision." Consider that Christ, who said that all the apostles had already seen the Father (John 14), was not a sophist. John said the same thing about the rest of the disciples in 1 John 2.[89] Nevertheless, they had seen nothing other than Christ's face in which the divinity of the Father was shining forth. Consider in what sense the still simple Thomas and Philip postulate the vision of the Father and its display by Christ, and, for that matter, Christ's response to the mind of those seeking him (John 14). There, when Christ said that the Father was seen through him, do not think that he was spoke vainly. Call this vision of the intellect, an idea, a

---

[88] John 1:18 : "No one has ever seen God. It is God the only Son, who is close to the Father's heart, who has made him known." And similar expressions in John 5:37, 6:46, 8:19, 12:45, and 14:7.

[89] John 14:7 : "If you know me, you will know my Father also. From now on you do know him and have seen him." 1 John 1:1.

conception, an understanding, or however you like. In the same sense grant that God was never seen before just as Christ himself said. Otherwise, Christ never introduced anything new, and he was promoting himself in vain by saying that the Father is seen through him. John would then be wrong to say, "We have seen the glory of Him, whom no one ever saw."[90] They saw nothing, but the glorious face of Jesus Christ. This syllogism is valid through a mechanism of God: by actually looking upon that face, Elohim was formerly seen as God, and this is now the face of Jesus Christ. Therefore, God is seen in the face of Jesus Christ. It is entirely true and proper that Christ is now substantively in God, just as the Word, which was God Himself, was with God. Always think of what sort was the witnessing of that face in the Law, and, comparing it to Christ's face, say now that God is more clearly seen. Do not forget: hear him calling out now to us from heaven, [115] "By seeing me, you see God. By seeing me, you see the Father." Raise the eyes of your mind and see. If God was able to place some sign in the world in which the light of God is properly seen, surely this was put there.

Perhaps you will make the objection that it is of too little benefit to see this external face. My response is that that is eternal blessedness its very self, if you see by believing (John 6 and 17). Just as with the gaze directed against the brazen serpent, so this gaze alone heals every bite of the devil (John 3).[91] But you unworthily gaze upon his face. Nevertheless, after you believe, you will never turn the eyes of your mind from it, and you will know that it is beneficial. For this vision alone will draw you entirely into heaven towards itself, and by brightening your darkness the light of his face will purge you from destructive error. "They

---

[90] John 1:18.

[91] John 3:14 : "And just as Moses lifted up the serpent in the wilderness, so must the Son of Man be lifted up," This quote is in reference to Num. 21:9 : "So Moses made a serpent of bronze, and put it upon a pole; and whenever a serpent bit someone, that person would look at the serpent of bronze and live." John 17:3 : "For the words that you gave to me I have given to them, and they have received them and know in truth that I came from you; and they have believed that you sent

gazed," he said, "upon him and they were made bright" (Ps. 33). "Illumine your face over your slave" (Ps. 118). "Raise the light of your face over us" (Ps. 4). "You will see and be illuminated" (Isa. 60). Did not Christ say that the eyes which see him are blessed? Most of the prophets are said to have seen God Himself face-to-face.[92] Therefore, if God is not seen in the face of Christ, they saw more than the apostles. As a result, Christ was talking gibberish when in this way he posited that the apostles were more blessed. Nevertheless, the apostles actually saw, and we see God's glory revealed in the face of Jesus Christ; indeed, the prophets saw beneath the veil and shadow of the angel with which like God the angel represented Christ for them. For certain people it was of too little benefit to see Christ with their physical eyes alone because they did not believe in him whom they saw. Still, it is entirely something else to see now with the inner eyes Christ's face shining in heaven because it cannot happen without faith. Indeed, those who are truly reborn in him see Christ dwelling within them. This inner vision gloriously transforms us into Christ [116] just as Paul said (2 Cor. 3).[93] From the standpoint of the inner man the light of Christ's face is the eternal glory and divine realization of blessedness. This act of greeting Christ is the greeting of his face, Psalm 41, and the illumination of his face, Psalm 43.[94] This vision is possessed of great power, but the illumination of the mind follows upon it if the vision itself is a divine realization. The eternal blessedness to come is a complete realization and vision of the divine light, a union with God. The vision of this eternal blessedness consists in the face of Christ that exists inside of us and makes us yet now its participants. Look at that face that was gloriously transformed on that mountain, at the sight of

---

me." John 6:40 : "This is indeed the will of my Father, that all who see the Son and believe in him may have eternal life."

[92] Ps. 33:5; 118:135; 4:6. Isa. 60:5.

[93] 2 Cor. 3:18 : "And all of us, with unveiled faces, seeing the glory of the Lord as though reflected in a mirror, are being transformed into the same image from one degree of glory to another."

[94] Ps. 41:10; 43:3 : "O send out your light and your truth."

which the light itself whereby God is light and Christ is the light of the world, is seen just as the light which illuminates the spirit of the viewer, and transforms him gloriously just as did the appearance of Christ.

From what has been said it is apparent that Christ is not only called God's image, but is also more than the image. For there is an image when there are two objects which have been depicted in a similar manner; of these two, one is called the image of the other. But in Christ there is something greater. If the angel Gabriel were to come to me in the form of a flying eagle, would I say this is the image of Gabriel? In fact, if it is called an image, it is more than an image; specifically, it is a certain representative expression, indeed, one that contains the hypostasis itself. In this way the Word, the person, or the face of Elohim was more than the image. It was God's very face, God Himself. It was a particular representation or form containing the very being of God. By a similar logic Christ is now more than an image and is a representation of the essence just as the apostle said in Hebrews 1. It is the impress of God's hypostasis, a sculptured representation of the divine essence itself. David and Moses called it תמונה, *temunah,* in Psalm 16 and Deuteronomy 4. Notice in what sense it is there called an image, when Moses said that they did not see the image of the speaker, the image, which later on David desired for us.[95] For, if you should now accept it as an image in that sense, you would be correct. There it was the very image in the form of a face. The image was the εἶδος, the display of the entity through the act of appearing (John 5). [117] In the same sense Christ is called εἴκων, the image of God, the representation of God (2 Cor. 4 and Col. 1).[96] Likewise, χαρακτήρ, a

---

[95] Heb. 1:3 : "He is the reflection of God's glory (*splendor gloriae*) and the exact imprint of God's very being (*figura substantiae eius*)." The Greek terms used are ἀπαύγασμα τῆς δόξης and χαρακτὴρ τῆς ὑποστάσεως, respectively. In Deut. 4:12 and in Ps. 16:11 the Hebrew terms תְּמוּנָה (temunah) and פָּנִים (panim) are used.with translation in LXX as εἶδος and πρόσωπον, respectively.

[96] These Greek terms, εἶδος (form) and εἴκων (image), are used in John 5:37; 2 Cor. 4:4; Col.

certain expression, sculpture, a representation of the hypostasis, that is, of the existence, the essence, or the substance of God because God is self-subsisting. From all this, the vision of God is proven. For by seeing the expression of that representation, I am said to see God just as if by seeing that eagle I would be said to see Gabriel. Otherwise, God would not be able to expose Himself in visible form. What Sophist is lunatic enough to diminish the power of God? As if God would be an inert log, incapable of self-manifestation and unable to communicate Himself to man. But, if He was able and willing to manifest Himself to man, this deed is through the veiled viewing of the oracle and the revealed face of Jesus Christ. Just as the solar face appears in the midst of the hugeness and the unapproached light, so in the midst of God's heights and profundities, His oracle appeared, being the person of Jesus Christ. I shall refrain from considering at this point the metaphysical images and invisible characters which the trinitarians posit among those notions of theirs. For they are ridiculous dreams that are unknown to scripture and they lack sense and understanding.

They make the objection that I place no notion of God among men, nor of angels or souls for that matter. I answer that I suggest that it is a manifest and transparent vision. We shall show the true essence of every notion that is in our soul in the following book, where we shall say that it is from the essence of light. We shall call that light which we see in the face of Jesus Christ through the illumination of the spirit, God Himself made visible to us through Christ. We say that this is the clear notion about God within us and that God is seen by us in Christ. God is the light, and we see that light in Jesus Christ's face. Or is this not the true vision of God and the true knowledge of Him through Christ? We shall show that the substance of the angels and souls is also from the substance of light and that it is seen in man's image. How otherwise could be seen those separated

---

1:15.

souls which John saw over the altar in Revelation 6?[97] [118] Nothing can be seen either in this age nor in the future except by virtue of light. The figure of a whole man was seen there shining forth in the soul because the soul itself holds man's true image and representation, just as Irenæus teaches in Book 2, chapters 33, 63, and 64. Philo teaches that the soul was formed after the image and example of the Word, and this has already been cited.[98] Therefore, the soul can be seen in the form of man. In fact, the angel can more easily consist in it and be seen in other forms, always by virtue of light, just as God is seen by virtue of light in Christ.

However, the sophists see with a certain clairvoyance; rather than see, they hallucinate. For them Christ was vainly made because they see God no differently than before. True Christians know and will always know that He was made the visible manifestation of God Himself. We know for certain that God is seen through Christ. We know that Christ in Thomas and Philip condemned the practice of seeking after God by other means: visions, conceptualizations, demonstrations. When He said that He was "the way," He proved that every means of knowing and seeing God existed in Him (John 14). That was God's decision and wish from eternity, to be seen in Christ alone. He wanted us to be ever gazing upon that mirror and to be illuminated in its presence by the Spirit so that our spirit, thus illuminated and containing that light, would be transformed to the same glory of Christ, would have been made a glorious copy of Christ (2 Cor. 3 and 4).[99] This is God's true intention which I confess to have through Christ whereby I enjoy Christ

---

[97] In Rev. 6:9 it is stated "under the altar" and not "above the altar."

[98] Irenaeus, *Adv. Hæreses*, lib. II, cap. 19, 33, 34 (PL VII, 773, 833, 835). According to Irenaeus the soul is made of a subtle substance so it can adapt to the body "just as water when poured into a vessel takes the form of that vessel" (cap. 19.6). In cap. 34.1 Irenaeus wrote: "it is plainly declared that souls continue to exist that they do not pass from body to body, that they possess the form of a man, so that they may be recognized, and retain the memory of things in this world."

[99] John 14:6. 2 Cor. 3:18 : "And all of us, with unveiled faces, seeing the glory of the Lord as though reflected in a mirror, are being transformed into the same image from one degree of glory to another; for this comes from the Lord, the Spirit." 2 Cor. 4:6 : "'Let light shine out of darkness,' who has shone in our hearts to give the light of the knowledge of the glory of God in the face of Jesus Christ."

and whereby I worship God with the spirit. Not apart from Christ, but with the same enjoyment with which I enjoy Christ, and with the same worship with which I worship Christ. "For whoever enjoys me, enjoys the Father;" "whoever worships me, worships the Father" just as "whoever sees me, sees the Father." He ought to be seen in the spirit because he is worshipped in the spirit; otherwise, Christ will say to us, "you worship what you do not know," [100] just as the Sophists worship what they do not know. Christ is the way and the light, and it is by the way that shines through him that one ought to approach God, to worship God, and [119] to see light that is God. The trinitarians have not entered upon this path. It is by an invisible path that they have their worship of an unknown God, nay, a three-headed monster. They nonsensically dream of a certain three-headed Cerberus, a kind of tripartite God, the three entities confined within one like three points within a single point. They reduce all the heavenly substances to the likeness of a mathematical point. They say that God Himself is like a point which has been repeated severally on the same surface or as if in one point there were three. Is this really how the Sophists see God outside of Christ? Is this really the conception which they are so proud of having about God? If in the face of Christ the natural splendor of God shines forth, if in the very flesh of Christ the substance of the divinity exists bodily, is not God seen there? How is it possible then that God was formerly manifested in the Word, now in the flesh, and, formerly as well as now seen eye-to-eye? Therefore, see and believe, reader. Otherwise, woe unto you.

Moreover, so that this vision of God may be made firmer in us, we should now talk about the hypostasis of the Word. But we have already shown sufficiently that this was the visible and substantive Word, the substantive light, and the face of Elohim, although it was flitting about under a cloud. There was a certain oracle subsisting and shining within a flaming cloud, and it was called "the glory of the

---

[100] John 4:22. Jesus said to the Jewish woman : "You worship what you do not know; we worship what we know."

Lord" and His majesty in the cloud. This was the oracle which was hidden by angelic wings, the oracle that was shaded over through which God gave His responses to Moses. It was the oracle within the recess of the house just as omnipotent Christ was hidden in a shadow. The Hebrew word proves that this is the meaning of "oracle." For from the word *dabar*, דבר, which is λόγος, comes *debir*, דביר, which is the oracle of the temple in Psalms 27, 3 Kings 6, and 2 Paralipomenon 3, 4, and 5.[101] Christ is the true oracle through which we receive the responses of God. He is the place of propitiation through which and in which God is made propitious to us. He is the shelter that protects us from all evil and on account [120] of which those whose sins have been covered, are blessed.[102] Just as Christ himself is now the oracle, so once he was in the temple, in the tabernacle, and previously the person of Christ was the oracle from which Adam, Abraham, Moses, and the others received responses. See how beautifully the entire Law lays out John's word, not only in the oracle of the cloud, but also in the light of the face of Elohim, and all the remaining ways. From the Law that hypostasis of the Word was gathered within the cloud, which was the seed of Christ's conception. It was the very substance of the Word, the substance of the cloud's archetype which was the substantive dew that watered earthly matter so that Christ would sprout therefrom (Ps. 71, Isa. 45, 55, 61, Ezek. 17, and Hos. 6).[103] Hence Christ is called

---

[101] These are references to the construction of the temple and especially to the statues of cherubim who were stretching their wings above the tabernacle. 2 Chron. 7-8 : "Then the priests brought the ark of the covenant of the LORD to its place, in the inner sanctuary of the house, in the most holy place, underneath the wings of the cherubim. For the cherubim spread out their wings over the place of the ark, so that the cherubim made a covering above the ark and its poles." The Hebrew term דביר, *debir*, was used to describe the inner sanctuary, chamber, of the house, and which was called in the case of the temple, the most holy place, קֹדֶשׁ הַקֳּדָשִׁים. The origin of *debir* from *dabar* is not confirmed by modern philology.

In 2 Chron. 5:14 it is stated that "the glory of the LORD filled the house of God."

[102] The same phrase is used by Servetus in the twenty third Letter to Calvin, *Christianismi restitutio*, p. 642.

[103] Allusion to the metaphorical "dew" or "rain" in Ps. 71:6; Isa. 44:3, 45:8, 55:10, 61:11; Ezek. 17:22; Hos. 6:3.

"God's seed" (Isa. 4, Zech. 3 and 6, and elsewhere).[104] The fact that everywhere in the Law it is said that God appeared and that He preceded the sons of Israel in a column of cloud by day and in a column of fire by night demonstrates the same hypostasis in the guise of a cloud. For "column" the Hebrew expression is עַמּוּד, *ammud*, which means "a standing" and "the taking of a position," from the verb עָמַד, ('amad) "he stood," "he took his position." It is clumsily translated there as "column," and the use of column there has no bearing on the subject. But at that time God used to appear in the conglomeration of cloud and fire that is in the essence of cloud or fire. The substance of the cloud, fire, and light was the same, and we do not mean any created, misty, elemental cloud, but one that was not created and super elemental, shining within. God was in the fire for God Himself is the fire.[105]

You will say that it follows, if the hypostasis or substance of the Word was as I have said, then it was corporeal and divisible as well. But this does not follow. If God exists in corporeal things and he brings corporeal things into Himself, from this it does not follow that He is corporeal. For God by His essence is a mentality that takes on any form. As in your soul there are the forms of corporeal and divisible things, so it is in God; it is in Him as a matter of His essence, but in you by accidence. God who lacks body as to Himself and is imperceptible, by a miraculous event that has been expressed to us has shown Himself through the Word to be perceptible and in the Word he was the spirit. This does not prove [121] the body in God, but rather shows that His is an ineffable mental intelligence that is capable of any form. His intellect is this amazing power such that in Him the

---

[104] Isa. 4:2 : "On that day the branch of the LORD shall be beautiful and glorious, and the fruit of the land shall be the pride and glory of the survivors of Israel." Zech. 3:8 : "I am going to bring my servant the Branch." Zech. 6:12: "Here is a man whose name is Branch: for he shall branch out in his place, and he shall build the temple of the LORD." The Hebrew term translated here as "branch," צֶמַח, means *sprout, growth,* and *process of growth.* .

[105] Servetus expresses here the biblical Hebrew concept of God as a fiery being.

logic of the body glows.[106]

The next book will plainly show that the visible forms in God have been placed apart from division and mutation. God is not divisible nor is the substance of the Word divisible since what is divisible is corruptible. Indeed, the bodiless image of an imaginary point is nothing in the nature of things nor could anything exist on the basis of those points as scientists *(physici)* teach. The substance of the angels is not the image of a point, likewise the substance of the souls. The very substance of the spirit of God from which the angels and souls emanate was not the image of a point, but the image of the substance of the prime breath and the archetype of this prime breath was in the Divine mind. In this substance of God which was the substance of the Word and spirit shown to the world, there are not parts nor can there be said to be a partition in the same way as with creatures. In the substance of God the parts and partitions are said according to the distribution of the dispensation. "God divided from the spirit which was in Moses and gave his portions to 70 men." In the mission of the holy spirit as well there were the "separated tongues of fire" and the individuals received their portion.[107] In this partition of the spirit, "the portion of each part is God" as the scripture says,[108] and the division did not pull apart the substance of the holy spirit. As the light of the sun is denser and yet distributed, though by its continuous nature conserved to its original nature, so even the light of God is finer; but sunlight is cast about, and the light of God is not. Whatever is in the world, if it is compared to the light of the Word and spirit, remains just a dense material that is divisible and penetrable. That light penetrates even the division of the soul and spirit; Paul is a witness for this.

---

[106] For the first time Servetus uses the Platonic concept of God as the intellect, mind, *Deus, mens omniformis.*

[107] Num. 11:17 : "will come down and talk with you there; and I will take some of the spirit that is on you and put it on them." Acts 2:3 : "Divided tongues, as of fire, appeared among them, and a tongue rested on each of them."

[108] Ps. 72:26 : "My flesh and my heart may fail, but God is the strength of my heart and my portion forever."

The light of God penetrates and fills the very substance of angel and soul just as sunlight penetrates and fills the air. The inner light of God penetrates and sustains even sunlight since it penetrates and sustains all worldly forms as a form of forms.[109] [122] We shall talk later about the spirit and light. It would be enough for now if we should address in the Word the true substance, the visible hypostasis which articulated *(referebat)* the man as the next book will vividly express this idea.[110] Not only was the form of Christ the man in the Word, but so was the

---

[109] Heb. 4:12 : "Indeed, the word of God is living and active, sharper than any two-edged sword, piercing until it divides soul from spirit, joints from marrow; it is able to judge the thoughts and intentions of the heart." This context is interesting because it illustrates Servetus's philosophy of light which is similar to that of Paracelsus. Paracelsus was a celebrated physician, theologian, and reformer of therapeutics, b. at the Sihlbrücke, near Einsiedeln, in the Canton of Schwyz, in 1493; d. at Salzburg, in 1541. He is known also as Theophrastus von Hohenheim, Eremita (of Einsiedeln), and Theophrastus Bombastus von Hohenheim. Paracelsus is the Latin form in common use among the German scholars of the time. In 1526 he was appointed, probably through the influence of Joannes Oecolampadius, the theologian, and Joannes Frobenius, the publisher, to the office of city physician of Basel, with which was connected the privilege of lecturing at the university. He was hated by those in authority because of his teaching, as well as his opposition to the prevailing Galeno-Arabic system, the burning of Avicenna's writings in a public square, the polemical tone of his discourses delivered in German, and his success as a practitioner. Paracelsus is a phenomenon in the history of medicine, a genius not recognized, who sought to overturn the old order of things. But he was not in touch with the humanist movement or with the study of anatomy then pursued, thus he stands alone and is misunderstood. He sought the cause of pathological changes, not in the four humors, blood, phlegm, yellow and black gall (humoral pathology), but in the entities, which he divided into *ens astrorum* (cosmic influences differing with climate and country), *ens veneni* (toxic matter originating in the food), the cause of contagious diseases, *ens naturale et spirituale* (defective physical or mental constitution), and *ens deale* (an affliction sent by Providence). The diseases known as tartaric, especially gout and lithiasis, are caused by the deposit of determinate toxins (tartar). Like the followers of Hippocrates he prescribed the observation of nature and dietetic directions. He postulated that in nature all substances have two kinds of influences, helpful (*essentia*) and harmful (*venena*), which are separated by means of alchemy. It requires experience to recognize essences as such and to employ them at the proper moment. His aim was to discover a specific remedy (*arcanum*) for every disease. Paracelsus may be considered the founder of modern *materia medica*, and pioneer of scientific chemistry. To him is due the use of mercury for syphilis as well as a number of other metallic remedies. He was the first to point out the value of mineral waters and native herbs. The light philosophy in Servetus's system is relegated to the secondary plan within his system of thought. The concept of the light as "the form of forms" (*Lux illa Dei, forma formarum*) is probably taken from Maimonides, *Guide*, Part I, chap. LXIX.

[110] Though this is the central point in Servetus's system he never discusses this manner of the generation of Jesus by God through his image or uncreated light, but by using the metaphor of a cloud which covered Mary with its shadow and served as a semen of the body of Jesus.

substantive seed of his conception. That man would not be said to truly be the son of God, if God had simply created him inside Mary without preserving the means of fathering from the substance of the father. The substance of the seed in the Word was the substance of God exhibited to us, and God was somehow made corporeal and human through the Word, once as a metaphor, but now in reality.[111] John the Evangelist relates that he felt the substance of the Word with his hands. Paul teaches that the divinity was placed bodily in Christ. The early theologians said that the corporeal Word was perceptible, tangible, and visible in a corporeal manner. You will say that the Word incarnate is tangible and palpable if you say that in other things the pure matter is not felt nor touched but rather that the form was tangible and the representation was palpable or the whole thus shaped was touched and felt. Let no one be surprised if we should say with John that we "touched with hands" the divinity of Christ since Paul says that it may be touched in other things (Acts 17).[112] Let no one be surprised if we should say that the Word of God when it was yet to be made bodily once had a corporeal face since the evangelists bear witness that even the holy spirit came down with corporeal appearance. This is not impossible for God who wished by fathering Christ to show his Word in this way. In a bodily manner God wished and was able to appear. With a corporeal appearance God came and stood upright before Samuel (1 Sam. 3).[113] The method is easy as we shall show.

The very hypostasis of the Word in the beginning of John's Gospel is declared, and based on what is said, "was," and because he teaches so, it was visible. John saw that Jesus Christ was once a man coming forth in the clouds of heaven with Daniel as witness, once leading the chariot of Ezekiel, riding a horse

---

[111] This is a radically new concept of the divinity and of Jesus.

[112] 1 John 1:1 : "We declare to you what was from the beginning, what we have heard, what we have seen with our eyes, what we have looked at and touched with our hands, concerning the word of life." Paul in Acts 17:27: "so that they would search for God and perhaps grope for him and find him – though indeed he is not far from each one of us."

[113] 1 Sam. 1:10.

among the myrtles of Zachariah, sitting on the throne of Isaiah and [123] overseeing every age. And since this was the artifice of a thinking and speaking God, he said it was λόγος. It was the articulating word just as if a word that was uttered from your mouth contained the form of a man through which all things would come to be. Christ once oversaw the world, and in his person the parable of Solomon introduced the Wisdom that was thus presiding. David declares the same thing through the utterance of the word, *Iah*, when he bids us to praise Christ in his name, which is יה, *Iah*, in other words, the existent, the essence, the hypostasis. "Exalt," he said, "he who rides his horse through inhabitable climes in His name, *Iah*" (Ps. 67). In Psalm 101, "The people who will be created, will praise *Iah*," that is, the existent one, who is Christ.[114] Christ himself teaches about the same hypostasis when he says, "I am, I am from the beginning, the eternal prince, having existence in God."

Moreover, so you may understand that in this certain stages in the manifestation of God and in the grace of Christ have been made for us, reader, first consider that God is *per se* incomprehensible, unimaginable, and incommunicable to us because He infinitely exceeds everything. Hence to form an idea about Him or to see Him is not possible for anyone unless He adapts Himself for us to our capacity by some appearance. Hence again in our spirit we would not possess His communication unless He were somehow to adapt Himself in the manner of our spirit, by a means that is inwardly subject to our perception. This divine means is the holy spirit in us, about which we shall speak later. For the time being we are

---

[114] Ps. 67:4 :" Lift up a song to him who rides upon the clouds (עֲרָבוֹת)– his name is the LORD (יה)." *Iah* (יה) is the abbreviation of the tetragrammaton. Servetus talks about the "inhabitable regions" (*inhabilitabilia*), the term which often is translated into Latin as cloud (*nubes*) which in Hebrew is expressed as '*arabot* (עֲרָבוֹת), the highest heaven, the term explained by Maimonides,

only concerned with the earlier manner of God's manifestation and appearance, which came to be by a certain divine image that was placed before us as we have already shown in many passages and as Christ himself indicated in John 5, 14 and elsewhere.[115] Secondly, consider that God according to this manner manifested Himself in visible form to Adam himself practically as a companion. However, having been hidden on account of sin, He later insinuated Himself without appearance by various ways into the spirits of men, always exercising pity towards the men in whom He had placed the law of nature by an inborn breath of divinity. By the speech-act too at some time [124] He manifested Himself just as if I were to make my voice heard among those who do not see me. By various means God drew wretched nature to Himself, the nature which was being held captive by Satan. In this way God at the time that the Law was given was made manifest to the entire people by the hearing of His voice. In the same way He spoke to many people after Adam all the way to Abraham. In Abraham another means of manifestation began: through vision (Gen. 15).[116] After Adam God first appeared to Abraham and to no one else before him. Thus, even on this basis you can infer that vision was a special gift. The first patriarch was presented with this privilege, and then his posterity, the divine prophets, who were said to see in the same way. Through the vision of Him God spoke everywhere, in a dream to some, face-to-face to others, exposing Himself in various ways. Still, the vision was always veiled, and in it there was a certain shadow that appeared through an angel. Ultimately, He was made clearly manifest to us beyond the mist and He was seen,

---

Guide, Part I, chap. LXXX. Ps. 101:18.

[115] John 5:37 : "And the Father who sent me has himself testified on my behalf. You have never heard his voice or seen his form." John 14:9 : "Whoever has seen me has seen the Father."

[116] Though Servetus does not mention Maimonides here, he follows the conclusion of this Jewish scholar expressed in *Guide*, Part I, chap. XXVII: "It is a common practice to refer to the words directed to the prophets by an angel in the name of God as if they were pronounced by God himself." This theory of Servetus is concerning the manifestations of God and is linked to another one, namely to his theory of God's names treated in the following book.

His face uncovered. "The Word was made flesh, and we saw His glory." We saw the glory of God in the face of Jesus Christ. We saw Christ, and in him we saw the Father. In him we saw the light, God Himself shining. And if only we had maintained this vision so that this internal vision and glorification, which yet makes us sharers of the glory to be through Jesus Christ our lord, would lead us all the way to that vision of eternal blessedness to be.

On the Divine Trinity

Book Four

in Which Are Shown
the Names of God, His Omniforming Essence,
and the Origins of All Things

Now that Christ has been seen, and in his face the Father, God, has been seen, it is not irrelevant to our subject to explain in the fourth Book the meaning of the divine names so that we, who proclaim Christ as our God, may show better the divine manifestation within him. We shall all now become acquainted with the omniforming essence of God, which has been explained with enough unanimity in the opinions of the ancients; we shall bring forward into the light the origins of things thus far unknown to the greatest philosophers.

The more distinguishing names of the divinity are יהוה, and אלהים. Elohim is a plural form, and it is by this name as the most common one that God is first so called. In fact, the name, Jehovah, is more particular to God. The name Jehovah, just as much as the name Elohim, contains the mysteries of Christ: Jehovah with respect to the essence, Elohim with respect to the appearance.[1]

Jehovah

The name, Jehovah, according to most people, means "essence," although

---

[1] The theme of Book IV corresponds to the theme treated by Servetus in his *De Trinitatis erroribus.* In Book V Servetus originally developed his theory of God's revelation on the basis of his theory of the divine names. The original concept was here, however, formulated with greater precision and enlarged by the Neoplatonic formulation of the *Corpus Hermeticum.*

others prefer the act of "generation."[2] Nevertheless, we say that by that name not only are both meanings understood, but, in particular, it refers to the essence. That means not the essence in a simple sense, but the essentiating essence or that which causes being. God is not like a point, but He is an infinite sea of substance, giving essence to everything, causing all things to exist, and sustaining the essences of everything. We leave to the Cabbalists their secrets regarding this name[3] and say just this, that as the letter *yod* with *scheva* indicates, it is a future *piel* in the active voice from the root, הוה, or rather היה by changing *yod* to *vav* and [126] short vowels into long ones, as frequently happens. And this especially happens in this case because the middle letter has a point, the *dagesh*, even though it is *piel* because *vav* is not in that instance considered a consonant, but a vowel. Because the vowel is *vav* and is without any syncopation, all the syllables of that name had to be pronounced by the Hebrews, yet the name is ineffable nor can it be so uttered unless you say the syllables by pronouncing them separately, *Je, ho, vah*.[4] But whether in that way or by making the *vav* into a consonant as we do, you would say Jehovah or Jova, and the fact remains that that name was uttered by many people in antiquity. Indeed, that name was informally applied to other things with a certain addition as is apparent in Genesis 22 and Exodus 17 where in one place it is

---

[2] Jehovah or Yahweh derives from the Hebrew word *hayah* (הָיָה) which has three meanings: 1. *to be, to exist*; 2. *to happen, to occur; to bring into being; to come to pass, to come about*; and 3. *to become, to come into being.* Servetus designates these three meanings by: *essentia simpliciter, essentiantem essentia,* and *esse facientem* (*generatio*).

[3] There was no cabbalistic influence on Servetus's thought. He emphatically rejected any such speculation and already in his *De Trinitatis erroribus* wrote: *"Stultissimaque res est aeternales eorum processiones ex illis verbis inferre, et in Cabbalistica illa metaphysica insanire"* (lib. II, 63r).

[4] Servetus explains the derivation of the tetragrammaton from the verb *hayah*, through the form of *hawah*, implying its meaning to the word יהוה (also spelled as יְהֹוָה or יָהּ). The name of God was too sacred to be pronounced, so while preserving it in the written text (kethibh), it was read (quere) as the word Adonai (אֲדֹנָי). The consonants of kethibh יהוה were punctuated with the vowels of quere אֲדֹנָי (namely, qameṣ, cholem, and shewa), that made the form impossible to pronounce יְהֹוָה . It is suggested that with vowels normal spelling of the tetragrammaton would be יְהֹוָה or יַהְוֶה.

called Jehovah-*ireh* and in another Jehovah-*nissi*.[5] Likewise, in Jeremiah 23 and 33 it is Jehovah-*zidkenu*, and in Judges 6, it is Jehovah-*salom*,[6] that is, God-vision, God-elevation, God-justice, God-peace, all things through Christ. Therefore, the name Jehovah is explained according to this use of the future form of *piel*, that is, "he will essentiate, he will cause to exist." Not only is God the one who is causing, but He also causes another to cause existence because the Father caused His son, who makes everything exist, and He gave essence to the son, who gives essence to everything so that the son himself may be the source of essence. We are taught that this is the actual meaning of that word by the authority of Jehovah Himself when He explains His name in Exodus 6, where, because He would make great things and give the power of doing this to man, He says that His name is Jehovah, which is the name of the one who does such great things and the one who causes another to act; and this name was not known to the patriarchs, although they knew the names, *El* and *Shaddai*. He said, "I appeared to Abraham himself, Isaac, and Jacob as *El Shaddai*, but I was not known to them by my own name, Jehovah."[7] Previously God had appeared to the patriarchs themselves and manifested Himself to them under the name, *El Shaddai* (Gen. 17, 28, 35, and 48). He always said to them, "I am *El Shaddai*."[8] From the meanings of these names in this passage of Exodus, it is inferred that a great many things were implied by the name, Jehovah.

The name שׁדי is [127] from the root שׁדד which means "to lay waste." The noun, שׁד, means destruction, a laying waste. Hence, God is called Shaddai as a

---

[5] In Gen. 22:14 : "So Abraham called that place "The LORD will provide" (יְרְאֶה). In Exodus 17:15 : "And Moses built an altar and called it, The LORD is my banner (נסי)."

[6] Jer. 23:6 and 33:16 : "And this is the name by which he will be called: "The LORD is our righteousness (צְדְקֵנוּ). " Judges 6:24 : "Then Gideon built an altar there to the LORD, and called it, The LORD is peace" (שָׁלוֹם, shalom and not salom as Servetus writes)."

[7] Exod. 6:2-3 . The Hebrew spelling is *El Shaddai* (אֵל שַׁדַּי) but Servetus spells the term *El Saddai*. Servetus follows here the explanation of Maimonides in *Guide*, Part II, cap. XXXV.

[8] Gen. 17:1, 28:3, 35:11, 48:3. Servetus is, however, aware that the name Yahweh (Jehovah) is used much earlier and not only in the indirect sense but also as pronounced by God himself (Gen. 15:7). He will explain this situation later.

destroyer or one who is able to lay everything to waste. This is clearly shown in Isaiah 13 and Joel 1, בשר משרי as "a laying waste by one who lays waste." This is where our translator has rendered the word destroyer as Almighty.[9]

Likewise, He is called *El*, "strong," whence *El Shaddai* is "mighty destroyer." God was first manifested to Abraham under this name in Genesis 17, where He said, "I am *El Shaddai*."[10] This was done in order that Abraham would be stronger by not fearing others and in order that, thinking himself always in the presence of God, most mighty, he would walk more perfectly in God's presence. Just as when He was angry with His enemies, God said such things to Abraham as a way of bolstering and supporting him: "Walk in my presence and be perfect." In fact, He says this to Moses in chapter 6, already mentioned: "Perhaps I was manifested to your fathers under the name of *El Shaddai*, perhaps they knew that I destroyed Sodom and Gomorrah; still, I did not declare to them that I was Jehovah, they did not yet completely know me as the one who gives essence, or the one who creates through another, or who grants to others the power to make miracles, as I shall presently do for Moses against the Egyptians."[11] Before Moses, the power to make miracles had been given to no one and thus the meaning of the name that implied this fact about God was known to no one, although that name had been heard by the patriarchs. The patriarchs did not know sufficiently whether Christ was Jehovah with such power of giving essence to all things or whether Jehovah was to give essence to Christ as one so powerful.[12]

---

[9] Isa. 13:6 : "Wail, for the day of the LORD is near; it will come like destruction from the Almighty!" The same in Joel 1:15 : "For the day of the LORD is near, and as destruction from the Almighty (וּכְשֹׁד מִשַּׁדַּי) it comes."

[10] Gen. 17:1: "When Abram was ninety-nine years old, the LORD appeared to Abram, and said to him, "I am God Almighty (אֲנִי־אֵל שַׁדַּי) walk before me, and be blameless."

[11] It is not a quote but a statement based on Exod. 6:2-8.

[12] Christ as a human personification of the Word, according to Servetus, is Elohim. He stated at the beginning of Bk V, 97r, of *De Trinitatis erroribus*: "The most prominent names of the divinity are Elohim and Jehovah, one is of Christ, and the other of the Father .... I have interpreted Elohim as God and his Word, but I said more clearly that Elohim was in person a man and in nature God."

At any rate, the perfect name of the one who essentiates this or causes to exist is declared by the very genesis of the cosmos, by the first passage in which that voice begins to be uttered by the holy spirit. For during six days of labor God was not referred to by that name just as not even Christ was so called while he lived on earth until he rested in heaven. Once the act of generation was complete, when the power to give essence, to make, and to produce had been given to His creatures, God, being still, was then called [128] Jehovah, "the one who causes to be" or "the one who gives essence through another" (Gen. 2).[13] There God is said to be the one who gives essence to the essences so that those essences may, in turn, give essence to others. He is Himself the source of all essence, the source of light, of life, "the father of the spirits," "the father of lights."[14] He gives essence to heavenly spirits; from Him flow the essential rays of divinity and the essential angels who, in turn, disperse His essence into other things.[15] God Himself is in them, and the very light of the Word shines in them. The Father has granted this power of giving essence entirely to Christ so that he may give essence to all other things. All things exist through Christ himself just as they are and consist in him, as Paul teaches. He bears, carries, and "lifts up all things with the word of his virtue" (Heb. 1). "All things in him have their substance, be they heavenly or earthly" (Col. 1).[16] The angels have been made parties to Christ's divinity, and they reflected that in the Law. God sends His light by means of the angels, and God Himself is this very thing: and Christ himself is the dispenser of his light, sending it from his substance, sending the spirit from his substance, and the angels minister to him. He sends the spirit through the angel, and this very thing is God Himself. The essence of God always shines there, the very spirit of God, the divinity itself, the light itself that is God.

---

[13] In fact the name Yahweh appears for the first time in Gen. 2:4.
[14] These are allusions to the names of God listed in Ps. 35:10; Heb. 12:9; and James 1:17.
[15] These are formulations which could be interpreted as an expression of Servetus's emanationism, contrary to other creationist statements.
[16] Statement based on Heb. 1:3 and Col. 1:17.

It is with this understanding that Jehovah is called Zebaoth, in other words, "the one causing the armies themselves" or "the essence of soldieries to exist."[17] Jehovah Himself gives essence to all the heavenly soldieries and armies with the splendor of His essence. Although, He says, there are countless numbers of soldiers without end and ten thousands of ten thousands, still, Jehovah Himself exists in them all (Ps. 67 and Dan. 7).[18] Hence it is a fact that the divinity's name is always in the names of the angels because His essence is in them. That universal and omniforming essence of God gives essence to men and all other things: His spirit from the beginning has been placed in us and has later been poured again into us abundantly. Therefore, God has the essences of infinite thousands, the natures of infinite thousands, but not by being metaphysically divided, rather by means ineffable. Wherefore, we reach a conclusion that is the opposite of what the trinitarian Sophists teach. For they place [129] three invisible, metaphysical entities in one essence and nature as if there were three points in one. We, on the contrary, say that there is only one entity, and this has the essences of infinite thousands and the natures of infinite thousands. Not only is God innumerable by reason of the things to which He is communicated, but also by reason of the modes of His divinity. The divine modes are ineffable in things and they have been preformed from eternity in God Himself. Nevertheless, to the extent that human frailty can, we shall here in some way explain these modes.

The principal divine mode is unique and the basis of all the other ones. This is the mode of the plenitude of the substance, the divine mode without measure

---

[17] Zebaoth, in Hebrew צְבָאוֹת (pronounced tze-ba-ot), was described in Servetus's *De Trinitatis erroribus* lib. V, 102r-102v: *"id est, militiae, quia essentia eius multitudinis numero militat, omnes illas militias et coelestes exercitus essentiae suae splendore munit, dicique potest Jehovah Zebaot, sicut dixi, Jehovah Elohim, quasi dicat, militias essentians, et inde provenit, quod divinitatis nomen nominibus angelorum est immixtum, quia eius essentia est eis immixta. Vides hic plures Deum habere essentias, non enim possunt dici plures res in una essentia, sed bene et converso: imo dico quod omnium rerum essentiae est ipse Deus, et omnia sunt in ipso."* Zebaoth is found in Isa. 47:2 : "The LORD of hosts (יְהוָה צְבָאוֹת שְׁמוֹ) is his name;" Jer. 10:16, 31:55, etc.

[18] Ps. 67:12 : "God gave the word; those who bore it were a great army (רָב צָבָא)." Dan. 7:10:

that exists in the body and spirit of Jesus Christ alone. The mode is twofold, and on this basis the one can even talk about two persons. It is the mode of the appearance of God in the Word and the mode of the communication of God in the spirit: the bodily mode and the spiritual mode. Both are substantive modes giving essence to other things in body and spirit, the source of every life, every light and spirit. This is God's eternal contemplation of things and His manifestation in accordance with this mode. From here like branches from a trunk, shoots from a root, leaves from a vine, come all other modes. There is another divine mode in accordance with the measure of the given spirit, for example, as in us and another one in angels. Again one spirit is inborn, one is added above and beyond through grace, and both are multiplex because of a particular division that is made through Christ. The final mode is that which exists in individual things according to their own, specific and individual forms. This is the final one; nevertheless, there is a certain divinity within things.[19] These mentioned modes of divinity are those which are available to us in our present state, for after the resurrection there will be others multiple and more subtle that we cannot know.

For the time being, in terms of the final mode in individual things, which now exists, by simply describing God's essence, we are saying that God Himself is the essence of all things. God is that which comprehends and contains all things.[20] God Himself [130] "sustains us" and "carries us" (Isa. 46 and 63). He "makes all things alive" (1 Tim. 6). "In Him we live, we are moved, we are" (Acts 17). "All things cohere in Him" (Col. 1). "Everything is from Him, through Him, and in Him."[21] All things are in Him; He gives being to things; and to every individual

---

"A thousand thousands served him."

[19] This context is extremely important for Servetus's systemic thought.

[20] Servetus is using the phrase *Deus ipse est comprehensio et continentia rerum omnium* which he will repeat later on pp. 132 and 271 comes from *Corpus Hermeticum* III.1. Besides this influence, the major influence on Servetus is that of Philo of Alexandria.

[21] Servetus is applying a remote idea from Isa. 46:4 : "even to your old age I am he, even when you turn gray I will carry you. I have made, and I will bear; I will carry and will save." Isa. 63:9 : "He redeemed them; he lifted them up and carried them all the days of old." 1 Tim. 6:13. Acts 17:28. Servetus paraphrases the verse of Col. 1:16 which refers to Jesus : "For in him all things

form He gives formal being. In His essence because He contains the forms of all things, He is, so to speak, the formal part of all things, especially by the particular manner in us, on account of which we are said to be parties to His divine nature. He is our share and our spirit's share so that we can rightly say not through the earthly possession of fields, but through the heavenly and divine possession: "Lord, my part and my portion" (Pss. 15 and 72).[22] Through Christ was set aside for us a helping, so to speak, of the divine spirit, and "we have all received from His fullness"[23] just as once a portion of the spirit of Moses was symbolically set aside for others. But in the other created things, it is not through the gift of the spirit, but by another, general logic that God is said to be. Thus, He sustains all things essentially so that, just as it exists *ex nihilo*, any given creation that is deprived of that sustaining help would return to nothing.[24]

The ancient Hebrews and philosophers taught this same thing. From the Hebrews the rabbi, Moses the Egyptian, cites this in Book I, *Perplexorum*, chapter 68, saying, "every being that exists is within the creator, and He is within all things; He helps and supports them through that mode which is called splendor or a certain secondary (reflected) light."[25] Aben Ezra teaches the same thing about Genesis as do all the others together with the prophets themselves.[26] All the old

---

in heaven and on earth were created, things visible and invisible, whether thrones or dominions or rulers or powers – all things have been created through him and for him."

[22] Ps. 15:5 : "Jehovah is the portion of my inheritance and of my cup." Ps. 72:26 : "God is the strength of my heart and my portion forever."

[23] John 1:16.

[24] It is a very clear formulation of Servetus's belief in creation and not emanation, and the necessity of continuous sustaining of the creation by God who gives it its essence, otherwise it would turn into nothingness: *"in nihilum redeat, sicut est de nihilo."*

[25] Moses Maimonides treats the same subject in chaps. 68, 69, and 72 of his *Guide to the Perplexed, Part I.* "He [God] and the things apprehended are one thing which is His essence" (Chap. 68). God is designated "as a cause and ground" (Chap. 69). "He [God] is the ultimate form and the form of forms" (Chap. 69). One cannot, however, confirm what Servetus ascribes to him, namely, the explanation of the sustaining of the world by the participation of the divine light. This idea has to be linked to the systems of Philo and of Proclus. But this specific metaphysics of light is one of the most original elements of Servetian thought.

[26] Ben Ezra, his full name Abraham-ben-Meir ben-Ezra, was a famous Spanish Rabbi (born in Toledo in 1092; died on his journey from Rome, or Rodez, to his native land, in 1167). He was a disciple of Juda ha-Levi, contemporary with Maimonides. He excelled in many fields of learning.

philosophers held this same opinion, so it will not be out of place to hear them at this point.[27]

On the basis of Pythagoras, Anaxagoras, and others, more ancient, and on the basis of the learned Zoroaster and Trismegistus, Plato in the *Parmenides*, *Cratylus*, and *Phaedo*, posits the one first being and states that all things are contained and cohere in one. And he adds that this same one and only thing that exists *per se* is beautiful and good, nor is anything else called beautiful and good save by its participation in this principle. Indeed, the closer they approach it, they are all the more beautiful. In fact, the one being is that which animates the cosmos, [131] ψύχωσιν, it is a type of mind, noun, that contains, ἔχουσιν, in itself all the natures of the cosmos so that everything coheres in it, and it gives them order, διακόσμουσαν, wherefore it is even called a cosmos, κόσμος.[28] Socrates in the *Cratylus* calls God the essence of nature, φυσέχην, because He carries and contains, ὄχει and ἔχει, nature itself, φύσιν.[29] By a natural order, all motions are led back to one prime mover, all natures to one nature, all lives to one first life,

---

He had to leave his city because of a disturbance against the Jews so he traveled through Europe, Egypt and Palestine. His main work is his *Commentary on the Sacred Books*, which is nearly complete (missing are the *Books of Paralipomenon*). His *Commentary on the Pentateuch* appeared in several revisions. It was published in Venice in 1526, thus it could be accessible to Servetus who cites it as demonstration that "many others" believed in creation *ex nihilo*. Aben-Ezra adheres to the literal sense of the Sacred Books and remains faithful to the Jewish traditions. But in his other works he follows the Cabbalistic views.

[27] So the assertions about the presumed pantheism of Servetus are erroneous.

[28] All scholars of the Greek thought admit today the dependency of Plato on Pythagoras and Anaxagoras, however, not so on Zoroastrianism and Hermetism. Their works were accessible to Servetus in their Christian editions. This error was shared by all the humanists of the Renaissance. The reference of Servetus to those three dialogues of Plato is confused. Plato did not recognize a personal, infinite God, through whom all beings have something divine. The concept of One is posterior to Plato and belongs to the Neo-Platonic school which begins with Plotinus (203-270 C.E.). The phrases like those used by Servetus can be found in the *Parmenides* dialogue where Plato ascribes to Parmenides (530-460 B.C.E.) his own theory of the subsisting Ideas and the two procedures proposed for their reflection in the world: imitation, μίμησις, and participation, μέθεξις, μετάληψις (*Parmenides*, 131a &ff). But Servetus says nothing about this thought of Plato. In *Cratylus* (430cd) Plato exposes the Ideas of Beauty and Good as the first ones. In *Phaedo* (92d) Plato states that the world of Ideas-Essences contains all the beings which are possible. The concept of the world as κόσμος and of a Demiurge who orders it is found, primarily, in *Timaeus*, 27a, 30b, 34a, etc.

through which and in which all other things live and are moved. All ancient authorities said that God lit everything up from chaos, and that by leading out of their materials that were, as it were, confused, He gave them visible and bright forms in the manner of His own beauty. He is beautiful and good, and He made the first light beautiful and good like Himself, and then He made everything else beautiful and good as the word of Genesis states. For the word, טוב, *thob*, in that passage means beautiful and good.[30] On the basis of the most ancient authorities, Iamblichus, Macrobius, and Philo His mind is the mother of all forms of things, and that it contains the formal shapes within itself, and that He granted to things symbols of His divinity, namely, spirit and light. For in Himself He contains that light with which He forms all things, and the spirit which He breathes into things.[31] Zoroaster had the same teaching in the *Oracles of Wisdom*, which are called μάγικα λογία.[32] The oracle of Apollo, cited by Porphyry in Book 10 of *On the*

---

[29] *Cratylus* 400b.

[30] It seems that Servetus took this idea from Ibn Ezra in reference to the meaning of "beautiful" which appears in Exod. 2:2, in addition to the idea of "good" which is found in Gen. 1:31.

[31] This is another confused reference. Iamblichus (ca 250–ca 330 C.E.) is a Syrian Neo-Platonist who authored several works and whose *De mysteriis Aegyptiorum* was well known during the Renaissance. Servetus could refer to certain phrases concerning the "higher soul" and the "highest triad" in Book VII, 2.3 and 6. More clear is the reference to Macrobius, another Neo-Platonist who flourished in the time of Theodosius II spanning the fourth and fifth centuries, and who was inspired by Plotinus and Porphyry, namely, to the commentary on *In somnium Scipionis* of Cicero, lib. I, cap. 14. The concept of the "symbols of the divinity" contained in things is derived from Neo-Platonism and goes back even to Zoroastrian and Hermetic writings. Servetus's modification is their identification with spirit and light. The concept that Wisdom, and not the mind as Servetus writes, identified with the eternal Logos is the mother of the Logos itself and of the world (her father is God according to Philo), derives from Philo of Alexandria. Wisdom contains in herself forms of everything (*De fuga et inventione*, 20:109).

[32] The so-called *Magical Oracles* or magical hymns, or divine chants, which were attributed in antiquity to Zoroaster or Zarathustra (who could have lived somewhere between the sixth and fifth centuries B.C.E.), were in fact composed, at least in their major part, in the second half of the second century C.E., and perhaps by Julian the Theurg during the time of Marcus Aurelius (A. J. Festugière, *Hermétisme et mystique païenne*. Paris, 1967, pp. 126, 302). There were many modern editions of this work, beginning with the Venetian edition by Patrizzi in 1593. Servetus could know it through the work of Valerius Maximus, *Factorum ac dictorum memorabilium libri IX*, known during the Middle Ages, but especially through the editions of 1539 and 1550. Valerius Maximus, ca. 20 B.C.E.–ca C.E. 50, was a Roman author about whom little is known. His *Nine Books of Memorable Deeds and Sayings* was written ca C.E. 30 and is a miscellany of anecdotes about a variety of subjects. The work was very popular, especially as a source for

Praises of Philosophy, openly states that God is the form, soul, and spirit of all things and He is not comprehended by the angels except by the reason with which He has decided to make Himself visible.[33] As Plutarch says in his *Isis*, as well as Proclus, the inscription of the goddess of wisdom among the Egyptians reads: "I am all that was, is, and will be. No mortal will so much as withdraw my veil."[34] He is truly Wisdom that contains all things in Himself. "God is wholly what you see, and wholly what you do not see," as Seneca said, and Lactantius quoted.[35]

---

writers and orators.

[33] This is not in the preserved fragments of Porphyry's book. Porphyry (ca 232/4-ca 305) or Porphyrios was born in Tyre [now Lebanon] or Batanaea [now Syria], and studied in Athens, before joining the Neo-Platonist group of Plotinus in Rome. In 263-268 Porphyry studied philosophy in Rome under Plotinus, who rescued him from a suicidal depression. In 301 Porphyry completed *The Enneads*, a systematized collection of the works of Plotinus, including a short biography. The name *Enneads* means "Nines", so-called because they were sorted into chapters of nine sections each. The *Enneads* became a book of great influence in the Hellenistic-Roman world, in the Islamic and Renaissance Christian worlds. Porphyry's student in turn was Iamblichus. Porphyry considered the salvation of the soul as the ultimate purpose of philosophy. He emphasized the mystic path of "flight from the body" and deemphasized the emanationist hierarchies of the Middle Platonists and Plotinus, and combined One and Intellect. He also represented the beginnings of the later Neo-Platonist tendency of organizing reality in triads. For Porphyry, Being, Life, and Intellect were phases in the eternal self-determination of the ultimate reality. There are many parallels between the Neo-Platonism and Indian Kashmir Shaivism philosophy. Kashmir Shaivism differs, however, from Neo-Platonism in that it is based on a monistic rather than a dualistic, Platonist view. The book of Porphyry *De laudibus philosophiae* is lost and was reconstructed in part on the basis of quotes in Lactantius, *Divin. inst.*; in Eusebius, *De praeparatio evang.*; in Augustine, *De civit. Dei*. The title given by Eusebius is *On the philosophy of the oracle*. The expression ἐκ λογίων was erroneously read in ancient codices as εὐλογίων, praises, eulogies. Such a reading was preserved by Julian Firmicus in *De errore profanarum religionum*, cap. 14 and by A. Steuco in *De perenni philosophiae libri X*, lib. III, cap. 14 (edited in Lyon 1540 and Basel in 1542). G. Wolff, *Porphyrii De Philosophiae ex oraculos haurienda librorum reliqiae* (Berlin: J. Springer, 1856, pp. 38-39, 143-147).

[34] Mestrius Plutarch (ca 46- ca 127) was a Greek historian, biographer, and essayist. He was born in the small town of Chaeronea, in the Greek region of Boeotia. He travelled widely in the Mediterranean world, and visited Rome twice. He was initiated into the mysteries of the Greek . god Apollo and served as one of the two priests of Apollo at the Oracles of Delphi. He left a huge body of writings, much of which are still extant and influenced ancient and modern thought. His work *Isis and Osiris* preserves this inscription in the temple of Atenea or Nit in Saïs, a town in Lower Egypt. He derived the etymology of Isis from the word ἰσμή, knowledge, thus the goddes would symbolize light, truth, and for this reason she was later confused with the goddess Ma, the daughter of the sun. This inscription is also preserved by Proclus in his *In Platonis Timaeum*, 30, where it is supplemented by a further text: "The fruit which I engendered has been the Sun."

[35] This is the phrase of Lucius Annaeus Seneca (4-65 C.E.) from his *Naturalium quaestionum libri septem ad Lucillum*, I pref., 13. Seneca was in Spain, in Cordoba, and was educated in Rome, and became famous as a playwright, an orator, and philosopher. He served as tutor to the

Plotinus makes the same point in his book *On Providence*. "The eternal mind [132]," he says, "in which all things cohere, though unmoved, builds everything else, and contains the natures of all things, and this world is its shadow and image."[36] Trismegistus, the father of the old philosophy, sang thus in the sacred sermon of Poimander: "The nature of all things, the glory of all things, and the basis is God, and in Him all nature coheres." To Tatius he said that the one God is everything, and it is "as if He had many bodies because there is nothing in the bodies which is not He." A little further on he said, "God is the basis, the embrace, and the container of all objects: He is the being of all objects." In his book entitled *"On how in God alone there is beauty and good"* he said: "Whatever exists is in

---

young Nero, and when Nero became Emperor in 54 C.E., he retained Seneca as his advisor. For several years, Seneca had a calming effect on the young emperor. After he retired in 62 C.E., however, he lost favor with his former pupil, and in 65 C.E., he was accused of conspiring against Nero and was forced to commit suicide. Lactantius cites Seneca many times in his *Divinar. institutionum*, lib. I, cap. 5, lib. VI, cap. 25 (PL VI, 136, 728) but not this phrase in a context of texts which are to demonstrate that the ancient writers were always monotheists, and that God should be adored "in the spirit," an idea which was cherished by Servetus.

[36] That is in the *Enneads*, III, 2.1, and in II, 9.8 (Plotino, *Enneadi*. Porfirio *Vita di Plotino*, traduzione con testo Greco a fronte, note e bibliografia di Giuseppe Faggin, (Milano: Rusconi, 1996). Plotinus (204/5 - 270 C.E.), is regarded as the founder of Neoplatonism. He is one of the most influential philosophers in antiquity after Plato and Aristotle. The term "Neoplatonism" was invented in the early 19th century by European scholars and was to indicate that Plotinus initiated a new phase in the development of Platonic tradition. Plotinus, however, regarded himself and thought that Plato needed to be interpreted in order to explore the philosophical position of Platonism and also to defend against those who had misunderstood and criticized him. He was born in Lycopolis. His interest in philosophy led him to the school of Ammonius Saccas in Alexandria. After ten or eleven years with him, Plotinus became interested in studying Persian and Indian philosophy and for that purpose he joined the military expedition of Emperor Gordian III to Persia in 243. The expedition was terminated when Gordian was assassinated by his troops. Plotinus then went to Rome in 245 and remained there until his death in 270 or 271. In Rome Plotinus was joined by Porphyry who arrived there in 263 and it was he who edited the Plotinus writings and divided them into six groups of nine. Ammonius Saccas was one of the Platonists who assumed that in some sense Aristotle's philosophy was in harmony with Platonism though it did not preclude disagreements between Aristotle and Plato. No wonder then that Plotinus adopted many Aristotelian arguments as compatible with Platonism and as useful for articulating the Platonic position. Plotinus's metaphysics is based on the assumption of the three basic principles: "the One" (or "the Good"), Intellect, and Soul. These principles are ultimate ontological realities and, according to Plotinus, they were recognized by Plato and by the entire subsequent Platonic tradition. Plotinus also recognized the One as the cause from which everything else derives including Intelect and Soul, and the process is not by an "emanation," though Neoplatonists sometimes used this language, but it should be understood as an atemporal ontological dependence.

God and contingent upon Him." In the same passage he said that God is everything and that God who makes everything makes it like unto Himself, just as every subject likens the object onto itself.[37] In the *Asclepius*, he said that God was everything in everything and was pantomorphic in appearance. He said that God's Word was the archetypal cosmos, the archetypal light, the archetype of the soul. "In everything," he said, "a certain image of God flashes out."[38] On this basis in the

---

[37] These are almost literal quotes from *Corpus Hermeticum*, lib. III, and lib. V, *"Discourse of Hermes to his son Tat."* The text reads: "For in all this there is nothing that He is not. He is both the things that are and the things that are not; ... He is apprehensible by thought alone, yet we can see Him with our eyes. He is bodiless, and yet has many bodies, or rather, is embodied in all bodies." In lib. VIII: "First of all things, and in very truth eternal and without beginning, is God, who is the maker of the universe; and second is the Kosmos, which has been made by God in his image, and is kept in being and sustained by God." All this was stated more elegantly and more succinctly by Servetus: *"Deus est principium, complexus, et continentia rerum omnium: est ipsum ese omnium."* Hermetica. *The Ancient Greek and Latin Writings which Contain Religious or Philosophic Teachings Ascribed to Hermes Trismegistus.* English translation, introduction and appendix by Walter Scott, forward by A.G. Gilbert, (Broughton Gifford, Melksham, Wiltshire: Cromwell Press, 1993); *Textos Herméticos*, introducción, traducción y notas de Xavier Renau Nebot, (Madrid: Editorial Gredos, 1999).

[38] Servetus gives a summary of *Corpus Hermeticum* (Part I or *Poimandres, lib. II*) where one reads: "Asclepius: What then is that incorporeal thing? Hermes: It is Mind, entire and wholly self-encompassing, free from the erratic movement of things corporeal; it is imperturbable, intangible, standing form-fixed in itself, containing all things, and maintaining in being all things that are; and it is the light whereby soul is illuminated. Asclepius: Tell me then, what is the Good? Hermes: The Good is the archetypal Light; and Mind and Truth are, so to speak, rays emitted by that Light. Asclepius: What then is God? Hermes: God is he that is neither Mind, nor Truth, but is the cause to which Mind and Truth, and all things, and each several thing, owe their existence."
The term *omniformis* or *pantomorphos* is absent from the first part of the Hermetic writings. Servetus derived the concept from Orphism, Philonian philosophy, as well as from Neo-Platonism, from Plotinus himself. In the *Enneads*, II. 4 there is a discussion of matter in a general sense as "the sense world" and an interesting doctrine for differentiation. From the discussion that it is matter that is a substratum for differentiation by accepting the Form, and since there are many Forms, therefore there must be intelligible matter in the intelligible world as well. "But since this intelligible world is absolutely indivisible, in a certain sense, however, it is divisible. And if the parts are separate from each other, any such division and difference are a condition of matter which in fact becomes divided and differentiated. And this intelligible world which is indivisible without parts, yet consisting of diverse parts, which form a unity, must reside in a matter as in a form of this unity: thus this unity must be conceived as varied and multiform (τὸ γὰρ ἓν τοῦτο τὸ ποικίλον νόησον ποικίλον καὶ πολύμορφον)." The term *pantomorphos* appears in the second part of the *Corpus Hermeticum, Asclepius,* where Trismegistus discusses the changing forms of the individual beings because they originate at different points of time and at places differently situated. The type of form, however, persists, implying that their ultimate source is the ideal, divine form: "but the forms change at every moment in each hour of the revolution of that celestial circle in which resides the god whom we

hymn of Poimander he sang: "God is holy, and His image is every nature." To his son, Tatius, he said that there is nothing in the nature of things that does not present before itself some image of divinity. It is presented to our eyes everywhere, and it thrusts itself upon us and insinuates itself into us, that is, the pantomorphic image of God, which itself is the image of light in all things.[39] Paul teaches the same things in Acts 17 when he says that in individual things God is nearly felt because He has been located in individual things. He quotes from Aratus: "We are the divine offspring," and states with Pythagoras that "we are a certain race of God" because we have the seeds of divinity in ourselves, truly born within us just as from the beginning the spirit of divinity was born in us. In the same place, the apostle says that "we live, are moved, and exist in God Himself."[40] In Him we breathe; our life and breath is in Him and is contingent upon Him. For this reason

---

have named Pantomorphos" (*Asclepius*, III).

[39] The first part of *Corpus Hermeticum*, lib. I *(Poimandres))*, ends with a hymn to God which begins thus: "Holy is God the Father of all," and which continues: " Holy art Thou, who by thy word has constructed all that is; holy art Thou, whose brightness nature has not darkened; holy art Thou, of whom all nature is an image." The following words of Servetus are a summary of lib. V which is addressed to Trismegistus's son, Tatius: "For God is ever-existent; and He makes manifest all else, but He himself is hidden, because He is ever-existent. He manifests all things, but He is not manifested; He is not himself brought into being in images presented through our senses, but He presents all things to us in such images. It is only things which are brought into being that are presented through sense. It is evident then that He who alone has not come into being cannot be presented through sense; and that being so, He is hidden from our sight. But He presents all things to us through our senses, and thereby manifests himself through all things, and in all things, and especially, to those to whom He wills to manifest himself." But there is nothing here about "omniformis imago" or about "omnibus lucis imago." These are Servetus's own elaborations on the theme.

[40] Acts 17:28 : "For 'In him we live and move and have our being'; as even some of your own poets have said, 'For we too are his offspring.'" These words were attributed to Epimenides of Crete (sixth century B.C.E. poet) or to Cleanthes of Assos (331-230 B.C.E.), a Stoic poet and philosopher, a disciple of Crates, later of Zenon. After the death of Zenon he became the leader of the school. After his death the Roman senate erected a statue in his honor in Assos. But as Servetus states the words quoted by Paul belong to a Hellenistic poet sympathysizing with stoicism, Aratus of Soloi (315-245 B.C.E.), a courtier of Antigonus II Gonatas (ca 319 B.C.E.-239 B.C.E.), a Macedonian king, the son of Demetrius I Poliocretes, and grandson of Antigonus I Monophthalmus), author of an astronomical poem in 1254 hexameters, *Phenomena*, to which belongs the *Hymn to Zeus* (Editio princeps, Venice, 1490). As to Pythagoras of Samos (ca 569 B.C.E.-ca 475 B.C.E.), it is well known that he did not write anything, but several works were ascribed to him in the epoch of the Alexandrian Neo-Pythagoreanism: *Symbols, Hymns, The Golden Verses*. The origin of this attribution of the phrase *nos esse genus quoddam Dei* is in note 102, Bk. V infra.

the ancients said that Jove was "airy" or that he was in the very air in which we live because the divine, life-causing breath is in the air. Paul paraphrases Aratus talking about Jove, and Aratus said that all things were filled with Jove. [133] "Jupiter is whatever you see, wherever you are moved."[41] They said Jove, based on the ancient tradition of the Hebrews, called God, Jova. Jova, which is an indeclinable noun, was given a declension and turned into Jove. Moreover, Jova is said for יהוה, Jehova, because the *shewa* in the first syllable is not uttered and the expression of the aspirate is left out as regularly happens in that language.[42]

In speaking to Asclepius about the spirit, Trismegistus said that the spirit of God fills everything and makes everything live and that the cosmos nourishes bodies and the spirit nourishes and sustains souls. In his third *Sermon* he said that this spirit, which makes everything live, came forth from a holy source. He said that the soul continues a dependent link with its own original source just as light and heat depend upon their source.[43] David had the same sense when in Psalm 103 he said, "lives fail when God withdraws His spirit."[44] Likewise, all Platonic philosophers affirm that God is the soul of the universe and that the spirit sustains and makes everything live in the universe. But regarding this universal essence and the forms of all things we shall say more later as we should first present some comments on the word, Elohim.

Elohim

In order that we may relate sure facts about the name Elohim, we must see

---

[41] The ancient philosopher Anaximenes (585-528) proposed an eternal protoelement which he calls air or breath: ἀήρ, πνεῦμα, as the primordial principle and origin of everything. Hence Cicero in *De natura deorum* I,10, and Augustine in *De civitate Dei*, VIII, 2, said that according to him the air is God or Zeus or Jupiter, as Servetus attests.

[42] Servetus's explanation of the origin of the name Jove from the Hebrew Jova or Jehova is very suggestive but it cannot be verified.

[43] Almost literal quote from *Asclepius*, III and lib. I (*Poimandres*).

[44] Ps. 103:29 : "When you hide your face, they are dismayed; when you take away their breath, they die and return to their dust." The following explanation by Servetus coincides more with Neo-Platonism than with Platonism. In a certain sense Plotinus would subscribe to it, but he does not say that God is the soul of the universe only that "by virtue of the universal soul this world is god" (*Enneads*, V.1.2).

what has appeared in God so that the name Elohim be consonant with what follows therefrom. The most ancient Hebrews in the *Bereshit rabbaa* or in the *Great Genesis* relate that from the beginning of the world there were the following things: the Messiah, the seat of God's glory, the city of Jerusalem, the garden of Paradise, the spirit of the just, the Law, and Israel, these seven things.[45] In truth there was from the beginning, along with the Messiah himself, the throne of divinity that was seen by Isaiah, the throne of exalted majesty (Isa. 6). This is shown to us in Deuteronomy 33, Jeremiah 17, and Psalms 92 and 102, where it is regularly said that the throne and the seat of God exist from the beginning. This very thing is the place of our sanctification which has been prepared from the beginning, as Jeremiah says in the passage. This very thing is the garden of heavenly paradise and the city of heavenly Jerusalem.[46] From the beginning the kingdom has been prepared for us, as Christ said, just as from the beginning that fire [134] in which the wicked will be punished, has been prepared (Matt. 20 and 25, and Isa. 30).[47] Notice in what sense the Hebrews spoke: the Messiah was "from the beginning." It is not in the manner of the trinitarian Sophists, but because his person and visible form were subsisting in God. Hence Rabbi Igzhac Arama said regarding Genesis: "Before the sun was created, the Messiah's name was subsisting, and it was already sitting on the throne of God."[48] I wish that our

---

[45] *Genesis Rabba, The Judaic Commentary to the Book of Genesis: A New American Translation I-III.* Translated by Jacob Neusner (Atlanta: Scholars Press, 1985). J. Theodore and C. Albeck, eds., *Midrash Bereshit Rabba: Critical Edition with Notes and Commentary.* 5 vv. (Jerusalem: Wahrmann, 1965).

[46] Is. 6:1; Deut. 33, there is mention of this here; Jer. 17:12; Pss. 92:2, 102:19. Maimonides explains in his *Guide* I. 9, the meaning of the term *kisse,* (כסא), *throne,* in the scripture as "the essence and greatness of God which are inseparable from his being."

[47] Matt. 20:23 and 25:46; Isa. 30:33.

[48] Isaac Arama (b. in Zamora 1420, d. In Naples 1494), Spanish rabbi and author. He was at first principal of a rabbinical academy at Zamora; then preached at Tarragona, and later at Fraga in Aragón. He officiated finally in Calatayud as rabbi and head of the Talmudical academy. Upon the expulsion of the Jews in 1492, Arama settled in Naples, where he died. He is the author of *"Akedat Yitzak"* (*Offering of Isaac*), a lengthy philosophical commentary on the Pentateuch (Salonica, 1522, Venice 1547). Servetus could have read the Venice edition. He also wrote a commentary upon the *Five Rolls,* and a work called *A Burdensome Vision,* about the relation of

191

Sophists had kept this interpretation.

The Hebrews prove in that passage, in Deuteronomy 33, that even the Law existed from the beginning "at God's right hand," and this because it is said to have been written by God's finger and in God's book, and it was thus brought down to earth from above. They argue as well that Israel existed from the beginning because they are called "the people of the age" or "an eternal people," one constituted from the beginning (Isa. 44), one that is sculpted in God (Isa. 49).[49] In the same way they prove on the basis of 4 Kings 19, Isaiah 37, 49, and Psalm 86 that the earthly Jerusalem was established from the beginning.[50] But because those things were the shadow of another truth, because we are substantively placed in Christ through the eternal spirit, we more accurately say that we are parties of Christ by a special means in him from eternity. The spirit of those who are regenerated in Christ is substantively in Christ, written down in the book of glory. These have eternity or a sharing of the eternity of Christ's spirit because they possess a portion of the substance of his spirit or of the substance of his breath. In this way it was fitting that Christ's royal throne was from eternity decorated for and destined for his people, who were chosen from eternity. What Christ said to the apostles, "You are with me from the beginning," "your names have been written in the heavens," "you are the people of the age," "you were sculpted in God," "your seats are from the beginning," tends to this point.[51] The heavenly city would not be said to have existed unless there were citizens in the city. See how great is the power of Christ's eternity and how great is the communication of that eternal divinity in us according to special forms and spirits.

---

philosophy to theology; also *The Hand of Absalom*, a commentary on Proverbs. Arama's writings were highly esteemed though he often copied from Rabbi Abraham Bibago, a philosopher from Huesca, without mentioning him. Arama's works were also esteemed by the Christian world. In 1729 M. A. J. van der Hardt, of the University of Helmstedt, published a dissertation under the title *"Dissertatio Rabbinica de Usu Linguæ in Akedat Ischak,"* on Arama's work, giving it in Hebrew with Latin translation.

[49] Deut. 33:2; Isa. 44:24, 49:5.
[50] 2 Kings 19:31; Isa. 37:32, 49:22; Ps. 86:5. The meaning of these texts is forced by Servetus.
[51] Allusions to John 15; Luke 10:20 and to references listed in note 47.

In fact, the spirits not only of the just, but also of other men and [135] of all things are from eternity bright forms in God as we shall soon say about the forms. Indeed, more particularly were those, who are among "the twelve times hundred forty four thousand times thousand of thousands" chosen and predestined in Christ himself (Rev. 21). From eternity an equal number of seats and residences have been prepared for them, and for each has been prepared his own spirit in God.[52] They were also real in God from the beginning and they were seen around that throne of majesty, that is, the cherubim and seraphim, the heavenly powers, the princes, and the governors of individual domains, each with his own throne, as Paul said in agreement with Daniel. They were the innumerable myriads of legions of spirits standing near and the ministering angels as well, as Daniel said. Ezekiel saw these things in God in chapters 1 and 10, where he says that he saw "visions of Gods." Mica saw nearly the same thing in the final chapter of 3 Kings, and likewise David in 2 Kings 22.[53] The voice of God's words was heard like the "sound of an army," Ezekiel being witness in that instance, and like the "voice of a multitude," Daniel being witness there (chap. 10).[54] This great majesty was seen and heard as a multitude in number, and in it the splendors of Christ's faces were shining forth, as the Hebrew idiom has it; the splendors of faces were shown by the angels, by the various faces of cherubim and seraphim, so many flashing eyes and forms of divinity there. These many things, I say, that were seen and heard in the heavens by Adam, Abraham, and other witnesses, must be called nothing other than *Elohim*, gods, Adonim, lords, Adonai, my lords.[55] Jacob saw this plurality in God and made note of it when he said that the Gods were revealed to him (Gen. 35). And also

---

[52] This is an imaginary figure. Rev. 7:4 and 14:1, 3 list the mysterious number of one hundred forty four. Chap. 21 mentions only the size of the wall of the celestial Jerusalem.

[53] Ezek. 1 and 10 describe an enigmatic vision of the "chariot of Yahweh," its wheel and cherubim. A similar vision of God is described in Dan. 10, but there are no indications of the crowds of cherubim or seraphim. Similarly erroneous are references to 2 and 3 Kings.

[54] Ezek. 1:24 : "I heard the sound of their wings like the sound of mighty waters, like the thunder of the Almighty, a sound of tumult like the sound of an army." Dan. 10:6 : "and the sound of his words like the roar of a multitude."

[55] Servetus interprets visions and biblical theophanies as strictly divine apparitions at the same

Abraham said: "Gods caused me to wander" (Gen. 20).[56] From this it is already obvious that Elohim contains many things in Himself. Verily Elohim was God; the form itself was Christ with the manifold ministry of the angels. In sum, Elohim is "one that has divinities like attractive forms;" is equivalent to "gods," "divine ones" or "the face of the Gods." That name was first given to God, and then to others who showed dazzling forms. [136] When the angels were sent to the ministry, they assumed the divine visage and were, therefore, called Gods, but it was under the person of Christ.[57]

The trinitarians have amazing visions regarding this name. For they say regarding the three entities that the word, "gods," is meant as if they were three gods, something which they themselves deny. Or were the three gods those that made Abraham go on his wanderings and were visible to Jacob himself? If they admit that they are three and that they are Gods, it follows that there are three Gods. Likewise the Jews, who would never allow those three entities in God, attribute the plurality of the noun, Elohim, to the idiom of their language in order to avoid the imputation of plurality in God, and they admit of no other mystery in this case. But, should they acknowledge the true Messiah, they will acknowledge that the mystery of God, Christ, and the angels is obvious in the word, Elohim, and that this is confirmed by the entire Law. For that idiomatic use of the plural is not rashly employed nor can it arise in the holy language without mystery. This is all the more so because other nouns in the plural are found throughout, just as in the passages cited, "the Gods made him wander," "the Gods appeared." The Gods are called "holy" in Joshua 24, "the living Gods," "the live Gods" in Jeremiah 10 and 23, "the Gods as judges" in Psalm 57.[58] In 2 Samuel 7 it is said that Gods went to

time explaining the plural of the term Elohim.

[56] This argumentation is based on Gen. 35:15 and 20:13 and many other verses where the term Elohim is used, which strictly translated means "gods" and which Servetus explains in light of his theological doctrine.

[57] Servetus is using the term *persona* to describe, as usually, the appearance, e.g. of angels. *Induebant personam divinam ..., sub persona tamen Christi.*

[58] These quotes from Josh. 24:19; Jer. 10:10, 23:36 have to be understood in the sense explained

redeem, that is, the heavenly powers went, God, Christ, and the angels. But now because Christ alone holds all the majesty in himself, his own, the Father's, the angels', as he himself says in Luke 9, it is appropriate that he is now called Elohim, as he has all the "divinities."[59]

Or, on the other hand, can there be any doubt that the name Jehova is applied to Christ? For there is no doubt that in the Law the Angel is called Jehovah. Therefore, *a fortiori* so is Christ: especially because that name was given to the angel as the prefiguration in the figure of Christ. Just as at one time Elohim and Jehova were the same thing because "God was the Word," so it is even now because Christ has been glorified in the manner of that pristine glory. Nevertheless, on earth that name was not given by the prophets to Christ when he was active: but Christ himself [137] attributed the divinity of Elohim to himself. But now he is the true Jehovah who causes everything to be, sustains everything, and confers his power to make miracles for his people.[60] He is the source of light that forms everything and pours the forms of things into our minds because at one time the forms of things were in God's wisdom, which is now Christ himself.

The Ideas or the Forms of All Things in God

Now, because we have on many occasions touched upon the language of the forms and because the knowledge of them guides us to a richer knowledge of Christ or rather to a richer exposition of God's essence and His names, we must now say something about them. The images or representations of all things from eternity were in God, in the wisdom, in the very Word of God, as it were, truly shining in the archetypal cosmos. For God saw everything in Himself, in His light,

---

in the note 56. In Ps. 57:1 in some versions there is the term "gods" but it is clear that it corresponds to "lords," "judges," "leaders."

[59] 2 Sam. 7:23 : "Is there another nation on earth whose God went to redeem it as a people, and to make a name for himself, doing great and awesome things for them, by driving out before his people nations and *their gods*?" Servetus clearly changes completely the meaning of the word, which means here "the leaders." The quote from Luke 9:31 refers to the transfiguration of Christ and is out of place here.

[60] The attribution of the name Yahweh or Jehovah to Christ can only be established by the application of various acceptations of the term *hayah*. Compare note 2.

that is, He saw the forms of all things, just as if in a mirror He beheld them shining within Himself. This was the received doctrine about God's wisdom from the origin of the cosmos, the one offered in sacred literature, the one which according to the tradition of our ancestors, the Chaldeans and Egyptians taught to the Greeks. According to the holy writings Job, Moses, David, Solomon, and others taught this. Zoroaster and Trismegistus, from whom, from Trismegistus especially, all the Greeks from Orpheus to Plato learned, taught the same thing. In the Poimander as in the Asclepius he taught that the shining forms of all things were contained in this first model of the cosmos which is the Word of God. Moreover, that first architect of the cosmos had a particular wisdom within Him, one that was filled with the forms and origins of things.[61]

Previously in chapter 28 Job taught all these words which had been written about the same wisdom in God Himself whereby He sees individual things and whereby He sees and arranges individual things under all of heaven.[62] See Solomon in Proverbs 8 regarding the same wisdom that orders all things from the beginning with God.[63] Baruch talks about it in the same way in chapter 3, and more broadly Jesus Sirach or Ecclesiasticus and the Book of Wisdom where wisdom is called the one and multiple spirit that contains all. It is taught that wisdom is the craftsman of all things like the carpenter who first holds the idea of [138] his house within

---

[61] Servetus accepts here the common belief among the Renaissance humanists about the antiquity of the Hermetic writings and Chaldean oracles and makes them the antecedents of the Orphic and Platonic writings. Moreover, Servetus follows the Philonic interpretation of the biblical texts. The ideas found in the Corpus Hermeticum: on the Word, Libellus (Pimander), 1,5; on the demiurge or the "second mind" that makes everything, I, 9-11; on the "archetypal man," image of the father, I,12. The idea of the "architect of the world" is not Hermetic but Philonic. Servetus seems to follow the *Asclepius* of the Hermetic writings.
[62] Job 28:24: "For he [God] looks to the ends of the earth, and sees everything under the heavens."
[63] Prov. 8:22-23 : "The LORD created me at the beginning of his work, the first of his acts of long ago. Ages ago I was set up, at the first, before the beginning of the earth." Prov. 8:29-30 : "when he marked out the foundations of the earth, then I was beside him, like a master worker; and I was daily his delight, rejoicing before him always."

himself.[64] Wisdom itself in chapter 8, which has already been cited, said, "I was a multitude in God's presence and I was His delights on every day,"[65] that is, the multitude of forms that produces individual products for the delights themselves. The Wisdom was "everything that existed, exists, and will exist."[66] It was λόγος, it was the amazing faculty of reason in which all things were shining visibly. The very Word of God is His wisdom, and for us the light of Christ's face is the light of understanding and the form of all things. It is God's Word visible and audible in the senses as well as in the intellect. From our own words the act of hearing perceives now this, now that form just as the faculty of sight does from vision. The Word of God, however, contains all things simultaneously: those that are seen, heard, and understood, indeed, even those things that are perceived by other senses.

The Word of God was called by the ancients, "the pantomorphous cosmos," "the archetypal cosmos," "the intellectual cosmos." According to his speeches addressed to Asclepius and his son Tatius, Trismegistus was taught by the Mind that "the pantomorphous cosmos" exists within God and that this lesser world was made in its likeness; and within God exists the idea of the cosmos which expresses the forms through individual bodies. By this logic all things exist and are contained within God.[67] Also Orpheus said that the essence of God was

[64] In Bar. 3:37-4:1 wisdom is identified with the Law and for this reason is privileged with Israel: "Afterward she appeared on earth and lived with humankind. She is the book of the commandments of God, the law that endures forever." The practical implications of wisdom are emphasized in Ecclus. where certain expressions point to the personification of wisdom. In the book of Wisdom of Solomon we find the high point in speculations of the Old Testament concerning Wisdom as personal entity. The New Testament identifies it with the Word. Servetus treats this subject with more precision in the *Letter 8* to Calvin and in the *Apology against Melanchthon.*

[65] Prov. 8:30 : "Then I was beside him, like a master worker; and I was daily his delight, rejoicing before him always." Vulgate translates this passage as : *"cum eo eram cuncta componens et delectabar per singulos dies ludens coram eo omni tempore."* From this Servetus deduced *"coram Deo eram multitudo."*

[66] Compare note 34 about the inscription in the Egyptian temple dedicated to Isis.

[67] Servetus is using Aesculapium for Asclepium. The title of the lib. XI of *Corpus Hermeticum* is *A Discourse of Mind to Hermes.* It treats the creation of the world by God as the source of everything and who has the forms of everything that exists. "God makes the Aeon, the Aeon

"pantomorphous" since it held all forms within itself. This is shown to us by the following reasoning: for He sustains the forms of everything and by sustaining in this way, He sees them in Himself as they appear in His light. We call these apparitions ideas.[68] The same conclusion is reached by another line of reasoning: because God places the appearances and forms of things in the minds of men. For man conceives the appearances of things according to the image of God. In the passage cited, the Mind thus teaches Trismegistus this fact in an informal manner. "Imagine," he says, "that you are understanding many things; next, imagine that God holds all understandings within Himself." For, unless you thus liken yourself unto God, you will not understand God. For a similar thing is recognized by that to which it is like.[69] Therefore, in God there are the appearances and the forms of things; if they are in us, we too are likened unto God. Seneca in his letter to [139] Lucilius said, "God has the examples of all things within Himself, the numbers and the modes: He is filled with their images, which Plato called the unchangeable ideas."[70]

But we do not have to look too far afield for evidence of this matter, all these things are sufficiently proven on the basis of the holy scriptures, if the very property of the light of God, who makes everything to appear and shine, is known to us through Christ. The life of every individual thing was shining in the Word (John 1).[71] In God's mind, before the things themselves were created, were the

---

makes the Kosmos, the Kosmos makes Time, and Time makes Coming-to-be .... The Aeon then is in God, the Kosmos in the Aeon, Time is in the Kosmos, and Coming-to-be is in Time ... . God is the source of all things; the Aeon is the power of God; and the work of the Aeon is the Kosmos, which never came into being, but is ever coming into being by the action of the Aeon .... For the things come into being in two different ways; the things that come into being in heaven are immutable and imperishable, but those that come into being on earth are mutable and perishable." These are Philonic and Middle-Platonic concepts.

[68] *The Orphic hymns: text, translation, and notes* by Apostolos N. Athanassakis, (Atlanta, Georgia: Scholars Press, 1988, reprint of 1977).

[69] These are almost exact words from lib. XI of *Corpus Hermeticum.*

[70] Servetus could read Seneca in the edition of Erasmus, Basel, 1528 and 1529. *Seneca's letters to Lucilius,* translated by E. Phillips Barker (Oxford: The Clarendon Press, 1932).

[71] John 1:4 : *"In ipso vita erat et vita erat lux hominum"* ("In him was life, and the life was the light of all people.")

ideas of things that were to be created. God recognized the appearances of the things, and He discerned them in His light within Himself when He said, "Let the earth produce animals according to their appearance, and let the earth sprout the plants according to their appearance."[72] In the same way, when we are about to build a house, a city, or something else, we conceive the forms with our mind, and these are from the light of God or like the light of God. This line of reasoning particularly moved Timæus of Locris, Archytas, and Plato.[73]

We think about things because the divine wisdom has been imparted to us, which, as Philo[74] said, is a certain "emanation of God's clarity, a whiteness of eternal light, a spotless mirror within us that relates all things to us in an image" (Wis. 7).[75] Jesus, the son of Sirach, when the books of the elders were opened, because he said that they were of a doctrine that was not to be despised, also teaches that there is in God a certain wisdom, in which God Himself, as in His own light, saw and reckoned all creation, all the drops of rain, and all the sand of the sea. This same wisdom has been poured into us, and we are granted a clear cognition of things thereby.[76] This tradition of the Hebrews is manifest. On the basis of the Law, Philo demonstrates the ideas in *Allegory of the Laws* by commenting on that statement of Moses to God: "Remove me from your book." When he spoke thus,

---

[72] The words of creation in Gen 1:24 and 11, changed.

[73] Timaeus of Locres, immortalized by Plato in his *Timaeus*. He features also in Plato's *Critias*. Later references to Timaeus of Locres from antiquity are by: Cicero in his *De re publica* I, X, 16), where he is described as an intimate of Plato; Proclus in his *Commentary on Plato's Timaeus* (II, 38, I). It is probably a pseudonym of Archytas of Taranto (400 B.C.E.-365 B.C.E.), a Pythagorean mathematician and philosopher and a great friend of Plato, author of *Harmony* and of *Diatribes* of which remain only some fragments. He was the ruler and the statesman, strategist and army commander-in-chief, under whose rule Taranto reached its peak power and wealth; it was the most important city of the Magna Graecia. Archytas was the author of a solution of the mathematical problem, a duplication of the cube. Servetus alludes then only in a general sense to the Pythagorean and Platonic philosophies.

[74] Servetus alludes to Wis. 7 and to the doctrine of Philo of Alexandria who considered wisdom in a three aspects: the attribute of God identical with his essence; an incorporeal being, archetypal world created by God; as an immanent entity in the world and in human beings. The concept of metaphysical light is not Philonic, but Servetus made an extensive use of it.

[75] Wis. 7:25-26 : "For she is a breath of the power of God, and a pure emanation of the glory of the Almighty; therefore nothing defiled gains entrance into her. For she is a reflection of eternal light, a spotless mirror of the working of God, and an image of his goodness."

Moses called the word of God a book in which were written down and inscribed the existence of all things.[76] Psalm 138, which is 139 for the Hebrews, nicely makes the same point where David, the prophet, speaks to God in this manner: "In your book all these things were written because up till now not one of them existed."[78] Ponder what that means: in the book of God all things are written before they exist. And Psalm 55: "You have numbered my wanderings; they are all in your book."[79] And in Psalm 49 God Himself said, "I know everything [140], and the entirety of the field is with me."[80] Based on ancient sources Plato wrote to Dionysius that everything is always with the king of universe.[81] In Revelation John teaches that the books of God are to be opened, and in them everything has been written so that individual judgments be rendered "according to what is written."[82] Obviously the book of forms and written entries is huge.

The first students of the church had the same opinion about the forms. Irenæus said that the forms of all things were first in God, that God had formed everything in advance within Himself, and that He had received the exemplar and image of all things from Himself (Book 2, chaps. 3 and 21). In Book 4, chapter 37, he said that God had received from Himself the substance of creatures, the exemplar of things created, and the model of all the adornments in the world. The Word of God, he said in the same passage, had, so to speak, outlines of things.[83] In

---

[76] This is a paraphrase of Ecclus, 1:1-10.

[77] Philo does not comment on this biblical text in any of his three treatises entitled *Legum allegoriae*.

[78] Ps. 138:16.

[79] Ps. 55:8

[80] Ps. 49:11-12 : "I know all the birds of the air, and all that moves in the field is mine. If I were hungry, I would not tell you, for the world and all that is in it is mine."

[81] Plato, *Letters*, II, to Dionysius, 312e.

[82] Rev. 20:12 : "Also another book was opened, the book of life. And the dead were judged according to their works, as recorded in the books." There are numerous allusions in the book of Rev. to the "book of life."

[83] Irenaeus, *Adv. Haereses*, lib. II, cap. 3, 2 : "Let them cease, therefore, to affirm that the world was made by any other; for as soon as God formed a conception in His mind, that was also done which He had thus mentally conceived." And cap. 9, 1 : "That God is the Creator of the world is accepted even by those very persons who in many ways speak against Him." Lib. IV, cap. 20, 1-3: "For with Him were always present the Word and Wisdom, the Son and the Spirit, by whom

his tract *Against Praxeas* Tertullian said that before the creation of the world, all things, having been arranged and made according to their own natures, had been in the very wisdom of God, but they lacked this alone: that they be recognized and contained in matter. The same things about the wisdom that contains the images of all things he repeated in his *Against Hermogenes*.[84] Clement of Alexandria in his *Stromata*, Books 4 and 5, displaying his opinion about the forms, he defined the form as λόγος θεοῦ, the Word of God. He said that there was a region of God that was difficult to grasp, which Plato, once taught by Moses, called the region of forms, χώραν ἰδεῶν, that it was the place which held all things pertaining to the universe. He said that the "mind of God was the place of forms" and for this reason, when a man contemplates the forms, he is almost made into God as much as the separated souls are visible gods when they are engaged with the divine

---

and in whom, freely and spontaneously, He made all things. to whom also He speaks, saying, 'Let Us make man after Our image and likeness;' He taking from Himself the substance of the creatures [formed], and the pattern of things made, and the type of all the adornments in the world." (PG VII, 119, 126, 256).

[84] Tertullian, *Adv. Praxeam*, VI : "Now, as soon as it pleased God to put forth into their respective substances and forms the things which He had planned and ordered within Himself, in conjunction with His Wisdom's Reason and Word, He first put forth the Word Himself, having within Him His own inseparable Reason and Wisdom, in order that all things might be made through Him through whom they had been planned and disposed, yea, and already made, so far forth as (they were) in the mind and intelligence of God. This, however, was still wanting to them, that they should also be openly known, and kept permanently in their proper forms and substances." *Adv. Hermogenem*, XVIII: "If any material was necessary to God in the creation of the world, as Hermogenes supposed, God had a far nobler and more suitable one in His own wisdom – one which was not to be gauged by the writings of philosophers, but to be learnt from the words or prophets." And "Now His wisdom is that Spirit. This was His counselor, the very way of His wisdom and knowledge. Of this He made all things, making them through It, and making them with It. 'When He prepared the heavens,' so says (the Scripture), 'I was present with Him; and when He strengthened above the winds the lofty clouds, and when He secured the fountains which are under the heaven, I was present, compacting these things along with Him. I was He in whom He took delight; moreover, I daily rejoiced in His presence: for He rejoiced when He had finished the world, and amongst the sons of men did He show forth His pleasure.' Now, who would not rather approve of this as the fountain and origin of all things-of this as, in very deed, the Matter of all Matter, not liable to any end, not diverse in condition, not restless in motion, not ungraceful in form, but natural, and proper, and duly proportioned, and beautiful, such truly as even God might well have required, who requires His own and not another's? Indeed, as soon as He perceived It to be necessary for His creation of the world, He immediately creates It, and generates It in Himself." (PL II, 161, 212).

forms or ideas.[85] He said in his *Discourse to the Nations*, that "From the beginning we were generated in God because everything was created in the Word." Therefore, should he say that the Word was born, he is doubtless saying that we were somehow born at that moment.[86] The act of generation is expressed there in manner of similarity to a person. He expresses the same opinion in Book 7 of the *Stromata* saying: "Before everything which was conceived, the Word of God was foremost, the master of those who were formed in it."[87] Origen's third *Homily on the Song of Songs* [141] says that among the heavenly there were the exemplars of everything so that, just as God made man after His own image, so He made other creatures in the likeness of other heavenly images. All these things of the world that are visible were previously invisible in God (Heb. 11). In the Homily on the first chapter of John he says that life, light, and the image of all things were in the Word to the extent as future progeny is in the seed.[88] Behold the true teaching that

---

[85] The passage of Servetus refers to the statement of Numenius (fl. ca 150 C.E.) who said that "Plato was a Moses speaking Attic." This statement was quoted by Clement of Alexandria, *Stromata*, I, 22. In Bk. IV, 25 Clement wrote: "Rightly, then, Plato says, 'that the man who devotes himself to the contemplation of ideas will live as a god among men; now the mind is the place of ideas, and God is mind.' He says that he who contemplates the unseen God lives as a god among men. And in the *Sophist*, Socrates calls the stranger of Elea, who was a dialectician, 'god:' 'Such are the gods who, like stranger guests, frequent cities. For when the soul, rising above the sphere of generation, is by itself apart, and dwells amidst ideas,' like the Coryphaeus in Theaetetus, now becomes as an angel, so it will be with Christ, being rapt in contemplation, ever keeping in view of the will of God; in reality." Clement follows here the reinterpretation of Plato by Philo of Alexandria and by Numenius. In *Stromata* Bk. V, 2 Clement wrote : "Also in the *Phaedrus* he says, 'That only when in a separate state can the soul become partaker of the wisdom which is true, and surpasses human power; and when, having reached the end of hope by philosophic love, desire shall waft it to heaven, then,' says he, 'does it receive the commencement of another, an immortal life.'" Servetus does not give an exact quote of Clement of Alexandria, PG VI, 230, 236.

[86] Clement of Alexandria, *Cohortatio ad gentes*, (PG VI, 3).

[87] Clement of Alexandria, *Stromata*, VII, 2 : "For ignorance applies not to the God who, before the foundation of the world, was the counselor of the Father. For He was the Wisdom 'in which' the Sovereign God 'delighted.' For the Son is the power of God, as being the Father's most ancient Word before the production of all things, and His Wisdom. He is then properly called the Teacher of the beings formed by Him." (PG VI, 298).

[88] According to Migne in *Patrologia Graeca*, Origenes has only two homilies on the Song of Songs (PG XIII,37-58). His tractate *In Cant. canticorum* is divided into four books (PG XIII, 83-198) but in book 3 the idea of Servetus does not appear. In Book I, 22 and Book II, 19 of the *Comment. in Ioannem* one can find approximate formulations to the formulation of Servetus of the seminal reasons (*rationes seminales*) (PG XIV, 58, 155, 478, 582).

was known to the first Christians as it was to the ancient Hebrews and the chief philosophers. In fact, even Augustine himself in the *Book of Eighty Three Questions*, question 46, and in many passages of the books of his *City of God* said that the form was λόγος, the reasoning faculty of the mind, the imagination. And, thus, there was in God truly the ideal reasoning, λόγος, the image that represents.[89]

At any rate, Ezekiel's vision in chapters 1 and 10, proves that this system of forms was in God. For there were wheels covered with living eyes, eyes that saw, just as with animals, and various faces shown among them. Although the prophet saw by reason of the mystery only four faces there, nevertheless, everything else always shines in God.[90] God Himself is full of eyes with which He contemplates everything that is, was, and will be, as something present for Him. His eyes and sources are infinite in the one essence of God. Indeed, according to the implication of the Hebrew expression, the very eyes of God are living sources, in which all things are seen as reflected in a mirror, and they flow into everything and in them all things exist. This is the book of God's scripture that contains the very existence of objects including "the hairs on your head," as Christ said. But let us in passing clarify that vision of Ezekiel because up to this point it has been poorly understood.[91] In it there is a fiery chariot from the North, sent by God through Christ, to burn up the city and roll the Jews swiftly into Babylon, as it is presented in chapters 10 and 43. Angry, God declares that they are to be carted off

---

[89] Agustine, *De diversis quaestionibus 83* liber unus, q. 46 *De ideis*, following the concepts of Plato (PL XL, 29).

[90] Ezek. 1:18 : "Their rims were tall and awesome, for the rims of all four were full of eyes all around." Ezek. 10:12 : "Their entire body, their rims, their spokes, their wings, and the wheels – the wheels of the four of them – were full of eyes all around." Ezek. 10:14 : "Each one had four faces: the first face was that of cherub, the second face was that of a human being, the third that of a lion, and the fourth that of an eagle." Servetus interprets very liberally the quotes from Ezekiel.

[91] Ezekiel 43:3 : "The vision I saw was like the vision that I had seen when he came to destroy the city, and like the vision that I had seen by the river Chebar" which was described in 1:18 and 10:12. Servetus wants to give a historical meaning to these visions of "God's chariot." This is a highly original interpretation.

to Babylon with force and suffering and this will be accomplished with fiery chariots, driven partly by men, partly by oxen, partly by lions and eagles. It is declared that they will be afflicted with different sorts of afflictions [142] by men, by cattle, by beasts and by birds. The wheels themselves are referred to as cartings or migrations that were sent to force the migration of that people. The voice was heard as that of plunderers, as that of troops. All those were filled with eyes that were intently gazing lest anyone of those to be taken captive escape. They sent out a clear bolt of lightning lest king Zedekiah himself or any of his people hide away, fleeing under cover of night. The wheels were swiftly moving with animals every which way lest anyone be able to escape by some route. It was the terrible vision of the angry God against the impious just as in a similar vision God is shown as angry against the Antichrist's followers (Rev. 4).[92] He is, however, complacent with others who give glory to Him, and He transports them into heaven in an angelic chariot. There are also animals there, full of eyes that intently gaze upon the chosen by Christ lest any of them perish. Indeed, those animals protect us from every harm, be it by man, beast, bird, or wild animal. All those eyes are always in Christ and in them everything shines out, but it is the chosen in particular who have been enrolled in the special book of life and who reign in His special kingdom.

Moreover, there are other arguments by which this exemplary reasoning in God is proven. For, if God made a microcosm in the image of some exemplar, the exemplar was already in God. Moreover, all things which are in the whole universe are contained in the microcosm. Therefore, the exemplar of the universe existed in God. In fact, the single exemplar of man contained all things just as all things are in Christ and just as in one soul there is the exemplar of many things. Likewise, whenever God gave the order to make certain things, He showed that their

[92] Servetus correlates the visions of Ezekiel with those of the Rev. 4:8 : "And the four living creatures, each of them with six wings, are full of eyes all around and inside. Day and night without ceasing they sing, 'Holy, holy, holy, the Lord God the Almighty, who was and is and is to come.'" These eyes may symbolize the divine omniscience as in Zech. 4:10 : "These seven are the eyes of the LORD, which range through the whole earth."

expressed form was visible in Him (Exod. 5, Num. 8, Ezek. 40 and 1 Para. 28).[93] In the very light of God all these things seemed to radiate, when God opened Himself or extended Himself in some way. For God it is not difficult, but natural and proper in the manner of a light that brings all things into a living state. These things were for Christ's glory [143] as was everything else that was figured in the light of God's Word, especially since no other notions exist in God or in Christ himself.

At this point I would take pleasure in asking my opponents whether they think that those notions, which they call qualities, are now in the soul of Christ.[94] In the future state of blessedness we shall have no other qualities or notions, but God's charity that presents us vividly the things themselves in their proper forms. For this is the particular property of His light. This reasoning is decisive, if you think well, if you understand well, how the angels see the future in God without interposing other species between God and the angels. So all theologians concede that the angels see in the Word and, thus, that in the Word are the forms of things.[95] In God, Samuel, who was called "the seer," saw the things which Saul had asked regarding the past and those things which would happen to him in the future (1 Sam. 9 and 10).[96] In God Micaiah saw the things that would be in war, the dispersal of Israel and the killing of Ahab (3 Kings, the last chapter).[97] In the visions of God, in the spirit and in God Himself, Ezekiel, while he was in Babylon,

---

[93] Exod. 25:40; Num. 8:4; Ezek. 40; 1 Chron. 28:11. These texts mention a previous design, pattern or model preexisting in the mind of God.

[94] Servetus refers to the qualitative notions or noetic species with which the scholastics explained the process of acquiring knowledge of things.

[95] These words may imply an allusion to the *Summa Theologiae* of Thomas Aquinas, I, q. 58, a. 1: "But as to the knowledge of the Word, and of the things he [angel] beholds in the Word, he is never in this way in potentiality; because he is always actually beholding the Word, and the things he sees in the Word. For the bliss of the angels consists in such vision; and beatitude does not consist in habit, but in act, as the Philosopher says (*Ethics*, 1, 8)." Servetus, however, nowhere mentions the name of Aquinas nor makes any reference to any of his works.

[96] 1 Sam. 9:6-9 : "'Come, let us go to the seer'; for the one who is now called a prophet was formerly called a seer." 1 Sam. 9:18-19 : "Then Saul approached Samuel inside the gate, and said, 'Tell me, please, where is the house of the seer?' Samuel answered Saul, 'I am the seer.'"

[97] 1 Kings, 22:14-23.

saw all the things which would be done in Jerusalem (Ezek. 8).[98] In the vision of God Balaam saw the things which would occur in the last times (Num. 24). To the same thing refer the first chapters of Jeremiah, Ezekiel, Amos, and many other places.[99] For the prophets, being called "the seers" for this reason, saw in themselves, in the spirit, in God, the future appearing in His light, sometimes by internal, sometimes by external vision, as God Himself declares (Num. 12).[100] This light was spread so widely that the very notions which we conceive with our own intellect are particular fragments of light and glittering images that illuminate the mind itself and present us everything like divine light. For without light nothing can be formed, represented, or seen.[101]

Now see this other piece of eyewitness testimony which proves most clearly the forms of light. Those visible images, after they have been sent from a given object into a mirror and then sent back into the eye, are particular fragments of light that carry in the foreground the form in question and the image of the object [144] which is seen in the mirror.[102] Because of God's great artifice an object that is not corporeal also contains within itself a bright image, form, and outline of the corporeal thing as it exists in God's truly incorporeal light, in which all things of the universe shine. In God there are no corporeal members, but the rays, so to speak, of all things bringing back the corporeal forms of all things as if reflected back in a mirror. Infinite rays, shining in infinite ways, originate in the immensity of His light without the real partition or division of God. In fact, this entire reflective process of rays and representations has its origin from above.

Moreover, so you may grasp through a familiar example how anyone could see future things in God, you should consider the following analogy. If, after

---

[98] Ezek. 8:3 : "And the spirit lifted me up between earth and heaven, and brought me in visions of God to Jerusalem."

[99] Num. 24:2; Ezek. 1:1; Jer. 1:2; Amos 1:1.

[100] Num. 12:6 : "'Hear my words: When there are prophets among you, I the LORD make myself known to them in visions; I speak to them in dreams.'"

[101] This is the statement of the fundamental principle of Servetus's cognitive illuminism in his epistemological system.

forming an idea about any thing, you reflect within on that notion, you would say that, as in the mirror of your mind, you were seeing that thing, even if it is absent or dead. Obviously this is because the light of your mind contains within itself the natural image of the thing just as if it were the appearance of light reflected back in a mirror. It is a natural image and a natural conceptualization, I say, just as you will soon understand from the natural and substantial form of the things themselves. The light of the divine Word contains the image and form of things, and in this light we see light, just as the prophet said.[103] For Trismegistus the same light of the Word is the archetypal light and the archetype of the soul,[104] and he is quite right in this because there cannot be any light in our soul that contains the image of things unless it is like that exemplary light from which even the souls themselves come, having the form of that body which they are to form. Nay, not only the souls themselves, but even the substantial forms of other things contain the form of the whole which they project into a mirror in an act that imitates that first exemplary light, in which everything began to shine and shines perpetually. If anyone were allowed to see openly God's very nature or Christ's full splendor, he would see in it everything which is, was, and will be, everything shining as form in it. [145] But this is granted not even to the angels but only in part and like a reflected knowledge for only in Christ it is direct. In this way one angel can see more than another in God and can advise another about future happenings as is apparent from the visions of Daniel and John.[105]

From all of these it follows that among the forms both divine and human, not only are there exemplary, but also substantial forms because there is a natural property in the forms to give representation and existence, and there is a natural affinity with the substantive form. Not only are all things represented in light, but it

---

[102] The reflected light is thus a carrier of the forms of the external object.

[103] It is an allusion to Ps. 35:9 : "For with you is the fountain of life; in your light we see light."

[104] Servetus reinterprets the statement of Trismegistus: "The Good is the archetypal Light; and Mind and Truth are, so to speak, rays emitted by that Light" (*Corpus Hermeticum*, lib. II).

[105] Angel Gabriel explains one vision in Dan. 8:15; in Revelation various angels participate in

is also in light that all things exist. That Word in which everything exists, is light (John 1 and Col. 1).[106] By seeing, God sustains everything in Himself and He sustains through the forms of individual things just as Plato taught after Trismegistus and Anaxagoras. Hence Plato's commentators, Plotinus and Proclus, posited in the divine forms not only exemplary, but even essential forms upon which everything created depends.[107] In the light of God there are the original forces of things, and then they are in the created light and elements. Like a product that is most similar to the first light and, like a seeded plot of land, light itself, once created, contains the formal properties of things and the virtues that are placed within the substantive forms. In the soul, too, there is a plantation of symbols that derives from light. Because of the nature of this same light and form, any given seed holds a certain formal property of the thing to be born just as the Word of God, which was the seed of Christ, held in itself his own formal nature and the seminal powers of all things. This is the first element, the first seed by which the

---

various visions of John.

[106] Servetus says *"Verbum illud, in quo omnia consistunt, lux est."* John 1:9 : *"Erat lux vera quae inluminat omnem hominem venientem in mundum."* And Col. 1:17 : *"Et ipse est ante omnes et omnia in ipso constant."*

[107] Anaxagoras (497-428 B.C.E.) was a Greek philosopher of Clazomenae in Asia Minor. He came from a noble family, but wished to devote himself entirely to science, so he gave up his property and moved to Athens, where he became an acquaintance of Pericles. But he was charged here by the political opponents of Pericles with impiety, that is, with denying the gods recognized by the state. He was acquitted but he felt compelled to emigrate to Lampsacus, where he died soon after. He is credited with bringing philosophy to Athens and he also was the first philosopher who introduced a noetic principle, νοῦς, which gives matter life and form. He postulated a two-fold world, one intelligible and the other derivative, perceptible. And it was the mind (intelligence) that arranged all things from the infinite and uniform stuff of the universe. He wrote down his doctrine in a work *"On Nature,"* of which only fragments are preserved (H. Diels, *Doxographi Graeci*). These fragments are really reconstructions made from various passages in doxographic literature (Jonathan Barnes, *Early Greek Philosophy* (London: Penguin Books, 1987, pp. 226-239)). Plato praised him but at the same time blamed him for not using this mind (intelligence) for detailed explanations, just as Plato did in his doctrine of the forms, but focusing on the natural processes (*Phaedo*, 97bc). Plotinus and Proclus made of νοῦς (or intelligence) the first derivative from the One to the matter and the sensible world through the universal soul. The activity of the intelligence produces the soul in a manner just as light derives from light and is multiplied in the ideas which constitute the noetic cosmos, the archetypal intelligible world of all things (*Enneads* V.1-9).

force is seeded into all elements and seeds.[108] Hence in the *Poimander* Trismegistus said, "The will of God that contains the Word that saw in itself the cosmos as something beautiful, has furnished on the model of its own exemplar the elements of nature and everything else with its own elements and its vital seeds."[109] Neither could plants nor animals be reproduced as they are with their forms in so consistent a manner from such tiny seeds and with such specificity unless there were in them [146] a certain preexistent, formal and ideal divine nature. A soul could not generate a truth by an internal change within itself if it did not have an inborn, divine implanting of truth. Therefore, in the soul and in other things there has been placed a certain plantation from the substantive seed of the Word, "in which there was the light and the life of everything."[110] The Word of God, which was the seed of the generation of the Christ and symbolically cast upon the earth as a seed, causes everything to generate and germinate, giving everything life with spirit and light. The relationship of everything to the one seed of the Word is an object of wonder. Just as when everything that produces, it first conceives the seed in itself before sending it outside into a fetus, so the seed of the Word was in God before it was conceived as a son in Mary.[111] This is a powerful argument since the generation of Christ is an example and prototype of all other acts of generations. It is the first cause itself that has caused an *a priori* deduction, from the cause to the effect, although we infer *a posteriori*, meaning from what is perceivable, from the effect to the cause. This was his prior deduction: that, just as there was the first seed of generation in God, before it was made the real son of God, so in other generations the creator wished that this order be preserved. Truly in God there was

[108] In the phrase *"In anima quoque est seminarium symbolum a luce"* it should be *symbolorum* instead of *symbolum*. Servetus establishes that the soul is a ground for formation of noetic symbols of all that is to exist by analogy with the divine Word and by virtue of the same light of God that is the primary source of formal properties of all things.
[109] This quote is a summary of statements in *Corpus Hermeticum* relating the formation of the universe, lib. I, the *"Poimandres."*
[110] John 1:4.
[111] Fundamental assertion of Servetus's Christology. He will develop it later in book II of *Dialogorum*.

the substantive seed of Christ, and in him the seminal natures and exemplary forms of all things.

The substantive forms of things proceed from the light after it has been created, and they contain the formal symbol of the uncreated light. To the extent that everything exists in light, the physical and the spiritual, so all things are seen outwardly in light, and in the light of the intellect all things are internally conceived. This is also true regarding the created light according to its own relationship and secondary nature. Hence, it was nicely said by Plato in *Timæus* that the notions themselves or the intellectual concepts of the mind have a certain natural affinity with the things themselves which they express. Indeed, it is an affinity based on the light therefore, he teaches that the forms of things exist from the light.[112] This is the mechanism of [147] natural affinity and natural image.

The forms of things depend upon light by which the images themselves, when they appear in the world, being reflected into the eye and penetrating even to the soul, are rays of formal light with respect to the intellect itself, which is also light, as they penetrate through a luminescent medium and impress there the image of an external object as the light itself. This image reflects the object itself in a natural manner by means of an affinitive and participatory process, which is a natural and formal symbol of the light. That light of your mind by which you see me within yourself, has an affinity with my own form when it is seen by you. This form of mine impresses its mark upon your soul. The light which connects the spiritual elements with the physical ones contains everything in itself and displays them openly for visualization by the eyes. The images which are situated in the soul are by nature shining, and they have a natural relationship of light with the external forms, the external light, and the essential light of the soul. This essential light of the soul holds the original plantation of those images as the symbol of divinity and of the light of the Word, in which the exemplary image of everything exists. Hence those images that are placed in the soul represent themselves in a natural way to the soul itself, however often the soul directs itself to them, nor is there any need here for some other new act of cognition.[113] In fact, from the incoming and the proper light of the soul itself the one light is brought together just as in other instances generally brightness comes together with brightness.

A separation is also possible or the destruction of the one with the other surviving just as in other matters the form is destroyed while the matter survives. Although images that approach the soul may be changed, the mind or the first substance of the soul still remains the same. Temporal objects, as Parmenides said, have a share in the eternal ideas, through which they are brought to fruition: nevertheless, although they be changed, the divine mind is not.[114] This is no more difficult a concept than the idea that in Christ human nature is one with the divine and that what was once human was changed with the divine nature ever remaining the same. Indeed, based on the fact that the mutation of the forms and bodies of this world is so fluid that they never remain in the same state, [148] *Timæus* concluded regarding those things which are defective and through their composition have an imperfect being, that there ought to be other things which remain intact and pure, and it is against these perfect objects that the imperfect are to be judged.

From here follows the Platonic paradox: bodies do not truly exist and in bodies there is no truth. If you say that this is Socrates, before you end your

---

[112] This is not an exact quote from *Timaeus*, 29b.

[113] Servetus explains by this relationship between the constitutive light of forms, images, external light, the soul, and the Word, the intellectual reflection and imaginative memory as the symbols of divinity and light of the Word residing in the soul.

[114] Parmenides (ca 530-460 B.C.E.) was a Greek philosopher and poet, born at Elea in Lower Italy, and is the chief representative of the Eleatic philosophy. He is considered a disciple of Xenophanes and wrote in opposition to Heraclitus. One more fact is known from his life, namely, that he stopped in Athens on a journey in his sixty-fifth year, and there became acquainted with the youthful Socrates. He wrote a didactic poem, *On Nature*, which survived in fragments and in which he exposed in mythical terms his system. It is characterized by an irreducible opposition between being and not being, permanence and change. Parmenides refuted all accounts of the origin of the world: *Ex nihilo nihil fit.* But it is an error to attribute to him Platonic concepts (such as participation, forms, divine mind, etc.) as Servetus does. Plato discusses the Parmenides doctrine and criticizes him for his "standstill universe" in *Theaetetus,* 181a, and in *Parmenides*

statement, the very thing that you have fingered no longer exists and has ceased to exist; therefore, this past thing does not exist when you assert that it is Socrates. Likewise, truth does not exist in bodies; for it would then be changed when the bodies change. Therefore, truth only exists in the mind's eye, and God alone is truth.[115] The statement of *Timæus* also follows: that the "intelligible world is always, and that it never is becoming;" the sensible world, on the contrary, "is always becoming and never is." For in no moment you could say, "This world is." For, before you finish your statement, the world has changed.[116] Therefore, this world is a "vanity of vanities" and an object that does not exist.[117] And it is the image and shadow of another thing that exists, namely, the intelligible world. Moreover, in an object which does not exist, there is no truth. Therefore, in this world there is no truth, and that which possesses truth "is not from this world,"[118] but, if any truth seems to exist in these things, it is rather the ephemeral image and shadow of the truth. For truth is the stable aspect of any given nature, and it is the unstained purity. This is the truth in a thing, the thing itself, which does exist. Truth in speech, truth in the mind, is something else, it is a conformity to something which exists.[119] Truth is the eternal Word of God with the eternal exemplars and essences of all things. Either way, Christ is truth.

---

and *Sophist.*

[115] Servetus summarized here the principal theme of the Plato's dialogue: the existence of two worlds, one ideal and true, which is perceived by the intellect, and the other one, the sensible and corporeal, changing and not perceived as true (*Timaeus*, 28a).

[116] *Timaeus*, 27d-28a : "We must in my opinion begin by distinguishing between that which always is and never becomes from that which is always becoming but never is. The one is apprehensible by intelligence with the aid of reasoning, being eternally the same, the other is the object of opinion and irrational sensation, coming to be and ceasing to be, but never fully real." *Timaeus*, 49d-e : "And in general we should never speak as if any of the things we suppose we can indicate by pointing and using the expression 'this thing' or 'that thing' have any permanent reality: for they have no stability and elude the designation 'this' or 'that' or any other that expresses permanence."

[117] Eccl. 1:2, 12:8.

[118] Servetus combines here the Platonic worldview with the Christian inspiration : "My kingdom is not from this world" (John 18:36).

[119] Servetus makes here a distinction between ontological truth and the logical truth : *"Veritas est naturae cuius vis constans et immaculata puritas"* And *"Alia est veritas ... conformitas ad rem quae est."*

From what has been said, it also follows that form exists within form, as for example, wheel in wheel, eye in eye, light in light. The one form of this man contains the forms that are infinite within God, just as one ray of light possesses the infinite sparks, and by which God for ever and ever contemplates all the things which are of this man: the sitting, the standing, the lying down, all the movements and all the parts including "the hairs [149] of his head." When David was contemplating that all things were thus in God, he said that the observance of this thing was amazing, beyond the comprehension of a human being (Ps. 138).[120] That this is not, however, difficult for God is demonstrated for this reason only: for, if the individual form of this man's parts, changes, and actions are in our soul in a potential sense and in an actual sense through the passage of time, why shall we not say that all these are always in God actually? All the more because the objects are not distinct in God, but rather all the beings shine forth in His light as numberless aspects in their infinite modes. All individual beings exist in the very form of the light in which they shine back, being always present for God and within Him.

I have treated somewhat broadly these matters regarding exemplars so that you would understand, reader, that what shines for ever and ever in his essence, meaning the first example of Christ, the head and basis of everything, the living exemplar and source of all life, was made without any change of God. He was special and the first substantive mode of divinity, the understanding, the living, the thing that injects life into things. By the arrangement by which all things now exist in God, everything was ordered before creation by nature. He is the only one, the companion, the son, and the heir, who can claim to be generated from God.[121] Not only was Christ by his standing first in God, but God presented Christ alone substantively; it was in him alone that He manifested Himself, when He thus put him alone in the fore, generating him from Himself with the plenitude of divinity

---

[120] Ps. 1:38:6 : "Such knowledge is too wonderful for me; it is so high that I cannot attain it."
[121] Two essential points of the Servetian doctrine of Christology: "The first substantive mode of

flowing thence to others. By every means you can imagine that the complete plenitude of divinity exists in the body of Christ, by those same means you must contemplate the divinity that was formerly apart, that now lives in the same form of man. And you have to say that this form is Jesus Christ who was once in the form of God. Just as in your soul there are the forms of other things, so there was once in God a wisdom as the soul of Christ that contained the forms of all things. In Christ there was life, and in him the life of others things shone forth (John 1).[122] In God there was the first shining of Christ, the sole basis of everything; later through it, in it, and from it in a secondary manner everything else [150] was shining, being dependent upon their own individual rank.

We call this wisdom the basis and guardian of the world, which God manifested at the creation, when He presented the Word as something visible to angels and men, and when He created everything through this presentation of Himself. Through the divinity which now exists in any given thing, God can now create a new world and appear through the creation hypostatically: so how much more could He do this through the divinity of Christ? If God received from Himself the figure and the substance of all creatures as we just stated, how much more did He receive the figure and substance of Christ? Without a change in Himself God is able here to present Himself to us as something visible and palpable no matter what the form because He contains in Himself all forms and all bodies essentially. Nevertheless as He contemplated the form of Christ from the beginning, He made it the first, the spring of life, which He laid open as a great mystery in the creation and incarnation. The cognitive process of God was the act that generated the son. There was not at that time a real son as distinct from the Father, but there was the natural knowledge of God that was already living. Just as by means of a mirror the reflection of an object placed before it is a natural consequence, so the reasoning of God was the natural reflection that gave natural

divinity" and "The only one who can claim to be generated from God."
[122] John 1:4 : "In him was life, and the life was the light of all people."

expression to Christ and held him in essence. This is the property of light, not only to express a form naturally, but to contain the substantive form in essence. If you can believe that God fathered a man from Himself, you will believe that the substance and form of a thing that is generated, has ever had existence from God. What person, who grants that other, secondary forms exist in him, will deny that this primary form is in God?[123]

The Bases of Natural Things

We have not yet provided satisfactory explanation of the glory of Christ's essence and his light if we do not derive the bases of natural things from him and show that he is the basis of everything. In this matter we need to review what we have said. The Word, in which everything exists, is the light; everything by reason of this same light exists in Christ; by his power everything is carried and [151] sustained (John 1, Col. 1, and Heb. 1).[124] All this can also be applied to the created light by analogy with the uncreated. By forming light God wanted there to be in the light the form and ability to form other things. Therefore, if everything exists through the light, and the light is that which gives existence to a thing, the light is the form of the thing. Moreover, the earthly material is called *tohu* and *bohu*, unformed and undifferentiated, because it was not yet made party to the light (Gen. 1).[125] Wherefore, you would again conclude that form exists from light. Not only forms and existence of things are from light, but so are souls and spirit because light is the life of men and the life of the spirit.

Light is the most beautiful of all things of this world and the other world. In the very form of light any given thing takes its existence, as it shines in it. Light

---

[123] The whole paragraph represents an elaborate argument in favor of the Servetian doctrine of the existence in all things and humans of the *symbolus deitatis*.

[124] John 1:4; Col. 1:17; Heb. 1:3.

[125] Gen. 1:2 : "the earth was a formless void." In Vulgate : *"terra autem erat inanis et vacua."* Servetus says : *"Informis et inconspicua."* Maimonides explains these Hebrew words, *tohu* and *bohu*, in an animistic manner making the astronomical bodies "living bodies and not dead ones like the elements." "And the earth was *tohu* and *bohu* : [It was] mourning [toha] and crying [boha] – which means that it, I mean the earth, cried woe and howled because of her evil lot." *Toha* and *boha* are Aramaic words. (*Guide to the Perplexed*, Part II.5).

alone gives form to heavenly, earthly, spiritual, and corporeal things, and it transforms them. From it proceeds the entire form of the world and all its adornment. The creator provided things with glowing forms lest they exist any further under that unformed, dark chaos. In everything that can be generated or corrupted, the approach of the sun towards us is the cause of generation, its withdrawal is the cause of corruption. The solar ray so governs the elements that one shining perfection of form can be seen. No thing can on its own emit the form and natural image of light into a mirror or into the eye without containing light formally within itself. This is a very powerful argument if you think about it correctly. The light is a visible form of all things. Whatever appears is light (Eph. 5).[126] Light itself transforms in various ways earthly and watery materials into glittering stones, glowing pearls, and everything else that is seen in its form through light. Light is in regeneration; it informs our spirit and transforms it as the light will substantively transform our bodies in the final resurrection. This reasoning proves the similarity of regeneration to generation as both derive substantively from light.

Christ's analogy also proves this conclusively. For Christ's body took its form substantively from the light of the Word by an engendering process of God, and in the resurrection it was substantively transformed just as on the mountain Christ's transformation was seen, having been made through light.[127] If Aristotle had known this, he [152] could then have understood that the formal basis of natural things was light, and that the divine manifestations were in things as prior bases. The bases of all things are in God, in Christ himself, who is the *alpha* and the ω. Aristotle could have understood that in spiritual substance light was the ἐνδελέχειαν of the soul, the act or continuous stimulation and life causing

---

[126] The quote from Eph. 5:8 is incongruous to the theme : *"eratis enim aliquando tenebrae nunc autem lux in Domino ut filii lucis ambulate."*

[127] Servetus interprets the biblical narratives of the birth, transfiguration on the Tabor mountain, and resurrection of Jesus in terms of the luminosity in order to infer the notion of the transforming power of light. This is the usual method of Servetus: he proceeds from the biblical

energy,[128] because light is the life of men, the life of our spirit so in the generation as in the regeneration. The form of fire is light; the form of water is glittering, and this is a quality of air as well. Light itself is the form of a solar body, and from it other things take their form. The form of Christ's glorious body is divine light that is also to be communicated to us (Phil. 3).[129] But the propagation of other things as well is unknown to Aristotle and all the Sophists, to whom the light of God's Word and spirit and the generation of Christ is unknown. For all things are propagated, generated, and produced by analogy with Christ.[130] In Christ's seed there existed the elements of our seed, our life, and our spirit. Within the glowing Word of God was and is spirit, life, and form of other things. All things exist through light, and without light nothing exists. There is no creature that does not reflect the creator and in which the creator's light does not shine; even Job knew this (Job 25).[131] Trismegistus said to his son Tatius, "Because everything else is bright through God, He Himself in turn shines through everything and in everything." And in a later passage he said, "God, the light, so crafted everything that we see Him shining in all things."[132] In his book *On the Sun* Julian claims on the basis of the very ancient opinion of the Phoenicians that this light is the true entelechy and the pure act, the image of the divine intelligence that has been extended through everything else, and it manifests the divinity itself in everything.[133] Christ wanted this, his light, to be perpetually prominent in our eyes

---

data to the philosophical speculations and conclusions.

[128] This is an express rejection of the principles of the Aristotelian philosophy in favor of the Neo-Platonic and Christian concepts of light.

[129] Phil. 3:21 : "He will transform the body of our humiliation."

[130] Another crucial formulation of the fundamental principle of the Servetian system: *"Nam per analogiam ad Christum omnia propagantur, generantur, et producuntur."*

[131] Job 25:3 : "Upon whom does his light not arise?"

[132] *Corpus Hermeticum*, lib. I.

[133] We do not find this allusion to Julian, the Apostate (331-363 C.E.), in the voluminous *Contra Iulianum Imperatorem* written by Cyril of Alexandria (380-444 C.E.) (PG LXXVI, 503-1158) which was known to Servetus. The allusion may be a generic conclusion from the work of Julian. He discussed the sun in his *Oration to the Sun* in three different ways: as a transcendental being similar to the Neoplatonic One presiding over the intelligible world; as Helios-Mithras, who controls the "intelligible gods" similar to the Platonic ideas; and as a visible sun, who is

so that there we would see him shining in everything. For this light is a certain propagation of the light of God's Word which resides within it, preserves its symbol in things, and makes them as one with it. [153] This light has been imparted to the sun, that received its life-giving power from the first light. The very light of the sun is variously distributed just like the light of Christ. Orpheus and the other ancients call the Word of God the φάνητα, or the appearing God, which appeared first from the infinite. This name was later also granted to the sun.[134] In the immensity of God Christ appeared first, just as the sun appears in the midst of the created light.

The variety of forms is variously combined by light. From the divine light and the acquired splendor of the soul one light is made, and from it there are the spiritual forms in us. From the light of the sun and the splendor that is born within the elements, one light is made, and from it there are the forms of bodies. The substance of the higher elements too, along with the earth itself, makes one material for things. These form the bases of natural things, the bases of the generation and corruption. Hot and cold are active within things, but they derive from light and splendor. I understand that solar light makes warmth and the watery splendor makes cold and it in turn, when congealed in celestial objects increases the force of the chilling effect. Just as there is life-giving warmth from the ordinary light of the sun, so from the moon, Saturn, and certain other celestial bodies and parts of the sky there is everywhere a moist dankness and cold death, just as from Mars there is a certain asphyxiating heat. The sun's clarity is one thing, the moon's clarity another. Fire is one thing, splendor something else. Christ, architect of the universe, who himself is the original basis and in whom all things exist, thus arranged these things in light: the heavenly and the terrestrial, the physical and the

---

revealing the world of sensory perception (*The Works of Emperor Julian* with English translation by Wilmer Cave Wright, (Cambridge, MA : Harvard University Press, 1962)), Vol. 1, pp. 360 ff.
[134] Servetus could read this in *Orphic Hymns* but the same is mentioned by Lactantius in his *Div. instit.* Lib. I, cap. 5 which refers to God, and not to the Word because he was "the first to appear from the infinite." Microbius, *op. cit.*, lib. I, cap. 17 explains that it "constantly renewed" thus he

spiritual. He created the materials of the elements and, drawing light itself from his resources, he substantively bestowed upon them the bright forms when they were combined.[135]

Based on what has been said this first inference can be made: nothing can now be created without the subject, but by virtue of light comes the formal propagation of things from things, the generations and the corruptions; and the form itself that is placed in the symmetry of the light and the elements, is produced substantively by the action of light and elements; and the elements themselves by means of the power [154] of the heavenly light are combined and governed. Therefore, all actions and transmutations come about in the first instance from light in bodily objects as in spiritual ones, in Christ as in us. In spiritual objects all energy is from light; spiritual light illuminates by giving essence to everything, and to light belongs the power to scatter demons, who, being dark, love darkness and hate light. Poimander said that in the divine mind light was the first appearance that overpowers the infinite realm.[136] In physical objects light also is the substantive form of everything or the origin of forms, active in everything as a principle by producing warmth, which is especially effective and active, while dryness is especially stagnant and passive. Cold and moist also arise from light or from the created splendor of water that has been imparted even to heavenly bodies. Colors derive from light in these lesser objects as is represented in a rainbow by light. We see that things are turning white after being washed with water. We see that whiteness is sometimes in a cold body, and that the splendor of water is increased by the process of congealing as with snow or hail: sometimes it is in a hot body as

---

refers to the sun.

[135] The term "architect of the universe" refers to the ideas of Philo of Alexandria and Prov. 8:30 : "then I was beside him, like a master worker; and I was daily his delight." The Hebrew text uses a word אָמוֹן which is translates as "artificer, architect, master-workman." The LXX translates this by ἁρμόζουσα, which is participle present feminine of the verb cognate to the Hebrew term.

[136] Lib. I of *Corpus Hermeticum* treats light as the primordial appearance of God, "That Light is I, even Mind, the first God." And "from the Light there came forth a holy Word, ... and the Word which came forth from the Light is son of God." The Word next fashioned the primordial chaos into the organized cosmos. But Servetus interprets this doctrine in his own way.

if the brightness of fire has been left behind after a complete incineration as with lime and ash. By the extinction of light or its suppression blackness is created as with soot, charcoal, and pitch. It is through this mode of light, when it has been suppressed, be it in a sin or in a demon, that blackness or a contracted obscurity exists. By a similar process the same judgment must be made about the other colors, all of which are contained in the substance of the thing just like the very form of light. A particular part of the form consists of the colors, although they may change, just as parts and elements are changed whether in the soul or the body. Hot and cold, moist and dry, are substances differentiated by Hippocrates, and they enter into the composition of everything. These substances are formal just like the colors, although, when they are manifested, they are called accidents. They are inserted into matter and make one form with the prior one.[137]

Secondly, it may be inferred that in the beginning God truly created *ex nihilo* and without preexisting material a two-fold heaven [155], a unique earth, and light just as the word of Genesis has it. Everything else was said to have been created later (Col. 1 and Rev. 10) because they were truly brought from non-being into being. Nevertheless, they were not created like in that first creation *ex nihilo* and without preexisting matter.[138] Truly there water was created at that event. From the water there were the heavens; from the water through the process of evaporation there was the air. From the air at last is made fire by way of cooked matter and light being warmed up by the air. In fact, flame itself is air set on fire. God did not create the luminary objects on the fourth day, but He did make them out of the solidified material of heaven. For in that passage there is the word, עשה, (for "to make,") which in Hebrew means, not "to make something *ex nihilo*," but "to shape and form something out of preexisting matter" as Rabbi Solomon, Rabbi

---

[137] Light is the universal formal cause which acts on four elements and their qualities. This seems to be an original Servetus idea.

[138] Col. 1:16; Rev. 10:6.

Abraham, and all the rest note there.[139] In the same way "the heavens were made,"
as the psalmist said, or the heavenly distinctions of spheres as Job said in chapter
37, where he says metaphorically that the heavens were made sturdy like a metal
mirror that has been cast.[140] Beyond the starry sky there are the spheres of the
seven planets, the seven governors of the physical world, the disposition of which
is wickedly said by some to be "fate." But Moses did not mention this lest the
ordinary folk lapse into idolatry of those "governors" or believe in the necessity of
fate.[141]

Thirdly it follows that Thales, the Milesian, who learned in Syria and Egypt
the teaching of Moses and Trismegistus, and was the first of all among the Greeks
to teach about nature, did not speak incorrectly when he said that everything came
from water because the earth is insufficient by itself and because the form of the
earth is from water.[142] Relying on Moses, Peter quite plainly teaches that heaven is
from water. "Heaven," he said, "and the earth were once from water and through
water they exist by the Word of God" (2 Pet. 3).[143] The same is indicated by the
watery splendor which has been imparted to the moon and everything else as well
as is taught by the etymology of the Hebrew expression. For in Hebrew "heaven"

---

[139] In the text there is an errata of עשה (to do, to make) to יצר (yatzar) which means to form, to
fashion, to give shape to preexistent substance. Servetus distinguished then between the verb
ברא used in Gen. 1:1 and the verb עשׂה used in Gen 1:16. Those rabbis mentioned by Servetus
are Aben Ezra (note 26) and the Commentaries on the Pentateuch (Bologna, 1482; Venice, 1525,
published in Hebrew) of the French rabbi Salomon Jarchi ben Isaac, Rashi (1040-1105) whom
Servetus will quote more explicitly in Dialogue II.

[140] Job 37:14-18.

[141] Obviously this opinion is not an invention of Servetus.

[142] The opinion about the influence of Moses and of Trismegistus (if one accepts his existence in
ancient antiquity) on Thales of Miletus (ca 625-548 B.C.E.) has no basis except an attempt to
derive the Greek philosophy from some presumed oriental thread of thought especially suggested
by the fact that he was of Phoenician origin and it was attributed to him that he traveled to Egypt
where he was supposed to study mathematics of the pyramids (Diels, A I,3,2). He proposed water
as the primary principle from which everything else was formed (Diels, Hi I,1).

[143] 2 Pet. 3:5 refers to the deluge and not to the creation. Gen. 1:6-9 talks about separation of
waters, but the overall meaning of Genesis rather supports the idea that water was the primordial
chaos or tehom from which everything else was formed.

is שמם, which means the same as water.[144] It was not doubted by the Hebrews that the firmament was made from water. God made the airy extension [156] from the waters that were evaporated by the spirit. As David said God made heaven by a process of extension, and it comes from water; its foundation is water (Ps. 103).[145] The whole breadth of heaven was produced from that foundation and located in it. Hence the foundations of heaven are said "to be shaking" when something tempestuous happens (2 Sam. 22 and Job 26).[146] Heaven was made by an extension teaches Isaiah in chapter 40 and Jeremiah in chapter 50. The Hebrew word, רקיע, rakija, means an expansion or extension.[147] For it was by an expansion or a certain extension that air was made from water. God called that airy expansion heaven when he commanded it to separate the waters from the waters, the rain waters from the waters that lay upon the earth. The waters that are above the heavens are vaporous waters hanging "above the mountains" in the clouds, and even the psalmist teaches this in Psalm 103, to which reference has been made. Therefore, water, although it is like a form in respect to the earth, nevertheless, supplies matter to higher elements and from those vice versa, it gains its formal force.

Fourth, it is settled that the earth was made before the sky. Moses first mentioned heaven out of respect (Gen. 1), but elsewhere he first mentions earth,

---

[144] No, water is *mayim* and heaven is *shamayim*. The similarity is a shear coincidence. Servetus does not follow even Maimondes who unequivocally stated that "God has brought the world into being out of nothing without there having been a temporal beginning." Also he interpreted the term "earth" used by the Genesis as meaning "the four elements." (*Guide*, Part II, cap. XXX).

[145] Ps. 103:2 : "You stretch out the heavens like a tent,"

[146] 2 Sam. 22:8 : "Then the earth reeled and rocked; the foundations of the heavens trembled and quaked, because he was angry." Job 26:11 : "The pillars of heaven tremble, and are astounded at his rebuke."

[147] Isa. 40:22 : "who stretches out the heavens like a curtain." There is no reference to extension of heavens in Jeremiah 50. The term *"rakiya"* means "extended surface, expanse." Hence it was used to designate the vault of heaven or firmament, which Hebrews regarded as solid and supporting waters located above it. Maimonides, *Guide*, Part II, cap. XXX, maintained that it was homonymous with *shamayim*, though its real meaning was different, conforming with the meaning "firmament of heaven" of Gen. 1:17 and 1:20.

saying, "When God made the earth and the heavens" (Gen. 2).[148] Likewise, based on the first chapter, it is certain that the firmament which is heaven itself was made after the earth. The center is by nature prior to the circumference. The Hebrews teach this: God first established the earth like someone making a circle, who, after fixing the center, then measures the circumference as Solomon said in Proverbs 8.[149] Psalm 101 follows the same opinion; David said to God, "You fixed the earth first, and the heavens are the work of your hands." In Proverbs 3 Solomon says, "The Lord with his wisdom founded the earth, and with his prudence he built the heavens."[150] In Isaiah 48 God says, "My hand founded the earth, and my right will measure the heavens."[151] In all these texts wherever the earth is sent to the fore, it is placed as the foundation. If heaven was made from water, it immediately follows that water is prior to heaven, and, therefore, earth as well because it was created at the same moment as water.[152] [157]

Fifth follows the exposition of what Paul said: "the third heaven is divine."[153] Heaven was created two-fold, and the third was not created. In the beginning God created two heavens as the noun in the dual, שמים, indicates. We accept that there are literally two heavens: the airy and the watery. In accordance with this meaning, Moses shows that these are the two heavens: the airy firmament and the region of waters.[154] He does not say anything about the angels there. Nevertheless, because the creation of the angels is contained in that passage, to some extent heaven can be called heaven of the angels, the chorus of the angels for

---

[148] Gen. 1:1 and 2:1.

[149] Prov. 8:23 : "Ages ago I was set up, at the first, before the beginning of the earth." For support of the argument that the earth was created before the rest of things.

[150] Ps. 101:25; Prov. 3:19.

[151] Isa. 48:13.

[152] One can observe in these paragraphs emphasis which Servetus puts on the central position of the earth in accordance with the geocentric doctrine propagated by Christianity.

[153] 2 Cor. 12:2 : "I know a person in Christ who fourteen years ago was caught up to the third heaven."

[154] The Hebrew word *shamayim* is in the dual form, but it is not used or understood in this sense. Rather like other words in this form is understood as plural different from the classic Arabic which preserved the dual forms. This situation occurs even in the case of parts of the body. Thus

they are the heavenly or ethereal substance in which there is the throne of God, the seat of God and the cherubim and seraphim. In this way Peter in Clement also explains the second heaven, calling the first heaven that which is apparent being both airy and watery. Christ agrees with this opinion when he teaches that heaven "was opened" when the angels, who are called the heavenly host, came down.[155] Peace was made in this heaven when Christ came and Satan fell from it like a lightening bolt. Therefore, whether by "heaven" you mean the entire firmament that is seen upwards or the crown of angels, being manifold, heaven is both. Everything that was created, and the angels too, is comprehended by the words, "heavens and earth," especially because all creatures are either of heaven or of earth. This is likewise indicated by the particle את, which is made of the first and last letters like the α and the ω; it is a particle that comprehends the whole when *he*, the demonstrative article, has been employed. In other words, it is as if the ancient author had said, "In the beginning God created the entire heavens and the entire earth and whatever is contained in them." That is how God explained the creation of everything in Exodus 20.[156] Hence according to chapter 2 of Genesis the armies of the angels are comprehended in the creation of the two heavens just as even in Psalm 32: "The heavens were made by the Lord's Word, and so also was all the army of them by the spirit of His mouth."[157] It is a fact that two heavens are indicated there besides the angels who are the ornaments of heaven as Job said in chapter 26.[158] Indeed, because the angels are the heavenly hosts and the ornaments of heaven, they obtain the name of heaven. Because of the fact that they are a particular substance resembling the heavenly airy substance, they were also

---

the base of the Servetus's speculation is shaky.

[155] Pseudo-Clement of Rome, *Recognitiones*, lib. I, cap. XXVII (PG I, 1222). Matt. 3:16; John 1:51.

[156] Exod. 20:11 : "For in six days the LORD made heaven and earth, the sea, and all that is in them," etc. *Aleph* and *Thav* are the first and the last letters of the Hebrew alphabet. Because both are in the article, Servetus arbitrarily interprets the saying "heavens and earth" as meaning to include everything that is in them.

[157] Ps. 32:6. The text mentions the "host of heavens" not the "host of angels."

[158] Job 26:13 : "By his wind the heavens were made fair."

simultaneously [158] created through the breathing of God as is gathered in the passages cited.

Now the third heaven is the heaven of divinity that lies beyond all these, being the inaccessible light in which the Father dwells, and it is called "the heaven of heavens."[159] Paul was taken into this third heaven. Christ dwells in this third heaven, and from him the angels, being far inferior, take their splendor inasmuch as they see only as much as is given to them through Christ. This glowing, fiery heaven is the lightening bolt of the Word, the universal exemplar of things, the divinity itself that is made accessible through Christ, just as God, who is in Himself invisible, has through Christ been made visible also to the angels (1 Tim. 3).[160] The angels used to see God under a veil as Isaiah teaches in chapter 6.[161] Up to this point there remains another most absolute means of vision, being after the final resurrection, when we shall see God as He is in a most withdrawn light that has never been seen by anyone, but by Christ alone, nor even by the angels themselves nor by the blessed souls. Up to this point the good angels are more to be blessed with us, just as the evil ones are more to be punished. Because these things exceed the present state and every human mind, we may return to those which have already been established through Christ.

Let us ponder God in the Word and the heaven which is within us. Christ has joined this heaven to us by making us kings in it so that we may reign among the heavenly. Hence the "kingdom of the heavens" is mentioned everywhere. This "third heaven" is truly one of fire, the other two being airy and watery with some participation of fire. Moses did not remember the "third heaven" in the creation just as he left out fire itself because of the great reason of the mystery. Paul mentioned the third heaven with great emphasis when he spoke about such

---

[159] This is a very common expression : 1 Kings 8:27; Deut. 10:14; Ps. 67:33, etc. 1 Tim. 6:16 : "It is he alone who has immortality and dwells in unapproachable light."

[160] 1 Tim. 3:16 : "He was revealed in flesh, vindicated in spirit, seen by angels, proclaimed among Gentiles."

[161] In a vision of Isa. 6:2 the seraphim were covering their faces and feet with the wings.

arcana.[162] Moses did not mention the fire in the creation at that time because the other elements combined with light itself were sufficient for the propagation of things because by a certain property fire is there where there are its material and light. We shall add another reason when we talk about Adam's sin, which fire's vengeance followed. There is even another reason: because the Jews did not know that the regeneration of Christ and his true fire were of the spirit.[163] The fire was [159] yet "to be sent unto earth" by Christ, a fire that would renew the old world.[164] For this same reason, Moses did not mention "the third heaven." "The third heaven" lacked a particular space, but "it is within us" and, like fire, it penetrates everything. The type of this "third heaven" is this fire which does not have a particular space like the other elements. Its space is where it has fuel, without which it cannot survive. Fire is among other elements so that, as it acts in them, it purifies them and raises them upwards to heaven on account of the power of the heavenly light in the light airy substance. Fire renews, purifies, and transforms everything; it is unable to be contaminated because it is always pure.

Based on the foregoing there is a sixth inference: water, air, and fire have another heavenly material that is distinct from earthly material. Among the Hebrews, Rabbi Eliezer the Elder once taught this. After him Rabbi Moses the Egyptian said that it was a "secret of secrets," it was the "arcana of the arcana of the Law," which the greater of Israel's wise men made known.[165]

---

[162] On the contrary, Maimonides teaches that in the story of the Genesis are mentioned four elements, including fire and not only implicated in the earth (Guide, Part II, XXX).

[163] Servetus describes the Jews as "animales Iudaei," an expression which is linked to the expression animalis homo in 1 Cor. 2:14, 15:44.

[164] Luke 12:49 : ""I came to bring fire to the earth, and how I wish it were already kindled!"

[165] Maimonides in his Guide, Part II, chap. XXVI wrote: "I have seen a statement of Rabbi Eliezer the Great, figuring in the celebrated Chapters (Peraquim in Hebrew) known as Chapters of Rabbi Eliezer, which is the strangest statement I have seen made by one who follows the law of Moses our Master ... He says : 'Wherefrom were the heavens created? From the light of His garment. He took some of it, stretched it like a cloth, and thus they were extending continually, as it is said: 'Who coverest Thyself with light as with a garment. Who stretches out the heavens like a curtain.' [Ps. 103:2] Wherefrom was the earth created? From the snow under the throne of His glory. He took some of it and threw it, as it is said: 'For He saith to the snow, Be thou earth.' [Job 57:6]" Maimonides after analysis of other similar passages in the Torah interprets them

I shall now demonstrate the same thing by many arguments because it is a subject that is unknown to all the philosophers and is connected with the knowledge of Christ. First: the material of the heavenly beings is one thing, that of the earthly something else. The creation of the earth and the permanent separation of heaven from earth prove this. The material of the earth was created there separately by God as was the material of water, and the atmosphere and entire heaven were made from the material of the water. Second: Christ's very generation proves this because it shows that there is an infinite distinction between those elements. For there are in Christ the three higher elements from the substance of the Father. Just as our paternal seed is watery, being full of airy and fiery spirit, so in Christ that cloud of God's oracle, being, as it were, watery, airy, and fiery, was the natural dew of Christ's generation that contained nothing earthly in it. In sum, in a fetus there is nothing earthly from the father, but from the mother as we shall show at greater length later.[166] Third: the meaning of the Hebrew word, שמים,

---

figuratively as "the prophetic vision of the true reality of the inferior first matter. And he concludes "Thus Rabbi Eliexer ... made it clear – I mean the fact that there are two matters, a high and an inferior one, and that the matter of the universe is not one. This is a great mystery, and do not think disdainfully of the fact that the greatest sages of Israel have made a clear statement about it. For it is one of the mysteries of being and a mystery of mysteries of the Torah." And later Maimonides repeats that Rabbi Eliezer wanted to say "the matter of everything that is on earth – I mean to say, of everything that is beneath the sphere of the moon – is one common matter, and that the matter of all the heavens and of what is in them is another matter and not the same as the one just mentioned." On the basis of such statements Servetus develops his own original doctrine of the creation of the universe and its nature.

[166] *Nihil in faetibus est a patre terreum, sed a matre.* Servetus's physiological theory was not objected to during the trial in Geneva. That theory is more complete than that of Aristotle and Galen in which the efficient cause of generation of the embryo is the masculine element, active; the feminine element, passive was limited to supplying the material for the embryo (Aristotle, *De generatione animalium*, I,18; II,3. Galen in *De foetus formatione* and in *De semine* admits formal and material causality of both the elements). According to Servetus the material is the element earth, coming from the mother. The other three come form the father. In Geneva objection to the Servetus theory was on the theological grounds, namely to its divine application that these three elements come from the substance of God in the generation of Christ. Servetus replied to this objection that "*Id item concedo, si utlimum* [i.e., substance of God] *de paternis elementis intelligas, dictum ob idealem eorum in Deo rationem.*" (*Sententiae vel propositiones excerptae ex libris Michaelis Serveti, XV; Michaelis Serveti responsio ad articulos Ioannis Calvini.* In *Defensio orthodoxae fidei de Sacra Trinitate* p. 502, 516 ; Robert-M. Kingdon, *Registres de la Compagnie des Pasteurs de Genève au temps de Calvin* (Genève : Librairie E. Droz, 1962, p. 33).

shows this for the heavens are said to be from water.[167] Moreover, the heavens have nothing [160] earthly; therefore, neither does water. Fourth: the other cited scriptures prove that the substance of heaven is watery and not earthly. Fifth: they prove the difference of the elements, which, being from the heavenly generation out of the three elements, we shall discuss in the books on baptism. For in baptism we are generated anew from "water, spirit, and fire" (Matt. 3, Luke 3, and John 3) so that through these we are made heavenly, although, having been born from the earth, we were previously earthly.[168] Sixth: this is proven by what we will say about the soul, in which are found the three higher elements. Seventh: this is proven by reason of the three heavens from which, after the manner of the three elements, the earth is always excluded. Eighth: the holy spirit, like heaven too, is indicated in scripture through the three higher elements; moreover, it is never indicated by earth, which is always contrary to heaven and spirit, just as the earthly is always contrary to the heavenly, and the carnal to the spiritual. Ninth: pure water can disappear entirely into a vaporous and airy spirit as if upwards into heaven. Earth, however, never does anything, but revert to ash, and it ever tends downward. Hence, Isaiah in chapter 51: "Sky dissolves into smoke, and earth into dust." In Ecclesiasticus 40 it says that what is of the earth, returns to the earth, and what is of water, returns to water.[169] Tenth: water was created with its splendor, but earth was without form. Eleventh: earth resists light and, like a dark demon, is unable to hold light. The co-mingling, however, of the other elements transforms it and makes it shine. Twelfth: earth is unable to hold both sound and spirit, but not so the other three elements. Thirteenth: earth alone is cursed as to Adam and is given as a source of food to the serpent. Fourteenth: based on the experiments of chemists it is plainly shown that earthly matter is always separate

---

[167] Compare notes 144 and 154.

[168] Matt. 3:11; Luke 3:16 : "He will baptize you with the Holy Spirit and fire." John 1:33 : "'He on whom you see the Spirit descend and remain is the one who baptizes with the Holy Spirit.'"

[169] Isa. 51:6 : "For the heavens will vanish like smoke, the earth will wear out like a garment." Ecclcus. 40:11 : "All that is of earth returns to earth, and what is from above returns above."

from other matter. Fifteenth: experience alone proves this proposition in all other respects because there has never been any observation of earth being turned into water or of water being turned into earth, no matter how you mix the two. For it is always the case that whichever one you choose, reverts to its origin. Because the followers of Averroes do not understand this, they say that all elements retain their integrity [161] in mixtures because the two materials have remained within them.

Now let us conclude that there are four bases for natural things: two being material and two being formal. The material ones are the two matters already mentioned: earth and water. The formal are solar light that heats and dries, and watery splendor that chills and moistens. Thus the four are called "primary qualities" and "four elements." But it is in two elements alone that there are the origins and excellences of qualities.[170] The basic qualities in fire are hot and dry; in water they are cold and moist. Of these there are in heaven two heavenly sources of heat: the Sun and the Moon. The light of fire is almost like that of the Sun, heating and drying; that of water is chilling and dampening, and the Moon has this property too because it has been given a power that is opposite to the Sun. The power of day has been given to the Sun, the power to heat and dry. To the Moon has been given the power of night, the power to chill and moisten through the absence of the Sun and by a certain inborn splendor of water, which it has. To this power are even added the properties of the other parts of heaven and stars. The Earth was created in itself without moderate temperature. Moreover, emerged from the waters, it was formed by light, dried out, and for that reason is called dry. In addition, because of its density, it powerfully retains from the waters an impressed cold. Therefore, the substantive form of the earth, as of all things which result from a mixture, derives from the splendor of water and heavenly light. The air as well is nearly devoid of the qualities in itself. For, after it was produced from water by a process of evaporation, it retained its cold and moist disposition

---

[170] There seems to be a certain incoherence with the previous statement in which Servetus defined only light as the formal element.

whereby through its blowing it chills even our natural property of warmth. But evaporation occurs from that which is hot, by which even the air quite easily heats up and is dried especially in the drying of the soil when it is scattered by the north wind.[171]

Finally, based on the foregoing, the ancient view is proved: all things are one, because all things are one in God, in whom, as the One, they exist. All things are one Trismegistus teaches throughout in the *Asclepius* and *To His Son, Tatius*. Melissus said that this totality of things was in the unchangeable and infinite One.[172] All other things that are mutable are reduced to this immutable One in the following manner. [162] Qualities or accidental forms, make one form with the prior form. Whatever derives from light, comes together with light into one. Whether it is heat or color or any other form, that would come to the body when it has been formed by light; it comes together into one with the prior form, with the very light which is the mother of forms. Thus the knowledge which is acquired by the soul comes together with the soul into one light; likewise, spirits come to one with the Spirit. All individual things come together into one with the Spirit and the light; the Spirit and the light are one in God; therefore, other things are also one in Him in accordance with a certain universal norm.[173] The forms of things, in which the things themselves exist as in the one being, are one in God, and in this way they make other things exist as one with God in the shadow of this truth, by which

---

[171] These are the views of nature representing the common knowledge at the time of Servetus.

[172] The fundamental affirmation of Parmenides of Elea (ca 510-ca 460 B.C.E.) was: Τὸ παρὰ τὸ ὄν οὐκ ὄν, τὸ οὐκ ὄν οὐδέν, ἓν ἄρα τὸ ὄν (praeter ens nihil, non ens nihil, ergo unum esse ens) (in Diels, ThO 7). Such a monistic view of Parmenides was understood by Plato (*Theaetetus*, 180b) and by Aristotle (*Metaph.*, I,5: 986b29). Parmenides is the representative of the Eleatic school of philosophy. He followed Xenophanes, his teacher, and Melissus of Samos (ca 470-ca 400) is his disciple. This affirmation is strongly confirmed in *Corpus Hermeticum, Asclepius* I : "All things are one, and the One is all things, seeing that all things were in the Creator before he created them. And rightly has it been said of him that he is all things; for all things are part of him."

[173] This universal norm is *Lux, mater formarum*. This transcendental unity which is expressed by Servetus does not affect the ontological order of things but only the formal because *rerum ideae, in quibus res ipse in esse uno consistunt, sunt unum in Deo*. Thus in spite of his Parmenidean orientation Servetus cannot be accused of being a pantheist.

Christ without mediation hypostatically is one with God.

One ought always to remember that in all things there are analogies to the very head, Christ. Likewise, always remember that there are various modes of the divinity as well as subordinations.[174] Therefore, the opinion of Parmenides and Melissus about the unique basis will be true in this way. Xenophanes, the teacher of Parmenides, plainly made this declaration when he said that the one basis is God.[175] Anaximander also said that there is a single, infinite basis for everything else. Democritus and Anaxagoras said that the substance of many bases was one, but that the forms were diverse. All these men knew the teaching of Trismegistus, that it concerned divine forms, and which was very near the truth, but Aristotle was unaware of it.[176]

Single is the basis, single the light of the Word;

pantomorphous is the light, as it is the head of everything;

Jesus Christ, our Lord, is the basis of God's creatures.

---

[174] Servetus again expresses his two principles: everything exists in analogy to Christ (*analogia ad caput ipsum Christum*) and everything is explained by various modes and subordinations of the divinity (*varios divinitatis modos et subordinationes*).

[175] Τὸ γὰρ ἓν τοῦτο καὶ πᾶν τὸν θεὸν (*unum et omne deum*) (in Diels, ThO 5).

[176] Servetus shows an excellent knowledge of the pre-Socratic philosophers : the ἄπειρον of Anaximander (610-547), the Νοῦς of Anaxagoras, and the πλῆρες (*plenum*) and σχήματα (atoms and their arrangements) of Democritus (472-370). He commits an error, however, assuming the antiquity of Trismegistus. He decidedly follows the Platonic doctrines and rejects the metaphysics of Aristotle.

On the Divine Trinity

Book Five

In Which

the Holy Spirit is Treated

We have postponed our discussion of the holy spirit until the hypostasis of the Word that was exposed by the utterance was known because at this point we shall make a discourse pertaining constantly to the Word with the intent of acknowledging the Spirit in the Word. Inasmuch as God's essence, to the extent that it is manifest to the world, is the Word, so, to the extent that it is communicated to the world, it is the Spirit, and the communication is connected with the manifestation. Inasmuch as there was in the Word the created man's primal form, so in the Spirit there was the created spirit's primal form. There was the Spirit in the archetype as a sure model of the breath, cohering for ever and ever in God, and, so to speak, coming forth from there. The Spirit was coming forth with the Word; by speaking, God was breathing. The substance of the Word and the Spirit was the same, but the mode was different. [1]

There are several analogies to this, if you first acknowledge this fact: being great, God, who is conformed in essence to all creatures and exhibited by them,

---

[1] The expressions used by Servetus *"idea princeps creati hominis"* and *"idea princeps creati spiritus"* do not refer to humans and to the human spirit in general but to the human Christ and his created spirit, which are, respectively, manifestation and communication of the Word and Spirit of God, that is God's substance understood as the Word and the Spirit without being two distinct trinitarian Persons, though they still represent the same essence or substance in the traditional sense. They represent only a different mode (*modus diversus*), God's essence manifested and God's essence communicated to the world.

has conformed Himself all the more to man and thereby exhibited Himself in essence through the Word and Spirit. For this reason the image of God's Word and Spirit was from the beginning our own word and spirit or our speech and respiration.[2] The spirit is in our speech, and the spirit actually does not differ from speech save in the manner of its dispensation, as with God. If by the power of God it should happen that, as I am speaking, you see a man in my voice, you would see the very thing which the expression itself indicates; you would say that there was in my visible speech the invisible spirit that is perceptible through hearing. You would also say that in the spirit was the word, located in spiritual substance. In the same manner the Spirit was in God's Word; [164] in the Spirit was His Word: a visible Word; a perceptible Spirit. Just as man was in God, so in God was man's Spirit. The entire mystery of the Word and the Spirit was Christ's shining glory. By breathing Christ, God breathed everything through him and filled everything, thereby already manifesting the fullness of His own Spirit.[3]

A second analogy to God's Word and Spirit is this: The image of that heavenly Word or of the oracular cloud is the elemental cloud that is a wind's substance which wholly passes everywhere with the wind. In this way God was the Word and the Spirit distributing variously the Word and the Spirit into the body and soul.

A third analogy for this is the seed of paternity, which is the spirit's substance, just as in Christ there was from the one divinity the seed of the Word and the substance of the Spirit. Scripture teaches these analogies; even the nature

---

[2] Servetus employs as synonyms the terms *verbum* and *sermo*, as well as *spiritus* and *halitus*. *Verbum* is the Word, pronounced announcement, speech; *Spiritus* is the breath or the breathed air. This correlation is a basis for further elaborations of Servetus's doctrine.

[3] The phrase used by Servetus, *Totum verbi et spiritus arcanum* ...was listed by Calvin in addition to the statements from *De Trinitatis erroribus*, lib II, p. 66v, as number six among the thirty eight errors of Servetus during the trial in Geneva. Servetus was accused of confusing the Persons of the Trinity to which he answered, *"... non potuisse confundi ea quae non erant separate,"* and *"Totum verbi et spiritus arcanum dico fuisse ad Christi gloriam, quia in eo est tota verbi et spiritus plenitudo."* (*Calvini Opera*, VIII, pp. 502, 515).

of things teaches them by bringing us from the creatures to the creator.[4] What is surprising, if God thus conformed Himself to man, when has He been conformed to all creatures? That pantomorphous essence conforms itself to us in the Spirit's essence. This pantomorphous essence was able to show itself as whatever sort it wished.

The display that holds the breathing, the Word that was uttered by breathing, truly was the Word that reflected in the cloud, was the seed of Christ's conception, holding the Spirit substantively within itself. Light is always considered common to the Word and the Spirit. The cloud of God's Word and Spirit was in its own internal substance the archetype of this other watery and airy cloud; and was a cloud, glowing as if of fire. This is entirely in one substance just as the three elements possess one first substance that is corporeal, spiritual, and shining. According to one mode of dispensation, this substance of the elemental cloud is a tangible, solid body; according to another, it is the blowing of the wind in the same substance that always possesses an innate light. According to one mode, God appeared in a cloud as the Word; according to another, He was breathing there, yet, according to both, He was always light, truly without deception. According to one mode, there was the Word in the flesh [165]; according to another, there was the Spirit in the soul; yet, according to both, there was always Light, truly substantively.[5]

Just as God was the Word, the Spirit, and the Light in the cloud, so now

---

[4] This illustrates the methodological approach of Servetus: biblical statements are the primary source and criteria of truth, empirical observation follows next as a naturalistic confirmation of the biblical original data, and the last are the philological analyses and the support found in the philosophical systems of various schools.

[5] This text presents Light as one of the substantive modes of God, equal to the Word and Spirit. But it is interesting to note that Light was always common to the other two modes of God : *Lux semper communis consideratur verbo et spiritui.* Servetus relates these three modes of divine existence with the three superior elements in accordance with the ancient cosmological theory: the cloud of the Word with water, the air or breath with the Spirit, the fire with the Light. Moreover, they are related to the body and soul of Christ, both of which are unique substantive modes of divine manifestation. That God is essentially fire and light we find in the Old Testament texts and this idea is taken up by the Hermetic literature. John also gives us to understand that the Word was the Light in God (John 1:1-9).

He is the Word, the Spirit, and the Light in Christ. In Christ God brought all those things together hypostatically and substantively, in the flesh and in the spirit. God joined His own uncreated Light with the created light in Christ, and there was one form just as from a solar and watery light we have said that one form is made. Also it is to the higher elements of the world's archetype that the lower are substantively joined in the generation of the one Christ. Thus, summarily speaking, a recapitulation of everything is gathered in Christ. The very body of Christ came into existence by mixing together the divine Word as the dew of Christ's conception with these created elements and earth through the action of God's Spirit. By implanting and coalescing the divine and human breath in his soul, the one hypostasis of his spirit, which is the hypostasis of the holy spirit, came into existence, making clear the true hypostasis of the holy spirit, which was always the divine breath.[6] The same Light was common both to the body and to the spirit, and it glorified the human elements that were taken up from Mary, in the one hypostasis with God. Thus you see how all things are one in Christ.

Notice that although the Word, the Spirit, and the Light can be the same in the archetype, and the same cloud can be watery, airy, and fiery, nevertheless, in Genesis the Word and the Spirit were mentioned before the Light; the water and the air were mentioned before fire. God used the dispensations of Word and Spirit before light appeared (Gen. 1) because the light of Christ had to be manifested later. Water and Spirit were mentioned there, not fire, which would soon come into being from light and Spirit. The Jews knew of two heavens, the watery and the airy, but not of a third, the fiery, which exists within us. With the Jews there was no rebirth "from water, spirit, and fire" through baptism. Christ, being the light of the world, exposed the true Light to us, which had been hidden from the Jews. Therefore, the fact that fire was omitted by Moses and that fire was sent to us, is not without mystery.[7] [166] The fact that God used the dispensations of

---

[6] This text was equally objected to by Calvin. Compare note 166 in Book IV.
[7] See notes 162 and 168, Book IV.

Word and Spirit before He manifested light, is not without mystery. God always gave man His Word and Spirit, but not His manifested Light. Through Word God then manifested Himself to man, and through Spirit He imparted Himself as if at that time He were hiding Christ's light. God did all those things through Christ, "who was then with God" in Word, Spirit, and hidden Light; who, when he later came, gave us rebirth through his speech and spirit, exposing his light itself and illuminating us with it so that the greatness of Christ's glory and his grace towards us would be apparent. To the extent that in the first generation God gave Word and Spirit to man before other living things, so later by means of His Word and Spirit He gave us rebirth through the gospel in the image of Christ, who was conceived by the holy spirit through the Word of God. Using from the very beginning these two dispensations, God created bodies with the Word, and by the Spirit He made them live just as "the heavens were made by His Word, and all their powers were made by His Spirit."[8] The matter of men was created by His Word, and the soul was introduced by His Spirit. At the resurrection, too, the body's parts are joined by God's Word or voice, and the soul is introduced by His Spirit (Ezek. 37).[9] Thus God distinguished these things, and thus we distinguish them. The functioning, dispensations, and modes of the Word and of the Spirit, which were the same thing as God, were once of this sort. Later through Christ, when the mysteries of God had been revealed, a broader distinction appeared on account of the divinity's richer manifestation; likewise, on account of additional things appearing in the body of flesh and in the created spirit. Through Christ the creature was joined to the Creator; the integrated matter was mixed and united with Him both in the flesh and in the spirit, being hypostatically one with God. This is the great mystery and our substantial union with the Father through the son!

---

[8] Servetus refers to the text of Ps. 32:6 but he manipulates the text adjusting it to his context. Previously he interpreted the text as meaning *exercitus eorum* (army of them), now he uses the original Latin text *virtus eorum*. Compare note 157, Book IV.

[9] In a vision of the dry bones : "Thus says the Lord GOD to these bones: I will cause breath to enter you, and you shall live" (Ezek. 37:6).

Moreover, we have already shown somewhere near the end of Book One against Lombard that the Spirit's dispensation was the same thing as God, not a third, metaphysical entity, and now we are going to demonstrate it again thus. For, just as God is said to have made through Himself [167] what He made with the Word, because "God was the Word," so, because "God is the Spirit," what scripture relates as done through His Spirit, it relates as done through God Himself. Just as the "holy spirit spoke," so "God spoke through the mouth of the saints and prophets" (Acts 3 and Heb. 1).[10] Therefore, what belongs to the domain of the holy spirit, is attributed to God Himself in terms of a particular mode. To receive the holy spirit is to receive power from on high by the attendance of a heavenly messenger (Luke 24; Acts 1).[11] The holy spirit is God's anointing; "God Himself anoints us," and "God is the Spirit" (2 Cor. 1 and 3).[12] When he says that the Spirit of God is in us, the apostle teaches that God Himself is the holy spirit in us because God said, "I shall dwell in them," and because he said, "you will be the temple of God," (1 Cor. 3 and 6; and 2 Cor. 6) or "the dwelling place of God in the holy spirit" (Eph. 2 and Isa. 57).[13] Whoever despises God, despises us "because He gave His Spirit in us" (1 Thes. 4). "Who lies to the holy spirit, lies not to men, but God" (Acts 5).[14] Likewise, that the holy spirit is a mode of divinity, and that his is the dispensation in and through Christ is proven by the fact that it is called "Christ's spirit" and "the son's spirit" (1 Pet. 1 and Gal. 4). Likewise, in Romans chapter 8 "God's Spirit dwells in you, and, if anyone does not have the spirit of Christ, he does not belong to him. But, if his spirit is the spirit of the

---

[10] John 4:24 : "God is spirit." Acts 3:18 : "In this way God fulfilled what he had foretold through all the prophets." Heb. 1:1 : "Long ago God spoke to our ancestors in many and various ways by the prophets."
[11] Luke 24:49 : "So stay here in the city until you have been clothed with power from on high." Acts 1:8 : "But you will receive power when the Holy Spirit has come upon you."
[12] 2 Cor. 1:21-22 : "But it is God who ... has anointed us, by putting his seal on us and giving us his Spirit." 2 Cor. 3:17: "Now the Lord is the Spirit."
[13] 1 Cor. 3:16, 6:19. 2 Cor. 6:16. Eph. 2:22. Isa. 57:15.
[14] 1 Thes. 4:8 : "Therefore whoever rejects this rejects not human authority but God, who also gives his Holy Spirit to you." Acts 5:3-4.

Father, who raised Jesus, etc."[15]

Because of these words, obviously speaking metaphysically about an invisible, real Son, Hilary in Book 2 and Book 8 of *On the Trinity* said that through the Holy Spirit sometimes the Father, sometimes the Son, sometimes a third entity was indicated.[16] In the beginning of his *Dialogues*, Athanasius made similar references to the threefold spirit of those three entities.[17] But, as far as I am concerned, everything is easy enough without metaphysical entities such as the fact that God's Spirit is said to be increased or diminished and, so to speak, divided, as God said to Moses, "I shall separate or split from your spirit, and from that I shall share with seventy men." Again later, "Separating or departing from the spirit, which was in Moses, and giving it to seventy men" (Num. 11).[18] Without diminution of this a portion of the spirit was given to him through the mode of divine distribution. This partition, augmentation, and diminution of God's spirit [168] must be accepted, we say, according to the modes of divinity, and also according to what was joined thereto, and which is truly divided. The division of

[15] 1 Pet. 1:11; Gal. 4:6; Rom. 8:10-11 : "But if Christ is in you, though the body is dead because of sin, the Spirit is life because of righteousness. If the Spirit of him who raised Jesus from the dead dwells in you, he who raised Christ from the dead will give life to your mortal bodies also through his Spirit that dwells in you."

[16] Hilary, *De Trinitate*, lib. II, 29 discuses the issue in a little different light : "Concerning the Holy Spirit I ought not to be silent, and yet I have no need to speak; still, for the sake of those who are in ignorance, I cannot refrain. There is no need to speak, because we are bound to confess Him, proceeding, as He does, from Father and Son . For my own part, I think it wrong to discuss the question of His existence. He does exist, inasmuch as He is given, received, retained; He is joined with the Father and Son in our confession of the faith, and cannot be excluded from a true confession of Father and Son; take away a part, and the whole faith is marred." In lib. II. 30 he wrote: The reason, I believe, why certain people continue in ignorance or doubt is that they see this third Name, that of the Holy Spirit, often used to signify the Father or the Son. No objection need be raised to this; whether it be Father or Son, He is Spirit, and He is holy. And in lib. VIII, 25 : "Now I think that it ought to be clearly understood that God the Father is denoted by the Spirit of God, because our Lord Jesus Christ declared that the Spirit of the Lord was upon Him since He anoints Him and sends Him to preach the Gospel." (PL X, 44 and 231).

[17] Athanasius, *Dialogi de sacra Trinitate*, I, 14 : "The Father too is the holy spirit, but is not the spirit of God." And later he distinguishes the three divine hypostases. Thus Servetus considers only a part of the text.

[18] Num. 11:17 : "and I will take some of the spirit that is on you and put it on them;" and 11:25 : "Then the LORD came down in the cloud and spoke to him, and took some of the spirit that was on him and put it on the seventy elders."

the ministries and operations are according to various dispensations (1 Cor. 12). That "the spirit was greater in Daniel than in others" is stated according to the dispensation (Dan. 6). Likewise, that the apostles were on more occasions "filled with the holy spirit" (Acts 2 and 4).[19] To give God's Spirit is the same as saying, "I shall give heart, understanding, and mind to them." Wisdom was given to Solomon, and it was the holy spirit, the spirit of wisdom. The spirit of wisdom, counsel, knowledge, piety, and other gifts is being given.

Not only on account of such a gift, but also because of the fact alone that He breathes our soul into us is it said that God gives us His Spirit (Gen. 2 and 6).[20] Our soul is a certain lamp of God (Prov. 20).[21] It is like a spark of God's Spirit, an image of God's wisdom, created, to be sure, but most like that spiritual wisdom and placed within it, having an inborn luminescence of divinity, a spark of that primary wisdom, and the very spirit of divinity. The spirit of divinity is placed within man, even after Adam's sin, so testifies God Himself in chapter 6, already mentioned. The dispensation of our own life is given and sustained through grace by His breath as Job said in chapters 10, 32, and other subsequent passages.[22] God breathed a soul into Adam's nostrils together with one airy blast, and for that reason he depends on it (Isa. 2 and Ps. 103).[23] God Himself sustains for us with His own spirit the breath of life by "giving a blast of air to the people who are on earth, and spirit to those who tread upon it," so that we may live, move, and exist

---

[19] 1 Cor. 12:5; Dan. 6:3; Acts 2:4 and 4:31.
[20] Gen. 2:7 : "Then the LORD God formed man from the dust of the ground, and breathed into his nostrils the breath of life." Gen 7:22 (and not 6 as Servetus says) : "everything on dry land in whose nostrils was the breath of life died."
[21] Prov. 20:27 : "The human spirit is the lamp of the LORD, searching every inmost part."
[22] Job 10:3 : "Does it seem good to you to oppress, to despise the work of your hands and favor the schemes of the wicked?" Job 32:8 : "But truly it is the spirit in a mortal, the breath of the Almighty, that makes for understanding." Job 33:4 : "The spirit of God has made me, and the breath of the Almighty gives me life." Job 34:14-15 . "If he should take back his spirit to himself, and gather to himself his breath, all flesh would perish together, and all mortals return to dust."
[23] Isa. 2:22 : "Turn away from mortals, who have only breath in their nostrils, for of what account are they?" Ps. 103:29 : "When you hide your face, they are dismayed; when you take away their breath, they die and return to their dust."

in Him (Isa. 42 and Acts 17).[24] Because God brings wind from the four winds and a gust from the four gusts, corpses are brought back to life (Ezek. 37). From the airy blast itself God introduces at that point souls into men, in whom was inborn the life of breathed air. Hence in Hebrew the word, "soul," indicates the same thing as the word, "breathing."[25] From air God, by introducing air with the soul itself, introduces the soul and a spark of divinity itself, which fills the air. The statement of Orpheus is true: "The soul is carried by the winds, and it enters from the whole by the act of breathing" as [169] Aristotle cites in his book *On the Soul.*[26]

Ezekiel teaches that the soul possesses something from the elementary substance, and God Himself teaches that the soul possesses something from the substance of blood. This matter I shall more thoroughly explain here so that you may understand that the substance of the created spirit of Christ has been joined in essence to the very substance of the holy Spirit. I call the air "spirit" because there is no other specialized word for atmosphere in the holy tongue. In fact, the thing indicates that the divine breath exists in the atmosphere, which the Lord's Spirit fills.

In order that you may have a complete idea of the soul and the spirit, reader, at this point I shall add the divine philosophy, which you shall easily understand if you happen to be conversant in anatomy.[27] Because of the substance

---

[24] Isa. 42:5 : "Thus says God, ... who ... gives breath to the people upon it and spirit to those who walk in it." Acts 17:28 : "For 'In him we live and move and have our being.'"

[25] Ezek. 37:9 : "Then he said to me, 'Prophesy to the breath, prophesy, mortal, and say to the breath: Thus says the Lord GOD: Come from the four winds, O breath, and breathe upon these slain, that they may live.'" Ezek. 37:14 : "I will put my spirit within you, and you shall live." In Hebrew the soul is *nefesh* and the breath is *neshama.* Maimonides in his *Guide* Part I, chap. XLI explains that *nefesh* is a homonym which also means life, Gen. 1:3; blood, Deut. 12:23; reason, Jer. 38:16; immortal soul, 1 Sam. 25:29; also will in various Psalms. This meaning of the term *nefesh* as blood gave Servetus a good biblical support for his discovery of the circulation of blood which he subsequently reports in this book.

[26] Aristotle, *De anima* I, cap. 5: 410b 28. Servetus accepts this concept of the soul ignoring the critique which was presented by Aristotle (W. K. C. Guthrie, *Orpheus and Greek Religion, A Study of the Orphic Movement,* (Princeton, NJ: Princeton University Press, 1993), pp. 57-59.

[27] This paragraph is the beginning of the most famous text of the *Restitutio* which refers to the description of the lesser blood circulation, the only one which was translated into many languages and which was the subject of many studies. But many of the popular versions of this

of the three higher elements it is said that the spirit's substance within us is threefold, being natural, vital, and animal.[28] Aphrodiseus calls them the three spirits, but actually they are not three, but spirits made distinct, anew.[29] The vital

---

text are not only defective in translation and do not render the correct meaning of the Servetian text, but are also incomplete and do not reflect the entire thought of Servetus. For example, the English translation by Charles O'Malley in *Michael Servetus. A Translation of His Geographical, Medical and Astronomical notes* (Philadelphia: American Philosophical Society, 1953), pp. 202-208; the Spanish translation by José Barón Fernández, *Miguel Servet. Su vida y su obra* (Madrid: Espasa Calpe, 1970), pp. 167-168. The Servetus text which existed in manuscript form since at least 1546 (R. H. Bainton, "The Smaller Circulation: Servetus and Colombo," Sudhoffs Archive für Geschichte der Medizin, 14 (1931), 371-374) indicates the absolute priority of Servetus in the discovery of blood circulation. Moreover, G. H. Williams suggested (*The Radical Reformation*, Philadelphia: Westminster, 3 ed., 1974, p. 584) that the obscure phrases of Calvin in his *Psychopannichia*, were written under the influence of his acquaintance with Servetus in 1534, though it was published in 1542 and 1545, and contains a veiled allusion to the Servetian idea of blood circulation.

[28] Servetus picks up here the old Greek doctrine of the four elements which was postulated by Empedocles, Aristotle, Hippocrates, and Galen. The superior elements are air, water, and fire; the inferior one is earth. The Latin term *spiritus*, as well as the Greek term *pneuma* and the Hebrew term *ruach* mean breath or what is breathed in. It was an ancient concept that the vivifying factor was in the atmosphere and was breathed in causing the organisms to become alive. It was a good naturalistic observation, but the real meaning of breathing and the role of the atmosphere could be explained only when we discovered the oxidative processes in living organisms and the biochemical mechanisms for the utilization of oxygen, contained in the atmosphere (air). Thus the term *spirit* also means a certain dynamism, vibration, activity and action, especially of God's effect on humans. And this was the meaning of the term in the Hebrew Old Testament and the Greek New Testament. The substance of God in the Old Testament was fire. The term *spirit* in modern theology is not well defined and is used to describe the "stuff" of God or his action. Also in the concept of the divine Trinity it has a special meaning describing the third person of the Trinity as the Holy Spirit. Servetus preserves the term *spiritus* to describe the three dynamic forces or currents within the living organism: the natural spirit (*spiritus naturalis*) or blood which is related to water; the vital spirit or air (*spiritus vitalis*), which is inhaled and elaborated in the arterial blood with its subtle elements; the animal spirit (*spiritus animalis*) or heat or fire which is produced in the brain and nerves associated with the mind and mental functions.

[29] Alexander of Aphrodisias (fl. ca 198-211) was a Peripatetic philosopher and commentator. He continued the tradition of writing commentaries on Aristotle's work established in the first century BCE by Andronicus of Rhodes, the editor of Aristotle's writings, which were designed for use in his school only. This activity reflected a revival of interest in Aristotle's philosophy. Aristotle's philosophy became neglected in the second generation after his death and remained overshadowed by the Stoics, Epicureans, and Academic skeptics throughout the Hellenistic age. Andronicus' edition of what was to become the *Corpus Aristotelicum* consolidated this renewed interest in Aristotle's philosophy. Alexander became known as the exemplary commentator throughout later antiquity and the Middle Ages He is also the last strictly Aristotelian one since the later commentators were members of the Neoplatonist schools and were concerned to integrate Aristotle's thought into the Neoplatonist philosophical system. Alexander of Aphrodisias does not talk about the three spirits but about the three understandings: "active," the divine one; "natural," equivalent to the "potential" of the scholastics; "actual" or acquired,

spirit is that which is communicated through the anastomoses from arteries to veins, once located in which it is called natural spirit.[30] Therefore, the first is blood, the seat of which is in the liver and the body's veins. The second is the vital spirit, the seat of which is in the heart and the body's arteries. The third is the animal spirit, the seat of which, like a ray of light, is in the brain and the body's nerves. In all of these there is the energy of one Spirit and God's Light.[31] The formation of a human being in the womb teaches that the natural spirit is communicated from the heart to the liver. For an artery issues forth, being joined to a vein through the umbilical cord of the fetus itself;[32] likewise, afterwards in our bodies artery and vein are always joined together. Adam's soul was breathed by God into the heart before the liver, and it was communicated thence into the liver. Through inhalation into the mouth and nostrils the soul is truly drawn inwards; moreover, inhalation is directed towards the heart. The heart is the first life principle, the source of heat within the body.[33] From the liver it draws the fluid of life, like fuel, and in turn it gives it life, just as water's liquid quality provides fuel for higher elements, and by the addition of light it is made from them into a life-source for germination.[34] From the liver's blood comes the soul's fuel by an amazing process of refinement, [170]

factual understanding. This is his interpretation of the corresponding theory of Aristotle (*De anima* III, 4. 429) which he presented in a fragment entitled *De intellectu et intellecto* of the now lost book *De anima*. Aristotle differentiated two understandings or intellectual functions, the passive and the active. Galen was the one who admitted the three "spirits" or *"pneumas."*

[30] Thus arterial blood is the vital spirit and venous blood the natural spirit. By the term *anastomosis*, Galen understood as a certain connection through the filaments between the arteries and the veins which facilitated the exchange of blood and *pneuma* (*De usu partium*, IV, and VI, 10; ed. Helmreich, Leipzig, 1907, vol. I, 201 and 332. English translation by M. T. May, 1968, Cornell University Press, vol. I, 208 and 303).

[31] *Unius spiritus et lucis Dei energia:* the energy of the unique spirit and light of God which unifies the three "spirits" vivifying and activating the body. Thus they are one "spirit." This represents a logical conclusion from the radical monotheism of Servetus and its repercussion in his cosmology and psychology.

[32] *Per ipsius foetus umbilicum.*

[33] *Cor est primum vivens, fons caloris in medio corpore.*

[34] This is a very instructive and original comparison. L. Garcia Ballester in his book *Galeno* (Madrid, 1972, p. 108) makes the following conclusion relative to this fragment from Servetus: "According to the established analogy, the umbilical cord performs the function of the roots in plants."

which you shall presently hear. Hence the soul is said to exist in the blood, and the soul itself is blood or a bloody spirit. It is not said that the soul primarily exists in the heart's walls or in the very body of the brain or liver, but, as God Himself teaches in Genesis 9, Leviticus 17, and Deuteronomy 12, in the blood.[35]

As to this fact, one must first understand the substantive generation of the vital spirit itself, which is composed and nourished from inhaled air and the finest blood. The vital spirit has its origin in the heart's left ventricle with the lungs particularly assisting in the generation of it. It is a thin spirit, which is worked with the force of heat, of bright red color[36] and of such fiery power, as if it were a bright vapor rising from purer blood, and holding within itself the substance of water, air, and fire. It is generated as a result of a mixing process that has occurred in the lungs, of inhaled air with worked, fine blood, which the heart's right ventricle communicates to the left. Moreover, this communication does not take

---

[35] Gen. 9:4 : "Only, you shall not eat flesh with its life, that is, its blood." Lev. 17:11 : "For the life of the flesh is in the blood; and I have given it to you for making atonement for your lives on the altar; for, as life, it is the blood that makes atonement." Lev. 17:14 : "For the life of every creature – its blood is its life." Deut. 12:23 : "Only be sure that you do not eat the blood; for the blood is the life, and you shall not eat the life with the meat." It seems that the association of life with blood was a universal theme in various cultures and hence the practice of bloody human or animal sacrifices to a divinity as the expression of the highest level of submission and redemption. Servetus does not hide his astonishment and admiration when analyzing the anatomophysiological aspects of the human being: *elaboratio mirabilis*. His approach to the naturalistic understanding of living organism is perfectly Galenic, but his genius allows him to combine it with the theological interpretation of the natural world in the Judaic tradition contained in the Hebrew Old Testament. Descartes adopted the same view of physical nature. But Servetus illuminates and enlarges this Hebrew worldview with the Neo-Platonic elements and develops his own, original worldview based on theology and science. For example, for Galen, the soul was an elaboration or mixture (*crasis*) of four elements whereas Servetus speaks of one "spirit" though operating in three different forms.

[36] *Flavo colore*, which perhaps should be translated as "yellow," "yellowish," or "golden yellow." O'Malley translated this term as *reddish yellow*. Trueta ("M. Servetus and the discovery of the lesser circulation," *Yale Journal of Biology*, 21,1948,1-15) translates it as "red." Barón Fernández translates is as "de color rojo claro" (of the bright red color), but he explains that Marcial uses the term *flavus* as "red," whereas Seneca talks about the *flavus pudor* (red blush). The key to proper translation is the usage of the Greek equivalent by Galen with whose writings Servetus was perfectly acquainted. B. Castelli in his well known *Lexicon Medicum*, published in Padua in 1762, states that the term *flavus* derives from the Greek ξανθός, and this term was used by Galen, which is the term designating bright red color, going into white, but much more intense than the term ὠχρός, pale, or pale yellow.

place through the middle of the heart's wall, as is commonly held;[37] rather, by a great mechanism[38] fine blood is kept in motion from the right ventricle of the heart via a long passage through the lungs. It is readied by the lungs and made red, and it flows from an arterial vein (pulmonary artery) into a venous artery (pulmonary vein).[39] Next in this venous artery itself (pulmonary vein) it is mixed with the inhaled air, and by the act of exhalation it is freed from the waste.[40] Finally, the entire mixture, a material suitable to become a vital spirit, is drawn hither into the left ventricle of the heart during the diastole.

The complex process of conjunction and the communication of the arterial vein (pulmonary artery) with the venous artery (pulmonary vein) in the lungs shows us that the communication and preparation of the blood does take place in the lungs. The arterial vein's (pulmonary artery's) remarkable size proves this: it would not be like that nor made that large, nor would it send so great a quantity of the purest blood from the heart into the lungs solely for the sake of their nourishment, nor by this logic would the heart serve the lungs especially because earlier in the case of an embryo the lungs themselves are normally supplied from elsewhere on account of the tiny membranes or [171] tiny heart valves, which are

---

[37] *Non per parietem cordis medium*: not by the interventricular wall (today it is called *septum interventriculare*). Servetus is here the first to announce that the interventricular membrane (interventricular wall) separating the right ventricle from the left ventricle is impermeable. He opposes the currently held view after Galen, that blood passes from the right ventricle to the left by passing through the pores in the separation. Galen supported his view by analogy with respect to the sizes of the vena cava which leads to the heart and of the pulmonary artery which comes from the heart, and of the aorta and pulmonary vein. "The openings which are visible in the heart, especially in the wall which divides it, have as a purpose the communication which I have described" (*De usu partium*, V, 17). After Servetus this opinion was contradicted by Vesalius in his second edition of *De humani corporis fabrica* (Basel, 1553). It seems there is no doubt that Servetus knew the first edition of the Vesalius' work from 1543, but he never mentions his co-disciple by name. If there were no contacts later, the convergence of the views should be attributable to the experiments which they performed together during the dissections in the prosectorium of Günther de Andernach.
[38] Servetus is using the expression *magno artificio*, just as Vesalius called the human body *fabrica*.
[39] Servetus is using the terms established in antiquity and used by Galen, *vena arteriosa* for the modern pulmonary artery, and *arteria venosa* for the pulmonary vein.
[40] The literal meaning of the term used by Servetus, *a fuligine*, is "from the soot."

not open until the moment of birth, as Galen teaches.[41] Therefore, blood is brought from the heart to the lungs at the moment of birth—indeed, so abundantly—for some other use. Likewise, air is not sent from the lungs to the heart just as it is, but rather after it has been mixed with blood through the venous artery (pulmonary vein). Therefore, mixing takes place in the lungs. The bright red color is given by the lungs, not by the heart, to blood filled with spirit. In the heart's left ventricle there is no place that is able to contain so great or copious a mixing process nor has its mechanical activity sufficient capacity to give it this bright red color. Finally, because it is devoid of vessels or mechanisms, the medial wall is not suited for the process of communication and refinement, assuming it can exude anything.[42] By the same process whereby there is a transfusion of blood within the liver from the *vena porta* to the *vena cava*, there also occurs in the lungs a transfusion of the spirit from the arterial vein (pulmonary artery) to the venous artery (pulmonary vein).[43] If one should compare all this with what Galen writes in Books 6 and 7 of *On the Use of the Parts*, he will understand deeply a truth that was not noticed by Galen himself.[44]

At any rate, the vital spirit is subsequently transfused from the heart's left ventricle into the arteries of the entire body in such a way that what is thinner seeks the higher elements where it is refined further, particularly in the net-like plexus (*plexus retiformis*) located under the base of the brain,[45] in which, as it

---

[41] This is one of the Galen's errors which is retained by Servetus, *De foetum formatione*, cap. 3., vol. IV. Discussion of this problem in García Ballester, *op. cit.*, p. 108.

[42] Servetus accepted another of Galen's assessments, namely, that the veins originate in the liver and constitute with it a system, just as arteries form a system with the heart.

[43] From the *vena arteriosa* to the *arteria venosa*.

[44] Servetus bases his discovery in an essentially Galenic system, but is completely aware of its novelty and does not hide it: *Si quis ... veritatem penitus intelliget, ab ipso Galeno non animadversam*. However, Galen admitted the existence of small anastomoses between the pulmonary artery and the pulmonary vein at the level of the lungs. The reading of chapters VI and VII (entitled *The Instruments of Pneuma*) in Galen's work, *On the Use of the Parts*, authorizes us to deduce that they existed not for the exchange of blood, but in order to aerate it before it could be used as a nutrient for the lungs, a condition necessary for the substantive conversion of the humor into the substance of the lungs (*De usu partium*, cap. VI and VII).

[45] *Plexus retiformis* or *rete mirabile* is the structure occurring in pigs at the base of the brain. Galen studied the anatomy of these animals and described these structures (*De usu partium*, IX,

approaches the rational soul's proper seat, it begins to change from vital spirit into that of the animal spirit. By the mind's fiery power it is more strongly refined, worked, and completed again within the tiniest vessels or capillaries, which are located in the choroidal networks (*plexus choroides*)[46] and contain the mind, its very self. These networks penetrate all the brain's inner parts and internally undergird the very ventricles of the brain that maintain the vessels that are folded upon themselves and interwoven all the way up to the origins of the nerves, in order to transmit into them the ability to feel and move. Although they are called arteries, these vessels, being very delicately woven together by a great miracle,[47] are, nevertheless, the ends of the arteries, [172] that connect with the origin of the nerves through the meninges.[48] They constitute a certain new type of vessel. For, just as with the transfer of blood from veins to arteries there is in the lung a new type of vessel derived from vein and artery, so in the transfer from arteries to nerves there is a certain, new type of vessel formed from the artery's sheath in the meninges, because, in particular, the meninges themselves continue their own sheaths within the nerves.[49] The sensitivity of the nerves does not exist in that soft material of theirs or in the brain. All the nerves terminate within the threads of the

---

4). In humans this structure is replaced by *circulus Wilsoni*, formed by the branches of the internal carotid artery.

[46] The brain is covered by a membrane with three layers called meninges: *dura mater*, *arachnoidea mater*, and *pia mater*. *Plexus choroides* are formed by the folds of *pia mater* which protrude into the cerebral ventricles, filled with capillary vessels. Servetus, in accordance with Galenic physiology, gives more importance to the cerebral ventricle than to the cerebral hemispheres.

[47] Servetus expresses his admiration of the complexity and intricacy of the human anatomical structures and their function.

[48] Servetus meant here the capillary vessels, like those present in the lungs, described by Galen (*De usu partium*, IV, 9) and not the connection between the meninges and the nerves which he mentions in the next paragraph. "Small arteries entering the brain tissue carry ragged sheaths of *pia mater* inward with them for short distances" (Elaine Marieb, *Human Anatomy and Physiology*, Menlo Park, CA: Benjamin/Cummings Science Publishing, 1998, p. 432).

[49] *Ita in transfusione ab arteriis in nervos est novum ... genus vasorum ex arteriae tunica in meninge: cum praesertim meninges ipsae suas in nervis tunicas servent.* The term *tunica*, from the Greek χιτών, was used already before Galen (*De usu partium*, IV,9). The blood vessels are covered by three membranes: *tunica adventitia*, *tunica media*, and *tunica intima*. The capillary vessel is just a single layer of cells called endothelium (Marieb, *op. cit.*, p. 691).

membranes that have the most refined sensitivity, and for this reason the spirit is always directed there. Therefore, from those small vessels of the meninges or choroids, as from a spring, a luminous animal spirit flows like a ray through the nerves into the eyes and other sensory organs. Conversely, luminous images of objects, perceived from without, approach and are sent by the same pathway into the same source as if penetrating within through a luminous medium.[50]

From the foregoing, it is sufficiently established that the brain's soft mass is not actually the seat of the rational soul because it is chilly and devoid of sensation. But it is like a residence for the said vessels so that they do not burst, and it is like a guardian of the animal spirit so that it not be blown away, when it is to be imparted to the nerves, and it is cool in order to moderate the fiery heat that is contained within the vessels.[51] Hence, it also happens that, by means of the aforementioned vessels, the nerves maintain in the interior cavity a common sheath

---

[50] Servetus describes nerves as a mass of soft material, and not as a hollow tube as described by Galen. In Servetus's explanation of the conduction of sensory signals the animal spirit is involved. It functions as "a luminous medium" (*lucidum medium*) which flows through the nerves to the sensory organs making them responsive to the signals coming from the outside, and then carrying "the luminous images of the things perceived" (*sensatarum rerum lucidae imagines*) inside, presumably to the seat of the soul located in the vessels of the meninges and choroid. It is interesting that Servetus explained the physiological mechanisms using the theological concept of the "spirit" which has its roots in the ancient theistic explanations of natural processes or phenomena. A somewhat similar but naturalistic theory of sensory perception, and rather mechanical, was developed later by René Descartes (1596-1650) in his *Discours de la méthode* (1637) and in the *Traité des passions de l'âme* (1649). Descartes postulated that the so-called "des esprits animaux" which are diversified corpuscles, like very "subtle wind" or a "pure and vivid flame," and migrate through the blood to the ventricles of the brain and from here through the nerves into the organs. They vary by diversity of their "agitation" and by diversity of their "parts." They are the cause of the "movements" or function of all the organs, including the sensory organs. These "animal spirits" are composed of the "most vivid and subtle parts of the blood" which are being rarified by the heat generated in the heart, and subsequently being carried to the cavities in the brain. Diversity of the "animal spirits" derives from the diversity of the organs from which the blood is transported into the heart. The soul, which is located in "the tiny gland in the middle of the brain" receives and sends all the "animal spirits" through the nerves and blood to all parts of the body, is a central place processing all signals (René Descartes, *Discours de la méthode. Les passions de l'âme*, Paris: Bookking International, 1995).

[51] Servetus did not recognize the role of the brain as the site of the functions which were ascribed to the soul. He considered the brain's function to be in cooling the blood which was heated in the heart. But he recognized the protective function of the cerebrospinal fluid contained in the subarachnoid space.

of membrane for the trusty protection of the spirit, and this comes from the thin meninx just as they have even their own exterior sheath derived from the thick meninx.[52] Also those empty spaces of the brain's ventricles, at which philosophers and doctors marvel, contain nothing less than the soul. But, as the waste received there,[53] and as the passages leading to the palate and nostrils, from which morbid secretions arise, prove, those ventricles, like sewers, were made primarily to receive the excretions of the brain.[54] And when the ventricles are filled in the described manner with phlegm such that the arteries of the choroids themselves overflow with it, then [173] suddenly apoplexy is produced. If a harmful humor blocks a region, and its vapor infects the mind, epilepsy or some other illness is produced near the region into which the humor has been expelled and collected. Therefore, we shall say that the mind is where we perceive it to be manifestly affected.[55] From excessive heat of those vessels or inflammation of the meninges one can observe deliria or frenzies of the brain. Wherefore, because of illnesses that occur, because of the nature of its localization and substance, because of the intensity of heat and the elegant beauty of the vessels that contain it, and because of the activities of the soul that occur there, we ever conclude that those small vessels are to be esteemed foremost because everything else is subservient to them and because the nerves that provide sensation are attached to them so that they gain their power from there. Finally, we reach this conclusion because we realize that the intellect labors in that region inasmuch as the arteries pulsate all the way

---

[52] This is a recognition of the two layers of meninges, *pia mater* and *archnoidea mater* beneath the *dura mater*.

[53] *Expurgamenta*. Even Galen observed these spaces or cavities in the substance of the brain, χώραι, but Servetus refers here to the four ventricles of the brain, two lateral, the third in the middle, and the fourth one in the back of the brain.

[54] It is interesting that he considered the ventricles, following Galen, as the storage of the waste products in the brain and at the same time the site of the soul. Erroneous is also his explanation of the origin of the mental diseases which he mentions.

[55] This statement represents an important principle of how to localize a specific mental function. The "rational soul" of Aristotle and of the Scholastics, or the "animal spirit" (*pneuma psychikon*) of Galen, the agent of the sensory function activated by nerves, does not have its location in the cerebral mass, but is spread in the whole of the nervous system.

up to the temples when we are in a state of deep contemplation. He who has not seen the place, will hardly understand it.[56]

These ventricles have been made for another, second reason: so that a portion of the air that has been inhaled through the ethmoid bone, by penetrating to their empty spaces and by having been drawn during the diastole from the very vessels of the soul may remake the animal spirit contained within and aerate the soul. In those vessels exists the mind, the soul, the fiery spirit that needs uninterrupted aeration. Otherwise, just like a fire outside, it would be confined and snuffed out.[57] Like fire, it needs back and forth blowing, not only to draw its fuel from the air, but also to expel its exhaust into the air.[58] Just as this external, elementary fire is joined to the dense, earthly body by their shared dryness and their shared form of light because it has the fluid of the body as its fuel, and is blown by the air and warmed and nourished, so the fiery spirit of ours and the soul is similarly joined with the body, making itself one with it and having its blood as its fuel; it is blown, warmed, and nourished by the airy spirit through the process of inhalation and exhalation so that it has a dual-natured food, the spiritual and the bodily.[59] By virtue of the place and spiritual warming it was just appropriate that

---

[56] This statement is a testimony to Servetus's empiricism and evidence that he performed dissections in Paris where de Andernach was teaching anatomy at the University of Sorbonne.

[57] Servetus follows the theory of four elements and of four qualities associated with them. With Galen (*De usu partium*, VI,7) he admits the existence of an innate heat which is maintained in the heart by being constantly aerated through respiration. Hence the double phase of *flabellatio* and *difflatio* which were erroneously interpreted as referring to the *systole* and *diastole*. Also the comparison with fire is Galenic in its origin, for this fire is the dynamic principle of nature and thus the identification which Servetus establishes between mind, soul, and igneous spirit (*mens, anima, igneus spiritus*). The point which Servetus tries to explain by using these naturalistic explanations is the influence of the "spirit of God" or of God by means of the "vital spirit" and by the "natural spirit" on the "animal spirit," that is on the life of the animated mind, in such a way that all the action, cosmic and human, even the most concealed and invisible, remains subjected to God-spirit as a mode of temporal expansion of the substantial mode of God's existence as Servetus teaches in many instances in *Restitutio*, pp. 129, 187,197.

[58] *Flabellatione et difflatione* is translated here as "back and forth blowing" in order to explain the renewal from the air and also the removal of wastes (*fuligo*).

[59] Servetus considers here the spirituality of our soul in its sensorial dimension. Just as the higher element fire in the external process is supported by two lower elements, fluid of the body and air, so our soul which is an igneous or luminous spirit is supported by two sources, "spiritual," the air, and "corporeal," the blood.

the same naturally luminous place of our spirit was infused by [174] another, holy, heavenly, luminous Spirit, and this was through the exhaling from Christ's mouth just as the spirit is drawn by us into the same place through inhalation.[60] It is fitting that, being the same, the site of our intellect and our shining soul is illuminated anew by the heavenly light of a second fire. For God first lit the lamp within us and turned the shadows that had there been generated anew into light as David says in Psalm 17 and 2 Samuel 22.[61] The same thing is taught by Elihu in Job, chapters 32 and 33. Also Zoroaster, Trismegistus, and Pythagoras taught the same thing as I shall soon show by citation.[62]

The formation and condition of the vessels also contribute to the mind's good quality in such a way that the soul is as much improved by their qualities as the vessels have been better arranged. Indeed, just as the light that has been placed there, is more and more illuminated by a good spirit, so it is obscured by an evil one. If a gloomy and vain spirit in the train of our luminous, animal spirit invades the vessels of the brain, then you will see demonic madnesses just as through a good spirit you will see luminous visions. Moreover, the vain spirit, which has nearby its seat in the abyss of fluids and in the cavities of the brain's ventricles, easily attacks those vessels. The vain spirit, the power of which is from air, freely moves in and out of those cavities with every breath of air we take so that it continually struggles there with our own spirit, which is placed within those vessels

---

[60] The spirit ("air") which we inhale is carried first to the heart. This inspiration and illumination is a continuous process of reinforcing the first inspiration caused by God in his creative act as described in Genesis. Servetus uses the physiological knowledge and explanations of Galen but supplements them with his theological teleological interpretations.

[61] Ps. 18:28 : "It is you who light my lamp; the LORD, my God, lights up my darkness." 2 Sam. 22:29: "Indeed, you are my lamp, O LORD, the LORD lightens my darkness." Job 32:8 : "But truly it is the spirit in a mortal, the breath of the Almighty, that makes for understanding." Job 33:4 : "The spirit of God has made me, and the breath of the Almighty gives me life." The Bible, which Servetus interprets in its literal and historical sense, is for him the ultimate and the first source of truth. Philology, philosophy, and empirical or "scientific" experience have only secondary importance and serve as instruments for his hermeneutics.

[62] Servetus alludes to the cosmogonies known to him which propose the primordial dark chaos at the beginning of the world and which was organized and brought into order, *cosmos*, by God-Light. We find them in *Magic Oracles* ascribed to Zoroaster and more detailed in the treatise of *Pimander* in *Corpus Hermeticum* as well as in some *Golden Verses of Pythagoras*.

like in a fortress. In fact, it assails our spirit from all quarters in such a way that it
could scarcely breathe unless betimes the light of God's spirit victoriously drove
the wicked spirit off.[63] See how appropriately the nature of mind, spirit, revelation,
and intellect suits that place, being both situated there and victorious, in the fight
over higher temptations such that I shall presently pass over the other temptations.
In a manner similar to inhaling, the love of God is awakened within the heart
through the holy spirit. In the heart there is, besides the principle of life, the
domain of the will and because of the temptations of the intellect and goads of the
flesh, the first source of sin, as agreed in Matthew 15.[64] But let us deal with the
things that are in the brain before we move on to the heart. Given the diversity of
those vessels in the brain, the actions of the mind are various just as [175] there are
various organs in the various ventricles, which I shall now set forth.

Once inhaled through a slender region, air travels through the ethmoid
bone that we have spoken of, towards the front ventricles of the brain located on
the left and right behind the forehead, and is communicated to that animal, fiery
spirit contained within the choroid's vessels.[65] There the choroid's capillary
arteries expand and draw in the air in order to aerate the soul. Just as the auditory
nerves and the nerves of the other senses do, so the two optic nerves come
together at the same capillaries and, the integrity of their shared membrane's
covering having ever been preserved,[66] they transport the bright images of
observed things to the most faithful and secure guardian of everything. For, if the

---

[63] Servetus is describing this "vain spirit" as "nequam spirtus" or "malum spiritus." In the mind
of Christians the term may produce confusion, but Servetus does not refer to demons, but to the
fact that the "spirit" (air) can be physiologically beneficial or harmful. Thus there is a
physiological basis, the "good air" or the "bad air" for our moral intentions, good or bad. The
luminous spirit of God is aiding us in the struggle through the action of the holy spirit. Servetus
distinguishes the spirit of God as God himself, the principle of the cosmic dynamics, and the holy
spirit as the divine principle, sanctifying and deifying.

[64] Matt. 15:18 : "But what comes out of the mouth proceeds from the heart, and this is what
defiles."

[65] These are obviously erroneous views concerning the passage of the air and its role in "moving"
the sensory and perceptive functions. Moreover, their localization is in the ventricles and not in
the nervous tissue of the brain.

[66] *Tegumento communis membranae semper servato.*

reflection and the spirit along with the soul were to wander around in those empty spaces, everything would be sent outside by blowing one's nose or, at least, by repeated sneezing. If the soul were there, it would not yet be in the blood because blood is not outside the vessels. Therefore, the mind is most securely located in the choroid's vessels.[67] The covering is a most secure one, and the main sensory nerves tend towards the vessels mentioned, which are located in a particular region within the frontal ventricles, such that in that place there is the beginning of common sense, a broad apprehension or imaging of the exterior senses in common that, once apprehended, begin there to be compared in turn and combined.[68]

Next, air that has been inhaled into the brain is transferred from the two anterior ventricles to the middle or to a certain common passageway into which they run together under the psalloid[69] and where there is the brighter and the purer portion of the mind, which thrusts out these seeds of forms, which were divinely placed in it from birth and can from the instant that images are apprehended, by a certain process of analogy, contemplate new objects or compose them, mix imagined things together, make inferences from one object to another, discern among them, and bring together the pure truth itself with God showing the way.[70] The smaller ventricle is there, the superior type of intellect because the choroidal arteries, which remake their fiery spirit during the diastole, are more abundant

---

[67] *In vasis ergo choroidum est mens tutissime sita.*

[68] Servetus refers to the localization of "common sense" as defined by Aristotle, *sensus communis*, (De anima, III, 2, 426ab), which today could be understood as the integration of perception. It seems that the physiology of perception described by Servetus was a common understanding in his time.

[69] *Psalloides, psalterium* or *lyra*, these are old terms used to describe the posterior part of the *corpus callosum*, a structure containing fibers connecting the two hemispheres of the brain including the commissure of the hippocampus. It corresponds to the *fimbria* of Galen (*De usu partium*, VIII,11). Servetus does not explain whether he refers to the third ventricle or the confluence of the two lateral ventricles.

[70] Servetus says "*lustrante Deo,*" an expression which could be interpreted as describing his gnoseological illuminism. Man could not arrive at "pure truth," the totality of the perceptive process, without some influence or illumination from God. This influence is effected actually through the aeration of the "fiery spirit" in the brain. Servetus, following Galen (*De usu partium*, VII, 14) and against Aristotle (*Hist. animal.*, III, 5) admits the localization of the process of thought in the brain though he missed the function of the neuronal tissue.

there and bring the perceptions of common sense to a faculty of reason that is more and more filled with light, that particular spiritual light penetrating within through the vessels, and the Divinity itself shining forth there. [176] The empty space in that region is not as great as in the other ventricles, so you could call it a passage rather than a ventricle or the long and sinuous path of investigation. It has been wisely constructed on account of the difficulty of its investigation.[71] The ventricle is smaller because so many excretions ought not to pile up where the part of the mind is purer and brighter. Moreover, what is generated there, easily slides directly into the adjacent *choana*,[72] so as not to block out the mind's lamp or act as an impediment to it. There are more vessels around the *conarium*,[73] more frequent pulsation of the arteries, a more powerful action of the mind and fiery spirit there. We also detect both internally and externally a stronger pulse in the adjoining temples when the intellect is working so that by this experience alone we are led to the very locus of the mind. Add the fact that the sense of hearing, which is the sense for learning, is nearer this region.[74] This construction of the human being is a most amazing thing.[75] Many long wrinkles are there, leading up to the cerebellum, so that by long discourse all complicated things can be investigated, and shadows can be illuminated with the assistance through the faculty of recollection of even

---

[71] We do not know whether Servetus refers here to the third ventricle, *aquaeductus cerebri* (aqueduct of Sylvius or mesencephalic aqueduct) or the fourth ventricle. The following text, however, suggests that Servetus refers most probably to the third ventricle.

[72] *Subiecta choana*. The term derives from the Greek word χοάνη which means *infundibulum*, "funnel," and refers to the *infundibulum cerebri*, a part of the brain joining the hypothalamus with the pituitary gland. In the Galenic system it served to eliminate waste, eventually through the nasal cavities.

[73] The *conarium* or pineal gland or *epiphysis cerebri*, called in Greek κωνάριον from its shape resembling a pine cone (κῶνος) (*De usu partium*, VIII, 14).

[74] *Sensus auditus, qui est sensus disciplinae*. The most important in the process of learning was the auditory sense and not the visual. The importance of the visual sense increased in modern times.

[75] This enthusiastic expression of Servetus reflects the attitude of the Renaissance and in his mouth it refers rather to an epistemological observation of a scientist rather than to a poetic élan. Servetus could be inspired by the expression found in Hermes Trismegistus, *magnum miraculum est homo* (*Asclepius*, 5) or even from his own "master," Champier, *maximum miraculum est homo sapiens* (Cl. Manzoni, *Emanesimo ed eresia: M. Serveto* (Napoli, 1974, p. 113). In any case it is a typical reflection of the Galenic tradition.

those things which were previously hidden in the memory. There, too, when our thought-process is focused, the warmth of inhaled air is in a certain manner retained there and increased by the *scolicoid*[76] as a doorkeeper, and by the sinuous *gluteae*[77] until the discourse has been completed and everything has been clearly explained, all our mind's arteries are being blown by it and throbbing under its impulse. Therefore, it is especially to the mind, which is fiery and shares in God's light, that the fiery region is suitable, once a concept, which is a ray of light and a certain luminous image, has arisen. Even external, perceivable images of objects which have been projected into the eye, are luminous[78] and are projected through a glowing medium by a luminous object or an object that has the form of light. Whence, even the mind itself is more and more illuminated.

The intellect is decorated by the faculty of sight, which shows us many different things, but it is also decorated by the objects of the other senses, all of which have some relationship [177] to our luminous spirit. The relationship derives from the substantive form of everything, which is light, and from the same spiritual manner in which it acts in individual objects. Sound and smell are like spirit; they are perceived like spirit, and like spirit they act within us. The perception of what we hear, occurs when the external spirit at the location of the eardrum strikes the internal spirit itself, in which is situated the soul's light and the confluence of spiritual harmony, which has been set in order by the diastole and the

---

[76] *A ianitore scolicoide.* From the Greek σκωληκοειδής, worm-shaped, and σκώληξ, a worm. Thus *a ianitore scolicoide* means by the "worm-shaped doorkeeper" and Servetus refers here to the part of the cerebellum known as *vermis*, a worm, and located between the cerebellar hemispheres and above the structures described by Servetus. Servetus follows, as usual, the description of Galen who considered it as the part able to control the passage of the *pneuma*, and not the pineal gland (body) (*De usu partium*, VIII, 14). The pineal gland was considered by Descartes as the site of the soul.

[77] *Sinuosis glutiis.* From the Greek γλούτια, the medullary tubercles near the pineal gland of the brain which correspond to the corpora quadrigemina located in the tectum above the mesencephalic aqueduct. The Greek term and its corresponding Latin term derive from the Greek γλούτος, buttock. This is an allusion to the "gluteal" form of the structures around the mesencephalic aqueduct which for Servetus as for Galen retained the inhaled air.

[78] *Rerum sensibiles species*: Servetus refers here to the images and not to the *species* in the technical sense of the sensorial perceptions according to the Aristotelian-scholastic theory.

systole. The process of what we smell, is nearly identical. Moreover, although they are more of the body, what is tasted or touched, nevertheless, have powers that are suited for altering the soul, the former through moisture, the latter through pressure, but both from the common form of light, from its diverse action upon the spirit. Due to light's property the whole substance acts upon the soul because it impresses on it the idea of the totality. The Sophists, who previously taught that nothing except qualities and tainted ghosts were seen either in God or in us, now see the substances themselves.[79] But by seeing light as substance in Christ we pursue the vision of true light in other things too.

Once illuminated by all aforementioned elements within the middle ventricle, and if the door-keeper grants admission,[80] the spirit heads for the fourth ventricle in the *parencephalis*, as does the luminous, reconstituted image which has been located in the light of the soul itself. In fact, as in the depth of the brain, those vessels tenaciously preserve there the treasure chest that is memory, and accumulate there what is discovered by sense or reasoning, not kept by walls, but retained in the soul's very substance as in some material. In that region the soul possesses stouter vessels of retained spirit lest memory dissipate too readily. I pass over the fact that, by this path, through the great nerves of the spine, the locomotive ability of the entire body is transmitted to the muscles with that animal spirit, as it were, radiating throughout. Thus, there are in the brain four ventricles and three inner senses. For the two anterior ventricles give rise to one common sense as the receptor of images. The middle one is contemplation and the final is memory. That is what we can say about the journey to the brain of the spiritual

---

[79] *Nisi qualitates et fucatas larvas.* Servetus opposes the explications based on the category of qualities. The sanctifying grace, for example, is not for him a quality. The senses themselves in some way reflect the substantive mode of recognizing the objects and not only by the qualities which we perceive inherent in them. And this is for two reasons: the light which Servetus defined as *mater formarum* (*Restitutio* 162) is the form of everything, and its connection with Christ-Light who is a substantive light in himself and through whom man may know all other substances.

[80] *Permittente ianitore*, see note 76.

portion of the inspired air, the brain's organs, and its powers.[81]

[178] The greater part of the inhaled air is conducted through the tracheal artery (trachea) into the lungs so that, having been worked out by them, it may cross over to the venous artery (pulmonary vein) where it is mixed with bright red and subtle blood, and is further elaborated.[82] Next the whole mixture is drawn during the diastole into the heart's left ventricle where it acquires its definitive form by the very strong, life-giving property of the fire contained therein, and it becomes vital spirit, while many impurities that are produced by that process having been exhaled.[83] The whole of this is like the material of the soul itself. Aside from this entire mixture there are still two other things in the soul: that living element, which is created by the act of breathing or produced in its own matter, and the spirit itself or divinity that is infused therein by the act of breathing.[84] All of this forms one thing, and one soul.[85] The medium which is mainly referred to as the soul, is the breath and the puff of air, both joined in essence with the spirit. Its substance is ethereal, being like that superelementary archetype and also like this inferior element:[86] one natural soul, the vital and the animal. Such is the entire nature of the soul, and the reason why the soul of all the flesh is in the blood, and why the soul itself is the blood, as God says. For by God's breath the gust of the

---

[81] *Media est cogitatio, et extrema memoria.* Perhaps Servetus understands here the term *cogitatio* not in its usual meaning as the ability to think, but as the ability to perceive the object in its totality since he differentiates in the brain three "inner senses" (*sensus interiores tres*) located in the four ventricles.

[82] Compare note 36.

[83] *Expiratis fuliginosis recrementis.*

[84] All these parts discussed until now constitute the biological or physical part of the soul considered as the "animating" part of the body. As to its origin Servetus is using both terms "creation by the act of breathing" and "production in its own matter" (*spiratione creatum, aut in sua materia productum*).

[85] Servetus accentuates unity of the soul though composed of various elements, similarly as he insisted previously on the unity of the three "spirits." By the same token a human being is one entity: *Omnia unum, et anima una.*

[86] The soul is connected with the archetypical spirit of God and with the vital spirit or the air which is breathed in and which is being transformed into the natural and into the animal spirit. The last is the spirit of the soul. Thus "spirit," blood, soul, are always related to the spirit of God, God understood as the cosmic spirit united with the human being and in the human being.

heavenly spirit or the ideal spark[87] has been infused through the mouth and nostrils into the heart and brain of Adam himself and into that of his children, and it has been joined in essence to that spiritual, bloody material within; it has been made soul within his innards (Gen. 2, Isa. 57, Ezek. 37, and Zech. 12).[88]

After the Chaldæans, the Academics, who said that a certain ethereal blast from God was joined to elemental air with the result that the divine mind could by this medium be infused into this dense body, taught that substances so dissimilar could come together in this manner. Holy scripture teaches this more clearly by referring to it frequently as God's breath and elemental breeze.[89] In *Timœus* Plato openly teaches that the soul's substance is a certain blending of elemental and divine substances, and that there is a certain third, intermediate substance that partakes of both. For the soul contains the symbol of divinity and of the elements of the cosmos. Otherwise, it would be impossible for the one soul to possess the force of the intelligible mind and the life-causing, governing [179] properties of bodies.[90] Hence it also happens that by listening with its senses in every instance the soul soothes the body because it loves its relation with it. Every now and then,

---

[87] *Illa coelestis spiritus aura sive idealis scintilla.* These are Neo-Platonic terms popularized by master Eckhardt who was also accused, unjustly, for pantheism when he used the term *scintilla animae.*

[88] Servetus calls this material in the blood spiritual because it is an airy vapor and a liquid as he stated previously. He cites the biblical texts to prove his point. Gen. 2:7 : "Then the LORD God formed man from the dust of the ground, and breathed into his nostrils the breath of life; and the man became a living being." Isa. 57:16 : "For I will not continually accuse, nor will I always be angry; for then the spirits would grow faint before me, even the souls that I have made." Ezek. 37:5 : "Thus says the Lord GOD to these bones: I will cause breath to enter you, and you shall live." Zech. 12:1 : "Thus says the LORD, who stretched out the heavens and founded the earth and formed the human spirit within."

[89] Academics or Platonists, members of the first Academy of the fourth century B.C.E. But this Servetian view is not found in the original Platonic doctrines.

[90] Plato expressed the interior conflict within man, the struggle between opposed tendencies in various ways: in *The Republic* using the concept of the tripartite soul; in *Phaedro* in the form of a myth about charioteer. He explains this in *Timaeus* using different categories saying that the demiurge created the souls "From the indivisible, eternally unchanging existence and the divisible, changing existence of the physical world he mixed a third kind of existence intermediate between them; again with the same and the different he made, in the same way, compounds intermediate between their indivisible element and their physical and divisible element: and taking these three components he mixed them into a single unity" (*Timaeus*, 35). Servetus accepts basically Plato's doctrine, but he insists on the unity of the soul.

when it reaches new heights, it is more affected by a higher relationship, the earlier one being ignored. It is said in *Cratylus* that the soul, ψῡχή, is "cooled by breathing," ἀναψυχη. And, nonetheless, it exists from the divine mind within man.[91] Just as the soul makes the body live, so by breathing God makes the soul live. Isaiah teaches that the spirit, which is from God, is rolled into the breeze, and that in this way God has made little "gusts," souls clothed in air. Zechariah said that, by a particular formation, the spirit of the soul was fashioned in the innards of men. The book of Genesis proves the same thing. For the breath of God is not said simply to be the soul, but rather with the inhaling of that breath the living soul is made within.[92] We shall show beyond what has already been shown so far that in the body's elements, just as in the seed, there is a substantive symbol of the soul yet to be drawn out. There are two things in the seed, and they are from the soul's essence, and they make a newborn's soul like unto his father's soul. They are the formal or forming ability and the spiritual material. The formal and forming ability is light itself and form.[93] From the seed the souls of other animate things are manifestly drawn out, human ones included, provided that the breath of the divine mind reaches the man himself; they are drawn out in the form which the nature of the seed requires, according to which the soul is formed. God's breathing takes place in the face of a human being through the mouth and nostrils, in the heart and the brain so that in this way the soul is formed in the form of a human being.[94]

Thus, like a potter, God is called a craftsman of the soul (Zech. 12). He fashions within their hearts the souls of individuals (Ps. 32). God is called the fashioner of light (Isa. 45).[95] For in light itself He forms in a real sense the substantive forms of things just as in the mind's light He forms ideas. Thus God formed the soul in light just as in light the soul itself subsequently forms and

---

[91] In *Cratylus* Socrates says: "The verb ἀναψύχειν means to cool, to refresh."
[92] Servetus alludes to the biblical texts already cited in note 88.
[93] *Formalis et formatrix est lux ipsa et idea.*
[94] Already earlier when talking about the physiology of the brain, Servetus says that the spirit, i.e., the air, is drawn to the same place as the heart and the brain.

fashions other images. Finally God is called the fashioner of everything (Jer. 10)[96] because He created nothing to which He did not give a particular form. God, being the fashioner of everything, gave a particular form even to the angels and the souls. With amazing craft and complex design God formed us inside and out even before we existed (Ps. 138).[97] First, by conceiving all things in His own mind God formed from eternity as exemplars the things in the form of his own light. Next, by bringing them forth to exist externally as individual things, [180] He gave them such a form as He had prefigured them in advance. If you should understand that this has been accomplished by a secondary process in our case, you will understand that Christ was the first who had in God his form, from which, once we have been formed in this external, created light, we received our own. In that created light, God forms everything both really and substantively by imparting to everything a token of His light and form, and by breathing into man in addition a wisp of spirit of the divine mind. The wisp of spirit which was transmitted to us by God is a kind of lamp or spark of light. God Himself is fire, and God is the spirit, by which the fiery and spiritual soul exists in our own fiery and airy, vital spirit. In light there exists the first form of all other souls and things, and in light there exists natural life, to quote John: light itself, by which "every man that is born in the world is illuminated" naturally, is of God (John 1).[98] In God's very luminous Word there exists the soul's source, and "in its light we see light" (Ps. 35).[99] It is magnificent how, according to this design, the holy spirit that was given to us in our rebirth, clings to our soul just as light clings to light, and fire to fire. It simply would not be called a rebirth of the spirit, if not for its likeness to that, God's first act of generation and breathing: and the new state of illumination is superior to the nature

---

[95] Servetus alludes to Zech. 12:1, Ps. 32:15, and Isa. 45:7.

[96] Jer. 10:16.

[97] Ps. 138:16 : "In your book were written all the days that were formed for me, when none of them as yet existed."

[98] Reference to John 1:9 : "The true light, which enlightens everyone, was coming into the world."

[99] Ps. 35:9 : "For with you is the fountain of life; in your light we see light."

of the old one.

Zoroaster, the Chaldæan, taught this already in his *Oracles of Wisdom*. He said there that, having been sent to us from on high by God's light, the soul seeks anew that light, is illuminated by it, and becomes fire all over again. "You must ascend," he said, "to that light and to the rays of the Father, from whence the soul was poured into you, the soul which is completely bathed in the mind's light, and which becomes a splendid fire through the Father's power."[100] In *Pimander* Trismegistus said, "Light and life are God, the Father, from whom man is born: therefore, if you see that you yourself exist from life and light, you will cross over to life and light again."[101] In his poems Pythagoras said, "Thus, have faith because the divine tribe belongs to men, to whom sacred nature shows everything by presenting light."[102]

That light is hidden from us, which extends itself to another greater light through the radiance of God. From that [181] light of Christ's life the soul's life advances to us at our generation as does the spirit's life at our regeneration. The manner is different just as it was with Christ himself; even the spirit is new. He himself, who was once the spirit of Elohim, is now the spirit of Christ's mouth, generating and regenerating (Ps. 103).[103] Nevertheless, it is one way in the case of one, another way in the case of the other. Regeneration is different from generation just as the spirit of grace is different from the soul that is born within. That spirit is God; the soul is not God, yet the soul is made God through this. The spirit of the soul is vital and its elements are corruptible. A new spirit's elements are incorruptible, being the same sort as those which Christ's vital spirit now

---

[100] Words of the Zoroastrian *Magic Oracles*, X.

[101] In *Poimandres*, I : "'But why is it that he who has recognized himself enters into the Good, as it was said in God's speech?' I answered, 'It is because the father of all consists of Light and Life, and from him Man has sprung.' 'You are right,' said he 'If then, being made of Life and Light, you learn to know that you are made of them, you will go back into Life and Light.'"

[102] Pythagoras :"Yet, do not fear, for the mortals are divine by race, to whom holy Nature everything will reveal and demonstrate." *The Golden Verses, op. cit.*, 63-64, p. 164.

[103] Ps. 103:30 : "When you send forth your spirit, they are created; and you renew the face of the ground."

possesses in heaven. According to God's direction the soul of all flesh is defined as follows: the soul is a particular, original and vital mist within the blood. Man's soul is a particular, original breath of the mind within the blood.[104] Moreover, the holy spirit of regeneration is together with the renewed elements of Christ, a new breath of the Divinity.

This is not to say, as you may fear, that our soul and the holy spirit of Christ are conjoined in essence and have an elemental substance of this sort just as the Word has the flesh joined to itself. Our soul's fire and our spirit's fire depend inseparably on that substance, and they are warmed and nourished by it just as we see that fire is warmed and nourished by fuel and air. And, just as a fire dies out when those elements fail, so the soul within us dies out, so to speak, because it has been deprived of vital activities.[105] In fact, if we put aside these worldly elements, the soul's substance, coming from God, considered by itself, is elemental, so to speak, like the angel's substance, too. For God's very spirit of God, which is the spirit of Christ's generation, from whom angels and souls proceed, contains that sort of elemental or superelementary substance within the archetypal world. Now Christ's spirit, made human, contains that very substance together with the human spirit. The spirit of our regeneration contains that substance because we are generated "from water, spirit, and fire" from heaven. [182] There uncreated things are understood simultaneously within the created objects themselves. And all these come together in the one substance of soul and spirit.[106] Consider what sort of

---

[104] The original Latin text: *"Anima est originalis quidam in sanguine vitalis vapor. Anima hominis est originalis quidam in sanguine mentis halitus."* Servetus always insisted that in regeneration one receives renewed elements plus *novus Deitatis halitus.*

[105] This phrase is consistent with Servetus's view that the human soul is immortal.

[106] All these affirmations together with the statement, "That spirit is God; the soul is not God, yet the soul is made God through this," infuriated Calvin in a written discussion during the trial in Geneva, cf. Kingdon, 43-44. Servetus responded in a letter conserved in the archives of Geneva: *"Verum est multa in unum coire, ut ossa, caro, nervi, anima, forma, spiritus in unum hominis substantialem coeunt."* And the ministers answered with this statement: *"Cum protulerit horribilem blasphemiam, ludibundus eam eludit. Convenit inter omnes multa in unum coïre. Sed nimis est consequential, animam effici Deum, ut res creatae et increatae in unam animae substantiam coeant, ut anima conjunctam habeat sibi elementarem Spiritum, sicut verbo unita est Christi caro. Quibus deliriis palam est omnia redemptionis mysteria profanari."* Servetus

substance Christ possesses today in heaven, what sort of breath is his, what sort is his vital spirit, which itself is the holy spirit that contains united hypostatically within itself these elements. For, just as God's Word exists hypostatically as man, so God's spirit exists hypostatically as man's spirit. Nevertheless, all the elements of his body and spirit were renewed, glorified, and made incorruptible through the power of resurrection. Through baptism and communion Christ imparts to us all those things, imparting himself entirely to us. The holy spirit is the very breath of Christ's mouth (John 20).[107] Just as when God breathed soul with air, so, at the same moment, Christ breathes the holy spirit with air.

In sum this is the point that must be contemplated: just as the soul is understood separately, when air or fire has been put aside, and, when it is with those elements, the soul is wholly one soul, one form, one entity, so, when the product of breath is put aside, the holy spirit is comprehended separately as a divine mode, and that is entirely the holy spirit, Christ's vital spirit, the one holy spirit. The addition of Divinity to individual things or the addition of things in God Himself does not change its name:[108] Divinity in a stone is stone, in gold it is gold, in wood, wood, in accordance with its own forms. Again in a superior way, Divinity in man is man; in the spirit it is spirit: just as the addition of man in God is God, and the addition of man's spirit in Him is the holy spirit.[109]

Yet not only does the holy spirit reside in Christ's breath, but it is also in the angel. Thus, we must see whether an angel is the holy spirit, and who is the other *paraclete*. The angel's ministry was added to the effusion of the holy spirit

---

interjected responding to the first part: *"Nos sumus facti dii, an non ob animae dona?"* and later to the second: *"Unde sequitur, dic pessime?"* (*Calvini Opera*, VIII, 518, 551).

[107] John 20:21-22 : "Jesus said to them again, "Peace be with you. As the Father has sent me, so I send you. When he had said this, he breathed on them and said to them, 'Receive the Holy Spirit.'"

[108] It is a new formulation of the Servetian principle.

[109] This formulation saves Servetus from the accusation of being a pantheist. Servetus clearly states: *"Deitas in homine est homo ..., adiectio hominis in Deo est Deus."* For that reason Christ is for Servetus God, because man was united with the Word. And *"adiectio spiritus hominis in eo est spiritus sanctus."* For that reason the holy spirit proceeds also from Christ, not from the son, because it is a breath of someone who is also God.

when the dove and the fire of the tongue was seen (Matt. 3 and Acts 2). By the same reasoning it is there called the ministry of the angel, just as those things which through God's Word come about in the Law, happen through the angels. In God's person an angel appeared to Moses in red fire (Exod. 3 and Acts 7). God's voice was uttered to Moses through an angel: "I am the God of your fathers."[110] In the angel's appearance there was God's substance [183] in the Word just as even above the apostles there was in Jordan God's substance in the spirit. "In the person of God" an angel was heard and seen by Abraham himself (Gen. 18 and 22), by Agar (Gen. 16 and 21), by Jacob himself (Gen. 31 and 32). The same thing happened in Joshua 5 and 6 and Judges 2 and 6.[111] God gives an explanation for this: because, divinity or God's name was in the angel, and God's voice was heard when the angel spoke (Exod. 23). Therefore, just as a voice was made through the angel, when from the heavens it said, "I am the God of your fathers," so a voice was made through an angel, when from the heavens it said, "This is my son." Thus, this is the holy spirit's voice (Matt. and Luke 3). That third entity was not able to say, "This is my son." Therefore, the holy spirit was not a third entity, but a dispensation of the Divinity through an Angel. Hence, after the holy spirit descended upon him, Christ said, "You will see God's angels ascending and descending above the son of man" (John 1).[112] It is said in one passage that "the angels" are descending, in another that "the spirit" is descending, and in another that "the holy spirit" is descending. In Acts 8 it is called "an angel" in the first passage, "the spirit" in the next, and "the spirit of the Lord" in the third.[113] Relying on the fact that it says regarding the *paraclete*, "He will announce the future to you," Isidore infers that an angel was meant because the word, angel, means

---

[110] Exod. 3:2 and Acts 7:30. Previously it was said that the expression "in the person of God" is equivalent to "as in the function of God." Also Exod. 4:5.
[111] Thophanies of Abraham, Agar, and Jacob always through an angel; as well as in the form of a "man standing ... with a drawn sword in his hand" to Joshua (Joshua 5:13) and of "the angel of the LORD [Yahweh]" to "all of Israelites" and later to Gideon in Joshua 2:4 and 6:12.
[112] In John 1:51 angels represent God and not the third Person.
[113] Acts 8:16, 29, and 39, respectively.

messenger and because the holy spirit makes many announcements through angels.[114] All the angels are ministers of the spirit (Ps. 102 and Heb. 1): "God makes the angels His spirits, and His ministers He makes fiery flames" (Ps. 103).[115] God made many revelations to good prophets through good angels just as He wanted to deceive the wicked through wicked ones (3 Kings 22 and 2 Para. 18 and Ezek. 14). Like a spirit, an angel enters a prophet's soul as with Ezekiel and Zechariah.[116] An angel is called a "spirit of falsehood," a "spirit of truth," and a "spirit of God." The angel addresses the centurion in the form of a man; as the holy spirit, he addresses Peter and others (Acts 10, 11, and 13).[117] It could not be said that the holy spirit was inside the Centurion inasmuch as he did not know Christ. In a man who has been born again, however, it is said that everything is through the holy spirit operating within. Hence in chapter 16 it is called a spirit and the holy spirit, and in the Macedonian man's vision an angel appears. In scripture separate mention is made of the angel and the spirit; in fact, they are the same thing, but, just as with the Word and the spirit, there is a difference with respect to mode. The Word and the angel were apparent in the human mode [184]; the spirit in the spiritual mode. And it is not surprising that an angelic spirit's word or deed was said to be of the holy spirit because an apostle's word or deed would be called the word or deed of the holy spirit. Therefore, it is not fitting to call an angel the holy spirit except in the sense in which the angel was once said to be Jehovah. What happened in the Laws according to God's Word, happened through an angel, but it is not for this reason that an angel is said to be God's Word except in the sense of

---

[114] Isidore of Seville, *Etimologies*, lib. VII, caps 2 and 5. It is true that the word παράκλησις means announcement or calling, but with a connotation of a calling for help. Hence the word *paraclete* indicates always the "one who called for help," intercessor or counselor.

[115] Ps. 102:20 : "O you his angels, you mighty ones who do his bidding, obedient to his spoken word." Ps. 103:4 : "O you his angels, you mighty ones who do his bidding, obedient to his spoken word." This is recorded in Heb. 1:7 : "Of the angels he says, "He makes his angels winds, and his servants flames of fire."

[116] 1 Kings 22:20-25; 2 Chron. 18:22; Ezek. 14:4-11.

[117] In Acts 10:1 and 11:12 a man, Cornelius, is mentioned, but an angel who appears to him and to Peter in a vision is not in the form of a man. Peter later addresses him as "the spirit told me." Also in Acts 13:2 : "the Holy Spirit said."

a shadow and his function, nor is an angel said to be God except in the sense of a shadow and his function. Far less do we attribute to an angel such divinity as did the Jews, by whom angels were revered as gods.[118] Wherefore, we conclude that neither in Christ's case nor in ours ought an angel be called correctly the holy spirit, but rather a minister to the holy spirit's tasks.

Therefore, the holy spirit, the consoler, who, Christ promises the apostles, will be in them, and who was given in Acts 2, is not understood primarily as an angel, although an angel may help there with a task. In place of his external consoler Christ promises the apostles that they will have another, inner consoler, a new holy spirit, which at that time did not exist, but was to be given after the resurrection and was gloriously to be imparted by an angel's service.

The holy spirit was rightly called "other than the son" for many reasons, even excluding from them the ministry of the angel. First because the spirit differed from the son as much as a blast of air does from a man; indeed, when the created breath has been removed, the holy spirit's substance materially differs from the son's substance. It could be called a being and a thing other than Christ except that the expression, "another thing," would strike you as odd. For then I would not grant that, as consoler, the spirit is something "other" than the son. In fact, just as Christ and the Father are one, "they are one" because they are in harmony, and because the Divinity is one and the same. Nevertheless, the holy spirit is distinct because the Divinity's mode is different.[119] In the Law a spirit of this sort was not given, one with this sort of essence, distinct and visible, yet coming together into one perpetual hypostasis with a human spirit. Therefore, it is more distinguished

---

[118] This affirmation would be abusive to the Jews if interpreted literally. In many ancient theophanies their beneficiaries adopt an attitude of adoration, because they believe that it is Yahweh who appears to them or Elohim or some important historical persons. Servetus gives a general explanation of the theophanies claiming that any theophany with a human face could only be the Word of God. The only mode through which God always shows himself is through the form and figure of a man.

[119] Servetus explained the text of John 10:30, "The Father and I are one," previously in Bk. I of *Restitutio*, p. 25, as well as in the Bk. II, p. 75, the other, parallel phrase of John 14:10, "I am in

now and can be called "other." Prior to the Word's becoming human, the holy spirit in itself was truly [185] the mode of the substantive divinity and thus not yet united hypostatically with man's spirit. Now it possesses a substantive and everlasting connection with Christ's human spirit. Christ likewise referred to that spirit as "other" than himself because he did not yet possess it, but it had been promised by the Father. Christ himself was to receive it at his resurrection, a new spirit of glory, and he would subsequently impart it to the apostles. He called it "other" on account of its high state of glory that had never been seen before. "He, whom you, apostles, have already received, will be different from the spirit." "It will be different from me myself. In fact, I will be different and a new man." "The taste of glory will be far different in it than it is now."[120] Thus he spoke: "He will glorify me."[121] The glory of the glorified Christ and of his new holy spirit was so great after the resurrection that with Peter as a witness the angels wanted to gaze, and, as if dumbstruck, marveled at it.[122] Because the angels themselves were the gods of the Jews, in the Law they had never seen such a dispensation of divinity. Through Christ a new knowledge of the holy spirit has been granted to the angels just as has been a new knowledge of God. The angels have learned certain details about Christ's kingdom, which they previously did not know (Eph. 3).[123] The kingdom of Christ that has been given to us, is a kingdom of the spirit; it is said that everything is made manifest to us "in the spirit," everything comes into being, and in this way everything comes into being through the holy spirit. The Father adorned His son with such great glory that he is not only "God from God," but he

---

the Father and the Father is in me." Now he treats still another text, "And I will ask the Father, and he will give you another Advocate, to be with you forever," John 14:16.

[120] Servetus attempts to summarize in very simple terms the meaning of his discussion by putting the words in Jesus' mouth.

[121] The quote is from John 16:14 : "He [i.e., God] will glorify me, because he will take what is mine and declare it to you."

[122] 1 Pet. 1:12 : "in regard to the things that have now been announced to you through those who brought you good news by the Holy Spirit sent from heaven – things into which angels long to look!"

[123] Eph. 3:5-10 : "the wisdom of God in its rich variety might now be made known to the rulers and authorities in the heavenly places."

is also "God from whom the other God proceeds." But, if it offends you to speak
of another God, say instead "another consoler" or another "person" of the
Divinity.[124] Christ is God, from whom other "gods" proceed and are generated.
For we are "gods" proceeding from him, and we have been "conceived from God"
(John 1).[125] But regarding the holy spirit why did Christ say, "He will not speak
from himself?"[126] Because the holy spirit would not provide anyone with
something discordant with God's Word. In Book 2 of *On the Holy Spirit* Didymus
explains it this way: "He will not speak from himself," that is, "not without me, but
the mode of divine inspiration will come from my will and the Father's will."[127]

We must turn for a little while to Christ's very origin [186] so that we may
through his gift have a drink from the very source. Ponder this for yourself, reader:
were He to be considered separately without Christ, God would in Himself be so
removed, and He would so transcend everything that He would have nothing in
common with us nor even with the angelic spirit, which He surpasses infinitely.
Ponder for yourself that neither the angels themselves see God nor do they have
any connection with His spirit except insofar as it is given through Christ because

---

[124] In his accusation during the trial in Geneva, Calvin selects only the penultimate phrase of
Servetus's paragraph stating that Servetus claims that Christ *"non solum sit ipse Deus de Deo,
sed et sit Deus de quo alius Deus procedat."* He omitted the next paragraph in which Servetus
clarified the situation: "another consoler or another 'person' of the Divinity…" For this reason
Servetus replied: *"Alium a Christo Deum dixi, alium deitatis modum. Hic insuper ibi adjeci:
Quod si hic loquendi modus te offendat, dicas aliam deitatis personam. Quid opus fuit te in
calumniam vertere id quod eodem loco ego jam castigaram ? Candidus ubique se ostendit
animus tuus.*" The pastors of Geneva accused him of allowing himself to admit "another God"
while ferociously attacking all pious people "who accept three real persons in one God."
Moreover, they state that Servetus interprets this "new mode of God" as "another person of God."
And they conclude that if the person or mode of the spirit "appeared suddenly during the
resurrection," then we have a "double error," of the origin, "because he assigns the beginning to
the holy spirit as the person from that moment," and of the reality of the other person, because
"he established another God." (*Calvini Opera*, VIII, pp. 502, 516, 538).

[125] John 1:12-13 : "But to all who received him, who believed in his name, he gave power to
become children of God, who were born, not of blood or of the will of the flesh or of the will of
man, but of God."

[126] John 16:13 : "When the Spirit of truth comes, he will guide you into all the truth; for he will
not speak on his own, but will speak whatever he hears, and he will declare to you the things that
are to come."

[127] In PL XXXIX, 1063.

"no one sees the Father except he alone and he to whom He wishes to reveal Himself." God is imparted to no one by the spirit except through Himself.[128] But there are divine means to obtain this vision and connection, the divine means whereby the Father manifests Himself to the world and shares of Himself through Jesus Christ alone. Just as He now shows those means to us, so, from eternity, He formed them in advance within Christ's wisdom. The divine and substantive mode is the holy spirit, the eternal mode being in God and its fullness being in Christ. The eternal mode was in God as a sort of preconception in His mind. The fact of the preconception of Christ's spirit in God is shown even from this point: if that portion or spark or measure or breath or mode of the spirit, which was in Peter or Paul, was once substantively in God, how much more so was Christ's very fullness? When the holy spirit is given to Peter and Paul, no change in God takes place nor is anything new really cut off from Him, but they are themselves changed because through the occurrence of their union and assumption they take up things which were prepared for them. The spirit which is given to them, is received from Christ, and in Christ it was prepared for them in advance. The preparation is immense and the means, inexpressible. "Neither did the eye see nor did the ear hear the things that were prepared for us."[129] Indeed, among the apostles there was the holy spirit's true substance, given according to a particular limit and prepared for them in this way from eternity. In fact, in Acts 2 and 4 it was said that "they were filled with the holy spirit" because at that time what was in them, filled and moved them in such a way that they would burst forth into amazing activities.[130]

---

[128] Matt. 11:27 and Luke 10:22 : "All things have been handed over to me by my Father; and no one knows the Son except the Father, and no one knows the Father except the Son and anyone to whom the Son chooses to reveal him."

[129] From 1 Cor. 2:9 : "But, as it is written, 'What no eye has seen, nor ear heard, nor the human heart conceived, what God has prepared for those who love him'..." It seems that it was a well known and used expression among the Jews already recorded by Isaiah : "From ages past no one has heard, no ear has perceived, no eye has seen any God besides you, who works for those who wait for him," Isa. 64:4. Moreover, the general expectation of the epoch was to "inherit the kingdom prepared for you from the foundation of the world," Matt. 25:34.

Nevertheless, the whole plenitude of the spirit was without limit not in them, but in Christ alone (John 3, Rom. 12, 2 Cor. 10, and Eph. 4).[131] Therefore, "according to the measure" we mean that one spirit was in this man here, [187] another in that man with you, another in that over there, and all were "one spirit."[132] Therefore, do not be surprised, if Christ called one "the *paraclete*" and the another "the spirit" because even you would call it one thing in this case, another in that case, and still other in another case. If you get rid of sophistic realities, everything will be easy.

So we can reach a conclusion by way of summation, the holy spirit is defined briefly as follows: the holy spirit is a substantive, divine mode, fitted to the spirit of angel and man.[133] Although the holy spirit substantively makes a unity with what is in Christ, with the sanctified creature of the spirit, nonetheless, in itself it is understood as pure divinity. According to the mode of dispensation, it is the "Divinity from the Divinity" just as in branches, leaves, and flowers there is divinity from divinity of the seed and root: just as in vine sprouts there is by a certain succession of divine distribution divinity from the vine's divinity. Therefore, the holy spirit truly is a substantive mode, distinct from the Father and the son and proceeding from both, perceptible, acting, saying and doing one thing here, another there. The holy spirit is distinguished from God, the Father, with the result that we may say that "God is in the holy spirit," just as "God was in the Word," and "God was in the light." The holy spirit is born from God just as from God is born the light. God is the holy spirit's Father just as He is the Father of light and

---

[130] Acts 2:4 : "All of them were filled with the Holy Spirit and began to speak in other languages, as the Spirit gave them ability." And Acts 4:31 : "And they were all filled with the Holy Spirit and spoke the word of God with boldness."

[131] The texts which indicate that "He whom God has sent speaks the words of God, for he gives the Spirit without measure," (John 3:34), whereas other texts indicate that the rest were given: "each according to the measure of faith that God has assigned," Rom. 12:3; "within the field that God has assigned to us," 2 Cor. 10:13; "according to the measure of Christ's gift," Eph. 4:7.

[132] 1 Cor. 2:10-11 : "These things God has revealed to us through the Spirit; for the Spirit searches everything, even the depths of God. For what human being knows what is truly human except the human spirit that is within? So also no one comprehends what is truly God's except the Spirit of God."

[133] Another succinct definition: *"Spiritus sanctus est substantialis modus divinus spiritui angeli at hominis accommodatus."*

the Father of glory. By the same figure of speech God is called the Father of Wisdom, the Father of the Word, if you understand that these things once existed without man.[134] God dwells in the spirit, and God is the spirit; God dwells in fire, and God is fire. God dwells in light, and God is light. God is in the mind, inhabits the mind, and God is the mind itself.

Perhaps you will object by saying, "Although from eternity time immemorial God's spirit contained the divine hypostasis alone or divinity's substantive mode like the first form of the elemental breath in God, and with the addition to it of the incarnation in one essence, it now has the elements of Christ's human spirit, it does not appear that His glory is greater than formerly, granted that after the resurrection it is greater than it was when Christ was active on earth." My answer: God's glory is neither increased nor diminished in itself; it is greater in us to the degree that it more greatly glorifies us. With Christ's resurrection God showed His power and glory to be so great that from corruptible, human elements He made [188] incorruptible ones, and for our own glory He so gloriously joined them to His own divinity with similar elements that in one and the same instant they substantively made one spirit with God, which is the holy spirit. Whatever is in Christ, is substantively one with God, insofar as he says, "I and the Father are one."[135] Just as Christ's body has been agglutinated in such way to God that it is substantively one with Him, so through him his spirit and man's spirit cling and adhere to God with the result that it is one spirit with Him (1 Cor. 6).[136] The spirit is given through Christ alone, and the spirit of Christ made human, has in this way been joined to us. Christ's own vital, eternal spirit is joined substantively to us just like the very flesh of Christ. But you will understand these points in the

[134] The phrase "God is the father of the holy spirit" caused opposition from Calvin in Geneva. Servetus defended this phrase using the words of Athanasius: *"Spiritum sanctum nasci ex Deo docuit Athanasius;"* and of Tertullian: *"Id ipsum docuit Tertullianum,"* (Cfr. lib. I, note 206). The pastors of Geneva followed Calvin amplifying Calvin's accusation to which Servetus replied: *"Nebulo iste sententias meas truncat, ut per fas et nefas mihi imponat,"* Calvini Opera, VIII, pp. 503, 543.
[135] John 10:30.

books *On Baptism* and *On Communion*[137] more thoroughly than can be related here. It is enough for now, if you understand that the holy spirit's substance is a divine substance which in and of itself is conjoinable to our spirit through Christ because of a particular bond, and that it thus sanctifies our spirit.

Having recognized the holy spirit's essence and the mission for our own sanctification, another mission must also be addressed here briefly. And on this subject we shall explain Christ's statement in (John 16): "The spirit as a *paraclete* will denounce the world regarding its sin, my justice, and the judgment against the enemy."[138] Such is the remarkable mission of the holy spirit. "The spirit will denounce the world regarding its sin because they do not believe in me." Evidently the spirit will prove that it is a noteworthy sin not to believe in him who, having been shown by the prophets and signs of heaven, performed so many and such great miracles for our salvation, who suffered so many and such great pains on our behalf, and who fulfilled so many and such great mysteries. It will evidently denounce the world "regarding my justice," declaring that I am just, I whom the world slanderously called unjust and fraudulent. The spirit will teach that I have done everything justly because I am received into my Father's presence, and I would not be received if I were unjust. Not only am I received, but I shall even remain there in perpetuity, and "you shall not see me hereafter."[139] This is my justice, and it must also be shared with you [189] so that by it I may bring even you into the Father's presence. Likewise, it will prove the world wrong "about the judgment" that was ritually carried out against Satan, not understood by them. It will teach that I lived according to the Law, and that I cast down the enemy, who was oppressing the world and holding it captive in hell. This Law's juristic power

---

[136] 1 Cor. 6:17 : "But anyone united to the Lord becomes one spirit with him."

[137] In pages 470 ff; lib. III of the Part IV.

[138] John 16:8-11 : "And when he comes [the paraclete], he will prove the world wrong about sin and righteousness and judgment: about sin, because they do not believe in me, about righteousness, because I am going to the Father and you will see me no longer; about judgment, because the ruler of this world has been condemned."

[139] John 16:16-19 : "A little while, and you will no longer see me ..."

is great. For it seems that, according to God's sentence, the demon held man captive and subject to Death by right: because he whoever had committed sin, had become a slave to sin. But the spirit will teach that the Demon has acted with iniquity in every instance, and that he always does act with iniquity by tempting with numerous seductive techniques the image that is beloved to God. Yet, though man was once justly punished by God, he has now been justly liberated through Christ's mercy. We shall more fully elaborate on these points in the book *On Original Sin*[140] because it is not the appropriate place here where we are discussing the holy spirit.

This point especially must be made: many people vainly torment themselves with questions concerning just how the holy spirit proceeds from the Father or from the Father and the son. Now I for my part make this declaration with great ease: "The spirit of truth is that which proceeds from the Father,"[141] or which the Father gives; for He is the primary source, and He "gives a good spirit to those who seek Him."[142] Notice, moreover, in what sense the word, "proceeds," is used there so that you are not wickedly taken in by an imaginary meaning. The Word, "proceeds," in that context is rendered in Greek as ἐκπορεύεται, namely, "sets out, goes out." There is no metaphysical, inner act of sending things out, but there is an act of going forth for God's works. There was no inner, material procession of the sort that Sophists fashion; rather there was an eternal preformation within the archetypal world such as later was his display. In the creation there was a remarkable and original display, namely, of the Word and of the Spirit. The modes of divinity were substantive with respect to the origin of all substantive things and Christ's generation. Truly before the creation there were neither movements of God within Himself nor was there any activity or passivity; there was no material

---

[140] In the first section of the Bk. I of *De regeneratione ac manducatione superna*, pp. 357-388.
[141] John 15:26 : "When the Advocate comes, whom I will send to you from the Father, the Spirit of truth who comes from the Father, he will testify on my behalf."
[142] Matt. 7:11 : "If you then, who are evil, know how to give good gifts to your children, how much more will your Father in heaven give good things to those who ask him!" Luke 11:3 : "Give us each day our daily bread."

generation or emanation or exhaling or breathing or production. No one was breathing and no one was being given breath. All of these words are representation of movement, activity, and receptivity. Therefore, the inner activities of those three, invisible entities having been disposed of, [190] we say that it is God's dispensation whereby He unites man's spirit with Himself. Truly this is "giving and sending the spirit:" when He takes a man unto Himself and unites his spirit to Himself. Because God does this through Christ, the spirit truly proceeds from Christ, especially if one considers that there is in him the entire, original plenitude of [the divinity].[143] We have said that divinity proceeds from divinity according to the mode of divine distribution. We grant that in terms of a creature's dispensation and in terms of a particular mode the language of "dispatches" has been attributed to God. It is said that, like an angel, the holy spirit visibly "sets out," "is moved," and "descends" (Matt. 3 and Acts 2).[144] But God's substance itself, which was in the angel, is not for that reason moved. God's Spirit, which fills everything, illuminates this or that man, thus moving him, in such a way that it is itself not moved. The holy spirit proceeds, sets out, and heads out from Christ's mouth because through the distribution of his own breath Christ bestows this gift upon us. The holy spirit proceeds from the Father and the son, and from the Father through the son. "Through Jesus Christ God pours the holy spirit into us (Titus 3).[145] Once the promise of the holy spirit has been received from the Father, Christ pours this gift into us (Acts 2).[146] As he was going on high, Christ received gifts from the

---

[143] Col. 2:9 : "For in him the whole fullness of deity dwells bodily." This text was explained by Servetus in Bk. II, p. 73 of the text of the *Resitutio*.

[144] Matt. 3:16 : "And when Jesus had been baptized, just as he came up from the water, suddenly the heavens were opened to him and he saw the Spirit of God descending like a dove and alighting on him." Acts 2:2 : "When the day of Pentecost had come, they were all together in one place. And suddenly from heaven there came a sound like the rush of a violent wind, and it filled the entire house where they were sitting." But there is no mention of the angel in the quoted texts.

[145] Titus. 3:6 : "This Spirit he poured out on us richly through Jesus Christ our Savior,"

[146] Acts 2:17-21 : "'In the last days it will be, God declares, that I will pour out my Spirit upon all flesh,' ..." This comes from Joel 2:28-32 : "Then afterward I will pour out my spirit on all flesh; ..."

Father, and "he has given them to mankind" (Ps. 67 and Eph. 4).[147] Christ received these upon his resurrection, since he did not have them previously because "he had not yet been glorified." The holy spirit of rebirth that glorifies and renews man, did not exist at that time (John 7).[148] The spirit itself, which is from the Father, is from Christ, as it was made his very own, essential and natural to him. Furthermore, Christ said, "Whom I shall send you from the Father" (John 15).[149] By sending from the Father Christ also sends from himself, and by sending from himself he sends from the Father because the Father is in him. First, Christ gave honor to the Father by saying that the spirit was to be given from the Father. Next, he added himself, saying that he would give himself. Although at that time Christ did not possess such a spirit, nevertheless, he said, "I shall send," "He will accept from me," and "He will announce to you." "Everything that the Father has, always belongs to me. Therefore, I have said that he will receive from me, that is, from [191] my substance and my divinity."[150] He will impress upon you the character of my substance and the form of the son that was received by me, and he will teach you the order that was already written, so that "one shall not speak apart from him." "From my own substance shall I share him" with you just as "I shall place my soul before you." The Greeks were wrong in not wanting to accept that the holy spirit comes from the son: because Christ is the only source from which the holy spirit emanates.[151] Truly the holy spirit is Christ's life, soul, and sense. It is Christ's spirit whereby we have Christ's very sense in such a way that we live by Christ's

---

[147] Ps. 67:18 : "You ascended the high mount, leading captives in your train and receiving gifts from people." These words were repeated by Paul in Eph. 4:8 : "Therefore it is said, 'When he ascended on high he made captivity itself a captive; he gave gifts to his people.'"

[148] John 7:39 : "Now he said this about the Spirit, which believers in him were to receive; for as yet there was no Spirit, because Jesus was not yet glorified."

[149] John 15:26 : "When the Advocate comes, whom I will send to you from the Father, the Spirit of truth who comes from the Father, he will testify on my behalf."

[150] John 16:14-15 : "He will glorify me, because he will take what is mine and declare it to you. All that the Father has is mine. For this reason I said that he will take what is mine and declare it to you."

[151] This is an allusion to another famous point of contention with the Greek concerning *Filioque*. Servetus summarizes his position which is fully admissible to the Roman orthodoxy: *Christus est unicus fons, unde spiritus sanctus emanat.* His explication, however, is not orthodox.

very life. Indeed, we may not be alive any longer by ourselves, but "Christ may live in us."[152] In us there is Christ's spirit, derived from his innermost substance, from his innermost heart, having been given with great love, and which for this reason is called "God's love in our hearts" (Rom. 5).[153] It was given to us from the innermost part of his heart so that through him Christ would truly be formed in our heart, and so that we would truly be transformed into his image. Because it was the son's spirit it was quite logical for Paul to show the Galatians that we were made sons through him. For he impresses upon us the very sibling relationship of God's son so that, as much as Christ's brothers, we may call him, "*Abba*, Father." The spirit itself contains the son's form as does the soul of a body. It makes the impression of the son within us; it forms the son within us, regenerating us thereby; for that reason it is called the spirit, ὑιοθεσίας, the spirit of filiation. Next, the body itself is added, and the blood, the flesh, and the bones, at the Lord's supper. This was never before given to anyone in the Law nor prior to Christ's resurrection. At that time no one was called Christ's brother or coheir to his kingdom, because the spirit, being of that sort, regenerating and glorifying, was not there yet, Christ not having been glorified yet (John 7). Hence after the resurrection Christ himself calls us his brothers (Matt. 28; John 20).[154]

Based on what has been said, a reason has been given for why the expression, holy spirit, is so frequently used in the New Testament and not in the Old. The reason for the difference is that there were sanctifications of the flesh in the Law, but not the sanctification of the spirit. In fact, at that time there was the

---

[152] Gal. 2:20 : "And it is no longer I who live, but it is Christ who lives in me. And the life I now live in the flesh I live by faith in the Son of God, who loved me and gave himself for me."

[153] Rom. 5:5 : "and hope does not disappoint us, because God's love has been poured into our hearts through the Holy Spirit that has been given to us."

[154] John 7:39 : "for as yet there was no Spirit, because Jesus was not yet glorified." Matt. 28:10 : "'Do not be afraid; go and tell my brothers to go to Galilee; there they will see me.'" John 20:17 : "But go to my brothers and say to them, 'I am ascending to my Father and your Father, to my God and your God.' "

spirit, but not as it is now: thus they neither knew the holy spirit "nor had they heard whether the holy spirit existed" (Acts 19).[155] It was a new expression or one that was unusual for them, [192] and the new powers indicated that it was something new just as it truly was a new spirit. Although that spirit which was among the prophets was Christ's spirit, nevertheless, it was a "different" spirit at that time; the dispensation of divinity was "different," and it operated "differently" among them than it does among us. Although we say that this holy spirit spoke through the prophets because it is eternal, nevertheless, they truly were sanctified differently than we are now, and they absorbed a "different" spirit or, rather, one that acted differently because Jesus Christ "had not yet been glorified" (John 7). They received the spirit of servitude out of fear while we have received the spirit of "God's sons" (Rom. 8 and Gal. 4). For that reason Christ calls them "slaves," while he calls us "friends" and "brothers" (John 15 and 20).[156] Therefore, the new spirit has been given in accordance with a new pact, and this is the reason for the expression's novelty.

Among the Jews there were references to a certain, material sanctification, which came about through an outer anointing and touching with the result that the object that [was] touched, was sanctified (Exod. 29 and Lev. 6).[157] Also by touching something impure, their own sanctity was contaminated (Lev. 5 and 11).[158] Among the Jews the flesh was sanctified, but now the spirit is holy. The anointing which we receive from Christ, is an anointing of the spirit (2 Cor. 1 and

---

[155] Acts 19:2 : "'Did you receive the Holy Spirit when you became believers?' They replied, 'No, we have not even heard that there is a Holy Spirit.'"

[156] John 7:39; Rom. 8:15; Gal. 4:5; John 15:14, and 20:17.

[157] Exod. 29; Lev. 6. These two chapters describe in detail ritual washings, anointing, making animal sacrifices, animal or grain offerings for atonement, etc.

[158] Lev. 5:2 : "Or when any of you touch any unclean thing – whether the carcass of an unclean beast or the carcass of unclean livestock or the carcass of an unclean swarming thing – and are unaware of it, you have become unclean, and are guilty." Lev. 11 lists animals which can be eaten by the Jews and those that are unclean and cannot be eaten, e.g., verse 4 : "But among those that chew the cud or have divided hoofs, you shall not eat the following: the camel, for even though it chews the cud, it does not have divided hoofs; it is unclean for you."

John 2 and Acts 10).[159] True Christians act from an inner anointing and sanctification which happens in the spirit and by the spirit. Therefore, we call the spirit holy, and we are baptized in the name of the holy spirit, which is unknown to the Jews, in such a way that, although dead in the Law and buried in the flesh, we might be ever mindful of the sanctification of the holy spirit alone. No Jew was ever born again "from water and the holy spirit." Sometimes a passage is read in which there is from a holy object a particular effect of the spirit of sanctification, a temporal effect, not the spirit of rebirth, the new holy spirit with its incorruptible elements. If in the Law it is ever said that God's spirit is in someone, it is not, as with us, taken as a reference to the holy spirit of rebirth, but rather as a reference to some intelligence, prophecy, or power (Exod. 28, 31, 35; Num. 24, 34; and Judg. 14).[160]

Holy scriptures refer even to a gust of wind as a spirit of God by virtue of its great effectiveness, [193] both in the literal and spiritual sense. For there was in that very gust of air a life-giving energy, and through such a mystery the true substance of the holy spirit was shown, that is, Christ's divine, life-giving breath itself. For this reason it is said that "God brings the wind out from His store-rooms" (Ps. 134; Jer. 10 and 51).[161] "God's spirit" is called that wind which was causing a stir over the waters in Genesis 1 at that time because it was great and

---

[159] 2 Cor. 1:21-22 : "But it is God who establishes us with you in Christ and has anointed us, by putting his seal on us and giving us his Spirit in our hearts as a first installment." 1 John 2:27 : "As for you, the anointing that you received from him abides in you, and so you do not need anyone to teach you. But as his anointing teaches you about all things, and is true and is not a lie, and just as it has taught you, abide in him." Acts 10:34-43 : Peter narrates at the occasion of the baptism of Cornelius how Christ abolished the old prohibitions of flesh in a new order of the spirit.

[160] In Exod. 28:3 : "And you shall speak to all who have ability, whom I have endowed with skill;" Of Aaron in Exod. 31:3 : "and I have filled him with divine spirit, with ability, intelligence, and knowledge in every kind of craft." The same of Bezalel in Exod. 35:31. In Num. 24:2 : "Balaam looked up and saw Israel camping tribe by tribe. Then the spirit of God came upon him." There is nothing related to the topic in Num. 34. In Judg. 14:6 the "spirit of God" is equated with a physical strength of Samson : "The spirit of the LORD rushed on him, and he tore the lion apart barehanded."

[161] Ps. 134:7; Jer. 10:13, 51:16 : "he makes lightnings for the rain and brings out the wind from his storehouses."

powerful in order to dry out the waters and heap them up, so to speak, into a pile (Ps. 32);[162] also, in order to produce an expansion of the airy firmament by the process of evaporation. In that context it is called "God's spirit" by reason of a complex mystery that was present already in God and would be present in Christ. The Hebrews also knew this. They themselves knew the energy of God's spirit that makes everything live, that activates and fills everything. In that instance God's spirit caused the waters to live so that they in turn would cause the earth to live for the generation of things. In the *Bereshit Rabba* as well, as they raised broader questions about the spirit, they said that "the spirit that stirred the waters," was the Messiah's spirit that stirs everything and makes it live from eternity.[163] Thus, without the illusions of our trinitarians that no one ever knew about anyway, they had the right idea. Instructed by the Law and by the prophets, those men knew that it would come to pass that God's spirit itself would rest above the Messiah, and that he himself from the beginning was the spirit, and that he was always active within things.

One more observation about this holy spirit of Christ remains to be made, namely, that, although there is no physical sanctification in us, nevertheless, in Christ's body there is a special quality so that he is said "to have been born of the holy spirit" and "by the holy spirit" (Matt. 1). He is of the holy spirit's substance just as he is of the Word's substance.[164] The substance of God's spirit contained in the archetypal world and even now contains the same elements of the Word that we have previously identified as being three higher ones or their substantive exemplar. The substance of the Word and of the Spirit was the same substance in

---

[162] This is Servetus's interpretation of the words of Ps. 32:6-7 : "By the word of the LORD the heavens were made, and all their host by the breath of his mouth. He gathered the waters of the sea as in a bottle; he put the deeps in storehouses."

[163] *Midrash Bereshit Rabba*, eds., Julius Theodor and Chanoch Albeck (Jerusalem: Wahrmann Books, 1965), vol. I, p. 56. Commenting on Gen. 1:2 it states: "And this is the spirit of the King Messiah."

[164] Matt. 1:18 : "she was found to be with child from the Holy Spirit." Matt 1:20: "'Joseph, son of David, do not be afraid to take Mary as your wife, for the child conceived in her is from the Holy Spirit.'"

God, God Himself thus displaying Himself. Also now, although Christ's flesh and spirit [194] truly are different, nevertheless, they have a true connection with elemental substance just as our own flesh and spirit have been bound together in this way. When it was in the sepulcher, Christ's flesh possessed separately its own divine substance in heavenly elements and in light's substantive form. Christ's very spirit, which he commended to God, as he was dying, contained then and still does contain separately our own regeneration's elements, which are the same as the Word's elements. And thus are the three superior elements common to the body and to the spirit in the manner of a shared bond whereby the soul is bound to its earthly body as much in Christ as in ourselves. But in us there are only elements created by virtue of being a creature of generation. In Christ they are both created and uncreated from the substantive propagation of creator and creature.[165]

Therefore, from the implication of that common and substantive bond between flesh and soul we obviously recognize that Christ's very flesh is born in Mary from the holy spirit's substance. Whatever is in Christ is holy: in him there is holiness of body and spirit, and immaculate flesh. In Christ alone were the sanctification of the flesh and the generation accomplished through the substance of God's spirit, and the substance of God's spirit was substantively imparted to the flesh itself. Therefore, regarding that paradox mentioned earlier, to the effect that truth does not belong to the bodies of this age,[166] Christ's body is not included because it is truth itself. In fact, the body itself is truly the spirit's food, and it is truly united with our spirit in one substance being bonded together in the spirit of regeneration. Christ's "flesh truly is more genuinely a food" than this, external

---

[165] These formulations of Servetus have to be correlated with those in other contexts: lib. IV, n. 169; Dial. II, n. 5. Servetus, pressed by Calvin, expressed himself more clearly: *Elementa creata quatuor in eo dico sicut in nobis: sed ei addo verbi substantiam, quam exemplarem fuisse dico, vim in eo exprimentem trium superiorum ut roris celestis... Tota caro, quidquid a deitate secernitur, est ex semine Davidis...* And these components form one essence *"Ut anima et caro sine confusione. Si substantialis fuit unio, una inde substantia resultat"* (*Calvini Opera*, VIII, 542-544).

[166] Servetus refers to the phrase in *Timaeus* which states that nothing temporal has a real being, really exists, Bk. IV, n. 116.

food.[167] In the case of the latter common food, there is no truth as the paradox indicates, but in the case of the former kind of food, there is truth in which there is a stable and immaculate purity. That is the true food of a particular life that lives forever, which is in us.

At this point could anyone doubt, if in Christ alone there was from the beginning the holy spirit, how the holy spirit descended upon him [195] in the Jordan? If so, my answer is: Before his resurrection Christ did not yet obtain God's full glory and power. They were kept for the resurrection by a certain dispensation of God. In the Jordan a new force and glory of regeneration through baptism was shown just as in his own rebirth Christ received a new spirit of glory. Through the incarnation there was a casting down of the highest, divine form into the lowest, servile garb, and through the resurrection there was the glorification. Therefore, Christ alone now contains hypostatically the whole glory of the Word and of the Spirit.[168] In him alone and from him alone there exists truly the holy spirit because it has been substantively placed within him and finally through his grace placed within us, and in this way we are substantively one with him just as he is one with the Father.

Again, if the holy spirit blends into one substance with our soul, who can doubt as to what that whole is? If someone does, my answer is: It is the soul, and it is the holy spirit. The addition of Divinity changes the name of neither its manifestation nor of the individual. There is a soul in the holy spirit, and the holy spirit exists within the soul. Just as God is in Christ, Christ is in God, and Christ is God remaining a man: thus by a sublime regeneration through hypostatic union, a soul becomes the holy spirit, and it remains soul just as man becomes God and becomes one with God. Moreover, the fact that, like fire compared to fire, light to

---

[167] John 6:55 : "for my flesh is true food and my blood is true drink."

[168] Another theme that was subject of discussion between Servetus and Calvin. It concerned the plenitude of Christ before the resurrection and in which sense he received through it a new spirit. Servetus maintained: *"Plenitudinem spiritus semper habuit Christus, sed ante resurrectionem non erat glorificatus. Ita dicitur novus spiritus ob novam gloriam. Imo totus ipse Christus est factus homo novus, nova omnia"* (*Calvini Opera*, VIII, 547-548).

light, that whole is one substance, is something you will obviously understand beyond what has already been said, if you consider Christ's entire vital spirit in which the soul and the holy spirit constitute one being. In fact, the very atmosphere, which we breath, is made substantively one with our soul after it has been joined in its essence within our heart to our own vital spirit. We have shown that derived forms are one with light's prior form. We have also said that the acquired concepts are in their essence one with the soul just as light is one with light, and spirit is one with spirit.[169]

[196] Just as Christ is one with God, so he said that we are made one with him through the holy spirit. Indeed, we are made "something else" greater. Within us a new internal, substantive, and immortal man is generated from flesh and bone, and he is substantively one with the soul. You will see this in baptism and communion because the reason for communion with Christ and chewing his flesh is not frivolous nor is the regeneration of so sublime a spirit frivolous. Christ shares substantively with us his own vital, eternal spirit just as he does his own flesh. He truly shares himself entirely with us.

Now is the time to give a true reason why Christ said, "This new spirit and the immortal life itself shall remain forever in us."[170] Formerly, the spirit was given according to circumstance to the Jews in the incorruptible elements of their soul. In us after regeneration there remains continuously Christ's spirit with the eternal elements such as they are in him, after he has been revived, just as his eternal flesh remains in us. God was not bound in this way with man before the incarnation as is now connected the spirit of Christ who became man. This was accomplished for our grace through his arrival so that in this way his humanized spirit would be bound with our spirit. In our own regeneration a true, incorruptible soul approaches our soul, and with an inner, incorruptible, everlasting man, the holy spirit inseparably remains in us. Christ's seed in us is called incorruptible as is the

---

[169] Compare Bk. IV, pp. 143 & ff.
[170] John 14:16.

"inner man" (1 Pet. 1 and 3).[171] Incorruptible is the man who was conceived not from blood nor from pleasure of the flesh, but from God (John 1 and 3, and 1 John 3).[172] On that basis John inferred that in this world we are of the sort that Christ is in heaven (John 4).[173] We are truly made into gods by participating in Christ's Divinity, being truly made "partners in divine nature," as Peter said.[174] As a shadow of this truth, it once was said, "I said, 'you are gods.'"[175] Our inner man is God from heaven and God's substance. [197] Now that this divine regeneration is recognized as a "regeneration from above," these details will be better understood. Then the inner, heavenly man will be understood; then a new progeny will be sent to heaven from on high. A special divine progeny of Christians will be born, at which Isaiah marvels.[176] Men who will never die again, will be born.

Before we put an end to this book, let us, as if gathering up what has been said, compare anew the Spirit to the Word as it once was and now is. God's manifestation was substantive in the world just as His communication was substantive. Just as God is logos, so God is spirit. With the Word He orders something to be made; with the Spirit He gives it life. The bodies of heaven and earth are created with the Word, given life with the Spirit, and at the same moment Light's form is posited within things. No thing exists without the Word; no thing without the energy of Spirit and Light has any inner force. Within the

---

[171] 1 Pet. 1:4 : "and into an inheritance that is imperishable, undefiled, and unfading, kept in heaven for you." 1 Pet. 3:4 : "let your adornment be the inner self with the lasting beauty of a gentle and quiet spirit."
[172] John 1:12-13 : "But to all who received him, who believed in his name, he gave power to become children of God, who were born, not of blood or of the will of the flesh or of the will of man, but of God." John 3:15 : "that whoever believes in him may have eternal life." 1 John 3:2 : "What we do know is this: when he is revealed, we will be like him, for we will see him as he is."
[173] John 4:17 : "Love has been perfected among us in this: that we may have boldness on the day of judgment, because as he is, so are we in this world."
[174] 2 Pet. 1:4 : "Thus he has given us, through these things, his precious and very great promises, so that through them you may escape from the corruption that is in the world because of lust, and may become participants of the divine nature."
[175] Ps. 81:6 : "I say, "You are gods, children of the Most High, all of you." This Psalm was quoted by Jesus in John 10:14 and many times by Servetus.
[176] Servetus applies to Christians, as did many other authors, the optimistic phrases of Isaiah concerning the power of Yahweh and blessing his own people (Isa. 45) or the new Jerusalem and

282

Word itself exist Spirit and Light. Spirit comes forth with the act of speech, and, just as we are unable to make speech without breathing, God breathes by speaking. For this reason it is called the "spirit of the mouth," "the spirit of the lips."[177]

Just as the Word's substance was made manifest and visible in Christ's physical elements, and just as his body contains substantively that substance, so the substance of God's Spirit is seen in Christ's spiritual elements, and his natural spirit substantively contains that substance. Just as in Christ, God's Word is substantively one body with the very substance of man (Eph. 2),[178] so, too, God's Spirit and the spirit of man are one spirit (1 Cor. 6).[179] God dwells in the son, and the son is God. God dwells in the holy spirit, and the holy spirit is God. Our own spirit itself is God; it goes forth and is born from God, just as Christ is God, having gone forth and been born from God: he in the primary instance, we in a secondary instance, but through him. From Christ's very mouth the spirit of regeneration advances into us. Christ grants us more than to the Jews this sublime gift of his physical and spiritual substance. Before Christ's coming, no hypostasis of the spirit was seen [198]. But Christ wanted it to be made manifest first in his own baptism, later after the glory of his resurrection in the apostles, so that in this way we would value more the effects and the grace of his arrival.[180] When Christ was seen and heard, the holy spirit was immediately seen and heard, and It was recognized internally within us as a consoler. Not only did we see the spirit as a dove and as

---

the new generation of the Jews (Isa. 60-62).

[177] Ps. 32:6 : "By the word of the LORD the heavens were made, and all their host by the breath of his mouth."

[178] Eph. 2:15-16 : "He has abolished the law with its commandments and ordinances, that he might create in himself one new humanity in place of the two, thus making peace, and might reconcile both groups to God in one body through the cross, thus putting to death that hostility through it."

[179] 1 Cor. 6:17 : "But anyone united to the Lord becomes one spirit with him."

[180] This phrase was objected to by Calvin since it implied that before there was in God no hypostasis or person of the holy spirit. One can deduce from reading the discourse of Servetus that Calvin did not understand the exact sense of the Servetus doctrine. Servetus taught that "the person in the Word is the visible hypostasis, but in the spirit it is perceptible hypostasis." To another objection of Calvin that such a concept of person scandalizes all the "pious," Servetus replied: "Piety consists in showing the error but not in a criminal accusation. You know that I had explained everything, yet you act against your conscience." (*Calvini Opera*, VIII, 546).

fire, but also through hearing (John 3), and within ourselves we perceived it (John 14).[181] Hence in Acts 2 "the tongues of fire" appeared, the "fierce sound was heard,"[182] and its effectiveness was perceived within.

Moreover, the Word's incarnation bears this resemblance to the sending of the spirit, and in this we are assimilated into God's son. As it comes down, the Word effects Christ's descent from heaven just as through the spirit's descent we descend from heaven. Likewise, we ascend with Christ. For Christ himself is called God's Word just as if that Word withdrew from God and came to many after it was made flesh. But truly it did not withdraw; rather, Christ ascended to God. In the same manner the spirit withdrew from Christ, so to speak, when it was sent to the apostles (Acts 2). But truly it did not withdraw; rather, we ascend to Christ himself as we start to sit with him in heaven. And there we already are reigning with him. May we reign always. Amen.

---

[181] By reading literally John 3:8 : "The wind blows where it chooses, and you hear the sound of it, but you do not know where it comes from or where it goes. So it is with everyone who is born of the Spirit." And John 14:17 : This is the Spirit of truth, whom the world cannot receive, because it neither sees him nor knows him. You know him, because he abides with you, and he will be in you."

[182] Acts 2:2-3 : "And suddenly from heaven there came a sound like the rush of a violent wind, and it filled the entire house where they were sitting. Divided tongues, as of fire, appeared among them, and a tongue rested on each of them."

[199] Two Dialogues
On the Divine Trinity

To the effect that there exists within it

not a mirage consisting of three invisible entities,

but the true manifestation of God's substance in the Word and its true

communication in the Spirit.

The First Dialogue

is concerned with the shadows of the Law, Christ's complement of

angels and souls, and hell's substance.

Michael. Peter.

Michael: The Elohim that was the creative force in the beginning with Moses, and the Word of John that was with God in the beginning, refer to Christ's one person.

Peter: Ah, here he is: it's the Servetus I've been looking for.[1] Well, well.

---

[1] The subject matter of these two *Dialogues* corresponds to the material discussed in *Dialogorum de Trinitate libri duo* whch Servetus published under his name in 1532. The text published in *Christianismi restitutio* is enlarged by many quotes and references. The beginning very similar, is, however, much more clearly stated in the 1532 edition : *"Necessario secundum scripturas, haec tria debent convenire, Logos, Elohim et Christus, quod ex sola collatione principii Genesis cum principio evaengelii Ioannis probatur."* The personage who introduces Michael in the

Why are you speaking to yourself all alone here?

Michael: I see that Christ is unknown to Christians. I see that those who do not know upon what the Christian faith rests, are called Christians, and in seeing this I groan. If Christ were to come today and declare again that he is God's son, again our Sophists[2] would crucify him. The one Christ is a single thing, a single being, and a single son. Theirs is a conjured up system, a fraudulent sophistry and an illusion based on the invisible.[3] Their salvation is illusory as is the death of that invisible entity. The notions of "idioms" whereby the angel is said to die in the hide of an ass [200] and the holy spirit to die in a mule are sacrilegious.[4]

Peter: And you place the seed of generation, meaning the cloud and the elements, in God?

Michael: Everything and the origins of everything are in God. The seed of generation is said to be in God as He generates, just as speech is said to be in God as He speaks. There was a seed in God, just as Christ is called God's seed, and the speech itself is called the seed: especially because all seeds were contained in that very speech. It is not accurate to speak of generation if those things which are the substantive components of generation are not borne in mind.[5] All the more so because Christ's relationship to God is the most excellent of all acts of generation being an outstanding example and the true prototype. What children receive from

---

original edition of *Dialogorum* is not Petrus but Petrucius. One could think that Servetus was influenced in writing his *Dialogorum* by Spanish convert Rabbi Moses Sefardi (who, after his baptism in 1106, assumed the name of Petrus Alphonsus) who also used in his *Dialogues* the character of Petrus and presented himself as Moses. His *Dialogues* were, however, published by Gymnicus in Cologne only in 1536, thus four years after Servetus's work was published. Servetus was very courageous in revealing his real name in the opening paragraph.

[2] By the term Sophists, Servetus means the scholastics including the reformers of the main Reformation movement, the so-called Magisterial Reformation. The "God's son" in Servetus's sense as a real human being, a biological son of God, and not as the metaphysical, invisible son of God, the second Person of the Trinity.

[3] This is an obscure phrase of Servetus: *"Ipsorum suppositum suppositium est, idioma sophisticum et invisibilis illusio."*

[4] This phrase is repeated many times in the *Christianismi restitutio*.

[5] Servetus makes an allusion to Luke 8:11 : "Now the parable is this: The seed is the word of God." Servetus's idea is based on the various meanings of the term *seed*. Servetus is especially concerned with the use of exact terminology : *"generationis substantialia."*

their fathers in other generations, Christ receives from God – children being from God's creatures, Christ being from the Creator. In scripture the seed of generation, the germ, the generative dew, and everything else are attributed to Christ. Otherwise, how do you say that the generation is from God's substance? If there were other things in God Himself, there was also in God, everything's true origin, the seed. If you acknowledge that everything was in God, you will obviously acknowledge that super-heavenly waters were in his archetype, fire in his empyrean, his spirit in the ether. Because of this you now remember that there was a divine display just as there was its preformation. We say that the spirit, Elohim, is like a breath of air; we say that in God there is fire, the watery cloud of God's glory, a fiery river, the rain of the Word, the dew, and the watering, for the purpose of generating God's true son, Jesus Christ. The manifestation of such things in God was not accomplished without mystery nor was God tricking His prophets with insubstantial sunlit specters when through the celestial spirit, fire, and water God's glory and majesty were declared.[6] The heavenly waters, the blow of air, spirit, and the radiance of fire were always apparent there in the cloud just as they are now apparent in the generations of others and in the sky. We have shown that that analogy to the Word is valid in the seed of our own generation, in the airy cloud, in speech, and in our breath.[7] There was divine substance, God Himself showing Himself in this way and presenting Christ's glory by exposing it; God, the creator, in this way wanted to conform Himself through Christ to His creatures. [201] Or was the omniforming essence unable to show itself such as it wanted?[8] If you are loathe to say that there is a seed in God, say that it was Divinity itself that acted in the seed's place. This grain or drop is not called a seed

---

[6] This is a new expression of the Servetian theory of the contribution of the three superior elements (air, fire, water) to the constitution of the generating seed of Christ. This was already visualized in the symbols of the Old Testament and conforming to the interpretation of the element earth as being material and passive. Compare Bk. IV, note 166; *Dialogorum* II, notes 5 and 18.

[7] See Bk. IV, pp. 152,162 concerning the Word as the *analogatum princeps*.

[8] *Essentia illa omniformis*. The Orphic and Neo-Platonic concept which Servetus already explained.

in the material sense, but in the sense of a formal idea, which itself is the truest seed in God.[9]

The Word was the seed in God, the seminal principle, the σπερματικός τεχνικός, as Philo said in his book, *On the Heir to Divine Things*.[10] If you are also loathe to say that there is a cloud in God, say that the divinity was within the cloud. The wisdom said of itself, "I have covered the earth like a cloud" (Ecclus. 24).[11] "Like a cloud shining inside a cloud," "inside the fog of the cloud," "inside a bright cloud" (Exod. 19 and Matt. 17).[12] Never was any cloud created without there existing, as an archetype, a true model of it, one referring to the cloud. Therefore, God, as He showed everywhere, was able to show men such a model, although even there was a separate, created cloud. I gladly concede, and I have even taught this point to others, that the cloud was created in those exhibitions of the God's glory, but I say that there was within itself a separate, uncreated, inwardly shining, super-elementary cloud, a Divinity itself that was showing itself thus. Inside the visible light, within it, God was the true light; God was the air within the air, the fire within the fire, the cloud within the cloud just as the true holy spirit was inside Christ's breath.[13]

Peter: You have asserted something else that I don't accept, that the Word no longer remains or that it was a shadow.

Michael: Far from having said that the Word does not remain, I might

---

[9] *Sed ratione formalis ideae, quae ipsa est in Deo verissimum semen.*

[10] Philo of Alexandria, *Quis rerum divinarum heres*, 24, 119, and also in *De aeternitate mundi*, 17, 85. Philo took the idea from the Stoics and applied it to his own philosophical system and his interpretation of the Hebrew bible (M. Hillar, "The Logos and its Function in the Writings of Philo of Alexandria: The Greek Interpretation of Hebrew Thought and Foundations of Christianity" in A *Journal from the Radical Reformation. A Testimony to Biblical Unitarianism*, vol. 7, no. 3 spring 1998, part I pp. 22-37; vol. 7, no. 4 summer 1998, part II pp. 36-53).

[11] Ecclus.24:3-4 : "I came forth from the mouth of the Most High, and covered the earth like a mist. I dwelt in the highest heavens, and my throne was in a pillar of cloud."

[12] Exod. 19:9 : "I am going to come to you in a dense cloud." Matt. 17:5 in the narrative concerning the transfiguration of Jesus : "While he was still speaking, suddenly a bright cloud overshadowed them."

[13] This elaborate interpolation is to support the doctrine of Servetus, already reported, concerning the Christian interpretation of the Old Testament theophanies.

instead have said, and I am on the point of saying, that today the same substance of the Word is in Christ's flesh. I say that the light that formerly shone in the cloud, is the Word's substance, and it is the natural glow of Christ's body. That Word, which once was the form of the man in essence, today preserves in the same man the same form, and the Divinity itself still exists within Christ in the form of man.[14] How will there be no everlasting nature of the divine form in him, if through him there is the form's everlasting nature in you?[15] The form is neither blended nor diminished; rather, its essence is perceived intact. [202] Furthermore, I say that the Word is not as it once was, because "it has been made flesh" and because the arrival of Christ made everything new. It is not according to a dispensation from the time of Moses, according to which it was in a cloud.

As to your second objection, that I have called it a shadow, as if it were the prefiguration of some future thing: just for the same reason as in any shadow there is a certain image. A shadow is a diminished form of light. What were shadows in the Law possessed at that time a diminished light and a certain nature: the likeness of another, more perfect object. All those shadows existed as there was the Word as well, and this indicates a certain imperfection of time. Those things which had not achieved perfection at that time, perished in a particular manner. Although what was once the Word's substance is now the same thing in the body of Christ, nevertheless, Christ was adumbrated or prefigured there.[16] For in the Law the types of things to come preceded the types which we can refer to as shadows. Now God is light in Himself, and He adumbrated Christ in the very substance of His own light and the Word, and He, who was seen in the Word, was once seen as in a shadow. For Philo the Word was a shadow. For this is what he said in his

---

[14] *Et in Christo adhuc est Deitas ipsa sub forma hominis.*

[15] Another expression of Neo-Platonic thought: the eternity of the form Christ-Logos in the man as an argument for the eternity of the divine form in Christ himself.

[16] In the original edition of *Dialogorum de Trinitate* Servetus explains better this objection: *"Necessitate coactus umbram vocavi, non aliter hoc mysterium explicare valens. Nec volo sic dicere quod Verbum fuerit umbra, quae transierit et non permaneat, imo eadem est nunc huius corporis, quae olim fuit Verbi substantia, fuit tamen Christus ibi adumbratus, et praefiguratus."*

second book of *Allegorical Interpretations* : σκιὰ Θεοῦ ὁ λογός αὐτοῦ ἐστί, in other words, "the shadow of God is His Word."[17] The shadow was the hidden form and model through the likeness of which, he said, man was made in God's image. In the beginning the prefiguration was more clear. Because of the sin the shadow and a certain obscurity increased. The shadow's condition no more takes away from God's Word than it does from God Himself. Nor do I detract from the angels, although I might say that Christ's shadow was in them. The shadow's condition actually has receded, but not on that account has the substance of the angels perished nor has that of God or that of the Word. The shadow exists then just as you would correctly say, if you were to compare us to the glory of a future age, that the shadow exists still in us. For "we now see in an enigma, but at that time it will be face-to-face:"[18] this glory that was already to us given through Christ prefigures another, greater glory in the future.[19]

Having made the comparison to our own situation, there was in the Law a diminished light; there were misty and obscure clouds which God placed then before Himself "as a shield" (Ps. 17 and 2 Kings 22).[20] [203] "The people living in the dark and in the region of death's shadow, saw a great light" that had risen for us through Christ (Isa. 9 and Matt. 4); likewise Luke 1: "It appeared to provide light for those living in the dark and death's shadow." [21] There you always see a shadow and dark, but here you see light that has been fully exposed. It has been

---

[17] It is not in Bk. II, but in Bk. III of *Legum Allegoriae*, XXX, 100. Philo says that there are two classes of mind, one that perceives the knowledge of God through created things "and which does not distinguish the cause from the things created as it would distinguish an abiding body from a shadow," and the other which emerged from all created objects and "receives a clear and manifest notion of the great uncreated, so that it comprehends him through himself, and comprehends his shadow, too, so as to understand what it is, and his reason [Logos], too, and the universal world." One can find here the influence of the "myth of the cave" described in the *Republic*, VII,514a.

[18] 1 Cor. 13:12 : "For now we see in a mirror, dimly, but then we will see face to face."

[19] Rom. 8:18 : "I consider that the sufferings of this present time are not worth comparing with the glory about to be revealed to us."

[20] Ps. 17:11 : "He made darkness his covering around him, his canopy thick clouds dark with water." 2 Kings (2 Sam.) 22:31 : "he is a shield for all who take refuge in him."

[21] The words of Isa. 9:2 cited later in Matt. 4:16 and Luke 1:79.

fully manifested in Christ, and it has been imparted to us in the spirit, and, subsequently, it will again be exposed in the glory of our full body through the bodily resurrection to come just like now with the resurrection of the spirit. The shadow once existed in the ceremonies of the Law and in other mysteries by analogy to the Word's higher mysteries that are concealed even in shadow, cloud, and mist with God. Christ was then in the hidden recess of the Most High and "in the shadow of the Almighty" (Ps. 90).[22] They were themselves all in shadow and dark because Christ was hidden in the Word's shadow and in the protection of the cloud. Moreover, this shadow of the Word lasted until, casting its shade over Mary, it ceased to be a shadow (Luke 1). In fact, until Christ's resurrection there was always something of the shadow just as in us up to the point of our own resurrection there is something of the enigma. Still the Divinity has been adumbrated in Christ's flesh, and it has not yet been glorified as is apparent in that adumbration and transfiguration on the Mountain in Matthew 17. Therefore, if the incarnate Word itself was, till now, in the shadow, how much more was it once in the cloud? Hence, while Christ lived on the earth, the shadows of the Law were not dissipated until the glory was entirely exposed in Christ and in his spirit. Therefore, we may join Paul in calling whatever was seen in the Law, a shadow, "but the body belonged to Christ" (Col. 2).[23] Nor did you introduce an infelicitous question, for I was just contemplating this very point when you heard me talking to myself.

Peter: What is the point you were making to yourself?

Michael: I was contemplating [204] the notion that the Word is the very person of Christ, and I was making a comparison between the Logos and Elohim, while relating everything to Christ.

Peter: It isn't accepted in our age that perceptible forms appeared in

---

[22] Ps. 90:1 : "You who live in the shelter of the Most High, who abide in the shadow of the Almighty."
[23] Cor. 2:17 : "These are only a shadow of what is to come, but the substance belongs to Christ. (*quae sunt umbra futurorum corpus autem Christi*).

God.[24]

Michael: This was accepted and known to everyone in the first church as is clear from Irenaeus and Tertullian. It was likewise with the ancient Hebrews, as I have already cited following Philo, Eusebius, and Jerome in other places. You read nothing else in the Law and the prophets.[25] They speak of God's manifestation, not a mirage. If God had wanted to give no understanding of His Divinity, it would have been pointless for Him to give man a longing for that very thing, especially to Moses and the others who wanted to see His face. It would have been pointless and illusory for the Law to teach so many things about this matter: God Himself would have been toying with us by showing Himself face-to-face. Christ himself would have been trifling with us to offer a vision of God. If you say that there is no substantive appearance of God and if you will say that there is no substantive sharing of Him, then God is shared substantively neither with the world nor with Christ, and then nothing other than a specter appeared in Christ. The ancient Hebrews, when referring to God with the words *temunah*, *zelem*, and *demuth*, were recognizing the first divine form and figure, in the image of which man was made; they call it Elohim's face.[26] In the first church of the Christians this was so commonly held that nearly all the heresies arose at that time from it. For Simon Magus, Menander, and Basilides, as cited by Ignatius, later Valentinus, Marcion, and Manichaeus and most of the rest attributed Christ as practically a specter, a human form alone that was once in the sky without a true body of flesh.[27] The

---

[24] Servetus does not refer to any specific doctrine of his time. He only compares early Christianity with the indeterminate Christianity of his time.

[25] Compare notes 51, 52, 54, 58, 98, Bk. III, *De Trinitate*. Based on these texts and at times twisting their meaning, and supported by his literal interpretation of the biblical texts, Servetus arrives at one of his fundamental formulations concerning God, namely, that God, invisible by his essence, became visible by his Word, which had eternally the same human form which was to be incarnated in Christ, and therefore is a "person," an aspect of God.

[26] For the concept of the form of figure of God and the meaning of these Hebrew terms see Bk. III of *De Trinitate*, pp. 93 and 103 of the *Restitutio*. Servetus gives his interpretation of the terms Elohim and the theophanies.

[27] Servetus points to the danger of the original Gnosticism which was, according to him, a corruption of the common belief in the Word or *Elohim* as the *temunah* or form of God. This Gnosticism amounted to the acceptance of various forms that emanated from the divinity and the

Sophists were brought by a hatred for these heresies to dreams about invisible entities and three points, as the kingdom of the Antichrist, who had his own advance parties, was approaching. This had been foretold by John that in this kingdom the three illusory spirits, which are Beelzebub's three sons, will prevail (Rev. 16).[28] After Athanasius and certain others, who were already the strong opposition for the Antichrist's kingdom, that attitude, whereby they might notice Christ's true manifestation, was never given the Sophists. [205] Read Tertullian at the end of his second book of *Against Marcion*, where he says that it was accepted by everyone in the early church that there was a human figure in the Word so that based on the testimony of the apostles even the Marcionites themselves held this belief.[29] Most illustrative is this testimony from the entire first church. In his book *On Christ's Flesh* and the one *Against the Jews*, Tertullian plainly teaches that the Word once had a human form and figure. Irenaeus teaches the same thing in Book 4, chapters 15 and 17. Many other passages in them are about the Word's human

negation that Christ had a real body. Simon Magus, the last representative of pre-Christian Gnosticism, is followed by Dositeus and Menander who are alluded to by Ignatius and cited by Clement in *Recognitions* as well as by Origen and by Irenaeus. Basilides, an Egyptian teacher and Valentinus also an Egyptian who taught in Rome, Marcion, a Greek who settled in Rome, all three in the middle of the second century, are known to us from the long passages in *Adversus haereses* of Irenaeus, in *Panarion* of Epiphanius, in the *Stromata* of Clement of Alexandria as well as from *Adversus Marcionem* of Tertullian. The dualism of Manichaeism, fully developed in the third century, shows an affinity to the previous Gnosticism as is keenly observed by Servetus.

[28] Rev. 16:13 : "And I saw three foul spirits like frogs coming from the mouth of the dragon." Though one could not deny that the opposition to Gnosticism was a partial factor in the formulation of the trinitarian dogma, it seems somewhat arbitrary to designate Gnostics as the precursors of the Trinity, unless one thinks, as Servetus indicated in another place, that the three divine Persons of the Trinity are comparable to the various *eons* which Gnostics recognized as intermediaries between man and the divinity.

[29] Terullian, *Adversus Marcionem*, lib. II, cap. XXVII (PL II, 316) : "Inasmuch as ye yourselves have now come to the belief that God moved about in the form and all other circumstances of man's nature, you will of course no longer require to be convinced that God conformed Himself to humanity, but feel yourselves bound by your own faith." Calvin and his pastors objected during the trial in Geneva to this interpretation of Servetus as well as to the following text, recognizing however, that "the son of God appeared to the patriarchs in the human form as a prelude to the incarnation," to which Servetus replied that this form existed in the divinity itself without being differentiated from God the Father except for being visible. And this again Servetus supports by the texts from Tertullian (*Calvini Opera*, VIII, 522).

form and the person in whose image they say Adam's body was formed.[30] Lest no one be so crude an anthropomorphist as to think that God in Himself is something corporeal; we have rightly said that He is incorporeal and invisible, but has shown Himself as a person because He is omniform. This manifestation was a pronouncement, a living representation, a shining of the Word.

Peter: I have been convinced that this genuine θεοφανίαν or apparition of God, was the shining of Christ. The λογός was truly the ideal reason brought out, the speech that relates, that represents. Therefore, return to your comparison of the logos and Elohim.

Michael: We know from Moses that in the beginning there was Elohim who created everything, and was seen as Elohim. We know from John that in the beginning there was the shining Word "through which all things were made."

Peter: What was before?

Michael: You are interrupting me!

Peter: I would first like to know what was prior such that everything else proceeded in order from there.

Michael: There was "the predetermined termination of the ages which God made in Christ," as Paul says.[31] Just as all things are now in God, so they were before creation in the same order in Him, and Christ was first of all: he alone was "the figure of God's substance and the visible brilliance of His glory."[32] What existed before, if it can be called "before," was the moment of eternity, so to speak; rather, in God's presence not "was," but "is" is said. By perceiving in His eternal reason a son that was corporal and visible to Him, God, by means of

---

[30] Tertullian, *De Carne Christi*, cap. IX (PL II, 772) and *Adversus Judaeos*, cap. IX (ibid, 622) : "For He who ever spake to Moses was the Son of God Himself; who, too, was always *seen*. For God the Father none ever saw, and lived. And accordingly it is agreed that the Son of God Himself spake to Moses." Irenaeus, *Adversus haereses*, lib. IV, caps. 5 and 7 (PG I, 985 and 991) in which it is said that Abraham knew the Father through the Word and for that reason "Your ancestor Abraham rejoiced that he would see my day; he saw it and was glad" according to John 8:56.

[31] Eph. 3:11 : This was in accordance with the eternal purpose that he has carried out in Christ Jesus our Lord."

pronouncing the Word in which there was spirit, made Himself visible [206] in the substance of such an external manifestation.[33] Through the same speech-act and through the same spirit He created a patrimony for the son in the form of this corporeal world, being the shadow of a better age. He created other men in the image of His son, giving Him children to be with him just as He said, "Behold me and the children whom God has given me."[34] Through speech and spirit God built all these things. All those things which He did through speech and spirit, appeared as the sort which were formed prior in His mind. Hence God gave to man speech and spirit; He shares Himself with him through speech and spirit so that man, educated by God's speech and spirit, would support his maker with speech and spirit.

Therefore, the first was the Word of God, a Word from the internal faculty of reason that was uttered for the generation of the son or was shown through His manifestation: "behold the personified Elohim, who creates the world." God simultaneously contemplates and utters the generation of the son by exposing the Word. And through that very Word of the son's generation He creates the world, to which the son is due as master. Whatever eternities you may imagine, there was already the divine design in them, a design which subsequently was the Logos and thereafter the flesh. God had in His wisdom already expressed man's form, which was later seen as Elohim and thereafter as Christ. Therefore, Elohim did not begin to exist in the beginning, but "he already existed in the beginning," as John says. There was previously the Word within the faculty of reason, but not shown through manifestation, as when it made itself visible in the creation. God is not said to change on this account, just as He would not even be changed, if He were now

---

[32] Heb. 1:3 : "He is the reflection of God's glory and the exact imprint of God's very being."

[33] Various paragraphs of Servetus's texts in which he expressed his understanding of the eternity of Christ were objected to during the trial in Geneva in proposition 27. Servetus complained that in answering him Calvin and the pastors omitted and twisted his assertions: *"haec verba ibi sunt adiecta, quae tu perfide omisisti, ut sententia mea videretur magis exosu,"* and *"Bene habent omnia, nisi esset tibi animus perversus"* (*Calvini Opera,* VIII, 517, 547).

[34] Isa. 8:18 cited in Heb. 2:13.

to make Himself substantively visible to you in a cloud or in a fire or in some other form. For He contains within Himself every form capable of perception which He wishes in presenting Himself to us. God, who shows them without any change in Himself, who "makes things visible that were once invisible," as the apostle says,[35] already had within Himself Christ and the ideas for other things. The Word existed before the world, but not with priority in a temporal sense because time did not exist, but in the sense of cause preceding effect. You must always keep this one point in mind: neither then nor now are there any differences of time in God's presence nor any intervals, but they are perpetual always and an eternity of the present. [207] Yes indeed, putting aside the temporal differences as concerning us, it must always be conceded that this corporeal son, Jesus Christ, who was made from Mary, comes from God since eternity and is generated before all ages through that utterance that was made in eternity. In eternity, before all times, Christ's reign is in place, as Paul teaches after Christ: the temporal differences are arranged later.[36]

Peter: Therefore, God begets the son by an act of will, not by an act of nature.

Michael: Between Athanasius and Arius, between Basil and Eunomius, between Augustine and Maximinus and all the rest of this ilk there was the fiercest inquiry into whether God's son was a son by nature or a son by the father's will. These are read in Athanasius, his book, *On Faith*, and in *Disputations against Arius*, in Basil's work, *Against Eunomius*, in Augustine's *Against Maximinus*,

---

[35] Heb. 11:3 : "By faith we understand that the worlds were prepared by the word of God, so that what is seen was made from things that are not visible."

[36] This paragraph represents a profound change in the trinitarian doctrine of Servetus in this edition of the *Dialogues* and in the entire *Restitutio* since the first publication of his *Dialogorum de Trinitate* in 1532. It can be illustrated by comparing the phrase which Servetus inserted in the margin of the first edition of Dialogue I : "God before the creation was not light nor the Word, nor the spirit, but something ineffable, and all these are the expressions of dispensation" (*Dialogorum de Trinitate*, 1532, I, A4). The equivalency of the Mosaic Elohim, historical Christ, and the Johannian Logos, the equivalency between the beginning of Genesis and that of the fourth Gospel required temporal manifestation more than the eternal preexistence of these forms or "persons" of God. The link was provided by the Neo-Platonic doctrine of *Deus omniformis*

Book 15 of *On the Trinity* against the voice of the Arians, in the 7th question *To Orosius*, and in other inquiries.[37] The Arians used to say that the Father begat the Son through free will, unconstrained by necessity or a law of nature, and that in this way He got His son. They were unwilling to grant that he was a son by nature lest he seem equal and coeternal with the Father because they always had an understanding about a certain, separate, real son. Athanasius, Basil, and Augustine were unwilling to grant that the Son existed through will lest he seem not to be coeternal and lest there be any change in God if He ever chose to exercise His will. But I say that the son was a man by nature and will. God did not at some point decide to will, but He eternally willed: and, as He willed through the act of contemplation, the one is a natural consequence of the other. Reasoning is natural as is cognition, will, and knowledge in God. According to these He decided naturally and willfully.[38]

Peter: Through a voluntary dispensation God was the Word seen externally. What was in Him?

Michael: By His own nature God is indefinable nor is He defined by us except as a cause of things, which is the utterance itself. By borrowing our

---

(θεός παντομορφος).

[37] Servetus refers to various discussions in the fourth century between the proponents of the trinitarianism and various forms of Arianism and Neoarianism. Eunomius (ca. 333 C.E.-ca. 393 C.E.) was a bishop of Cyzicus (ca.361). He was a disciple and secretary of Aeetius and adopted his extreme Arianism. His followers were called Eunomians or Anomoeans [from the Greek word = unlike], named so because of their denial of a substantial similarity between God the Father and God the Son. Eunomius taught that by definition God was unbegotten and that the Son, begotten of the Father, could not therefore be equal to the Father. Basil the Great refuted him in his work *Against Eunomius* (364). The Eunomians were condemned at the First Council of Constantinople in 381. Discussion between Arius and Athanasius in Athanasius *Expositio fidei catholicae*, equivalent to lib. X of his *De Trinitate* (PG XXVI, 292), and in *Disputatio Athanasii cum Arrio coram probo iudice*, which is attributed today to Virgil of Tapso (PL LXII, 167); between Basil and Eunomius in Basil's *Adversus Eunomium*. (PG XXIX, 467-669); between Augustine and Maximinus in Augustine's *Contra Maximinum ep.*, his *De Trinitate* lib. XV, cap. XX , and in *Ad Orosium praesbiterium contra priscillianistas et origenistas*, q. 7 (PL XLII, 743, 1087, 669).

[38] The Arians and Servetus talk only about a man, the son of God, while the trinitarian dogma proposes the Son as the second Person. Servetus suggests a very original mediation between the two camps: that God always, since eternity voluntarily wants to manifest himself and communicate substantially and this is natural for God.

expressions from other contexts we say that certain natural things are in God.[39] [208] We say that He is the light, the spirit, the mind endowed with reason, that He is all-knowing and fills everything. It shined in Him naturally that which He Himself first wished to be. You cannot think otherwise about God. For this would mean, if we exclude Christ, to understand God, what was not granted even to the angels. Therefore, naturally and willfully there was Logos, the ideal faculty of reasoning, and the utterance, Christ's shining with God, his light with God.

Peter: Why was darkness apt to precede light? Even before the sin? Moses teaches this in Genesis 1 and Paul in 2 Corinthians 4 as if darkness was the first beginning.[40] The sound is heard in the darkness, and it is the Spirit's voice: therefore, the Spirit, which reaches the ear without light, differs from light.

Michael: Insofar as light was apparent in God Himself, it was from light that was not apparent. So also light is said to be created from darkness. For the same reason says the Apostle, "Invisible things were themselves made visible" (Heb. 11).[41] Damascius Platonicus relates that the Egyptians called the first beginning "unknown darkness" because it was, above all, conception. Hence, Manichaeus, when he incorrectly devised a material darkness, hit upon the idea that his race of darkness came from an evil beginning.[42] God, who always sees

---

[39] In the original *Dialogorum* (1532, B6v) Servetus wrote: *"Dolendum, quod philosophicis loquendi consuetudinibus sic simus imbuti, ut in Dei mysteriis cognoscendis efficimur caeci, et velimus Deo ipso videri sapientiores. Primo hoc notandum, abusive Deo tribui naturae nomen, nam id quod cuique rei a nativitate innatum est, et proprium, dicitur eius natura. Unde hanc Christi carnem, quia ex Deo nata est, naturam habere divinam usque ad mortem oportet clamare. Deus tamen in seipso nullam habet naturam nec originem, qualem habet eius filius. Nulla Deo convenit naturae ratio, sed quid aliud ineffabile."* Calvin objected to the last paragraph of Servetus (*Calvini Opera*, VIII, 545).

[40] Gen. 1:3 : "Then God said, 'Let there be light'; and there was light." 2 Cor. 4:6, but in another context : "For it is the God who said, 'Let light shine out of darkness,' who has shone in our hearts to give the light of the knowledge of the glory of God in the face of Jesus Christ."

[41] Heb. 11:3 : "By faith we understand that the worlds were prepared by the word of God, so that what is seen was made from things that are not visible.

[42] Damascius Platonicus (462-533) belongs to the last generation of the Neo-Platonic philosophers associated with Plato's Academy. He had been made head of Plato's Academy in 520 and he was still head when the Christian emperor Justinian closed it in 529. At the same time Justinian under the influence of the clergy closed all the other Hellenic schools. When Justinian became emperor, his troops were fighting against the armies of the Persian king. It was

everything, in Himself, in His own light, there never was darkness, but was the true light from which He brought out this light of the world by saying "Let there be light!" Sound's spirit is like light coming from a luminous source, and in the soul it merges with light into one. Finally, He Himself will be exposed as light. In fact, He now exists in light, in a light that is innate to water or air to be sure, but does not appear to us.[43] Although created sound's spirit differs from created light, nevertheless, the Spirit is the light in God. And in the soul itself there is one substance of spirit and light, and it is like God.

Peter: In the cited passage, Paul is discussing Christ's true light, which shines in our hearts and before it there was only darkness.

Michael: If you go back to the beginning, I have already said that light was appearing from a state of non-appearing. [209] By this mechanism God's son himself or the Word itself was light from light, visible light from invisible light. Likewise light is said to exist mystically from darkness because Christ's light shines for us from darkness, from a darkness that existed before his arrival.[44] The prototype for this is indicated in that created light which was given after darkness because it was thus to be given in the shadow of Christ's true light. In the mystery there existed in the world darkness before light, just as we existed in darkness before Christ's light gleamed for us through the good news. Behold, the created

---

natural that Damascius, Simplicius and five other members of the Academy, when forced out of Athens, went to Persia to serve in the court of the Persian King Khosrow I, when Khosrow and Justinian signed the peace treaty in 532. It is not completely clear what the terms of the treaty were in regard to the philosophers who had gone to Persia. Agathias, the Byzantine poet and author of a history of his own times, wrote of these events after the death of Justinian in 565: "... *the terms of the treaty would have guaranteed to the philosophers full security in their own environment: they were not to be compelled to accept anything against their personal conviction, and they were never to be prevented from living according to their own philosophical doctrine."* Damascius, dominated by a strong skeptical tendency, admits the unknowable reality of the One, and that all the rest are merely appearances, *tenebras incognitas.* Mani, Manes or Manichaeus was crucified in 273, therefore could not influence Damascius.

[43] For the spirit of light, water, and air, one should understand in this context wave or vibration. We can imagine ultimately as if Servetus were establishing this reduction of the waves of the elements to the luminous vibrations in accordance with his theory of light as the *mater formarum.*

[44] These are reflections on Gen. 1:4; Ps. 111:4; Acts 26:18; 2 Cor. 4:6.

light itself was the shadow of Christ's light. By the same mystery it is proven that the Word itself is a shadow, and it gleamed for us from darkness. That Word which was never clearly seen, adumbrated the very body of Jesus Christ, which in God is now a corporeal, luminous, and visible truth, under cover of a certain obscurity. Therefore, the Word is not now the sort it once was because it does not exist according to that dispensation to which in the time of Moses it was the oracle within the cloud's mist. For, as is written in 2 Paralipomenon 6, "God, who used to live in mist," now lives in Solomon's temple, which is Christ's body (John 2).[45] If the Word is now the sort it once was, it follows that the Law is as it once was, and that it is a veil over the face of Moses. For, by analogy, to the greater things happen the lesser ones.[46] If now such is the Word, where is that oracle? Where is the Lord's glory that appeared there? Is not the fullness of all those things in Christ's body? Have not all of those things been transferred to Christ through the adumbration of Mary? You do not note sufficiently how great was the impact of Jesus Christ's arrival and the nature of innovation of everything that took place with the New Testament. The Word is new just as the spirit is new. "All the old things have been remade as shadows, and, behold, everything has been made new" (2 Cor. 5).[47] Christ is a new man, a new name, a new food. We have a new reign, a new heaven, a new land, a new everything.[48]

Peter: How is it possible that he is eternal and always new?

Michael: The spirit is called new [210] because of the invocation of creation and because of the new glory, and it exists eternally in God's substance. From Paul's perspective Christ is called "a new man" because he exists from God

---

[45] 2 Chron. 6:1 and John 2:21 : "But he was speaking of the temple of his [Christ's] body."

[46] Again Servetus repeats one of his fundamental principles : *Nam per analogiam ad superiora fiunt haec inferiora.*

[47] 2 Cor. 5:17 : "everything old has passed away; see, everything has become new!" And Wisd. 5:9 : "All those things have vanished like a shadow, and like a rumor that passes by."

[48] References to Rom. 6:4; Gal. 6:15; Eph. 4:23; Rev. 21:5.

and man in one substance and one body (Eph. 2).[49] And he himself is eternally Logos and Elohim in God's substance.

Peter: You are of the opinion that the Logos and Elohim are ever the same.

Michael: When I hear from John that the shining Logos is called a referential faculty of reason; and that at another time it was the light of Elohim's face, necessarily I think of Christ's face because the entire Law places this image before my eyes, as I said sufficiently in Book 3. Extremely crucial for this point is the force of Christ's words: "Who sees me, sees the Father."[50] On the basis of those, we can thus infer that, if God was made manifest in the flesh, by seeing that flesh God is seen. Therefore, in this face of Christ, God is seen, and whoever once saw the face of Christ, saw God. Moreover, God was once seen within the oracle, and what was seen, was Elohim's face. Therefore, it follows that the Logos, Elohim, and Christ's face are the same thing in the person.[51] In chapter 12 John teaches that the glory of God which Isaiah saw in chapter 6, was Christ's glory. This same point is proven on the basis of what John writes about light in the Gospel and his Letter.[52] For the Word was that light by which God is light, and the same light was the light and glow of Elohim's face (Ps. 4, 35, 43, 66, 88, 89, and 118).[53] John saw this same light, glow, glory, clarity, and radiance in Jesus Christ's face because he said, "We saw his glory" (John 1). Peter bears witness that he saw the same thing on the mountain in the transfiguration of Christ's face (1 Pet. 2). Paul teaches that he saw the same thing in Christ's face, and that it was seen (Acts

---

[49] Eph. 2:15, but out of context : "He has abolished the law with its commandments and ordinances, that he might create in himself one new humanity in place of the two, thus making peace."

[50] John 14:9.

[51] *Idem in persona*. For Servetus, "person" means an aspect, appearance.

[52] John 12:38-41, using the words of Isa. 6:10, concludes : "Isaiah said this because he saw his glory and spoke about him," implying Jesus. Characteristic for the fourth Gospel and 1 John 1:5-7, 2:8-11 is the use of terms light and darkness.

[53] There are in these psalms various references to the face of Jehovah or a luminous semblance.

and 26; 2 Cor. 4).[54] Therefore, the Logos, Elohim, and Christ, who is "the word's light," were the same thing. The light itself was seen in the beginning by Adam himself as Elohim's face; afterwards it hid behind the cherubim as Isaiah teaches. It had been covered, and "human darkness did not grasp it." We were blurry-eyed because of our transgression of the horrible edict and, together with Adam, affected with shame such that we could not bear the brightness [211] nor dare direct our eyes to that face out of fear of death because of the cherubim standing before us with a flaming sword. For this reason the most merciful prophet, Jesus, was brought to us in order to remove the fear of the fiery sword and of the transgression. We are taught this in Deuteronomy 18, with which Hebrews 12 and Exodus 20 are in agreement.[55] At that time the people were unable to endure the terrible vision of fire. But now without any fear we gaze, our eyes uncovered, upon God's glory at Jesus Christ's face. In fact, we always possess it in the spirit like an illuminated mirror so that even we are transformed by the spirit into the same image and glory (2 Cor. 3 and 4). From this passage of Paul make the following analogy. Just as Elohim's face used to shine on high, so the face of Moses was luminous because of his association (Exod. 34). Just as Elohim Christ's face was veiled by a cloud on high, so even Moses placed a veil over his own face so that others would not be allowed to see his face or understand Christ's mysteries.[56] How skillful is this association of mysteries! Just as that light was Elohim's face externally imparted to the very face of Moses, so the light of Christ's face is being shared internally with us so that we may there see God's glory in Jesus Christ's face. We are always reaching this one conclusion, namely,

---

[54] John 1:14; 1 Pet. 2:9 : "who called you out of darkness into his marvelous light." Paul in his conversion, Acts 9:3 and 26:13; 2 Cor. 4:4.

[55] Heb. 12:18-21 mentions the scenes from Deut. 18:16 and Exod, 20:19.

[56] 2 Cor. 3:13-14 : "not like Moses, who put a veil over his face to keep the people of Israel from gazing at the end of the glory that was being set aside. But their minds were hardened. Indeed, to this very day, when they hear the reading of the old covenant, that same veil is still there, since only in Christ is it set aside." This is an allusion to Exod. 34:33 while Christ is the "image of God." 2 Cor. 4:4 : "In their case the god of this world has blinded the minds of the unbelievers, to keep them from seeing the light of the gospel of the glory of Christ, who is the image of God."

that the light, Logos, Elohim, and Christ are the same, that for the ancients there is a shadow, but for us there is truth, and for us everything is new. "The old had passed and now everything is new."

Peter: If everything old was a shadow, the old heaven was a shadow of the new heaven, and the old earth was a shadow of the new earth, and the old man a shadow of the new man.

Michael: And the spirit was a shadow, the air a shadow, the fire a shadow, the waters a shadow, and the whole world a shadow. The old earth compared to the new is shadow and darkness, *tohu* and *bohu*.[57] The new earth has been glorified as Christ's flesh, and our flesh will be transformed and made new in its likeness. In Christ's very flesh and in his spirit there are heavenly elements that make heaven new. Christ dispenses to us in regeneration new waters, new air, and new fire because when we are generated and made anew "from water, spirit, and fire." [212] These things are substantively new from eternity in God. The waters above the heavens mentioned in Genesis can be taken literally as rainwater; nevertheless, they refer to those superheavenly waters of the archetypal world contained in the cloud of the Lord's glory that were to be the flower of Christ's natural generation and the Divinity's true rain.[58] They also relate to the new, superheavenly waters of our own regeneration and to the future, heavenly irrigation in our own spirit. The spirit of these internal waters of our regeneration is the same Divinity and substance that was in the archetype's waters that generated Christ. This very Divinity was adumbrated in these created waters with a specific similarity of substance. In these created waters, just as in air and fire, there is a symbol of the Divinity as a shadow, which, within the elements of Christ is the true shadow of the Divinity imparted to us at baptism. This entire world and whatever is in it, contains a specific shadow of the Divinity, and there is the

---

[57] Or *unformed* and *empty*, the biblical terms used to describe the primordial chaos, Gen. 1:2 : "the earth was a formless void."

[58] In the Manuscript of Paris, the word *ros*, dew, is used and not *flos*, flower.

Divinity in them just as there is a shadow of Christ's Divinity.[59]

Peter: The world has divinity even though it has been placed in evil?

Michael: The world was made good and beautiful by God, and everything was placed within God.[60] Through the intermediary of light and form everything is one with God in the shadow of His truth whereby Christ without any mediation is truly consubstantial with God.

Peter: By this secondary process it must be understood, as Trismegitus says, that the world is consubstantial with God, is the second God, and is the son of God.[61]

Michael: He said that the world's very form is λόγος, and that God's son is like the world, thus taking it to be without a head. But from our perspective the notion of son refers to Christ, who is the world's head. Without thinking about Christ, whom not even the angels knew at that time, Zoroaster also said that the Father of the omni-form world is omni-form God.[62] It seems that this demon, Pimander, meant to teach the truth, but did not know Christ, or, whatever he had known about him in the Word, he shrewdly meant to hide by attributing the Word's divinity to himself, just as the angel attributed it to himself when he was in the presence of Moses. [213] Trismegistus was another Balaam who was truly knowledgeable about many things, but for all that he was deluded into idolatry. When he speaks in many passages addressed to Tatius about God's image, he

---

[59] But there is no pantheism in his risky phrase: *Mundus hic totus, et quae in eo sunt, quandam deitatis umbram continent, et est in eis deitas, velut umbra deitatis Christi.*

[60] According to the meaning of the Hebrew word טוב, *thob* (Gen. 1:10, 12, 18; compare Bk. IV, note 30).

[61] Thus in *Poimandres*, VIII, 1 : "For seeing that the Kosmos is the second God, and an immortal being, it is impossible that a part of that immortal being should die." And again in X, 14 : "The Kosmos is contained by God, and man is contained by the Kosmos. The Kosmos is the son of God." In XII, 16 : "The Aeon is an image of God, the Kosmos is an image of Aeon." The same in *Asclepius*.

[62] The term omniform is not the idea of Zoroaster, but one expressed by Servetus, which comes from the three or four instances when in the *Magic Oracles* it is said that in the things were posited the seeds of the fiery bond with majestic love, and that the paternal mind scattered the symbols throughout the world (*op. cit.*, II, VII, X).

declares that it is the world's omni-form image. But more correctly we say that it is Christ's image, wherein the whole world is contained, just as the forms of many things are contained in your soul. The wisdom formed in God Himself was the likeness, insufficiently known to them as such, of the holy and omniscient soul of Christ. In the wisdom were the models of all things in the manner in which they exist now in Christ's soul. There are not now in Christ's soul those qualities or created notions, but the actual, original forms and that very soul contains, hypostatically united with itself, even God's wisdom together with the individual knowledge of all things.[63] Zoroaster and Trismegistus said that the world was a great God.[64] We say that Christ is a great God, the world's lord, omnipotent. In this they fell short of contemplation of the first, true model because they gave priority to the world, though the world was made for man's sake. Jesus Christ, the world's maker, was and is substantively in God more genuine than the world, and through him the world exists secondarily in God.

Peter: The demon, Pimander, did not want such future glory for man to be revealed because he preferred being worshipped by man to showing that man should be worshipped by him.

Michael: Concealing the truth in a few cases, he said that many truths were worthy of admiration.[65]

Peter: He said that nature's elements had been bedizened with vital seeds, and even Augustine confirms this in Book 3 of *On the Trinity*.[66]

Michael: This same point is shown in the holy scriptures.

Peter: By what arguments?

---

[63] Here Servetus advances more his christological doctrine with respect to the one expressed in *Dialogorum de Trinitate* of 1532. Not only did Word preexist Logos, Elohim as the person of the omniform God, but the Logos itself is this being omniform about which Neo-Platonism is concerned. By this he confirms in a way not very different from that of Augustine the Platonic or Stoic ideas about *rationes seminales*, as he indicates later.

[64] Compare notes 61 and 62.

[65] It is a mixed praise of the hermetic wisdom which he described earlier as another "Balaam" and "deluded into idolatry."

[66] Augustine, *De Trinitate*, lib. III, cap. IX, entitled, *The Original Cause of All Things is from*

Michael: The principles and elements of natural things were already formed in God in the very order in which they now exist so that they would provide other things with their force. It is plainly shown that after creation too, the Divinity's divine condition was communicated to these elements.[67] We infer first that God is in the atmosphere. For it was by the special process of God's breathing that the atmosphere was separated from the water (Gen. 1). [214] In the atmosphere there was the divine breath, and for this reason the atmosphere itself is called "God's spirit." For this reason God is called "spirit" because He makes everything live with His airy spirit. The soul is brought out through that breath of air. In that breath of air that holds the Divinity's breath, the true and substantive divinity of Christ's breath which breathed from the archetype into everything is adumbrated in a certain symbolic way, thereby filling everything. This first seed-source within the Divinity's breath, containing the shadow of Christ's divinity, is next diffused and disseminated in combination with light, from the atmosphere to other creatures. Through God's spirit in the beginning it made the waters live by its activity for the very purpose that by their watering they, in turn, would cause the seeds to live. From the air, the rain waters take that very token of the Divinity and, by the waters, everything else born of the earth is, in turn, made to live, receiving a token of the same life-giving Divinity and form of light. In the seeds of things that very thing contains various properties, seminal principles, [*rationes seminales*] and efficient forces able to bring about the reproduction of similar forms according to the Divinity's luminous form as given by Christ. Nothing exists in the world that has life or any force without the Divinity and a token of Christ's light. "In him there was life," and "everything exists through him." And, just as the life of other things exists in him, so in him there exists the force of other things.

God, where he describes the transfer of causality through the seeds (PL XLII, 877-879).

[67] This is proposition number 34 extracted from Servetus's book and objected to by Calvin. In it Servetus affirmed that in created things there is divinity substantively, and that all is filled with divinity. Servetus responded to the objection by quoting Irenaeus and by insinuating that if things are not in God, then Calvin would move and live in the demon. This is the substantive presence of God, because "this by which we are sustained is a substance." (*Calvini Opera*, VIII, 550).

Not only were all things brought to life and caused to sprout by means of waters by that token of Christ's Divinity, but they adumbrated the greater life-giving property of other waters and the germination of Christ, who alone is the model seed that makes us, like the frond on the vine, sprout in him through the regenerating waters. Therefore, that ancient divinity of air, water, and other things was a shadow. From the beginning Christ himself through the spirit and light imbued everything, not with a single token, but with various tokens of his own divinity and with vital seed sources. These tokens were variously dispersed from thing to thing, and they introduced to everything the Divinity's various properties according to the inherent forms.[68] Aristotle, the first to try, [215] was never able to account for the four qualities alone for such varied results in the generation of species nor, as he admits, could Galen, who imitated Plato after him.[69] Whether they wish to or not, they are forced to acknowledge the properties of the forms or species, which were sufficiently proven by older authorities and were located within the universe of things. Hence, Thales said that everything was "full of gods." The aphorism of Empedocles has long trumpeted: everything exists in everything potentially by means of a token of light that contains the forms of things, by means of a token of the Divinity, whereby God is said to be everything in everything.[70] This was Empedocles' thinking: if God is in a stone and a piece of

---

[68] In this speculation of Servetus the air (atmosphere) is identified as God's spirit, breath, principle of life, and movement as represented in Gen. 1 and it is fused with the concept of Christ-Logos as the spirit and life "through whom everything" exists as it is represented in John 1 and by Paul in addition to the concept of the omniforming Logos, which, in the form of tokens of divinity (*symbolus deitatis*) or seminal principles (*rationes seminales),* is disseminated and distributed in everything else imparting inherent forms. Is this pantheism, as some scholars claimed?

[69] It is difficult to evaluate what Servetus meant by this phrase, but it seems that he claimed that neither Aristotle nor Galen could account for the generation of such a variety of species, the former from his four qualities, and the latter by imitating Plato.

[70] Servetus took from Aristotle (*De anima* I,5:411a7) this phrase about Thales of Miletus (ca 625 B.C.E.–ca 548 B.C.E.). He did not know the statement of Diogenes Laertius (*Lives of Eminent Philosophers,* I.27) about Thales : "the world is animate and full of divinities [δαιμόνων]." The thoughts attributed to Empedocles (ca. 490 B.C.E.–435 B.C.E.) were interpreted by the Orphics and Neo-Platonists. He formulated them in his two poems *On Nature* and *Purifications.* He postulated that everything originated from the four elements; one could thus say that, according

wood is in God, a piece of wood is in the stone. God Himself, who is stone within a stone, is wood within a piece of wood because by His forms He gives essence to everything. Democritus, Anaxagoras, and the rest thought the same thing, when they said that everything existed simultaneously, i.e., in God. Democritus explained that everything was simultaneously possible. For Anaximander there was a blending of everything just as there is a maelstrom in chaos, as Hesiod and Aristophanes related.[71] Truly, there was no confusion in God. Only, according to them, a confusion or a blending of things existed in the beginning, when the external arrangement of bodies had not yet been accomplished or there did not exist a material organization. That was how they conceived of it within God, just as it is said that there is in man's mind a chaos of many things because the ideas exist simultaneously. Furthermore, in matter that is susceptible of many forms, there is said to exist a potential chaos of many forms, as in the Divinity itself. For a special power exists within bodies both for acting upon the soul and for bringing it forth.[72]

Peter: I think it is true that through that shared token of light and divinity the body acts upon the soul and vice-versa because there also exists between the

---

to his doctrine, "everything is in everything." Or according to a preserved fragment, "From the one is born the multiplicity of things" (*Empedocles*, Helle Lambridis, Tuscaloosa: The University of Alabama Press, 1976, p. 68. Walther Krantz, *Vorsokratische Denker*, Berlin: Weidemann, 1949, 31 B 17). He developed, however, a complete, naturalistic and cyclic cosmogony resembling in general terms speculations of modern physicists.

[71] Anaxagoras (ca. 500-428 B.C.E.) says clearly that "everything is in everything" in the sense that in "everything are contained all other things" (Krantz, *op. cit.*, 59 B 9) because he admits the existence of indefinite multiplicity of similar elements (*principia homoeomerias*, ἀρχὰς τῶν ὄντων τὰς ὁμοιομερείας) arranged in a variety of ways. For Democritus (ca. 472-360 B.C.E.) there existed in the beginning fullness (solid being) and emptiness (*plenum et vacuum*, τὰ ναστὰ καὶ τὸ κενόν). This fullness was penetrated by emptiness and was split into an infinite number of particles, atoms, which are the origin of all things (Aristotle, *Metaph.*, I 4:985b4). Anaximander (ca. 610-547 B.C.E.) admits as the origin of everything something that is indeterminate (ἄπειρον), something nebulous like the biblical chaos, which became organized by a process of separation and association (Aristotle, *Phys.*, III 4:203b13). Servetus knew these doctrines from Aristotle and compared them with the cosmogonies in Hesiod's *Theogony* and *Works and Days*, as well as in Aristophanes' *Birds*. For early Greek philosophy see Jonathan Barnes, *Early Greek Philosophy*. (Harmondsworth: Penguin Books, 1987).

[72] Servetus does not reject the creation of the soul; he admits only the formation of the material elements of the soul starting with the primary corporeal elements as he explains in Bk. V.

309

soul and the body a sharing of the three higher elements.

Michael: The soul is greatly affected by the body. The mind's disposition follows the body's temperature, as Galen teaches in his extraordinary book.[73] The soul is variously afflicted through the body's diseases. In the soul itself and in any given substantive form, there exists the body's form: and in it there are seed-sources for outlining and regulating the body. In the body, too, there exist elements and certain potent particles for drawing out and bringing forth the soul and the substantive form. [216] Unless this force and capacity for drawing out and bringing forth the soul were present in the elements, God would not have said, "Let the earth and the water bring forth animals." "The earth," said Pimander, "bore animals which it had possessed within itself." For the earth had already been watered by the waters, and it had already obtained light's form, and thus it had been equipped with divine and vital seeds.[74] Hence God said to Cain, "When you cultivate the earth, it will not give you its own strength from within it."[75] Likewise from the same token of spirit and light it follows that, just as there are various properties hidden within bodies, so in souls there are various concepts placed there by no teacher, and are all "full of gods."

Peter: If these bodies act upon souls, all the more will the heavenly bodies, which are all the more "filled with gods," that is, imbued with divine properties through the office of the light that coheres from the beginning and forever with them, act upon and influences them.

Michael: We have already shown that in bodies as in spiritual things light enjoys primacy and an efficaciousness of form. Created light has the Divinity's most effective token of all through the operation of which it forms all things

---

[73] The title of this treatise is *The Faculties of the Soul Derive from the Complexity of the Body*, which was written in the last years of his life (he lived between 130-200 C.E.) and in which he follows the teaching of Hippocrates.
[74] This is a summary of the ideas presented in the treatise, *Corpus Hermeticum*, Libellus I *The Poimandres*.
[75] Gen. 1:12 : "When you till the ground, it will no longer yield to you its strength; you will be a fugitive and a wanderer on the earth."

substantively, through which it transforms corporeal and spiritual things, through which it flows into all things and endows any given thing with unique properties of its own form. It possesses the most effective token of uncreated light being its first-existing and beautiful image and by the nature of which all things are likened unto God and are beautiful.[76] The image of uncreated light is this created light placed within it that adumbrates it, that prefigures another, future and more exalted light of Christ. And, when this light shines openly after the final judgment, the sun's light will be blotted out, and it will pass away like a shadow. Therefore, this light and its divinity is a shadow.

Peter: What about fire?

Michael: Fiery light or fiery luminescence differs from the sun's purer light in this respect: it is always combined with glowing air or smoke. Because flame is nothing but heated air, in the fire is gathered the same token of the Divinity as in the air. Besides, and for a more exalted reason, there is in the divine air a fire kindled into a more divine state like a new fiery spirit coming off God and bringing with itself a heavenly light and prefiguring another, greater fire of the holy spirit as was given by that fire of the archetype. [217] Fire before other things is a living substance. It penetrates everything else. It is always active in other elements, purifying them and elevating them into the sky because of the atmosphere's thinness combined with heavenly light. Fire is that which joins heavenly light with elemental matter, raising it to heaven. Fire is the only element that is immutable, although it renews all other elements, it always tends towards the sky, and has been given like a celestial gift for the special use of mankind though other living beings do enjoy its use as much as man does.[77] It is fitting, then, that God is said to be fire and spirit: formerly in shadow, now in truth. Now, indeed, God kindles within us His spirit's fire, which this elemental fire conveys as shadow.

---

[76] This is one of the most impressive formulations of Servetus concerning light as the transcendental factor for the beauty and similarity of the cosmos to the divinity.

[77] Fire as a celestial gift is used exclusively by humans: *"Ignis ... est quasi celeste donum, ad hominis usum peculiariter datum."*

Peter: In the end, it is your conclusion that in every spirit there is some shadow.

Michael: We have already stated that the invisible sound's spirit is a shadow of what will be the visible and luminous spirit. Slavery's spirit was once given to the Jews, and it was a shadow of this new spirit of regeneration, which is the spirit of true filiation. From the previous Book, it is established that the Jews possessed a certain shadow of the true spirit.[78] The fact that "God's Spirit agitated the waters" shows that the Spirit's shadow also existed at the moment of creation. At that time God filled the world with an airy spirit that contained God's breath. Just as Elohim's spirit was at that time communicated to the world through an external breathing, so now Christ's spirit has been given us internally through his own, true breath with the result that the former was the external figure of this internal truth. Wherefore, to satisfy now your question about the prior shadow, I conclude that God Himself and His Word and His Spirit and His Light and His angels adumbrated Christ's mysteries. Things of heaven and earth adumbrated Christ. In men and other creatures Christ was adumbrated. If you pass from Adam, Abel, Enoch, and Noah through all the patriarchs, kings, priests, and prophets, you will find in them Christ's shadow. [218] Not only was the shadow in the person of the fathers, but it was also in their services, just as the pastor, the farmer, and the vintner were the shadow of Christ, the true pastor, the true farmer, the true vintner. In the very fruits of the earth, in animals, stones, pearls, metals, treasures, springs, rivers, wells, rain, clouds, thunder, lightning, and winds, Christ's mystery was figured. In the food of Paradise, in the manna, in Aaron's staff, in the wooden tabernacle, in the bronze serpent, in the arc of the covenant, in the vessels of gold, silver, or whatever other materials, in the stone that produces water, in the stone temple, in the angular stone, in the lion, the eagle, the turtledove, the dove, the calf, the lamb, and all other things, Christ was adumbrated. All those things adumbrated Christ, and they were all contained in Christ. He is the beginning and end of all things; in him is the model, the form, and the fulfillment of all things.[79] No mineral, animal, or plant is of any use to us as food, drink, medicine, bodily ornament, or sensual pleasure without being adumbrated in Christ, and he alone offers them to us. You will subsequently see all these in the inner man. After the ultimate resurrection, too, his word's light will offer us all benefits.[80] He is clothing, food, and drink for the "new man;" he is shelter from the boiling summer and turbulent weather; he is a bulwark, the strongest tower: formerly in shadow, now in truth.

That the "shadow's nature" may be more confidently proven, take note, too, that all ritual and worship of God were "shadow." The entire Law's ritual was carnal, prefiguring another, spiritual law which, through Christ is true ritual and worship of God. God was never truly worshipped in the Law nor was He truly made manifest. Just as God cannot be seen outside of Christ, so He cannot even be worshipped thus. Christ himself demonstrates this in John 4, when he says, "Now is the first time when God is worshipped in truth." God was formerly worshipped in shadow, not in truth, with the worshipped angels adumbrating Christ.[81] [219] In shadow, He was worshipped in the temple of stone and the wooden tabernacle where a mist of God's glory appeared. But now because God's temple is Christ himself, we ought to worship there and with a spiritual worship, just as Christ

---

[78] Compare Bk. V of *Christianismi*, pp. 191-192.

[79] Other beautiful expressions of the very Pauline and Renaissance christocentric formulations.

[80] This is christocentric mysticism which reaches a high level of ignoring everything mundane and "transcending all knowledge" since they are nothing but a premonition of other things and celestial experiences by a principle of analogy to which they aspire.

[81] This phrase together with another indicated in note 118 of the Book V, was an object of a severe censure by Calvin during the trial in Geneva: *"Nos quoque fatemur sub figuris ostensa fuisse patribus quae palam nobis in Christo fuerunt exhibita. Sed hinc sacrilega sua commenta perperam infert Servetus, "adoratos fuisse angelos" a sanctis ut deos. Nam de pura unius Dei adoratione non minus recte edoctus erat Abraham, quam quivis nostrum. Nimis ergo indigna est contumelia, angelos fuisse ipsorum deos, et in lege Deum nunquam fuisse vere adoratum."* Servetus based his defense on the texts in which angels were mentioned as gods; but he had to be more precise, as in other instances, about the meaning of the term Elohim. He stated that the angels were adored as gods but not in truth because in comparison with our truth people operated in a shadow (*Calvini Opera*, VIII, p. 549-550). The study of these arguments clearly indicates that Calvin and Servetus could not understand each other because they operated on different levels and used different terminology.

appears and dwells internally within us. Whosoever hunts for a vision of God outside Christ or, perhaps, for worship of God outside Christ, worships in the manner of Jews, Saracens, and Pagans with the result that they make Christ superfluous to us. We ought to worship and know God as He wished to show Himself to us: "I affirm that I am seen and worshipped in Christ alone." I declare that generally the path to God exists in Christ just as he said that he was the road: "Who worships me, worships the Father." "Now is the time," or in other words, "Through my offices the world is allowed to worship the Father in me as true worshippers in spirit and truth." I would like you to contemplate the fact that Christ in Thomas and Philip condemned all efforts to seek God through other ways, visions, and mental exercises. But let us consider him again: generally he wished and showed that he was to be worshipped in this way. Those arguments about vision are valid with respect to worship because worship presupposes vision. "He, who worships me, worships the Father just as whoever sees me, sees the Father."[82] That which is worshipped in the spirit ought to be seen in the spirit. He ought to be seen where he is worshipped and in the manner he is worshipped. Otherwise, even now Christ will rightly say to us, "You worship what you do not know."

The vision of God was once a shadow, just as was the worship; that face, which Moses saw, was Christ's shadow. He saw an angel that was adumbrating Christ. They all had faith in God and Christ as shadow. Abraham, when he believed in God, believed in Christ via a special shadow. The one to whom he gave his faith, adumbrated Christ, and he saw Christ to be via a special shadow. He actually saw an angel, and in him he saw the future of Christ's brightness because, in a man's form, the angel was cloaked in the Word's light. This light was λόγος, reason, representing Christ.

Peter: Were not the angels who would be man's ministers created in man's form? [220] And if so, when were they created?

---

[82] Servetus is citing John 2:23, 12:45, 14:9.

Michael: As He creates the world through His word, God also readies His helpers through His spirit (Gen. 2; Ps. 32; Job 26 and 38).[83] The actual substance of the angels bears a certain likeness to that substance which was the luminous, elemental substance of the Word and the Spirit or its elemental archetype. The substance of angels and souls emanated by a certain gust of breath from the very substance of Christ's spirit. Just as God is fire and spirit, so He makes His breath and "fiery flames into His angels" (Ps. 103).[84] Therefore, an angel's substance, because it is fiery and spiritual, can easily take any given form.

Indeed, the fact that angels were created in man's image for a particular reason is shown by the fact that, like the substance of souls, the substance of angels derives from the image and substance of Christ, the man. Then there is the fact that God said to the angels, "Let us make man in our form and shape," as if such were already the form, shape, and image of angels.[85] Thirdly, there is the fact that they once looked to God they saw an angel in man's image: "an angel face-to-face" as Gideon says.[86] Fourth, Stephen's face is said to be "like an angel's face." Fifth, the angel is to be man's helper, and he would thus be better suited to help him in everything. Sixth, the soul has this form, and it is almost like an angel. Seventh, it is the most complete of all images, shapes, and forms, even those which are formed in angelic light, and God chose it for Himself and His minions. Read of the fine benefits of this body and its individual parts in Galen's books *"On the Function of Parts"* of the human body.[87] In fact, these benefits will be far better, indeed, the best of the best, after the resurrection, and they will even be sought by the angels themselves because these qualities are now like a shadow of what will be. It is the duty of angels to be near men, as is shown by the fact that God began with man, when He said, "Let us make men." [221] For He had not previously

---

[83] Gen. 2:7; Ps. 32:6; Job 26:4, on the "spirit" or creative breath, not in Job 38.

[84] Ps. 103:4 : "you make the winds your messengers, fire and flame your ministers."

[85] Gen. 1:26. See the explanation in Bk. III, note 61.

[86] Judges 6:11-13.

[87] Galen, *De usu partium*, 17 books (English translation by M.T. May, Cornell University Press, 1968).

spoken to the angels, although, "rejoicing," as Job said, in the creation of individual things, they, as His helpers, were ever awaiting His commands.[88] Moreover, God summoned the angels for man's creation, not as artists at liberty, but showing that He would need their service for His work to be accomplished. Before the angels man is a dear object to God because Christ, His son, is the true man in God, and man was made in his image and allowed before angels to share in the true physical and spiritual substance of Christ. For this reason the angels are like man's teachers and helpers. The craftsmanship in man's make-up is far superior to that of the angels, and man's glory will be greater than that of the angels. It will come to pass that the angels worship man, just as it is written: "Let all God's angels, too, worship him."[89] Thus, from the beginning the good angels, conforming themselves to the Creator's will, began to care for and love man as a thing precious to God. But the bad angels, vain and proud, were tainted by a jealousy for our dignity. They resented the fact that the earthly man was to be elevated before them by the Word and was to be worshipped by them, although they, arrogant because of the beauty that was their gift, wanted to ascend higher than everything and be equal to God, to be like unto the Most High, just as man has been made God's equal and like unto the Most High. It was a source of great annoyance to them that fragile, earthly man was to be preferred to the ethereal angel. They saw that power over all other creatures had yet been given, not to an angel, but to man. Moreover, an angel was made a servant to men. Therefore, while they pretended to do God's work, they began secretly to go around and make plots so that by oppressing us they would come to the fore. Then, first the woman was led astray by the serpent, and through her, as if through an instrument of the devil, man was led astray too, and made subject to the demon.[90] He brought every sort of evil unto man because of the devil's jealousy, pride, wrathfulness, and

---

[88] Job 38:7 : "when the morning stars sang together and all the heavenly beings shouted for joy."
[89] Heb. 1:6.
[90] This is a pejorative representation of a woman *"mulier, tanquam diaboli instrumentum,"* but not shared by Servetus.

greed. The evil demon stamped upon us all these qualities as his brand along with many others happenings as a circumstance of our flesh. [222] For that, even the demon is already now being tortured, and he will be more fiercely tortured later with fire.[91]

Peter: Therefore, the angel's sin existed when man had already been created.

Michael: On the sixth day, God saw everything that He had made, and it was good. On the seventh day, there was a hallowed state of rest. On the eighth or at the week's beginning the sin was consummated just as at the week's beginning there was through the resurrection a restoration to a heavenly state. Because man was located in paradise, the demon was driven to a state of discontent; on the seventh day he was forced to be resting, but on the eighth he killed him. For that reason, therefore, as a sign of redemption, the eighth day was made memorable through circumcision just as the seventh was by rest.[92] On the day when the first man was born, the second man died. And on the day when the first man died, the second came back to life.[93]

Peter: Can good or bad angels grow or decay?

Michael: Because they fell from grace, they will not return ever to the first rank. Nonetheless, in that state their punishment may be increased or decreased. We see that at the flood the punishment of the wicked angels was raised to the level of the prison of the abyss. As Christ said, "some are worse than others."[94] Satan, who was cast out by Christ, must even now be cast out of heaven. For he still circulates among the heavenly, and he still holds a heavenly status. The more

---

[91] Servetus repeatedly drives this point that demons will be tormented more later.

[92] The computation of days corresponds to the Hebrew and Christian tradition. The first day of the week in the Hebrew tradition is the Christian Sunday, and the Hebrew holy day is Saturday, the seventh day of the week. The circumcision on the eighth day is explained, according to the Lev. 12:3 by Maimonides, but without these mystical references (*Guide*, Part III, cap. XLIX).

[93] A curious chronology, doubtless motivated by the mystical attitude of Servetus. Thus Adam would be created and Christ died on Friday, on Sunday Christ was resurrected and Adam would die, that is, sin, on Monday.

[94] Matt. 12:45.

the demon affects us, and the more people he subjects to his rule, the more he is and will be tortured. Among tyrants and the greedy there is an example of those who, the more they possess, the more they will suffer, the more they labor, and the greater the punishment they ready for themselves. This is the way it is with the rule of demons among men. They have been blinded by a hatred for men and driven by a desire to rule us. Furthermore, the demon has succeeded that even the good angel, because of sin, turned against man. For man is driven from the garden of delight through the agency of the good angel as if by an angry parent. The cherub has been placed there with a flaming sword lest others be allowed to see Elohim's face as Adam had once seen it in the angel. Adam's vision was a shadow. Had Adam not sinned, it would have remained for Christ himself to be made gloriously manifest later to Adam and his kin without dying because "the Word was still with God" for that purpose. [223] The tree of the knowledge of good and evil, which previously had been forbidden to man, had to be given through Christ to a second Adam. And through him Adam would have seen God more clearly than he previously had through the angel. Oh, how wonderful is God! He wanted to grant His full manifestation and glory to Christ. In fact, He sent the angels out even in Christ's shadow so that Christ's glory would later be distinguished as being above the angels.

Peter: Is the substance of angels and souls material and divisible?[95]

Michael: A substance that is penetrated by another substance and retains within itself another substance, can be called material. The ancients taught that the substance of angels and souls, to the interstices of which God's light penetrates, was of this nature. Likewise the soul penetrates but in different manner than God's light, and, like actual matter, it takes upon itself various, luminous forms. Separated souls retain a form that is like us because they are substantively conformed to man's shape. The soul's substance is not only divisible, but it also suffers pain of a sort that we experience by that division, although everything that is divided, may, like air that has been divided, soon coalesce. Holy scripture teaches that individual souls feel pain, suffer injury, and undergo various torments because of the punishment of sensation. Excepting God, everything is divisible, and His light touches upon the division of everything, and it penetrates everything, as the apostle says.[96] These are Philo's words, with which he teaches in his book *On the World* that the substance of angels and souls is material: "The soul's form is not fashioned with the same elements with which everything else is formed. But it possesses a purer matter, upon which angelic nature is based."[97] Likewise, these are Clement of Alexandria's words in Book five of the *Stromata*: "The Stoics say that God is body and spirit in essence just like soul and angel, and you will find all this in our own scriptures. What they say about God, we understand about wisdom, which was created or formed within God Himself. Just so do we understand angels, whom Plato calls fiery men."[98] Therefore, the ancients were not wrong to say that angels and souls were spiritual bodies of a special, very fine, nearly incorporeal substance.

Peter: Do they eat some kind of food?

Michael: Not like we do. They feast on the invisible food of divinity. That food deeply penetrates them and somehow causes a division. For it is analogous to

---

[95] The question mark is added as it is suggested by the context.

[96] This is not exactly a Pauline idea, but Servetus might have in mind expressions like the one in 1 Cor. 4:5 : "Therefore do not pronounce judgment before the time, before the Lord comes, who will bring to light the things now hidden in darkness and will disclose the purposes of the heart."

[97] Philo of Alexandria, *De opificio mundi*. But the quote comes from the treatise *Quod Deus immutablis sit*, X.46. Philo refers to the fifth element from which are made the heavens, angels and ideas.

[98] Clement of Alexandria, *Stromata*, lib. V., cap. XIV (PG VI, 252). Plato never spoke about angels, they were oriental inventions, very prominent in Hebrew mythology. However, in *Faido*, 107e, Plato mentions through Socrates "guardian spirit" which every human has: "And so it is said that after death, the tutelary genius of each person, to whom he had been allotted in life, leads him to a place where the dead are gathered together; then they are judged and depart to the other world." In *Statesman* 271d and in *Epinomis* 984e he mentions "the divine spirits, and air-born race, holding the third and middle situation." "Daemons" or "divine spirits" in the classical sense were intermediate creatures between mortal and immortal. They served as interpreters and messengers of men's prayers and offerings to the gods, and of the gods' requitals to men (Plato, *Sympos.* 202d). Good mortals might become daemons after death (Eurip. *Alc.* 1003; Plato, *Cratyl.* 398b) and they were charged with the guidance of mankind (Plato, *Laws* 713d).

the food of our own bodies. All the more so because our bodies will feast upon the same food after the resurrection. [224] Taste, hearing, and other senses are not missing once the souls are separated from the body. Scripture and the most ancient oracles teach that the divine have a type of food. We grant this, if by food we mean a type of restoration. The soul is refreshed with air. [99] It has been said that the airy substance of the demons is refreshed by fumigations, and that the spirit is refreshed by the spirit. The demon, as Christ said, has no rest in hot and filthy regions, but in moist ones like pigs and men that lead a life of pigs. [100] Certain base emotions are attracted to specific humors in us, and in consequence the demon seeks those humors. He thirsts for the blood of sacrificial victims, and he is hungry for their scent. That is the material demon's food according to Athenagoras, Tertullian, Clement of Alexandria, Lactantius, Eusebius, and many others from among the great authorities. If, in general, he were to eat nothing, he would not be condemned by God "to eat dirt." [101] Heavy, earthly food is a heavy penalty for a light, airy body. Because he was condemned by God "to eat dirt," he prefers moist dirt to dry. Likewise, he has seen to it that dirt to be eaten by him is vaporized with fumigations. By that process the imposter gets himself praised like God and takes care of his own weakness. After all, he is forced to do this: not for nourishment, but because he was unworthy of the previous food of divinity. This is the punishment that was meted out to him because, being perhaps envious of his earthly glory, he deceived earthly man. For this reason he was ordered to creep upon the earth. It is not wholly accurate to say that the demon eats dirt as a food source, but rather that he feeds upon and consumes it and labors around it. In his hunger for matter the demon is like fire, and thus he always delights in fiery

---

[99] *Aëre reficitur anima* : the mechanism of aeration of the soul and blood circulation which Servetus explained before.

[100] Servetus alludes to the parable like narrated in Matt. 12:43.

[101] Gen. 3:14 and Isa. 65:25. This was the belief of certain church fathers in addition to relating the notions of the old demonologies, like Clement of Alexandria in *Stromata*; Lactantius in *Divin. Institut.* (lib. II, cap. 17; PL VI, 341); Eusebius in *Hist. eccl.*, and in *Praeparatio evang.* lib. IV, cap. 23, PG XXI, 3061); Athenagoras, (*Apology*, 24-25); Tertullian, (*Apologeticus adv. Gentiles*, cap. 22, PL I, 404).

sacrifices. Nothing prevents the demon's substance from being tortured or refreshed by this element: he is alternatively tortured by dryness and refreshed by moisture so that he hates light but loves darkness. [102]

It has been proven among all those who teach the basics of magic, that demons are sustained in a certain manner by fumigations and blood.[103] In fact, by that same logic God has ordered that blood be offered, fiery sacrifices consummated, and that various fumigations be undertaken for Him to divert His peoples from the magic and idolatry of the Egyptians. [225] Scripture shows that the smell and gentle perfume of incense or the burnt sacrifice is pleasing to good angels too. Angels have recommended, however, that these offerings be made not to them, but to God (Judges 6 and 13).[104] Demons, too, have often been forced to admit as true the fact that they are divisible bodies and are somehow soothed by food. Their oracles teach this. Following Pherecydes, Plutarch relates this, as does Marcus according to Psellus, and as Porphyry, and Proclus, and Chalcidius and others do.[105] In his *A Bundle of Myrrh* Rabbi Abraham confirms this same thing for

---

[102] There is a certain similarity between this text and the one in the *Fourth Letter to Calvin*, p 583 of *Christianismi Resitutio*.

[103] Probable allusion to the commentary on Lev. 17:7, though Servetus never cites the author, of Nachmanides (Rabbi Moshe ben Nachman, 1194-1270). He was a Spaniard, and both a physician and a Torah scholar. Unlike the rationalist Maimonides, Nachmanides had a strong mystical bent. His biblical commentaries are the first ones to incorporate the mystical teachings of the kabbalah. Nachmanides could be regarded as one of the first Zionists. He moved to the Holy Land during the Crusades after he was expelled from Spain for his polemics. In his work *Pirch Ha Tora le-Ramban* (C. B. Chavel, ed., Jerusalem, 1962. p. 92) he stated that this practice of fumigations "refers to the fumigations which the magicians offer to daemons ... as it was demonstrated experimentally in the acts of magic."

[104] Judg. 6:20-21, 13:15.

[105] The Neo-Platonists Proclus (410-485) and Chalcidius (beginning of the fourth century) in quotes non identifiable. The latter probably in the preserved text in *Fragmenta philosophorum graecorum*, (Mullach, ed., Paris, 1867, vol. II, cap. 119 and 128). Pherecides of Siros (seventh to sixth centuries B.C.E.) is a pre-Socratic philosopher praised by Aristotle (*Metaph.* 1091b) who was the author of a cosmogony of semiorphic inspiration (Krantz, 7). Servetus could read the reference to *Isis and Osiris* of Plutarch and to *Oraculorum Philosophia* of Porphyry. Servetus also could find in Eusebius who discusses these ideas about demonology in *Praeparatio evangelica*, lib. V, cap. 5 and lib. IV, cap. 7; (PG XXI, 323 and 250). Michael Psellius was a famous Byzantine statesman, philosopher, and monk of the eleventh century, a minister to the empress Theodora. From him comes the idea to make Orphism a precursor of Christianity, which was so influential during the Renaissance and affected Servetus as well, and of Zoroastrianism, the commentaries on whose writings he also published. The reference here is to *De operatione*

the Jews following Josephus and Philo.[106] Out of our own theologians both Augustine and Basil the Great, following those already cited, teach that angels have a special, spiritual body.[107]

Peter: I want to learn something about the origin of souls because you appear to be making souls older than angels.

Michael: I have said that the soul's substance is a breath drawn by God from this ethereal, elemental substance and at the same instance brought together into one space: and at that moment it begins once it is breathed by God into a prepared body. I have said that a soul consists of purer blood, that it is a luminous mist, simultaneously elemental and ethereal, and as elemental it is watery, airy, and fiery at the same time.[108] Hipparchus, Democritus, and Leucippus, said that the soul was fiery, agree with this opinion. Anaximenes and Diogenes, who claimed it was airy, Hippon, who claimed it was watery, and Critias, who said it was of blood, also agree with this notion.[109] Empedocles and Plato, opined that it

---

daemonium (cap. 9), a dialogue on the action of the daemons between Timothy and a certain Thrax, who narrates his conversations with a certain Marcus, a monk from Mesopotamia who converted to Manichaeism (PG CXXII, 839-842).

[106] This reference to Josephus is perhaps in the *Jewish Antiquities*, lib. XIII, cap. 11. On Philo of Alexandria, Harry Austryn Wolfson, *Philo: Foundations of Religious Philosophy in Judaism, Christianity, and Islam*, (Cambridge: Harvard University Press, 1947), vol. I, p. 370. Abraham Saba was a Spanish rabbi, a disciple of Isaac de Leon, who, after his expulsion from Spain, found refuge in Portugal from where he was expelled again in 1496 and finally ended in Fez in Morocco. His work *A Bundle of Myrrh* or *Zeror ha-Mor*, a commentary on the Pentateuch has a mystical tendency and even cabbalistic, was published first in Istanbul in 1514, and later in Venice in 1543. Servetus could read any of these two editions. The mentioned idea is in fol. 100b of the edition of Cracow, 1585.

[107] In the *Fourth Letter to Calvin* Servetus also refers to Augustine (*De Genesi ad litteram*) and Basil (*Homil. in Hexameron*) who believed that daemon had "a substantive body penetrable by the light," a spiritual body.

[108] Servetus summarizes here his concept of the soul and its natural or elemental basis which he explained in Book V, p. 169 & ff. when he postulated the role of the pulmonary respiration in the continuous renovation of the soul. The elemental composition of the soul excludes participation of the element earth as the lowest element, non-spiritual.

[109] The philosophical speculations concerning the soul could be accessible to Servetus from the manuals available in his epoch, but also from reading of some more philosophically oriented church fathers such as Lactantius, Eusebius, Clement of Alexandria who have preserved them. Michael Psellius seems to be a particular source for Servetus through his treatise *De animae celebres opiniones* (PG CXXII, 1093-1045). Hipparchus of Nicea (190-125 C.E.), Greek astronomer and mathematician, considered the founder of trigonometry, who compiled a star

consisted of all the elements, will also share this opinion. Pythagoras and Philolaus,
said that it was made up as a harmonious combination of them, also share it.[110] So

---

catalogue in which he gave the positions of some 850 stars and classified them according to their
magnitude on a scale of 1 to 6. Ptolemy later incorporated this knowledge into his *Almagest*.
Hipparchus also found the distance to the Moon using the parallax method, and, independently of
Kiddinu of Babylon, discovered the procession of the equinoxes by comparing his observations
with those of Timocharis 150 years earlier. He extended Apollonius of Pergas work on epicycles
and eccentrics by offsetting the Earth from the center of the planets' orbits and thus explaining
the different lengths of the seasons. With the atomists Leucippus and Democritus he postulated
the fiery nature of the soul. Leucippus and Democritus considered the soul material composed of
spherical atoms, very subtle, called σύγκρίματα which through respiration are nourished by the
atoms of fire scattered in the air. From Anaximenes (ca. 585-ca. 520 B.C.E.) this fragment is
preserved: "Just as our soul, being air, maintains our bodies united, so also the breath (*pneuma*)
and the air surround the whole cosmos" (Diels, A4, 13). He understands by the term "air" not
the atmosphere but the primordial protoelement. Similarly, Diogenes of Apollonia in Crete, who
was a pupil of Anaximenes and contemporary with Anaxagoras, makes air the primal element of
all things; but he went further and regarded the universe as originating from an intelligent
principle, by which it was vivified and ordered, a rational as well as sensitive soul, but still
without recognizing any distinction between matter and mind. Diogenes wrote several books on
cosmology *Peri Phuseos*. Hippon of Samos (fifth century B.C.E.) is listed by Aristotle
(*Metaph*ysics 983b22) as one the philosophers who made water the first principle of the universe,
reviving the old idea of Thales of Miletus. Critias (460-403), an Athenian philosopher,
rhetorician, poet, historian, and political leader, was a relative and friend of Socrates and Plato.
He is a personage in various dialogues of Plato: *Charmides, Timaeus, Critias*. Nowhere does the
idea ascribed to him by Servetus appear.

[110] The idea that the soul is a harmonious combination of all elements derives more from the
second generation of Pythagoreans (Philolaus, Antiphon, Hiketas) than from Pythagoras himself,
which was criticized by Plato. Philolaus of Croton (470-385) is one of the three most prominent
philosophers in the Pythagorean tradition. He wrote one book, *On Nature*. Philolaus considered
that the cosmos and everything in it is made up of two types of things, limiters and unlimiteds.
Unlimiteds are undefined by any structure or quantity; they include the Presocratic material
elements such as earth, air, fire and water but also continua such as space and time. Limiters set
limits in such unlimiteds and include shapes and other structural principles. Limiters and
unlimiteds are "fitted together" or "combined in harmony," which can be described
mathematically. The musical scale is Philolaus' primary example of such a harmony. The cosmos
comes to be when the unlimited fire is fitted together with the center of the cosmic sphere (a
limiter) to become the central fire. Philolaus was the precursor of Copernicus in moving the earth
from the center of the cosmos and making it a planet, but in Philolaus' system it orbits not the
sun but rather central fire. Philolaus also developed a medical theory in which there was an
analogy between the birth of a human being and the birth of the cosmos. The embryo is
conceived of as composed of heat and then as drawing in cooling breath upon birth, just as the
cosmos begins with the heat of the central fire, which then draws in breath along with void and
time from the unlimited. Philolaus posited a strict hierarchy of psychic faculties, which allows
him to distinguish human beings from animals and plants. He believed that the soul was a
harmony of the physical elements of the body. Plato mentions Philolaus in *Phaedo* (85d) and
adapts his metaphysical scheme for his own purpose in the *Philebus*. Plato criticized his doctrine
of the soul because it was not compatible with the idea of the soul's immortality and
transmigration. Philolaus' idea was closer to that of Empedocles (ca. 490-ca. 435) who claimed
that "the soul is born when the elements are mixed together and it dies when they separate"

does Alcmaeon, when he says that it is an ethereal substance, and Critolaus, who says it is a fifth essence, and Posidonius, who says it is a form.[111] Heraclitus, the naturalist, calls it a spark from the stars; Heraclitus of Pontus says it is light. Those, too, who say that the soul was grafted in humans will also agree as will those who say it is from God.[112]

In fact, the soul is all these things. Possessing a token of elemental substance, it is an ethereal substance derived from Christ's archetype just as there is within it a token of God's spirit and light. This inspired substance, which is called created, and which has been introduced together with the divinity, [226] a certain spiritual light conveying the divine form immanent in God Himself, and by whom, once inhaled, is illuminated; with each new act of breathing it coalesces again substantively with God into one light through the holy spirit.[113]

(Krantz, B9.26.7). But in a poem entitled *Purification* Empedocles states: "For it is not blood nor blended breath which provides the substance and principle of our souls: from these the body is compounded, earth-born and mortal; but the soul has come here from elsewhere" (Plutarch, *On Exile*, 607CE). And he embraces the notion of metempsychosis. The statement of Servetus concerning Plato does not reflect exactly Plato's view of the soul which is a mixture of the divine, immortal part (reason), and the mortal part (*Timaeus*, 69-70; *Faedrus*, 247c; *Alcibiades*, I, 130a; *Faedrus* 247c). According to Plato it is not the soul that maintains the harmony of the elements or of the compounded human being, but virtue (*Republic* 431c; *Phileb* 19ad; *Laws*, 689c).

[111] Alcmaeon of Croton, a Pythagorean physician of the fifth century B.C.E. (Krantz, 22B). In spite of what Servetus says, the theory of the souls as an ethereal pneuma was postulated by a peripatetic eclectic Critolaus of Phaselis (ca. 220-ca. 133 B.C.E.), according to Tertullian, *De anima*, cap. 5. Posidonius of Apamea (ca. 131-ca. 51 B.C.E.) studied under the Stoic philosopher Panaetius of Rhodes. He traveled widely in the western Mediterranean region and he made scientific studies relating to astronomy, geography and geology. Some time after 100 B.C.E. Posidonius became the head of the Stoic School in Rhodes. He also held political office in Rhodes. From his works only titles of a dozen of his treatises survived. Servetus could get the information about him in Cicero and in Tertullian.

[112] Fragments of Heraclitus on the soul in Krantz, 22B. Not Heraclitus of Pontus, but Heraclides of Pontus (387-312 B.C.E.). He was a pupil of Plato and he also studied with Aristotle and with Speusippus who was Plato's successor as head of the Academy. When Speusippus died in 339 B.C.E. Heraclides returned to Pontus. In his work *On the Nature of the Gods* Heraclides proposes composition of the soul from subtle luminous particles. Cicero, in his *De natura deorum*, in these words described the works of Heraclides: "[he] filled volume after volume with childish fictions."

[113] The preceding page was an object of a severe critique by Calvin: "After having amassed many delirious, perverse, and pernicious views on the substance of the soul, he concludes that the soul derives from God and his substance; still more, that with its inspiration there was conferred on it a divinity and that with each breathing it unites substantially with the light of God through the action of the holy spirit." To which Servetus replied: "Omit the expression 'from the substance of God' and you will find that the rest is true and the only one who is delirious is you, Simon

Peter: Democritus and Anaxagoras have easily come to agreement on this point according to their citation in Aristotle.[114]

Michael: The former thought that the soul and the mind were basically the same in man; the latter held the opinion that they were different in that the soul was animating and the mind was discerning. God is the first mind, the property of which is born within us, and because of this property and because of the soul the mind is called rational. As if it were a separate entity too, the new mind overcomes the soul like a new spirit, substantively making unity with the soul. Paul separates the mind from the spirit when he calls the mind a shared intellect and the spirit as something additional through an external impetus (1 Cor. 14).[115] At any rate, the mind is the soul, and the mind is also like a part of the soul. The spirit is the soul, and the spirit is like a part of the soul.

Peter: How were we in Christ before the angels?

Michael: In the eternal spirit of regeneration. Those who were regenerated again existed before the angels through Christ's dignity and gift. Although according to the period in the state of material creation angels did go before us, nevertheless, there is in us a certain dignity which came before them, and through it we existed in Christ before time and without beginning. Everything that has been created, existed previously in God through the simple nature of form alone. The individual spirits of the chosen existed in a different manner: they existed in their own substance, in their own breath through a different mode, in Christ's throne. Although the gift of the divinity exists in good angels as it does in us, there is,

---

Magus." The Genevan pastors in turn insisted: "The astonishing ferocity of this man to accuse of delirium with Simon Magus whoever does not want to be identified as a Manichaean with him." In reply Servetus still attempted to clarify their opinions: "I teach openly the creation of the soul on pp. 178, 225, 260, and others of *Restitutio*. And I said that the angels and the souls have a similarity with the substance of the spirit from which they emanated" (*Calvini Opera*, VIII, 506, 518, 550, 551).

[114] Quoting Aristotle indicates the source of Servetus' information.

[115] Paul distinguishes the spirit and the mind in 1 Cor. 14:14-15 : "For if I pray in a tongue, my spirit prays but my mind is unproductive. What should I do then? I will pray with the spirit, but I will pray with the mind also; I will sing praise with the spirit, but I will sing praise with the mind also."

nevertheless, a distinction. While the angels have been created with a degree of uniformity, souls have been breathed by God separately and with a unique nature, a circumstance which proves that souls are superior. And this is shown by the additional, superior gifts granted us such that we are made brothers, joint-heirs, and co-regents with Christ. The same point is made by the fact that God does so many and such marvelous things for our sake, not for the sake of the angels. In fact, He has made everything for us, even the angels themselves.

The spirits of the regenerated ones are consubstantial and coeternal with God. [227] Hence, we usually say that the saints came down from heaven because "no one goes up to heaven without first having come down from it."[116] They came down from heaven through the life-causing spirit, having been taken up into heaven through the same. Those who were already in heaven earlier, have come down. The community itself "came down from heaven and from God" (Rev. 3; Heb. 12).[117] If you believe that the spirit's spark given to this man in his regeneration is God's true substance, you ought to believe that it was completed from before time for him, such a share having been taken from Christ's fullness from before time.

For God does not change, although even now He takes a portion of it from Himself. But this man does change when he is taken up to it as he goes up to the throne that has been readied for him. As many thousands as have been chosen, an equal number of spirits and an equal number of thrones have been prepared for them.

Peter: You said that Christ's one and only substance was in God, yet now you are putting more spirits in Him.

Michael: Christ's holy, eternal spirit is one, although it contains the substances and measures of many spirits. On the day of your regeneration he makes with your spirit one new spirit in you; one with the other person's, and still

---

[116] John 3:13.
[117] Rev. 3:12; Heb. 12:22.

one with still another person's. The spirits of God's chosen have been distinguished among themselves, but they are one spirit in God. That spirit is one and several; it has various measures of dispensation and maintains joined together what is actually divided within us. In a special way a particular part of Christ's spirit has been apportioned to us, and a new spirit is created in us, it being a new creature. Just as Christ's spirit has the essential and incorruptible breath, so, when it is imparted to us, it inwardly restores our own spirit in conformity with its own incorruptibility. For the resurrected Christ's spirit does not any further take on a corruptible substance. This is the spirit "of grace and truth,"[118] the shadow of which was in that breath innate to Adam. Thus do we call even the old soul a shadow, and thus do we say that its divinity was a shadow of the new divinity's spirit. That breath of Adam's animating soul is like steam and smoke that arises from a purer fire and seeks another fire. That breath was given to man as a particular shadow in a diminished [228] and hidden light, prefiguring another, purer and more luminous spirit that would exist in man. A fiery property lies hidden in smoke and wherever it is, it is easy to ignite a more vivid fire, just as in our own soul something is kindled through God's breath. In other respects the soul is an extremely delicate vapor that is wafted into its surroundings in such a way that after death it is a shadow of the man when he was alive, but not a truly living thing.[119]

Peter: Hence after death the ancients called the living's souls "shades" just as in the holy scripture the soul is called "death's shadow."[120]

Michael: After death they are called shadows because they are deprived of life's quality and because they are shadowy ghosts of the living. The ancients, possessing an appreciation of justice, but not knowing about the resurrection of the bodies that was to come through Christ, believed that these shadows would be

---

[118] John 1:14.

[119] Somewhat ambiguous phrase: *"Est anima ipsa vapor admodum fragilis ..., ut post mortem sit umbra viventis, non res vere vivens."*

[120] It is usually called "umbra mortis" in Hebrew, Isa. 42:7; Luke 1:79.

judged without their bodies. Hence, the Pythagoreans related many fantastic stories about the punishment of souls. But this fault can be forgiven in them because they could know about neither the resurrection of bodies nor the nature of the judgment to come. Hence, relying upon Socrates, the Platonists were convinced that there existed a perfect state wherein souls were separated from bodies. Many are engaged in this very error today.[121] In fact, it is an unnatural state for souls to be outside bodies, and this is shown by the fact that souls are naturally attracted to bodies and receive something, on an essential level, from the body's substance. Souls are naturally and originally integrated into a body, and they are shaped in the manner of a body. They would never have been separated any further from the body, had Adam not sinned. A soul is warmed in a body by life's warmth, and it resists separation. Though we know that the mentioned separation does happen at an appropriate time, nevertheless, when there is exceptional need for cleansing [of the body], it takes place at great suffering for the soul.[122] In fact, even Christ's soul was naturally grieved because of its separation from the body, even though it knew that it would shortly be restored to an immortal and glorious body. Hence, the souls of murder victims grieve when they undergo a kind of casting off of the body (Rev. 6).[123] In Genesis 4 God told Cain that Abel's "blood had a voice" because his soul, which exists in the blood, was complaining that it

---

[121] Orphics, Pythagoreans, Platonists recognized, though with some differences, immortality of the soul and its transmigration or metempsychosis (Plato discusses this in *Faedo* and in *Timaeus*). Transmigration was understood as a certain sanction measured to the souls independent of the body, and those which were not sufficiently purified were to be reincarnated in new successive bodies. Servetus calls this doctrine an honest "fable." Socrates treats the theme of immortality of the soul in *Apology*, 40c-41c, and more extensively in *Faedo*, 80b-c and other dialogues of Plato. It is not possible to know whom Servetus had in mind by referring to his contemporaries. Perhaps, he referred to the standard Catholic doctrine adopted by Protestants as well. From his silence one may infer that he was not aware of the recent discussions over the immortality of the soul triggered by the publication of the *Tractatus de immortalitate animae* by Pietro Pomponazzi in Padua in 1519.

[122] These are Aristotelian concepts namely, that the soul is the substantive form of the body and therefore it is naturally integrated with the body (*ad corpus naturaliter ordenata*, *De anima*, II,2 414a22). Servetus's Platonism thus can be qualified as relative.

[123] Rev. 6:10 : "Sovereign Lord, holy and true, how long will it be before you judge and avenge our blood on the inhabitants of the earth?"

had been deprived of its body.[124] [229] Finally, if, after resurrection, there will be a more perfect state of the soul with the body, it immediately follows that the separated soul's state is not the most perfect.

But to return to the subject of shadows, regarding the soul's shadow you will more broadly approve my discussion about shadows if you reach the conclusion that God Himself, His Word, His Spirit, His Light, His angels, souls, men, animals, heaven, luminaries, stars, elements, and whatever other creations there are prefigured Christ's mystery in a special shadow. Not only things, but actions, such as the first act of creation, the inspiration of the soul, the sanctification of the sabbath, the building of paradise, circumcision, sacrificial offering, the ordering of the kingdom and priestly office, and everything else were all shadows.

Peter: Do souls retain their senses after death?

Michael: Separated souls are made by natural deprivation more insensate so that, like delicate shadows, they may be stirred up by "guardian spirits,"[125] being on their own account scarcely capable of anything: souls that are at rest are said to be "sleeping." They, nevertheless, do have senses and a voice (Luke 16; Isa. 14; Ezek. 32). Take, for example, the voice of the souls of the murder victims that called out to God in Genesis 3 and Revelation 6 and 20.[126] Pimander says that, as a soul's components, the physical senses flow back to their own sources.[127] Thus, it happens that a separated soul's senses suffer pain as is stated in the mentioned chapter 16 of Luke.

Peter: If the holy spirit existed hypostatically in Christ's separated soul, as the Word existed in the flesh, which was, in turn, born from the holy sprit, why do we not say that the holy spirit, like the Word, was made incarnate in the flesh?

---

[124] Gen. 4:10 : "What have you done? Listen; your brother's blood is crying out to me from the ground!"

[125] *Ut quasi leves umbrae a geniis agantur,* the only case where Servetus refers to these strange beings. Thus the allusion and the sense of the phrase is incorrect.

[126] Luke 16:22-30; Isa. 14:10; Ezek. 32:21; Gen. 4:10; Rev. 6:10; Rev. 20:4.

[127] A nonspecific allusion to *Poimandres,* lib. I of *Corpus Hermeticum.*

Why do we not say that, because the son's form is in the Spirit as it is in the Word, the holy spirit is the son just as the Word is the son?

Michael: That very fact shows beautifully that there is not a material difference between the Word and the Spirit, but rather in the mode of manifestation and communication. Obviously, it further shows that the Word is not actually called a real son, but rather a personal son.[128] In the Word there exists the son's form; in the spirit of the chosen there is now the son's form; in the flesh there is the son's form; in the soul there is the son's form; in the substantive shape there is the son's form, but the form in earthly matter of the whole of any given man or the image of the whole is the son's form; likewise, [230] with the remaining substance of the three elements. Yet, not for that reason do we say that there are so many sons in one son. Rather, we say that every one is a unique son. Because it is said that the Word rather than the spirit was once the son, a distinction is made based upon the mode. For the Word once appeared in the "person" and figure of the son to be, and the spirit was acting latently. Therefore, we say in that instance "the son;" likewise, the Word was made incarnate rather than the holy spirit because the spirit relates more to the soul. Nevertheless, the spirit was actually made human. We are all said to be made God's sons, although our own spirit is not said to be God's son. Nevertheless, in the spirit there does exist a type of filiation, a υἱοθεσία. Thus, Christ himself, not his divinity, not the divinity of the Word or the Spirit, although once the son's form, the son's visible person was in the Word, it is said to be entirely and materially God's son.[129]

---

[128] Calvin objected to this distinction which he correctly qualified as " the focus of his impious dogmas" because it destroyed the real distinction between the three Persons by rejecting the understanding that in God there is a real hypostasis that would be something else than his image or his own representation. This traditional view is rejected by Servetus who admits hypostases in God but understood them as modes: "I beg you, read carefully my texts and adopt the heart of a Christian, praying that the truth be revealed to you. You do not understand yourself and cry out as a blind man in the desert. For by harboring so ardently a spirit of vengeance, wisdom does not have access to your malicious soul." (*Calvini Opera*, VIII, 501, 515, 537).

[129] Thus the Word is the son because it really was incarnated as the son of God in Mary and to him pointed all its personal manifestations in the Old Testament. But, on the other hand, nothing would prevent us from calling the Spirit the son, but this would create confusion. The spirit is the

To understand that that form was not formerly the material son, but rather an exemplar of the son, take this comparison. The form of this man, Solomon, exists in the soul, in the corpse, in substantive form, and in matter. The divine form is one, and it molds matter, shape, and soul into one being. This form existed under a particular shape and substance in David's seed according to the token that was imparted as seed-source consisting of the Divinity, light, and the elements. Yet, we do not for that reason say that the form existed in David's seed as David's son. Instead, we say that the entire man, Solomon, was David's son who, inside a particular seed-source composed of light's form and in elemental substance, existed previously within David's seed.[130]

This is the most accurate analogy. We conclude by the from-result-to-cause argument that Christ was wholly God's genuine son, and that in a substantive and formal way he existed previously in God. Christ existed in God in light's first formal and essential image and in the Word's super-elemental substance that contains the human seed's full power. As the craftsman of all things, Christ places upon the generation of everything else the particular image of his own generation. Regarding Christ, no difficulty can arise that you would not dispose of by this comparison. As is well known, all the scriptures teach us thus that this man is [231] God's son: the creator himself is recognized from what he has created, so that the blindness of our own scientists regarding a material distinction of three invisible points must be regretted.[131]

Therefore, regarding Christ's soul it must be said that it was of a similar nature, that it contained the son's form with the divinity of the Word and Spirit, and that it was substantively one soul, just as Christ is one with God. Christ's soul,

---

author of our filiation which, however, refers to everything that exists.

[130] This analogy is based on the one already established earlier: the Word acted as the semen for Jesus, but we call "son" only a man who was constituted by it, and not a man when he still is *"in lucis ideae seminario quodam et elementari substantia."*

[131] Servetus is using the term *"mathematici"* translated here as "scientists." He meant by this "scholastics." The three invisible points cannot be distinguished in reality, the less so the three Persons invisible.

going down in essence to those below, contained in substance within itself the
hypostasis of the Word and Spirit, although the flesh remains in the grave: the
former being in the spiritual mode, the latter is in the physical. Christ's soul lived a
life like our own, and in it was "the source of all life" (Ps. 35).[132] God, who
breathed into him a human soul like our own, at the same time breathed
measurelessly into him the entirety of his eternal divinity. Subsequently, by
breathing the holy spirit into him as He breathes it supplementally into us, God
breathed anew the entirety of his divinity via a different dispensation, and He
renewed his earlier spirit through the resurrection because a new spirit, which the
spirit given him in the river Jordan adumbrated, was also given him.[133] Thus, to
return to the matter of shadows, consider that not only did the old spirit of the
Jews adumbrate the new one, but Christ's earlier spirit itself also adumbrated in
him another future spirit of more exalted glory. Likewise, that breathing in of his
living soul prefigured and desired yet another glory of God, just as David's soul
desired and "thirsted" for it by being a representation of it (Ps. 41 and 62).[134] The
spirit of God's sons, which is God, yearns and thirsts and aches for Christ's other
"future glory to come in us" (Rom. 8 and 2 Cor. 5). And, like the shadow of some
other entity, it indistinctly represents as in a mirror the other one (1 Cor. 13 and 2
Cor. 3).[135] See how great is the prefiguration of Christ's mysteries!

---

[132] Ps. 35:9 : "For with you is the fountain of life; in your light we see light."

[133] Another statement objected to by Calvin together with the one discussed in note 168 to Book
V (p. 195 of the *Restitutio*). Servetus supported his claim by texts of John 1:16 and 3:34 because
already John the Baptist cried out "From his fullness we have all received" and "He whom God
has sent speaks the words of God, for he gives the Spirit without measure" [i.e., to Christ]."
Servetus admits this plenitude of Christ from the beginning but not his glorification before the
resurrection. He acquired then a new glory and a new grace. As usual, Calvin distorts the texts of
Servetus in order to make the condemnation easier (*Calvini Opera*, VIII, 506, 517, 547-548).

[134] Ps. 42:2 : "My soul thirsts for God, for the living God. When shall I come and behold the face
of God?" And Ps. 62:1 : "O God, you are my God, I seek you, my soul thirsts for you; my flesh
faints for you."

[135] Rom. 8:21 : "the creation itself will be set free from its bondage to decay and will obtain the
freedom of the glory of the children of God." 2 Cor. 5:6 : "So we are always confident; even
though we know that while we are at home in the body we are away from the Lord –." 1 Cor.
13:12 : *"videmus nunc per speculum in enigmate tunc autem facie ad faciem nunc cognosco ex
parte tunc autem cognoscam sicut et cognitus sum."* 2 Cor. 3:18 : "And all of us, with unveiled

Peter: The "shadow's" condition does not prevent in any way Christ's soul from being called God.

Michael: Christ's soul is God; Christ's flesh is God just as Christ's spirit is God, and just as Christ himself is God. In Christ there is a soul like our own, and in it there is God in essence. In Christ there is a vital spirit like our own, and in it there is God in essence. In Christ there is flesh like our own, and in it there is God in essence. Christ's soul [232] is eternal; Christ's spirit is eternal; Christ's flesh is eternal, and they are all in the divinity's proper substance.[136] Christ's soul in the divinity's proper essence breathes from eternity the full gift of the soul to the world, and from that there is a portion of the divinity in our own soul. The holy spirit is found nowhere unless it has been given by Christ. Otherwise, there would be life outside of Christ, and not everything would be made to live through him. In him alone exists every source and the entire divinity, being the substantive divinity of body, soul, and spirit. His flesh was born from God's substance, possessed of the divinity's essence, and the substantive form of God's light. His soul eternally contains the essential life-spark whereby other souls received their breath together with a particular token of it. Likewise, there exists in him the new spirit of glory by the breath of which a new man's spirit is inspired upon being regenerated again because it makes man's spirit incorruptible, heavenly, and godly and much more exalted than happened through the soul's first inspiration. For our first soul was not God. However, when it comes over us, Christ's spirit, which is God, makes it

faces, seeing the glory of the Lord as though reflected in a mirror, are being transformed into the same image from one degree of glory to another."

[136] Together with other words taken out of context indicated in note 84, Book I and in note 95, Book II, this paragraph constitutes objection no. 9 of Calvin during the trial in Geneva: "Inexcusable is this heretical error of Servetus ... for he confuses two natures. He reduces to nothing the true humanity. Add to it that he makes possible a particular divinity ... " "Thus his first truth is not to distinguish between the two natures of Christ." Servetus responded: "The first truth and justifying faith is to believe with certainty that this man is by nature the son of God." Thus it becomes obvious again what is the nucleus of the Servetus systemic doctrine (*Calvini Opera*, VIII, 502, 516, 539-540). Servetus was, however, more orthodox than his opponents are willing to admit and certainly his doctrine was in contrast to that of the Socinians who denied that he contributed to their heritage. Faustus Socinus wrote : "We deny that Servetus was our progenitor, it is not from him that we derive our thought concerning God and Christ, and the

God and joins it more tightly with God and makes one with God through a special process, thereby freeing it from death and slavery.

But that token of godliness can, in a certain manner, be taken away from the soul. Then the souls of the impious, which by God's judgment have been sent with their bodies to the horrible darkness, will be stripped of God's light, of His token, and of His properties, just as Christ says: "Even what they have is taken from them" (Matt. 25 and Luke 19). However, "it is given and will be given more fully" in the case of us who keep what has been given.[137] Just as through his spirit Christ now regenerates and transforms us into a state of incorruptibility so that the incorruptible spirit is daily increased and kept whole in Christ after the body's death, so also in the age to come the divinity's substance, which also in corporeal terms is natural in Christ alone, will radiate from him into us, transforming and glorifying our bodies by sharing his divinity and light (Phil. 3).[138] Thus, like rivers from their source and limbs from a head, we shall always depend on him as now and forever we depend on him. [233]

Peter: On this basis is inferred a reason for distinguishing why the fathers were formerly said to die, whereas by being placed in the resurrected Christ we no longer die, but still live with him in eternal life, as Christ himself teaches in many passages of John.[139]

Michael: Although there was hope for life among the faithful patriarchs, nevertheless, they did not reign, as we do now with Christ when once that through Christ the immortal, heavenly kingdom has been brought to earth. Those patriarchs did not share in Christ's incorruptible substance, as we do. We have stated that the soul's elements are themselves corruptible, and for that reason that the soul is

---

difference between him and us is not small" (*Bibliotheca Fratrum Polonorum*, I, 535a).
[137] Matt. 25:29; Luke 19:26.
[138] Phil. 3:21 : "He will transform the body of our humiliation that it may be conformed to the body of his glory, by the power that also enables him to make all things subject to himself."
[139] John 4:14 : "but those who drink of the water that I will give them will never be thirsty. The water that I will give will become in them a spring of water gushing up to eternal life." John 6:35: "I am the bread of life. Whoever comes to me will never be hungry, and whoever believes in me will never be thirsty."

dispersed into its surroundings, deprived, so to speak, of its own substance. Subsequently, having in a certain manner been subjected to evil demons because of Adam's sin, it was drawn below to the underworld, never again, so to speak, to be restored to the body, which it had corrupted. This is all the more so because the flesh was polluted and thus made mortal, and it would no longer live as it once did. Therefore, there is great need for grace and pity so that someone may renew everything for life and may cleanse the flesh because it cannot live in God as it is. Indeed, through his own death and resurrection, by giving life to the spirit in the moment of death and by glorifying the flesh in his resurrection, Christ has made everything available without requiring recompense from us.

Peter: Certain people say that after his death Christ's soul by fighting with demons in hell experienced amazing suffering.

Michael: By his death Christ consummated all sufferings. He did not go down to hell to suffer there anew, nor was he less than Lazarus, whose soul was compassionately led by the angels to Abraham's bosom. The strength of Christ's soul always bested demons by afflicting, harming, and, especially, by terrifying them. It is said that Christ endured certain things which he suffered in his limbs, in the manner in which he suffered persecution from Paul.[140] Add the fact that on the very day of his death the thief's soul was placed in paradise as a sharer in the glory of Christ's soul. Therefore, paradise already existed in his soul. After death Christ's soul, [234] having by God's spirit been miraculously brought to life, went down to the underworld with glory and power to rescue thence pious souls. Rising up thence, the body itself also went up to heaven in the full realization of glory and power.

Peter: These two mysteries are fulfilled in us in a like order.

Michael: Christ gives us life and glorifies us in spirit before he did it in body. He will glorify us in body at the final resurrection. At this point, when we rise again in baptism as a token of his death, he glorifies us in spirit. Likewise,

Christ communicates to us his spirit, before his body just as we have the baptismal rite before the communion rite. In Christ's baptism his entire spirit is given to us just as in communion his entire flesh is given to us. The spirit's incorruptible elements, such as Christ in heaven now has, are given to us when we are truly and incorruptibly regenerated by the power of Christ's resurrection, "in water, spirit, and fire." Through this new spirit our very soul attains true immortality, a taste of that true, immortal glory, and our spirit is made one with God. These are facts, not fancies, just as it is true that Christ has been brought back to life in us.[141] At the Lord's supper Christ's incorruptible flesh is itself joined to our new spirit, and this flesh is an incorruptible food of the "inner, incorruptible man." Thus, our own "inner man" is gathered from Christ's flesh and bones, and through his spirit and our own it is compacted into one element so that in this way our own life is "stored up in Christ," and our inner man is rendered incorruptible and immortal.[142] For this reason, not only is it said that there is no death for our "inner man," but that there is even no death for the total man; it is rather a special type of rest and slumber, because the "inner man" always remains alive and whole, and the spirit remaining alive and whole, entrusted and rendered into God's hands is to be restored with its soul total and whole. This new spirit is not dissolved at death into the surrounding environment, nor is it handed over to the evil demon, but rather, stored up in Christ, it is kept whole, just as it was during man's life, and in paradise and in the kingdom of heaven it ever reigns with Christ. We are truly alive in Christ in this manner; we already live an eternal life, [235] and Christ does live in us. The separated souls of those who lived in Christ, already reign with him, the rest being

---

[140] Heb. 9:4-5; 1 Cor. 15:9; Gal. 1:13.

[141] Note that Servetus always takes literally the biblical texts and as a result, the other imprecise formulations on the natural immortality of the soul in another context in which he refers to its biological or material elements become overridden. The spiritual immortality which is conferred by sharing the same spirit of the resurrected Christ in the baptism also affects the body. *Vera haec sunt, non imaginaria, sicut vera res est, quod Christus resuscitatus in nobis est.* Servetus considers seriously the process of divinization of individual Christians about which are concerned the biblical texts, especially Paul.

[142] Allusions to Pauline phrases, well known, Gal. 2:19; Col. 3:3; 1 Cor. 15:44.

kept in the underworld, as John teaches in Revelation 20.[143]

Peter: Did Christ's descent to hell bring nothing to souls held there?

Michael: He broke Satan's bonds; he loosed hell's bonds; and for most he softened the pain that Satan inflicts. By rising again and raising many with him he gave all the hope of rising again.[144]

Peter: Of what nature were hell's tortures, and in what manner has Christ changed them?

Michael: When he went to hell, the souls were not being tortured as they ought to have been, nor now are they so tortured, nor are even the demons themselves. Still, as Christ says, "a fire has been readied for the devil and his angels."[145] Hell's tortures result from the deprivation of life, and for that reason Peter calls them "death's tortures" (Acts 2) and David (Ps. 17).[146] Pain takes many forms, or there are many pains which are for that reason called "pains" there. The nature of the present hell is quite different from the future damnation of gehenna, as you will hear next. For hell and the whole of the demon's dominion over men will be destroyed, but the demon himself needs fiercer punishment. The current nature of hell is connected with the grave and fits the punishment of Adam who was deprived of life and was subsequently sent to hell when the devil was given power over man. Therefore, there exists in that place a natural and inborn yearning for life that arises from having already tasted it; the torture arises from the loss of so loved a thing. Just as, when we die, we are horrified, become despondent, and grieve, so, as Job says, we are gripped with horror, despondency, and grief as long as we are held by death.[147] David was aware of these tortures of death and hell just as everyone else engaged in thus cleansing and washing away Adam's sin through

---

[143] Rev. 20:6 : "Blessed and holy are those who share in the first resurrection. Over these the second death has no power, but they will be priests of God and of Christ, and they will reign with him a thousand years."

[144] Matt. 27:52-53.

[145] Matt. 25:41.

[146] Acts 2:24 : "*quem Deus suscitavit solutis doloribus inferni.*" Ps. 17:4 : "The cords of death encompassed me; the torrents of perdition assailed me."

[147] Job 10:22 : "the land of gloom and chaos, where light is like darkness."

death and hell, was. Wherefore, it is said in Psalm 48 that they have been led from hell through Christ's agency, and that they have been "freed from hell's power" because hell did have power over them.[148] Those who died prior to Christ's death, have been led to hell just as if they had been handed over to oblivion by God, with the exception of those few to whom a faith in Christ's coming gave comfort. Hence, "the land of perdition and oblivion" is commonly called "the grave" (Ps. 87).[149] The same expression for hell and the grave was used in holy scriptures such that one went "to the grave" and "to hell" at the same time. Hell followed death, as John said.[150] Just as the body drew the soul to sin and made it subject to perdition, [236] so with the body as a grave the soul is subjected to death and hell in darkness.

There are other torments of hell besides. For among the wicked hell's torture is manifold in accordance with the nature of death, and for this reason, while the agony of death lasts, it is called "the torment of death." Hence (as Peter and Jude both teach following the Old Testament) the souls of the giants, as if drowning daily under the mist of tartarus, are tortured with water, just as they drowned when they were dying.[151] The souls of the Sodomites undergo punishment by fire whereby they perished, as if after their death the manner of death to which they were condemned, remains impressed upon them. Their souls suffer from water and all the more from sulfurous fire because, as we said, in these waters are other, internal waters which drown, and in external fire there is internal

---

[148] Ps. 48:15 : "But God will ransom my soul from the power of Sheol, for he will receive me."

[149] Ps. 87:5-6.

[150] There is no such idea in John nor in 1 John or 2 John, nor in Revelation. Perhaps Servetus had in mind phrases like: "The poor man died and was carried away by the angels to be with Abraham. The rich man also died and was buried. In Hades" (Luke 16:22-23).

[151] There is mention in 3 Macc. 2:4 that the giants were destroyed by flood. The author of 1 Pet. in 3:18-20 mentions that Jesus, after his death, went to proclaim to the spirits in the underworld of those who perished during the flood in the time of Noah. In 2 Pet 2:5 again the flood is mentioned as punishment of the ungodly. There is a vague reference in Jude 5 and 14-15 to punishment of the "ungodly" and even to angels who are "kept in eternal chains in deepest darkness for the judgment of the great day."

fire which is scorching their souls. [152]

   To all this one has to add the activity of demons, whose function is to
rekindle the fire. The souls thus feel so much their own torture by fire that they
appear to desire the taste of water (Luke 16).[153] It is the sort of fire that tortures
and devours and burns souls with the punishment of sensation, as Christ and David
say in Psalm 48.[154] It is said there that hell removes the wicked, and this cannot be
taken as referring only to the seizing of the corpse in the grave. Hence, in chapter
24 Job says, "Just as summer takes away snow, so hell takes away the sinner."[155]
Even for little children who have died, there is a particular torture in hell, just as in
their death there was for them a particular youthful pain. That dark horror of the
demon alone is enough to bring punishment to the little child who is already
terrified by the darkness. For every deed in life there is in hell another, new torture
for the soul, a certain worm and remorse from a guilty conscience. Even Paul
perceived this in 1 Corinthians 3, where by "fire" he understood every class of
affliction whereby the quick and the dead are affected by a certain repetition for
their deeds in life such that each person is tortured through the same means by
which he sins.[156] Sin, as God says, always "lies at the door," and after death hell is
ever before the eyes of the wicked.[157] The more an individual vaunts himself
through pride and luxury, the more he is there humiliated, worn down, and
afflicted with weariness (Isa. 14; Ezek. 32; and Rev. 18).[158] [237] This worm does

---

[152] In 2 Pet. 2:6-10 and Jude 7 Sodom and Gomorrah are mentioned as punished for their sins
and burned to ashes. The idea is that the punishment of the souls imitates the agony of death of
the bodies.
[153] Luke 16:24.
[154] Ps. 48:14 : "Like sheep they are appointed for Sheol; Death shall be their shepherd; straight to
the grave they descend, and their form shall waste away; Sheol shall be their home."
[155] Job 24:19.
[156] 1 Cor. 3: 13-14 : "the work of each builder will become visible, for the Day will disclose it,
because it will be revealed with fire, and the fire will test what sort of work each has done. If
what has been built on the foundation survives, the builder will receive a reward. If the work is
burned up, the builder will suffer loss; the builder will be saved, but only as through fire."
[157] Gen. 4:7 : "If you do well, will you not be accepted? And if you do not do well, sin is lurking
at the door; its desire is for you, but you must master it."
[158] Isa. 14:11-15; Ezek. 32, describes all the vengeance God will exert on other nations with each
Israel was warring; Rev. 18:2-3.

not die among the wicked, and their sin is always directed against them.[159] Wherefore even hell is given a name derived from the verb, to ask, שְׁאוֹל, *Sheol*, because in hell there is a certain inquisition into the deeds of one's life down, as Christ says, "to the last penny."[160]

There is another method of torture in hell that occurs before and after Christ's resurrection. Those who did not know that Christ would come had torture arising from their own life, that is beyond hope because they dwelled in the land of oblivion and had no hope for resurrection (Ps. 87 and Isa. 38).[161] However, Christ's descent into hell took away that desperate situation. In fact, as Matthew said, at that time he led the patriarchs and prophets, who formerly awaited him, out of hell. Isaiah predicted this in chapters 43 and 49, as did Zechariah in chapter 9 and David in the passages already cited.[162] When he rose from the dead, Christ took away from them all grief, just as now among those who have been truly regenerated because they have attained the spirit once separated from them, there does remain from death no torture, but the perpetual joy of life in Christ with the expectation of another, full life to come of the body. Death's pain does not remain among the saints, although in dying they suffer physical pain. As there was for Christ only "death's pain" in terms of the flesh, not hell's subsequent, dark pain, but rather God's great light together with the soul, so it is even for us who have truly been born again. For every one else, however, a horrific and dark hell follows death because they are all by nature "anger's children" due to Adam's sin, unless they wash it away. Nonetheless, when he went down to hell, Christ caused for

---

[159] Reminiscent of a phrase in Ps. 50:3 : "For I know my transgressions, and my sin is ever before me."

[160] Sheol, שְׁאֹל, or שְׁאוֹל, underworld. Cognitive is the verb שָׁאַל, to ask, to inquire. Matt. 5:26: "Truly I tell you, you will never get out until you have paid the last penny."

[161] Ps. 87:4 : "I am counted among those who go down to the Pit; I am like those who have no help." Isa. 38:18 : "For Sheol cannot thank you, death cannot praise you; those who go down to the Pit cannot hope for your faithfulness."

[162] Isa. 43 and 49 refer to the new people of Israel. In Zech. 9:9 : "Rejoice greatly, O daughter Zion! Shout aloud, O daughter Jerusalem! Lo, your king comes to you; triumphant and victorious is he, humble and riding on a donkey, on a colt, the foal of a donkey" Servetus wanted to see a prophecy of Jesus as well as in the previous texts.

them the hopeless pain of death in hell partly to be alleviated by the hope of resurrection and partly to be commuted into a fear of other punishments, the whole matter being postponed for future judgment, but made clear to them at that time. In chapter 4 of his First Letter, Peter teaches this fact, saying "The good news was declared to the dead as well so that in terms of the flesh they be judged as men, but in the spirit live with God."[163] The good news of the arrival and resurrection, which Peter was discussing there, was for the dead so that [238] even those in hell would recognize Christ as their judge and "genuflect in his name."[164] The declaration of the good news that is manifested through Christ's descent to those in hell, to the dead, reaches the point that those who await the resurrection of the flesh and the judgment, have within them a spirit placated in God. Christ, who "died and lives, is Lord of the dead and living" (Rom. 14). The dead "strive to please him" (2 Cor. 5). Those in hell "genuflect in his name" (Phil. 2). They praise him from beneath the earth (Rev. 5).[165] Hell's gloomy horror was actually made bright by the light of Christ's entry, and that horror is so far away because Christ himself endured the gloomy horrors there. Christ, the savior, brought this hope and salvation even to those kept in hell. Christ, savior of all, there offered himself, offering, because it is within him, freedom from that prison.

Peter: Do you think that he is called "savior of all" for that reason?

Michael: He is called savior and judge of all, and it is said that he died for everyone for the following reason: by taking away death and hell and offering life in their place Christ himself forgives everyone for Adam's original sin, which in itself consisted of eternal death and hell's horror for everyone, so that everyone, restored to life by him as judge, would be justly judged not for Adam's deed, but for all their own deeds, although the good and bad alike used to be judged there by demons.[166]

---

[163] 1 Pet. 4:6.
[164] Phil. 2:10.
[165] Rom. 14:9; 2 Cor. 5:9; Phil. 2:10; Rev. 5:13.
[166] This means that before Christ all, good and bad, remain under the sign of sin as slaves of the

341

Christ is for a second reason called savior of all, just as he is called creator of all: the spirit of divinity was from the beginning placed inside everyone, and it derives from his own breath (Gen. 2 and 6).[167] Now this spirit internally establishes a certain rule of conscience, which brings all peoples to salvation or damnation (Rom. 2 and Acts 10).[168] On this basis Christ will raise up all peoples and demand an accounting for his gifts to them: more will be demanded from him to whom more has been given.[169]

"Christ is called the savior of all, but especially of the faithful" (1 Tim. 4).[170] Here is the third and the most important reason for his saving action. In that passage we must take special note of the strength of the expression "especially" (*maxime*). For Christ shows his own salvation's power particularly in those of us who have been reborn again, and even in the old patriarchs who were faithful to him. By his grace and his resurrection's power he now keeps us with him lest we be led down to hell. [239] And by rising up he led the patriarchs, who had already been led down there, out of hell with himself. Everyone else he left in hell until judgment day, certain ones yet in need of cleansing, others needing to be punished thereafter by his just judgment. For beyond what the wicked already suffer, there remain other punishments for them to suffer in body and soul, when they are condemned in the final judgment.

Peter: Those who are to be condemned do not yet know for certain, although they may be fearful.

Michael: They cannot know it for certain because even others, who are not to be punished, may be kept there and tortured with them. When they are brought to judgment, then they will be stupefied because they did not know that such

---

demon; now being pardoned the original sin, justice can be done acceding to one's proper actions.
[167] Gen. 2:7, 6:11.
[168] Rom. 2:14; Acts 10:1.
[169] Matt. 25:29.
[170] 1 Tim. 4:10 : "For to this end we toil and struggle, because we have our hope set on the living God, who is the Savior of all people, especially of those who believe."

condemnation was in store for them. There they will plead in various ways; there will be "weeping and the gnashing of teeth." Then "the sheep will be separated from the goats" which were not previously separated.[171] They are all ignorant of what is contained in God's closed judgment book. Yet at the judgment the books will be opened, and hell will produce its dead for judgment to be passed then on them all and on the demons as well (Rev. 20).[172]

Peter: Why does Christ speak of Abraham's exalted bosom if he was suffering hell's pain and horror?

Michael: Truly did Abraham, just like David, feel this horror as he was dying. Truly before Christ's death paradise was not open, and the power of death and hell was ever harsh until Christ came and broke it and tied it fast, tearing up its trappings (Matt. 12; Mark. 4; Luke 11).[173] When Christ rose from hell, he made the saints who believed in him, rise with him (Matt. 27). At that time he plundered hell's principality and powers (Col. 2) in order to abolish them completely in the final judgment (1 Cor. 15).[174] The demon's booty consisted of pious souls, which Christ, the victor, frees as he takes the patriarchs with him into heaven's kingdom. Hence, according to Matthew 8, Luke 13, and Hebrews 11, the heavenly kingdom is granted by Christ to them because he made them partners in his resurrection.[175] Christ, having obtained his kingdom through the resurrection, at that moment he took the patriarchs and prophets into his charge because they kept their faith in

---

[171] Matt. 25:30-32 : "All the nations will be gathered before him, and he will separate people one from another as a shepherd separates the sheep from the goats, and he will put the sheep at his right hand and the goats at the left."

[172] Rev. 20:12-14.

[173] Matt. 12:29; Luke 11:22, not in Mark 4.

[174] Col. 2:15 : "He disarmed the rulers and authorities and made a public example of them, triumphing over them in it." 1 Cor. 15:24 : "Then comes the end, when he hands over the kingdom to God the Father, after he has destroyed every ruler and every authority and power."

[175] Matt. 8:11 : "I tell you, many will come from east and west and will eat with Abraham and Isaac and Jacob in the kingdom of heaven." Luke 13:28-29 : "There will be weeping and gnashing of teeth when you see Abraham and Isaac and Jacob and all the prophets in the kingdom of God, and you yourselves thrown out. Then people will come from east and west, from north and south, and will eat in the kingdom of God." Heb. 11:8-16 : "By faith Abraham obeyed ... By faith he stayed for a time in the land ... as did Isaac and Jacob... Therefore God is not ashamed to be called their God; indeed, he has prepared a city for them."

him from long ago just as because of that faith he is now taking us into that kingdom.

Peter: Even before the resurrection Christ teaches about the excellence of Abraham's breast (Luke 16).[176]

[240] Michael: This is true for many reasons. First because his glory was already at hand; second, because the patriarchs, having an expectation of liberation through Christ, knew about the time through the prophetic spirit, especially because at that time John the Baptist had come down to them as an eye-witness of him. Thus, because Christ was already present as a liberator, they had a great measure of consolation and enjoyed a great degree of solace. Third, in contrast with the punishment of others, the bosom of Abraham for the pious provided comfort of his glory. Fourth, the demon in hell was constrained by certain laws. For just as for the impious there was then and is now variation in the punishments in hell, so with greater reason the good were kept apart from the wicked. It is clear that a distinction among the impious was introduced, as it is evidenced from the separation between the giants and the Sodomites. This is also the case with other instances of wickedness (Isa. 14; Ezek. 32).[177] Therefore, the difference between the good and the wicked was all the greater. Fifth, good angels were always among the pious as guardians bringing solace with their divine radiance. Thus, Christ says that the soul of Lazarus was "carried by angels" to Abraham's breast. The demon's power over his breast was limited because of the Patriarch's extraordinary faith with the assistance of good angels. In his *On the Exultation of Samuel*, Philo understands that the "gods" who go up from earth are the good angels who protected his soul with their own blessed soul. After Moses had been buried on the mountain by an angel, a guardian angel led him down so

---

[176] Luke 15:20-24 in a parable of Lazarus.

[177] Isa. 14:20 : "You will not be joined with them in burial, because you have destroyed your land, you have killed your people." In Ezek. 32 are differentiated various levels of punishment for the enemies of Israel.

that at Christ's transfiguration he appeared on the mountain with Elijah.[178] Sixth, Abraham's breast was separated from the others not only in recognition of his faith, but also because a place had been made for it so that during the intervening hiatus others would not be able to come to that place. Finally, God, who fills everything, fills even hell by offering solaces to whomever he wishes. Because God was Abraham's God, Abraham lived there in God in his grace. God's wisdom offered solace to the faithful even in hell (Eccclus. 24). The divine wisdom's renown was always known even in hell (Job 28).[179]

Peter: Where do you think was that place for Abraham's breast?

Michael: Just as we have said that a grave is hell, so we say that [241] the grave is Abraham's breast as if there were a special communication of souls in the grave.[180] Everywhere there is a place with room enough for souls, whether they are to be tormented or comforted. Scripture teaches that graves are places where souls are guarded so that it is said that souls are led to the grave in connection with the body, which by their nature they love. The gospel teaches that demons loiter around grave sites (Matt. 8; Mark. 5; Luke 8). This is because, just as they are drawn to souls, they congregate at grave sites.[181] When Christ said that those who are in graves would hear his voice, he did not consider souls apart from graves. By their nature souls seek a body; those which sinned in a body, grieve in its presence

---

[178] *On the Exultation of Samuel*, the title mentioned by Servetus is not listed among the works of Philo of Alexandria. Perhaps he refers to Philo's *De Ebrietate* XXXVI, where Philo describes how the soul of Solomon was in state of exultation and delight not produced by wine because he "drank no wine or intoxicating liquors to the day of his death," but because his soul was filled with "grace" and "he was enrolled among the ranks of the divine army which he will never leave in consequence of the prudence of the wise captain." Reference to Moses is an allusion to Matt. 17:1-9.

[179] Ecclus 24: 29 : "For her [wisdom's] thoughts are more abundant than the sea, and her counsel deeper than the great abyss." Job 28:22 : "Abaddon and Death say, 'We have heard a rumor of it with our ears.'"

[180] *Quaedam animarum communicatio.* The following explanation is more in the Aristotelian style of natural affinity than in the Platonist tradition which considered the body a "tomb" of the soul."

[181] Matt. 8:28 : "two demoniacs coming out of the tombs met him." Mark 5:2 : "immediately a man out of the tombs with an unclean spirit met him." Luke 8:27, in connection with "the man possessed by demon."

and grieve that they have been robbed of it. This is especially true in the Law because souls were not yet, like now, taken up into the heavenly kingdom. It is not illogically stated that, whoever approaches a corpse, approaches a soul (Lev. 21; Num. 6).[182] It was said that souls were going down into the pit (Isa. 38; Ps. 29, 48, etc.).[183] In those days, souls were afflicted with a corpse as an insult, and according to the passages cited this was hurled against them by the prophets as a punishment (Isa. 14; Ezek. 32; et passim).[184] The prophets everywhere threaten revenge and punishment whereby corpses would lack graves and be consumed by beasts. This would be a ridiculous form of punishment, if it had nothing to do with souls. Improperly buried, Elisha's corpse was miraculously discovered for his soul's benefit. Moses was buried by an angel lest to his holy soul's grief the demon be able to abuse it as an object of idolatry for others. For holy souls grieve, when we commit idolatry around their corpses.[185] A grave used to be something holy and inviolable. Not without mystery is the solemn prayer about the grave of Abraham and his family found in scripture. Not without reason were pious men affected by the graves of their ancestors and forebears (Gen. 47 and 49; 3 Kings 13). It was believed that some peace greater than in the company of the wicked was there. Likewise, the soul had a greater expectation of rising again together with the pious.[186] It was believed that good angels were guardians there, [242] where the souls of their forebears were under guard. Because the family of ancestors, being sure and proven to God and descended from Abraham, was

---

[182] Lev. 21:11; Num. 6:6.

[183] Isa. 38:18; Ps. 29:3, Ps. 48:14.

[184] Compare note 177.

[185] The miraculous discovery of Elisha's body is described in 2 Kings 13:21. About the dead Moses it is said that "no one knows his burial place to this day" Deut. 34:6. Servetus uses a tradition reported by Jude 1: 9 : "But when the archangel Michael contended with the devil and disputed about the body of Moses, he did not dare to bring a condemnation of slander against him, but said, 'The Lord rebuke you!'" The source of this tradition is unknown to Talmud and to the Midrash.

[186] Gen. 47:30 and 49:29 concerning the death of Jacob. 1 Kings 13:31 concerning the death of a prophet.

unique, everyone is led back to the bosom of Abraham, the parent, just as those who kept his faith and piety, and who were buried with him.

There is meant the peace about which the angel spoke to Daniel, when it said, "As your lot, you will be at peace at the end of days."[187] Likewise, the same thing is said about other pious men because they have been placed among their people: they rest with their own according to lot of neither anyone else nor the wicked. In this way what is written in Wisdom chapter 3 was true at that time. "The souls of the just are in God's hand, nor will the torture of death touch them. They are in peace after death," and "theirs is the hope of complete immortality."[188] Wisdom said that it had penetrated the earth's lower parts, saw them sleeping there, and gave them light as they placed their hope in the Lord (Ecclus. 24).[189] Although they would be in hell, nevertheless, Elisha and Jonas asked God to accept their souls and allow them to be placed there in a place of repose. And this was a shadow of the true repose that would exist among those in heaven through Christ. Hence, by a heavenly voice John was bidden to write something novel: "Blessed are they who hereafter die in the Lord, that they truly rest from their labors." "Hereafter," he said, or "presently" or "finally," ἀπορτι, "from this time," to distinguish it from the old repose. Christ often used the same expression to emphasize that, after the time of his resurrection, there would be a new kingdom.[190]

Peter: Are you saying that in the age to come certain sins can be forgiven, after the dead are in this manner punished, cleansed, and saved through fire?
Michael: For some their sins are forgiven in this age, for some in an age to come, for others still neither in this age nor in the age to come, as says Christ in Matthew,

---

[187] Dan. 12:13.
[188] Wisd. 31:1 and 4.
[189] Ecclus. 24:5 and 12.
[190] Rev. 14:13. The same Greek term and the same idea are used in Matt. 23:39, 26:29 and 64; John 13:19, 14:7.

chapter 12.[191]

Everything is forgiven now for those who believe in Christ, God's son. Thus, born again in him, they feel no pain from hell because of his exalted grace. Christ's baptism takes original sin's guilt away from them. They live a heavenly life in a body, as well as after the body is cast aside, once they have been truly born again in the living Christ and revived with his spirit. Nonetheless, even among this group [243] some will be reckoned "least" because of their transgression of the "least commandments," as Christ said.[192] Whoever has built something superfluous upon Christ's foundation, will be punished with the fire of affliction, whether in this age or in death, thus being "saved through fire," as Paul said.[193] Yet, as for those who have not pursued this regeneration and are now held in hell awaiting liberation in the future at his hands (after all, many among the Jews and Gentiles were found to be pious), their sins will be forgiven in the future judgment. Sins arising from Adam's sin, which have manifested themselves in us prior to the era of complete recognition, and which tie us to death in body and bring hell as a companion, will be taken away in the future age, just as had happened with Adam's own, original sin. It is truly fitting to say that this sin along with many other sins will be forgiven with Christ as judge, and that unclean flesh will be cleansed. For it is said that, after everyone, including children, Jews, and Gentiles, along with Adam, paid his debt through the pains of death and hell, Christ by raising them from the dead will later remove the sin of death, destroying death itself and hell and saving them "through fire," so to speak. Christ made the same point himself: "You will not leave there until you make the smallest repayment, no matter how small" (Matt. 5; Luke 12).[194] For those who are now held in hell's

---

[191] Matt. 12:32 : "Whoever speaks a word against the Son of Man will be forgiven, but whoever speaks against the Holy Spirit will not be forgiven, either in this age or in the age to come."

[192] Matt. 5:19 : "Therefore, whoever breaks one of the least of these commandments, and teaches others to do the same, will be called least in the kingdom of heaven; but whoever does them and teaches them will be called great in the kingdom of heaven."

[193] 1 Cor. 3:15.

[194] Matt. 5:26; Luke 12:59.

prison, are being afflicted with suffering for even their smallest misdeeds. This is what it means "to settle a debt down to the last penny." There, as he himself says, Christ acts for the remission of sins, about which Paul also spoke, and he says that "through fire" we are purged of them.

Still for those remaining men who will be condemned for more serious crimes arising from the act of premeditation, their sins will be discharged not even in the coming age. Those who knowingly and with sure malice resist the good spirit in its activity are the ones meant here. The one who refuses to render faith to Christ, will clean away this sin's filth neither in death nor in resurrection; instead, at the resurrection he will suffer eternal punishment. The same thing awaits those who with an obstinate lack of contrition commit other sins. For example, sins against the spirit, such as when someone, aware of his own sin, refuses to repent.[195]

[244] Peter: If we all pay for Adam's sin with death, why was it necessary for Christ to pay the same price on our behalf with his own death?

Michael: Christ's death creates the very fact that we can pay that penalty: without it we were all held in everlasting hell, never to rise again. Furthermore, Christ more effectively pays other penalties on behalf of those of us who have been born again because by his death he so rescues us from hell's death that we do not detect so much as a whiff of hell, which everyone else has felt and continues to feel. Christ by rising weakened hell and freed certain people thence. In his final resurrection he will free everyone from death and hell; death and hell will be utterly destroyed.

Peter: How is hell destroyed?

Michael: After the resurrection there will no longer be a hell. None of the demon's power will extend to mankind. Like a gravesite hell exists now under the demon's monarchy. That monarchy will be destroyed, and the demon will be

---

[195] Matt. 12:31; Mark 3:29; Luke 12:10.

tortured mightily. The devil has not yet been cast into "the fire which has been readied for him," as Christ says.[196] Death itself, which was the devil, the cause of our death, and hell itself, which was the devil keeping us in hellish regions, will both through Christ be cast into "the lake of fire" (Rev. 20).[197] Death and hell will then perish as John explains in that passage. There will be a death of death, and hell will be cut away, as Paul says following Hosea.[198] The demon's sway over mankind will then be entirely destroyed: his entire "sovereignty and power," as Paul said.[199] It will exist neither above nor below, nor shall hell exist in the manner it does now: God's fire will burn hell itself down to its very depths (Deut. 32).[200]

Peter: Will not even the elements survive?

Michael: Neither heaven nor earth nor the other elements; not the light of the sun nor the moon, as John says following Isaiah: "All these ancient bits will pass away, and everything will be made new." Everything will be broken down by fire, as Peter said.[201] Then in God we shall breathe the new ethereal substance of the three higher elements. All this earthly matter, mixed with others and distributed in precise measure within the bodies of people, will be glorified. [245] Everything is so arranged in proportion, everything that was created for mankind, so that nothing superfluous remains. Mankind is everything's end, and God is mankind's end. God made everything for man and through Christ, who is the Alpha and Omega. Jesus Christ's face alone was from eternity substantively the prince in God, and he gathered all these faces according to his own image into one so that they are all one in God, and mankind's face in God alone remains in substance with

---

[196] Matt. 25:41.
[197] Rev. 20:10.
[198] Hos. 13:14 : "O Death, where are your plagues? O Sheol, where is your destruction?" cited in 1 Cor. 15:55 : "Where, O death, is your victory? Where, O death, is your sting?"
[199] Eph. 1:21.
[200] Deut. 32:22 : "For a fire is kindled by my anger, and burns to the depths of Sheol."
[201] Isa. 60:19 : "The sun shall no longer be your light by day, nor for brightness shall the moon give light to you by night; but the LORD will be your everlasting light, and your God will be your glory." 2 Pet. 3:12 : "Since all these things are to be dissolved in this way, what sort of persons ought you to be in leading lives of holiness and godliness, waiting for and hastening the coming

the angels. Nonetheless, we shall know all those things which now exist in the world, in God's appearance as well as the more sublime things that he will make available.

From the discussion about "shadows" up to this point you infer how the entire world, death, and hell go by as a shadow. That death that previously reduced us down to a shadow, was itself a shadow. It was a shadow of the other, eternal death that would exist in the final judgment. For that reason John calls the latter, a second death (Rev. 20 and 21).[202] Illnesses, too, that we here suffer, are shadows of affliction yet to come. When the demon, that was death and sickness to us, is taken away, Christ will then remove all sickness. The earlier hell of fire that contains and torments our shades, was a shadow, going by as a shadow. There is another, eternal hell that was prepared before time, being a divine fire where souls will not be tortured by the devil, but where people and devils will be tortured by God's judgment, and the devil will have no power over mankind.

Peter: What will this fire be like?

Michael: That fire was prepared before time, and it is God Himself who is the fire. For no creation whatsoever is as old as God.[203] God was shown to Moses in fire, and fire everywhere went out from the Lord for vengeance, declaring that He was an avenging fire that consumed in His judgment. It suits the most powerful judge to possess in himself the means to punish the wicked rather than to have those means reside in someone else. He is, therefore, the beginning and end of all things so that, just as everything stems from Him, so everything that remains, returns to Him albeit by differing circumstances.

If Origen had understood this point, he would not have said that the

---

of the day of God, because of which the heavens will be set ablaze and dissolved, and the elements will melt with fire?"

[202] Rev. 20:6 and 21:4.

[203] *Ignis ille ab aeterno paratus est ipsemet Deus.* It is possible that Servetus depends for these ideas on Sefer Torat ha-'Adam of Nachmanides (Ch. B. Chavel, *Kitbe Moshe ben Nahman*, Jerusalem, 1963, vol. II, p. 285). Nachmanides also talks about a subtle fire that "is not a body, does not have limits and is not contained in a space ..., and which is a river of fire that flows from the Throne of the glory."

demons were to be saved on the basis of the fact that they would return to their origin.[204] To be sure they will return, but [246] to God Himself by going into fire. God's spirit itself will kindle that fire, according to Isaiah, chapter 30,[205] with the result that the demons that sinned against God's spirit, will be tortured by the spirit, just as the souls will be tortured with the pain of their biting conscience. This will be the fire of revenge from the Lord's face as it will be "His might's glory" (2 Thes. 1).[206] It is said that God's face burns like a "devouring fire," and that it is set for judgment (Isa. 30 and 66).[207] With His aspect of virtue alone will He torture and inflict pain upon the wicked. The holy spirit itself, which you have accepted, will be your torture, if you ill serve it. God Himself is a consuming fire that burns away everything evil, body and soul. Christ himself will then be a torture to demons, just as they were a torture to us. For this reason in the Gospel the demons cry that they are being tortured by Christ.[208] He will be death to death and perdition to perdition. God Himself will bring darkness to the wicked, just as the same cloud of God was light for the Israelites and darkness for the Egyptians (Exod. 14).[209]

As for the fire with which the wicked will be punished after the

---

[204] Origen did not propose an eternal fire or an infernal punishment. He postulated *apocatástasis* that is, universal restoration through a purifying fire in order to begin a new cosmic phase. All sinners, including demons will be saved. God himself, and in another instance he says his Logos, will be this mysterious purifying fire, but not the material, external fire (Origen, *On the First Principles*, lib. I, cap. V, 2; lib. II, cap. X, 3; lib. III, cap. V, n. 3, VI, 4-6, (PG XI, 166, 235, 327, 337)). Also in *Contra Celsum*, lib. IV, 20 (ibid., 514). *Origen on the First principles*, English translation by G. W. Butterworth, (Gloucester, Mass.: Peter Smith, 1973).

[205] Isa. 30:30 : "And the LORD will cause his majestic voice to be heard and the descending blow of his arm to be seen, in furious anger and a flame of devouring fire."

[206] 2 Thes. 1:6-9 : "For it is indeed just of God to repay with affliction those who afflict you, and to give relief to the afflicted as well as to us, when the Lord Jesus is revealed from heaven with his mighty angels in flaming fire, inflicting vengeance on those who do not know God and on those who do not obey the gospel of our Lord Jesus. These will suffer the punishment of eternal destruction, separated from the presence of the Lord and from the glory of his might."

[207] Isa. 30:30 and 66:15 : "For the LORD will come in fire, and his chariots like the whirlwind, to pay back his anger in fury, and his rebuke in flames of fire."

[208] Mark 5:6-7 : "When he saw Jesus from a distance, he ran and bowed down before him; and he shouted at the top of his voice, 'What have you to do with me, Jesus, Son of the Most High God? I adjure you by God, do not torment me.'" Luke 8:28.

[209] Exod. 14:20.

resurrection, scripture does not call it hell, although, to be sure, it could be called hell in a mystical sense. It is everlasting paradise's fire which is said to have been prepared thus before time as an archetype.[210] Here, he will torment demons, body and soul, thrusting upon them the foulest stench, the most hideous sights, sounds, tastes, and touches, as is wont to happen to those who with dysfunctional senses declare sweet things bitter and perfumed scents foul. Moreover, the blessed ones' experience will be the opposite: all their senses will be filled with glory's sweetness; their mind's light will be new, clear their understanding of those things which previously appeared puzzling, because of the true illumination of Christ's divinity that brings everything before us. Because of sin Christ allowed only this much: we were handed over to the hands of wicked judges in order to make clear his own justice, but in the resurrection the most just judge will himself examine every act of every person by reading them in his own ledger. In fact, he will present it to each person to read as it truly is. Every aid offered by angels will then end, as will the hindrance of demons once they have individually brought forth those in their trust who are to be judged in Christ's presence. [247] Christ alone, who fulfills every office, will bring us before God, the Father, so that in Him there will be the fulfillment of everything, and so that Christ will then be "everything in everything," keeping in his bosom all of us in God. The world began from Christ alone, and it will end in Christ alone, who is the Alpha and the Omega. Thus, ending this, my last discourse on the shadows, I say that the body, the soul, death, hell, all earlier judgments, everything that is understood, all knowledge, what has been seen, heard, smelt, tasted, or touched, all activities of angels and demons, just like heaven, earth, sun, moon, and everything else that was transitory, have gone by as a shadow, and that there was nothing genuine in any of these. Rather they were a shadow of this great, permanent truth.

---

[210] The phrases that follow seem to be copies almost textually from the aforementioned places in Origen's writings. In any case it is Servetus' original interpretation of the *ignis aeternus et inextinguibilis* of Matt. 3:12, 18:8; Mark 9:47; Luke 3:17.

In Christ alone is there truth and eternity.

In him alone is their complete fulfillment and our complete salvation.

May God alone before everything be always blessed. Amen.

The Second Dialogue
concerning the Divine Trinity
wherein the manner of Christ's generation
is explained, showing that he is not a creature
nor is he of limited power, but rather is truly to be worshipped and is
the true God

Peter: I decided to asked you some other questions, which was why I first was looking for you, but I put it off for a while because listening to you was such a pleasure as you spoke about the great prefiguration of Christ's mysteries, his fulfillment, and his permanent truth. Still I have questions about some other topics, which I did not understand previously. Now, if it is no trouble to you, please explain what remains.

Michael: If it is not trouble to me? It is always a pleasure to discuss Christ and to subject his mysteries to serious inquiry. I work very hard to know him; I think day and night, calling upon his pity and asking for a revelation that grants true understanding.

Peter: You said that there existed in all creatures certain aspects that were analogous to the manner of Christ's generation. Take this moment to explain this. Teach me about the manner of Christ's generation and make his full godhead wholly manifest. For the Sophists say that Christ, the man, was a pure creature of limited power and was not to be worshipped with the same worship with which we are bidden to worship God alone.

Michael: "At the name of Jesus everything of heaven, earth, and hell genuflects" (Phil. 2). Hell's powers worshipped this same Jesus (Mark 5). All the apostles worshipped him (Luke 24). All the angels worship him (Heb. 1). According to John 5, this Jesus is to be honored with every honor with which the Father is honored. [249] In fact, the Father cannot be honored, worshipped, seen, or understood save through him (John 14).[1] Therefore, the Sophists are lost throughout heaven. Jesus is the one who gave that instruction on worship because it was his wish to be worshipped alone. The Sophists are committing the foulest error regarding the name applied to him, "humanity," itself or the phrase, "pure man," itself as you will soon see. This same man, whom they demeaningly call a creature, you will today come to know, not as a creature, but as the creator of everything, after you notice these three degrees of dispensation in him. The first of these is the Word with God. The second is the coming forth into the world. The third is the return to the Father. To begin with, according to the dispensation whereby the Word was with God, there is no question of there being a creature because the Word was God Himself before creatures existed. Christ's reflection in God was God appearing in that glory whereby Christ was to be glorified.

Peter: It has been clearly shown that "reflection" was the word used there because every λóγος, every utterance, and every wisdom is the natural reflection of any given thing. Likewise, because in the Book of Wisdom wisdom was called a reflection, and Christ, who was there reflecting, is called the reflection or the refulgence by the apostle. Likewise, because as Elohim he was thus in the person there reflecting and appearing. The church's first doctors and the heresies prevalent then all confirm that this person in the Word was most clearly shown in the scriptures.[2] Fine. Let this first degree be more than sufficiently explained. Now go to the second degree.

Michael: Christ came forth, not in a creature's manner, but was conceived and begotten from the holy spirit (Matt. 1 and Luke 1). He who has not come from the male parent's substance cannot be called a son. You are said to have come from your father's substance because of the elements of your father's seed, which

---

[1] Phil. 2:10; Mark 5:6; Luke 24:52; Heb. 1:6; John 5:23, 14:9.
[2] About this concept of the "reflection" in wisdom and in Paul see note 3 of Book II. In the thinking of the primitive Christians it was common to understand this manifestation of the Word as wisdom, and that Christ the man would be the end of this divine dispensation. Servetus wrote to Calvin at length in his *Letter* no. 8. This theme was also treated very briefly by Servetus in *Dialogorum de Trinitate*, 1532, Bk. II, B4.

exist from your father's substance, and in which even his soul's and his form's seeds exist. With Christ it is the same. Actually, it is more so with Christ, who is the model of the process. Christ's flesh exists from God's substance, and in it God is seen. Christ's flesh [250] has God's being, and it is a godhead in a body. You will think that the generation of this flesh is a source of wonder, if, keeping the physical principles of the generation of creatures in mind, you recognize that all these are fulfilled through the Word. For all those were in the Word.[3]

Peter: Was that flesh which Christ took from Mary, pure creature?

Michael: Christ's flesh, such as it was in the grave, possessed in substance a divine form. Besides the divine form of light, that flesh had the archetype's elemental substance, truly divine elements, God's substance. The building blocks of his flesh were taken from Mary's womb as was the purest blood, it being pure creature. In our case, the embryo's flesh is fashioned from the mother's blood, once it has been altered by the male seed's formative power. In Christ's case his embryo was similar, and the alteration of the mother's blood, when affected by that uncreated seed, was also similar. The three superior elements are from both parents in Christ as in us. Still, in Christ, as in all creatures in general, the earthly matter is wholly from the mother alone. Earth is everything's mother, and the earthly element always derives from the mother. Nothing earthly derives from the father that would intrude upon the make-up of a begotten human being. It was no different with Christ. If there is any earthly element in our own paternal seed, it is the keeper of the spirit contained therein, and it goes around the outer shell of that membrane which is called the χόριον.[4]

The paternal seed, which was the Word, substantively contained in Christ the elemental substance of water, air, and fire, in other words, the superelemental

---

[3] Servetus modifies partially his doctrine exposed in the cited passage of *Dialogorum de Trinitate*, 1532, and explains these "natural principles" of generation in accordance with Galenic science in order to elucidate how generation is accomplished by the Word of God, which in the case of Jesus assumed the function of the semen.

[4] *Chorion*, the membrane that envelopes the fetus in the womb, described by Galen (*De usu*

substance, which in our case is contained in our own paternal seed. That same seed, in which exists the particular property of the species and of the individual according to the token of light and spirit which has been placed as a seed-source within it, performs manifold functions in all of us just as well as in Christ. It contains the substance of the higher elements and is mixed with the earthly material that is taken from the mother, as if it were a separate kind of matter. Likewise, it behaves like a craftsman and technician because the seed source of the form has been placed within it, [251] and it is the special source for producing a new form and soul. Thirdly, in it there is a spirit, which unites with the spirit held within the vessels for the purpose of bringing the body to life after it has been shaped. It does not burst out, nor does the seed's spirit dissipate into the outer atmosphere after the embryo's shaping has taken place, as certain people say. Instead, it is held within the vessels, as Galen explains in his book *On the Seed*[5] to which contribute the encasing of the secondary membranes and enclosure by the curved structure of the uterus so that the spark of fire confined therein may heat up and be active. This fiery strength of the seed, having a token of divine form, soul, shape, and light, is that formative capacity and that causative essence of natural forces, which in the first book, *On Natural Potentialities*, book 1 of *On the Causes of Pulse*, and in his book, *On the Substance of Natural Potentialities*, Galen after Aristotle and the other philosophers, often looked for, but ultimately admitted he did not know.[6]

God so determined that the path to all truth and the manifestation of all things was through Christ, who is "the path," "the light," and "the truth," and "in whom all wisdom's treasures are stored."[7] Even natural science's treasures are

---

partium, XV.4).

[5] In his book *On the Seed*, Περὶ σπέρματος, libs. I and II, and in cap. XIV of *De usu partium* Galen corrects certain theories of Aristotle concerning embryology and contained in his *De generatione animalium*. Galen rejected the view of Aristotle that the paternal seed does not contribute any material for the generation and that its *pneuma* evaporates while it communicates its potential to the maternal material. Servetus follows Galen.

[6] Neither Aristotle nor Galen could explain in any of those treatises the forces and mechanisms of which governed the reproductive process.

[7] John 14:6; Col. 2:3.

stored in Christ. Adopt this resolution for yourself: the very Divinity that was in Christ's generation brought about what in the generation of other things the paternal seed is wont to bring about. In fact, every other seed derives its forces from the seed that is the Word.

Peter: Just as we go from the generation of other things to that first generation, so we return from that generation to the others. The generation of other things will be better recognized, if the natural composition of Christ's body is recognized insofar as he is a natural son, naturally conceived.

Michael: Having been thoroughly taught by Christ a philosophy which is not subject to doubt, we say that light's force is everything's shaper.[8] Furthermore, that there is an innate light and that there is a light coming from the outside. The solar ray, which from the earth's mud gives rise to living animals, proves this point. Just as the ray, containing a force conjoinable with another, acts upon the earth in a manner to give life, where a certain union occurs, so it is in the union of male and female, and in the union of the divine light. The life of all things [252] is a kind of union, whether we speak of the corporeal or the spiritual. It is necessary that in a subject two forces always be united, the one which it has and the other from the outside in order to produce one third thing. Moreover, we will say in a little while what kind of union and blend it is, not only in Christ, but also in us. For the time being we say that, once a union or a blend of seeds has taken place with earth, a formative capacity, drawing itself out of that coalescence, produces and fashions animals and even plants.[9] In the case of animals, it causes the first forming of particular basic parts with their vessels. First, the umbilical vessels of the fetus stretch from the uterus of the mother, as we observe in anatomy, in the direction of the natural liver and the life-giving heart. The nutrient's first conversion into blood is performed by the liver itself, and this is due to the power of fiery vital (life-

[8] *Nos a Christo indubitatam philosophiam edocti, dicimus, formatricem omnium esse lucis vim.*
[9] Besides his discovery of the pulmonary circulation, Servetus is operating within the worldview he inherited from the Hellenistic and scholastic traditions. He applies, however, his discovery to the explanation of the generative processes. The role which he assigns to light has a remote

giving) spirit and formal light located within the liver itself.

In Christ's case both these elements were from God's substance. Christ's vital spirit within his own arteries and the substantive form of his embryo's liver were God's substance. Therefore, it follows that, when blood was being formed in the liver by them, there was and is in Christ's very blood the divinity hypostatically joined with him. In Christ's very blood there exists the substance of God's spirit and the divine light's substantive form. Hence, it is said to be God's blood on which depends the world's redemption.[10] It is the "true, real, and substantive drink" for our soul and for the "inner man."[11] Christ's blood is God just as Christ's flesh is God, and Christ's soul is God. Nor is the nature of the bones, ligaments, and other organs any different because in all these there is His own form of light. For in Christ, as in us, that same formative, fiery force by drying out earthly matter through the mechanism of heat and giving it the hardness of bones endows solid parts with formal light.

Peter: Hence, Christ's divinity is complex and is wholly gathered into the parts. Not because it is actually divided up, but because by a miraculous dispensation it is active in individual parts and mixes itself with them.

Michael: Christ's very constitution is truly divine, [253] and it derives from God's substance through many mechanisms.[12] First, because, as the substantive form in body and blood, it possesses the Word's truly divine light. Second, because in the very flesh and blood it holds the archetype's three divine elements that come from the Father's substance. Third, just as bloody matter taken from the mother, though created, has been luminously transformed and glorified

---

affinity with the ideas popular during the Renaissance, especially those of Paracelsus.
[10] On the margin, Servetus wrote *Sanguis Dei* as the subtitle for the following paragraph.
[11] Allusions to Eph. 1:7; Col. 1:14; John 6:54-56.
[12] We translate here the term *plasma*, used by Servetus, as constitution because it does not refer to a particular element or physiological process, but to the corporeal assembly, to the whole vivified body. Servetus seems to have borrowed the term from Irenaeus who uses it in this sense: *"Suum plasma in semetipsum recapitulans"* (*Adv. Haereses*, lib. III, cap. XXII,1); *"Ab initio plasmationis nostrae in Adam"* (ibid., lib. V, cap. I,3) (PG VII,219 and 293). Servetus teaches that not only the formal element of Jesus is divine but also the material.

361

from incarnation into God as light, so his food and drink, by which his blood and flesh were fortified daily, was correspondingly transformed. Fourth, because there is as yet within the flesh the vital, divine spirit, which is also a natural spirit. Fifth, because in its very soul the body holds the Word's light in essence as well as the archetype's elemental substance together with this corruptible, elemental substance that we have prior to resurrection. Sixth, because a new, divine regenerating spirit of glory exists in him after resurrection alongside all the incorruptible substance. Seventh, because this divinity is not new, but was wholly Christ's very body from before time in God as a person as was his spirit in substance, as well as the Word itself in the substance of the spirit. Eighth, because the "glimmer of his face" and spirit shown forth truly is that light by which God is light so that God is seen in him and imparted to us by his agency. Ninth, because the entirety of God's power and all God's trappings are in him so that everything exists and lives in him.

To the same extent that the universe's light, which "separates day from night,"[13] is solidified in the one solar body and yet scatters from it into other things, so that primary and substantive God's light coalesced, so to speak, into the one body of Jesus Christ from which it subsequently radiates into us. Even the sun's light takes its existence in God's light, and it maintains its token in material things. As in the sun's case we say that there is primal light and in other things other lights of lesser and varying degrees, so it is in Christ so that he is always everything's "chief and head."[14]

Peter: Now I am starting to see the analogies.

Michael: In whatever manner you can imagine that one thing is truly joined to another or truly exists in it, be it heat, color, light, [254] shape, soul, spirit, element, in all the same manners God truly exists in Christ so that everything's model is in Christ's very body and soul. On the other hand, in every manner you

---

[13] Allusion to Gen. 1:14.
[14] Allusion to Eph. 1:22 : "And he has put all things under his feet and has made him the head over all things for the church." 1 Pet. 5:4 : "And when the chief shepherd appears, you will win the crown of glory that never fades away."

can think, that the external body is maintained and supported by a power within, and caused to live in a union of essence, in the same ways Christ exists in God, is supported by Him, and is caused to live by Him as a model of everything. In every manner you can imagine that one thing derives from another, such as a stone from a mountain, or waters from rock, or as the scripture of the Law, the Word, the light, the angels, derive from God, or yourself from your father's loins, so in all the same manners Christ derives from God and is a model of every derivation. He derives from God and "glows like a lamp," shining and flashing from an invisible light (Isa. 62). He derives from the internal mind's hidden, divine intellectual faculty. For this reason he is said to glow, to flash, and to glimmer, being visible light from an unseen source.

Peter: I wish the Nicaean fathers had said that he was "light from light" in this sense.[15] But they wanted to tear God apart and cut the invisible ray, made really distinct, from the visible. Thus, they were confused by their own invisible confusion because they failed to recognize that Jesus, the human being, was God's biological son. They did not want to see Christ's openly shown light, just as Sophists even today deny this vision. But continue with your analogy of Christ's origin.

Michael: Christ came and proceeded from his father, just as you do from your own father. The paternal seed of Christ's conception did the same thing for him that your father's created seed does for you so that all filiation is truly derived from Christ himself, just as "all paternity comes from God, the Father."[16]

Peter: The comparison between our filiation and that of Christ is most

---

[15] Allusion to *lumen de lumine* of the Nicaean creed. Isa 62:1 : "For Zion's sake I will not keep silent, and for Jerusalem's sake I will not rest, until her vindication shines out like the dawn, and her salvation like a burning torch." Servetus draws attention to this text in *Dialogorum de Trinitate*, 1532, concerning the use of the terms λάμπας and παύγασμα in LXX, see note 2.

[16] Rom. 8:15-16 : "When we cry, 'Abba! Father!' it is that very Spirit bearing witness with our spirit that we are children of God." Eph. 3:15 : "For this reason I bow my knees before the Father, from whom every family in heaven and on earth takes its name." Servetus's originality consists here in demonstrating that the most suitable analogy is that of universal paternity of God, because of his real intervention in the natural generation of Christ.

appropriate. If we were made after his image, our filiation is in the image of his filiation.

Michael: Things of heaven and earth relate to Christ by analogy. [255] The analogy to Christ's generation exists in the soul and the holy spirit. The angels were breathed by and proceed from God in Christ's image. They receive from Him the superelemental substance and the Divinity's image. The winds are blown in his image and the clouds and rains are made. This solar light is Christ's image. By analogy to Christ and in his image minerals are produced, plants grow, and animals reproduce. By analogy to Christ, mixtures are made and he is the model of every mixture and union. In everything begotten and created there is an analogy to Christ.[17]

Peter: Expatiate upon the similitude in the case of minerals.

Michael: In the production of a given mineral, metal, or stone, there is Christ's likeness, if you should see his flesh separately as it was in the grave. The production of any given mineral takes place in this manner. It is by the power of a heavenly, warming light, a light that comes down through higher elements and is located within them, a light that is through them shared with the earth so that earthly matter is boiled down and given shape together with the other elements that are mixed with it; and a visible, glowing form is imparted to it, bringing it utterly into one substance. In the earth's bowels those minerals are formed, just as Christ's flesh was rendered thus in his mother's bowels. The earth is everything's mother, and there exists in everything an earthly element deriving from the mother.[18] The higher elements will be blended with the earth during the formation of our own flesh and of the bodies of everything else, and those elements are given form by light. You might say that it was no different in Christ's body. For his flesh has this divinity made corporeal just as this stone or this gold physically has an inborn flash of light. Always bear in mind that any body's substantive form is light,

---

[17] This the fundamental principle which culminates his doctrine of the analogy : *In omnibus genitis et creatis est ad Christum analogia.*

and that it has a divine idea placed within.[19] This is the state of affairs with all things, and it is by analogy with Christ. From this point it is obviously being shown to us that the divinity of Christ is first.

Peter: What about plants?

Michael: Plants sprout [256] and grow in similarity to Christ. For example, just as the power of heavenly dew through the accidence of a sown seed's force, or even without it, by watering earthly matter, like a seed, and transforming it by the power of spirit and light, causes plants to sprout, so it happens even with Christ (Isa. 45 and 55).[20] Thus Mary's womb became a garden whither descended the rising sun's dew and caused Christ to sprout forth (Ps. 71; Isa. 61).[21] David's last words confirm the similarity of Christ to the sprouting of plants. The confirmation is found in 2 Samuel 2, where it is said that the sprout comes from the earth through the agency of light and rain, and thus does salvation sprout forth. Zechariah shows the same thing in chapter 3 and 6, when he calls Christ himself a "sprout." Jeremiah also says, "I shall cause David's seed to sprout."[22] It is through a great mystery that in Christ's case there exists the sprouting of heavenly and

---

[18] Again Servetus expresses his concept of *terra mater*. Compare note 3.

[19] These concepts are more Neo-Platonic than scientific. Aristotle never would have attributed the function of a "substantive form of bodies" to light.

[20] This is a literal interpretation of Isa. 45:8 and 55:10-11 : "Shower, O heavens, from above, and let the skies rain down righteousness; let the earth open, that salvation may spring up, and let it cause righteousness to sprout up also; I the LORD have created it." And "For as the rain and the snow come down from heaven, and do not return there until they have watered the earth, making it bring forth and sprout, giving seed to the sower and bread to the eater, so shall my word be that goes out from my mouth; it shall not return to me empty, but it shall accomplish that which I purpose, and succeed in the thing for which I sent it."

[21] Ps. 71:6 : "May he be like rain that falls on the mown grass, like showers that water the earth." Isa. 61:11 : "For as the earth brings forth its shoots, and as a garden causes what is sown in it to spring up, so the Lord GOD will cause righteousness and praise to spring up before all the nations."

[22] The quote is in 2 Sam. 23:3-4 : "The God of Israel has spoken, the Rock of Israel has said to me: One who rules over people justly, ruling in the fear of God, is like the light of morning, like the sun rising on a cloudless morning, gleaming from the rain on the grassy land." Zech. 3:8 and 6:12. Jer. 23:5 : "The days are surely coming, says the LORD, when I will raise up for David a righteous Branch, and he shall reign as king and deal wisely, and shall execute justice and righteousness in the land." And Jer. 33:15 : "In those days and at that time I will cause a righteous Branch to spring up for David; and he shall execute justice and righteousness in the land."

earthly matter within one growth. That this is the seed, the sprout, and the branch that sprouted from heaven's dew and earth's fruit, explains Isaiah in chapters 4, 11, 45, 53, 55, and 61.[23] This is that same sprout miraculously bursting forth from the planted marrow of the lofty cedar (Ezek. 17 and 34; Jer. 23 and 33; Hos. 6).[24]

Jesus Christ is the very sprout, the branch from Isaiah's stock, the model and prototype of every generation and sprouting. To the Sophists the meaning of this sprouting into the one form of Jesus Christ, however, is a joke. They prefer remaining ignorant of these great deeds of God to having God commingle in so many ways with His creature.[25]

Peter: In what respects is the human being more like a plant?

Michael: There are those who say that the top of the trunk tends downward and that the roots beneath the ground are like hair. Others declare that the heart of the plant is in the trunk's middle. But in plants there are no faculties or motions of heart or brain, only of the liver. There are no arteries or nerves in them, but nourishing veins. In trees there is only the faculty of the liver that draws unto itself, that nourishes, and that allows growth up to a set limit. Therefore, man is like a plant in respect to the veins of the liver. A tree's roots are the portal veins bringing nourishment. When these come together into one structure, they continue in the two-fold trunk of the vena cava, and then into the branches. [257] That

---

[23] Phrases used by Isaiah in 4:2, 11:1, 45:8, 53:2, 55:10, and 61:11 which talk about "the branch of the LORD," "A shoot ... from the stump of Jesse," "Shower, O heavens, from above," "For he grew up before him like a young plant, and like a root out of dry ground," "the rain and the snow ... from heaven." Isa. 61:11 : "For as the earth brings forth its shoots, and as a garden causes what is sown in it to spring up, so the Lord GOD will cause righteousness and praise to spring up before all the nations."

[24] Ezek. 17:22 and 34:27. Jer. 23:5 and 33:15 quoted in note 22. Hos. 6:3 : "Let us know, let us press on to know the LORD; his appearing is as sure as the dawn; he will come to us like the showers, like the spring rains that water the earth."

[25] Servetus rejects the doctrine of the "Sophists" which introduces an unsurpassable barrier between God his creatures, that is, the popularly accepted doctrine of traditional Christianity, but at the same time he makes allusion to the little used concepts of "analogies" which Paul, Irenaeus, and other ancient writers applied to Christ. There is also here a veiled reference to the Calvinist doctrine of the absolute chasm between God and his creatures, which was the object of many statements in *Institutes of the Christian Religion* and polemics of Servetus in his *Letters to Calvin*. In fact Calvin selected several points in this context in his *Defensio* (*Calvini Opera*, VIII, 503, propositions XIII-XV, XXI).

dense part which you see in the root of a plant or between the root and the trunk, is like the liver.[26]

Peter: As with plants, is there a vegetable soul in the liver whereby the embryo lives?

Michael: In the holy language it is not called a soul save in those instances where there is breathing. Thus, we say that there is no soul whatsoever in plants. The ability to draw nourishment and grow occurs through the specific power of inborn heat together with the divinity of form located there. In this way fire practically grows on its own by drawing its nourishment. Life is said to exist in plants, but not as a soul's life; rather, there is the formal life of heat like when we say that fire lives or dies in a lamp. In fact, some assert that stones and other items possessing a catalytic power in medicine not only live, but even experience age, sickness, and death, which we feel occur every day even with wine.[27]

Peter: Therefore, is not the embryo's soul or life, whereby it is likened to plants, similar to our own?"

Michael: Not at all, because the embryo does not have its own soul. The embryo is said to live with a vegetal life before God breathes a soul into it. But the nature of a tree's roots is different. For nourishment reaches the liver through the umbilical cord. And thus the tree's roots are not the portal veins, but are rather like the tentacles of an octopus with respect to the vascular connections or, as Hippocrates calls them, the κοτυληδονες of the mother's womb. From there many vesicles insert themselves into secondary ones, and merge into two pairs of vessels, which enter the fetus through the umbilical cord. When a baby is born, the bonds of the mother's vascular connections are broken and cleansed through a washing away of the filth of the afterbirth like a newly transplanted tree. And you will see

---

[26] This is a very imprecise analogy though of Galenic origin. There are manifest here its limitations in view of the Aristotelian doctrine that Servetus denies the existence of a soul in plants, in conformity with the scriptural language, but in contrast to *De anima* of Aristotle.
[27] Servetus establishes a dichotomy in his analogical concept of life. On one side there is God, Christ and animated beings who respire, on the other inanimate vegetative beings which act as living ones due to the physical, natural force of heat and on the basis of chemical reactions.

these mysteries in the heavenly birth, like a new tree through baptism's cleansing being transplanted into Christ, given a new soul, and receiving a new food.[28]

Peter: Is not the heart the first living organ, if the embryo lives a vegetal life through the liver before the heart executes its function of the diastole and systole.

Michael: That is not wholly the liver's life. For it is supported from a different source. Although that life exists solely from the seed's power, it is not [258] the soul's life. In the uterus the embryo is animated by the mother's soul and heart. For the arteries which enter the fetus itself through the umbilical cord, take their source from the heart and pour vital spirit into the fetus.[29] The life-giving heat of the maternal vital spirit together with the seed's innate power make the embryo live with a vegetative life and at that time without another soul. Therefore, though it cannot be absolutely said that it is the heart that lives first in a chronological order, it is, nonetheless, what is alive in principle, and is living before all things by means of a true soul.

Peter: When is a man's true soul breathed into him by God?

Michael: When a man starts to breathe, at the moment of birth. There is no breathing in the womb or exhaling. The fetus does not live by its own soul, but by the mother's soul, as if it were a part of the mother. As we have said, it lives because the vital spirit enters through the umbilical arteries. The benefit of the soul that is contained in these arteries, does not cease until the person is born.

---

[28] This analogy between the birth of a child and the transplantation of a tree is inspired by Galenic sources. The application of this analogy to the birth of a Christian in baptism constitutes a part of the original Servetus intention to establish radical analogies among the religious phenomena. The reference to Hippocrates is to the Aphorisms V, 45 (Émile Littré, ed., 1844, vol. IV, p. 548) which Servetus could read in the edition of Rabelais of 1537 or in the edition of all the works of Hippocrates edited by Jano Cornario (Basel; Froben, 1546). Galen describes those vessels named by Hippocrates as κοτυληδονες, "terminals of the vessels reaching the uterus" (De usu partium, XV, 5).

[29] Servetus does not tackle the correlative problems associated with the fetus such as the question of abortion. His text, however, indicates clearly that he would approach it in positive terms. Moreover, these embryological and physiological doctrines of Servetus were not commented on until now by the experts in medical sciences who focused their interests only on the discovery of the pulmonary circulation.

Therefore, the fetus lives in the womb through the constant benefit of this spirit. It is the same with a branch that in its fruition grows on a tree and then is transplanted to become a new tree.[30]

Hence, the prophet calls to God, "I have been thrust upon you from the womb, and in a new way am I placed within you" (Ps. 21).[31] A person is brought to life through God's breath upon the soul. The soul's substance easily makes this point because we have shown it to be respiration and breath. The soul is not called differently in the holy scripture or in Hebrew. In Latin, too, the soul takes its name from the fact that it is called in Greek ἄνεμος or wind. What Orpheus said, that the soul is carried by the wind,[32] that it enters through respiration, and that it lives from air and with air, is not at odds with the scripture. The same thing is shown to us from Ezekiel and others. In making a soul, God inspires his breath (Isa. 57).[33] Through breathing the soul is sent into Adam's mouth and nostrils, and it is thus sent into his descendants and preserved through the act of breathing. Therefore, when the fetus is in the womb, and it has neither inhaling nor exhaling, it thus has not even its own soul. How could the soul be in the heart, if the heart does not have diastole or systole? Neither the heart nor the lung moves at that time. The valves of the heart or those membranes [259] for the openings of the vessels are not opened until a person is born. No vital spirit is generated there in the heart. Rather, there is only that which is infused from the mother. Therefore, how could its own soul be there at that time? There is no vital spirit of its own in which the soul could reside, until it is born a person. The inspiration of the divine soul, the opening of the heart, and the introduction of the spiritual blood takes place at that

---

[30] This is a reply to the traditional Catholic doctrine according to which the spiritual soul is created by God individually in the first moment of the fertilization of the egg.
[31] Ps. 21:10 : "On you I was cast from my birth, and since my mother bore me you have been my God."
[32] *Animam vento feri*. With this expression Servetus refers to the Orphic quote preserved and criticized by Aristotle in his *De anima*, I, cap. 5. Compare note 26 of the lib. V *De Trinitate*.
[33] Veiled allusion to Isa. 57:16 : "For I will not continually accuse, nor will I always be angry; for then the spirits would grow faint before me, even the souls that I have made."

moment through a great bit of artistry.[34]

For at the moment of birth according to such or such a position of the stars, such or such a soul arrives. The celestial influence that brings a soul's inclination, temperament, and other, innate qualities, is at that moment stamped upon the whole life.[35] It is not accurate to call what is in the womb a son because it is not actually a person. It is called a son out of a certain expectation and anticipation of the seed, just as Christ was the son in the time of the Law. The entire time under the Law is like a pregnant mother who has not yet acquired her son.[36]

Peter: Before the soul is breathed into the fetus, is there an active power in the fetus that bursts the fetal sack?

Michael: What else could there be? The chick bursts the egg's shell before it breathes. Various plants break walls and stones through their own movement in order to make way for themselves.

Peter: The analogy to the Head is constant in the generation of plants and animals.

Michael: The generation of all animals is Christ's image. Not only of those which are created from the seed of their parents, but even of those that sprout like worms. This too can be inferred from our previous discussion on the sprouting of plants. For through the activity of celestial light and rain there is always a generation in earthly matter of the sort that we see in Christ. The holy scripture

---

[34] These speculations of Servetus represent a good example of how a scientist attempted to combine the religious doctrines with his naturalistic, though limited, experience. Servetus did the best within the framework of the Galenic level of anatomical and physiological knowledge.

[35] This is one of the few occasions when Servetus mentions astrology in the *Restitutio*. He had given many years before in Paris public lectures on astrology for which he was brought before the court and defended himself in tractate *Disceptatio pro astrologia*, 1538. It was reprinted by Tollin in Berlin in 1880, translated into English by Charles O'Malley in 1953 and into French by F. Rude and P. Cavard in 1958 and by Jean Dupèbe in 2004 (Michel Servet, *Discussion apologétique pour l'astrologie contre un certain médecin*. Texte établi et traduit par Jean Dupèbe, Genève, Librarie Droz, S.A., 2004). It is important to emphasize that Servetus always leaves our will a choice and does not make it dependent on the blind arrangements of the celestial bodies. They have only an inducing (*inducens*) and not determining effect.

[36] This comparison at the level of history and theology is a culmination of Servetus' analogical

says that we are worms, just as Christ calls himself a worm (Ps. 21).[37] In addition, there is this other, true analogy in the generation of all animals: just as all things that reproduce from a seed inside themselves prior to sending it forth to create a fetus, so in God there was the seed of the Word before the son was generated in Mary.

[260] Peter: The Sophists have no such thoughts. Where scripture does not say, they say there is a son.

Michael: Just as God's Word, which holds substantively every seed's power, was the dew of Christ's natural conception in the virgin's womb, so is even the seed used in the conception of animals; just as the sun and man produce a man, so God and man produced Christ. The body's preparation is always needed, just as the preparation was accomplished in Mary. Preparation is required by the soul's nature, which, coming together from outer and inner substance, is created or produced by God by the introduction of air within. Thus the soul lives in the body insofar as it can get pure air as well as pure fluid from the body, by which it is warmed and nourished, so to speak.[38]

Peter: Souls are drawn somehow or other from the body, as they are from the earth and water, said Moses, and from the seed, just as the souls went out from Jacob's thigh and Abraham's loins.[39]

Michael: Because of the power of the seed paternal character shines in the son's soul because the soul gains something from the seed. Our own soul gains something from the seed just as Christ's soul gains from the seed of the Word. Just as in the seed there is a substantive token of the soul to be drawn out, so there is in the body's elements formative light, formal shape, divine dispensation, and

---

approach.

[37] Ps. 22:6 : "But I am a worm, and not human; scorned by others, and despised by the people." Also Job 25:6 : "how much less a mortal, who is a maggot, and a human being, who is a worm!" And Isa. 41:14 : "Do not fear, you worm Jacob, you insect Israel!"

[38] The soul which is the air lives only if it can breathe the air, but it is created by God.

[39] Servetus refers to the obscure texts. Gen. 32:25 talks about a force located in the hip of Jacob when he struggled with the "angel of God." Gen. 17:6 and 35:11 talk about kings and nations as offspring of Abraham

spiritual matter together with the various formal aspects that are accidental to a soul. There is one soul, drawn from elements of seed and blood and breathed by God. The soul is one, having many lives. In Genesis 2 God's one breath is called נשמת חיים, *nismat hajim*, "the breath of lives."[40] One is the breath of many lives that makes men live with the life of the body and the life of the spirit: the vegetative life, the sensate life, and the intellective life. God said that even the one soul lives many lives. If it is a fact that the souls of brutes are drawn from a seed, and that we have many aspects in common with them, then it will also be a fact that our own souls are by some process drawn from a seed.[41]

Peter: So is there some kind of divinity, godliness, or of immortality in the souls of brutes? For that is what those following the teaching of Trismegistus Numenius, Plotinus, Porphyry, and Iamblichus, together with the other Pythagorians believe.[42] [261] Indeed, they held this all the more because there is some token of intelligence in these animals, and that comes from God. The soul is breathed into their nostrils just as it is into our own. As with man God draws the spirit from them upon their death, as the prophet witnesses. Also, God gives them his spirit so that they may live (Ps. 103).[43] This was essentially the discourse of

---

[40] Servetus, faithful to his method of literal interpretation, attempts to show that the one soul introduced in the text of Gen. 2:7 and which is called by the scholastics after Aristotle "the substantive form," produces three levels in which life is expressed and admitted since the writings of Plato: the vegetative life, the sensate life, and the intellective life.

[41] Servetus makes a good observation that the "soul" must be somehow connected to the biological inheritance. So he as a scientist probably was not so sure about the immortality of the souls either.

[42] This is a general statement indicating that Pythagoreans, as well as Hermetics, Platonists and Neo-Platonists admitted a certain "divinity" in everything, including the souls of the animals. Numenius (flourished in the middle of the second century C.E.) is the most important link between the Neo-Pythagoreans and the Neo-Platonists who were represented later by Porphyry (233-304 C.E.) and Jamblichus (250-330). The doctrines of Numenius were available to Servetus through the writings of Eusebius of Caesarea, his *Praeparatio evangelica*, lib. XI, and of Plotinus, *Enneads*, III,8,3 and IV,8,8. From Porphyry Servetus knew *Oraculorum philosophia* and *Isagoge*. From Jamblichus, *De mysteriis Aegyptiorum*.

[43] The *spiritus* is equivalent to *aer* in the texts such as Ps. 103:29-30 : "When you hide your face, they are dismayed; when you take away their breath, they die and return to their dust. When you send forth your spirit, they are created; and you renew the face of the ground."

Pythagoras, and he believed that God's judgment held sway over wicked souls.[44]

Michael: The souls of brutes are drawn from the power of the created light, in which we said there existed a life-giving ἐνδελέχεια.[45] Thus, they are mortals, just as everything else is subject to corruption according to the nature of its form. God imparts to them His spirit in the universal energy of airy breath by giving to them inhalation and exhalation. Just as in other things the energy of God's spirit and light varies, nevertheless, a particular substance's immortality does not follow, but rather only the form's immortality.

In fact, Trismegistus strenuously denied that every death was a corruption or destruction, but instead he held that in death individual things disappeared through a separation of their components. The ancient philosophers, Xenophanes, Anaxagoras, Democritus, Leucippus, Empedocles, Parmenides, and many others together with Pythagoras followed him in this opinion. They did not believe that anything could dissolve into nothing. Their error was in the understanding of the forms.[46] In the case of an extinguished candle we see how easily the form of created light is reduced to nothing. We see the same result when we close a window. As light is undone, so we see that the substantive forms of things which come from light, are undone. Trismegistus, having had an understanding of the single, divine idea, which is the basic form, placed the immortality of everything in it. The cosmos, he said, and everything that is in it, have a share in the divinity and are one with God, being immortal, incorruptible, and eternal, as if it would be

---

[44] In the system of Pythagoras souls were undergoing successive stages of reincarnation as a process of purification.

[45] *Entelechy* or *act*, one of the most technical terms of Aristotle. Servetus adopts the concept, but he applies it to his system and links it to the concept of light as the vital act which in turn was borrowed from Orphism and Platonism.

[46] Servetus believed, as all in his epoch, that Hermes Trismegistus was anterior to pre-Socratic philosophers. All these mentioned philosophers, Xenophanes and Parmenides (Krantz, 22B63, 31B17), (Parmenides who believed in immobility, in spite of admitting a cyclic palingenesis), Leucippus and Democritus (the atomists, according to Aristotle *Met*. 1,4.985b4, Krantz, 68), they agree with Pythagoras, the Orphics, and Hermetics in the eternity of Being, whose changes, however, they could not explain.

unspeakably wrong for that in which there was God, to perish or be corrupted.[47]
For us, however, just as it does not follow from the fact that God is immutable,
that all those things which are in Him, are immutable, so neither does it follow
from the fact that He is incorruptible, that all those things that are in Him, are
incorruptible. Just as [262] the unification of a soul with a body does not prevent
that body's corruption, so the token of the divinity does not prevent the form's
destruction. We say that forms which come from created light perish in their
entirety, but not that they perish such that their own forms do not remain in God.
We thus admit that everything's eternity is dependent upon God because the forms
for everything are always in God, be of those things which exist, or of those which
do not exist. To Him everything is alive. Nonetheless, generations and corruptions
occur through time, and those things, the forms of which are destroyed, perish.[48]

To some extent Trismegistus can be forgiven, if we say that he considered
this transitory shape of things as a thing of no significance, but contemplated the
idea alone. In this book, *On Regeneration*, he said that, if we leave out the
transitory and deceptive form of the cosmos, it ought to be reformed in accordance
with the pure idea of God. Then man's true eternity, which he posited not in
brutes, but particularly in men, is gained in the soul's own substance. Hence, in
speaking about generalities he said to his son, Tatius, that everything was one in
God, especially intelligent bodies, which live through activity and eternity, and of
which the soul is good, such that, like God's mind with which they are united, they
are thus not separate from the intelligible good and are able to accomplish what
they wish beyond fate. A little further on he says "The man who takes God, is

---

[47] Trismegistus wrote in *Poimandres*, libellus VIII : "I must explain in what way the soul is
immortal, and by the working of what sort of force of the composition and dissolution of the
body. For death has nothing to do with any of them. The word 'death' is a mere name, without
any corresponding fact. For death means destruction; and nothing in the Kosmos is destroyed.
For seeing that Kosmos is the second God, and an immortal being, it is impossible that a part of
that immortal being should die; and all things in the Kosmos are parts of the Kosmos."
[48] The last sentences are a typical example of Servetus's reasoning. It is a cross between the Neo-
Platonist inspiration and Aristotelian approach. Here the concept of the "form" though connected
to the concept of *symbolus*, is closer to the Aristotelian μορφή than to the Platonist εἶδος.

immortal beyond all others, fashioned according to the divine essence, and is the only one whom God approaches and to whom God reveals the future."[49]

Peter: Let us get back to the analogy of our own manner of generation. Is the seed of generation from the father alone in Christ's case and in our own?

Michael: In Book 2 of *On the Generation of Animals* Aristotle says that the female seed has nothing to do with procreation.[50] But Galen disputes Aristotle with many arguments in Book 2 of *On the Seed*. The woman has her own reproductive vessels, just as the man does, and they are fashioned by nature with the same skill, and the race of man and woman are both productive of seed. Furthermore, there is no procreation through the man's contribution of seed alone. Then, the fetus is likened in soul and body to the mother just as the father, whether in character, temperament, face, or all other distinguishing features.[51]

[263] In Leviticus 12 and Psalm 50 God Himself teaches that the woman makes seed and conceives through her own seed. Genesis 3 is clearer where it says that the woman's seed is a man, Christ.[52] Christ is "from David's seed" through Mary and Joseph, that is, through lineage and through adoption. Hence, Matthew and Luke report that Joseph was "from David's house and family," being a son of David, and that through him Christ was a "son of David" and "David's seed." For

---

[49] In *A Secret Discourse of Hermes Trismegistus to His Son Tat, Concerning Rebirth* (*Poimandres*, libellus XIII) : "The mortal form changes day by day; it is altered by a lapse of time, and becomes larger and smaller; for it is an illusion." The regeneration (rebirth) begins when one learns not to form representations under the figure of a three-dimensional body and reaches the glimpse of the "intelligible world" : "When a man is born again it is no longer a body of three dimensions that he perceives, but the incorporeal." In libellus XII we read: "Every living creature is immortal. But more than all the rest, man is immortal; for he can receive God, and hold intercourse with God. With man alone of living creatures God associates."

[50] Perhaps there is no decisive difference between the theory of Aristotle and that of Galen : the mother supplies the material by the cold character of her nature, and the sperm provides the heat thus it is the principle and motor and gives form to the embryo. It seems that Servetus developed these concepts further and later will apply them to the theory of the incarnation of Jesus.

[51] Servetus makes a good observation concerning the transfer of psychological features from the father as well as from the mother.

[52] These are very weak biblical bases for the assertion of Servetus. Lev. 12:2 : "If a woman conceives and bears a male child, she shall be ceremonially unclean seven days." Ps. 50:5 : "Indeed, I was born guilty, a sinner when my mother conceived me." Gen. 3:15 : "I will put

according to the Law the seed of a man who is determined to be by name from a given person's house or family, is declared that man's son, although he may not necessarily be born from him.[53] John teaches that we are born from the blood of man and woman, meaning from the "seed and sexual intercourse" of both (John 1). Yet Christ was not thus conceived from his parent's blood nor from sexual intercourse. Here there truly is a difference. We are conceived in Christ's image, excepting the nature of original sin. The glowing cloud's heavenly dew, as it overshadowed the virgin, mixed itself with her seed and blood without lust of the flesh, and it transformed human matter into God, the holy spirit breathing there without measure so that the man, Jesus Christ, a branch from Isaiah's stock, took root there in the life-giving spirit.[54]

Peter: Thus the point already made about the mixture in Christ.

Michael: It is better referred to as a mixture of matter with matter and a union of soul or form. It is called a mixture of the divinity in instances when there is a diversity of parts or forms.[55] Christ is the exemplar of every mixture and union; he is the prototype that was better known to the ancients than the Sophists. For the ancients taught that there was a mixture of the divinity in Christ, but the Sophists today deny this. They cannot understand that one form was generated in Christ from the higher and lower, from the paternal and maternal elements because in all these things we see nothing else. In these created things you see that the element earth has been raised to heaven through the mixing of other, heavenly elements. This fact indicates to us the heavenly mixture in Christ. In Christ there was a

---

enmity between you and the woman, and between your offspring and hers (*semen tuum et semen illius*)."

[53] Such is the meaning of the genealogies of Jesus based on the lineage of the ancestors of Joseph (Matt. 1:1-16; Luke 3:23-38).

[54] John 1:12-13 : "he gave power to become children of God, who were born, not of blood or of the will of the flesh or of the will of man, but of God." Servetus always ascribes the condition of sin to the beginning of any human birth. Thus here is an analogy between the generation of man and Christ broken.

[55] Servetus talked about this distinction in terminology already in *De Trinitatis erroribus*, VII, 113r and in *Dialogorum de Trinitate* (1532) II, B6r. He stated that "the ancients talk about God mixed with human rather than united" a mixture of human with God.

mixture of heavenly elements with the earthly and a union of the divine form. [264] Or rather, that mixture or union of uncreated with created light at that time was complex. The divinity was mixed and united with Christ. It was mixed due to the variation in parts and because the superior elements which derived from God's substance were mixed together with the corresponding human elements of earthly matter which were taken from Mary. And the divinity also was hypostatically united with Christ by reason of the elements, the soul, and the form. The archetype's superelemental substance made its substance one with this elemental substance spiritually in the soul, on the one hand, corporeally in the flesh, on the other. Furthermore, the essential divine light of Christ's soul and the substantive form of Christ's body are God's light and divine form substantively united with him.[56] Thus, Christ is every mixture and union's exemplar and prototype. Within himself he not only blends and unites human components; he also combines into one true substance the divine components with the human. He contains every union and mixture as much in soul as in body.

Peter: You have also said that the analogy of Christ's conception was in terms of the soul and the holy spirit.

Michael: That the substance of the soul and the substance of the holy spirit in similarity to Christ is made from God and man has been sufficiently established by what has already been said. The soul's substance is as much elemental as it comes from God just as Christ is an elemental body and from God. Just as God's Word was made flesh in Christ, so God's breath was made soul in Adam. You would say the same thing about the holy spirit, in which there is an even greater likeness to Christ, because our soul is not God in the same way that Christ and the holy spirit are God. As we said at the end of Book 5,[57] the holy spirit came down into the souls of the apostles in nearly the way the Word came into the flesh. The substance of Christ's spirit is elemental and divine just as the substance of Christ's

---

[56] In this final explanation of the nature of Christ Servetus did not use the terminology which he himself postulated.

body is elemental and divine. God's true Spirit makes one spirit with that of man, and this is generally called the holy spirit, just as God's Word made one being [265] with the flesh, which is generally called the son. Just as the holy spirit is said to proceed from God, so the son said, "I have proceeded from God."[58]

Peter: As once the son's face was in God, so also was the holy spirit's face in him.

Michael: In God's treasury are, as Christ said, "things old and new."[59] In the previous dialogue I sufficiently laid out for you the old shadows, but now I will explain how everything is new.

The ancients received a spirit different from our own so that you could say the face of the present truth was there. Nonetheless, you had a true, divine inspiration just as there was God's true and substantive Light in the Word.

The similarity between the son and the spirit is not like that between the Word and the Spirit. Like "God's Word," "God's Spirit" can be truly understood as to be in the body of flesh and prior to the body of flesh. The son, however, is truly ever the body. Properly speaking, the holy spirit just as the Word is only the name of the divinity, while the son is properly the name of the man. Just as the name of the *word* was imparted to the man so that the man himself, Christ, is called God's Word, so the name *holy spirit* is imparted to man's spirit so that it is wholly called the holy spirit. The *Spirit* and the *Word* mark the dispensation in God; the designation, the *son,* on the other hand, is more substantive or somewhat more material. The son was conceived materially and corporeally in Mary through the Word and the Spirit. The son contains the Word and the Spirit in himself as body and soul or form and breath.[60]

---

[57] *Christianismi,* Book V, p. 191ff.

[58] John 8:42.

[59] Matt. 13:52 : "Therefore every scribe who has been trained for the kingdom of heaven is like the master of a household who brings out of his treasure what is new and what is old." And Song 7:13 : "The mandrakes give forth fragrance, and over our doors are all choice fruits, new as well as old, which I have laid up for you."

[60] This analogy derives from the designation of the terms which Servetus explained. God conceived his son in Mary through his Word and spirit. It "became" the body of Jesus, and being

This relationship alone should have prompted the Sophists to a recognition of the true, real son because he hypostatically contains in himself the Word and the Spirit. The holy spirit, therefore, as we have already said regarding it and rightly so, is the substantive mode of the divinity and is in simple terms understood as pure divinity. By sharing the divinity in this way, the name of the holy spirit is shared with the creature itself. It is imparted to the human and angelic breath. In fact, the holy spirit exists originally and naturally in Christ's breath alone.[61]

Peter: The Word's Light was formally united with matter; it is not, therefore, said to have been made flesh.

Michael: "The Word was made flesh;" "the Word was flesh;" "the Word existed as flesh;" the Word [266] was substantively united and mixed with it. John used the Greek word, ἐγένετο, to render the Hebrew expression, היה. The old Greek translation, Septuagint, suggests this because it always renders the Hebrew with this Greek term. Therefore, the Word properly speaking "was flesh," "existed as flesh," and "was made flesh."[62]

Light is the form of matter, which transforms matter, and it is substantively united with matter, not only in Christ, but in all other creatures, which are formed and shaped in Christ's image. Moreover, so that you may have a fuller understanding as to what "has been made flesh" and how much it differs from what has been united with the flesh, you must with respect to the Word consider these

---

light at the same time, it was his "substantive form" which was communicated substantively to his soul. And because of this, for having the same substance of the two first "dispensations" of God, the man Jesus is hypostatically the Word of God and the holy spirit.

[61] One should not forget the distinction which was established by Servetus between the holy spirit and the Spirit of God.

[62] In lib. VII of *De Trinitatis erroribus* 113r-113v Servetus is more precise about this idea and indicates that the sense of the expression *factum est* should be the same as of the expression in Genesis *and there was light*. The text of Servetus reads: *"Item, non dixit Ioannes, Verbum caro factum ad mentem illorum; sed Verbum caro fuit, Verbum caro extitit, et haec est proprisssima significatio, ὅ λόγος σάρξ ἐγένετο. Nam illud quod erat Verbi persona, est nunc ipse Christus."* And he continues: *"Sunt enim duo consyderanda, res et persona, res ipsa Deus, et dispositio Verbum, et Deus erat Verbum, et omnia proprietas in ratione Verbi transivit ad hominem qui est nunc in Deo, eo modo quo antea Verbum erat apud Deum, et cum hoc res ipsa omnino in homine est unita et inmixa, quia Deus erat in Christo, mundum reconcilians."*

points: form, element, and light, these three being common to the body and the soul. To the extent that it was the form or the person and prefiguration of the man, it is said that the "Word was made flesh" and, so to speak, moved like a person into the flesh such that what was once attributed to the Word's person, is attributed to the person of flesh because they are the same person. This is all the more significant because the Word does not yet on its own make its own person, but rather does so together with the flesh.[63]

In the seed's elemental or superelemental substance the Word has been made man because its elements have by some means been made corporeally into the flesh's elements and spiritually into the soul's. Yet, insofar as the Word is light's essence and the formative power of bodies, it is said to be united with the flesh's matter or to have been hypostatically and substantively united with human nature so that the whole combination is the one man and the one flesh of God. It is also united on a spiritual level in the soul so that it is wholly one soul and so that Christ's soul is one with God. You will find in our own seed, like a shadow, a similar manner of incarnation, and that it follows the same three modes. For our seed is made flesh according to the nature of man's form and the substance of the elements, and it is mixed with flesh; and also the nature of its light is there united in body and soul.[64]

Peter: Through that incarnation is God said to be made into a man?

Michael: Our seed is said to have been made man because like a shadow it reflects the similarity and mode whereby God, the Word, was made man. [267] God, the Word, was man in person, and this person is now a true man. Thus, God is said to have been made man, not in a straightforward sense, but in regard to His person.[65] Just as the Word was made this flesh, so the Word was made this man,

---

[63] This means that since the incarnation the Word of God alone is not the person or manifestation of God but together with the humanity of Jesus. The Word ceased to be the person of God and now Christ is his person for he incorporates the Word and the holy spirit in himself.
[64] The complex paragraph that repeats the same statement but differentiates the stages in the Word until it is identified with Jesus.
[65] The Word of God is eternally a man as a person though not truly: God was not made man

who is a true man, but not a man in the connotative sense. Making the flesh a participant in God's substance, the Word is a participant in the flesh so that one man is a participant in both substances and both natures. Such is God's incarnation so that in one flesh God and man are one. Let God, the Word, be made man, and let man assumed by God be made God. Aaron's rod, which was cast incarnate onto the ground, shows us another reflection of this incarnation; for it existed as flesh and was made flesh, although the staff's substance remained just as the Word's substance remains. The serpent, itself made flesh, was called a staff just as the man, Jesus, is now called God's Word (Rev. 19).[66]

The placement of the divinity in his flesh increases his dignity, but does not change his appearance.[67] This flesh is called God, and it remains genuine flesh. The flesh was itself made the Word just as the Word was made flesh. In fact, Athanasius, the leader of the Sophists, said in his book, *On the Faith to Theophilus*, that the flesh was made the Word, but that the Word was not made flesh. He said that the divine nature was mixed with human, and that the human nature was not mixed with the divine.[68] These are ridiculous ravings. The earlier generation, which had seen and understood God's grandeur, had perished, and in its place others, ignorant of the master, as was once said in a similar circumstance in Judges 2, had risen up.[69] If there is a mixture and a union, if the placing of the Divinity does not change the appearance, but increases the dignity, this is wholly flesh; the whole Word is genuine man. Soul is holy spirit; angel becomes holy

---

simpliciter, but only his "person" or manifest aspect which was and is his Word.

[66] Allusion to the story narrated in Exod. 7:9 and in Num. 21:8-9. Servetus does not interpret the story that the rod appeared as a serpent, but that it was incarnated as a serpent, i.e. it was a serpent without ceasing to be a rod. In the same way the Word in the man Jesus who for this reason is the substance of God. Servetus alludes also to Rev. 19:13 : "He is clothed in a robe dipped in blood, and his name is called The Word of God."

[67] This is another fundamental principle of the Servetus intellectual system: *Positio deitatis in carne eius dignitatem auget, speciem non mutat*, which he repeats in many other formulations.

[68] Athanasius, *De Trinitate*, lib. VIII (PL LXII, 285-286).

[69] This is a repetition of the idea of the "fall of the church" after the first generation so emphasized by the Anabaptists. From this derives the urgency of the "restoration." Servetus applies to this situation the text of Judg. 2:8-10 : "Moreover, that whole generation was gathered

spirit. Both the soul remains, and the angel remains. The Word is made flesh, and the Word remains. The Word has not been annihilated, nor has it converted to flesh by some "transelementation." Rather, it is unformed matter, transformed by the Word, so that the entire combination [268] is the Word as flesh. To the very substance of the Word is added the participation of the transformed flesh forming one hypostasis, one substance, one body, and one, true man.[70]

Jesus Christ is one man who holds within himself a divine and human nature. By bringing them together in one body and in one new man he holds both within himself, as Paul said in Ephesians 2.[71] Obviously, Christ was a new man because the world had never before experienced a man of such a nature. Not even today can the world know this man because it does not want to believe that a man was fathered by God. Our own inner man is derived in this new man's image from God and man in one substance. There is one spirit in us from the divine and human spirit. There is in us one substantive soul derived from our own elemental substance and that breathed into us by God. The result of mixing the superelemental archetypical substance and this elemental substance is one substance in Christ. In Christ created and uncreated light formed one substance. Were you to think separately about the world's entire soul or about that Spirit which makes everything live, you would see that there is one substantive soul in Christ that results from both it and the human soul. The combination of divine elements with human ones never splits the unity of being any more than does the combination of soul or spirit with the human body. With our own bodies this will be clear after the resurrection, when we will share in Christ's divinity and be one

to their ancestors, and another generation grew up after them, who did not know the LORD or the work that he had done for Israel."

[70] Servetus refrains from using the term "person" which could lead to equivocation. He rejects the process of "transelementation" as well as later he will reject transubstantiation. He prefers the term mixture to the term union and admission that the matter would disappear in one way or the other.

[71] Eph. 2:15-16 : "He has abolished the law with its commandments and ordinances, that he might create in himself one new humanity in place of the two, thus making peace, and that he might reconcile both groups to God in one body through the cross."

with God according to the nature of our bodies. This very fact is now shown in the unity of the spirit because we are made one spirit with him. It is also shown in what Christ said, "The Father and I are one."[72] The unity with God of all elements, created and uncreated, of body, soul, and spirit, is inferred simply from this statement, "The Father and I are one." Christ is substantively one with God thereby making us substantively one with him.

Peter: The Sophists do not have this understanding of the unity of Christ's substance, [269] but instead create an agglomeration in order to avoid the existence of a fourth person among their divine things in case if it is a substance.[73]

Michael: They do not understand that this word, *homoousios,* that they bandy about, must refer to the fact that Jesus Christ is said to be *homoousios,* meaning, consubstantial with God. They call it a hypostatic union without understanding that it is truly a hypostatic union, meaning, a substantive one. For, if the union is substantive, a single substance is the result therefrom. They are incapable of understanding that it is the generation of a single seed and a single form that was sung of by the prophets. They are incapable of understanding that one shape was generated from a higher and lower substance, from the paternal and maternal substance. They are incapable of understanding that the Word's substance and the substance of the flesh are one substance just as a husband's substance and a wife's substance come together in the single flesh of the embryo. Through the mystery whereby a husband and wife are one in the one flesh of their child, God and man are one in Christ. In Paul's opinion the mystery is great because God was made manifest "in flesh."[74] Great is the mystery because that flesh is *homoousios* with God and joined to Him in one hypostasis. Thus, God came together with human nature to raise it up by fathering for Himself a son as a human being. The one Christ recapitulated the human and the divine in the mass of his one body just

---

[72] John 19:30. This theme Servetus treated before in Book I. Latin formulation: *"Divinorum cum humanis coniunctio nunquam scindit entis unitatem magis, quam animae, aut spiritus cum corpore."*

[73] Servetus discussed this risk of the *quaternitas* in *Christianismi,* lib. I, 39.

as everything else is one in him. The created and the uncreated are one in him. God and man are one in him. Heaven and earth are one in him.

The *Letter to Epictetus* by Athanasius, upon which Epiphanius and Cyril showered the greatest praises, shows how destructive has been the error in this matter. There it is vehemently denied that Christ's body forms a single substance with the Word. They say that hell vomits such things forth because they are themselves motivated particularly by an hellish madness.[75] In their own defense the Nicaean fathers cite Theognostus and Dionysius of Alexandria, as Athanasius reports in their *Decree against Eusebius*.[76] Nevertheless, they plainly teach there that Christ, the man, was of the same essence with God, or that he made one substance with Him. Origen and Cyprian taught the very same thing even earlier, [270] as I cited in my First Book. In explanation of the statement, "I and the Father are one," they said that the man was one with God. Here are the words from Origen's Third Book *Against Celsus*: "Christ's mortal body, and the human soul contained in it, possessed with God not only a communion, but a unity such that through a participation in the divine nature they have been changed and transformed into God."[77]

Peter: You say that Christ does not differ from us in appearance.

---

[74] Reference to various texts: Rom. 16:25; Eph. 5:32; Col. 1:26.

[75] *Epistola ad Epictetum* of Athanasius cited in note 189 of *Christianismi* lib. I. This letter is cited by Epiphanius, *Haereses*, lib. III, t. II, Heresy 27, 3-13, who describes this heresy among the testimonies of the consubstantiality of the body of Christ with the divinity (PG XLII, 643), and by Cyril of Alexandria who unmasked this heresy when Nestorians tried to falsify it for their own use (*Epistula 40* to Acacio of Mytelene, PG LXXVII, 182).

[76] That is in his *Epistola de decretis Nicaenae Synodis*, n. 25 (PG XXV, 459-462), in which he praises the teaching of Dionysius of Alexandria against the Sabellians, and of Theognostus who wrote *Hypotyposeis (Outlines)* without being afraid, as Athanasius wrote, using the term *ex substantia patris*, i.e. the substance of the son originates from the substance of the Father "just as brightness from the light and water from the vapor." Besides this mention of Theognostus by Athanasius there is no account about him by either Eusebius or Jerome. Athanasius mentions him as an *eloquent* or *learned man* and as *the admirable and zealous*. Theognostus seems to have belonged to the catechetical school of Alexandria, and to have flourished there in the latter half of the third century, ca. 260 C.E. Photius mentions that he was a disciple of Origen, or at least a devoted student of his works. He wrote a work in seven books, the title of which is given by Photius as *Hypotyposeis (Outlines)*.

[77] Origen, *Contra Celsum*, lib. III, 41 (PG II, 465). On Cyprian compare note 122 of Book I.

Michael: That is because the appearance is the same, and the true man's form is the same. As I said already, God's presence does not change appearance especially because Christ's divinity will be granted to us. God's presence not only does not change appearance, but, furthermore, neither does it break up the unity within an individual.[78] In fact, divinity itself makes a unity for every manifestation and individuation. Our flesh will be transformed at the resurrection. We will not for that reason, however, be of a different appearance than we are now. Porphyry, who said that his rationality and mortality constitute the distinction specific to a human being's appearance, would say that the appearance would be a different, but I say that after the resurrection the appearance and the individuation are the same, just as the individuation of a child and an old man are the same, granted the matter, form, and soul have undergone a change from childhood to old age. Those who follow Porphyry, might even say that after being born again through baptism we are of a different appearance than before because at that moment our soul gains divinity and incorruptible substance.[79] Therefore, we must say that despite the acquisition of divinity the appearance is not changed, whether in the soul or in any aspect of a human being. Thus, Christ is of the same appearance as us because he is truly a human being.

Peter: God causes and sustains this unity in everything.

Michael: God alone is the unity allowing any given thing to be one in one form. Otherwise, without unity the parts would collide, so to speak, into dust and nothing unless they were sustained by it.

Peter: Therefore, everything is made up of parts, nothing being simple or a being in itself.

Michael: By a universal law everything is put together because of God or

[78] Servetus amplifies here the principle postulated previously, see note 67: *Deitatis positio non solum non mutat speciem, sed nec individui solvit unitatem. Imo deitas ipsa omnem speciei et individui unitatem facit.*

[79] Servetus seems to forget that Porphyry refers to the specific conceptual distinctions and not the real though one could talk about the real distinctions between these concepts so differentiated specifically.

is stable through Him. "Everything exists because of Him. Everything is because of Him, through Him, and in Him." God alone is a being *per se*. God alone exists as pure simplicity, form, and essence. From Him everything else receives its composition, [271] constitution, formation, and dependence. He alone is the life that gives life to everything else and constitutes in their modalities, even angels and souls. For this reason, Trismegistus said to Tatius that God is "encompassing the constitution of all things."[80] Hence, everyone else after him has said that the forms alone, from which every thing draws its existence, are simple. In Jeremiah 10 God is called everything's life, everything's fashioner, and that which gives essence to everything, even those things of heaven which we tended to express with the phrase, Jehovah Sabaoth.[81] Therefore, even heavenly bodies draw their essence and constitution from Him. Angels and souls exist from His substance.

Peter: The constitution of Christ's flesh is amazing, and it is a model of everything else's formation. Thus, it obviously follows that it had descended from heaven.

Michael: Christ's flesh, which corporeally holds the Word's substance, its substantive vital, divine Spirit, and the substantive form of God's Light is truly heavenly from heaven and from God's substance. It is the Word's flesh, God's flesh, having eternal existence. Christ's words, whereby he declared that he and his flesh had come from heaven, are plain (John 6).[82] The metaphor symbol of manna from heaven makes the same point. The manna's descent ought to be referred to Christ's flesh because through that food, the manna, the flesh was represented as food. Likewise, "the second man, Christ, descended from heaven, the celestial man" (1 Cor. 15).[83] The one we saw going up, is "the one who earlier had come down" (Eph. 4). Christ's very body and flesh owned origin of their "glory in

---

[80] Compare notes 20 and 37, Book IV. "It is God that is the author of all, and encompasses all, and knits all things together" (*Corpus Hermeticum*, VIII).

[81] Jer. 10:16 : "for he is the one who formed all things, and Israel is the tribe of his inheritance; the LORD of hosts is his name."

[82] John 6:38-51 and 3:13.

[83] 1 Cor. 15:47. On the manna as the Eucharistic type, John 6:31 and 49.

heaven to which it is now glorified" (John 17). The very Christ's flesh is the food which God the Father promised in John 6, previously cited.[84] It is shown there that God is the father of this food that was vouched for and marked by Him, and the divinity's full measure was pressed upon it. God is the father of this food, the father of this flesh, although the Sophists deny it. "This flesh is a vine, and his father is a farmer" (John 15).[85] Therefore, God the father of this vine, is the father of this flesh, and the father of true man.

If Christ's flesh [272] were not heavenly from God's substance, if it were not a corporeally divinity, it would not have been conceived out of God, and thus it would not be God's son. If this were not so, it would not be said that the flesh had an incorruptible form, and that it could not undergo corruption. If this were not so, the structure of so great a body of the church could not be made from Christ's very flesh into one flesh. If it were not divine, it would not be impartible to the many in one communion, nor would it make us into God's members. Nor would by suffering that punishment for us that flesh be sufficient to reconcile man and God or to renew what exists in heaven and earth. There is no clearer proof of this than if you were to consider carefully that this flesh was conceived and born out of God. For, if it were conceived from God, it has a godly substance through its natural origin. There is no doubt that in Christ's flesh the mystery is great, if God is seen in that flesh and the Divinity has become corporeal.[86] Those who do not acknowledge that Christ's flesh is consubstantial with God, in vain make the nonsensical claim that they are defending Christ's divinity, because they defend impossible chimeras, not Christ. There is no more convenient means whereby in the reign of the Antichrist Satan was able to obscure Christ's divinity than by making, under the supposition of an invisible son, Christ, the man, into a purely

---

[84] John 17:5 and 6:33.
[85] John 15:1.
[86] These ideas of the "celestial body" of Jesus were doubtless inspired by the contemporary Anabaptist sources which Servetus does not mention (Hofmann, Ziegler, Schwenckfeld), but he deduced them from the scriptures and philosophical principles independently. They served later to support his doctrine of divinization by the communion.

created being. May God protect all Christians from such an insanity![87]

Peter: So, then, we ought not to concede that Christ, the man, is creature?

Michael: The true Messiah, Jesus, who was crucified, shared in the nature of God and man such that he could not be called a creature, but rather one that partakes of creatures. The apostle gives an elegant teaching on this point (Heb. 1, 2, 3, and Ps. 44). For the anointed one is before all those that share in him, before all creatures, and he himself was made to share in them. Christ who sanctifies, and we who are sanctified, share in the same form and are from the same God. Thus, in this passage he calls us "brothers." Indeed, it is proper that, if in his capacity as our salvation's prince and pontiff, he were to save us, he would, as Paul says there, be as we are, one that shares in flesh and blood.[88] Moreover, that he shares in all creatures, is emphasized by the statement in Colossians 1 that he was first born of them, [273] and in Revelation 3 that he was the "beginning of God's creatures."[89] He shares in God and man just as you share in your father and mother. He shares in creator and creature.

Peter: It appears that even in the holy spirit there is a share of creature.

Michael: Macedonius, Eunomius, and the other metaphysicians were mistaken about that fact when they said that the holy spirit was pure creature.[90]

---

[87] The "reign of the Antichrist" is the Roman Catholic pontificate and by extension any Christianity that adheres to the trinitarian confession according to the Nicaean formula which Servetus considers alien to authentic Christianity which he intends to "restore."

[88] Servetus is referring to various statements in Heb. 1:5 and 13:2, 9, 14, and to Ps. 44:7.

[89] Col. 1:15 and Rev. 3:14 : "the origin of God's creation."

[90] Bishops Macedonius of Constantinople and Eunomius of Cyzicus, disciple of Aëtius, were the principal representatives of the movement called under a general term as Neo-Arianism, which was rejected by various fathers of the church such as Basil and Gregory of Nyssa. Macedonius (d. after 360) was a bishop of Constantinople from 342 up to 350, and from 351 until 360. He inspired the establishment of the Macedonians, a sect of his followers which was suppressed as heretical in 374 by pope Damasus and in 381 by the First Council of Constantinople. They gradually ceased to exist as a distinctive sect. Eunomius (died ca. 393), one of the leaders of the extreme or "anomoean" Arians, who are also called Eunomians, was born at Dacora in Cappadocia at the beginning of the fourth century. He studied theology in Alexandria under Aëtius, and afterwards came under the influence of Eudoxius of Antioch, who ordained him deacon. On the recommendation of Eudoxius he was appointed bishop of Cyzicus in 360. Here his expressions of extreme Arianism led to complaints, and Eudoxius was compelled, by command of the emperor, Constantius II, to depose him from the bishopric. During the reigns of

Because of their sophistries they were ignorant of the dispensation of such mysteries and the human spirit's glorification realized through Christ such that the new spirit is one with God. Just as God's Word is man hypostatically, so God's Spirit is hypostatically man's spirit. Just as the Word's name is imparted to man, so the holy spirit's name is imparted to man's spirit. Christ's incorruptible breath is contained in the holy spirit's substance. Christ's spirit, which was God, is said to have been renewed at his resurrection, because it was one spirit integrated from the divine and human spirit; and it is said to have been renewed because of its new glory and because of the new creature of incorruptible breath, which Christ's holy spirit contains substantively within itself.[91] Christ does not now breathe corruptible air as he did before his suffering. He breathes his incorruptible spirit in our hearts and the divinity itself in one hypostasis, imparting all this to us by his breath.

Peter: Therefore, the "Father's person is called one thing, the son's another, and the holy spirit's something else."[92]

Michael: According to the manifestation, the manner of speaking, the

---

Julian and Jovian, Eunomius resided in Constantinople consecrating schismatical bishops. He then went to live at Chalcedon, was banished in 367 to Mauretania and recalled back to Constantinople. In 383 the emperor Theodosius, demanded a declaration of faith from all religious leaders and punished Eunomius for continuing to teach his doctrines by banishing him to Halmyris in Moesia. Afterwards he resided at Chalcedon and at Caesarea in Cappadocia, from which he was expelled for writing against the local bishop Basil. He died at his birthplace, Dacora, about 393. His writings were held in high reputation by his followers and dreaded by the orthodox, so that several imperial edicts had to be issued for their destruction. His first apologetic work (from 360-365), has been recovered from its refutation by Basil. A second apology, written about 379 exists only in the quotations given from it in a refutation by Gregory of Nyssa. His exposition of faith demanded by Theodosius is extant, and has been edited by Vallesius in his notes to the 1648 edition of Socrates' *History of the Church*. The teaching of Aëtius and Eunomius maintained that between the Creator and created there could be no essential, but at best only a moral, resemblance. Eunomius carried these views to a practical issue by altering the baptismal formula of baptizing in the name of the Creator and into the death of Christ. The Eunomians were condemned by the Council of Constantinople in 381. (John Chrysostom, *On the Incomprehensible Nature of God,* translated by Paul. W. Harkins, (Washington, DC: Catholic University of America Press, 1984), Thomas A. Kopecek. *A History of Neo-Arianism,* (Cambridge, MA: Philadelphia Patristic Foundation, 1979), Richard Paul Vaggione, *Eunomius of Cyzicus and the Nicene Revolution,* (Oxford, New York: Oxford University Press, 2000)).
[91] These concepts correspond to those commented previously in notes 60 and 70.
[92] These are not the words of the Nicaean formulation but of the so-called Athanasian creed though of later origin. Various forms of it can be found in PG XXVIII, 1582 &ff.

nature of the activity, the particular mode or the manifold dispensation it is said that "one thing is the Father's person, another thing is the son's person, and still another thing is the holy spirit's person." The distinction is genuine too, depending on the nature of the creature implied thereto.[93] Although the holy spirit is understood as pure divinity, it is always a special mode of godhead, and its attachment to Christ's created breath "does not change its appearance," as I have said, nor does it change the holy spirit's name.

On this basis you may infer the whole idea of the Trinity: "The Father is God; the Son is [274] God; the Holy Spirit is God." "The Father is not the Son; nor is the Son the Holy Spirit; nor is the Holy Spirit the Father."[94] It is according to the person's property that the Father is visible to us as the son, and that the son is inwardly visible to us as the holy spirit. The son differs from the Father really as does holy spirit from the son, but the difference is not one of substance because they have the same Divinity's substance. The Father is the source of all dispensation and divinity, being simply God without any creature admixture or participation, being incomprehensible in Himself. The son has the Father's divinity together with the participation of the corporeal aspect of a creature nature. The holy spirit has the divinity of the Father and of the son, receiving a share of the creature nature from the son, through whom it proceeds and comes to us.[95]

Therefore, it must be conceded that in the holy spirit there is at the essential level a sharing of the creature nature or a communication. It possesses a hypostatic communication with airy breath that is not corruptible, but incorruptible, that is of the same sort as that which substantively exists in Christ

---

[93] Servetus admits thus only a real distinction between the persons *ratione adiunctae creaturae*, that is God the Father is really though not substantively distinct from the man-son. But Servetus understands the internal distinction between these persons only as a modality: *modis quibusdam, dispensatione multiplici*.

[94] From the Athanasian credo. These are orthodox formulations of the Trinity thus differentiated by capital letters. In the next paragraph Servetus resumes his interpretation of persons.

[95] The most radical position taken in this text by Servetus is in the last sentence in which he asserts that the holy spirit also "receives a share of creature," but it is deduced logically from the premises he presented in previous pages.

and in the truly regenerated, whose spirit is truly renewed and made incorruptible through the power of Christ's resurrection. It is by a miraculous process that, through resurrection and regeneration, God turns something corruptible into something incorruptible. This is done by God through grace's great mystery through Christ, the mediator, so that we understand that Christ denies us none of those things which exist within himself; rather, he gives himself wholly to us in spirit and body. Hence, we understand that we, who in terms of the spirit, now rise up resuscitated and are truly made shareholders in Christ, being already incorruptible within and truly sharing in the incorruptible substance of Christ's flesh, to be resuscitated in terms of flesh.[96] Just as now, when in spirit we rise again through baptism, we are incorruptibly glorified by the spirit, so, rising again in the flesh, we will be glorified according to the flesh in Christ's image when he rises again in [275] glory.

Peter: You said that the third mystery of Christ's resurrection, which is already manifest, would be a source of wonder.

Michael: After the incarnation and death there followed Christ's awesome and glorious resurrection through which that which was of the creature nature and that which was of humanity, that is which was vulnerable and mortal, was completely lost as if it were something accidental. There is nothing of the animal in Christ, but "his body is wholly of the spirit."[97] Through resurrection Christ's flesh attained "that glory that the Word possessed with God" (John 17).[98] Just as someone might say that through the incarnation "the Word was made flesh" and made into a creature, so, on the other hand, by the same logic, he might say that because of the resurrection the flesh ceased to be a creature.

---

[96] The incorruptible substance of Christ's flesh, divine in origin, became incorruptible only after its resurrection. The Christian participates in his spirit through baptism.
[97] 1 Cor. 15:44.
[98] John 17:5 : "So now, Father, glorify me in your own presence with the glory that I had in your presence before the world existed."

Peter: Naturally, for how else could the state of being a creature be put aside?

Michael: At the resurrection of our own bodies we shall put aside that state of being creatures, just as now at our spiritual regeneration our "inner man" is made God. In a future age the substantive form of our bodies will not be the form of created light. Therefore, by that logic we shall put aside our being a creature because that being is named according to the form just as "form is that which gives being to an object."[99] And thus, the once created form's being has been put aside in this way, that being of a creature will be put aside. The substantive form of Christ's body does not now have any relation to created solar light such as before the resurrection Christ had, not only in the flesh, but also in the soul, just as we too now do. Just as in the final resurrection this corruptible light of sun and moon will be destroyed, and no other light will survive save the stark clarity of God's essence (Isa. 60 and Rev. 21 and 22),[100] so the quality that accrues to Christ came about at his resurrection with the result that, Christ's raised body has only the substantive form of God's uncreated light [276] of the same sort as the divine Word's substantive light ever was.[101]

Just as in the case of these lesser things a greater light removes the lesser, so at that time it will happen that only Christ's light will remain there, just as that light alone existed in the archetype before the sun's light was created. This light, which is easily destroyed, is itself fragile, and this world, formed in it, is fragile. We see that nothing is more easily destroyed than a candle's light and a sound's

---

[99] *Quia ipsum esse, ab ipsa denominatur forma, sicut forma est, quae dat esse rei.* This is clearly an Aristotelian concept.

[100] This is a curious adaptation of the mysterious texts of the Old and New Testament. Isa 10:19 : "The sun shall no longer be your light by day, nor for brightness shall the moon give light to you by night; but the LORD will be your everlasting light, and your God will be your glory." Rev. 21:23 : "And the city has no need of sun or moon to shine on it, for the glory of God is its light, and its lamp is the Lamb." Rev. 22:5 : "And there will be no more night; they need no light of lamp or sun, for the Lord God will be their light, and they will reign forever and ever."

[101] To follow the reasoning of Servetus one must not forget his affirmation that the light is the substantive form, symbol of the divine idea of every being (compare notes 9 and 19), and his division of light into two classes: the interior (*insita*) or divine light, and the exterior

spirit.[102] Thus, this light will not survive then nor will created sound's spirit. Just as those things that will remain in the future age now have a substance that is already permanent, such as that of the elements of matter and of the soul itself, so those things too, which will be annihilated, are now being annihilated, such as the created light's forms and the created sound's spirits.[103] Neither what we now see, nor what we hear, nor what we taste, touch, or smell, will survive at that time. Instead, we shall see, hear, smell, taste, and touch God. Therefore, we shall have to shed the mortal condition. Nonetheless, the individual aspect will be called the same because the divine form remains the same with the soul, although, as we said in the case of the child and the old man, everything else may be changed. Before the resurrection Christ's flesh was not as it is now. Even living, it would have been changed and transformed, just as at the moment of the final resurrection living bodies will be changed and transformed. As Paul says, the flesh's true transformation will be a conversion into a divine form.[104]

Peter: Therefore, it is not the same flesh if it is not the same, created form.

Michael: The flesh is the same, and it is the same uncreated form. The divinity's placement in the place of any given form neither changes an object's appearance nor does it destroy the individual aspect; instead, it keeps it from destruction. The identity chiefly derives from the divine form's presence and the soul.[105] Light's form derives from the divine form and exists through it, manifesting it according to circumstance. Fragile, created light will fade away merely at the divine form's very bright manifestation. Therefore, just as greater light now makes vain the lesser, so it will be at the resurrection because of the

---

(superveniens) or created.

[102] Spiritum soni. Servetus means here by this term the vibrating air, the wave produced by sound.

[103] Servetus admits matter and soul to be everlasting.

[104] Again Servetus is using the biblical texts to support his speculations. Rom. 8:11 : "If the Spirit of him who raised Jesus from the dead dwells in you, he who raised Christ from the dead will give life to your mortal bodies also through his Spirit that dwells in you." 1 Cor. 15:53 : "For this perishable body must put on imperishability, and this mortal body must put on immortality."

[105] This is the Servetian formulation of the "principle of identity": Identitas principaliter est ab

great power of divine light that transforms and glorifies everything. [277] Lesser light will not survive in the greater's presence.

This line of reasoning is consistent with experience and scripture's authority.[106] God teaches us through experience what lasts and what does not, what will be destroyed and what will not. If someone is unmoved by these points, let him say that the created light will remain together with the uncreated. We say that it will not survive because it is fragile, vain, and, furthermore, because created light's source, the sun, will not itself remain. What is annihilated is not capable of resurrection. In fact, it would not then be called a resurrection, but rather another *ex nihilo* creation. Finally, we trust the scripture, which plainly teaches that no light whatsoever, whether the sun's or the moon's, will remain. Indeed, there ought to be no further argument at all over whether it is the same flesh, when Paul says that at the resurrection individuals will not have the same body as before, but that God will give them a body as He wishes (1 Cor. 15).[107]

Peter: The glory of Christ's resurrection is great, and our own resurrection will be analogous. Our flesh "will be transformed, and it will be made to conform with Christ's glorious body" (Phil. 3).[108]

Michael: You plainly see already that Christ's glory was consummated in God and separate from a creature's being. If his divinity is set aside, no man can be understood with reference to Christ such as the Sophists say with respect to the existence of human nature in him or to being pure man. If you remove the divinity, the unity and essence of the man in him is melted away. Therefore, when we say "man" and "Christ's flesh," we also understand divinity in those instances.[109]

---

idea divina manente et ab anima.
[106] Another formula which summarizes the three criteria of certainty in the Servetian system: *Ratio est cum experientia et scripturae auctoritate.*
[107] 1 Cor. 15:38 : "But God gives it a body as he has chosen, and to each kind of seed its own body."
[108] Phil. 3:21 : "He will transform the body of our humiliation that it may be conformed to the body of his glory."
[109] The sense of this explanation is that one cannot talk about the divinity and humanity of Christ as about the two natures united in one divine Person as is maintained by the orthodox. The man

Peter: "In terms of flesh Christ was conceived from David's seed"[110]: therefore, was the flesh created?

Michael: You saw that the divinity of Christ's flesh is truly substantive. Indeed, because that which is separate from "spirit," is called "flesh," one can sometimes understand by the word, "flesh," that the matter which is flesh, was created. Christ is said to have been made from David's seed in terms of flesh, in other words, as a creature of flesh or as human matter. Alternatively, it could be according to the flesh because the whole, which is from human propagation, is held in the flesh, and some component is imparted to the spirit from the flesh. Still, [278] it is true that Christ's flesh is not pure creature. "Humanity" contemplated by the Sophists, which for them is pure human being, pure creature, does not exist in Christ. That is because in him there does not exist a human being's created form, just as it will not exist even in our own case after resurrection. Assuming for a moment that there is in him created light's form as there was, when he was active on earth, still there would not exist in him that sort of pure human. For, if you take away the divinity, a soul is not a soul, and flesh is not flesh, and man is not man. Therefore, if you take away the divinity, there is nothing that would be a pure human being in Christ. If in other things you take away the divine form, a stone would be called nothing, as would gold, flesh, soul, and man, because the form that gives specific and individual being to something, and which gives the form's being to a created form, is divine.[111] Well then, if you exclude his divinity, there is no form in Christ nor man. Christ himself is an eternal sea of forms who through the forms made himself to be adumbrated in all things and by a particular, secondary process has produced what the original divinity first produces really and

---

Christ is divine, for he is the son of God, for he is substantively God, for he is the Word of God and the Spirit of God as his substantive form (in the Servetian sense) and his soul, as well as his principle of identity.

[110] Rom. 9:5.

[111] *Cum idea divina sit, quae dat esse specificum et individuale, et quae ipsi formae creatae dat esse formae.*

substantively in him alone.[112]

The person who rejects comparisons with created things and various lines of connection between creatures and creator, will never know Christ, especially because Christ himself, as beginning, as first born and head of all creatures, maintains himself in relation to creatures as the head does to the limbs.[113] Form is inseparable from any given thing just as divinity is inseparable from the son of God. It is inseparable just as it is said by certain people that a quantity is inseparable from a measured thing or that an image is inseparable from the thing depicted.[114] In fact, the idea itself is the thing's measure; the idea is the image; the idea is the unity. The form of any given thing receives temporally this image or this function from the same idea which shaped it in the first place. Therefore, light's temporal form does not have that eternal quality that will exist after resurrection.

Peter: That fact makes the glory of Christ's resurrection the more illustrious.

Michael: So great is the glory and power of Christ's resurrection: he has been so taken unto God that no one could contemplate anything greater in God. The son was then made [279] more like his Father, made incorruptible in every aspect, glorious and powerful in a more sublime way than before. His return from man to God through resurrection was made such as was his departure from the Word to flesh at his incarnation. Christ himself gives abundant testimony to this. For he said that the son of man would rise up "to where he had been before" (John 6). He also said in John 16 that he would return "to the same place from whence he had come." In John 17 he said that he would return "to the same glory."[115] Just

---

[112] Servetus emphasizes the cosmic function of Christ and underscores that without divinity he is *nec forma nec homo*.

[113] The thought is expressed in a beautiful Latin expression: *Nunquam Christum cognoscet qui rerum creatarum analogias despicit*.

[114] These comparisons are not modal but essential.

[115] References to John 6:62, 16:28, and 17:5.

as "he came from heaven on high," so "he would return to it" (Ps. 18).[116] The divine had come down to the human so that the human might go up to the divine. This man, Jesus Christ, was transported to such glory and power that you could identify none greater. That Jesus who was crucified, is himself God's equal. God's power is no other than he who is therefore called God's "power, force, and strength."[117] In fact, by reason of his greater gifts Christ has now been glorified with a greater glory than was the Word's glory. There never before was such a glory as that of the holy spirit of regeneration. For this reason, even the heavens were made new and incorruptible, although they were previously corruptible. There is among us too, a new and heavenly kingdom. Christ's resurrection and the creation of a new man within us has more craft in it than the entire previous creation of the world because whatever was associated with it, was made corruptible, but whatever is associated with this new state, is incorruptible. There it was but a shadow; here there is truth.

Peter: If Christ has God's full power, he is not something finite.

Michael: The one who has all God's power, to whom belongs everything that God has, is not a finite thing. On the contrary, he is infinite in understanding, power, duration, and presence. Christ has not been limited by the physical requirements of a single space, but exists without spatial motion, wherever he wishes. Beyond a body subject to measure, there is a "spiritual body" in the "new heaven" that fills "with its plenitude" all "higher and lower things" (Eph. 4).[118] He is the one who said that he fills "heaven and earth" (Jer. 23).[119] In fact, that was Christ's shadow. Christ who fills everything, [280] fulfills that prophecy by every means of fulfillment. "On account of this man, God made the world, and the world

---

[116] Ps. 18:7, but originally it refers to the course of the sun.

[117] Rev. 7:12.

[118] Successive allusions to 1 Cor. 15:44; Rev. 21:1; Isa 65:17, and Eph. 4:10. One has to understand the ubiquitous presence of the body of Christ resurrected in the transcendental sense as it surpasses the limits of space; through divinization it belongs to a different category of reality.

[119] Jer. 23:24.

is filled by him," says Peter in Clement's eighth Book.[120] That "he came down to the netherworld's lowest regions and went up to the highest heights" in order to fill everything, was Paul's testimony.[121] "He walks upon the wings of winds" (Ps. 103). "He rides through those ethereal zones occupied by angels," the ערבות *araboth* (Ps. 67). "He sits upon the earth's course," and "with his palms he measures heaven, with his hand the sea's waters" (Isa. 40).[122] According to Philippians 4 even now Christ is among us just as he once was, when in Jeremiah 23 he said, "I am God near at hand." Just as before, now "heaven, is his seat, and the earth is a stool for his feet."[123] In fact, then were shown things as metaphorical signs which now really exist and are truly fulfilled in him. Just as he once "walked through the midst of Israel's camps," now too Christ walks in our midst (Deut. 23).[124] Christ is now walking "in the midst of the candelabra;" in other words, he walks in the midst of the churches as Revelation plainly teaches: "Behold, God's tabernacle is with men, and it shall reside with them." Our own "atrium is within," a place where Christ truly dwells among Israel's sons (Ezek. 43).[125] "I shall place," he says, "my sanctuary in their midst, and it will be my dwelling among them" (Ezek. 37).[126]

Christ is not, as some think, in a particular spot in heaven. His place is not to be sought among the elements nor the stars nor in a "third heaven." Christ did not take up a station in a fixed region of heaven, but above all the heavens, and he is within us. Those who take Christ away from us with the evidence of place "at the Father's right hand," have a carnal understanding.[127] Rather, this ought to

---

[120] Clement, *Recognitiones*, but the quote seems rather from lib. II, n. XXVIII (PG I, 1222) : *Propter quem cuncta praeparaverat.*

[121] In Eph. 4:9-10 : "'He ascended,' what does it mean but that he had also descended into the lower parts of the earth? He who descended is the same one who ascended far above all the heavens, so that he might fill all things."

[122] Ps. 103:3, Ps. 67:4, 33. Isa. 40:22, 12.

[123] Jer. 23:23. Isa. 66:1 cited in Acts 7:49.

[124] Deut. 23:14.

[125] Rev. 1:20 and 21:3; Ezek. 43:5.

[126] Ezek. 37:27-28.

[127] This is the formula of the creed taken from many places in the scripture which appears for the

demonstrate that he is not at the Father's right hand. Nevertheless, they think that Christ is "a human being, like an animal," and that God's right hand is something fixed. Or surely they think that Christ's flesh is located in heaven to be a display for the benefit of heaven's winged occupants. Well, we say that Christ is in that heaven where angels do not reach. He is in the "third heaven" where and from whence "he fills everything." Outside every place [281] and outside every finite body there is his "spiritual body" in a "new heaven," which "is within us."[128] In Christ alone there is God, and in him there is the source of every divine quality. God breathes nowhere, save through Christ's spirit. He addresses no one, save through Christ's voice. He shines upon no one, save with Christ's light. Weaving us together by a miraculous bond into a single unit, Christ's body is impartable to many through communion "with the result that we are his body's members," made from his flesh and his bones.[129] Christ's body and the church's body are one flesh, just as a man's flesh and that of his wife are one flesh. Just as Eve came from Adam's flesh and bones, so the church comes from Christ's flesh and bones. In Ephesians 5 Paul proclaimed "the great mystery in this."[130] Another, similar mystery is "God's manifestation in the flesh" (1 Tim. 3).[131]

Behold, three like mysteries: Adam and Eve are one flesh; Christ and the church are one flesh; God and man are one flesh. Paul made note of these three mysteries at the same time when he said, "The husband is the wife's head, Christ is the husband's head, and God is Christ's head" (1 Cor. 11).[132] As to this union of head and body, it would otherwise be a monstrosity in every case, should you detach the one from the other. Please notice the similar nature of these three mysteries. As God is made one flesh with man through incarnation, so a wife melds with her husband to form a single flesh in the form of their progeny, and Christ

first time in Ps. 109:1 and then in Matt. 26:64; Mark 16:19, etc.
[128] 2 Cor. 12:2.
[129] Eph. 5:30.
[130] Eph. 5:32.
[131] 1 Tim. 3:16.
[132] 1 Cor. 11:3.

through the act of communion, truly creates a single flesh with the church.

Therefore, the error of those who say that Christ is not eaten and seek to have him locked up and held in a single, solitary region of heaven, is manifest. Those who do not know Christ, do not even know where God is.[133] We never had anything in the world from God except for Christ, nor will we ever have anything until the day of judgment, when Christ will present us face-to-face with God, the Father. In John 14 Christ amply provides all these points for your consideration, provided you read his words attentively. For, just as in considering his vision there follows the inference from Christ's statements, so it is in considering his path and place: "Do you not believe that the Father is in me? The Father, [282] who remains in me, accomplishes everything." Now this would not be true, if without him the Father were to accomplish different deeds in different places. Just as "everything was made through him," so everything is now made through him, and "without him nothing is made." Neither in heaven nor on earth does anything exist without him (John 1). He is every thing's essence as we said about *jehovah*. He is *jehovah* and the basis of natural things.[134] The splendor that is the form of any given thing, exists because of Christ and within Christ. "Everything exists in him" (Col. 1). He bears, holds up, and carries everything with "the power of his word" (Heb. 1). "He made us, and he supports us, and carries us" (Isa. 46, 63). "In him we live, are moved, and exist" (Acts 17). "He makes everything live" (1 Tim. 6). With his own spirit he supports, "creates, and recreates everything's life" (Ps. 103). He is our life and the "length of our days" (Deut. 30).[135] Finally, without Christ nothing can come into being, be seen, or be heard. This light which you see

---

[133] *Deum ubi sit, nesciunt, qui Christum ignorant.* Servetus will base on various expressions of this concept his attack on the eucharistic doctrines of Luther and Zwingli in the last part of *Christianismi restitutio.*

[134] John 14:2 and 1:3. It does not mean that Christ is the same as God, in the most veiled sense of the term Jehovah. But he is *jehovah* (with minuscule) according to the etymology accepted by Servetus in lib. IV, 125-127 : "Father caused His son, who makes everything exist, and He gave essence to the son, who gives essence to everything so that the son himself may be the source of essence."

[135] Allusions to Col. 1:17; Heb. 1:3; Isa. 46:4, and 63; Acts 17:28; 1 Tim. 6:13; Ps. 103:29, and

with your eyes, is Christ's splendor or a certain likeness of his light, residing within him. The sound that you hear, is Christ's spirit. In the world nothing has been created in which the Creator does not shine and is not active. God Himself has been mixed with the all the world's things. He is the very form of Christ's splendor and Christ's life-causing spirit.[136]

Peter: Therefore, in seeing a given object, not only is God seen, but so too is Christ?

Michael: Yes, even by those who believe that Christ's light is dispersed in the object. Nevertheless, God is seen first and foremost in Christ. In any given object God is almost "touched" (Acts 17),[137] but in Christ He is touched foremost. In all creatures a certain scent of God's power is detected, but this is foremost in Christ. God is in everything, but foremost in Christ, in whom alone exists the true and natural union, god-making, hypostatic, and awesome. In all things there is a token of Christ's divinity, a secondary dispensation of his divinity and a secondary, created light. In Christ, however, there is the full and substantive divinity and original, uncreated light itself. In him there are the first forms of things [283], that is to say, in his mind, then in the objects themselves. The first forms, as before creation they existed within God's wisdom and in a similar manner as they exist in a soul, so now are within Christ's infinite mind and in Christ's very soul. In Christ's soul there is the recognition of all things, even the "hairs on a head." In him there is the entire fullness of all things. In him there is the primal concept of everything, and in him there are actually the bases of all things. Essences flow from Christ into all creation's objects : divinity and the ideal forms themselves variously radiate from him like the light from a second sun.[138] Innumerable are the shades in

---

Deut. 30:20.

[136] Servetus is using the expression *Omnibus mundi rebus immixtus est ipse Deus* and does not say *unitus* as he before distinguished between a mixture and a union. Compare note 55.

[137] Acts 17:27 : "so that they would search for God and perhaps grope for him and find him – though indeed he is not far from each one of us."

[138] This is evidently a concept inspired by the Platonist-Philonic philosophy but applied to the Christian doctrine of Christ.

corporeal and spiritual objects, just as there are many shades of our own solar light. In fact, even after resurrection, there will be no sunlight. Nonetheless, there will be the various shades of God's clarity and glory just as one star differs from another in brightness. Christ will always be like the sun, and everyone else will ever after be located in his rank. "Each and every one will be in his own place, but Christ is foremost" (1 Cor. 15).[139] As now all the divinity's fullness exists in Christ, so the same divinity was ever in a man's form.

Peter: The Sophists think only of the simple predestination of Christ, the man, when they say that in God we, too, have an equal, predetermined end.

Michael: You will presently and without difficulty see, based on their own statements, how seriously they are mistaken. If you consider individually each member on its own, you will attain the most complete assessment of the head. As each of us possesses different gifts, so each has been predestined from before time in different ways. One substantive seat of light and glory has been readied since before time for one person, another for another. Therefore, in our case predestination is neither straightforward nor of only one cast. Now what will you say about the head? In him we have been predestined. In him we are all contained. Upon him we all depend. As now the ranks of objects are diverse in God, so since before time they existed in him, and Christ is chief of all the ranks.[140]

Think that this ranking is eternal in God and that Christ has been established over all things. Truly we cannot have an *a priori* understanding of what the λόγος was in God, [284] unless we begin *a posteriori* by crossing the threshold, by going first through Christ. In this matter an error has been committed by all the Sophists. For this reason I say that we ought to have an understanding of

---

[139] 1 Cor. 15:23.

[140] These considerations introduce the next paragraph in which Servetus explains his methodology, namely, not to begin with the Son of God, the second Person of the Trinity which would indicate a certain *a priori* approach, but with the man, Jesus, son of God, in whose predestination all mankind and all things were in a certain way predetermined. With a similar recommendation Book I of the *Christianismi restituio* was begun as well as *De Trinitatis erroribus*. This represents the essence of his Christianity.

402

Christ that he was God's first thought or His ideal reason. In Christ we must think that there is the very fullness of God's light, and say that this fullness, formerly, by the same token, was in the form of Logos and Elohim. We ought to regard Christ as the unique goal such that the Word's whole mystery was once the glory of the man yet to be. Without changing Himself God wished and was able from before time to reveal that He was of this sort. Without changing Himself God loves some more and others less, but most of all, He loves Christ. Without changing Himself, God is united with some more and less with others, but most of all with Christ. There is no change in God, but rather in the very objects, which, according to their status, come near to God. Ineffable are the means whereby God sustains everything, unites Himself to everything, and is active in all things. Moreover, Christ is he who effectuates everything in every instance, and God does this through him. Who would deny that God was able to do this through Christ, when He was able to create a new world through the divinity which exists in any given object, and when He was able to make the very thing function within everything? How much more does Christ perform "all works in all things" now that "the entire fullness of divinity is in him"?[141]

Peter: Therefore, in the devil and in man, does he effect the act of sin, the sin itself?

Michael: Stoics and magicians would have to admit this with their "enslaved judgment," but it is not satisfactory to conclude, based on the fact that God is active within us, that our judgment is a slave. For God acts in us to the end that we act freely.[142] It is an awesome design, and the modes of divine activity are

---

[141] Col. 2:9 : "For in him the whole fullness of deity dwells bodily." The text is discussed by Servetus in Book II of *Christianismi restitutio*. The emphasis on "the divinity which exists in any given object" used here for a specific purpose together with several other texts provided the occasion for an easy accusation of Servetus of pantheism.

[142] Among those two categories differentiated by Servetus one does not have to understand only the Stoics who were selected because of their submission to a natural fatalism, but especially the Calvinist doctrine of predestination which Servetus attacked at every occasion. Servetus used frequently the term *magus* and *magia* in reference to Calvin as an insult in his *Letters to Calvin* as well as during the trial (*Opera Calvini*, VIII, 515-553).

variable just as His power and spirit are manifold. As if an act were not declared a sin, He sustains it in its natural condition and acts according to the deed's essence: nonetheless, the good spirit gives succor, bidding that it not be done. God hates the deed, yet He does not deny the native ability to do it. Such does He wish to be the device of free ability, to which is ascribed the ability of committing sin. Just as God is free, so, [285] in different ways, He shares that free ability as he wishes.[143]

We would conclude that free will is a slave in the Creator Himself, were we to see that nothing but a servile will reflected in creatures, especially in those that are God's true image, and in whom the divine mind shines.[144] If Christ fully has a free will, we too have something because, genuinely partaking of him in everything, we enjoy the gift of his spirit and freedom. But, I will save those issues for another occasion.[145] For the time being, lest there be any deficiency in Christ's glory, we steadfastly make this assertion: Christ himself has a free will. Just as he is free to do anything, so he is freely able to restore those of us who today are bewitched with a "servile will," to a state of sound mind.

Peter: They are affected by this reasoning: What God previously conceived and ordained, cannot now be any different.

Michael: It is by a false supposition that they suppose the issue of time to have relevance for God, and it is for this reason that they make their false inference. What happens now, God not only conceived before time, but He sees in His present: He sees it happen freely and that is how He ordains it.[146] Otherwise, not even Christ would be free in his own actions because God previously recognized and ordained the actions according to their own nature. From the very fact that from God's perspective there is nothing awaiting existence, Philo in his

---

[143] *Sicut Deus liber est, ita liberam illam facultatem, ut vult, varie communicat.*

[144] A good argument for a free will in humans.

[145] Servetus cautiously says: *Si Christus habet plene liberum arbitrum, et nos aliquid habemus.* At other occasions he mentions that at least at certain occasions we feel free, e.g., pp. 54, 301, 568 of *Christianismi restitutio.*

[146] These are allusions to the doctrine of Lorenzo Valla mentioned in *Christianismi restitutio*, lib II, 55.

404

book, *On the World*, concluded that it is with providence that there exists free will in man, in whom the divine mind is reflected.[147]

Peter: How did the son obtain glory and power through resurrection if it was already his by birth?

Michael: The fact that a son may immediately possess everything that belongs to his father, is not a fact of nature. Rather, by nature all the father's glory and estate are owed to the son. This is confirmed in death according to the will. Christ did not by divine dispensation fully obtain all of the Father's power and glory until the will was confirmed by his own death, and he was glorified through his suffering. Now, after the glorification Christ came to possess everything so that no name, no glory, no power, and no honor can be given to God without it also accruing to him. Although you can give a special name that only suits God, the Father, [286] such as calling Him "ungenerated" and "Christ's father," nevertheless, another name, which would reflect His glory or power with respect to us, suits the son just as the Father. In fact, it is bestowed upon the Father through the son. Their name is necessarily one just as they are one. He is truly God, the omnipotent Creator, and he is truly *jehovah*.

May he alone, who reigns in unity of substance and spirit with God, the Father, have the glory, the authority, and all the power for ever. Amen.

---

[147] Philo of Alexandria (ca. 20 B.C.E.- 50 C.E.), *De opificio mundi*, LI, 146 : "Every man in regard of his intellect is connected with divine reason, being an impression of, or a fragment or a ray of that blessed nature." And in LII, 149 : "Accordingly, Moses says, that 'God brought all the animals to man, wishing to see what names he would give to each.' Not because he knew that he had formed in mortal man a rational nature capable of moving of its own accord, and in order that he might be free from all participation in vice. But he was now trying him as a master might try his pupil, stirring up the disposition which he had implanted in him." Philo of Alexandria was published for the first time in Latin in 1520 in Paris and the first printing of his works in Greek appeared in 1552. Servetus was able to introduce the Greek terms of Philo into his opus.

APPENDIX
List of Works Published by Servetus in Publication Order and Their Translations[1]

Declarationis Iesu Christi Filii Dei libri quinque authore Michaele Serveto alias Revves Tarraconensi. In Stuttgart manuscript of 119 pages (in Stuttgart, Haupstaatsarchive, 1763, Bü. 25). This is a copy of the original manuscript. It was most likely a sketch for the Servetus' first book *De Triniatis erroribus.* The manuscript was first transcribed by Marian Hillar and Ángel Alcalá and published in Latin with Spanish translation by Ángel Alcalá in Miguel Servet *Obras Completas,* (Col. Larumbe Clásicos Argoneses 24, Zaragoza : Prensas Universitarias de Zaragoza, 2004). Spanish translation, *Cinco libros de declaración sobre Jesús el Cristo hijo de Dios,* Vol. II.-1, pp. 3-113. Vol. II-2, Latin text, pp. 535-625.

De Trinitatis erroribus, libri septem. Per Michaelem Serveto, alias Reves ab Aragonia Hispanum. Anno M.D. XXXI. [Haguenau, 1531]. Published by the press of Johann Setzer (Secerius). Several copies are preserved in various libraries. Reprinted in Regensburg in 1721. The book was translated in 1620 into Dutch by Reiner Talle (Regnerus Vitellius, 1558[9]-1619[20]). *Van de Dolinghen in de Drievvldigheyd, Seven Boecken, Eertijds in Latijn beschreven Door Michiel Servetus, gheseyt Reves van Aragonien, Spaenjaerd ...,"* Amsterdam, 1620; into English in 1932 by Earl Morse Wilbur, *On the Errors of the Trinity. Seven Books. By Michael Serveto, alias Reves, a Spaniard of Aragon MDXXXI.* In *The two treatises of Servetus on the Trinity .... Now first translated into English by Earl Morse Wilbur, D.D.* (Cambridge: Harvard University Press; London: Humphrey Milford; Oxford University Press; Harvard Theological Studies, 1932); Catalan translation by Ana Gomez Rabal, *Dels errors sobre la Trinidat,* (Barcelona: Edicions Proa, S.A., 1999). Spanish translation by Ana Gómez Rabal, with collaboration of Ángel Alcalá, *Siete libros acerca de la Trinidad,* in *Obras completas, op. cit.,* 2004, Vol. II-1, pp. 143-381. Latin text, Vol. II-2, pp. 627-781.

Dialogorum de Trinitate libri duo. De Iusticia regni Christi, capitula quatuor. per Michaelem Serveto, alias Reves, ab Aragonia Hispanum. Haguenau, 1532.

---

[1] Bibliography of extant works by Servetus was collected by Madeline E. Stanton in: Fulton, John Farquhar *Michael Servetus, Humanist and Martyr; with a Bibliography of His Works and Census of Known Copies, by Madeline E. Stanton.* (New York: H. Reichner, 1953). Marian Hillar, *Michael Servetus: Intellectual Giant, Humanist, and Martyr,* (Lanham, New York, Oxford: University Press of America, 2002), pp. 263-268. Ángel Alcalá, *Miguel Servet* (Zaragoza: Caja de Ahorros de la Inmaculada de Aragón, 2000), 91-92.

Published by Johann Setzer. A second pamphlet on the Trinity of 19 pages, to which he added a treatise of 25 pages, *De Iusticia regni Christi, capitula quatuor*. Several copies preserved in various libraries. Reprinted in Regensburg, 1721. Translated together with *De Trinitatis erroribus* by Earl Morse Wilbur (1932). All three works were reprinted: Servetus, M., *De Trinitatis erroribus libri septem*, 1531. *Dialogorum de Trinitate libri duo*, 1532. *De Iusticia regni Christi, capitula quatuor*, 1532. Minerva G.m.b.H., Frankfurt a.M. 1965. Spanish translation by Ana Gómez Rabal and Ángel Alcalá, *Dos libros de diálogos sobre la Trinidad. Cuatro capítulos sobre la justicia del reino de Cristo.* in *Obras completas, op. cit.*, 2004, Vol. II-1, pp. 383-482. Latin text, Vol II-2, pp. 783-853.

Claudii Ptolemaei Alexandrini geographicae enarrationis libri octo. Ex Bilibaldi Pirckeymheri tralatione, sed ad graeca & prisca exemplaria à Michaële Villanovano iam primum recogniti. Adiecta insuper ab eodem scholia, quibus exoleta urbium nomina ad nostri seculi morem exponuntur .... Lugduni, ex officina Melchioris et Gasparis Trechsel fratrum, MDXXXV (1535). Several copies are preserved in various libraries.
Humanist erudite, linguist, mathematician and geographer, Willibald Pirckheimer (1470-1530) published Ptolemy's geography with new maps in Strasburg in 1525. The Greek original of the work was published in 1533 by Erasmus in Basel. Servetus reedited, corrected, and supplemented Pirckheimer's edition using also the Greek original and several previous editions. *Claudii Ptolemaei Alexandrini geographicae enarrationis libri octo.... à Michaële Villanovano secundó recogniti .... Prostat Lugduni apud Hugonem à Porta, MDXLI,* Lyon 1541. Book is dedicated to Servetus's protector, Archbishop Palmier. Fragments were translated into English by Charles David O'Malley, *Michael Servetus. A Translation of his Geographical, Medical and Astrological Writings with Introductions and Notes,* (Philadelphia: American Philosophical Society, 1953), 15-37. Spanish translation by Ángel Alcalá, *Ocho libros de la narración geográfica,* in *Obras completas, op. cit.,* (2005), Vol. III, pp. 5-101. Latin text, Vol. III, 303-373.

In Leonardum Fuchsium apologia, autore Michaele Villanovano. Lyon, 1536. There is a facsimile copy of the work done by Oxford University Press, 1909. This is a response by Servetus to the work of Leonard Fuchs, *Apologia*, in defense of his friend, Symphorien Champier, a known Galenist and antiarabist. Its English translation was published by Charles David O'Malley, *Michael Servetus. A Translation of his Geographical, Medical and Astrological Writings with Introductions and Notes,* (Philadelphia: American Philosophical Society, 1953), 38-54; Spanish translation by Ángel Alcalá, *Apología contra Leonardo Fuchs. Disertación sobre la Astrología*

(Villanueva de Sijena, 1981). A new translation by Ángel Alcalá, *Apología contra Leonardo Fuchs*, in *Obras completas, op. cit.*, Vol. III, (2005), pp. 103-118. Latin text, Vol.. III, pp. 375-389.

Syruporum universa ratio, ad Galeni censuram diligenter expolita. Cui, post integra de concoctione disceptationem, praescripta est vera purgandi methodus, cum expositione aphorismi: Concocta medicari. Michaele Villanovano authore. Parisiis Ex officina Simonis Colinaei. 1537. (Several editions of the work appeared, in Venice in 1545; in Lyon in 1546, 1547, 1548). English translation of the work was published by O'Malley, Charles David, *op. cit.*, (1953), 55-167. Spanish translation by Ángel Alcalá, *Tratado de los jarabes*, in Obras completas, op. cit., Vol. III (2005), pp. 119-253. Latin text, Vol. III, pp. 391-483.

Michaelis Villanovani in quondam medicum apologetica disceptatio pro astrologia, Paris 1538. It was also reprinted by Henri Tollin in 1880. Its English translation was published by Charles David O'Malley, *op. cit.*, 168-188. Spanish translation by Ángel Alcalá, *Apología contra Fuchs. Discurso en pro la Astrología*, (Villanueva de Sijena, 1981). French edition with Latin text and translation by Jean Dupèbe, *Discussion apologétique pour l'astrologie contre un certain médecin*, (Genève: Librairie Droz S.A., 2004). New Spanish translation by Ángel Alcalá, *Discurso en pro de la astrología contra cierto médico*, in *Obras completas, op. cit.*, Vol. III, (2005), pp. 255-277. Latin text, Vol. III, pp. 485-500.

In 1542 Servetus appears as the editor of the Bible of Santes Pagnino. The most important disciplines in this period were theology and medicine. Theology was studied through the Bible in the Latin translation, and the texts of Galen in the Arabic translation were the basis for medicine. There were several editions of Bible translations including the Complutensian Polyglot Bible, the publication of which was coordinated by Cardinal Francisco Ximenes de Cisneros in cooperation with the most distinguished scholars in Europe such as Vergara, Coronel y Lopez de Zúñiga in Spain, Erasmus in Holland, Calvin in Geneva, Santes Pagnino in Lyon and Sébastien Castellion in Switzerland. Santes Pagnino (1470-1541) was a Dominican monk from Lucca, a pupil of Savonarola (1452-1498, who was hanged and burned in Florence for heresy and critique of church practices), an erudite in Hebrew and classical languages. Pagnino became a professor of classical languages at the College of Oriental Languages, founded by Pope Leo X. He dedicated twenty-five years to the translation of his Bible from the original languages into Latin, which was first published at Lyon in 1527/1528. This edition is said to be the first to be divided into chapters. The next edition appeared in 1541 in Cologne edited by Melchior

Novesianus and then was corrected by Servetus and published by Hugues de la Porte in 1542 as *Biblia Sacra ex Santis Pagnini tralatione, sed ad Hebraicae linguae amussim novissimè ita recognita, & scholiis illustrata, ut planè nova editio videri possitt. Accessit praeterea liber interpretationum Hebraicorum, Arabicorum, Graecorumque nominum, quae in sacris literis reperiuntur, ordine alphabetico digestus, eodem authore. Lugduni, apud Hugonem à Porta. M.D. XLII. Cum privilegio ad annos sex.* Servetus added a preface and notes to the Pagnino Bible recommending in the prologue the study of the history of the Hebrews for a better understanding of the Bible. He accused biblical studies of not reaching for the literal and historical sense but searching in vain for the mystical meaning. The prologue and notes of Servetus to this edition were translated by Ángel Alcalá, *Prológo y notas a la edición de la Biblia expurgadas por la Inquisición*, in *Obras completas op. cit.*, Vol. II-2 (2004), pp. 489-509.

There was another edition of the Bible of Pagnino *in octavo*, the same year, probably edited by Servetus, too. *Biblia sacra ex postremis doctorum omnium vigiliis, ad Hebraicam veritatem, & probatissimorum exemplarium fidem. Cum argumentis, indice, & Hebraicorum nominum interpretatione. Lugduni, Apud Hugonem à Porta. 1542.* This edition of the Bible contains an appendix *Summa totius sacrae scripturae, librorum videlicet veteris et novi testamenti* which is ascribed to Servetus. It was translated by Ángel Alcalá, *Rsumen de toda la sagrada escritura, o sea, de los libros del Viejo y del Nuevo testamento* and published in *Obras completas, op. cit.*, Vol. II-2 (2004), pp. 511-518. Latin text, Vol. II-2, pp. 855-861.

Christianismi restitutio. Totius ecclesiae apostolicae est ad sua limina vocatio, in integrum restituta cognitione Dei, fidei Christi, iustificationis nostrae, regenerationis baptismi, et coenae domini manducationis. Restitutio denique nobis regno coelesti, Babylonis impiae captivitate soluta, et Antichristo cum suis penitus destructo. M.D. LIII. 734 pp. 8°. It ends with the initials M.S.V
There is also a reprint of the fragment of *Christianismi restitutio* by Giorgio Biandrata, an Italian physician who obtained his degree in Montpellier (here he was a fellow student with Rabelais), became a personal physician of the Italian-born wife of King Sigismund of Poland. Later he returned to Italy and was forced to leave Italy around 1553 for his religious convictions, he returned to Poland and Transylvania. *De Regno Christi Liber primus. De Regno Antichristi Liber secundus. Accessit tractatus de Paedobaptismo, et circuncisione. Rerum capita sequens pagella demonstrabit. Ioan. 15. ver 14. Vos amici mei estis, si feceris quaecunq ego praecipio vobis. Albae Juliae. Anno Domini 1569.*
The first known translation of the *Restitutio* is that by a Pole, Gregorius Paulus

(Grzegorz Paweł), who translated some chapters into Polish and published them in Pińczów already in 1568! *Okazanie Antychrysta y iego Królestwa ze znaków iego własnych w słowie bożym opisanych, których tu sześćdziesiąt. [The advent of Antichrist and his kingdom, according to his own signs, of which there are sixty, as described in the Word of God.]*
The book was reprinted by Christoph Gottlieb von Murr (1733-1811) in Nürnberg in 1790 and this edition was reprinted again by Minerva G.m.b.H., Frankfurt a. Mein, 1966. Von Murr made a page-for-page reprint of the Vienna copy of the manuscript (now at the Harvard University Library).

The German translation by Bernhard Spiess, *Wiederherstellung des Christentums,* (Wiesbaden: Verlag von Chr. Limbarth. 1892, 1895, 1896), 3 vols.

The Spanish translation was done in two separate books, one containing only the *Christianismi restitutio,* the second, the rest of the Servetus book. Miguel Servet, *Restitución del Cristianismo.* Primera traducción castellana de Ángel Alcalá y Luis Betés. Edición, introducción y notas de Ángel Alcalá (Madrid: Fundación Universitaria Española, 1980). Miguel Servet, *Treinta cartas a Calvino. Sesenta signos del Antichristo. Apología de Melanchton.* Edición de Ángel Alcalá (Madrid: Editorial Castalia, 1981). New Spanish translations by Ángel Alcalá, *Treinta cartas a Calvino,* in *Obras completas, op. cit.,* Voll. III, (2005), pp. 3-140. Latin text, Vol. III, pp. 255-352. *Sesenta signos del reino del Anticristo,* in *op. cit.,* Vol. III, pp. 141-155. Latin text, Vol. III, pp. 353-361. *Apología contra Felipe Melanchton,* in *Obras completas, op. cit.,* Vol. III, pp. 157-254. Latin text, Vol. III, pp. 363-426. New Spanish translation by Ángel Alcalá of the *Christianismi restitutio* will appear in Vols. V and VI of *Obras completas, op. cit.,* (2006).

There is also a Portuguese translation (in a manuscript) of a part of the *Christianismi restitutio (De mysterio Trinitatis, et veterum disciplina, ad Philippum Melanchthonem, et eius colegas, apologia) Aplogia a Felipe Malnchthon e a suas colegas sobre o mistério de Trinidade e sobre os costumes antigos* as part of the dissertation by Elaine Cristine Sartorelli *O Programa de Miguel Servet para a Restitução do Cristianismo; Teologia e Retorica na Apologia a Melanchthon,* presented at Universidade de São Paulo, Facultade de Filosofia, Letras e Ciencias Humanas (São Paulo, 2000).
There is a Polish translation of selected fragments of Servetus' works: Michał Servet, *Wybór pism i dokumentów.* Opracował, wstępem i przypisami opatrzył Lech Szczucki. Teksty tłumaczyli Andrzej Kempti et al., (Warszawa: Książka i Wiedza, 1967).